NETWORKING

BASICS

NETWORKING BASICS

SECOND EDITION

PATRICK CICCARELLI, CHRISTINA FAULKNER, JERRY FITZGERALD, ALAN DENNIS, DAVID GROTH, AND TOBY SKANDIER

with
FRANK MILLER

WILEY

John Wiley & Sons, Inc.
New York • Chichester • Weinheim • Brisbane • Toronto • Singapore

PUBLISHER	Don Fowley
EXECUTIVE EDITOR	John Kane
MARKETING MANAGER	Christopher Ruel
SENIOR EDITORIAL ASSISTANT	Tiara Kelly
SENIOR PRODUCTION MANAGER	Janis Soo
ASSOCIATE PRODUCTION MANAGER	Joel Balbin
CREATIVE DIRECTOR	Harry Nolan
COVER DESIGNER	Ngieng Seng Ping
COVER PHOTO	Christian Riekoff/Photo Researchers, Inc.

This book was set in Times New Roman by Aptara, and printed and bound by Courier Westford. The cover was printed by Courier Westford.

To order books or for customer service, please call 1-800-CALL WILEY (225-5945).

Library of Congress Cataloging-in-Publication Data

Networking basics / Patrick Ciccarelli . . . [et. al].—2nd ed.
   p. cm.
   Includes index.
   ISBN **978-1-118-07780-1** (pbk.)
1. Computer networks. I. Ciccarelli, Patrick.
   TK5105.5.N466865 2012
   004.6—dc23

                              2011051141

Printed in the United States of America

10 9 8 7 6 5 4 3 2

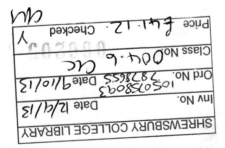

Patrick Ciccarelli, CCNP, CCDP, MCSE, and M.A. in Instructional Technology, is the founder and CEO of Nethos, a San Francisco–based network consulting company. Patrick is a former regional instructor for the Cisco Networking Academy, an international program that prepares individuals for a career in networking. Patrick is also co-author of *MCSE 2002 Jump-Start: Computer and Network Basics* and CCDP*: Cisco Internetwork Design Exam Notes,* both from Sybex.

Christina Faulkner has nearly 20 years of experience as an educator. With Patrick Ciccarelli, she was one of the first regional instructors for the Cisco Networking Academy. She is currently the Technology Coordinator for the Hayward Unified School District.

Dr. Jerry FitzGerald is the principal in Jerry FitzGerald & Associates, which he started in 1977. He received his PhD in business economics and a master's degree in business economics from the Claremont Graduate School, an MBA from the University of Santa Clara, and his bachelor's degree in industrial engineering from Michigan State University.

Alan R. Dennis is currently a professor at the Kelley School of Business at Indiana University, where he holds the John T. Chambers Chair of Internet Systems, which honors John Chambers, the founder of Cisco Systems and a groundbreaking developer in networking technology. He has written numerous books on data communication, system design, and networking. He is the publisher of *MIS Quarterly,* a scholarly quarterly lodged in the Information Systems department at Indiana University.

David Groth is a full-time author and consultant. He is the author of Sybex's best-selling *A Complete Study Guide, PC Chop Shop: Tricked Out Guide to PC Modding,* and is coauthor of *Cabling: The Complete Guide to Network Wiring, Network Study Guide: Exam N10-003, i-Net Study Guide: Exam IK0-002, CompTIA Network Certification Kit (Exam N10-003),* and coeditor of *A Fast Pass.*

Toby Skandier is in technical education development and delivery for Sprint Corporation. He is the author of CliffsTestPrep *CompTIA A, Network Administrator Street Smarts: A Real World Guide to CompTIA Network Skills,* and coauthor of *Network Study Guide: Exam N10-003, CompTIA A Complete Study Guide.*

Frank Miller has nearly 30 years experience designing, developing, and delivering technical training materials. He has worked with computer networking for nearly 20 years, with experience that includes Unix and Linux networks, AppleTalk, LAN Manager, various generations of Novell's NetWare, and every version of Microsoft Windows networking since the first days of Windows for Workgroups. He has written numerous books and training materials that are used by various schools and professional organizations in the United States and around the world.

PREFACE

Today's students have different goals, different life experiences, and different academic backgrounds, but they are all on the same path to success in the real world. This diversity, coupled with the reality that these learners often have jobs, families, and other commitments, requires a flexibility that our nation's higher education system is addressing. Distance learning, shorter course terms, new disciplines, evening courses, and certification programs are some of the approaches that colleges employ to reach as many students as possible and help them clarify and achieve their goals.

The second edition of *Networking Basics* offers specially designed suite of services and content, which helps address this diversity and the need for flexibility. *Networking Basics, Second Edition* content puts a focus on the fundamentals to help students grasp the subject, bringing them all to the same basic understanding. Content from *Networking Basics, Second Edition* has an emphasis on teaching job-related skills and practical applications of concepts with clear and professional language. The core competencies and skills help students succeed in the classroom and beyond, whether in another course or in a professional setting. A variety of built-in learning resources allow the students to practice what they need to perform and help instructors and students gauge students' understanding of the content. These resources enable students to think critically about their new knowledge and apply their skills in any situation.

Our goal with the second edition of *Networking Basics* is to celebrate the many students in your courses, respect their needs, and help you guide them on their way.

LEARNING SYSTEMS

To meet the needs of working college students, the second edition of *Networking Basics* uses a learning system based on Bloom's Taxonomy. Key topics are presented in easy-to-follow chapters. The text then prompts analysis, evaluation, and creation with a variety of learning aids and assessment tools. Students move efficiently from reviewing what they have learned, to acquiring new information and skills, to applying their new knowledge and skills to real-life scenarios.

Using this learning system, students not only achieve academic mastery of *concepts* in networking courses, but they also master real-world *skills* related to that content. The learning system also helps students become independent learners, giving them a distinct advantage in the field, whether they are just starting out or seeking to advance in their careers.

ORGANIZATION, DEPTH, AND BREADTH OF THE TEXT

Modular Format

Research on college students shows that they access information from textbooks in a nonlinear way. Instructors also often wish to reorder textbook content to suit the needs of a particular class. Therefore, although *Networking Basics, Second Edition* proceeds logically from the basics to increasingly more challenging material, chapters are further organized into sections that are self-contained for maximum teaching and learning flexibility.

Numeric System of Headings

Networking Basics, Second Edition uses a numeric system for headings (for example, 2.3.4 identifies the fourth subsection of Section 3 of Chapter 2). With this system, students and teachers can quickly and easily pinpoint topics in the table of contents and the text, keeping class time and study sessions focused.

Core Content

The topics in *Networking Basics, Second Edition* are organized into 12 chapters.

Chapter 1, "Networking Fundamentals," introduces PC networks and their importance to modern businesses. The chapter begins with an overview of the development of PC networks and the Internet. It compares and contrasts peer-to-peer, client/server, and directory service–based networking models and explains the roles of low- and high-level protocols in network communication. Students are also introduced to local area networks (LANs), campus area networks (CANs), metropolitan area networks (MANs), and wide area networks (WANs).

In Chapter 2, "Network Standards and Models," students are introduced to the standard models used to describe networking technologies and the standards bodies that produce them. Students are provided with a detailed look at the Open Systems Interconnection (OSI) model and learn why the model is important. The chapter also compares the OSI model to two other commonly used models: the Internet model and the TCP/IP, or Department of Defense (DoD), model. The chapter gives the students a baseline for understanding and comparing network technologies, software, and devices.

Chapter 3, "Network Protocols," looks at the Data Link layer and Network layer protocols in detail, including applicable published standards. It discusses protocols in the context of their role in network communications. The chapter looks first at lower-level protocols, focusing on and comparing the Ethernet and Token Ring protocols. It then moves on to network protocols, with a comparison of the TCP/IP and AppleTalk protocols suites, which are the protocols that students are most likely to encounter in real-world networking applications.

Chapter 4, "Network Architectures," provides students with a detailed look at common network architectures, including peer-to-peer, client/server, directory service, and hybrid architecture models. It includes an overview of the security models used in each of these network architectures and the relationship between logical and physical network models. Students learn the basics of developing a network design to meet an organization's operational requirements.

Chapter 5, "Network Topologies," compares and contrasts common logical and physical topologies. Students are given guidelines for selecting the most appropriate topology, based on network requirements, including when a hybrid topology is the best solution. As a way of discussing the technologies involved with each topology, students are introduced to the access methods used by each, including a detailed comparison of Carrier-Sense Multiple Access/Collision Detect (CSMA/CD) and other wired/wireless topologies as representative access types.

Chapter 6, "Network Media and Devices," provides a detailed discussion of wired media types, network connection devices, and Internet connection devices. The chapter compares and contrasts the use of coaxial (coax), unshielded twisted-pair (UTP), shielded twisted-pair (STP), and fiber-optic cable in both legacy and current network applications. Students learn to recognize the various cable types and, given network requirements, how to choose the most appropriate cable types. Students also learn how to choose appropriate connection devices based on network requirements, with a detailed look at bridge and router operations.

Chapter 7, "Transmission Control Protocol/Internet Protocol (TCP/IP)," puts special and appropriate emphasis on the TCP/IP protocol suite. Students learn about the importance of TCP/IP as the de facto standard for nearly all current PC networking applications. The chapter looks at representative TCP/IP packets to introduce how addresses are used and then discusses addressing requirements. Students learn about the need for name resolution and the most common name resolution options. Students also learn about the requirements for configuring computers to support TCP/IP, using Microsoft Windows as a representative example operating system.

Chapter 8, "Network Servers and Services Fundamentals," focuses on the role of the network operating system (NOS) in a network environment. Students compare and contrast popular options, looking at Microsoft Winders Server, Apple Macintosh, with a special focus on Mac OS X, Unix, Linux, as well as history of Novell NOS. The chapter includes a look at interoperability issues students might encounter in a heterogeneous networking environment and introduces virtualization and virtual machines.

In Chapter 9, "Enterprise Networking Services," the role of network servers is expanded to include larger network environments, including the Internet. This chapter discusses networking requirements in the context of network analysis and design. Students learn what questions they need to ask and what information they need to gather, as well as how to apply what they have learned to create a viable network design. The chapter takes a broad-based approach, showing the dependencies between technical requirements, user and manager requests, and budgetary constraints.

Chapter 10, "Wireless, Remote, and Wide Area Networking," broadens students' exposure to network environments by introducing additional networking options. Students learn about the current state of wireless networking standards and ways in which wireless networking can be integrated into a network design. The chapter compares the use of dial-in and Internet-based remote access configurations with the benefits and drawbacks of each. The chapter introduces WAN connectivity methods currently in use, and how to make design choices based on network requirements.

Chapter 11, "Network Security," discusses issues critical to all networks. Students learn about the most common threats to network security and how to avoid them. They also learn about recovery requirements for after a network has been attacked. The chapter looks at both what can be done through network and client software, such as user and password management, and through hardware devices that help protect a network, such as firewalls. Students learn about encryption and its use in data communications. They also learn about the threat that viruses pose, and available anti-virus tools and countermeasures.

Chapter 12, "Network Management," describes management roles and requirements, as well as how these might be delegated in a large organization. The chapter focuses on key management and support areas, such as backup and restoration, network monitoring, performance tuning, and software change management. Students are introduced to several management tools and learn about the use of technologies based on Simple Network Management Protocol (SNMP).

This second edition has been updated and modified in response to user suggestions:

All images and screenshots have been updated to reflect new networking and operating software.

- *Chapter 3* includes a new In the Real World feature on 802.16 Wireless MAN. Content on legacy technology IPX/SPX was removed.

- *Chapter 4* introduces cloud networking and virtual hosting. This chapter also has a new section on choosing network architecture with list of advantages and disadvantages.

- *Chapter 5* has been revised to include less information on ring topology and more information on wireless network topologies.

- *Chapter 7* now includes a further explanation of IPv6 concept and enhancements, with parameters.

- *Chapter 8* has been updated with Windows Server 2008 and 2008 R2 information. New sections are included on group policy and virtualization. The section on Novell NetWare has been cut down.

- *Chapter 10* includes a new section on accessing wireless networks and cloud computing.

- *Chapter 11* was revised to include a section on VPN security.

PRE-READING LEARNING AIDS

Each chapter in the second edition of *Networking Basics* features a number of new learning and study aids, described in the following sections, to activate students' prior knowledge of the topics and orient them to the material.

Do You Already Know?

This bulleted list focuses on *subject matter* that will be taught. It tells students what they will be learning in this chapter and why it is significant for their careers. It also helps students understand why the chapter is important and how it relates to other chapters in the text.

The online assessment tool in multiple-choice format not only introduces chapter material, but it also helps students anticipate the chapter's learning outcomes. By focusing students' attention on what they do not know, the self-test provides students with a benchmark against which they can measure their own progress. The pretest is available online.

What You Will Find Out and What You Will Be Able To Do

This bulleted list emphasizes *capabilities* and *skills* students will learn as a result of reading the chapter and notes the sections in which they will be found. It prepares students to synthesize and evaluate the chapter material and relate it to the real world.

WITHIN-TEXT LEARNING AIDS

The following learning aids are designed to encourage analysis and synthesis of the material, support the learning process, and ensure success during the evaluation phase.

Introduction

This section orients the student by introducing the chapter and explaining its practical value and relevance to the book as a whole. Short summaries of chapter sections preview the topics to follow.

In the Real World

These boxes tie section content to real-world organizations, scenarios, and applications. Engaging stories of professionals and institutions—challenges they faced, successes they had, and their ultimate outcome.

In Action

These margin boxes point out places in the text where professional applications of a concept are demonstrated. An arrow in the box points to the section of the text and a description of the application is given in the box.

For Example

These margin boxes highlight documents and websites from real companies that further help students understand a key concept. The boxes can reference a figure or the Toolkit found at the end of each chapter.

Career Connection

Case studies of people in the field depicting the skills that helped them succeed in the professional world. Profiles end with a list of "Tips from the Professionals" that provides relevant advice and helpful tools.

Summary

Each chapter concludes with a summary paragraph that reviews the major concepts in the chapter and links back to the "Do You Already Know" list.

Key Terms and Glossary

To help students develop a professional vocabulary, key terms are bolded when they first appear in the chapter and are also shown in the margin of the page with their definitions. A complete list of key terms appears at the end of each chapter and again in a glossary (with brief definitions) at the end of the book. Knowledge of key terms is assessed by all assessment tools (see below).

Toolkit

An end-of-chapter appendix that contains relevant documents and examples from real companies.

EVALUATION AND ASSESSMENT TOOLS

The evaluation phase of *Networking Basics*, *Second Edition* learning system consists of a variety of within-chapter and end-of-chapter assessment tools that test how well students have learned the material and their ability to apply it in the real world. These tools also encourage students to extend their learning into different scenarios and higher levels of understanding and thinking. The following assessment tools appear in every chapter of *Networking Basics, Second Edition*.

Self-Check

Related to the "Do You Already Know" bullets and found at the end of each section, this battery of short-answer questions emphasizes student understanding of concepts and mastery of section content. Though the questions may be either discussed in class or studied by students outside of class, students should not go on before they can answer all questions correctly.

Understand: What Have You Learned?

This online posttest should be taken after students have completed the chapter. It includes all of the questions in the pretest so that students can see how their learning has progressed and improved. The posttest is available online.

Summary Questions

These exercises help students summarize the chapter's main points by asking a series of multiple-choice and true/false questions that emphasize student understanding of concepts and mastery of chapter content. Students should be able to answer all of the Summary Questions correctly before moving on.

Apply: What Would You Do?

These questions drive home key ideas by asking students to synthesize and apply chapter concepts to new, real-life situations and scenarios.

Be a . . .

Found at the end of each chapter, "Be a . . ." questions are designed to extend students' thinking and are thus ideal for discussion or writing assignments. Using an open-ended format and sometimes based on web sources, they encourage students to draw conclusions using chapter material applied to real-world situations, which fosters both mastery and independent learning.

INSTRUCTOR AND STUDENT PACKAGE

Networking Basics, Second Edition is available with the following teaching and learning supplements, all of which are available online at the text's companion website, located at www.wiley.com/go/ciccarelli/networkingbasics2e.

Instructor's Resource Guide

Provides the following aids and supplements for teaching a networking basics course:

- *Sample syllabus:* A convenient template that instructors can use to create their own course syllabi.
- *Teaching suggestions:* For each chapter, teaching suggestions include a chapter summary, learning objectives, definitions of key terms, lecture notes, answers to select text question sets, and at least three suggestions for classroom activities, such as ideas for speakers to invite, videos to show, and other projects.

PowerPoint Slides

Key information is summarized in 10 to 15 PowerPoint slides per chapter. Instructors can use these in class or may choose to share them with students for class presentations or to provide additional study support.

Test Bank

This includes one test per chapter, as well as a midterm and two finals: one cumulative, one noncumulative. Each includes true/false, multiple-choice, and open-ended questions. Answers and page references are provided for the true/false and multiple-choice questions, and page references are provided for the open-ended questions. Questions are available in Microsoft Word and computerized test bank formats.

Student Project Manual

Online *Networking Basics Project Manual* contains activities (an average of five projects per textbook chapter) designed to help students apply textbook concepts in a practical way. Easier exercises at the beginning graduate to more challenging projects that build critical thinking skills.

MSDN Academic Alliance—Free 3-Year Membership Available to Qualified Adopters!

The Microsoft Developer Network Academic Alliance (MSDN AA) is designed to provide the easiest and most inexpensive way for universities to make the latest Microsoft developer tools, products, and technologies available in labs, classrooms, and on student PCs. MSDN AA is an annual membership program for departments teaching Science, Technology, Engineering, and Mathematics (STEM) courses. The membership provides a complete solution to keep academic labs, faculty, and students on the leading edge of technology.

Software available in the MSDN AA program is provided at no charge to adopting departments through the Wiley and Microsoft publishing partnership.

As a bonus to this free offer, faculty will be introduced to Microsoft's Faculty Connection and Academic Resource Center. It takes time and preparation to keep students engaged while giving them a fundamental understanding of theory, and the Microsoft Faculty Connection is designed to help STEM professors with this preparation by providing articles, curriculum, and tools that professors can use to engage and inspire today's technology students.

Contact your Wiley rep for details.

For more information about the MSDN Academic Alliance program, go to: **msdn.microsoft.com/academic/**

Note: Windows Server 2008, Windows 7, and Visual Studio can be downloaded from MSDN AA for use by students in this course.

ACKNOWLEDGMENTS

Taken together, the content, pedagogy, and assessment elements of *Networking Basics, Second Edition* offer the career-oriented student the most important aspects of the information technology field as well as ways to develop the skills and capabilities that current and future employers seek in the individuals they hire and promote. Instructors will appreciate its practical focus, conciseness, and real-world emphasis.

Special thanks are extended to Michael Goldner of ITT Technical Institute for acting as an academic adviser to the text. His careful review of the manuscript, significant contributions to the content, and assurance that the book reflects the most recent trends in Networking, were invaluable assets in our development of the manuscript. We also thank Carol Jankura and Thena Berry for all of their valuable contributions to the revision and hard work in preparing the manuscript for production.

We would especially like to thank the following reviewers for their feedback and suggestions during the text's development. Their advice on how to shape the second edition of *Networking Basics* into a solid learning tool that meets both their needs and those of their busy students is deeply appreciated:

- Debra Taylor, Forsyth Technical Community College
- Donald McCracken, Kaplan University
- Kin Lam, Medgar Evers College
- Shahed Mustafa, DeVry College of New York
- Mark J. Puig, Chippewa Valley Technical College
- Patrick Seeling, University of Wisconsin—Stevens Point
- Andrei Szabo, Queensborough Community College—CUNY

BRIEF CONTENTS

CONTENTS

NETWORKING FUNDAMENTALS

What Do You Already Know?

- What is a network?
- Where did the Internet come from?

For additional questions and to assess you current knowledge of networking fundamentals, go to **www.wiley.com/go/ciccarelli/ networkingbasics2e.**

What You Will Find Out	What You Will Be Able To Do
1.1 The roots of networking and why it is important.	Trace the development of PC networks and the Internet.
1.2 The network models commonly in use today, their components, and how they are structured.	Describe the different network models and components.
1.3 How data is transferred within networks.	Identify communication components and protocols used in a network.
1.4 The different types of networks.	Understand the differences in the different types of networks commonly in use today.
1.5 What networking may look like in the future.	Recognize the trends that are changing the way businesses and organizations use networking technologies.

INTRODUCTION

There was a time, not that long ago, when networked personal computers (PCs) were the exception. Now, not only have networks become the rule for business, home networks have also become common. Why? In short, networks, which consist of computers connected together so that they can communicate, enhance both business and personal productivity by enabling users to share resources.

In this chapter, we first explore the reasons behind the growth of networks, with a quick look at the roots of PC networks and the Internet, and some of the advantages and disadvantages of networks. Then you'll learn some fundamental network concepts, including the basic components of a network, the roles that different network devices play, and the two primary network models in use today. Next, you'll be introduced to the topic of data communications and protocols. The chapter then turns to a discussion of the three main types of networks you'll likely encounter, and concludes with a look at some of the major trends that will impact the future of networking.

1.1 UNDERSTANDING THE NEED FOR NETWORKS

Network
Computers connected in such a way that they can communicate with each other.

Dumb Terminal
A **dumb terminal** is effectively a screen, a keyboard, and a box having only enough computing power to receive, send, and display text and graphics with all data storage, processing, and control occurring at the mainframe.

Server
A **server** is a computer that stores and provides resources, data, and services to the network.

Modern **networks** grew out of what has been referred to as "mainframe sensibilities." Many of the earliest network designers and developers came from a mainframe background. In a traditional mainframe computer environment, like the one shown in Figure 1-1, **dumb terminals** connect to a central mainframe computer.

A PC network is similar in that the computers are electronically connected. Most networks have one or more specialized computers, called **servers** that act somewhat like the central mainframe. The biggest difference is that PCs are smart terminals that have their own processing and memory.

1.1.1 Network Roots

To understand the need for a PC network, we need to take a closer look at its roots. Mainframe computers brought computers from the realm of government-only to businesses, though only the biggest business could afford to take advantage.

The introduction of the PC resulted in a revolution in how businesses, and eventually homes, operated. The PC brought computers to small business and to the individual user. However, information technology (IT) professionals coming from a mainframe background saw some fundamental problems. PCs represented isolated pockets of data and made sharing information difficult for users. They also saw them as a potential security risk, because anyone who has physical access to the computer has access to its data.

Figure 1-1

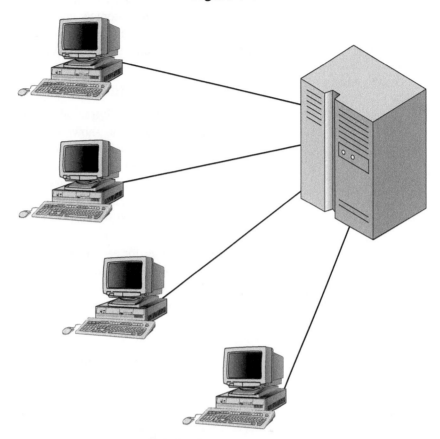

A mainframe computer and terminals.

TIPS FROM THE PROFESSIONALS

Going Full Circle

The need for shared communication has continued to evolve, and in some ways we have come full circle. Modern Cloud computing is similar to the old mainframe and dumb terminals used prior to PC networking. Cloud computing has data and applications stored on the "Nebulous Web" via Web service providers who provide everything from simple file storage to Software As A Service (SaaS) and computation using large Super Computers.

The term *Cloud* comes from the symbol used in network diagrams to represent the Internet. For users, Cloud computing provides convenient, on-demand network access to a shared pool of configurable resources, without the need for expensive or complicated physical and logical network architectural infrastructure.

The first PC networks grew out of a desire to resolve these problems. They provided for shared storage, and in most cases centralized storage, enabling information sharing. Most also had centralized security as a way to limit access to authorized personnel only.

1.1.2 Network Benefits

A network, for our purposes, is a set of PCs and other devices connected so that they can communicate, as shown in Figure 1-2. The biggest benefit of PC networks is that they facilitate resource sharing. Primary among these shared resources is shared data, making sharing information and working together easy for network users. In fact, for most business networks, the original justification was consolidating and sharing data.

Network resources start with data, but they don't end there. Networks also let users share hardware resources, such as printers, so that you don't need a separate printer for each user, which has been a driving factor for both business and home networks. Another shared resource that has become more important in recent years, and is often the primary reason for home networks, is sharing a high-speed Internet connection.

Figure 1-2

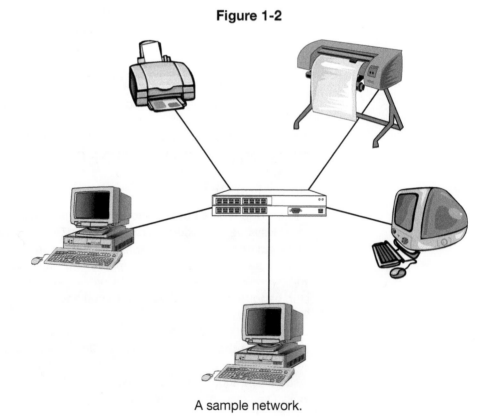

A sample network.

Networks are also a communication and support tool. Most businesses would be lost without e-mail, and in many cases e-mail is implemented internally as a network resource. Most operating systems also have utilities to enable remote troubleshooting and even remote control of computers.

Other PC network benefits relate to security. Most networks have built in **authentication mechanisms.** Most networks rely on usernames and passwords for authentication, but others use advanced methods, even biometric devices that authenticate a user based on physical features such as fingerprint or retinal scan.

Authentication mechanisms
Authentication mechanisms are ways that the network can validate who is and who isn't allowed access to the network.

Not only does security control who can access the computer, it also lets you manage what a user can do after he or she connects to the network. This includes access to shared data and resources, but also who can make changes to computer configurations or install new software.

1.1.3 Network Concerns

The network's greatest benefit is also its greatest potential concern. Sharing information can be a dangerous thing, if it gets to the wrong person. Business plans, materials costs, or customer lists, in the wrong hands, can be devastating. Personal information in the wrong hands can lead to identity theft. If you are going to have a network, you have to protect it.

Maintenance and support are also concerns. Networks require ongoing support and regular maintenance, which includes both network hardware and software. It means keeping the network up-to-date and running and fixing problems as they occur. Networks have given rise to a new job category, that of **network administrator,** who perform such tasks as insuring that data is backed up on a regular basis, because losing a computer that holds everyone's shared files can be much more serious than losing a single computer's data.

Network administrator
A **network administrator** is an IT expert specializing in the upkeep and support of networks.

That brings us right back around to security. The security tools available depend on the type of network. Part of network maintenance includes reviewing and maintaining security. **Wired networks** have different issues than **wireless networks.** Different network models and different networking products have different ways of implementing security. Knowing what is available and what is applicable to your situation is critical so you can put it to use.

Wired networks
Wired networks consist of PCs and servers, which are physically connected by cables.

Wireless networks
Wireless networks use radio transmission instead of cables to communicate.

1.1.4 The Internet

The Internet plays a key role in many modern networking configurations. A case could be made that the Internet is one of the most important developments in the history of both information systems and communication systems. It has also been a breeding ground for the design and development of new information and communication technologies, with many PC network innovations tracing their roots directly to the Internet.

The Internet is essentially a network of networks using a common communication protocol, Internet Protocol (IP). In 1969 the U.S. Department of Defense started the Internet as a network of four computers called ARPANET. By 1987, the U.S. Internet joined to its Canadian equivalent and supported approximately 11,000 servers. That number grew to nearly 200,000 servers by the end of 1989. In the early 1990s, most of the individual country networks were linked together into one worldwide network of networks. By the end of 1992, more than 1 million servers were on the Internet.

Originally, commercial traffic was forbidden on the Internet. That changed in the early 1990s, allowing commercial networks to begin offering commercial online services. Commercial growth quickly overshadowed the traditional government, university, and research use of the Internet. In 1994, the U.S. and Canadian governments stopped funding their few remaining circuits and turned them over to commercial firms. No one knows exactly how large the Internet has become, but estimates suggest more than 500 million computers and 1 billion people are on the Internet.

Today, the Internet serves as the world's largest portal to information, commerce, and entertainment.

IN THE REAL WORLD

Running Out of Addresses

For the past two decades computer networks have used the Internet Protocol version 4 addressing scheme to identify computers on the Internet. That system had a total of two to the power of 32, or four billion two hundred ninety-four million nine hundred sixty-seven thousand two hundred ninety-six (4,294,967,296), addresses. We have exhausted that supply, and according to the Internet Assigned Numbers Authority (IANA), the organization responsible for the global coordination of the DNS Root, IP addressing, and other Internet protocol resources. On February 1, 2011, the IANA allocated two blocks of IPv4 addresses to APNIC, Asia's regional Internet registry (RIR). At the same time, it was agreed that the five remaining IPv4 address blocks would be divided amongst the RIRs, which means that IANA's stock of IPv4 addresses is now exhausted. We are now moving to the IPv6 addressing system, which has two to the 128th power or the equivalent of enough addresses for almost every grain of sand on the earth.

SELF-CHECK

1. List two benefits of modern networks.
2. How are PC networks similar to older mainframe networks? How are they different?
3. Why is security for PC networks a concern?
4. What are some of the access control methods used to protect networked information?

Apply Your Knowledge   How would you use biometrics to improve security of a computer network?

Project 1.1

Understanding the basic networking standards, including the OSI, DoD, and Internet networking models is important. These models provide common terms for describing network operations and ways of describing and comparing network components.

Complete **Project 1.1: Understanding Key Concepts** in the online Network Basics Project Manual.

This project reviews common networking terms and terms relating to standards.

1.2   UNDERSTANDING NETWORK BASICS

Networks are used to make work and communication more efficient. A network connects computers, but can also connect other devices such as shared printers, removable media drives, scanners, and other equipment. In order to understand networks and how they work, you need to start with the basics.

1.2.1 Understanding Networks

Node
A **node** is a uniquely identifiable device.

Networks enable people to share resources, including printers, hard disks, and applications, which can greatly reduce the costs of providing these resources to each person in a company. Networks are built around this idea, connecting shared sources resources to their consumers. Several terms are used to describe these network devices, including hosts, nodes, workstations, peers, servers, and clients. Any device capable of communicating on the network is also referred to generically as a **node.**

NETWORKING FACT
PEERS VS. CLIENTS AND SERVERS
Peer-to-peer networks are non-centralized networks made up of connected stand-alone computers that simply share communications.   Client/server networks most closely resemble the older mainframe networks in that a central server provides data storage, resource access, and services to the client computers connected to the network.

1.2.2 Understanding Network Components

Network system
The path over which servers and clients communicate.

A typical network like the one in Figure 1-3 has three basic hardware components: one or more servers or host computers (including microcomputers and mainframes), clients (PCs), and a circuit or **network system,** which is the path over which they communicate. The term *cable plant* is becoming

Figure 1-3

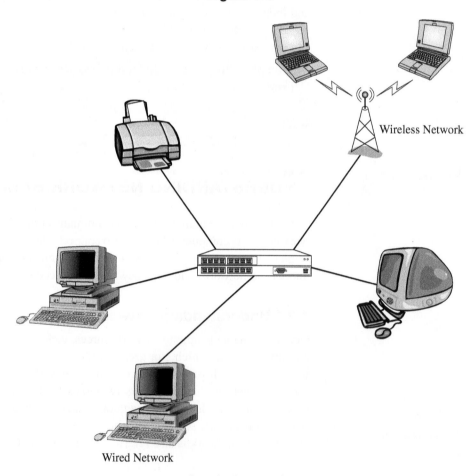

Wireless Network

Wired Network

A typical network.

less descriptive of the network transmission media (the media carrying the network signal), however, with the increasing popularity of wireless networks. In addition, servers and clients also need special-purpose network software that enables them to communicate.

The server stores data and software that the clients can access. You can have several servers working together over the network with client computers to support the business application. The client is the input–output hardware device at the user's end of a communication circuit. It provides users with access to the network, the data and software on the server, and other shared resources.

Strictly speaking, a network does not need a computer designated specifically as a server. Most modern client computers are designed to support the dual roles of both client and server, sharing resources to the network and, at the same time, accessing resources from the network.

The circuit (cable plant or transmission media) is the pathway through which the data or information travels. Traditional wired networks typically use copper wire, although **fiber-optic** cable and wireless transmission hybrid systems are common. There are also devices in the circuit that perform special functions such as hubs, switches, routers, bridges, and gateways.

1.2.3 Recognizing Network Device Roles

Figure 1-4 shows a small network that has four client PCs and three specialized server PCs connected by a hub or switch and cables that make up the circuit. In this network, messages move through the hub to and from the computers. All computers share the same circuit and take turns sending messages.

Each computer, client, or server has a **network adapter,** or **network interface card (NIC).** In the case of a wireless network, the network adapter sends and receives radio frequency messages, not that different from a walkie-talkie or cell phone. The network adapter also determines the low-level protocol used by the computer to communicate on the network. Network adapters running on one **protocol** cannot communicate with network adapters running on a different protocol. High-level protocols, implemented and managed through software, control functions such as how computers recognize each other and how messages are formatted. We discuss protocols more in Section 1.3.

In older networks, **hubs** are used as central points where the cables leading out to network PCs come together. A hub is simply a connection point that does not provide any sophisticated control. In current networks, you are more likely to see a **switch** rather than a hub. From the outside, both look much the same, but a switch is a more sophisticated communication device that helps control and manage the data passing between the PCs.

Figure 1-4 also shows a **router.** The router enables computers on one network to communicate with computers on other networks, but at the same

Fiber-optic
Fiber-optic cables consist of thin transparent plastic or glass fibers that transmit information using light (laser) signals.

Network adapter
A **network adapter** is the hardware that enables a computer to connect to a network.

Network interface card (NIC)
Network interface card is another name for a network adapter.

Protocols
Protocols define the way in which devices communicate on a network, things like signal strength and format.

Hub
A connection device that allows multiple connections to the network.

Switch
A connection device similar to a hub but more sophisticated, including functionality that allows it to control and manage data transmissions.

Router
A **router** is a device that connects two or more networks.

Figure 1-4

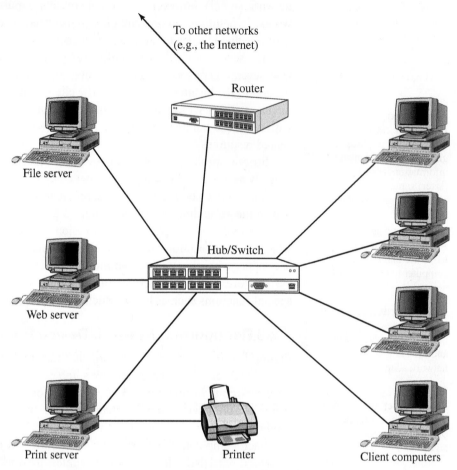

To other networks
(e.g., the Internet)

Router

Hub/Switch

File server

Web server

Print server

Printer

Client computers

An example network.

Gateway
A connection device that is used to connect networks and devices that would not otherwise be able to communicate with each other.

time provide a level of isolation between the networks. Routers are a key part of the Internet, which is, at its core, a massive set of interconnected networks. A **gateway** is used to connect dissimilar networks and devices. For example, a gateway can be used to connect PCs on a LAN to a mainframe computer.

Bridge
A device used to connect two or more physical networks.

Like routers, **bridges** connect a network to other networks. Bridges do not provide the same level of isolation as routers, but can be used in some situations where routers cannot be used. Another device, called a **brouter,** combines the functionality of a bridge and router in the same device.

Brouter
A connection device that transmits both routable information, such as protocols, and non-routable information, such as data.

1.2.4 Recognizing Network Models and Software

The two basic network models are called the client/server and peer-to-peer models. Physically, little differentiates the two. From the information you have so far, the network in Figure 1-4 could follow either model.

Client/server network
A network model that connects multiple PCs, called clients, to a single computer, called a server, which distributes data and resources to the network.

Directory services network
In a **directory services network**, everything on the network, including users, computers, and shared resources, are maintained in a centralized directory.

Peer-to-peer network
A **peer-to-peer network** is a small network in which individual PCs are connected directly to one another without the use of separate servers.

Workgroups
Workgroups is the term that Microsoft uses to refer to peer-to-peer networked computers.

Peer server
Peer server refers to the PCs in a peer-to-peer network that act as both client and server.

Client operating system
A **client operating system** is the control program installed on the client PC.

Server operating system
The control program installed on the server, also known as a network operating system.

A **client/server network** is the model that most closely matches the mainframe network model. One or more computers are designated as servers, providing resources to the network. The rest of the computers are clients, consuming those resources. The identifying feature of a client/server network is that you have centralized control over network security. Clients, or more accurately, the user working at the client, must be authenticated and allowed access to the network. You can also control the resources to which the user has access, as well as the level of access. For example, some users might be able to read from or write to a server, while other users can only read data.

An enhancement that grew out of the traditional client/server network is the **directory services network.** These networks are designed to make managing today's rapidly growing networks that can include hundreds or even thousands of clients, servers, and network users, easier. Copies of the directory are usually maintained on multiple servers to provide redundancy in case of failure and to optimize network performance.

In a **peer-to-peer network,** you still have shared resources, but you don't have centralized control over access to the network or its resources. Also, peer-to-peer networks are, by design, small. Microsoft recommends that peer-to-peer networks, also known as **workgroups,** be limited to no more than twelve nodes. In a peer-to-peer network, the network client computers act both as clients and as servers and are sometimes referred to as **peer servers.** Individual users control what is made available to the network and the level of access allowed. A possible point of confusion is that computers can be running a server operating system, such as Windows 2000 Server, but the network can still be configured as a peer-to-peer network with the server operating system implemented in a peer server role.

1.2.5 Understanding Servers and Clients

You might find taking a little closer look at servers more useful. The basic difference between clients (which include peer servers) and servers is the software that they run. Clients, as you might guess, run a **client operating system.** It enables them to access the network and in most current versions, to act as a peer server. Common client operating systems include Microsoft Windows XP, Windows Vista, and Windows 7.

Servers run what is called either a **server operating system** or **network operating system.** Either one enables the computer to act as a server, by running the software necessary for central security management. Server operating systems typically include a client interface and can be used like a network client, if necessary. Familiar examples are Windows Server systems such as Windows 2003 Server and Windows Server 2008, as well as most Linux versions. Some older network operating systems enabled a computer to operate in the role of server only. The only interface provided was one for server configuration and network management. The best-known example of this type of server operating system is Novell's NetWare.

Understanding that peer servers are not limited to peer-to-peer networks is important. You can deploy peer servers on client/server and directory services–based networks to provide additional resources, shared drives or files, and even web services. For example, you might configure client computers with attached printers as peer servers acting as print servers.

IN THE REAL WORLD

The Growing Role of Networks

New computers are now built with the network in mind. For instance, a network adapter is now considered standard computer hardware and in most cases integrated into the computer. Furthermore, all current PC operating systems have client software, and usually built-in server software components, as a critical part of the operating system.

Portable (laptop and notebook) computers take this a step further. Not only do laptops have a built-in wired network adapter, nearly all new laptops also come with a wireless network adapter, giving you an option of connecting to either type of network. Some also include a telephone modem, which is the device that lets a computer communicate over standard dial-up telephone lines.

Another innovation is the inclusion of a webcam or forward-facing camera in most laptop computers and more recently in many smart cell phones allowing for video communications via Voice over IP (VoIP). Many messaging programs such as Yahoo Messenger, Windows Live, and Skype take advantage of the enhanced communication system.

Another indispensable part of this evermore connected environment is the Internet. The desire to connect to the Internet, which is a massive (and primarily PC-based) network, has been a major factor in PC, Tablet, and smart phone sales. If you have any doubt of the Internet's influence, think about this question. When was the last time you saw an advertisement for a business or service that didn't include the address of its website?

SELF-CHECK

1. Compare the roles of network clients and network servers.
2. How is a router used in a network?
3. Compare the client/server, directory services, and peer-to-peer network models.

Apply Your Knowledge Describe how you use your computer at home. Do you have more than one computer? Are they interconnected? Do you have an Internet Service Provider (ISP) and broadband Internet?

Project 1.2

An important part of understanding network fundamentals is the ability to recognize common network components.

Low-level protocol
A system of rules for how network connection is achieved.

Complete **Project 1.2: Identifying Basic Components** in the online Network Basics Project Manual. Use the drawing from Project 1.2 as a guide to draw a representation of your own home or business network.

1.3 UNDERSTANDING DATA COMMUNICATIONS

Token ring
A network method in which packets of data were passed around a network from PC to PC until the packet reached its intended destination. Although outdated in copper wired networks, a variation of the Token Ring protocol is used as the principal protocol in Fiber Distributed Data Interface (FDDI) networks.

ARCNET
An acronym for Attached Resource Computer Network. ARCNET is an outdated networking protocol that was used in the 1980s for office automation tasks.

Ethernet
A protocol defining the wired connections within a network.

Data communications is the movement of computer information from one point to another by means of electrical or optical transmission systems. This is in contrast to the broader term *telecommunications*, which includes the transmission of voice and video (images and graphics) as well as data and usually implies longer distances. The line between the two has tended to blur in recent years, with telecommunications often a key part of data communications. Data communications networks facilitate more efficient use of computers and improve the day-to-day control of a business by providing faster information flow. They also provide message transfer services to allow computer users to talk to one another via electronic mail, chat, and video streaming.

1.3.1 Low-Level Protocols

Low-level protocols control the physical process of data communication. The first network protocols were **Token Ring, ARCNET,** and **Ethernet.** Each protocol used a different method for computers to access the network, and computers using one protocol could not (and still cannot) communicate directly with computers using a different protocol. The protocols also have an addressing method that ensures that each computer on the network is uniquely identifiable. This address is coded into the network adapter and known as a Media Access Control (MAC) address.

The most significant of the three protocols was (and is) Ethernet. Robert Metcalf, then a graduate student at Harvard University, first drew the concept for Ethernet on a piece of paper as part of his PhD thesis. Today, Ethernet is the most widely used access method for computer networks.

1.3.2 High-Level Protocols

High-level protocol
The rules for how data is transferred from one device to another.

Addressing
How computers identify and recognize each other on a network.

Handshaking
The process used by computers for establishing a connection to each other.

Connection
The process of having two computers recognize each other and open a communication channel.

High-level protocols operate at the software level and control things such as message formatting, which is how messages are broken up into smaller pieces known as packets for transmission and then reassembled at the other end. They control **addressing** and **handshaking,** two processes in establishing a **connection** between computers. Establishing a connection looks something like starting a conversation by placing a telephone call to another person.

Over the years, a number of higher-level protocols were developed (see Table 1-1), which led to some confusion and problems in getting different computers to communicate with each other. Apple computers used their own proprietary protocol, known as AppleTalk, on its networks. For several years, Novell exclusively used another protocol, known as IPX/SPX on its networks with the PC client software providing IPX/SPX support. Microsoft originally used a limited protocol known as NetBEUI, but early on realized that to grow, Windows needed broader-based communication support and began including its own AppleTalk and IPX/SPX compatible protocols as part of the operating system.

The Internet was based from the beginning on a different protocol, Transmission Control Protocol/Internet Protocol (TCP/IP), which is actually a suite of different protocols, each supporting different communication roles. In the last several years, however, TCP/IP has become the de facto standard for all computer networking applications, including PC networks. Current versions of Microsoft Windows and Novell NetWare both default

Table 1-1: High-level protocols

Protocol	Description
AppleTalk	Apple Computer proprietary protocol. This protocol is no longer in use.
IPX/SPX	Novell proprietary protocol, originally required on NetWare networks.
NetBEUI	Protocol originally used by MS-DOS and Windows network software.
TCP/IP	Protocol suite developed for use on the Internet and currently used on the Internet and PC networks, including Windows, Linux, and NetWare networks.

to installing TCP/IP as the only protocol in use on computers running their operating systems. Linux, on the other hand, has used TCP/IP since its inception.

A word of warning when discussing a TCP/IP network—in TCP/IP terms, a router is called a *gateway*. Because of this, when discussing network devices, you need to understand the network protocol used on the network and the context in which the term is used.

IN THE REAL WORLD

How Protocols Work Together

Like so many other computer-related terms, the exact definition of the term *protocol* depends on its context. Are you taking about a low-level protocol or a high-level protocol, what's the difference, and why does it matter? As you have learned, low-level protocols handle the physical communication process. You can think, then, of high-level protocols handling the logical communication process.

To get a general idea of how they work, look at a relatively simple example. You want to retrieve a file from a file server. To do so, you have to locate the file server on the network, establish a connection with the file server, request the file, accept it from the server, and then close the connection when finished.

The whole process is handled through a series of standard messages, defined by the different protocols used to communicate. Each of these messages is routed through the computer to the network adapter where it is converted into an electronic signal as shown in Figure 1-5.

Figure 1-5

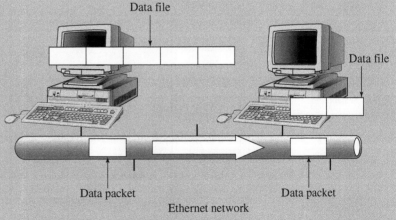

Network communication.

(continued)

IN THE REAL WORLD　　*(continued)*

The computer at the other end receives the electronic signal and converts it back into data that the computer can recognize and use. Actually, every computer will see the data, but all of the computers except the destination computer (identified through a unique address) will ignore the data.

High- and low-level protocols exist at different layers of the OSI network model. Figure 1-6 details the interconnections between those layers. We will discuss the OSI model in more detail in Chapter 2.

Part of the problem is that the blocks of data, known as packets, that can be sent between the computers are a specific size limit, defined by the low-level protocol used. There is also a limit set by the high-level protocol, which will be no larger than the low-level protocol's physical limit. To get around this, the high-level protocol breaks the data, the file in this case, into pieces small enough for transmission and formats them with all of the control information needed before passing them to the network adapter. It also numbers the packets so that the receiving system knows the proper order and can reassemble them back into the original file.

Figure 1-6

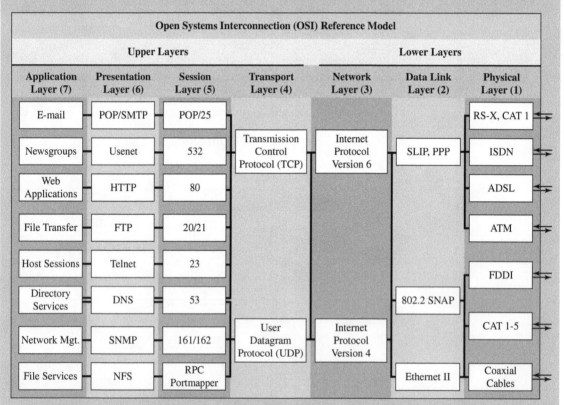

The Open Systems Interconnect Model (OSI).

SELF-CHECK

1. Define data communications.
2. How have newer systems taken advantage of the merging of data communications and telecommunications?
3. Compare the role of low-level and high-level protocols.

Apply Your Knowledge Why do you think Microsoft abandoned its original network communications protocols of NetBEUI in favor of the TCP/IP protocol suite?

Project 1.3

Open the Command Prompt window on your computer (on a Windows computer, click Start > Run.)

Type "cmd" and click OK.

After you have the command prompt window up, type "ipconfig /all" and press Enter.

Record all the information it provides.

1.4 COMPARING TYPES OF NETWORKS

The four main categories of networks are:

- **Local Area Network (LAN):** It's a relatively small network of computers, printers, and other devices in a single building or floor.
- **Campus Area Network (CAN):** A network spanning multiple LANs but smaller than a MAN, such as on a university or local business campus.
- **Metropolitan Area Network (MAN):** It's a high-speed internetwork of LANs across a metropolitan area.
- **Wide Area Network (WAN):** It traditionally connects LANs using the public switched telephone network, but more commonly connects through the Internet.

Significant differences exist among local, campus, metropolitan, and wide area networks. In addition to covering different sized geographic areas, they have varying installation and support costs associated with them.

Devices used in LANs can be relatively inexpensive and easy to maintain. Larger networks require more sophisticated networking equipment and additional support. The investment in a MAN or WAN is not only based on installation and equipment costs, but also on the costs of long-term support and on-site administration. Most larger networks require at least one full-time, on-site administrator plus additional support staff. In many cases, a single person handles all LAN-related issues. Often, in very small offices, one person may take on the responsibilities of network support in addition to his or her regular work. Other small- to medium-size offices hire consultants to provide technical support they cannot provide themselves.

In addition to these network types, working in something of a supporting role, are backbone networks. These provide a high-bandwidth path for communicating between networks. There are also network technologies implemented as part of these networks and based on technologies developed initially for the Internet.

In fact, the Internet has led to the demise of many traditional backbone networks. Today, because of the easy access to the Internet and lower costs for high-bandwidth Internet access, companies can connect to remote or distant locations without spending lots of money. A person working on a small local network with Internet access can share documents and files with people all over the planet, and access servers at distant locations. The global reach of the Internet allows this kind of connectivity without the high cost of installation and support associated with private wide area networks. Security is provided through use of **virtual private networks (VPNs).**

Virtual private network (VPN)
A private communication path over the public Internet acting as a secure encrypted network within a larger or public network.

1.4.1 Local Area Network (LAN)

Local area networks (LANs) play an important part in the everyday functioning of schools, businesses, and government. LANs save people time, lower equipment costs by centralizing printers and other resources, and allow sensitive information to remain in a secure location. Recently, LANs have been used as tools to improve collaboration between employees and for job training using audio and video.

A LAN connects computers and other network devices so that the devices can communicate with each other to share resources. Devices on a wired LAN are connected using inexpensive cable. Due to limitations in distance, performance, and manageability, a LAN is usually confined to a single office or floor of a building. In Figure 1-7, several computers are connected via a cable to a hub/switch. The lines from the computers to the hub/switch are the cables that allow data transmissions to pass from one computer to the others.

Many new local area networks are being installed using wireless technologies. Wireless LANs allow users to connect to network resources without the need for cabling or wiring. Computers can be configured to communicate directly with each other so that no other connectivity equipment is required. More commonly, wireless networks use an **access point (AP),** which acts as a central access point (working similar to a hub or switch) and can also connect a wireless network to a wired network.

Access Point (AP)
A designated point of entry within a network where wireless devices send and receive transmissions.

Figure 1-7

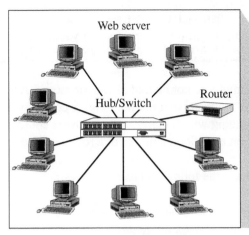

Local area network (LAN) at the Records Building— one node
of the McClellan Air Force Base backbone network.

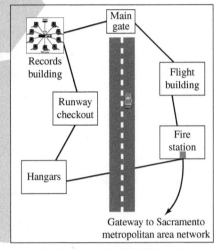

Backbone network at the McClellan Air
Force Base—one node of the Sacramento
metropolitan area network (MAN).

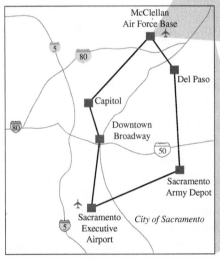

Metropolitan area network (MAN) in Sacramento—
one node of the wide area network (WAN).

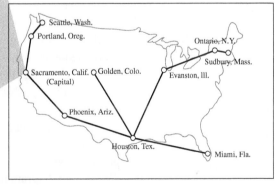

Wide area network (WAN) showing Sacramento
connected to nine other cities throughout the U.S.

Comparing network types.

A company network might be configured as one or more LANs, depending on the size of the company and the building. A company that is located in a multistory building with hundreds of employees could have a LAN on each floor. Between each floor, a bridge or a router is used to connect the LANs.

Local area networks have the following characteristics:

- They are used within small areas (such as in an office building).
- They offer high-speed communication—typically 100Mbps or faster.
- They provide access for many devices.
- They use LAN-specific equipment such as hubs, switches, and network interface cards.

1.4.2 Campus Area Networks

IN ACTION:
NETWORKING
AT HOME

Many people are installing Home Area Networks (HANs), which are effectively identical to LANs. These networks allow home users to connect a variety of electronic devices such as computers, peripherals, telephones, video games, TVs, "smart" appliances (computerized devices), and home security systems. They also let all of these computers and devices share a single Internet connection.

A campus area network (CAN), sometimes called a Corporate Area Network, is a computer network connecting several LANs within a building or small geographical area such as a university campus or corporate park. A CAN is larger than a LAN but smaller than a metropolitan area network (MAN).

1.4.3 Metropolitan Area Networks

A metropolitan area network (MAN) is made up of LANs that are interconnected across a city or metropolitan area, typically spanning up to 75 miles, like the one shown in Figure 1-7. MANs are popular as a way of allowing local governments to share valuable resources, communicate with one another, and provide a large-scale private phone service. MANs are also appealing to fairly large regional businesses that want to connect their offices for the same reasons. Although MANs are very expensive to implement, they offer a high-speed alternative to the slower connections often found in WANs because of the MANs' higher-performance cable plant and equipment.

Backbone network
A large central network.

Traditional MANs connect through a **backbone network (BN).** A BN can be used to connect LANs to form MANs, but can also connect other BNs, MANs, and even WANs. BNs typically span up to several miles and provide high-speed communication, commonly up to 100 to 1,000 Mbps. The second diagram in Figure 1-7 shows a BN near Sacramento, California that connects the LANs located in several buildings at McClellan Air Force Base.

Figure 1-8

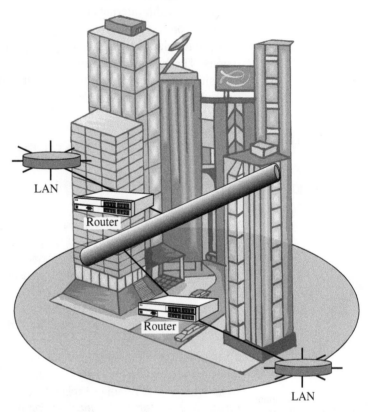

MAN connections.

Figure 1-8 takes a closer look at MAN configuration. The LANs are standard LANs with a router used to connect to the MANs, typically with just one connection to each site. Creating a new MAN connection requires purchasing or leasing existing cables from a telecommunications company (the least-expensive option) or having new cables installed, which can cost hundreds of thousands of dollars. MANs can also use shared space on fiber-optic lines.

MAN networks have the following characteristics:

- Sites are dispersed across a city and perhaps the surrounding area as well.
- With the advent of MANs, historically slow connections (56Kbps–1.5Mbps) have given way to communication at hundreds of megabits per second and even gigabit speeds.
- They provide single points of connection between each LAN.
- They use devices such as routers, telephone switches, and microwave antennas as parts of their communication infrastructure.

In recent years, there has been a tendency toward linking LANs through high-bandwidth Internet connections instead of building or buying MANs. Another option you sometimes see for MAN connectivity is leasing space on communications satellites, such as those used for satellite TV transmissions. The biggest problem with this option is that connections can be sensitive to weather conditions, with the connection becoming degraded or even lost during heavy rains.

IN THE REAL WORLD

Choosing Your CAN Connection

Once upon a time universities and large corporations had only a few options for their campus-wide network connections. They could work with a regional carrier or local telephone company, or they could lease expensive dedicated lines and connection equipment. That meant working with only one available vendor who had few restrictions on the rates it charged for hooking up networks.

Things have changed. Within the United States and most developed countries, multiple communication carriers, including public and private telephone companies, data communication companies, and cable providers are competing for your business. In most cases, you are no longer required to purchase or lease your connection equipment from your carrier. The benefit of this competition is lower costs for communication lines and connection equipment. The drawback is that you no longer have a single vendor when you have problems, which is why universities and corporations all have their own information technology department with their own network administrators.

This competition has helped drive down the cost of using the Internet and the creation of an **Intranet** for private use within the organization.

Note that Internet Service Providers (ISPs) are happy to lease the bandwidth, and the connection is made using stable, established, and well-understood technologies. When problems arise, most ISPs are willing to provide diagnostic and troubleshooting assistance, though sometimes at an added cost.

Intranet
A private internal computer network that uses Internet Protocol technology to securely share part or all of an organization's information with its authorized users. It often consists of a web interface used to distribute notices, announcements, and appropriate internal proprietary information. (Discussed in Section 1.4.4)

Long-haul transmission lines
Telephone cables or other communications methods within a wide area network used to transmit over long distances.

Regional carriers
Regional telephone companies.

1.4.4 Wide Area Networks

A wide area network (WAN) interconnects two or more LANs or MANs. Traditionally, a LAN becomes a WAN when it connects across the public telephone network often using lines leased from local telephone companies. These connections involve lines known as **long-haul transmission lines** because they are designed to carry traffic over long distances and require coordinating services from multiple **regional carriers.** They can also be connected through fiber-optic cabling or, less frequently, wireless technologies. WAN connections run over telephone cables because they cover a wide geographical area—they may span cities, states, or even continents.

FOR EXAMPLE

LOOK AT FIGURE 1-7

Figure 1-7 shows how LANs, MANs, CANs, and WANs differ. Look at the lower right image and notice how the sample WAN connects to nine cities across the continental United States.

Interconnecting LANs and MANs over great distances, often crossing both land and water, requires a lot of coordination and sophisticated equipment. In most cases, local telephone companies provide the physical cable connection. When connections are required across the globe, telecommunications companies usually provide satellite connectivity.

The majority of WANs communicate at speeds between 56 Kbps and 1.5 Mbps, although speeds up to 9.953 Gbps are available. At one time, WANs were considered low-speed connections, but this is rapidly changing as the availability of high-bandwidth connections increase and the associated costs drop.

WANs have the following characteristics:

- They can cover a very large geographical area—even span the world.
- They usually communicate at slower speeds (compared to LANs).
- Access to the WAN is limited—a LAN usually has only one WAN link that is shared by multiple devices.
- They use devices such as routers, modems, and WAN switches, connectivity devices specific to LANs and used to connect to long-haul transmission media.

By connecting many LANs using WANs, organizations enable their users to share information. WAN links are how the Internet was created and continue to make up the Internet today. Ironically, the Internet has been replacing more traditional connection methods, especially in new WAN implementations.

1.4.5 Internet Technologies

Technologies developed for the Internet have been a major evolutionary factor in how LANs are implemented and used. Two common terms are intranets and extranets.

An intranet is a LAN that uses the same technologies as the Internet, such as using web servers like the one shown in Figure 1-9 to facilitate internal communications, but it's open to only those inside the organization. Sometimes it includes a mix of private and public access. For example,

Figure 1-9

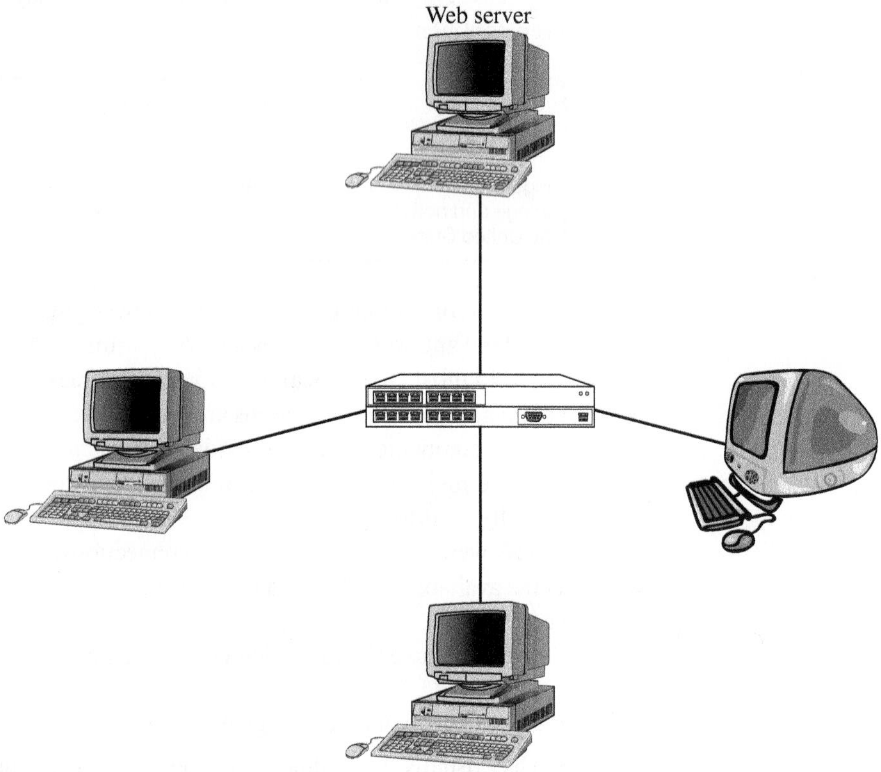

Web server

Intranet with Web server.

although some pages on a web server may be open to the public and accessible by anyone on the Internet, some pages may be on an intranet and therefore hidden from those who connect to the web server from the Internet at large. Sometimes an intranet uses a completely separate web server hidden from the Internet. The intranet for the Information Systems Department at Indiana University, for example, provides information on faculty expense budgets, class scheduling for future semesters, and discussion forums.

Extranet
A private network that allows for specific external users to access it over the Internet.

An **extranet** is similar to an intranet in that it, too, uses the same technologies as the Internet but instead is provided to invited users outside the organization who access the network from the Internet. It can provide access to information services, inventories, and other internal organizational databases that are provided only to customers, suppliers, or those who have paid for access. Typically, users are given passwords to gain access, but more sophisticated technologies such as smart cards or special software may also be required. Many universities provide extranets for web-based courses so that only those students enrolled in the course can access course materials and discussions.

IN THE REAL WORLD

Growing Your Network

The basic network types are not the only network configuration options. The truth is that network configurations are very flexible and a significant number of networks use some variation or combination of network types.

For example, a LAN is not necessarily a single, stand-alone network. They're usually described and drawn that way for simplicity's sake, but the key to describing a network as a LAN is the fact that it occupies a small geographic area.

Consider a situation where a company occupies both floors in the building shown in Figure 1-10. The most common configuration is to have each floor as a semi-autonomous network. A vertical backbone is used to connect the networks. A router on each floor is used to connect that floor's network to the backbone. The network configuration as a whole would be referred to as a routed LAN. It is definitely a

Figure 1-10

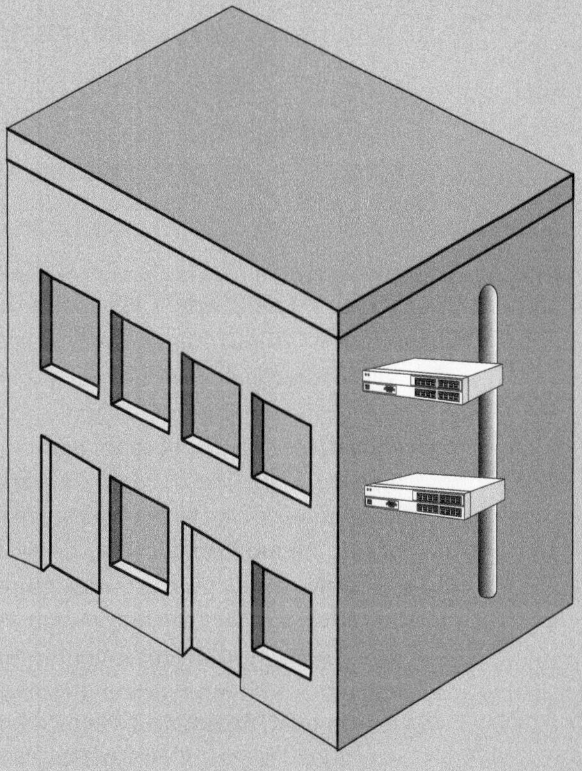

Vertical backbone.

(continued)

IN THE REAL WORLD   *(continued)*

LAN, given the very small geographic region involved, but routed to provide a level of isolation between the floors while still enabling them to communicate.

Unlike the backbone in a MAN, the company doesn't purchase the vertical backbone or lease it from a telecommunications company. Instead, the company installs it as part of its corporate network infrastructure. In many cases, the backbone is simply a fiber-optic cable run between the floors. The routers are designed to make one connection to a fiber-optic line and another to a wired network. By some definitions, the connection device would be called a brouter, rather than a router, but the term brouter is not commonly used in modern network descriptions. In some configurations the connection might be made with a bridge instead of a router.

SELF-CHECK

1. Compare characteristics of LANs, CANs, MANs, and WANs.

2. How are intranets and extranets similar? How are they different?

Apply Your Knowledge Can you identify any of these network types in your community? Describe it and explain how it fits into one of these models.

1.5 THE FUTURE OF NETWORKING

Network technologies continue to change and expand at an ever-increasing pace. New devices and technologies, such as tablet computers and smart phones, increase the need for networking methods with more flexibility and broader scope. The future of networking will be focused on virtualization, integration of new technologies, resource sharing, and greater efficiency in bandwidth usage to allow for faster data exchange.

Data communications and computer processing go hand in hand, but many feel that we have moved from the computer era to the communication era. As such, allowing communication across multiple platforms and between locations is becoming more and more critical for networking. Three major, interrelated trends driving the future of communications and networking are as follows: pervasive networking, integration of voice, video and data, and expanded information service.

1.5.1 Pervasive Networking

Pervasive networking means that communication networks will one day be everywhere; virtually any device will be able to communicate with any other device in the world. This is true in many ways today. To see this, you don't need to look any further than today's cell phones. **Smart phones,** such as the iPhone, Blackberry, and Android are essentially small PCs that allow network access through Bluetooth, wifi, and cellular networks. Not only can you place calls, you can browse the Web, check e-mail, and even check in with your PC. **Media players,** first designed as a replacement for portable tape or CD players, now support a full range of multimedia services. The boundary between your television tuner and computer is disappearing. Common household devices, including heating and cooling systems, windows, light switches, water heaters, heaters, and even appliances like dishwashers, are being designed so that a central computer can network with and control them.

Helping to drive this change is the rate of increase in data transmissions, or the available **bandwidth.** For example, in 1980, the capacity of a traditional telephone-based dial-up communication was about 300 bits per second (bps). By the 1990s, data was routinely transmitted at 9,600 bps, and by 2000, dial-up modems could transmit at 56 Kbps and digital subscriber line (DSL) at 1.5 Mbps over that same telephone line. Speeds in multiple Gigabyte per second (Gbps) ranges are available on the most recent DSL lines and through cable television carriers. Speeds of 10 Gbps wireless transmission are also promised in the near future. As speeds have gone up, the relative costs have gone down. A major benefactor has been the Internet, with ever-increasing Internet circuit bandwidths and subscriber connection speeds. In many regions, telephone and cable television companies are the primary **Internet service providers (ISPs),** the companies providing the doorway to the Internet.

Between 1980 and 2000, LAN and backbone technologies increased capacity from about 128 Kbps to 10 Mbps or 100 Mbps. Backbones are soon expected to routinely be running at 10 Gbps. The changes in WAN have been even more dramatic, from a typical rate of 56 Kbps in 1980 to 622 Mbps over a high-speed circuit in 2000, with most experts now predicting a high-speed WAN or Internet circuit able to carry 25 Tbps (25 terabits, or 25 trillion bits per second) in a few years, maybe even higher.

The term broadband communication has often been used to refer to these new high-speed communication circuits. **Broadband** is a signaling method that uses a wide range (or band) of frequencies. The wider (or broader) the bandwidth of a channel or frequency is, the greater the information-carrying capacity. *Broadband* is a relative term, but its true technical meaning has become overwhelmed by its use in the popular press to refer to high-speed circuits in general.

Smart phone
Any device capable of placing phone calls and advanced computing functions including web browsing, e-mail transmission, media playing, document viewing, and scheduling.

Media player
Small portable digital device used for playing audio and video files.

Bandwidth
The capacity on a given network for data transmission.

Internet service providers (ISPs)
Companies providing Internet access for a fee.

Broadband
Type of high-speed data transmission circuit.

1.5.2 The Integration of Voice, Video, and Data

A second key trend is the integration of voice, video, and data communication, sometimes called convergence. In the past, the telecommunications systems used to separately transmit video signals (such as cable TV), voice signals (primarily telephone calls), and data (including computer data and e-mail). One network was used for data, one for voice, and one for cable TV.

This practice began changing rapidly in the late 1990s. The integration of voice and data is largely complete in WANs. The carriers, such as AT&T, provide telecommunication services that support data and voice transmission over the same circuits, and hardware manufacturers provide the infrastructure needed to meet the changing definition of data. One of the fastest growing consumer and business service areas is the cable television industry, with cable service providers offering cable television, Internet access, and telephone service all over the same lines.

The integration of video, voice, and data was somewhat slower in LANs and local telephone services, but it's rapidly changing. Most companies have successfully integrated both on the same network, though some still lay two separate cable networks into offices, one for voice and one for computer access. Early roadblocks included legal restrictions and the bandwidth requirements for video.

1.5.3 New Information Services

A third key trend is the provision of new information services on these rapidly expanding networks. The Internet has changed the nature of computing so that now, anyone with a computer can be an information publisher. You can find information on virtually anything on the Internet. Never before in the history of the human race has so much knowledge and information been available to ordinary citizens. The challenges society faces as individuals and organizations are threefold:

- Assessing the accuracy and value of information
- Assimilating the information to determine its usefulness
- Using the information effectively

Application service providers (ASPs)
Companies that develop and sell applications that are used over the Internet.

Today many companies are beginning to use **application service providers (ASPs)** rather than developing their own computer systems. An ASP develops a specific system (for example, an airline reservation system or a payroll system), and a company purchases the service, without ever installing the system on its own computers. It uses the service the same way you might use a web hosting service to publish your own web pages rather than attempting to purchase and operate your own web server.

Information utilities
Companies that sell information services.

ASPs are now evolving into information utilities. An **information utility** is a company that provides a wide range of standardized information services, the same way that electric utilities today provide electricity or telephone utilities provide telephone service. Companies would simply purchase most of their information services (such as e-mail, Internet, accounting, payroll, and logistics) from these information utilities rather than attempting to develop their systems and operate their own servers. We are already starting to see some movement in this area with various services such as file transfer and storage and public e-mail already available.

IN THE REAL WORLD

Future Shock?

Not only are networking technologies changing rapidly, the rate of change is also increasing. One place you can see this change is the integration of voice and video in computer operating systems and in PC networks. It's visible when you purchase a new flat screen TV or Blu-Ray Player that has its own Internet connection. Companies such as NetFlix, Blockbuster, and Pandora stream movies and music directly to your television, computer, or smart phone. As a result, you can watch TV while you work, or connect your computer as your television tuner and video recorder.

Businesses use streaming video (video transmissions over the network) as an information tool and for employee training. Voice over IP (VoIP) equipment, the technical term for Internet-based telephone service, is both inexpensive and readily available from a wide variety of retailers, including chain discount stores. New smart phones and tablets have both a forward-facing and rear-facing camera, making the dream of video telephone calls a reality for the average consumer. For many companies and individual consumers, their ISP is also their telephone company. Most young people today no longer have a land line telephone. Their cell phone is literally their connection to the world.

All of the major news services now offer video clips along with traditional print stories, and many television networks let you watch recent programs that you may have missed on broadcast TV from their websites. You can purchase both audio and video files from commercial download services, including full-length theatrical movies. You can even distribute your own audio and video files through podcasts or social networking sites.

SELF-CHECK

1. Describe the process of convergence.

2. What is an information utility and how has it evolved?

3. What challenges do organizations face in relation to the information made available by the Internet?

Apply Your Knowledge   How has convergence and the use of VOIP changed the cost of long distance telephone communications?

SUMMARY

Section 1.1

- Many of the earliest network designers and developers came from a mainframe background.
- PC networks grew out of the need for information sharing.

Section 1.2

- Printers, hard disks, and applications can be shared.
- Any device capable of communicating on the network is also referred to generically as a node.

Section 1.3

- Low-level protocols control the physical process of data communication.

- High-level protocols operate at the software level.

Section 1.4

- A LAN connects computers and other network devices so that the devices can communicate with each other to share resources.
- A metropolitan area network (MAN) is made up of LANs that are interconnected across a city or metropolitan area.

Section 1.5

- Pervasive networking means that communication networks will one day be everywhere.
- The integration of voice, video, and data communication is called convergence.

ASSESS YOUR UNDERSTANDING

UNDERSTAND: WHAT HAVE YOU LEARNED?

 Go to **www.wiley.com/go/ciccarelli/networkingbasics2e** to evaluate your knowledge of transaction and locking support.

Measure your learning by comparing pre-test and post-test results.

SUMMARY QUESTIONS

1. Broadband includes a wide range of frequencies to increase the volume of data communication. True or false?

2. Which of the following refers to a network deployed in the smallest geographic area?

   (a) WAN
   (b) MAN
   (c) CAN
   (d) LAN

3. What is the primary shared resource on large PC networks?

   (a) Data
   (b) Audio speakers
   (c) Scanners
   (d) None of the above

4. A _____ is a device used to connect network devices like computers and printers.

   (a) Node
   (b) Router
   (c) Switch
   (d) Gateway

5. What is the device used to connect two or more LANs?

   (a) Node
   (b) Router
   (c) Hub
   (d) Server

6. Which network model does not support centralized security?

   (a) Client/server
   (b) Directory services
   (c) Peer-to-peer

7. Microsoft Internet Explorer is an example of a Web server. True or false?

8. What is distinctive about fiber-optic cable compared to other transmission media types?

   (a) It carries digital data.
   (b) It uses radio-frequency communication transmissions.
   (c) It contains copper wire.
   (d) It uses glass or plastic to carry the data signal.

9. What is the term used to refer to any uniquely identifiable device on a network?

   (a) Node
   (b) Host
   (c) Server
   (d) Gateway

10. What is the device that makes a physical connection between a computer and the network cable in a traditional wired network?

    (a) Switch
    (b) Network interface card
    (c) Brouter
    (d) Access point

11. What is the most commonly used low-level protocol on PC networks?

    (a) ARCNET
    (b) Token ring
    (c) Ethernet
    (d) NetBEUI

12. Which of the following is defined by a high-level protocol?

    (a) Physical connection to the network
    (b) Signal strength
    (c) Connection procedures
    (d) Cable plant structure

13. Which protocol is the de facto standard for PC networking?

    (a) IPX/SPX
    (b) AppleTalk
    (c) NetBEUI
    (d) TCP/IP

14. What type of network would you use to connect various locations in San Francisco through existing phone company-owned cables?

    (a) CAN
    (b) LAN
    (c) MAN
    (d) WAN

15. An extranet is a network that uses Internet technologies to allow access to invited users from outside the organization. True or false?

16. What is the term referring to the integration of voice, video, and data communications?

(a) Convergence
(b) Pervasive networking
(c) Information utility
(d) Extranet

17. What is an ASP?

(a) A company that provides public access to the Internet.
(b) A company that develops specific systems and services.
(c) A company that provides telecommunication infrastructure for purchase or lease.
(d) A company that designs and develops connection devices.

18. Which of the following refers to a private communication path over a public network?

(a) BN
(b) MAN
(c) ASP
(d) VPN

19. What is the device used to connect a wireless and wired network?

(a) Access point
(b) Switch
(c) Gateway
(d) Modem

20. Why would you deploy a peer server on a peer-to-peer network?

(a) Peer services provide centralized access authentication.
(b) Peer servers are dedicated sources services optimized for peer-to-peer use.
(c) Peer servers act in the role of both server and client.
(d) Peer servers cannot be used on other types of networks.

APPLY: WHAT WOULD YOU DO?

You are working with a team designing a network for a large organization. The team is gathering information about network requirements and trying to make some initial design considerations. The company has five offices in St. Louis and additional offices in Dallas, Los Angeles, and Seattle.

1. What are issues that will help determine the types of connections needed between the offices?

2. Describe the general network design and the role of connectivity devices.

3. Why would a directory services network more likely meet the organization's needs than a peer-to-peer network?

BE A NETWORK CONFIGURATION ENGINEER

You are a consultant currently specializing in small-to-medium businesses. You want to expand your business to include home network design and implementation.

1. What network issues are similar in small businesses and home networks?

2. What are additional issues might you need to deal with in a home network?

3. What is the potential impact of pervasive computing developments on home network design?

4. Why might you configure the network as an intranet?

KEY TERMS

Access point

Addressing

Application Service Providers (ASPs)

ARCNET

Authentication mechanisms

Backbone network

Bandwidth

Bridge

Broadband

Brouter

Client operating system

Client/server network

Connection

Directory services network

Dumb terminal

Ethernet

Extranet

Fiber-optic

Gateway

Handshaking

High-level protocol

Hub

Information utilities

Internet Service Providers (ISPs)

Intranet

Long-haul transmission lines

Low-level protocol

Media player

Network

Network adapter

Network administrator

Network Interface Card (NIC)

Network system

Node

Peer server

Peer-to-peer network

Protocol

Regional carriers

Router

Server

Server operating system
(or Network operating system)

Smart phone

Switch

Token ring

Virtual Private Networks (VPN)

Wired networks

Wireless networks

Workgroups

NETWORK STANDARDS AND MODELS

What Do You Already Know?

- What are standards and why are standards important?
- What are some of the networking models in use today?

For additional questions and to assess you current knowledge of networking standards and models, go to **www.wiley.com/go/ciccarelli/ networkingbasics2e.**

What You Will Find Out	What You Will Be Able To Do
2.1 The role of network standards.	Explain why network standards are important and how they are developed.
	Identify major standards bodies and their general responsibilities.
2.2 The OSI model.	Describe the purpose of the OSI model and why it is important.
	List and describe each of the layers in the OSI model.
2.3 TCP/IP (DoD) and other models.	Compare and contrast the OSI, TCP/IP (or DoD), and Internet models.

INTRODUCTION

This chapter discusses the role of network standards and introduces the major standards bodies. Perhaps the best known of these is the Open Systems Interconnection Reference model (the OSI model), which helped change the face of network computing; however, it is not the only network standards model. Two other closely related models are the TCP/IP model, also called the DoD model, and the Internet model.

2.1 UNDERSTANDING THE NEED FOR STANDARDS

Standards come about through various means and for a variety of reasons. Some standards are carefully and clearly defined and documented. Examples of this type of standard include the specifications for how a network interface card (NIC) might connect to a network cable plant. Other standards are more a description of accepted practices made after the fact. For example, the various desktop operating systems use a common look and feel, but no general standard with guidelines exists that each vendor is required to follow.

The primary reason for network standards is to ensure that hardware and software produced by different vendors can work together. Standards mean that customers are not locked into one vendor. They can buy hardware and software from any vendor whose equipment meets the standard, like the network shown in Figure 2-1. In this figure, you see a mix of software and hardware working together to form a small network, and even connecting the network PCs to the Internet.

NICs from one vendor can communicate with NICs from another vendor. All modems, as long as they are built to the same standard, are functionally the same. Standards help to promote more competition and hold down prices. You can focus on quality and cost instead of manufacturer name when making your purchase decisions.

2.1.1 Understanding the Standards Process

Formal standard
A standard developed by an official industry or government body.

There are two types of standards: formal and de facto. A **formal standard** is one that has been defined by one of the standards organizations. For example, there are formal standards for applications (such as websites and e-mail), for protocols, and for physical hardware. Formal standards typically take several years to develop. One potential problem is that technological innovations can outpace standards, making them less useful.

Figure 2-1

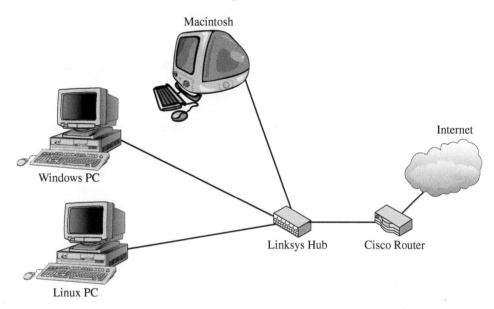

Mixed vendor environment.

De facto standards
Unofficial standards that
emerge in the marketplace.

De facto standards are those standards that are supported by several vendors but have no official standing. For example, Microsoft Windows is a product of one company and has not been formally recognized by any standards organization, yet it is a de facto standard. In the communications industry, de facto standards often become formal standards after they have been widely accepted.

In some cases, a standard can fall into both categories. The TCP/IP protocol suite is based on formal standards, and it defines the standard for protocols used on the Internet. There is no formal standard, however, defining which protocol should be used on PC networks. For businesses and universities to connect to the Internet, they had to implement TCP/IP. Rather than using multiple networking models, most adopted TCP/IP for their PC networks as well. Before long, the vast majority of PC networks were using TCP/IP, making it the de facto standard for that application.

Standardization process
The formal process by which
standards are developed.

Specification stage
The first stage of the
standardization process in
which the problem is defined.

**Identification of choices
stage**
The second stage of the
standardization process in
which potential solutions are
identified.

The formal **standardization process** has three stages: specification, identification of choices, and acceptance. The **specification stage** consists of developing a nomenclature and identifying the problems to be addressed. In the **identification of choices stage,** those working on the standard identify the various solutions and choose the optimum solution from among the alternatives. **Acceptance stage,** which is the most difficult stage, consists of defining the solution and getting recognized industry leaders to agree on a single, uniform solution. Large investments of time, money, and products are often at stake. As a result, the standards-making processes are not immune to corporate politics and the influence of

Acceptance stage
The final stage of the
standardization process in
which a solution is adopted
as a standard.

national governments. Often, manufacturers will release products based on draft standards, standards that have not yet made it through the full acceptance process.

2.1.2 Recognizing Standards Organizations

Formal standards are proposed, developed, and maintained through standards organizations. The major standards organizations have defined areas of responsibility. Some of the largest and most important standards organizations include:

- **International Organization for Standardization (ISO):** The ISO makes technical recommendations about data communication. The ISO website home page is shown in Figure 2-2. The national standards organizations of each ISO member country comprise the ISO membership. In turn, ISO is a member of the International Telecommunications Union (ITU), whose task is to make technical recommendations about telephone, telegraph, and data communication interfaces on a worldwide basis.

- **International Telecommunications Union-Telecommunications Group (ITU-T):** This is the technical standards-setting organization of

Figure 2-2

ISO home page.

the United Nations. Representatives from about 200 member countries comprise the ITU. Membership was originally focused on just the public telephone companies in each country, but ITU now seeks members among public- and private-sector organizations who operate computer or communications networks or build software and equipment for them. The ITU-T, then, is the part of the ITU that coordinates standards for telecommunications.

IN THE REAL WORLD

Building an Industry on a De Facto Standard

Some 30 years ago, the personal computer industry was a very different world. Only a few manufacturers—most notably Apple Computer, Radio Shack, and Commodore—made home and hobby computers. Commodore had even made an attempt to get desktop computers into businesses with its PET line of computers. The term "personal computer" had yet to be coined to describe these computers designed for individual use.

This terminology changed with the introduction of IBM's personal computer, nicknamed the PC. The IBM branding make companies suddenly take notice and PCs began making their way to business desktops. At the time, rather than being the standard, IBM's PC was simply one standard among many. No formal desktop computer standard existed.

What IBM did when it released the PC was revolutionary. If IBM had patented the technologies in the PC as proprietary, then other companies would have had to license the technology to build their own versions. Instead, IBM decided to make the PC an open standard, released it publicly, and welcomed other companies to build their own versions of the PC, referred to at the time as PC clones.

The industry still didn't have a formal standard, but it had a de facto standard that manufacturers could agree upon in the IBM PC. Soon, a flood of PC-standard computers were on the market. Before long, competition drove down prices and soon made computers readily affordable. Non-PC systems, like the Apple Macintosh, had to drop their prices, too, just to remain competitive. It wasn't long before IBM became a minor player in a marketplace that it helped invent.

Today's consumers continue to benefit from that early decision. Computers grow steadily more powerful while prices continue to drop. Computers are everywhere, and a part of everyday life, thanks in no small part to a de facto standard.

- **American National Standards Institute (ANSI):** The ANSI is the co-ordinating organization for the U.S. national system of technical and non-technical standards. ANSI has about 1,000 members from public and private organizations in the United States. ANSI is actually a standardization organization, not a standards-making body. It accepts standards developed by other organizations and publishes them as American standards and coordinates development of voluntary national standards that comply with international recommendations. ANSI is a voting participant in and the U.S. representative to the ISO and the ITU-T.

- **Institute of Electrical and Electronics Engineers (IEEE):** This professional society in the United States includes a Standards Association (IEEE-SA) that develops various standards, but is best known for its standards for LANs. These standards include the most commonly used for wired networking (Ethernet IEEE 802.3) and wireless networking (IEEE 802.11). Other countries have similar groups; for example, the British counterpart of IEEE is the Institution of Electrical Engineers (IEE).

Request for Comment (RFC)
The documents in which formal standards are developed and published.

- **Internet Engineering Task Force (IETF):** This organization sets the standards that govern how much of the Internet operates. The IETF is unique in that it doesn't really have official memberships; anyone is welcome to join its mailing lists, attend its meetings, and comment on developing standards. Standards (including those defining TCP/IP) are developed and published through **Request for Comment (RFC)** documents.

 SELF-CHECK

1. Compare formal and de facto standards.
2. Why are standards important to an industry segment like networking?
3. List the major standards organizations relating to data communications, networking, and the Internet.

Apply Your Knowledge The 802.11n wireless standard has been used for some time now. Is it a de facto standard, a draft standard, or has it been ratified as a formal standard?

2.2 UNDERSTANDING THE OSI MODEL

The Open Systems Interconnection Reference model (OSI model) helped change the face of network computing. Before the OSI model, most commercial networks used by businesses were built using nonstandardized technologies developed by individual vendors. This made expanding networks difficult and cross network communications nearly impossible because the technologies used by one vendor could not communicate with those developed by another vendor. To combat this problem, during the late 1970s, the ISO created the Open System Interconnection Subcommittee to develop a framework of standards for computer-to-computer communications, which completed the seven-layer OSI model in 1984. The use of a layered standard makes developing software and hardware that link different networks much easier because software and hardware can be developed one layer at a time.

You will probably never use a network based strictly on the OSI model because it never caught on commercially in North America. Some European networks use it, and most network components define their purpose and use based on this model.

So, why does it matter? It is used as a commonly accepted and understood frame of reference for discussing network equipment and network-related issues. Other models you will encounter, such as the Internet model, are usually described in terms of the OSI model. Also, questions about the OSI model are on the network certification exams offered by Microsoft, Cisco, Novell, CompTIA, and other vendors.

2.2.1 Understanding How the OSI Model Works

The seven layers of the OSI model are the Application, Presentation, Session, Transport, Network, Data Link, and Physical layers. These layers make up a framework that defines the way in which information passes up and down between physical hardware devices and the applications running on user desktops. Figure 2-3 shows the relationship between the layers and a brief overview of the function of each.

Each layer of the OSI model is independent from every other in its purpose and responsibilities. Each must do its own job and must be able to move information between the layers above and below it. In this way, the model creates a modular system where functions can be isolated to their respective layers. Each layer makes design and development easier and also aids developers and network engineers alike in troubleshooting problems that arise within a network.

Following the movement of data through the OSI model is easy. When two devices want to communicate with each other, data will be sent from the Application layer of the source computer or device. The data, in the form of a packet, continues down the layers of the OSI model until it reaches Layer 1, the Physical layer. From there, it begins its journey as electrical impulses onto the physical network.

The Physical layer is where data joins with the transmission media and is transmitted over cables or through the air. The transfer physically occurs as an electrical signal, modulated light, or radio waves. When the data reaches the destination device, it travels back through the OSI model until it is fully processed and usable.

Figure 2-3

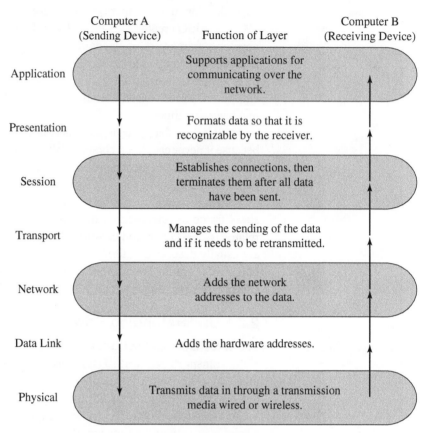

OSI model functional diagram.

Encapsulation
The process by which header and trailer information is appended to a data packet as it passes from computer to computer over a network.

Header
The set of information that is added to the beginning of a data packet.

Trailer
Information that is added to the end of a data packet.

Decapsulation
The process by which the header and trailer information is stripped from a data packet.

When a user wants to access information on another computer, the user's computer must request conversation with the destination computer. As part of its request (and any subsequent messages), it needs to add the information for the recipient computer to understand how to process the information. The process of adding information to data as it passes through the layers is known as **encapsulation.**

This process is shown in Figure 2-4. As the data moves down through the OSI layers, header and trailer information is added to the packet. The packet **header** describes the packet, including the source and destination computers and something about what the packet contains. The **trailer** identifies the end of the packet and usually includes data that helps identify transmission errors when they occur. The data inside the packet does not change during the encapsulation process. At the destination device, the header and trailer information is put through a process sometimes referred to as **decapsulation,** leaving just the original data.

Figure 2-4

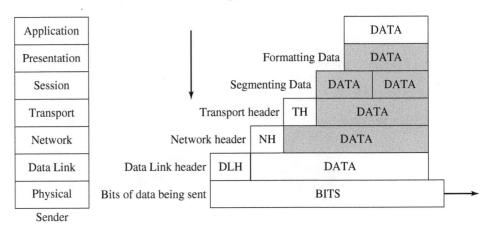

The OSI model encapsulation process.

This process repeats at every computer sending or receiving data and for every packet sent through the network. The process is generally the same for other networking models.

2.2.2 Understanding the OSI Layers

Part of each layer's job is to perform specific functions for processing the data before it is passed on to the layer above or below. For the source, that means each layer processes the data and prepares it for the layer below it, ending with transmission on the network. The process is reversed as the destination prepares the data for application processing or display.

You can think of the services provided by each layer as horizontal and vertical communication relationships. The data transfer between layers in the same device represents a **vertical relationship** between the layers. **Horizontal relationships** exist between the corresponding layers in different devices. This relationship is known as **peer layer communication.**

Vertical relationship
Communication from one layer to the layer above or below on the same device.

Horizontal relationship
Communication from one device to another on the same layer.

Peer layer communication
Another name for horizontal relationships.

The Application Layer

The **Application layer** allows the end user's access to the network by providing a set of utilities for application programs. Protocols functioning at the Application layer work with the applications you use to communicate over the network.

Five categories of services are very common to most Internet and network users, although other services do exist. The five most common categories are:

Application layer
The network layer that houses the applications that allow users to access the network.

- Files services
- E-mail services
- Network printing services

Figure 2-5

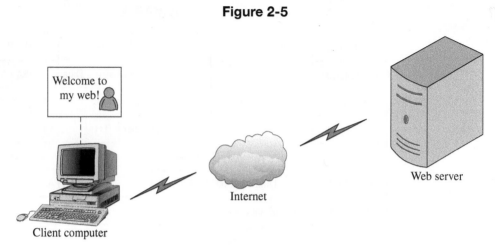

Application layer (HTTP).

- Application services
- Database services

Simple Mail Transfer Protocol (SMTP)
A communication protocol used to define how e-mail is sent and received.

Hypertext Transfer Protocol (HTTP)
A linking protocol that is used for accessing web pages over the Internet.

File Transfer Protocol (FTP)
A transmission protocol used for sending files.

Examples of protocols from the TCP/IP suite that are needed for applications to work on a network are **Simple Mail Transfer Protocol (SMTP)** to send e-mail to another person, **Hypertext Transfer Protocol (HTTP)** to access web pages while surfing on the Internet (Figure 2-5), and **File Transfer Protocol (FTP)** to download a file from an FTP server, a file server that is based on Internet technologies. These examples are only a partial list.

Equating the purpose of the Application layer with computer applications or programs is a common mistake. Business productivity software, for example, does not inherently run at the Application layer, although the software may make use of network services. For example, a word processing application might use e-mail or network printing services.

The Presentation Layer

Presentation layer
The network layer that makes data viewable by the user.

The **Presentation layer** formats the data for presentation to the user. It accommodates different interfaces on different terminals or computers so the application program need not worry about them.

The Presentation layer has three main jobs:

- Data presentation
- Data compression
- Data encryption

Data presentation
Formatting data so that it is readable by the recipient.

Data compression
Resizing the data to speed transmission.

Data presentation ensures that the data being sent to the recipient is in a format that the recipient can process. This function is important because it enables the receiving device to understand the information from the sending device. **Data compression** shrinks large amounts of data into smaller pieces. This allows data to be transferred more quickly across a network.

Figure 2-6

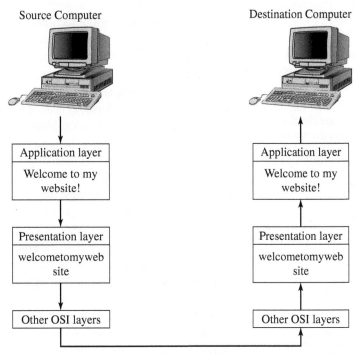

The Presentation layer.

Data encryption
Making data unreadable by unintended recipients.

Data encryption uses algorithms to modify the data based on an encryption sequence or key. Encryption is important because it helps to hide information from unintended disclosure. Encrypting sensitive data before transmission is a common practice. Various encryption methods are used resulting in various levels of protection.

Look at the Presentation layer example in Figure 2-6. The source computer is sending a text document to the destination computer. At the Application layer, this data looks like a normal sentence with formatting intact. When it reaches the Presentation layer, the text data is compressed, transformed, and possibly encrypted, and then sent on through the remaining layers.

At the destination computer, when the information reaches the Presentation layer, it is returned to its original format (with spaces and formatting), and then sent on to the Application layer.

Session layer
The network layer that controls the communication between computers.

The Session Layer

The **Session layer** is responsible for initiating, maintaining, and terminating each logical session between computers. The Session layer also handles dialog control and dialog separation.

Session initiation
The process that sets up the parameters of the connection between computers.

Session termination
The process that closes down the connection between computers.

Session accounting
The process that handles billing for sessions.

Dialog control
The service responsible for determining which computer is sending and which is receiving at any given time throughout the session.

Simplex
Data flows in only one direction.

Half duplex
Data flows in both directions, but only in one direction at a time.

Full duplex
Data flows in both directions at the same time.

Data separation
The process of bookmarking packets to allow for sessions to be recovered.

Transport layer
The network layer responsible for moving data, ensuring that it is received without errors.

Session initiation must arrange for the desired and required services between session participants, such as logging onto circuit equipment, transferring files, and performing security checks. **Session termination** provides an orderly way to end the session, as well as a means to abort a session prematurely. Some redundancy may be built in to recover from an unexpected broken or interrupted transport connection. The Session layer also handles **session accounting** so the correct party receives the bill when billing by session time or data volume, as is done with some WAN connection methods.

To understand the Session layer's basic functions, think of your telephone. When you dial a number and the other person answers, you create a connection. When you start speaking with the person at the other end, you initiate a session. You terminate the session by hanging up. You would be responsible for related charges, though if the person on the other end is on a cell phone, additional charges may also apply at the other end.

Dialog control is responsible for determining which device participating in the communication will transmit at any given time and controlling the amount of data that can be sent in a transmission (as in Figure 2-7). Transmission types managed through dialog control include simplex, half duplex, and full duplex. In **simplex** communication, the information moves in only one direction, as in a broadcast (think TV or radio). **Half duplex** lets the two ends communicate, but one at a time, like using a walkie-talkie. **Full duplex** enables the two ends of a conversation to communicate simultaneously, usually through separate send and receive channels.

Data separation is the process of inserting markers into packets to ensure that if a loss of packets or other problems happen during transmission, the conversation can recover and continue. These markers let the Session layer know what data it needs to retransmit.

The Transport Layer

The **Transport layer** deals with end-to-end issues, such as procedures for entering and departing from the network. It establishes, maintains, and

Figure 2-7

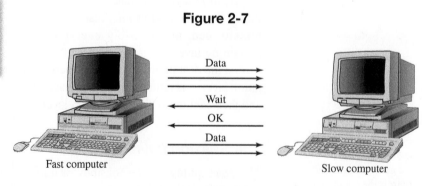

Fast computer

Slow computer

Dialog control.

TIPS FROM THE PROFESSIONALS

In actual practice, the distinctions in the Session, Presentation, and Application layers are often blurred, and some commonly used protocols actually span all three layers. For example, SMB—the protocol that is the basis for file sharing in Windows networks—functions on all three layers.

Flow control
The process that limits the number of transmissions sent at one time to avoid overloading the receiving device.

Connection-oriented transmissions
Transmissions that require an acknowledgement of receipt from the receiving computer.

Ack
Acknowledgement message sent by the receiving computer in a connection-oriented transmission.

terminates logical connections for data transfer between the original sender and the final destination. It is responsible for obtaining the address of the destination computer (if needed), breaking a large data transmission into smaller packets (if needed), ensuring that all the packets have been received, eliminating duplicate packets, and performing **flow control** to ensure that no computer is overwhelmed by the number of messages it receives. Flow control keeps the source from sending data packets faster than the destination can handle. The Transport layer can also perform error checking, but this function is normally performed by the Data Link layer. The Transport layer manages two types of transmissions, connection-oriented and connectionless.

Connection-oriented transmissions, shown in Figure 2-8, have the receiving device send an acknowledgement, or **ack,** back to the source after a packet or group of packets is received. If no ack is received, the sending system can assume the packets were lost and retransmit, or the destination

Figure 2-8

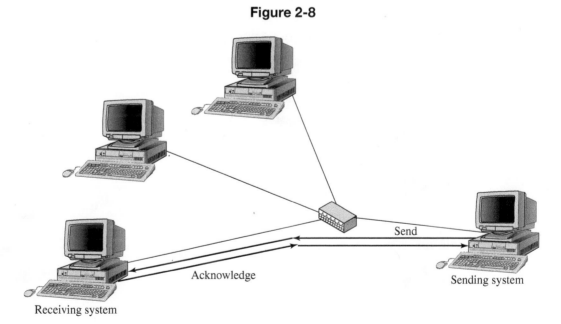

Connection-oriented transmission.

Reliable transport method

A transmission that ensures the error-free receipt of packets.

can request a retransmission if it detects that it missed a packet in sequence. This type of transmission is known as a **reliable transport method.** Because connection-oriented transmission requires the additional response traffic, it has often been considered a slower method than connectionless, although this point tends to be moot in today's faster networks.

Connection-oriented transmission features include:

- Reliability
- Relatively slower communication
- Packets are resent if a packet is unrecognizable or is not received.

Connectionless transmissions

Transmissions in which no response from the receiver is required.

Connectionless transmissions (see Figure 2-9) do not have the receiver acknowledge receipt of a packet. Instead, the sending device assumes that the packet arrived. This approach allows for much faster communication but is less reliable than connection-oriented transmission.

Connectionless transmission features include:

- Little or no reliability
- Faster transmission
- Packets are not retransmitted (because transmission errors are not detected)

The TCP/IP protocol suite, at this layer, includes examples of both connectionless and connection-oriented protocols. We introduce these a little later in the chapter, but a detailed discussion of these protocols is beyond the scope of this chapter.

Figure 2-9

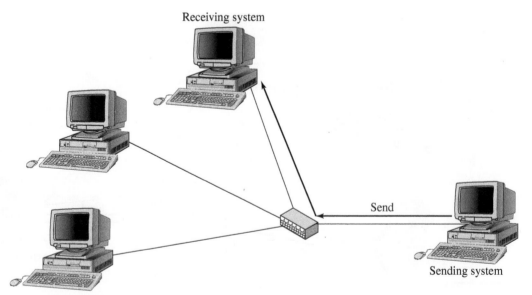

Connectionless transmission.

Figure 2-10

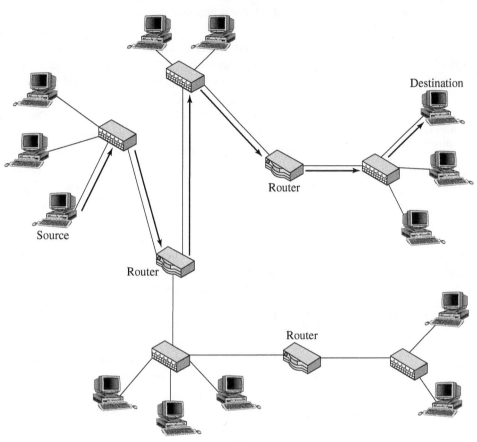

A routed packet.

Network layer
The layer that handles routing of packets from one computer to another.

Datagrams
Another name for the packets of data that are moved around the network.

Routing
The process of determining the path required to deliver packets to their destination.

The Network Layer

The **Network layer** is responsible for the addressing and delivery of packets, also known as **datagrams,** and performs routing. **Routing** is the process of finding a path through the routers, connecting networks into an internetwork so that packets are delivered to the correct network and finally to the correct computer, as shown in Figure 2-10. Routing ensures that the packet is delivered to and through the appropriate router. Notice that the path that the packet takes only passes through other networks when they are part of the path to the next router.

NETWORKING FACT

A protocol is considered routable if it uses addresses that include a network part and a host part. Any protocol that uses physical addresses isn't routable because physical addresses don't indicate to which network a device belongs.

Physical address
The unique identifier of the network card attached to a computer.

Logical address
The unique network identifier assigned to a computer.

Source routing
A routing technique in which the routing information is included in the packet being routed.

Hop
The intervening routers in a path of routers through a network.

Routing table
An internal table that routers use to determine the best path to send a packet to its destination.

Routing protocol
The protocol used by routers to define how the routing path is chosen.

Each computer has a **physical address,** which is coded on the network card, and a **logical address** that is assigned through the system networking software. Both are unique addresses. The Network layer relies on the logical address for routing purposes. When a packet arrives at the Network layer, the Network layer adds source and destination addresses through encapsulation. The destination computer can be on either a local network or on a remote network, in which case, the packet must be routed to arrive at the right destination.

Routing can be handled in two basic ways. One is **source routing,** where the addresses of all of the routers along the way are embedded in the packet, and the packet follows the specified path. However, the more common method is to have each router along the way direct the packet to the next router, or **hop,** in the path. In order to do so, it checks the next destination address and compares it against an internal table, called the **routing table,** to choose the best path. A counter is decremented each time the packet crosses a router. When the counter reaches zero, the router assumes that the packet is lost or stuck in a loop, and the packet is discarded.

Routers can use various algorithms to determine the best path. Most often, the decision made on the shortest path is based on the number of hops to the destination. However, routers can also take into consideration factors such as the bandwidth and traffic levels on alternate routes and make routing decisions based on current network conditions. The **routing protocol** used by the routers determines the way routing is managed. Alternate routes aren't an issue in Figure 2-10 because only one path exists between the source and destination systems.

A router is the primary piece of hardware working at the Network layer, which is why routers are sometimes called Layer 3 devices. Brouters also operate, at least partially, at the Network layer. Some switches, identified as Layer 3 switches, also operate at the layer. Devices that a packet passes through on its way to the destination device are called intermediate systems. Intermediate routers need to deal with the packet only up to the Network layer of the OSI model, as shown in Figure 2-11.

Figure 2-11

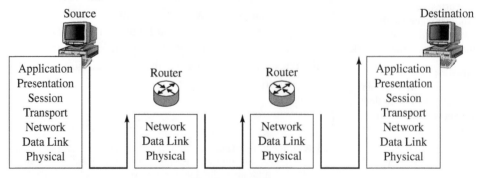

Route operation.

Data link layer
The layer of the OSI model responsible for transmitting data over the network cable.

Transmission circuit
The physical conduit over which data travels within a network.

Frames
The data packet combined with its header and trailer information.

The Network layer also has the job of making sure the data packet is compatible with the network it is entering. For example, if a network's media requires shorter packet lengths, then the routers can break up and reformat the packets so that the network they are entering can handle them.

The Data Link Layer

The **Data Link layer** manages the physical **transmission circuit** in the Physical layer and transforms it into a circuit that is free of transmission errors (as far as the upper layers are concerned) by performing error detection, correction, and retransmission. It also converts data packets into **frames,** which is the data packet plus the encapsulating information, including layer 2 addresses (see Figure 2-12). The Data Link layer is made up of two sublayers, each providing services. These are the Logical Link Control (LLC) sublayer and the Media Access Control (MAC) sublayer.

Logical Link Control (LLC)
Provides the interface between the media-access method and Network layer protocols.

Media Access Control (MAC)
Sublayer is responsible for the connection to the physical media and physical address.

LLC type 1
Connectionless service on the LLC sublayer.

LLC type 2
Connection-oriented service on the LLC sublayer.

> **FOR EXAMPLE: FRAMED PACKETS**
>
> Figure 2-12 illustrates the elements of the framed packet.

The **Logical Link Control (LLC)** sublayer bridges the **Media Access Control (MAC)** sublayer to the upper-layer protocols through connectionless and connection-oriented services. The IEEE 802.2 standards define LLC standards. The LLC sublayer supports a connectionless service **(LLC type 1)** that assumes that data has arrived correctly at the destination. It also supports a connection-oriented service **(LLC type 2)** that checks that a message arrives correctly. Because of the additional overhead for LLC type 2 and the fact that connection-oriented service is already provided at the Transport layer, LLC type 1 is most commonly used.

The MAC sublayer adds the device's actual physical address, called the **MAC address,** to the packet. The frame then has all the addressing information necessary to travel from the source device to the destination device. Why is the MAC address necessary? It is necessary because it is the address used to locate the destination computer after the packet reaches the correct local network.

MAC address
The unique identifier of the network interface card attached to a computer.

The MAC address is permanently hard-coded on the network interface card (NIC) by the manufacturer (as in Figure 2-13). It is a unique hexadecimal address with six pairs of hexadecimal digits and is not duplicated anywhere in the world. The first six digits are assigned to (and identify) the NIC manufacturer. The last six are a unique value assigned by the manufacturer.

Figure 2-12

Header	Destination MAC	Source MAC	Destination address	Source address	LLC header	Data	CRC	Trailer

Completed frame.

Figure 2-13

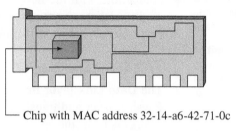

└─ Chip with MAC address 32-14-a6-42-71-0c

MAC address.

The Physical Layer

Physical layer
The layer that controls the rules for data transmission, including electrical currents, types of cables, and transmission speed.

The **Physical layer** defines the rules by which data is transmitted, such as voltages of electricity, number of bits sent per second, and the physical structure of the cables and connectors used. This is the layer for which the most, and clearest, operational standards are defined.

The NIC operates at this level and converts data into transmission signals. The signals generated depend on the network connection medium. These transmissions can be analog or digital, though both types transmit binary data. The Physical layer defines both the transmissions and the rate at which these transmissions are sent.

Figure 2-14

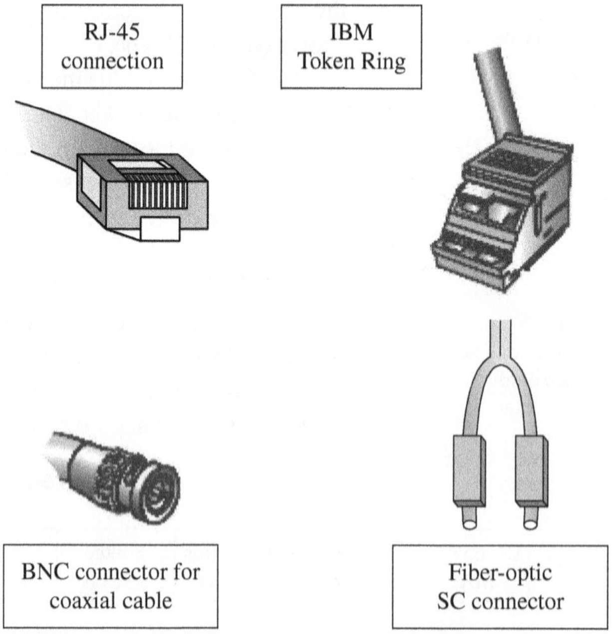

RJ-45 connection	IBM Token Ring

BNC connector for coaxial cable	Fiber-optic SC connector

Sample connectors.

Table 2-1: Selected IEEE Standards

Standard	Name	Description
802.3	**Ethernet**	Most commonly used networking standard with support for speeds ranging from 10 Mbps to 10 Gbps in current implementations.
802.5	**Token Ring**	Originally developed by IBM and used primarily on IBM networks and mainframe connections. Token Rings are still used for certain applications such as factory automation, but they are rarely used in business networks.
802.11	**Wi-Fi**	Wireless networking standards including 802.11b and 802.11g, the two standards most commonly used by PC networks and compatible devices.

The Physical layer also manages the way a device connects to the network media. For example, if the physical connection from the device to the network uses coaxial cable, the hardware that functions at the Physical layer will be designed for that specific type of network.

All components, including the connectors, (see Figure 2-14), will be specified at the Physical layer as well.

The most commonly used standards are those defined by the IEEE. The three most common IEEE network standards are listed in Table 2-1.

IN THE REAL WORLD

Practical Consequences

Most network addresses do not implement functionality from all layers of the OSI model. Hubs are dumb connection devices and only operate at the Physical layer. Routers, on the other hand, are more sophisticated and implement functionality through the Network layer. The communication protocols operating at the network clients and servers implement all seven layers. At least, that's how it usually works. For every rule, there's usually at least one exception.

The NetBEUI protocol is an example of a protocol that does not implement all of the layers of the OSI model. NetBEUI has no equivalent of the Networking layer. What's the consequence of this? Because you don't have a Network layer, you don't have logical network addresses. That also means that you can't support routing. Routers ignore NetBEUI frames because they don't have source or destination network addresses. The routers have no idea what to do with them, so they do nothing. Frames are trapped on the network segment on which they are generated.

(continued)

IN THE REAL WORLD   (continued)

What does this mean to network communications? It means that if you need to communicate with a computer located on a different network, you must use a protocol other than NetBEUI, like AppleTalk or TCP/IP. Both of these do include Network layer functionality, and because of this, can support routing.

Because of this limit, computers deployed in a routed network and running NetBEUI commonly also run one or more additional protocols. There were other justifications for multiple protocols, as well. Some applications were written to use functionality specific to a communication protocol. In other words, you might need AppleTalk to run one application, but need NetBEUI to run another. Internet access and Internet applications required (and still require) TCP/IP.

This reliance on multiple protocols could get to be a problem, especially on computers with limited resources. Each protocol that you load at the computer adds to the memory overhead. Performance suffers. Background traffic increases because of "housekeeping" traffic required by the protocols. On some older systems, if you tried to run too many simultaneous protocols, your computer wouldn't be able to do much of anything else.

All these limits, consequences, and reliances make it easier to see why the industry has settled on a de facto standard, doesn't it?

Tips from the Professionals

The concepts of standards and protocols can be difficult to understand in real-world concepts. Imagine two baseball teams, one from Japan, and one from Argentina. The game's standards would be the general rules of sportsmanship and orderly behavior of the players. The protocols would be the actual rules of baseball. Neither team could speak to each other directly (as in an IBM PC and an Apple Macintosh computer), but by following the standards and protocols they would be able to play a great game of baseball. By following the communication protocols in this chapter, all sorts of devices would be able to collaborate and work together.

SELF-CHECK

1. List and describe the seven OSI model layers.
2. List and describe common IEEE Physical layer standards.

Apply Your Knowledge What is a practical application of Half-duplex communications and why would it be used?

Project 2.1

A formal standards organization can develop standards, or they can come into being through common acceptance and use. Standards have been an important part of network design and development. They help to ensure interoperability between different manufacturers' products. They provide standard, accepted terms for describing network functions and network activity. In short, they provide a standard language for discussing networking. Three common network model standards are the OSI model, the DoD model, and the Internet model.

Complete **Project 2.2: Comparing Network Models** in the online Network Basics Project Manual to understand each of these models, how they are structured, and what occurs at each level.

2.3 UNDERSTANDING OTHER NETWORK MODELS

The OSI model is the one most commonly referenced from a theoretical standpoint or when discussing networks in general, but is rarely seen in real-world applications. For that, we need to look at two other, nearly identical standard models, the TCP/IP model and the Internet model.

The Internet we know today was made possible by the creation of the TCP/IP model. The U.S. Department of Defense built the ARPANET network to link its defense installations to several major universities throughout the United States. By the early 1970s, ARPANET was becoming difficult to manage, so it was split into two networks: one for military use, called MILNET, and the other for nonmilitary use. To link the two networks, a new method of connecting networks, called Internet Protocol, IP for short, was invented. The designers of IP designed IP to allow for tens of thousands of networks to communicate via IP.

TCP/IP model
Transmission Control Protocol/Internet Protocol, the protocol used by the Internet.

DoD model
Alternate name for the TCP/IP model referring to its having been designed by the U.S. Department of Defense.

The four-layer **TCP/IP model** is technically known as the **DoD model** because the U.S. Department of Defense (DoD) funded the original project from which TCP/IP was developed. The Internet model evolved from the work of thousands of people who developed pieces of the Internet. The Internet model has never been formally defined, but it is generally accepted as a five-layer model. The two models are nearly identical, which is understandable because the Internet is based on the TCP/IP protocol suite, so it reflects the structure of that suite and its underlying model.

2.3.1 TCP/IP Model

The **DoD model** is considered a working model because it was used as the basis for the development of the TCP/IP protocol suite. For documentation

Figure 2-15

OSI Model	TCP/IP Model
Application layer Presentation layer Session layer	Process layer
Transport layer	Host-to-Host layer
Network layer	Internet layer
Data Link layer	Network Interface layer
Physical layer	

TCP/IP and the OSI models.

Process layer
The TCP/IP layer responsible for how applications on both ends process data.

Host-to-Host layer
The TCP/IP model layer responsible for controlling the communication between network devices.

Hosts
Network devices.

Transmission Control Protocol (TCP)
The protocol used to create connection-oriented services in the TCP/IP model.

User Datagram Protocol (UDP)
The protocol used to create connectionless services in the TCP/IP model.

Internetwork layer
Another name for the Internet or Network layer in the TCP/IP model.

Internet layer
The layer of the TCP/IP model responsible for addressing devices and routing data between networks.

purposes, the TCP/IP suite of protocols is often mapped to the more contemporary OSI model. The TCP/IP model does not have clearly defined layers, but it is possible to compare the functions of the layers of the DoD model to that of the OSI model, as you can see in Figure 2-15. From the comparison, a four-layer DoD model can be derived. Some overviews of TCP/IP include a Physical layer as part of the stack that is not defined as a part of the DoD model. TCP/IP leaves the physical connection to manage itself.

The Application or Process Layer

The Application layer of the TCP/IP model, also known as the **Process layer,** handles the way applications at both the source and destination devices process information as it is sent and received. The Application layer of the DoD model maps to the Application layer, Presentation layer, and most of the Session layer of the OSI model.

The Host-to-Host or Transport Layer

Like the OSI model's Transport layer, the DoD's **Host-to-Host layer** manages the data flow between devices and the type of transmission as either connection-oriented or connectionless. The name comes from TCP/IP terminology in which network devices are referred to as **hosts.** TCP/IP uses two protocols to provide this service. The **Transmission Control Protocol (TCP)** provides reliable connection-oriented service. The **User Datagram Protocol (UDP)** provides the less reliable connectionless service.

The Internet Layer (Network Layer)

You might sometimes hear the Internet layer called the Network layer or the **Internetwork layer.** No one name is more right or wrong than the others. Defining the **Internet layer** by the primary protocol referred to at this layer,

Internet Protocol (IP)
The protocol used to assign unique addresses to devices on the Internet.

Internet Protocol, is easiest. The **Internet Protocol (IP)** serves several functions, the foremost of which is to provide a hierarchical addressing scheme used to identify devices on the network, so that every device on the Internet has a unique address. IP addresses also let you configure your own network so that each node is uniquely identified. The Internet layer relies on the hierarchical addressing of IP to route data independently of the type of network media like the Network layer in the OSI model.

Network Interface layer
The layer of the TCP/IP model responsible for routing data inside a single network. Replaces the OSI Data Link layer.

The Network Interface Layer

The **Network Interface layer** manages the transmission of data within a network. After the Internet layer routes the packets to the correct network, this layer makes sure that the data is sent to the correct device, functioning like the OSI Data Link layer.

2.3.2 Internet Model

Internet model
Five layer network model most commonly used.

Although the OSI model is the most well-known network model, the one that dominates current hardware and software is the simpler five-layer **Internet model.** The two models have very much in common (see Figure 2-16). The Internet model collapses the top three OSI layers into one layer. The biggest difference between the Internet and TCP/IP (or DoD) model is that the Internet model, unlike the TCP/IP model, does include a Physical layer.

The Application Layer

The Application layer is the application software used by the network user and includes much of what the OSI model contains in the Application, Presentation, and Session layers. It is the user's access to the network. By using the application software, the user defines what messages are sent over the network.

Figure 2-16

OSI Model	Internet Model
Application layer Presentation layer Session layer	Process layer
Transport layer	Host-to-Host layer
Network layer	Internet layer
Data Link layer	Network Interface layer
Physical layer	Physical layer

Comparing the OSI and Internet models.

The Transport Layer

The Transport layer in the Internet model is very similar to the Transport layer in the OSI model. The Transport layer:

- Is responsible for linking the Application layer software to the network and establishing end-to-end connections between the sender and receiver when such connections are needed.
- Provides tools so that addresses used at the Application layer (Internet Universal Resource Locator, or URL address) can be translated into the numeric IP addresses.
- Is responsible for breaking long messages into several smaller messages to make them easier to transmit.

The Network Layer

The Network layer is responsible for the end-to-end transfer of messages from the sender to the final destination. The Network layer in the Internet model performs the same functions as the Network layer in the OSI model. It performs routing, in that it selects the next computer to which the message should be sent and can find that computer's address if it doesn't already know it.

The Data Link Layer

The Data Link layer is responsible for moving a message from one computer to the next computer in the network path from the sender to the receiver. The Data Link layer in the Internet model performs the same basic functions as the Data Link layer in the OSI model:

- It controls the physical layer by deciding when to transmit messages over the media.
- It formats the messages by indicating where they start and end.
- It detects and corrects any errors that have occurred during transmission.

The Physical Layer

The Physical layer in the Internet model, as in the OSI model, is the physical connection between the sender and receiver. Its role is to transfer a series of electrical, radio, or light signals through the circuit. The physical layer includes all the hardware devices (such as computers, modems, and hubs) and physical media (cables, satellites, and radio frequency). The physical layer specifies the type of connection and the signals that pass through it.

2.3.3 Groups of Layers

The layers in the Internet model are often so closely coupled that decisions in one layer impose certain requirements on other layers. The Data Link

IN THE REAL WORLD

Troubleshooting by the Layers

Just why is all this talk about layers important? After all, they're just logical models, right? That's true, but these layers represent divisions that hardware manufacturers and software vendors use when developing new products. Consider the Internet model. Someone can develop new software or enhance existing software that operates at the Application layer knowing that the processes at the underlying layers, as well as the interface to those layers, is already defined. The role of a router is already clearly established. You know exactly what is expected of a network adapter.

These defined layers, and their relation to standard hardware and software, can also help you when problems arise. Consider a problem where a network computer can communicate with other computers on the local network, but can't communicate with computers on other network segments. That problem immediately gives you a starting place for your troubleshooting. How? It's a routing problem because you can't make the hop from one network to another. Now you can start asking other questions. Can other computers on this network communicate with other networks? If not, the problem is likely related to the router. If they can, then it's something with this computer, maybe an address configuration problem.

Take it down a level. You have a computer that can't communicate with any other computer on the network. This time you probably want to start your search at the Physical or Data Link layer. The network adapter may have failed, or the computer may simply have become disconnected from the cable.

You may not specifically step through the layers when problems occur, but even so, understanding the layered structure can help you direct your troubleshooting efforts. Not responsible for troubleshooting? Then an understanding of the Internet model can help you explain your problem in terms that make sense to you and the technician.

layer and the Physical layer are closely tied together because the Data Link layer controls the Physical layer in terms of when the Physical layer can transmit. Decisions about the Data Link layer often drive the decisions about the Physical layer. For this reason, some people group them together and call them the Hardware layers. You can see this in Figure 2-17.

The same is true of the Transport and Network layers. They are so closely coupled that sometimes these layers are called the Internetwork layers. When you design a network, you often think about the network design

Figure 2-17

OSI Model	Internet Model	Groups of layers	Examples
Application layer Presentation layer Session layer	Process layer	Application layer	Internet Explorer Netscape Navigator Web servers and pages TCP/IP suite protocols (HTTP, FTP, etc.)
Transport layer	Host-to-Host layer	Internetwork layer	TCP/IP suite protocols (TCP, UDP, IP)
Network layer	Internet layer		
Data Link layer	Network Interface layer	Hardware layer	NIC Cable plant NIC device drivers
Physical layer	Physical layer		

Grouping layers.

in terms of three groups of layers: the Hardware layers (Physical and Data Link), the Internetwork layers (Network and Transport), and the Application layer. The same groupings of Hardware, Internetwork, and Application can also apply to the OSI model and less to the TCP/IP model (because of its lack of a Physical layer).

SELF-CHECK

1. Compare the OSI, TCP/IP (or DoD), and Internet models.
2. How are Internet layers organized into groups?

Apply Your Knowledge Why do you have both connection-oriented and connectionless transmissions at the transport layer? Can you think of an example of connectionless protocol use? Why is it used in this example?

Project 2.2

Microsoft and other operating system manufacturers build network components into their operating systems. You can view and manage the status of these networking components. Many components also have parameters that you can configure to control how your computer communicates on the network. Part of understanding these network components is knowing how they are related to each other.

Complete **Project 2.5: Mapping Network Components** in the online Network Basics Project Manual to understand how network components are related to each other.

SUMMARY

Section 2.1

- Standards are necessary to make sure that devices and applications from different vendors can work together.
- Standards can be either formal or de facto. Official governing bodies develop formal standards. The market place develops de facto standards.

Section 2.2

- The OSI model is the model most commonly used to describe network hardware and software.

Section 2.3

- The TCP/IP model has only four layers, while the Internet model has five.
- The Internet model is currently the dominant model in hardware and software.
- The primary difference between the TCP/IP and Internet models is that the Internet model includes the Physical layer defined in the OSI model.

ASSESS YOUR UNDERSTANDING

UNDERSTAND: WHAT HAVE YOU LEARNED?

 Go to **www.wiley.com/go/ciccarelli/networkingbasics2e** to assess your knowledge of network standards and models.
Measure your learning by comparing pre-test and post-test results.

SUMMARY QUESTIONS

1. A de facto standard is one that emerges in the marketplace, but has no official standing. True or false?

2. What standards body developed the OSI model?
   (a) ISO
   (b) ITU-T
   (c) IEEE
   (d) ANSI

3. Which of the following is used to develop and publish Internet standards?
   (a) DoD
   (b) ITU
   (c) RFC
   (d) IETF

4. ANSI is a U.S. standards-making body. True or false?

5. Which layer of the OSI model is responsible for routing?
   (a) Data Link layer
   (b) Transport layer
   (c) Session layer
   (d) Network layer

6. Which of the following terms is used to describe a connection where both ends are able to communicate simultaneously?
   (a) Full-duplex communication
   (b) Reliable transport method
   (c) Connection-oriented transmission
   (d) Half-duplex communication

7. The connectors used to attach a NIC to a network cable are defined at what layer of the OSI model?
   (a) Data Link layer
   (b) Physical layer

    (c) Transport layer

    (d) Network layer

8. What is the MAC address?

    (a) Logical address defined at the Internet model Network layer.

    (b) The address used to determine the route taken through an internet-work.

    (c) A value used for data encryption by the Internet Application layer.

    (d) The globally unique address hard-coded on a network adapter.

9. The Internet network model consists of how many layers?

    (a) Four

    (b) Five

    (c) Seven

    (d) Ten

10. What is the most commonly used network physical standard?

    (a) 802.11

    (b) 802.5

    (c) 802.3

    (d) 802.2

11. Which of the following are associated most closely with the OSI model Application layer?

    (a) E-mail services

    (b) Logical addresses

    (c) Connection-oriented transmissions

    (d) Dialog control

12. Which OSI model layer is NOT represented in the DoD network model?

    (a) Physical

    (b) Network

    (c) Transport

    (d) Presentation

13. Which protocol is most closely associated with the Internet model Internet layer?

    (a) TCP

    (b) UDP

    (c) IP

    (d) HTTP

14. Which Host-to-Host layer protocol provides connection-oriented service?

    (a) TCP

    (b) UDP

    (c) IP

    (d) HTTP

APPLY: WHAT WOULD YOU DO?

You are setting up a home network at your house for two desktop computers and three laptop computers with wireless network interface cards.

1. What equipment would you buy, and why?

2. How would you set up the home network and what protocols do you use in your home network?

3. Which layers of the OSI model do you think are the most important for your home network and why?

For each of the following, identify the layer primarily responsible for the requested action in both the OSI model and the Internet model.

1. The source file is encoded in seven-bit ASCII code. The destination system expects the file in EBCDIC.

2. The network is an Internet environment. Clients in Chicago need to access content in New York. The packets need to cross several hops to make it to the server.

3. You need to order the correct cables for connecting client computers to the hubs.

4. The word processing application needs to be designed so that users can e-mail documents in progress.

5. The MAC address is hard-coded in a removable ROM. You can change the physical address by changing the ROM.

For each description, identify the correct standards organization.

1. Accepts standards developed by other organizations and publishes them as U.S. standards.

2. Developed the OSI seven-layer model.

3. Developed standards for Token Ring and Wi-Fi.

4. Publishes Internet standards as RFCs.

BE A NETWORK ADMINISTRATOR

Choose Components

A friend wants to network his family's computers and entertainment devices in his home. He's asked you to help him shop for components. Explain how standards ensure that different vendors' devices will work together.

Troubleshoot the ISO Layers

You work for a company with a series of small LANs interconnected using the ISO model. Your boss is having trouble with his network connection.

He can communicate with his printer, which is on the same network segment, but can't communicate with his boss's computer on another network segment. Using your knowledge of ISO layers, determine how to begin troubleshooting the problem.

Apply Standards

Explain the significance of specifications defined by standards at the Internet model Physical layer?

KEY TERMS

Acceptance stage

Ack

Application layer (DoD and Internet)

Application layer (OSI)

Connectionless transmissions

Connection-oriented transmission

Data compression

Data encryption

Data Link layer (Internet Model)

Data Link layer (OSI Model)

Data presentation

Data separation

Datagram

De facto standard

Department of Defense (DoD) model

Decapsulation

Dialog control

Encapsulation

File Transfer Protocol (FTP)

Flow control

Formal standard

Frames

Full duplex

Half duplex

Header

Hop

Horizontal relationship

Hosts

Host-to-Host layer (DoD)

Hypertext Transfer Protocol (HTTP)

Identification of choices stage

Internet layer

Internet model

Internet Protocol (IP)

Internetwork layer

LLC type 1

LLC type 2

Logical address

Logical Link Control (LLC)

Media Access Control (MAC)

MAC address

Network Interface layer (DoD)

Network layer (Internet)

Network layer (OSI)

Peer layer communication

Physical address

Physical layer (Internet)

Physical layer (OSI)

Presentation layer (OSI)

Process layer (DoD)

Reliable transport method

Request for Comment (RFC)

Routing

Routing protocol

Routing table

Session accounting

Session initiation

Session layer (OSI)

Session termination

Simple Mail Transfer Protocol (SMTP)

Simplex

Source routing

Standardization process

TCP/IP model

Trailer

Transmission circuit

Transmission Control Protocol (TCP)

Transport layer (DoD and Internet)

Transport layer (OSI)

User Datagram Protocol (UDP)

Vertical relationship

3
NETWORK PROTOCOLS

What Do You Already Know?

- What is a protocol?
- How do you use a protocol?
- What are the most prominent protocols currently used?

 For additional questions to help you assess your knowledge of access methods and network protocols, go to **www.wiley.com/go/ciccarelli/ networkingbasics2e.**

What You Will Find Out	What You Will Be Able To Do
3.1 The role of protocols.	Define and describe protocols.
	Identify where protocols fit in networks.
3.2 How protocols help with access.	Identify and define protocol standards.
3.3 Compare network protocols.	Identify and describe the major protocols currently in use.

INTRODUCTION

Networking terms are tricky. Context makes all the difference. Protocols are no different. If the conversation turns to protocols, the first thing you need to know is which protocols you are discussing. Most networks have several different protocols in use. You have protocols that manage access to the network, protocols that manage traffic between computers, protocols that manage and update routers, and maybe even protocols that manage special applications like virtual LANs.

The most commonly used protocols can be defined in terms of OSI model layers. We look at the two critical types of protocols that are present in every network at the Data Link and Network layers. The Data Link layer protocols are known as **access protocols** or access methods. The Network layer protocols are known as **network protocols** or communication protocols. We can also look at protocols from the context of defined standards, because each protocol is defined through one or more published standards.

3.1 UNDERSTANDING THE ROLE OF PROTOCOLS

IN ACTION:
UNDERSTANDING
PROTOCOLS

Get a feel for what a protocol is.

Access protocols
Communications procedures used at the Data Link layer on all networks.

Network protocols
Communications procedures used at the Network layer.

Before we begin taking protocols apart and discussing what they do, having a common understanding of what they are is helpful, at least in the context of this chapter. A protocol, in simple terms, is a set of rules a computer uses to communicate.

3.1.1 Understanding Communication Requirements

Consider the two people in Figure 3-1. They have a basic, but common, problem. They simply can't understand each other. So, what do they need in order to be able to communicate? They either need a common language, one that they both speak, understand, and agree to speak, or they need a translator who understands and speaks both of their native languages.

Figure 3-1

Confused speakers.

The preferred solution, if possible, is for both to speak a common language. Communication goes faster with less opportunity for confusion. With a translator, communication goes slower (at least twice as long) because of the time needed to translate the content. Something also has a chance of being lost or confused in translation.

The same is true of computers. For two computers to communicate, they must either have at least one language (protocol) in common or a translator. If a translator is required, performance suffers because of the processing overhead needed to convert data from one protocol to another.

3.1.2 Identifying Protocols by Role

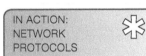

IN ACTION:
NETWORK
PROTOCOLS

Understand where protocols fit in networks.

Most network devices must support at least two protocols, a Data Link layer protocol used for network access and a Network layer protocol used to manage higher-level communication requirements. To understand why two protocols are needed, we need to look at their roles in network communication. To do so, we take a typical network computer and break it out using the OSI model.

Despite the wide range of variations you might see, we can describe a typical computer based on the technologies currently in use. It's running the current, or a recent, version of the Windows operating system. It is connected to an Ethernet network wired as a physical star and configured to use TCP/IP. Take a look at Figure 3-2.

Moving down through the OSI model, you can see that a data packet is wrapped up in layers like an onion. Layers are added as the data moves down through the **protocol stack,** the protocol software components running on the computer. The protocol stack consists of different protocols in the **protocol suite.**

Protocol stack
The group of protocols surrounding a data packet that is added and removed as the data stack moves through the layers of the OSI model.

Protocol suite
A group of network protocols used as a group, like TCP/IP.

Each layer performs various functions, wrapping the message content with control information on its way down through the stack. In our example, at the Data Link layer, our message is encapsulated in an Ethernet frame and sent out on the network cable (represented by the Physical layer). The process is reversed at the receiver end, unwrapping the layers until you finally reach the original message.

In an Ethernet network, all of the computers on the network segment will receive the message, except possibly for areas where MAC address filtering blocked the message. For the computers that are not the addressed recipient, the packet never makes it past the Data Link layer. The destination address, which is a MAC address, is checked at the Data Link layer, and if the address on the packet doesn't match the address on the computer, it's ignored.

Decisions may need to be made at higher levels of the OSI model. You can configure a computer to concurrently run multiple protocol suites, such as TCP/IP. Each protocol encodes data that uniquely identifies a packet as having been generated by that protocol. As the packet moves up through the

Figure 3-2

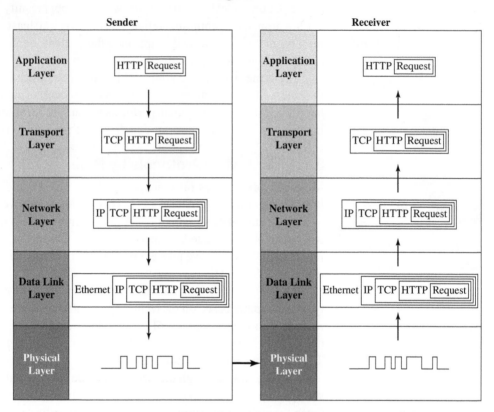

TCP/IP protocol stack use.

OSI model, it is checked first against the protocol configured as the computer's default protocol. If there's no match, the packet is checked against all other protocols running on the computer until a match is found and the packet is processed based on that protocol's requirements. If no match is found, an error is noted and the packet contents ignored.

3.1.3 Transmitting Digital Data (Digitally)

This chapter focuses on LAN access and data transmission, so you might find it interesting to know something about how digital data is transmitted, a process known as digital transmission.

Digital transmission is the transmission of binary electrical or light pulses with only two possible states, a 1 or a 0. The most common voltage levels range from a low of +3/−3 to a high of +24/−24 volts. Digital signals are usually sent over a wire of no more than a few thousand feet in length. To successfully send and receive a message, both the sender and receiver have to agree on:

- **Voltage levels:** The voltage ranges used represent 1s and 0s.
- **Encoding method (digital signaling technique):** How information is represented as voltage levels or electrical current changes.

- **Data rate:** How fast the sender can transmit data.
- **Unipolar signaling:** The voltage is always positive or negative. The unipolar technique uses a signal of 0 volts (no current) to transmit a zero, and a signal of +5 volts to transmit a 1.
- **Bipolar signaling:** The voltage varies from a plus voltage to a minus voltage.

Nonreturn to zero (NRZ)
This telecommunications binary code schema represents 1s and 0s with separate significant voltage conditions (for example, 1 as positive voltage and 0 as no voltage). No other conditions are recognized in this code.

Return to zero (RZ)
This telecommunications code always returns to 0 volts after each bit before going to +5 volts (for a 1) or −5 volts (for a 0) for the next volt.

Figure 3-3 shows four types of digital signaling techniques. The unipolar technique, at the top of Figure 3-3, uses a signal of 0 volts (no current) to transmit a zero, and a signal of +5 volts to transmit a 1.

In bipolar signaling, the 1s and 0s vary from a plus voltage to a minus voltage. The first bipolar technique shown in Figure 3-3 is called **nonreturn to zero (NRZ)** because the voltage alternates from +5 volts (indicating a 1) and −5 volts (indicating a 0), without resting at 0 volts. The second bipolar technique is called **return to zero (RZ),** or **double current signaling** as it sometimes is called in Europe, because you are moving between a positive and negative voltage potential.

Figure 3-3

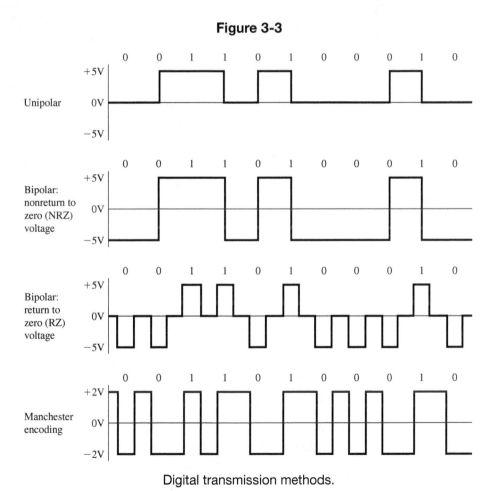

Digital transmission methods.

IN THE REAL WORLD

Decisions, Decisions

So, how do you decide what protocols to use? You'll need to consider them one by one. All of the computers on a network segment will use the same Data Link layer access protocol. If you have an Ethernet network, all computers use Ethernet. In a Token Ring network, they all use Token Ring, and for a wireless network they use Wireless Access Protocol (WAP).

What about the Network layer and above? First, you need to understand that you aren't limited by your access protocol. All current communication protocols support all current access methods, that is, either Ethernet, Token Ring, or wireless networking. The requirement is that all of the computers that need to communicate must have at least one protocol in common. For most networking requirements, that protocol is TCP/IP, which is the current de facto standard for PC LANs. However, it's not the only protocol in use.

Suppose your network includes a legacy NetWare server that uses IPX/SPX as its only communication protocol suite. That means that any and all clients that need to access the server directly must also have the IPX/SPX protocol suite or its equivalent which realistically means clients with both TCP/IP and IPX/SPX.

Other options are available, depending on your exact network needs and service resources. For example, you can configure most Windows server versions as a NetWare gateway, giving Windows clients indirect access to NetWare resources through that gateway.

Manchester encoding
A special type of unipolar signaling in which the signal is changed from high to low or from low to high in the middle of the signal.

Ethernet uses **Manchester encoding,** where a change from high to low is used to represent a 0, whereas the opposite (a change from low to high) is used to represent a 1. Manchester encoding is less susceptible to having errors go undetected, because if no transition is in midsignal the receiver knows that an error must have occurred.

SELF-CHECK

1. In general terms, what is the purpose of access and network protocols?

2. What is Manchester encoding?

Apply Your Knowledge   Why are protocols necessary and how do they allow different devices with different operation systems to communicate?

3.2 COMPARING ACCESS METHODS

The Institute of Electrical and Electronics Engineers' (IEEE) 802 standards define the network access methods used in PC networks. The 802 standards include not only access methods used in PC networks, but also low-level protocols used for other types of data communications. In fact, the 802 standard is an overview of the standards that define the Physical layer and MAC sublayer connections of LAN and MAN devices. All of these 802 standards are compatible and work together at the Data Link layer, that is, as you move above the MAC sublayer into the Logical Link Control layer, which in itself is defined through an 802 standard.

3.2.1 802 Standards

IN ACTION:
PROTOCOL
STANDARDS

Get to know the standards governing protocols.

Here we take a brief look at the 802 standards. The goal is to give you a brief overview of the types of protocols defined by these standards. No 802.13 standard is not in this list because there is no 802.13 standard. The numbering jumps from 802.12 to 802.14.

802.1: LAN and MAN Bridging and Management

The **802.1 LAN and MAN Bridging and Management** standard defines the way in which a networking device, such as a bridge, selects a path to connect local area networks and metropolitan area networks.

802.2: Logical Link Control

Destination service access point (DSAP)
The first byte of the LLC extended two-byte address which indicates whether the destination address is for a single or group of computers.

Source service access point (SSAP)
The second byte of the LLC extended two-byte address which indicates the address of a single computer.

The **802.2 Logical Link Control** standard defines the upper portion of the Data Link layer, known as the Logical Link Control (LLC) sublayer, which uses the Logical Link Control protocol. The LLC protocol is responsible for providing connection-oriented service. The LLC protocol uses an extended two-byte address. The first byte indicates a **destination service access point (DSAP)**. The second byte indicates a **source service access point (SSAP)**.

802.3: CSMA/CD Access Method

The **802.3 Carrier Sense Multiple Access/Collision Detection (CSMA/CD) Access Method** standard, the 802.3 standard, is the access method that is the basis for Ethernet. CSMA/CD and Ethernet are commonly used interchangeably, but Ethernet technically defines the cable and CSMA/CD defines the way that the cable is accessed. CSMA/CD requires that all devices on the network must listen to the cable before it can transmit (carrier sense). Only one device on the network can transmit at a time. So if a device senses a transmission already on the wire, it must wait. After the line is clear, any device can send its message (multiple access). If two computers transmit at the same time, a collision occurs and both must retransmit (collision detection).

IN THE REAL WORLD

CSMA/CD: Then and Now

The 802.3 Ethernet standard of Carrier Sense Multiple Access/Collision Detection was implemented in the early days of networking for use on hub-based Ethernet networks.

On switched networks, it is turned off as part of the auto-negotiation process that configures the line speed and duplex parameters. Most switches are of the store-and-forward type, and hosts do not send packets directly to the intended receiving host. Instead machines send their packets to the switch, which will store them in its internal memory. When each packet has been received in full and checked for validity, it will be forwarded to the destination port. In the event that two packets need to be sent through the same port (the port the receiving host is connected to), they will be queued up and sent one after the other.

802.4: Token Passing Bus Access Method

The **802.4 Token Passing Bus Access Method** standard was developed to provide the benefits of Token Ring without the physical requirements of a ring. An 802.4 network is physically installed in a line or tree-shaped cable. Logically, the data actually travels through the wires in the form of a ring. 802.4 is not used in LANs or PC networking. It is used, however, in some specialized manufacturing control systems.

802.5: Token Ring Access Method

IBM originally developed and trademarked Token Ring. The **802.5 Token Ring Access Method** standard was developed to describe Token Ring. Although Token Ring can use a physical ring cabling, the most commonly used topology is physical star, logical ring.

Under the 802.5 standard, devices take turns transmitting data. They are able to transmit if they receive an empty token. The data they have to transmit is placed in the token and passed on to the next device in the network. The token travels around the entire network looking for the device it is addressed to until the destination device receives the token. The destination device takes its message out and replaces it with a response to the source device. After the source device gets the token back and takes out its own message, the next computer in the ring gets a chance to use the token to transmit.

802.6: DQDB Access Method

The **802.6 Distributed Queue Dual Bus (DQDB) Access Method** standard was developed for metropolitan area networks. This standard uses two parallel cables in a bus-network topology. Each of the two cables in the bus transmits in a different direction so devices can send messages in either direction for bi-directional communication. The bus has a head (a terminating device) that generates cells (fixed-size data packets) that travel throughout the network until they reach the end of the cable.

802.7: Broadband Local Area Networks

The **802.7 Broadband Local Area Networks** standard specifies the design, installation, and testing necessary for broadband transmissions, which allow for multiple transmissions using different channels at the same time. The broadband bus topology creates a full-duplex medium that supports **multiplexing.**

Multiplexing
A communication method that allows multiple signals to transmit simultaneously across a single physical channel by varying length of transmission, frequency used, or both.

802.8: Fiber-Optic Local and Metropolitan Area Networks

The **802.8 Fiber-Optic Local and Metropolitan Area Networks** standard states the recommendations for configuring and testing fiber-optic LANs and MANs. The testing specified under this standard ensures the integrity of the fiber-optic cabling.

802.9: Integrated Services

The **802.9 Integrated Services (IS)** standard defines a unified access method that offers IS for both public and private backbone networks, such as FDDI. It also defines the MAC sublayer and Physical layer interfaces. The 802.9 standard allows for internetworking between different subnetworks— networks that are a part of a larger network and are connected with bridges, routers, and gateways.

802.10: LAN/MAN Security

The **802.10 LAN/MAN Security** standard defines the assigning of unique Security Association Identifiers (SAIDs) for the purpose of security within and between LANs and MANs.

802.11: Wireless LANs

The **802.11 Wireless LANs** standard identifies a group of standards developed for wireless LAN technology. It defines communication between two wireless clients or a wireless client and an access point. It uses the 2.4GHz frequency band to transmit at up to 2Mbps. The 802.11 standard uses various specific transmission methods, depending on the particular substandard. 802.11b and 802.11g use the same transmission method.

The **802.11a** standard was the first high-speed wireless standard and extends 802.11. 802.11a defines transmissions that utilize the 5GHz frequency band with 54Mbps of wireless throughput. The standard was not commonly used.

The **802.11b** standard was the basis for most of the early wireless devices. 802.11b uses the 2.4GHz frequency band for communication and allows for up to 11Mbps of throughput to be transmitted. Upon the release of 802.11b devices, wireless networking became popular both at home and in the workplace.

The **802.11g** standard devices support and provide connectivity to 802.11b devices on the network because they are communicating within the same frequency band.

In October 2009 the **802.11n** standard was adopted to improve communications throughput over the previous version (802.11g). The 802.11n standard adds 40 MHz channels to the physical layer, effectively doubling the available channel width offered in previous versions. The new standard also adopts the multiple-input multiple-output (MIMO) technology, which offers communication through multiple antennas, thus handling a higher throughput of information. On the MAC layer, the 802.11n standard adds frame aggregation, a technology that reduces processing overhead for the protocol.

802.12: High-Speed LANs

Demand Priority Access Method
This media access method places the responsibility for network access control to the hub from the workstation; the hub is responsible for determining the priority for routing communications over the network.

The **802.12 High-Speed LANs** standard defines how the Physical layer and MAC sublayer support 100Mbps signal transmission using the **Demand Priority Access Method,** which puts the responsibility for transmissions on the hub. Devices request permission to transmit, and the hub determines the order of the transmissions and provides access to the network. Demand priority also allows for devices to be assigned a priority status so that their transmissions take precedence over other transmissions. This method allows for higher bandwidth transmissions between devices.

802.14: Cable TV Access Method

The **802.14 Cable TV Access Method** standard provides a reference for digital communications services over cable television networks using a branching bus system. The MAC and physical characteristics follow the 802 standards, including connectionless and connection-oriented communications.

802.15: Wireless Personal Area Network

Wireless Personal Area Networks (WPANs)
Describes short distance wireless networks.

Bluetooth
A peripheral connection standard that allows devices such as cell phones, pagers, and PDAs to communicate.

The **802.15 Wireless Personal Area Network** standard is under development by the IEEE and focuses on **Wireless Personal Area Networks (WPANs).** A WPAN can include mobile devices such as PCs, personal digital assistants (PDAs), cell phones, pagers, and much more. The 802.15 standard that was adopted in 2002 utilized a portion of the Bluetooth specs. A group of manufacturers independently developed **Bluetooth** as a peripheral connection standard so that their devices could interoperate. Bluetooth and 802.15 are fully compatible. Today, Bluetooth is gaining popularity and can be found in devices such as PDAs, cell phones, headsets, and standard computer peripherals such as printers.

802.16: WirelessMAN™

The **802.16 WirelessMAN™** is a group of broadband wireless communications standards for MANs developed by the IEEE. 802.16 standards are expected to enable multimedia applications with wireless connection and have a range of up to thirty miles.

3.2.2. Focusing on LAN Access

More than likely, you will encounter only Ethernet used as access methods on PC LANs. Here we put special emphasis on IEEE 802.3, IEEE 802.5, and IEEE 802.11b, 802.11g, and 802.11n. You're also likely to see Bluetooth in use, but for peripheral connections, not for PC networking.

Connecting with Token Ring

We start with 802.5, the IEEE standard based on IBM's Token Ring. Token Ring standards have remained relatively unchanged for more than a decade. During the same period, higher-speed Ethernet networks have replaced Token Ring as the popular choice for PC LANs. You may still see some Token Ring installations, but those that you do see will most likely be part of a legacy network or a link to an IBM mainframe or minicomputer. Fiber Distributed Data Interface (FDDI) has almost the same topology as Token Ring LAN technology, because it uses the same ring base network topology, but it doesn't use the IEEE 802.5 Token Ring protocol as its basis.

Figure 3-4 is an example of a hybrid network that includes Token Ring. When you find a network like this, rather than spending too much time trying to decide how the network might develop, you need to focus on what you have and how you need to support it. In this case, you need to support both logical bus and logical ring networks configured as a single network segment and connected by a bridge.

Determinant access method
This network method makes it possible to trace packets as they pass through the network.

Media Access Unit (MAU)
A unit in a Token Ring topology which passes packets to computers on the network.

One of the advantages of a Token Ring network is that it's a **determinant access method,** which means you can trace the token's path through the network. Determining where the packet is possible, and given its current location, you know where it will be going next. It always follows the same path in the same order. Token Ring is also somewhat self-healing in case of errors, using **Media Access Units (MAUs).** Most MAUs are able to block a computer that is not responding or is corrupting packets. Also, if a computer becomes temporarily disconnected from the ring, in most cases, when reconnected, it will pick up where it left off.

Disadvantages of Token Ring are cost and performance. As Token Ring has fallen out of favor, the necessary hardware is harder to buy and more expensive. Most hardware purchases are made to replace failing hardware,

Figure 3-4

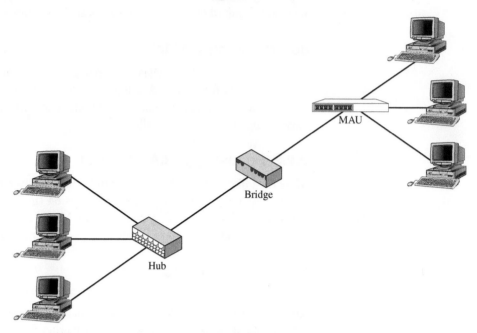

Hybrid network.

not to deploy new networks. Token Ring performance is severely limited compared to recent Ethernet versions. Token Ring networks operate at either 4 Mbps or 16 Mbps with no revisions to these standards under consideration.

Connecting with Ethernet

Various Ethernet versions are, by far, the most commonly used in current networking configurations. Figure 3-5 shows a typical simple Ethernet network. At a quick glance, it looks identical to the hybrid network in Figure 3-4.

Why is Ethernet so popular? The most common implementation is 100 Mbps Ethernet, but 1 Gbps and faster versions are gaining in popularity as hardware prices continue to drop and equipment becomes more readily available. Most hubs and switches are designed to compensate automatically for different versions. For example, the most common hubs provide concurrent support for both 10 Mbps and 100 Mbps Ethernet. The hub detects the speed when the computer is connected and makes the necessary conversions so that the computers can communicate.

The biggest advantages are in cost, availability, and performance. The hardware needed is relatively inexpensive, and most computers come with 100 Mbps Ethernet integrated into the motherboard or already installed as

Figure 3-5

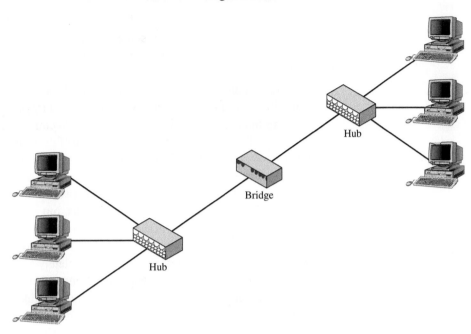

A simple Ethernet network.

a network adapter. Hubs and switches can be purchased from nearly any store that sells consumer electronics. Standards are already available for 1 Gbps and faster Ethernet. The 802.3x standard defines 100 Mbps Ethernet, commonly called Fast Ethernet, and the 802.3z standard defines 1 Gbps Ethernet, or Gigabit Ethernet.

The biggest disadvantage with Ethernet is that performance can suffer as the network size increases. The more computers you have on a cable segment, the more likely collisions will occur. The problem can be lessened substantially by replacing hubs with switches and setting up collision zones through the use of bridges and routers.

Any time you have two or more computers on the same cable segment, collisions can occur. If more than one device sends a message at the same time, a collision occurs. This collision spreads throughout the segment in which it occurred. Thus, all the devices learn about the collision and must back off from transmitting. The devices wait a pseudorandom amount of time and retransmit. This time is known as the **backoff.**

The backoff period is based on a binary algorithm. When a device has waited its allotted time, it then listens to the line again before it sends a message, which is often referred to as the **listen before transmit method.** The delays resulting from collisions and backoff times can have a noticeable impact on network performance as the number of collisions increases.

Backoff
A random amount of time each system on a network must wait before attempting to transmit when a collision has been sensed.

Listen before transmit method
The process by which a system senses traffic on the network before attempting to transmit at the end of the backoff period.

Connecting with Wireless LANs

Wireless LAN standards, specifically the current 802.11n standard, are quickly becoming the rule in some networking applications. You can find wireless LANs in company networks when installing a wired network is difficult or when you want to provide easy access for portable computers. Even more common are wireless LANs used for home networks, both because they are easy to implement and because they provide an easy way to share an Internet connection between multiple computers.

Ease of implementation is obviously one of the primary benefits of wireless LANs. Another benefit is cost, especially in most new computers. Wireless networking support is a hidden cost because most laptops and many desktop computers come with a wireless network adapter already installed.

Wireless LANs do have their drawbacks, but how serious they are depends on how the network is used and how much effort you plan on investing in setting up your network. Security is the biggest problem because wireless LANs are, by default, almost completely unsecured. That means, depending on your network's range (with ranges steadily increasing) someone outside of your company (or home) might be able to connect into your network. They could just be piggybacking on your Internet connection, but if you are using less than secure resource sharing methods, it could give them access to sensitive information.

IN THE REAL WORLD

Household Networking Hazards

Older wireless phones or wireless baby monitors might interfere with 802.11 wireless routers in your home.

The problem is that the wireless network (card and router) runs on the same nominal frequency as most cordless phones (2.4GHz). The FCC actually set up 11 channels around the 2.4GHz band numbered for the 802.11 standard. Each one has a slightly different frequency. The default channel for wireless cards and routers is normally channel 6. However, the software for the router and card allows you to use any channel from 1 to 11, but normally, you should use channels 1, 6, or 11. The reason that you don't get interference all of the time is that the cordless phone is frequency agile. It will try each channel to find the clearest signal. If it decides to use the channel your wireless network is using, interference will occur. Newer wireless phones use 5.8GHz or 6.0 GHz and won't interfere with your wireless network.

SELF-CHECK

1. Which 802 standard access methods are currently used in PC networking applications?
2. What is backoff?
3. Why are wireless networks considered insecure?
4. What is Bluetooth, and how does it differ from Wi-Fi?

Apply Your Knowledge What are some of the methods used to make wireless networks more secure?

If you have access to wireless communication on your computer, describe how you would link your computer to an available wireless access point. How would you link your computer to another wireless device? If you have Bluetooth on your computer or have a Bluetooth cellular phone, describe the process of linking two Bluetooth devices. (*HINT:* Take a look at your Bluetooth device documentation.)

Project 3.1

The IEEE 802 standards define the network access methods used on PC networks. You need to be able to recognize these standards and how each applies to network access requirements. All of the 802 standards are compatible and work together through the Data Link layer of the OSI model.

Complete **Project 3.2: Recognizing IEEE** in the online Networking Basics Project Manual to understand the 802 standards.

3.3 COMPARING NETWORK PROTOCOLS

Network protocols define how devices and even applications communicate. Prior to the development of protocols, no intercommunication existed between devices. The protocols used on your network have an impact on both how the network functions and its ability to communicate with other networks.

For example, a protocol that is available for all Windows machines is NetBEUI. It is very fast, but it is seldom used because it is not routable. Another formerly common protocol suite, Internetwork Packet Exchange/ Sequenced Packet Exchange (IPX/SPX), which was developed as a part of Novell's system of communication within a NetWare client-server environment, could be routed, but only to communicate with other NetWare networks and not on the Internet. It too is seldom used because Novell no longer sells or supports NetWare. Additionally, Microsoft has not included nor supported IPX/SPX in its operating systems beginning with Windows Vista.

Part of the problem is that a single protocol can't independently provide complete intercommunication. It must work with other protocols, operating at different layers of the OSI model, to provide complete end-to-end communication. When a set of protocols works together, it is called a protocol suite or **stack.**

Stack
A group of protocols that work together at different layers of the OSI model.

Two important protocol suites used in internetworking are:

- **Transmission Control Protocol/Internet Protocol (TCP/IP):** The most common of all network protocol suites, the standard in today's networks, and the protocol suite used for communication on the Internet.
- **AppleTalk:** Designed for communication between devices using the Mac OS and often found within the educational arena.

IN ACTION:
NETWORK
PROTOCOLS

Identify the major network protocols in use today.

In recent years, TCP/IP has become the protocol of choice even in NetWare networks and for computers using various versions of the Mac OS. Each of these protocol suites implements a set of rules that provides a unique method for intercommunication between devices. The protocols within each suite function at layers within the OSI model from layer 2 (the Data Link layer) through layer 7 (the Application layer). Because the TCP/IP and IPX/SPX protocol suites were developed before the adoption of the OSI model, they do not map perfectly to its layers.

When deciding what protocol or protocols to use, keep in mind that you should minimize the number of protocol stacks running on any one client and that computers must share a common protocol in order to communicate. As a result, if clients need to directly access a legacy NetWare server, IPX/SPX will be required. TCP/IP will be required if the clients need to support Internet access. Also, any protocol dependent applications, ones that rely on a specific protocol being present in order to work, will fail if that protocol is not available. For example, some older multiplayer PC games relied on SPX for the clients playing the game to communicate. Remove IPX/SPX (or NWLink, as the case may be) and you eliminate the possibility of multi-user play.

3.3.1 Using the TCP/IP Suite

The TCP/IP suite was developed for use on the Internet. Its origins lie in the first RFC, which is discussed in Chapter 4. It is also known as the DoD or ARPANET protocol suite. Its name comes from two of the main protocols

Figure 3-6

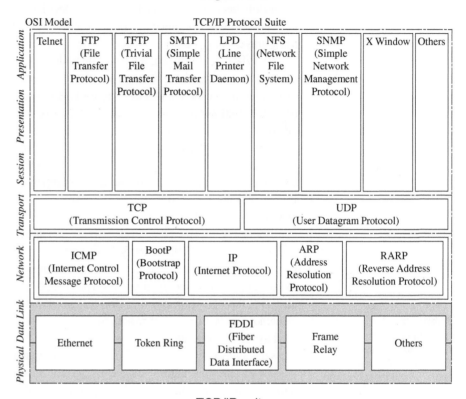

TCP/IP suite.

within the stack: Transmission Control Protocol and Internet Protocol. TCP is responsible for connection-oriented communications using error checking, and IP is implemented in the addressing system used to identify devices.

Although developed for use on the Internet, you can use TCP/IP to build LANs, MANs, and WANs. TCP/IP is the most widely implemented protocol suite and is used within a variety of platforms, including Unix, Windows, and the Macintosh. Even though it doesn't map directly to the OSI model, Figure 3-6 shows how protocols in the TCP/IP protocol suite relate to that model.

Notice that TCP/IP is designed to work with a wide range of physical access methods. In fact, the TCP/IP standards provide the links for physical access, but don't define physical access methods.

Recognizing TCP/IP Features

The TCP/IP suite offers a number of features and benefits, including interoperability, flexibility, and multivendor support.

We discuss interoperability first. TCP/IP has become the standard protocol suite because of its capability to connect LANs, WANs, and the Internet. As more LANs connect to the Internet, TCP/IP is quickly becoming the most universally available protocol today.

TCP/IP's flexibility comes from the wide variety of protocols built into the protocol suite. These range from protocols that manage the mechanics of connection-oriented and connectionless communications, up through protocols that support specialized applications such as file transfers and delivery of web page content.

Another big benefit of the TCP/IP suite is the fact that almost all network software vendors support its use. Apple, DEC, IBM, Novell, Microsoft, and Sun are just a few of the many companies that support the suite. In fact, finding a manufacturer that doesn't support TCP/IP is much more difficult than one that does.

Both a benefit and a drawback of TCP/IP is its addressing scheme. The IP addresses used by TCP/IP identify a two-part address: a network address and a host address. The network address identifies the network to which the host belongs and is used for routing purposes. The host portion of the address uniquely identifies the computer or other device on that network segment. A second value, known as the **subnet mask,** identifies which portion of the address is used as the network address and which is used as the host address. An IP address manually configured on a Windows XP computer is shown in Figure 3-7.

Subnet mask
A portion of the IP address that identifies which part of the 32 bits is the host address and which part is the network address for the system.

As you might imagine, manually configuring addresses for a LAN with hundreds, or even thousands, of hosts would be a daunting task. As a result, TCP/IP supports automated address assignment through the **Dynamic Host Configuration Protocol (DHCP)** service.

Determining what address can be used for any given system depends on another protocol, the **Internet Protocol,** or IP. The current standard used primarily for access to the Internet is IPv4. This protocol defines a 32-bit naming convention. The Internet has enjoyed a huge growth since the inception of IPv4 more than 20 years ago. As available IPv4 addresses have been assigned, the IPv4 address space is filled to capacity. The Internet is migrating to the next version of the IP protocol, IPv6.

Dynamic Host Configuration Protocol (DHCP)
This service dynamically assigns network addresses from a central host.

IPv6 offers a number of advantages over IPv4; most importantly is the use of 128 bit addresses. The number of host addresses possible with 128 bits multiplies the number of possible addresses by a magnitude of millions. The number of unique addresses available using IPv6 is 340,282,366,920,938,463,463,374,607 trillion. All newer networking equipment and operating systems now include the IPv6, and some countries like China have already converted to its exclusive use.

Internet Protocol (IP)
This network protocol defines unique addresses for each computer that communicates on a network.

Identifying the TCP/IP Protocols

The easiest way to categorize the many protocols of the TCP/IP suite is according to where they operate within the OSI model. Each protocol

Figure 3-7

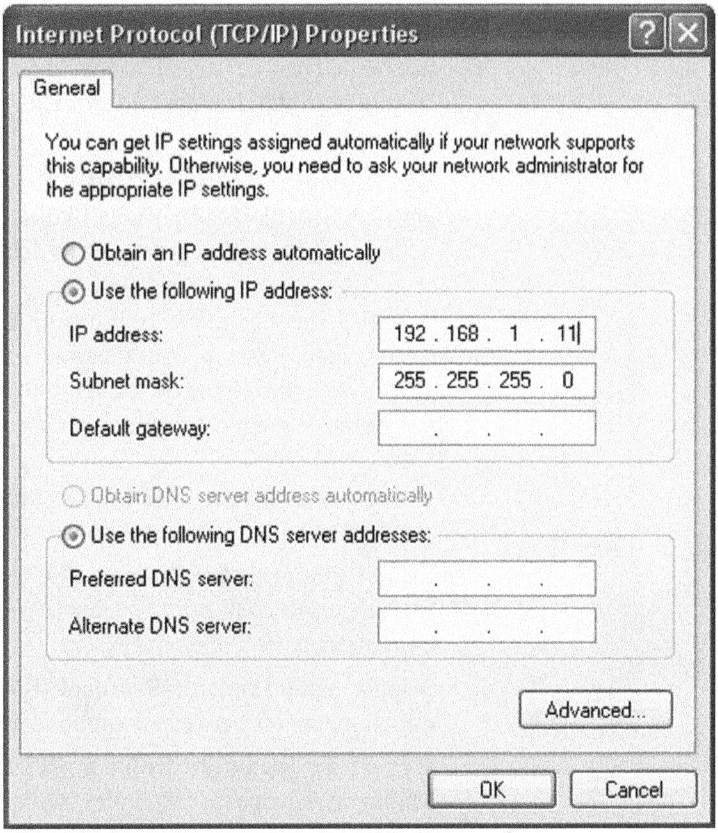

Manual IP address.

in this stack operates at one of three layers: the Network layer (also known as the Internet layer in the TCP/IP model), the Transport layer, or the Application layer.

The Network layer protocols are:

- **Internet Protocol (IP):** Provides for network identification through addressing and connectionless delivery of packets.
- **Address Resolution Protocol (ARP):** Provides a device's MAC address from its IP address.
- **Reverse Address Resolution Protocol (RARP):** Provides a device's IP address when the MAC address is known.
- **Internet Control Message Protocol (ICMP):** Management and troubleshooting protocol that provides support through error and control messages.

The Transport layer protocols provided with TCP/IP are:

- **Transmission Control Protocol (TCP):** Provides connection-oriented packet delivery services that include error checking and sequence numbering, with the destination device responding with a receipt on packet delivery.

- **User Datagram Protocol (UDP):** Provides connectionless packet delivery services that send packets without any type of error checking, sequence numbering, or guarantee of delivery.

TCP/IP Application layer protocols include the protocols operating at the OSI model Session, Presentation, and Application layers. TCP/IP includes a wide variety of protocols used to support different network services. Some of the most commonly used application protocols include:

- **File Transfer Protocol (FTP):** Protocol, service, and application that provides reliable file transfer between TCP/IP hosts.

- **Trivial File Transfer Protocol (TFTP):** Used for file transfer over the Internet using UDP, but requiring acknowledgement (through TFTP) for each packet before the next is sent.

- **Simple Mail Transfer Protocol (SMTP):** Protocol used to transfer e-mail messages between computers using TCP as its delivery protocol.

- **Hypertext Transfer Protocol (HTTP):** Used to access Hypertext Markup Language (HTML) files (web pages) over the Internet or through an intranet, allowing for rapid, reliable data exchange.

- **Domain Name System (DNS):** Protocol and service used for host name to IP address resolution.

- **Telnet:** Protocol and application that provides remote terminal emulation services in clear text.

- **Dynamic Host Configuration Protocol (DHCP):** Protocol and service used to automatically provide IP address and other TCP/IP configuration settings for host computers.

- **Simple Network Management Protocol (SNMP):** Protocol enabling remote configuration, monitoring, and management of network devices, services, and resources.

Some operating systems' implementations of the TCP/IP protocol suite support only a portion of the full protocol stack. Several protocols and services are considered optional, letting you enable or disable them as necessary. You should disable any protocols not needed or used on your network. For example, if not needed, you should disable FTP to avoid allowing unauthorized access to your network's computers.

TIPS FROM THE PROFESSIONALS

Many utilities associated with the TCP/IP protocol suite help network administrators troubleshoot network connections. Some of the most often used are:

- PING (Packet Internet Groper) uses the Internet Connection Messaging Protocol (ICMP) to test the connection of a node on the network and to measure the time required for messages sent from the host to reach the intended node or host.

- IPCONFIG is used to test the protocol stack on a particular node, and depending on the switch used (Remember the IPCONFIG /all command that you used in Chapter 1?), can deliver different functions. (Note that the equivalent command for Linux/Unix systems is IFCONFIG.)

- TRACERT is used to actually follow the route (Trace Route) a data packet takes from the source device to the destination, and shows the devices (routers) that packets travel through and the time from node to node. Using it to troubleshoot **bottlenecks** (areas of the network where data flow is slow due to congestion or lack of adequate resources) is quite useful.

3.3.3 Using AppleTalk

AppleTalk is the proprietary protocol suite developed in the mid-1980s for use with Apple Macintosh networks. It is a multilayer architecture that is built into the Macintosh operating system. Because of this, all Macintosh computers are capable of networking right out of the box. Windows server computers also support AppleTalk as a way of providing resources to Apple Macintosh clients. Recently, changes have been made to the suite to improve its communication capabilities. Unlike the TCP/IP and IPX/SPX protocol suites, the AppleTalk protocol suite was developed with the OSI model in mind and maps directly to the OSI model.

Features and benefits of AppleTalk include ease of addressing and built-in mechanisms for limiting network traffic.

The network portion of an AppleTalk address is manually configured by the network administrator, although **device numbers** are dynamically assigned, using 8 bits or the numbers 1–253. The numbers 0, 254, and 255 are reserved. This dynamic addressing happens when a device is turned on. A device chooses a random number from the range available and sends out a message asking if it is being used. If a device replies that it is using that address, another address is tried. If no one responds to the advertisement of this number, the device maintains it as its address. It then saves this address in RAM.

Device numbers
A random number selected by a device in an AppleTalk network that uniquely identifies that system on the network.

Zones
A logical group of clients within an AppleTalk network, used to route broadcasts appropriately within the given zone, and prevent other broadcast messages from crowding network traffic.

Devices located within an AppleTalk network are assembled into logical zones. These **zones** block the broadcasts that are sent within the network. Each zone can then be connected to an interface on a router. The router can block the broadcasts, but can provide information about all of the connected zones to the user. In this way, traffic is limited while access is provided to all devices throughout the network.

One reason that this is important is because AppleTalk is the "chattiest" of all protocols. Devices using AppleTalk send broadcast messages every 10 seconds. These constant broadcasts, which can be limited only by layer 3 devices such as routers, dramatically affect network performance. If you implement an AppleTalk network, be sure to limit the number of devices within the broadcast domain by using a router.

Identifying AppleTalk Protocols

AppleTalk protocols were designed as a client-distributed network system to provide the sharing of resources within the Macintosh environment. As with SAP in the IPX suite, AppleTalk clients use broadcasts to find out what services are available to them.

Phase 1
A type of AppleTalk network in which one physical network and one logical zone is supported.

Phase 2
A type of AppleTalk network in which one physical network and multiple logical zones are supported.

Two versions of AppleTalk are currently available: Phase 1 and Phase 2. **Phase 1** AppleTalk supports one physical network with one logical network or zone. **Phase 2** supports one physical network with more than one logical network and multiple zones. The zone provides the boundary for automatic device number assignments, so you can have up to 253 devices per zone.

AppleTalk protocols are described as Data Link layer protocols, mid-layer protocols, and upper-layer protocols. Protocols operating at the Data Link layer are:

- **EtherTalk Link Access Protocol (ELAP):** Provides physical access to an 802.3 (Ethernet) network.

- **AppleTalk Address Resolution Protocol (AARP):** Used to retrieve a computer's physical address for packet delivery.

- **LocalTalk Link Access Protocol (LLAP):** Apple's combined Physical and Data Link layer protocol supporting multipoint connectivity in a bus topology wired as a daisy-chain. It supports dynamically addressed workgroups with up to 32 computers per workgroup.

- **TokenTalk Link Access Protocol (TLAP):** Provides physical access to an 802.5 (Token Ring) network.

LLAP was originally based on the LocalTalk protocol suite, which was used with Apple brand computers before the development of AppleTalk.

Four middle-layer protocols are operating at the Network and Transport layers of the OSI model. These are:

- **Datagram Delivery Protocol (DDP):** Provides what is described as best-effort, but not guaranteed, delivery. There are two types of DDP, **Short DDP** and **Long DDP,** depending on the range required for the packet.

- **Routing Table Maintenance Protocol (RTMP):** Protocol used to manage and maintain AppleTalk routers and pass routing table information between the routers.

- **Name Binding Protocol (NBP):** Matches device names to network addresses, similar to DNS on a TCP/IP network, allowing for user-defined logical naming conventions.

- **AppleTalk Transaction Protocol (ATP):** Provides reliable transport services between computers or applications, including keeping track of application transactions.

Short DDP
Used to send packets to computers on the same network.

Long DDP
Used to send packets between different networks when routing services are required.

Upper-layer protocols are implemented at the Session, Presentation, and Application OSI model layers. AppleTalk supports five upper-layer protocols:

- **AppleTalk Data Stream Protocol (ADSP):** Protocol responsible for establishing connections, sequencing, and packet flow control and can be used as an alternative to ATP, but without transaction tracking.

- **AppleTalk Session Protocol (ASP):** Implemented specifically at the OSI Session layer, it provides Session-layer services.

- **Printer Access Protocol (PAP):** Protocol used to support shared and network printers and print job management.

- **Zone Information Protocol (ZIP):** Protocol responsible for keeping track of network numbers and zones, matching network numbers to AppleTalk network zones.

- **AppleTalk Filing Protocol (AFP):** Supports file sharing, file transfer, and end-user printer sharing to Macintosh and non-Macintosh clients.

Windows servers support the AppleTalk protocol suite as a way of providing services and resources to Macintosh clients in a Windows network. More recent versions of the Mac OS use TCP/IP instead of AppleTalk as their primary protocol suite.

IN THE REAL WORLD

The Growth of TCP/IP

Many people have said again and again that TCP/IP is the protocol of choice for most current PC LANs. One of the driving factors for this has been the explosive growth of the Internet. In the early days of the Internet, only a few technophiles knew of its existence, let alone tried to access it. Now, Internet access is one of the primary motivations for first-time computer buyers. However, that's not the only reason. Internet access alone can't account for all of its growth.

The other primary motivation for switching networks over to TCP/IP is interoperability. TCP/IP has been the default protocol for UNIX computers for years. Its introduction into Windows, NetWare, and Apple Macintosh networks has made it easier for these different platforms to share files and other resources. Heterogeneous networks, once a network administrator's worst nightmare, have become relatively easy to set up and maintain.

That doesn't mean that the Internet hasn't also been an important factor for company and other organizational LANs. A website has become a matter of necessity for credibility in today's ever more web-driven marketplace. E-mail, sent and received through the Internet, has become a key tool for both professional and personal communication. Think about it. When was the last time you saw a business card that didn't include an e-mail address? Not only that, more and more companies are using the Internet for their communication backbone for wide area networking.

SELF-CHECK

1. What are some of the most common Application layer protocols?
2. How are unique computer addresses assigned in TCP/IP, IPX/SPX, and AppleTalk?

Apply Your Knowledge How will the advent of the newer IPv6 protocol affect these address assignments? Will a computer have both IPv4 and IPv6 addresses?

Project 3.2

1. Find Your IP address and information about your Network Interface Card (NIC).
   - Find the "My Computer" icon on your computer and right click on it. Choose properties.

- Within the Properties window, choose "Device Manager." (Note that this is in a different location on Windows XP than on Windows 7.)
- Choose the "Network Adapter" section and list all the properties of each of your network adapters (NIC) by right clicking on each one and choosing properties from the drop down menu.
- You will find interesting information under the "Advanced" tab.

2. Identifying your configuration.

- Push the Flag Key and the "R" key at the same time to open the run command.
- Type "cmd" in the window and OK to open the command prompt window.
- At the C:\> prompt type "ipconfig /all". (Note that there is a space between the ipconfig and the /all.)
- Note the information.
- What is your IPv4 address?
- Do you have an IPv6 address? If so, what is it?
- What is your physical address (MAC address)?
- What is your default Gateway address?
- Is DHCP enabled? If so, what is the IP address of your DHCP server?

SUMMARY

Section 3.1

- Protocols are components that allow computers to communicate.
- Protocols can be understood through the OSI model, with each layer of the model represented by one or more protocols.

Section 3.2

- The IEEE standards committee defines the 802 standard. The 802 standard includes methods for various types of data communications.

Section 3.3

- The TCP/IP suite was developed for use on the Internet.
- The IPX/SPX protocol suite was developed for use with Novell NetWare networks.
- The AppleTalk protocol suite was developed for Apple Macintosh networks.

ASSESS YOUR UNDERSTANDING

UNDERSTAND: WHAT HAVE YOU LEARNED?

 Go to **www.wiley.com/go/ciccarelli/networkingbasics2e** to evaluate your knowledge of access methods and network protocols.

Measure your learning by comparing pre-test and post-test results.

SUMMARY QUESTIONS

1. AppleTalk is a single, monolithic protocol that handles all network communication requirements for computers running a Mac OS. True or false?

2. Which TCP/IP protocol is responsible for providing connection-oriented transport?
   - (a) ARP
   - (b) FTP
   - (c) TCP
   - (d) UDP

3. Which of the following is an example of a PC LAN access protocol?
   - (a) TCP/IP
   - (b) NetBEUI
   - (c) Ethernet
   - (d) Token Bus

4. Manchester encoding is the digital transmission method used by Ethernet. True or false?

5. You can have two or more access methods share the same physical media segment. True or false?

6. The Logical Link Control standard is defined by which IEEE standard?
   - (a) 802.1
   - (b) 802.2
   - (c) 802.11
   - (d) 802.15

7. Bluetooth is compatible with which IEEE standard?
   - (a) 802.5
   - (b) 802.11
   - (c) 802.13
   - (d) 802.15

8. The RARP protocol does what?
   (a) Maps a known IP address to a MAC address.
   (b) Maps a known MAC address to an IP address.
   (c) Maps a known IP address to a host name.
   (d) Maps a known host name to an IP address.
9. Which TCP/IP protocol provides clients with access to HTML files?
   (a) HTTP
   (b) FTP
   (c) SNMP
   (d) DHCP
10. Which TCP/IP network provides terminal emulation?
   (a) DNS
   (b) Telnet
   (c) TFTP
   (d) SNMP

APPLY: WHAT WOULD YOU DO?

You are hired as a network administrator. During your initial network inventory, you determine that all computers on the network are configured for either 10 Mbps or 100 Mbps Ethernet. Also, all computers have both the IPX/SPX (or NWLink) and TCP/IP protocol stacks installed and enabled. All network servers are running either Windows NT Server or Windows 2000 Server.

1. At the Network layer and above, from a protocol standpoint, what is necessary for a client and server to communicate?
2. When is it required that you have clients running the IPX/SPX protocol stack?
3. The network is wired as a physical star with computers running 10 Mbps and 100 Mbps Ethernet mixed throughout the building. What is necessary when selecting a new hub to replace one that has failed?
4. What is a potential drawback of having computers run more than one protocol stack?
5. What happens if a computer configured to use TCP/IP as its primary protocol and IPX/SPX as its secondary protocol receives an IPX/SPX packet?

Your network is currently wired as a 16 Mbps Token Ring network. You are preparing to expand the network. The new network is being installed as 100 Mbps Ethernet. You will not be upgrading the Token Ring network at this time.

1. What must you do for the old and new segments to communicate?

2. Both the Ethernet and Token Ring network adapters are designed to use RJ-45 adapters. What would you expect to happen if you connect a computer to the wrong type of network?

3. What is a potential disadvantage of the Ethernet network that is not a problem on the Token Ring network?

BE A NETWORK ADMINISTRATOR

Optimizing Your Network

Your company network includes 16 Mbps Token Ring, 10 Mbps Ethernet, and 100 Mbps Ethernet clients. Each client type is currently connected to its own isolated cable segment. Client computers are configured to use both TCP/IP and IPX/SPX. Most client computers need to support Internet access.

1. How can you optimize the network's available bandwidth, based on the technologies currently in use?

2. What is the potential performance bottleneck in the upgraded network configuration?

3. How can you reduce the possibility of this happening?

4. What determines whether or not a network protocol is needed on a client computer?

5. In the current environment, which protocol would you most likely configure as the default (or primary) protocol and why?

6. What change could you make to the network protocols to improve client performance?

7. Using other research references, if necessary, describe the steps you would take, both hardware and software, to optimize the network. Choose the best available access method and network protocol from those currently in use on the network. Include any potential pitfalls that you'll need to watch out for when removing or disabling support for any protocols currently in use.

KEY TERMS

Access protocols

Backoff

Bipolar signaling

Bluetooth

Demand Priority Access Method

Destination service access point (DSAP)

Determinant access method

Device numbers

Dynamic Host Configuration Protocol (DHCP)

Internet Protocol (IP)

Listen before transmit method

Long DDP

Manchester encoding

Media Access Unit (MAU)

Multiplexing

Network number

Network protocols

Nonreturn to zero (NRZ)

Phase 1

Phase 2

Protocol stack

Protocol suite

Return to zero (RZ)

Short DDP

Source service access point (SSAP)

Stack

Subnet mask

Wireless Personal Area Networks (WPANs)

Zones

NETWORK ARCHITECTURES

What Do You Already Know?

- What is network architecture?
- What types of network architectures are available?
- How do you secure network architecture?

For additional questions to help you assess your knowledge go to **www.wiley.com/go/ciccarelli/networkingbasics2e.**

What You Will Find Out	What You Will Be Able To Do
4.1 What network architecture is.	Explain the evolution of architectures.
	Recognize common network server types.
	Understand why planning your network architecture is important.
4.2 What a peer-to-peer network is.	Recognize the features of peer-to-peer networks.
	Understand peer-to-peer network security issues.
	Understand the principles behind implementing a peer-to-peer network.
4.3 What a client/server network is.	Recognize the features of client/server networks.
	Choose the right client/server network for you.
	Understand client/server network security issues.
	Understand the principles behind implementing a client/server network.

4.4 What a directory services network is.	Recognize the features of directory services networking.
	Choose the right directory services network for you.
	Understand directory services networking security issues.
	Understand the principles behind implementing a directory services network.
4.5 What a hybrid architecture is.	Recognize the hybrid architectures.
	Understand how to segment your hybrid architecture into workgroups.
	Understand the basic advantages and disadvantages for each network architecture discussed in this chapter.

INTRODUCTION

If you want to understand PC networking, you need to understand how the various components of a network interconnect and how they interact.

As software development has improved over the past several decades, computers have become better at interacting on a network. The way in which computers interact on a network is known as the **network architecture.** The physical design, the nuts and bolts of how network devices connect to one another, is known as the **network topology.** This chapter focuses on network architecture models.

The three types of network architecture models that are the most common in current use and therefore are important for you to understand are peer-to-peer, client/server, and directory services. You will sometimes see references to additional architectures: the **hybrid network,** which is actually a network employing a combination peer-to-peer and client/server networking. You may also hear references to **cloud networking.** In cloud networking, an organization offers IT-related services, like hosting applications, to clients. Cloud networking requires an investment in LAN and WAN technologies and specialties in network management. The end result is that clients do not have to make an investment in these core functionalities, and the offering organization can provide a valuable service. The type of architecture appropriate for an organization depends on several factors, including geographical locations, the number of users, special application needs, and the amount of technical and administrative support available.

4.1 UNDERSTANDING ARCHITECTURE BASICS

The network's architecture influences a network's design, the computers included in the network, and how these computers interact with each other and with the user. If you know the architecture on which a network is based,

Network architecture
A method of describing the logical design of a network of computers and how they interact.

Network topology
Describes the physical connections between devices on a network.

Hybrid network
A network architecture that makes use of a combination of other types of architectures.

Cloud networking
A service that combines LAN, WAN, and management functionality necessary to offer IT-related capabilities as a service to clients.

Host-based networks
A network architecture that relied on a central server to control all communications and clients that were capable of very minimal processing.

IN ACTION: EVOLUTION

Network architecture evolved from host-based networks.

Telnet
A software application that allows a user to log on to a remote computer as if the user was sitting at that computer and using its resources.

Economies of scale
This microeconomic term refers to the increase in efficiency of production as the quantity of goods increases.

you have a general idea of how resources are shared on the network and of network security structure.

Despite the differences between network architectures, they all share common features; for instance, all networks:

- Come from the same common roots.
- Involve connected computers so that they can communicate.
- Are based on the same set of hardware devices.
- Use the same communication protocols.

4.1.1 Architecture Evolution

The very first data communications networks developed in the 1960s were **host-based networks,** with the server (usually a large mainframe computer) performing all processing functions. The clients (usually terminals) enabled users to send and receive messages to and from the host computer. The clients merely captured keystrokes, sent them to the server for processing, and accepted instructions from the server on what to display, usually a simple text stream.

This very simple architecture often worked well. In fact, it is still in use in some applications. If you've ever used a terminal (or a PC with **Telnet** software), you've used a host-based application. There is one point of control, because all messages flow through the one central server. In theory, they are **economies of scale** because all computer resources are centralized. However, when you consider the high cost of host systems and relatively low cost of microcomputers, microcomputer-based LANs quickly became a more cost-effective option.

Cost isn't the only issue with host-based networks. The server must process all messages. As the demands for more and more network applications grow, many servers become overloaded and unable to quickly process all the users' demands. Prioritizing users' access becomes difficult. Response time becomes slower, and network managers are required to spend increasingly more money to upgrade the server. Unfortunately, upgrades to the mainframes that usually are the servers in this architecture are "lumpy." That is, upgrades come in large increments and are expensive (e.g., $500,000 or more for "minor" upgrades).

PC networks grew out of a desire to bring the shared resources and common applications of a host-based network to desktop computers. Manufacturers based much of the communication infrastructure on that used in host-based networks, but designs varied by manufacturer. Some manufacturers, such as Novell, tried to emulate the host-based network as closely as possible using a PC as the network's central server. Others, such as 3Com and later Microsoft, opted for a more distributed design with multiple servers. Today's architectural models evolved from these early designs. PC networks continue to be a vibrant, rapidly changing environment.

The late 1980s saw an explosion in the use of PCs and PC-based LANs. Today, more than 90 percent of most organizations' total computer processing power now resides on LANs rather than centralized mainframe computers. Why this shift? It was fueled in part by low-cost, popular applications such as word processors, spreadsheets, presentation graphics programs, and managers' frustrations with application software on host mainframe computers. Most mainframe software is not as easy to use as PC software, is far more expensive, and can take years to develop or even to make incremental changes. In the late 1980s, organizations still using host-based computing had development backlogs of two to three years for any new application. New York City, for example, had a six-year backlog. In contrast, managers could buy PC packages off the shelf or develop PC-based applications in a few months.

These and other advantages led to ready (if not always appropriate) acceptance of available network architectures. Then, as now, many organizations depended on retailers or consultants to recommend networking solutions. Although organizations still rely on retailers or consultants, consumers are more likely to have some PC network experience. Employees and management staff have both a better understanding and increased expectations. As organizations had a better idea of their needs and made requests and suggestions to LAN software manufacturers, LAN features changed to meet their needs. In the process, network architectures also changed with specific models developed to meet the needs of different business sizes and segments.

4.1.2 Common Server Types

Network servers are a critical part of any network. How the servers are deployed and interact with other computers on the network depends on the network architecture. Knowing what types of servers you might find on a network and the role of each is important.

Servers might be dedicated to these roles, or configured as peer servers, acting as both a client and server. Some of the most common network servers are listed here. Servers you are likely to encounter include:

- **File servers:** File servers offer users a central location to save files. The security control access to these files depends on the network architecture and server configuration. In many configurations, files stored on a file server are secure because they require a user to log in with a unique login name and a unique password.

- **Print servers:** Print servers make shared printers available to network users by allowing users to print simultaneously to the server. The print server stores the **print jobs,** documents waiting to print, in a **print queue,** which is a storage location, until the printer is available. The file containing the print queue is often referred to as the **spooler file,** and the process of queuing the print jobs often referred to as **spooling.**

IN ACTION: RECOGNIZING SERVER TYPES ✳

Many networks share common server types.

File server

A server on a network whose primary function is to serve as a repository for network user files.

Print server

A server on a network whose primary function is to control network user access to shared printers.

Print jobs

Files sent to the print server by a network user, waiting to access the printer.

Print queue

A collection of files awaiting access to the printer on a printer server.

Spooler file

A file on a print server that contains the list of print files waiting to be printed.

Spooling

The process by which files waiting to be printed on a print server are ordered to provide access to the printer.

Messaging server
A server on a network whose primary function is to manage messages between network devices, for example, e-mail and broadcast messaging.

Application server
A server on a network whose primary function is to hold and manage application executables, files, and data.

Web server
A specialized application server whose primary function is to serve content to clients through the Internet.

Virtual hosting
The method by which one system is able to serve as a host for multiple domain names, thus allowing several systems to share a single IP address and the host system to share resources, such as memory, processor cycles, etc.

Bandwidth throttling
The method by which client demand for access to a web server can be regulated to manage access in times of high demand.

Server-side scripting
A method of providing a unified look and feel for web pages through the hosting server.

- **Messaging servers:** These servers answer requests for e-mail by clients or route mail messages to appropriate mail servers. These servers are more commonly seen on larger networks that manage their own mail accounts. Smaller networks more often use mail services provided by Internet Service Providers (ISPs).

- **Application servers:** Application servers provide services to the network clients or support enterprise-based applications. Some application servers keep data and the application on the same computer, but it varies by application. Application servers are specific to the applications they support, such as database servers or business-related applications. For example, websites use at least one application server: a web server. Depending on the website, additional application servers may be used in a supporting role, such as a database server storing content used by the web server and hosted websites.

- **Web servers:** This type of application server's primary function is to serve content to clients through the internet. Web servers can help an organization by providing a single interface through which multiple websites can be accessed from one address, referred to as **virtual hosting.** Web servers can also help with organizing how demand from clients is handled through **bandwidth throttling.** Additionally, a web server can help you unify the look and feel of web pages for your clients through **server-side scripting.** Lastly, web servers allow organizations to host and share large files.

The most common server types are file and print servers. These server types are usually first deployed on a network, with others implemented over time as needed. Some companies never have a need to go beyond offering just file and print services.

With application servers, you need to understand the specific server types and the services that they provide to the network. Web servers give users access to information over the Internet or through a private intranet. A database application is an application that stores information formatted for efficient storage and data access.

In some cases, a computer may be configured to support multiple server types. For example, small networks commonly have the same server acting as both a file server and a print server. Most server types, such as database servers, are recommended not be configured to also host other services.

4.1.3 Evolving Network Connections

Just as coming up with a blueprint before constructing a building is essential, deciding on a network architecture before setting up a network is equally important. The technologies that make up a network are not of much good used separately. People who want to use a network to solve a problem or improve a process need the different components to function as one. A network architecture provides the blueprint for designing and implementing a network.

An important part of implementing a network is matching the network's size and capabilities to the company's needs. In the early days of PC networks, networking was seen as a solution best suited to large companies, while smaller companies struggled along with stand-alone PCs. With time, the number of networking options increased while costs decreased, making PC networks more readily available to most, if not all, companies.

Networks also tend to evolve over time. As companies grow, so do their networks. Today, companies of all sizes are using networks so employees can communicate and work more efficiently. In some companies, a day's work may involve collaborating with coworkers located in offices around the world. These companies require networks that will support thousands of users who need to access information across the company. These large networks are called **enterprise networks,** like the one shown in Figure 4-1.

Enterprise networks can be enormous, with thousands of users and possibly hundreds of servers. Each office location may look like a single or multiserver network, except that each location will be connected to the rest of the corporate WAN. Wide area networking has become a testing ground for new client-server applications, which are capable of communicating between distant servers. Such wide area networking extends the client-server model across many LANs, involving several servers to fulfill a user request.

Enterprise networks
A large network that contains multiple servers and typically integrates wide area links.

IN ACTION:
REASONS TO PLAN
YOUR NETWORK

What can happen if you fail to plan your network?

Figure 4-1

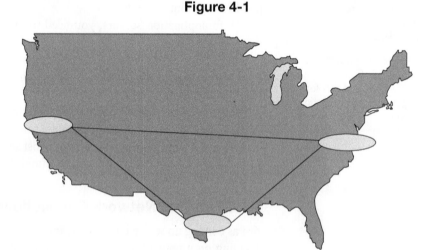

Enterprise network.

IN THE REAL WORLD

Why You Need to Plan Your Network

Quite often, organic terms are used to describe networks. Doing so isn't that inaccurate when you consider that the most networks look like something that grew up in place rather than something carefully planned and designed. Such growth is especially true of older networks that have gone through multiple generations of hardware, software, and various network administrators, each with their own idea of the "best" network design.

The network grows with the company. Even though network growth is something that should be carefully planned and implemented, more often than not, it just happens. Computers are added as new employees are hired. Additional cable is laid and new hubs are added in as necessary. The cable plant branches and intertwines until it sometimes becomes difficult to figure out just what goes where.

The lifecycle often goes something like this. The company starts out with a simple network, maybe no more than one or two file servers and a few clients. Other servers get added—a mail server so the company can handle its own e-mail, a database server to handle a custom database application, maybe even a Web server for internal communications. Eventually, these servers get consolidated into a secure server room for their protection.

Software features and available technologies change. The company upgrades the cable plant and pulls new cable throughout. They might upgrade hubs and other hardware at the same time, and if not, they save that for later to spread out the costs.

The end result, more often than not, is a mess. Crawl spaces are filled with cable going nowhere and more than likely no one person knows what is or isn't actually used. Troubleshooting cable problems becomes a nightmare, often making it easier to just run yet another new length of cable rather than trying to locate and fix the correct one. Network communication is routed through different cable and support hardware, often mixing specifications that weren't designed to be mixed, and as a result, intermittent problems become a common feature of the network.

What's the solution? More often than not, the best solution is to start over. Pick an appropriate network architecture, select appropriate hardware, identify the hardware that you can reuse, and rewire the network. However, this time, you label the new cable and once everyone has migrated to the new network, you pull out the old cable so that it's no longer a source of confusion. The solution is neither cheap nor easy, but you will probably find that it is will pay for itself over time in improved reliability and performance.

SELF-CHECK

1. What are the two most common server types?

2. What is the basic purpose of network architecture?

Apply Your Knowledge > Create a network between two computers by creating a workgroup and joining the two computers to it. Share a file so that both computers can access it.

Project 4.1

The three network architectural models currently used in network design are peer-to-peer, client/server (or server-based), and directory services (or directory-based). Although peer-to-peer networks are still often found in smaller companies, many larger companies have shifted from the client/server model to the directory services model. Peer-to-peer networking is the model almost exclusively used when setting up home networks.

As you work through this chapter, complete **Project 4.2: Comparing Network Architectures** in the online Networking Basics Project Manual to be able to recognize network architectural model features and common architectural models.

4.2 EVALUATING PEER-TO-PEER NETWORKING

Peer-to-peer network
A network architecture in which each computer can act as both a server and a client.

Macintosh Plus
An Apple computer that offered an early version of peer-to-peer networking.

Windows for Workgroups 3.11
An early Microsoft Windows version that supported peer-to-peer networking.

Workgroup
A logical peer-to-peer network grouping.

A **peer-to-peer network** is a design in which any computer can act as both a server and a client with no central security control. In peer-to-peer networks, users share their computers' resources, making them available to other users. Peer-to-peer networks were available as early as 1984, when Apple Computer unveiled its **Macintosh Plus,** which was capable of networking with other Macintosh computers without the use of a server. Microsoft also introduced peer-to-peer networking capabilities in 1992 with the release of **Windows for Workgroups 3.11.** In fact, the term Microsoft most commonly uses to describe a peer-to-peer network is a **workgroup,** which is a logical peer-to-peer grouping identified by a **workgroup name.**

To allow sharing of resources in Linux/Unix in a peer-to-peer networking architecture you have to configure each system to allow networking and to be able to identify other systems. All Linux/Unix networking is done through the TCP/IP protocols and doesn't require services like Macintosh Plus or Windows for Workgroups 3.11. After your Linux/Unix system is configured to be visible on networks (by defining the **host name**)

Workgroup Name
A name used to uniquely identify a workgroup on a network.

Host name
A unique identifier assigned to a device on a network used to access the device.

Host name resolution
A process through which a host name identification is connected to an IP address, thus allowing communications between systems and devices on a network.

IN ACTION:
RECOGNIZING
PEER-TO-PEER
NETWORKS

Key features of peer-to-peer networks.

Decentralized resource sharing
A term referring to sharing resources from peer servers and individual users' computers rather than from centralized sources.

and is able to identify other systems (through **host name resolution**), sharing of resources is as easy as permitting user's access to your system or being granted access to another system.

The most basic peer-to-peer network allows people to share resources such as folders, printers, and CD-ROM drives. What does this mean in practical terms? Peer-to-peer networking lets one user access a file or printer connected and/or shared on another user's computer across the network, thereby reducing costs associated with a centralized server or multiple printers. The most popular peer-to-peer networks have advanced to the point that peer-to-peer networks are accessible over the Internet for use in online gaming, virtual reality, and peer-to-peer file sharing applications.

4.2.1 Understanding Peer-to-Peer Features

Peer-to-peer networking enables **decentralized resource sharing.** Specific characteristics include:

- It allows users to share many resources from their computers, including files and printers.
- It's best suited to groups of 12 or fewer users, though some manufacturers suggest configurations with up to 20 users.
- It's decentralized so that user files are not stored in a central location.
- It allows computers (and users) to communicate easily.

Peer-to-peer networking is built into the operating system software on your computer. After the software is configured on each workstation, users are responsible for making their specific information available to others (sharing it) and managing the access to that information. A sample peer-to-peer network is shown in Figure 4-2.

When users are participating in the same peer network, they belong to a workgroup. The workgroup is assigned a name, which may represent users who work in the marketing department or the group of people who sit in the cubicles in the northeast corner of the building. Because this group is local, based on workgroup name, membership isn't necessarily related to the computer's physical locations on the network. The workgroup name makes remembering who is participating in the peer-to-peer network easier, which is important when you have multiple workgroups on the same network.

4.2.2 Choosing a Peer-to-Peer Network

When considering your networking needs, you should consider your users' needs and what is available in your environment. You may have a business that does not have the necessary network hardware and cabling to support a

Figure 4-2

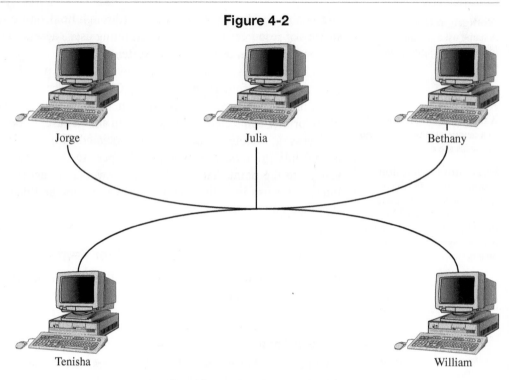

Sample peer-to-peer network.

Hidden costs
Refers to the operational
costs of running a network
that are not readily apparent.

**Total cost of ownership
(TCO)**
The complete cost of
operating a network including
the costs of hardware,
software, maintenance, and
administration.

complex networking solution. Peer-to-peer networks are uniquely suited to situations with significant budgetary constraints preventing client-server or directory-based model. Keep in mind, however, that a peer-to-peer network assumes a certain level of computer literacy because users are expected to handle their own resource sharing. If users don't have that level of expertise, then some type of client/server model might be more appropriate.

You will sometimes see cost listed as a peer-to-peer networking advantage when compared to other network architectures. The problem is that this purported advantage usually doesn't account for **hidden costs,** such as the added cost of supporting users and correcting their mistakes. The total cost of a system can be difficult to calculate. The **total cost of ownership (TCO)** includes the cost of equipment and software, as well as the cost for managing the technology. For example, a peer-to-peer network might include a specialized server, such as a web server and a network peer. The management costs include items such as the time that users spend managing the technology and correcting problems resulting from inappropriate shares. Look out for these hidden costs, which are often overlooked.

Peer-to-peer networks are best suited to very small businesses or to support a small, autonomous group within a larger company. However, migration paths from peer-to-peer networking to other architectures are available, so some companies will start out with a peer-to-peer network and then move to a different network architecture as their needs change.

4.2.3 Securing a Peer-to-Peer Network

Share-level security
A security method used in peer-to-peer networking, with access permissions based on password-protected resource shares.

IN ACTION:
PEER-TO-PEER
NETWORK SECURITY

Understanding a method for securing the peer-to-peer network.

Peer-to-peer networks sometimes use **share-level security,** which gives the users the authority to assign passwords to the local resources on their computers.

Share-level security allows a person who is sharing a resource to implement security with a password, or by not assigning a password, the person can let anyone on the network use the resource. In some older operating systems, assigning a password to protect the resource required that the password be given to all the people who needed to be able to access that resource. Passwords that are shared seldom stay secret, or secure, for very long.

The same password could be assigned to every resource, but doing so would be like a building manager creating the same key for every apartment in the building. Figure 4-3 demonstrates a better security scheme, which is to use a different key for each apartment. In peer-to-peer networking, assigning each resource a unique password minimizes the security risks. The drawback, however, is that managing the passwords can be more difficult. For example, users not only have to remember multiple passwords, but they would also have to remember the resources with which the passwords are associated. This often results in users keeping a password list handy in a desk drawer, taped under the keyboard, or even posted on a display screen for all to see.

More modern operating systems do a better job at security. Windows 2000 and XP Professional, Macintosh OS 9 and OS X, and Linux

Figure 4-3

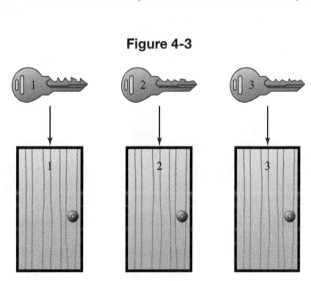

Peer-to-peer security.

User-management
A feature available in some PC operating systems that allows the user to assign unique user name and password combinations for resources available on that system.

all support a **user-management** feature that allows you to assign separate usernames and passwords for each individual. But once again, users and their passwords are being created and managed individually on each workstation. You can also manage security through groups of users, but group management is usually more trouble than it's worth at this level. This decentralized model of a peer-to-peer network makes for a cumbersome system because you have to create user accounts for each user that needs access on each computer sharing resources. When passwords change, they have to be manually changed on each computer.

Windows XP supports two basic file sharing configurations. One, the default, is known as simple file sharing. With **simple file sharing,** you can share folders and their contents to designated individual users or all the members of your workgroup. You can control access to the data, but the same permissions are granted for all designated workgroup members. If you want to control access permissions by user or group, you need to disable simple file sharing through the computer's folder options.

Simple file sharing
A Windows XP files sharing method in which some or all designated workgroup members have the same access permissions.

4.2.4 Implementing a Peer-to-Peer Network

Implementing a peer-to-peer network typically involves three steps:

- Install network hardware.
- Configure the peers and workgroup members.
- Share resources to the network.

The basic hardware requirements are common to most LANs without regard to the network architecture. You need a network adapter installed in each network member and a communication path. Nearly all computers come with an Ethernet network adapter integrated in the motherboard circuitry, so for a wired network, you just need to lay the cable plant and connect the computers. Figure 4-4 shows these requirements. Most laptops ship with wireless networking built-in, often eliminating the need for a physical cable plant.

Figure 4-4

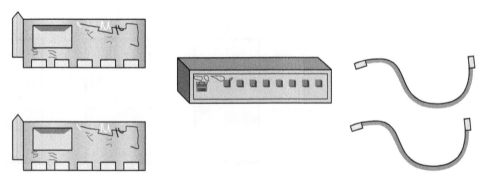

Network hardware requirements.

To configure network members, you configure the network communication properties, which depend on your communication protocol, and identify the computer as a workgroup member. Each operating system has its own method of configuration for peer-to-peer networking. Even though configuring every operating system for peer-to-peer networking is out of the scope of this chapter, the following example should give you a basic idea of the information and methods you will need in your own environment. The property screen used to configure a Windows XP computer as a workgroup member is shown in Figure 4-5. Open the System properties from the Control Panel, select the Computer Name properties, and click Change to change the computer name and workgroup membership. This is also where you configure membership in an Active Directory domain. We discuss directory services networking in Section 4.4.1 of this chapter.

The procedures for sharing resources depend on the operating system and version. Share-level security or access permissions by user are specified when you share the resource, but can be changed later as necessary. A detailed discussion of procedures for resource sharing is beyond the scope of this chapter.

Figure 4-5

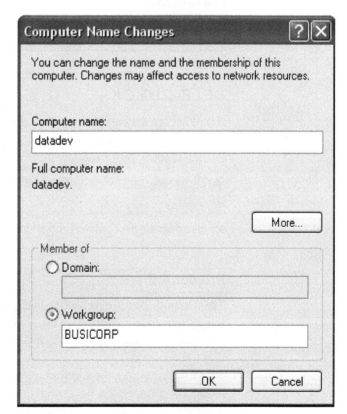

Configuring a workgroup name.

FOR EXAMPLE

BIRTH OF A NETWORK

Busicorp started out as a small custom print shop. Over the years, the business has grown to offer not only printing services, but also reproduction, editing, and graphics services. The company has Internet access through a cable modem, and the company's six employees use e-mail addresses provided through the ISP. The problem is that each employee has to log in through the same computer, the only one with access to the Internet, to check or send mail.

All of the computers run Windows XP Professional and have built-in Ethernet network adapters. The employees all have quite a bit of computer experience and can manage their own computer's configuration requirements and install and configure applications when needed.

The owner wants to make collaborating on projects easier for employees. He needs to make sharing files and graphics easier as well. Security isn't a serious issue, except for files stored on one computer. He is the only employee that should have any access to that computer. He also wants everyone to have access to a high-speed, multifunction printer that is connected to one of the computers and used for most print jobs. However, he wants to keep this cost to a minimum.

This situation is ready-made for peer-to-peer networking. You have a small number of employees who need to share resources and don't really have a need for centralized control. A peer-to-peer network would let employees share project files and the multifunction printer. Employees would also be able to share the Internet connection so that anyone could manage e-mail from his or her own computer. The only thing needed is the network hardware to connect the computers.

What about the one computer that has sensitive files? For the time being, the best solution would likely be to simply not connect it to the network. Doing so is the surest way of protecting it against unauthorized access.

SELF-CHECK

1. What are the basic criteria for selecting peer-to-peer networking?

2. What are the two security methods supported in a peer-to-peer networking environment?

3. What are the basic steps for implementing a peer-to-peer network?

Apply Your Knowledge Take a look at your own computer. How would you set up a peer-to-peer network on your own system?

Project 4.2

The defining feature of a peer-to-peer network is that it has no centralized resource or security management. A peer-to-peer network lets users share resources from their computers and manage access security, if any, themselves.

Complete **Project 4.3: Exploring a Peer to Peer Network** in the online Networking Basics Project Manual and explore the different procedures for sharing resources from a computer running Windows 7.

4.3 EVALUATING CLIENT/SERVER NETWORKING

Companies have traditionally chosen the client/server architecture instead of peer-to-peer because it better meets their needs. Companies and other organizations have also found additional cost savings in client/server networks. Client/server network architectures centralize resources, data, and security. One reason for added security is that securing important information is easier when it is located in one place. Centralization also makes protecting information easier in the event of a fire or other disaster. Client/server architectures offer a performance improvement over peer-to-peer networks by taking advantage of the processing capabilities of workstations, along with the power of servers. In a client/server network, both the client and the server can process information simultaneously.

4.3.1 Understanding Client/Server Networks

Client/server network
A network model that closely matches the mainframe network model, with servers providing resources to the network and clients consuming resources. A defining feature of this type of network is centralized security control. Also known as a server-based network.

The **client/server network** architecture is a centralized model for data storage, security, network applications, and network administration. The client/server architectural model, along with its more recent variations, is the most common networking architectures in use today. Many companies that started with peer-to-peer networking quickly outgrew that model and had to find better networking solutions. Most end up installing some kind of client-server network.

Characteristics of client/server networks, also referred to as server-based networks, include:

- They're based on a scalable model that can support small networks of a few (less than ten) users up to large networks with thousands of users.
- They employ specialized servers that provide services to the client workstations.
- They provide shared services such as print and file services.
- They allow a high level of security based on access permissions.
- They can be centrally managed by a network administrator or a team of network administrators.

Server applications
Specialized applications that run on server NOSs and provide resources or special services to network clients.

A simple client/server network is shown in Figure 4-6. The client/server model requires network servers designed and implemented for that role. The computers used as servers are often (but not always) more powerful than the network's client computers. They also run special software or operating system versions that enable them to act as a network server. In this model, most applications run locally at the client with data stored on central file servers. In some cases, the network might include **server applications,**

Figure 4-6

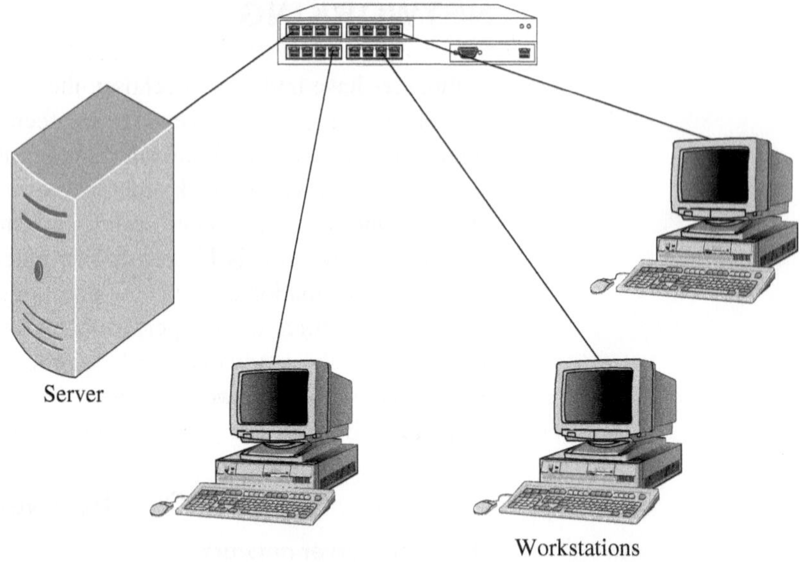

Sample client/server network.

which are simply applications designed to run at the server and provide some service to the network, such as database and web servers.

As a company grows, it is likely that the server it started with will become less capable to meet user demands. When performance begins to degrade, it often becomes necessary to dedicate servers to specific roles, with each running different applications and performing specific tasks. It is not unusual for a large company to have two or more servers dedicated, for example, to responding to users' login requests. Other services include acting primarily as file servers, while others provide print services to the network.

4.3.2 Choosing a Client/Server Network

IN ACTION:
RECOGNIZING
A CLIENT/SERVER
NETWORK

The basic characteristics of a client/server network.

Most companies use some type of server-based network, either based on the traditional client/server model or on the directory services model discussed later in this chapter. Planning and selecting the right client/server technology is not always that easy. There are several possible variations on the basic model, as well as recent enhancements providing even greater control and flexibility.

The basic criteria for selecting a client/server network are:

• Files need to be stored centrally.

• Security is important to protect sensitive and valuable data.

• Users will need access to the server applications, shared data, and other resources.

- One or more network administrators will be managing the server(s).
- It has too many users for a peer-to-peer network.

Server hardware expense has become less of an issue as computer costs have dropped while the processing power and hardware resources in the typical computer have improved. However, the hardware necessary for some specialized servers, such as for a high-volume database application, can still be relatively expensive. This issue relates to the specific application, not the network architecture.

4.3.3 Securing a Client/Server Network

Client/server networks are more secure than peer-to-peer networks by design. First, servers centralize resources on a network making managing resource access through user and group accounts easier. The network administrator or administration staff and not individual users manage the user accounts and the resources the users have access to. Finally, servers offer stronger security features such as sophisticated authentication systems. Let's revisit the earlier example comparing network security to keys and apartments.

In Figure 4-7, the apartment tenants Sue, Julia, and Bethany live in the same apartment building. When they moved in, the apartment manager gave each person a separate key that was unique to her apartment. The apartment manager keeps track of who has what key. If someone loses a

Figure 4-7

Revised security example.

key, the apartment manager will reissue a duplicate only to the person who was originally assigned the key.

This analogy applies to coworkers Sue, Julia, and Bethany at work. They each have been assigned a password. The names they use to log onto the network, called user or login names, and their passwords differentiate one from the others. When the network administrator grants one of them permission to use a resource, they have been given a "key." The key applies only to that user.

Most server-based networking products also let you define groups of users. When you grant access permissions to groups, the same permissions are granted to the group members (unless explicitly blocked). Group access makes sense in a network environment because you will often have groups of users doing similar tasks and needing similar access permissions. When you need to make changes, you can make them to the group rather than each individual user, providing for more efficient use of network administrators' time and efforts.

IN ACTION:
IMPLEMENTING A
CLIENT/SERVER
NETWORK

What are the issues involved in implementation?

Segment
(1) A physical network division within a larger physical network.
(2) A term sometimes used to refer to datagram fragments at the Transport layer of the OSI model.

4.3.4 Implementing a Client/Server Network

Except for the additional servers, the network hardware required for a client/server network is generally the same as for a peer-to-peer network. The difference is not so much in the type of hardware required but in the volume of hardware. More computers means more NICs, more cable, and more hubs. If the network becomes large enough, you might need to use routers to break the network into smaller **segments,** which are individual network sections designed so that most of the traffic generated remains local to that segment. As the network grows, you may also need to include wide-area connection hardware in the network design.

In general, implementing server-based networks is not as simple as implementing peer-to-peer networks. You can design server-based networks in many ways. Likewise, hardware and software for servers can be configured in many ways. Selecting the right design depends on your organization's size, the network requirements, and the cost. Traditional client/server networks are used less often as a network architecture; they're most often seen in older networks of companies that haven't had a need or the budget to migrate to newer architectural models. Still, even in newer architectures, you might see individual servers that operate on the client/server model. This model is commonly seen, for example, in database servers.

Implementing a Single-Server Network

When a company outgrows its peer-to-peer network, it usually adds a server and converts the network into a client/server network. Many companies, knowing that they are too large for a peer-to-peer architecture, start out with this design. You saw a simple example of a single-server network in Figure 4-6. The network capacity and the number of users that the network can support will depend on various factors such as the network operating system, the software that runs on the network servers, and the server hardware configuration. Network servers are typically designed to support hundreds of users, but they realistically can provide optimum support for a significantly smaller number.

Other requirements placed on the server may further reduce the server capacity. When you configure a network with a single server, not only is that server responsible for processing user logins and handling user security, it typically also acts as a file and print server. You also have a potential problem in that the server represents a **single point of failure,** that is, if the server fails, so does the network.

Implementing a Multiserver Network

Seeing companies, even small businesses, deploying client/server networks based on multiple servers, known as a **multiserver network,** is more and more common. One reason is avoiding the potential problems that could result from a server failure on a single-server network. Also, because servers can provide a variety of functions, you'll often see multiple servers with each providing different services. The number of users found on this type of network varies widely by company, but often reaches hundreds or even thousands of users, though at the higher end of that range they can become very difficult to manage.

Many companies go to a multiserver design, like the one in Figure 4-8, because it provides better user support. That is because separating services across multiple servers improves performance and reliability. Each server can be optimized to run a particular service. If one server fails, other servers continue to function normally and, in some cases, can even take over for the malfunctioning server. Notice that the network configuration is more complex than that of a single-server network and can grow to become even more complex with time and added requirements.

This model can be expanded over a wide area by connecting individual LANs, as shown in Figure 4-9. Users can access not only the servers in their own local networks, but in the remote networks as well. Typically, you want to keep the resources that a user most often needs local to that user to minimize network traffic and management concerns.

A multiserver network is shown in Figure 4-9; note that it's more complex than the single-server network.

To get a better idea of what is happening with client-server models over WAN links, consider the following example based on Figure 4-9. Julia, a user in San Francisco, needs information from Sue, a user in Washington, DC. Julia sends an e-mail message routed through a messaging server on her local network. The message is forwarded through the network in Chicago, finally arriving at the messaging server in Washington and through that server to Sue. In this multiserver example, you have e-mail servers deployed in each local network. Typically, you would also have, at minimum, a server in each location to process users' login requests and evaluate access security.

Single point of failure
In the context of networking architectures, a term that refers to a resource that, when it fails, causes the network as a whole to fail.

Multiserver network
A network that implements multiple servers in various roles.

Figure 4-8

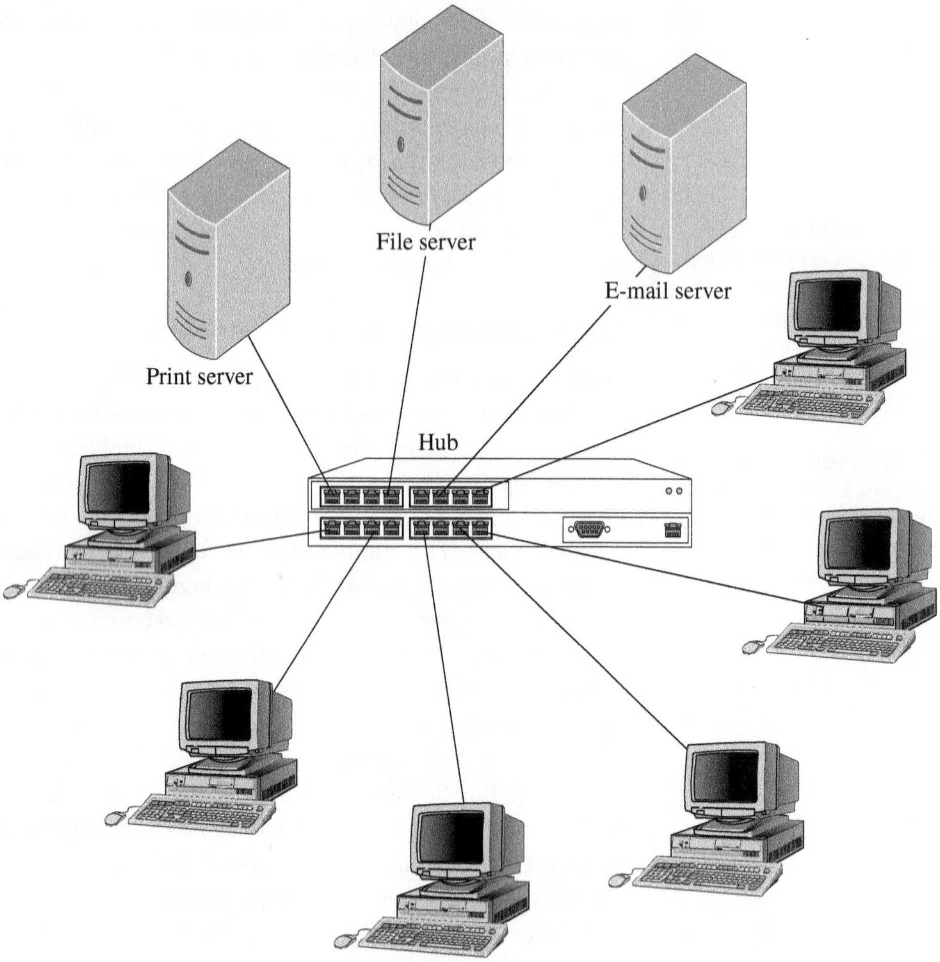

File server

E-mail server

Print server

Hub

A simple multiserver network.

Figure 4-9

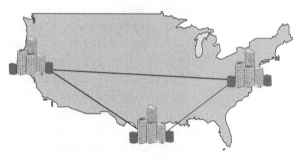

A wide area network (WAN).

IN THE REAL WORLD

Growing Your Network

Each server in a multiserver network means more costs (for computer hardware and software) and more management overhead. Not only do you have the cost of the computer, which is often the smallest investment, you also have the cost of the operating system and any additional server applications. Why go to the expense? Because you need to if you want to have an efficient and reliable network.

How do you determine the best time to expand you network? Some companies avoid that decision as long as possible, sometimes until they are forced to make the decision while the network is down and waiting for the server to be repaired. A better way is to monitor network activity in order to determine the cost of downtime as a monetary justification, and also the perceived server performance, which is the key to keeping your users satisfied. When any load becomes too much or too much of a risk for a single server, it's time to expand.

SELF-CHECK

1. Why is having a single server a potential risk?
2. What are the potential disadvantages of a server-based network?
3. What is an indication that server capacity has approaching its physical limits?

Apply Your Knowledge On your Windows Server, open Task Manager by pushing "Ctrl+Alt+Del" and choosing it from the selection window that appears.

Select the Performance Tab and observe the capacity of your server.

4.4 EVALUATING DIRECTORY SERVICES NETWORKING

Many people see directory services networks as an evolutionary development from the traditional client/server network root. Immediately popular, directory services networks have quickly replaced many, if not most, traditional client/server networks, especially in larger companies and large enterprise networks. However, this statement is not meant to imply that directory services architecture is limited to large networks. In fact, directory

Heterogeneous networking
Environments that have a mix of hardware platforms, operating systems, and server applications.

IN ACTION: RECOGNIZING DIRECTORY SERVICES NETWORKS

What are the characteristics of directory services networks?

Directory services networks
A centralized network architecture model that provides support for centralized user, security, and resource management. Also known as a directory-based network.

Directory-based networks
A centralized network architecture model that provides support for centralized user, security, and resource management. Also known as a directory services architecture.

Object model
A directory model in which all network models are treated as objects that can be clearly defined and described.

Directory object
A directory services network entity, such as a user or computer.

Resource servers
Any server that provides shared resources to a network.

services architecture scales from the very small to the very large, meeting most organizations' networking needs. Directory services networks provide greater flexibility, enhanced security, and are, by design, well-suited to **heterogeneous networking** environments where you have a mix of hardware platforms, operating systems, and server applications.

4.4.1 Understanding Directory Services Networking

Like a client/server network architecture, **directory services architectures** (also known as **directory-based networks**) are based on a centralized model for security and resource management. Directory services networks are built around an **object model** where everything in the network is treated as a **directory object,** that is, an entity that belongs to the directory. These objects include the servers that manage login processing and security, **resource servers** that provide resources to the network, users, groups, security definitions, and even directory services-aware applications. The two major networking software manufacturers, Microsoft and Novell, have migrated their server products to a directory services network model.

The easiest way to understand a directory services network is to look at a specific example. Microsoft refers to its implementation of directory services as **Active Directory.** Active Directory uses domains, which are groups of directory services objects, as security boundaries. A simplified sample is shown in Figure 4-10. Understanding that this organization is logical and not physical is important.

Figure 4-10

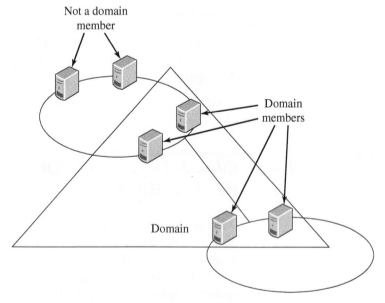

A sample domain.

Active Directory
Microsoft's directory-based network architecture.

Domain member
A directory object assigned to a domain, typically referring to a user or computer.

Member server
A directory-based network server.

Domain controller
A directory-based network server responsible for maintaining the directory of network objects and managing user authentication and authorization.

Audit
The action of tracking and recording network activity, usually in regard to user activity.

Domain members, users and computers assigned to that domain, can be physically located anywhere on the organization's network. A domain resource server for example, is commonly referred to as a **member server,** which includes any server that is part of the domain except those that manage the directory and security functions such as user logins. Everything within a domain is managed through a centralized security model, and an object such as a user or computer can belong to one domain only. Access to resources within the domain, as well as the user's rights and privileges within the domain, are based on a single login. Network administrators can also define resource access between domains, giving you more flexibility in managing large organizations and providing a way for organizations to work together and share resources.

The characteristics of directory services-based networking are as follows. They:

- Are based on a model that scales from very small to very large organizations, including wide-area enterprise networks.

- Use specialized servers, sometimes referred to as **domain controllers,** that process user authentication and authorization.

- Use a logical security boundary, called a domain, that centralizes security and resource management.

- Provide flexible security for shared resources, including management of server applications designed for use in a directory services environment.

- Provide a high level of security with detailed control over rights and permissions and the ability to **audit,** to track and record, user activity on the network.

- Are centrally managed, from a logical standpoint, but network administrators can be located anywhere on the network as long as they have access to domain controllers.

The domain controller (network security server) is key to the network design. In an Active Directory network, you define a domain by promoting a Windows server to the domain controller role. The domain controllers maintain the directory containing all domain objects, including security definitions. As shown in Figure 4-11, changes made to any domain controller are automatically propagated to other domain controllers, keeping all copies of the directory synchronized, which means that any domain controller can authenticate user logins and authorize user access to domain resources. It also means that keeping at least one domain controller up and running at all times is critical to the network, so you should strive to have at least two domain controllers for any domain, no matter how small.

In addition to user authentication and authorization, Windows servers acting as domain controllers can also support other roles including that of file server, print server, or even running server applications. However,

Figure 4-11

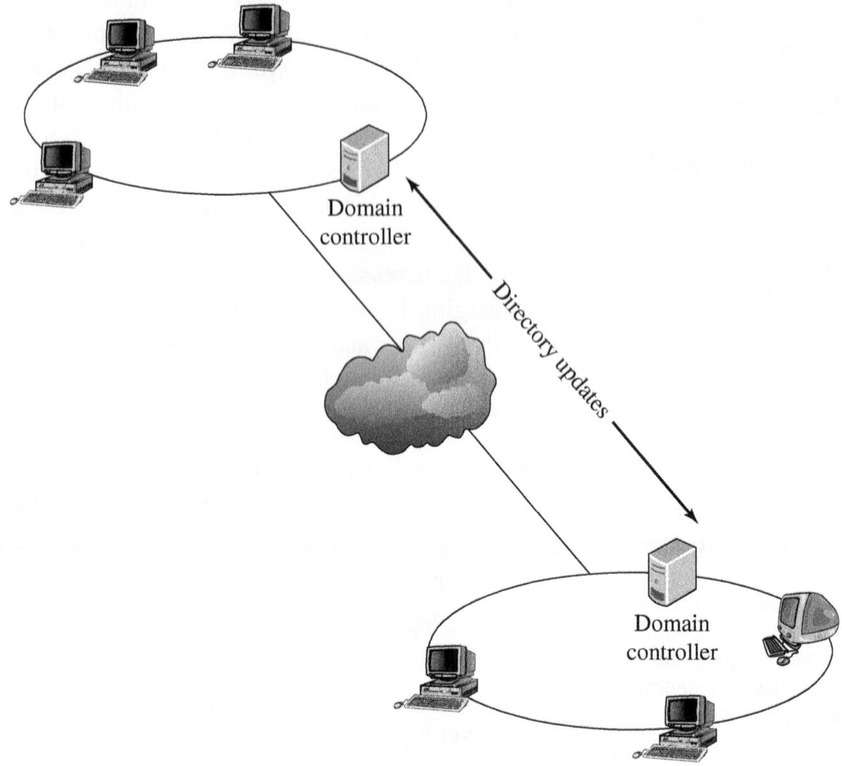

Domain controllers.

doing so is discouraged in all but the smallest of networks because a great deal of overhead is involved in supporting user access. When you force the server to support other roles as well, overall domain performance usually suffers.

4.4.2 Choosing a Directory Services Network

Organizations began deploying directory services-based networks even before the software on which they are based was officially released, acting as live test cases for the software manufacturers. Though not a strict requirement in every case, because most companies upgrade to the most recent versions of their chosen server operating systems, they also migrate to a directory services networking environment. The greater flexibility, enhanced management capabilities, and enhanced security are primary motivating factors. Another important factor is that manufacturers are gradually phasing out support for earlier server software versions, and with it, support for more traditional client/server networking models.

Basic criteria for selecting a directory services network are:

- You need to support more users than a peer-to-peer networking architecture can easily support.
- A need exists for centralized management of network resources.
- Security is a primary concern, and you need detailed control over security and access management.
- You need to define multiple logical security boundaries with different security and management requirements for each.
- One or more domain administrators will be managing the networks domain(s).

Making some changes, such as moving a computer from one domain to another, are relatively easy. However, careful planning is required because other changes, such as moving users or changing domain names, can be relatively difficult. In this environment you want to avoid letting administrators just learn as they go. Mistakes can be disastrous and expensive. Even though small domains can be relatively easy to maintain, the number of management options can quickly become confusing as you move beyond the most basic administrative activities.

4.4.3 Securing a Directory Services Network

As already stated, one of the key features of a directory services network is the high level of security. Both network servers and clients are configured as part of the directory of the domain, which makes it possible to organize them into groups and centrally manage local security and computer properties. You can see this in Figure 4-12, which shows how you would add a Windows XP computer as a member of a domain. When you make this change, you will be prompted for the name and password of a user who is authorized to make this change. Whether or not any user can join computers to a domain depends on the Windows Server version on which the network is based. For security reasons, with Windows 2000 Server, not everyone can join a computer to a domain. With Windows Server 2003, any user can join up to ten computers to a domain. You will also have to restart the Windows XP computer before the change takes effect.

You also have various ways of organizing users into groups available, with the end effect of making managing resource access significantly easier because most management requirements can be handled as a group, rather than at the individual user level.

Current versions give you control over user passwords, giving you a way of raising the bar on network security. Not only can you require all users to have passwords, you can also set requirements as to password length and complexity. Current Windows Server versions require **complex passwords**

Complex passwords
A user password that is designed to be difficult to guess, typically requiring at least three of the following: uppercase letters, lowercase letters, numbers, and non-alphanumeric characters, and to be of a minimum significant length, like six characters.

Figure 4-12

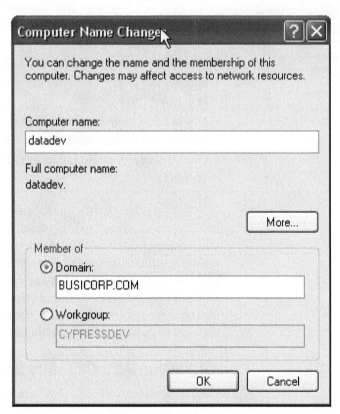

Domain membership.

by default, which means passwords require a mix of numbers, letters, and non-alphanumeric characters. You can even check automatically for passwords that appear to be too easily compromised.

You define the resources to which a user has access through group members and permissions granted explicitly to the user. The user gets access to all of the domain's resources, including directory services–aware applications, through a single login. This access includes applications such as database applications, messaging or mail servers, and web servers. You can even define resource access permissions across domain boundaries, but still managed through the same single user login, making security a relatively simple matter from the context of the domain user.

4.4.4 Implementing a Directory Services Network

The network hardware requirements are the same as for a client/server network and depend on the network's size and complexity. Because domains are logical definitions, membership is not restricted by physical locations or routed network boundaries. There is, however, a limiting factor. When

IN ACTION:
IMPLEMENTING A
DIRECTORY SERVICES
NETWORK

What are the primary
concerns with implementing
a directory services network?

Domain tree
A group of hierarchically
related domains.

Root domain
The uppermost domain in a
domain tree and the root of
the domain hierarchical
structure

Forest
A logical group of domains.

joining a computer to a domain, the computer must be able to communicate with a domain controller for that domain. Also, users need to be able to contact a domain controller when logging in and when accessing domain resources. Because of this requirement, when a domain is spread across wide area links, you will typically want to place a domain controller in each geographic location, like you saw in Figure 4-11. Keep in mind that doing so increases the background traffic across the links because of the need to keep the domain controllers synchronized, but this traffic is usually minimal.

A key part of the design process is designing your domain or domains. Your domain design will determine how you manage network security and access. This process can sometimes become very complex. A detailed discussion of domain design is beyond the scope of this course, but we need to mention a few key points. When designing a multiple domain environment, each domain must have a unique name, as shown in Figure 4-13. Also, you have a hierarchical domain structure, with parent and child domains. This structure is sometimes referred to as a **domain tree.** The uppermost domain is known as the **root domain.** Domains can also be organized into larger entities that are effectively groups of domains, known as **forests.**

You can see this in the domain structure in Figure 4-13. The root domain in this case is Busicorp.com. This name will be used as the name suffix for all member computers in that domain. You also have two child

Figure 4-13

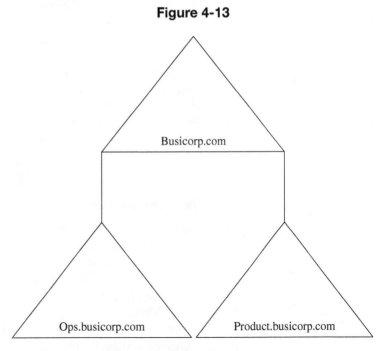

Hierarchical domain structure.

IN THE REAL WORLD

Considering Migration

Busicorp has grown too large to continue working as a peer-to-peer network. You're ready to make the jump into a network architecture designed for larger organizations.

So, just what does this mean? It means that you're going to make the jump from peer servers to real network servers and operating systems such as Windows Server 2008. However, you don't want to jump straight into a new environment without first considering the changes. You need to determine what you need as a domain structure. You'll be able to get by with a single domain. Most organizations, even those that have deployed multiple domains, could truthfully get by just as well (maybe better) in a single domain.

Moving to a new environment also means that your security structure, and with it your network culture, is going to change. You are moving from distributed to centralized security and resource management, which means users no longer have complete control over their computers or the resources hosted on them. As their computers join the domain, domain administrators are added to the local security structure and have the ability to make changes directly to the client computers. Even though doing so means less work for your users in the long run, some users might have trouble adjusting to this change and to the idea that someone else has access to their computers and control over their security. On the plus side, it means that new hire employees don't need to be quite as computer literate because they won't be responsible for things like resource sharing or security management.

Changing network environments is a major shift that impacts all network users. Going into the process, you need to expect that it's going to require an adjustment period as employees get used to the new environment and accept that some employees may never fully embrace the changes. Employees will have to learn to live with the changes, like it or not, after the administrative functions are centralized.

Tips from the Professionals

Often businesses have offices far away from their central headquarters, and as often as not they are connected to headquarters via a simple dial-up telephone connection, if connected at all. This can make use of the domain controller in a Directory Services network slow, difficult, and prone to lost data. Therefore, it is customary to have a domain controller in each remote location to allow users faster log on and access to the shared material found on domain controllers. Generally these controllers are synchronized with the headquarters domain controller during off peak network time, as in the early morning hours when users are unlikely to be accessing the server. In the event that no communications connection is available with headquarters (imagine an office on a deserted island), you can still use some methods to have domain controllers at those sites. You simply install Active Directory on the server before shipping it to the remote site. You can then periodically update and synchronize that server's Active Directory from restored backup media that has been shipped to the site on removable media.

domains, Ops.busicorp.com and Product.busicorp.com. You might create these child domains, for example, so that you can have different management and security structures for different divisions within an organization, while still letting users in those different divisions share resources and work together in a collaborative environment.

You also must determine how your network's physical design impacts the logical design. The network's physical design will impact factors such as placement of domain controllers and resource servers. In most cases, you will want to try to keep resources physically close to the users who most often need access to improve performance and to keep network traffic, especially over potentially slower wide-area links, to a minimum.

As a final word on domain names, as long as you keep the domain private (don't expose it directly to the Internet), you don't have to register your domain name. Names used on the Internet, such as Microsoft.com, must be registered and can be used only by the entity (person or company) to which it is registered. If you want to put a public face on your organization, such as a publicly accessible Web server, you need a registered domain name. However, even if you do register the name you use on your network domain, exposing your domain directly to the Internet is strongly discouraged because it opens a vast number of potential security holes. Access to the Internet should always be protected by a firewall, which filters all traffic into and out of your network, or similar security devices. Many networks set up multiple layers of security devices between themselves and the Internet.

SELF-CHECK

1. What is the role of a domain?

2. Describe the basic security model of a directory service network.

Apply Your Knowledge   What is the relationship between the logical and physical network designs in a directory services network?

4.5 RECOGNIZING HYBRID ARCHITECTURES

In today's ever-changing network environments, seeing variations and combinations of the basic networking architectures described in this chapter is possible. Organization structures often require flexibility and a certain amount of innovation in designing a network that's a match to operational requirements. For example, in large organizations in which client/server or directory services network architectures are implemented, small, independent groups of people may find working efficiently without getting bogged down in the structural overhead difficult. **Hybrid network architectures** allow various standard network architectures to coexist on the same network. Small groups of users can easily share files and other resources without requiring the intervention of the network administrator.

Hybrid network architecture
A network architecture that makes use of a combination of other types of architectures.

4.5.1 Using Hybrid Architectures

Hybrid networks incorporate the best features of workgroups in peer-to-peer networks with the performance, security, and reliability of server- or directory-based networks. In large corporate networks, users often do not have the ability to share files. The information technology department will typically provide users with the ability to use their workstation and nothing more. Users won't be able to make changes to their workstations. The reason for this tight security is to prevent the introduction of illegal applications and viruses, and to simplify workstation support.

IN ACTION:
RECOGNIZING
HYBRID ARCHITECTURE

Key characteristics of hybrid networks.

The specifics of how you can implement a hybrid network vary between manufacturers. The basic idea is that hybrid networks provide the centralized services of servers, but they also allow users to share and manage their own resources. A sample network is shown in Figure 4-14. After a user in a workgroup logs in to the network, the user doesn't have to have any other interactions with the server while accessing shared files in the workgroup. However, this configuration is supported in limited situations only. Windows Server 2003, for example, does not support a hybrid network based on this configuration.

The advantages of hybrid networks include the following:

- Server applications are centrally located and managed.
- Users can assign local access to resources on their computers.
- Users can manage resources without requiring assistance from the network administrator.

The disadvantages of hybrid networks include the following:

- Network access can become burdensome for the users.
- Users may need to remember multiple passwords.

Figure 4-14

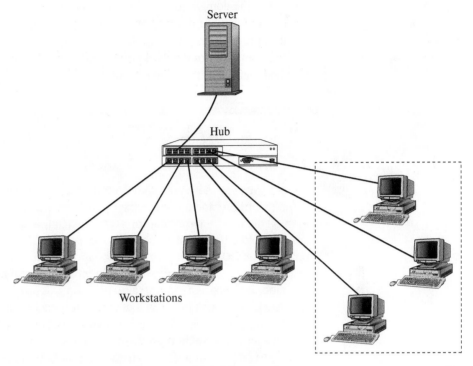

Hybrid network.

- Files can be duplicated and changes overwritten between the computer with the shared folder and the server.
- Files saved on the workstation are not backed up.

Before deploying a hybrid architecture, you need to consider your requirements and the capabilities of your primary network architecture carefully. You may find that configuring the requirements through features provided in your server- or directory-based network is just as easy and definitely more secure.

4.5.2 Separating Workgroups

One design you might see is to have a peer-to-peer network that resides on the same physical network as a server- or directory-based network, but not taking part in the logical security structure. For example, you could do this with Windows XP computers by configuring them as workgroup members rather than as domain members. Because the computers are not taking part in the domain, they are neither restricted nor protected by domain security, so workgroups can become a security risk. You might consider using an internal firewall to segregate the workgroup off its own screened subnet as a way of protecting both it and the domain.

Another justification for separating workgroups is that you don't want the rest of the domain to be aware of or have access to whatever the workgroup members are doing. For example, you might use this structure to isolate a product design group. In that case, not only does the firewall protect the domain from the workgroup, but it also protects workgroup members and their work from the domain.

IN THE REAL WORLD

Working Within Your Architecture

Directory-based networks like Microsoft's Active Directory provide different options for grouping users and computers. One of these is through the user of **Organizational Units (OUs),** which are like containers that hold other directory objects, like users and computers. One key point about OUs is that from the standpoint of the administrator and security, they can be a somewhat autonomous logical boundary within the larger boundary of the domain.

What this means to you is that you have a way of setting up a structure that is functionally similar to a workgroup environment without leaving the security protections and control of the domain. You can delegate rights and permissions, including administrative level permission, within an OU so that they apply only to the objects in the OU. You put your workgroup members and their computers (and no one else) into an OU and set up security to meet their specific requirements. As a protective measure, ultimate control and responsibility can be maintained at the domain administrator level, giving the administrators the ability to override anything done at the OU level, if necessary.

4.5.3 Choosing an Architecture

Now that you have an understanding of the different types of network architectures available, how do you choose what is best for your environment? Your selection will be based on a number of factors including, the:

- Number of users that will be connecting to the network
- Knowledge level of users
- Way the network will be used
- Level of security your network requires
- Amount of capital you have available to spend on your network resources

Table 4-1 provides a brief summary of each of the architectures covered in this chapter as well as a list of the primary advantages and disadvantages for each one.

Table 4-1: Primary Characteristics of Network Architectures

Architecture	Primary Characteristics	Advantages	Disadvantages
Peer-to-peer	• Every system can act as client or server. • Every user is responsible for managing his or her own system. • Security is maintained on the user side.	• Most effective for small networks with less than or equal to 12 users. • Low cost—cost is limited to the price of a new client.	• Not effective for large groups of users greater than 12. • Relies on user savvy for network administration. • Security not managed centrally.
Client/Server	• Processing happens on the server side. • Clients responsible for processing messages to and from only the server. • Security is centralized. • Most network resources are centralized.	• Security is managed in a central location. • Data is stored centrally.	• High cost of set up and upgrades. • Requires specialized knowledge to administer.
Directory-based	• Security boundaries are defined through logical domains and not limited by physical locations as long as communication paths exist. • Supports heterogeneous networking environment. • Management responsibilities can be delegated to multiple administrators, managers, or users.	• Flexible, highly secure environment. • All network resources are centrally managed. • Users can use a single authentication key to access network resources.	• Flexible management can quickly become highly complex. • Network administrative servers can be potential single points of failure.
Hybrid	• Can allow small groups of users to collaborate on files. • Combines the ease of peer-to-peer networking with the high security of client/server or directory services architectures.	• Server applications are centrally located and managed. • Users can use network resources as if they are local. • Users can manage resources.	• Network access can become burdensome for the users. • Users may need to remember multiple passwords. • Active files can become out of sync between the server and local versions. • Local files are not backed up.

SELF-CHECK

1. In general terms, what is a hybrid architecture?

2. When setting up both a directory-based and peer-to-peer network on the same physical network, how can you minimize the potential security risks inherent in the peer-to-peer network?

Apply Your Knowledge How would having a domain-based network improve security for your connected peer-to-peer networks? Give two examples.

SUMMARY

Section 4.1

- A network architecture is the method for describing the logical way in which computers are able to communicate with each other.

- Networks evolved from host-based networks, relying on mainframes for central processing, to a variety of architectures that allow you to customize your network to your needs.

- Some networks make use of servers dedicated to specific functions including file management, printing, messaging, applications, and web servers.

Section 4.2

- Peer-to-peer networks allow any system to serve as a client or a server.

- Peer-to-peer networks enable decentralized resource sharing across the network.

- Peer-to-peer networks are best suited for workgroups of 12 or fewer users.

- Peer-to-peer networks assume users have a basic knowledge of computing. They rely on the user to perform most of the network administration.

Section 4.3

- Client/server networks centralize resources, data, security, and administration.

- Client/server networks are the most common architecture in use today in organizations.

- Client/server networks are more secure than peer-to-peer networks.

- Client/server networks can use more than one server dedicated to a single service, like web, print, and application servers.

Section 4.4

- Directory services networks are highly secure.

- Managing a directory services network requires a specialized skill set.

- All resources within the directory services network are viewed and centrally managed as objects.

- Users must be able to access the directory services management server in order to log in or access any resources within the network.

Section 4.5

- Hybrid architectures are combinations based on standard network architectures.

- Each architectural model has its advantages and disadvantages.

- Each architectural type has advantages and disadvantages.

ASSESS YOUR UNDERSTANDING

UNDERSTAND: WHAT HAVE YOU LEARNED?

 Go to **www.wiley.com/go/ciccarelli/networkingbasics2e** to evaluate your knowledge of network architectures.

Measure your learning by comparing pre-test and post-test results.

SUMMARY QUESTIONS

1. In which network type do network users take responsibility for resource sharing and access security?

   (a) Peer-to-peer
   (b) Client/server
   (c) Server-based
   (d) Directory-based

2. A disadvantage of host-based computing is that there is no central control. True or false?

3. On what kind of server would you most likely expect to find a spooler file?

   (a) File server
   (b) Print server
   (c) Messaging server
   (d) Application server

4. A network architecture provides the blueprint for designing and implementing a network. True or false?

5. A workgroup is a logical peer-to-peer grouping. True or false?

6. A peer-to-peer network should be limited to no more than how many users?

   (a) 6
   (b) 12
   (c) 20
   (d) 10,000

7. Which of the following is NOT a feature of a client/server network?

   (a) Centralized security management
   (b) Centralized resource management
   (c) Dedicated administrative personnel
   (d) User control of resources

8. How are computers organized for security management purposes in a directory-based network?

   (a) By physical location in the network
   (b) By domain membership

    (c) By network address

    (d) By workgroup name

9. Which of the following is considered a disadvantage of a client/server network?

    (a) Managing data storage and backups is difficult.

    (b) It is the least secure network architecture.

    (c) It requires dedicated management staff.

    (d) User accounts are managed locally on each network computer.

10. When designing a traditional client/server network you must consider the number of users, _____, and geographic location.

    (a) Resource requirements

    (b) Transmission media

    (c) Communication protocol

    (d) Domain names

11. The topmost domain in a hierarchical domain structure is known as the root domain. True or false?

12. A forest is a group of servers in a server-based network. True or false?

13. In a directory-based network, resource servers are also known as what?

    (a) Domain controllers

    (b) Member servers

    (c) Organizational units

    (d) Child domains

14. Domain membership is determined strictly by a computer's location on the physical network. True or false?

15. What is the logical security boundary in a directory services network?

    (a) A domain

    (b) A hybrid network

    (c) A subnet

    (d) A firewall

16. What is a hybrid network?

    (a) A network containing heterogeneous computers.

    (b) Another name for a peer-to-peer network.

    (c) A network architecture that combines two or more standard architectures.

    (d) A security boundary in a directory services network.

APPLY: WHAT WOULD YOU DO?

For each of the following, identify the network architecture or architectures (peer-to-peer, client/server, or directory services) that most closely match the specified requirements.

1. Users must be able to share resources from their computers and manage resource security.
2. You have slightly more than 50 users, but want to keep the network design as simple as possible.
3. You need central control over network resources.
4. You want to be able to differentiate security boundaries.
5. You want to use a distributed security model.

You need to implement a network that will have three physical locations connected by wide area links. For security purposes, you want to divide users by four departments, but users from each department are in each of the physical locations. Each department has very different security and resource requirements.

1. What type of network architecture should you use?
2. How can you organize users for security purposes?
3. In general, how will access security be managed?
4. How do you identify computers that are part of each department?

BE A NETWORKER

Directory-based Networks

Research features of directory-based networks as implemented by Microsoft. Compare and contrast the architectural model with the host-based mainframe architecture used in earlier networks, pointing out key similarities and differences.

Describe the impact on users of migrating from a small single server-based network to a directory-based network with multiple servers in different roles. Also describe the impact on network designers and administrators.

KEY TERMS

Active Directory

Application server

Audit

Bandwidth throttling

Client/server network

Cloud network

Complex passwords

Decentralized resource sharing

Directory object

Directory services networks

Directory-based networks

Domain controller

Domain member

Domain tree

Economies of scale

Enterprise networks

File server

Forest

Heterogeneous networking

Hidden costs

Host name

Host name resolution

Host-based networks

Hybrid network

Hybrid network architecture

Macintosh Plus

Member server

Messaging server

Multiserver network

Network architecture

Network topology

Object model

Peer-to-peer network

Print jobs

Print queue

Print server

Resource servers

Root domain

Segment

Server applications

Server-side scripting

Share-level security

Simple file sharing

Single point of failure

Spooler file

Spooling

Telnet

Total cost of ownership (TCO)

User-management

Virtual hosting

Web server

Windows for Workgroups 3.11

Workgroup

Workgroup name

CHAPTER

5

NETWORK TOPOLOGIES

What Do You Already Know?

- What is a network topology?
- What is a network bus?
- How do physical and logical topologies differ?
- When is it appropriate to mix topologies in a single network?
- What is media access control?

For additional questions and to assess your current knowledge of network topologies, go to **www.wiley.com/go/ciccarelli/networking basics2e**

What You Will Find Out	What You Will Be Able To Do
5.1 Comparing physical network topologies.	Identify the most appropriate topology, given networking requirements.
5.2 Comparing wireless network topologies.	Explain the access methods used by wireless topologies.
5.3 Understanding other topology issues.	Identify situations when it is appropriate to use a hybrid topology.

INTRODUCTION

Network topology refers to the structure of a network, how connections are made between network computers. Make sure you don't confuse the physical topology with the logical network architecture. The same logical architectural model can be implemented using various physical topologies.

A **physical topology** is a description of the layout of the network media that interconnects the devices on a network. The physical topologies that are implemented today include the bus, ring, star, and mesh. A **logical topology** defines the way in which devices communicate and data is transmitted throughout the network. This chapter introduces both wired and wireless topologies.

The type of physical topology you choose for your network is important because it affects how devices communicate. Some of the factors to consider when choosing a topology include:

- Cost: Both the initial installation cost and ongoing maintenance cost.

- Scalability: Whether or not the topology has the capacity to grow to meet your long-term needs.

- Bandwidth capacity: Making sure that an implementation of the topology can handle your traffic requirements.

- Ease of installation: The easier the network is to install, the more likely it will go right the first time.

- Ease of troubleshooting: Downtime is expensive and directly impacts the bottom line.

Network topology is a hardware issue. Even though Windows operating systems are sometimes used in examples, especially when discussing setting up and connecting to a network, the information about network topologies applies equally to other operating systems and to non-PC (and even non-computer) network hardware devices.

5.1 COMPARING PHYSICAL NETWORK TOPOLOGIES

Physical topology
The layout of the cables connecting the network devices.

Logical topology
The way in which devices communicate and data is transmitted.

Topology
The structure of a network.

Hybrid topologies
Networks that use more than one topology in their physical structure.

When implementing a wired network, your network **topology** determines how you wire your physical cable plant. One thing to remember is that you are not restricted to a single topology. You can find many examples of networks, especially older networks that have gone through multiple upgrades, that employ a variety of network topologies. You will also find networks that use a mix of wired and wireless topologies.

A good place to start a discussion about network topologies is with the traditional topologies. They were originally used in creating host-based networks and carried over as companies moved to PC networks. We'll be discussing four wired topologies: bus, ring, star, and mesh. You may also hear mention of networks having **hybrid topologies,** which simply means that it employs more than one topology in its physical structure.

5.1.1 Bus Topology

A physical **bus topology** utilizes a single main cable that runs throughout the network and to which devices are attached. A physical bus topology

Figure 5-1

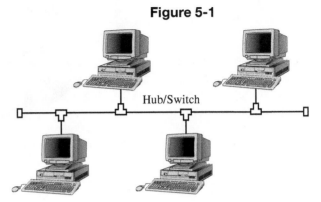

Hub/Switch

Bus topology sample.

Bus topology
A single main cable to which all devices are attached.

Terminator
A passive device attached to each end of a coaxial cable in a bus topology to absorb the signal when it reaches the end of the line.

Coaxial cable
A type of cable which has a single conductor surrounded by an insulator, a metal shield, and an insulating cover.

Thinnet
A bus topology that uses a thin coaxial cable.

BNC connector
A type of RF connector used to connect coaxial cables.

10Base2
A bus topology Ethernet network that uses thin a coaxial cable. Also known as Thin Ethernet or Thinnet.

Thin Ethernet
See 10Base2.

looks something like a rail line, a long unbroken path with stations along the way where trains can take on and drop off passengers and cargo. The main cable segment must end with a **terminator** that absorbs the signal when it reaches the end of the line, as shown in Figure 5-1. Without a terminator, the electrical signal that represents the data would reach the end of the copper wire and bounce back, causing errors on the network. You would end up with multiple, overlapping signals on the line with no way to differentiate between them or to isolate and process the correct signal.

Networks that have a physical bus topology use a **coaxial cable,** which has a single conductor surrounded by an insulator, a metal shield, and an insulating cover. Most implementations use a thin coaxial cable (RG-58), often referred to as **Thinnet** in an Ethernet network, that connects to the network interface card (NIC) using a **BNC connector,** shown in Figure 5-2. As you can see in the Figure 5-1, you can connect two or more computers in a daisy-chain fashion. Terminators are installed on both ends of the cable.

The Institute of Electrical and Electronics Engineers (IEEE) 802.3 standard sets the length of a cable segment and the number of devices on an Ethernet bus network. For a Thinnet network, also referred to as **10Base2** or **Thin Ethernet,** the maximum segment length is 185 meters (about 600 feet) with no more than 30 devices per cable segment. The standard for determining the number of devices and segments per cable is known as the 5-4-3 rule. You may use up to four repeaters to join a maximum of five segments (three of which can be populated with devices), for a total cable length of 925 meters (3035 feet). This is shown Figure 5-3. The total number of nodes allowed is 150.

FOR EXAMPLE

5-4-3 RULE

Figure 5-3 illustrates the 5-4-3 rule for networking. As you can see, the segments must be arranged so that you alternate segments with and without devices.

Figure 5-2

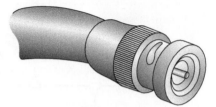

BNC (bayonet connector) plug

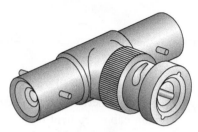

BNC T connector

BNC connectors.

Figure 5-3

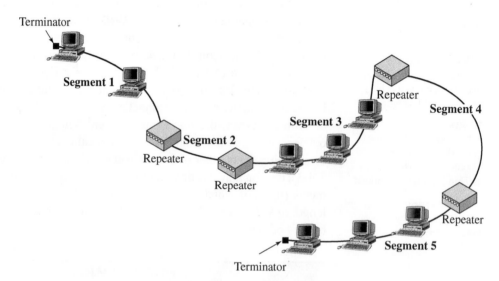

10Base2 cable segments.

Repeater
An electronic amplifier used to increase the strength of an electronic signal as it moves through the cables.

Thicknet (RG-59 Coaxial Cable)
See 10Base5.

Thick Ethernet
See 10Base5.

10Base5
A bus topology Ethernet network that uses thick coaxial cable. Also known as Thick Ethernet or Thicknet.

Gauge
The measurement of the diameter of the copper core in a coaxial cable.

A **repeater** is, in effect, a simple amplifier. It takes whatever signal is on the cable (including electronic noise or unwanted background electronic signals) and amplifies it before passing it on to the next segment.

Another, less common, option is **Thicknet (RG-59 Coaxial Cable)**, which is also known as **Thick Ethernet** or **10Base5.** The 10 refers to the 10 Mbps bandwidth of the cable, whereas Base indicates that the transmission type is a baseband transmission. Thicknet cabling uses a heavier **gauge** coaxial cable than Thinnet and is sometimes used as a backbone network. Installing and working with Thicknet is extremely difficult because of the cable's unusual size and stiffness.

The maximum cable segment length for Thicknet is 1,625 feet (500 meters) with a maximum of 100 nodes per segment. You can have up to four repeaters joining five segments for a total cable length of 8,125 feet and up to 300 nodes.

Understanding the difference between a cable segment and a network segment, or sub network, is important. Cable segments like those in Figure 5-3 are all part of the same network segment. Hosts on any of the segments have the same network address. The repeaters are effectively invisible to the network. Network segments are separated by routers and have different network addresses.

All devices packets on an Ethernet network are received by all devices on the network (all cable segments) at effectively the same time. Each device must open the packet and check the destination address to determine whether or not it is the desired recipient. Also, all devices have (in theory) equal access to the network. Any device can transmit at any time, as long as the network is available (not currently carrying any traffic).

Advantages of a bus topology include:

- Thinnet networks are relatively inexpensive to install.
- You can easily add more workstations.
- Bus networks use less cable than other physical topologies (but the cable can be more expensive).
- The bus topology works better with smaller networks.

Disadvantages include:

- If the cable breaks, the network is down (all devices lose network access).
- Access time and network performance degrades as devices are added to the network.
- Maximum bandwidth for Thinnet is no more than 10 megabits per second (Mbps).
- As you add devices, all devices are temporarily prevented from using the network.
- Locating problems, such as cable breaks, shorts, or bad terminators, is difficult.

Legacy network
Existing installations that haven't been migrated to a different topology.

Carrier Sense Multiple Access/Collision Detect (CSMA/CD)
A method of accessing a network used to manage conflicts by detecting and preventing collisions.

Thinnet networks were, at one time, the most common type of PC network. Now, nearly all bus networks are **legacy networks.** Purchasing new NICs that include a BNC connector is difficult. When found, they're more expensive than newer, higher performance NICs. The same is true of cable and connectors. For most network consultants and support technicians, the biggest reason for moving away from bus networks is that it is so difficult to troubleshoot. Unless you have specialized test equipment, finding cable or NIC problems is a slow, tedious process.

One of the most important functions of the Data Link layer is to provide a way for packets to be sent safely over the physical media without interference from other nodes attempting to send packets at the same time. The two most popular ways to do this are CSMA/CD and token passing. Ethernet networks use an access method known as **Carrier Sense Multiple Access/ Collision Detect (CSMA/CD).** CSMA/CD is a multiple-access method that manages conflicts through collision detection.

IN THE REAL WORLD

Talking on the Bus

Imagine the network as a meeting with a heated discussion where everyone wants to talk. The folks around the table are polite enough to wait until the current speaker finishes, but as soon as that happens, they try to come in with their comments. Two, three, maybe more, all start talking at the same time. No one can understand what anyone is saying, so they negotiate who gets to speak. As soon at that person finishes, it happens again, and so on.

CSMA/CD operates as the mechanism by which the nodes negotiate speaking order. Only one node is allowed to transmit on the network at a time. As nodes attempt to send data, they listen to see if the line is clear. If a transmission is already in progress on the network, they wait and then attempt to retransmit.

The biggest problem with this method is relatively easy to see. The more nodes you have on the network, the more devices you having trying to transmit. As the number of collisions goes up, so does the number of retransmissions, which adds to the problem. You eventually reach a point where collisions become so prevalent that performance noticeably suffers. It can get bad enough that users notice and complain about slow access.

When does this happen? That's part of the problem. You can't always accurately determine in advance when you're going to reach the tipping point. It depends on the number of devices on the network and the level of network activity. If a network is running close to its limit, it will become noticeable at peak traffic periods, such as when everyone is starting up their computers and trying to log on first thing in the morning.

Let's break down what that mouthful means. First, all devices are connected to and monitoring the bus at all times (Multiple Access). When a node wants to transmit, it waits for the bus to become available (Carrier Sense). If two nodes try to transmit at the same time, a **collision** occurs and both transmissions are corrupted so that nothing gets through. The nodes recognize this (Collision Detection) and both wait a pseudorandom time period before trying to transmit again. After the timeout, a node waits for the bus to become available and tries again.

Collision

When two computers try to send packets over the network at the same time, the signals will collide with each other and the transmission will be garbled.

5.1.2 Ring Topology

Ring topology

A network in which the nodes are connected in a continuous circle, passing data from one to the next in order.

As its name implies, a **ring topology** is a topology in which the stations are connected in a ring (circle) and in which the data flows in one direction in a circle, from station to station (see Figure 5-4). It has no beginning or end, so there is no need for terminating the cable, which allows every device to have an equal advantage accessing the media. There are two kinds of ring topologies: single ring and dual ring.

Figure 5-4

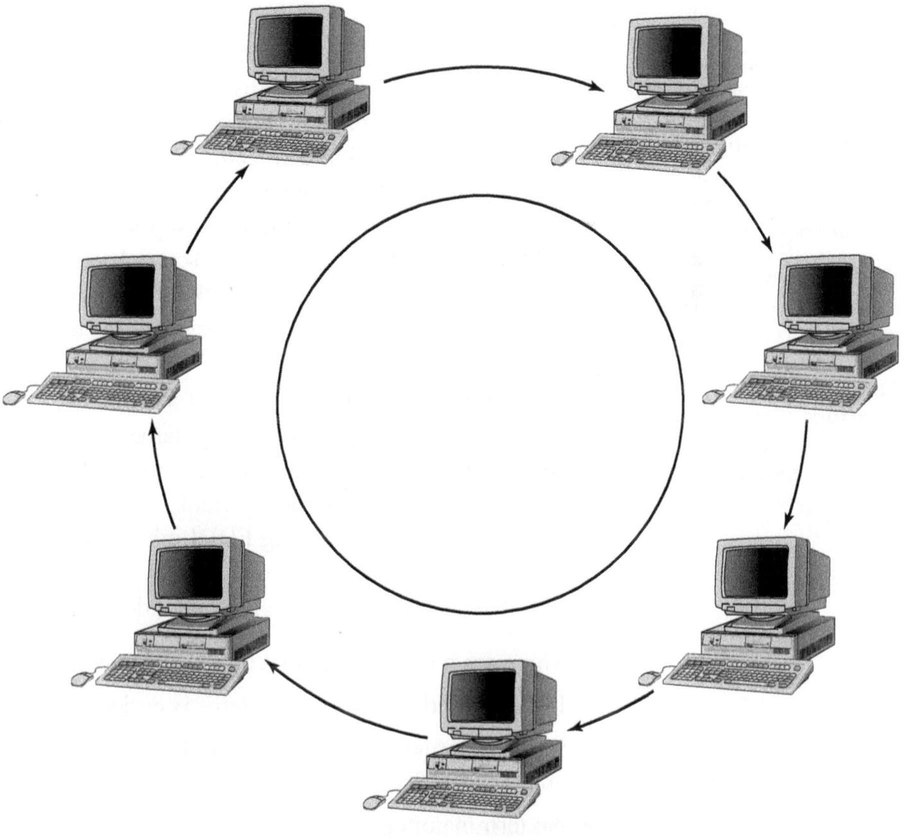

Single ring topology.

TIPS FROM THE PROFESSIONALS

Buying the Ring

Although ring systems are still used today, finding replacement parts and individuals who have sufficient knowledge to manage them is difficult and expensive. Newer physical star, logical ring systems are easy to install and manage, and are very inexpensive. Should you be presented with an older **802.5 Ring** topology, you should recommend that it be replaced.

Token Ring
A topology in which a data packet was sent around a ring of computers until it reached its intended destination.

IEEE 802.5
IEEE standard name for Token Ring topology.

Counter-rotating rings
The two rings in the dual-ring topology that send data, each in a different direction.

Redundancy
Duplicate transmission paths.

Fiber Distributed Data Interface (FDDI)
A dual ring topology that uses fiber-optic cable.

IBM originally developed **Token Ring** preferred topology for IBM equipment. Today high-speed Ethernet networks have replaced many Token Ring networks.

As technology evolved, a dual-ring topology was developed. This topology uses **counter-rotating rings** (see Figure 5-5). All of the devices connect to both rings. Not only does this let more packets travel over the network, it also provides **redundancy.** The network continues to communicate even if one of the rings fails.

The most common dual ring implementation is **Fiber Distributed Data Interface (FDDI),** which is a technology similar to Token Ring. However, where Token Ring uses copper wire to carry electronic signals, FDDI uses modulated light carried through fiber-optic cable.

FDDI was designed as a high-speed network and was most often used as a building or campus backbone network. It is still used in this implementation and, in rare circumstances, as a metropolitan area network (MAN) backbone.

The biggest drawbacks to FDDI are that the cable and network hardware are relatively expensive, easily damaged, and more difficult to install than copper wire cables (or wireless networks). However, those drawbacks often are outweighed by the fact that it is more difficult to physically tap into a fiber-optic line, making FDDI inherently more secure, and that it is immune to electrical interference.

Advantages of a ring topology include:

- There are no collisions, making communication more reliable.
- Locating and correcting problems is easier with devices and cable.
- In most implementations, failing devices can be automatically detected and isolated from the ring.
- No terminators are needed.

Figure 5-5

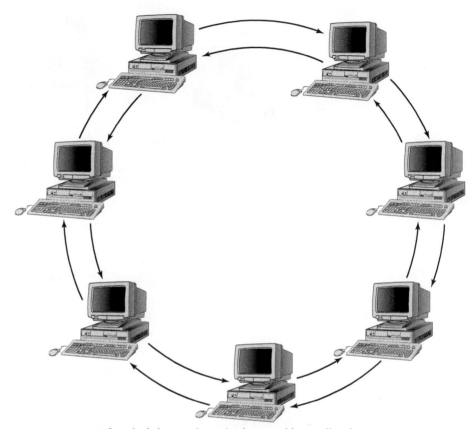

In a dual-ring topology, the data travel in two directions.

Dual-ring topology.

Disadvantages include:

- A ring network requires more cable than a bus network.
- A break in the cable will bring the entire network down in some implementations.
- As you add devices to the ring, all devices are temporarily prevented from using the network.
- Equipment can be difficult to locate and relatively expensive.

Star topology
A network topology in which network devices are connected to a single hub.

5.1.3 Star Topology

A physical **star topology** gets its name because it is installed in the shape of a star, like spokes in a bicycle wheel. The star topology is, by far, the one most commonly seen in modern network implementations. As bus and ring

Figure 5-6

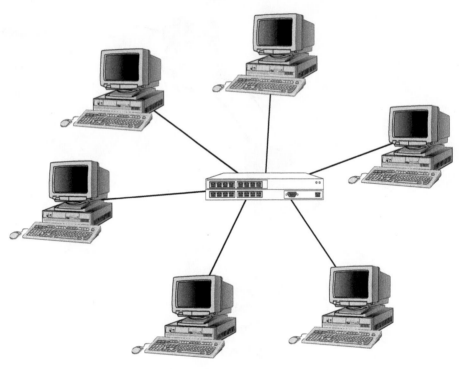

Star topology.

networks are phased out or upgraded, they are most often replaced by some kind of star. Each device in a star network is connected to the central hub with its own cable. Although doing so does require more media, the media is relatively inexpensive and very easy to install.

FOR EXAMPLE

LOOK AT FIGURE 5-6

As you can see, a star topology is made up of a central connection point, a hub (or switch), where the cable segments meet.

Extended star topology
A star network with multiple hubs connected to the central hub.

If a star network is expanded to include one or more additional hubs connected to the main hub, as shown in Figure 5-7, it is called an **extended star topology.**

Advantages of a star topology include:

- Adding more devices is easy as your network expands.
- Hardware is relatively inexpensive and easy to install.

Figure 5-7

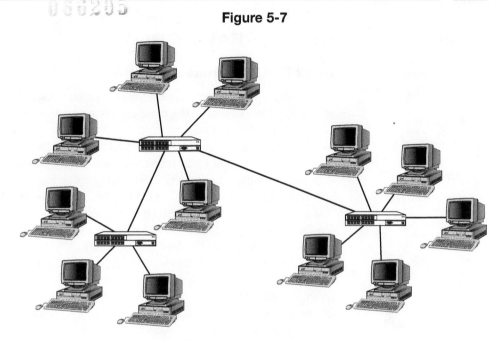

Extended star topology.

- The failure of one cable or one cable break will not bring down the entire network.
- The hub provides centralized management.
- Finding and fixing device and cable problems is easy.
- A star network can be upgraded to support faster network transmission speeds.
- It's the most common topology, so numerous equipment options are available.

Disadvantages include:

- A star network requires more media than a ring or bus network.
- The failure of a single central hub can bring down the entire network.
- The failure of one hub in an extended star affects all devices connected to that hub.

Nearly all new network installations, including home networks, use some form, of physical star. Extended stars can be expanded to include hundreds or even thousands of devices and can support speeds exceeding 1 gigabit per second (Gbps). Most star configurations use copper wire **twisted pair cable,** but some high-speed versions use fiber-optic cable. Some of the earliest star configurations used coaxial cable, but coax-based stars are now almost never seen.

Twisted pair cable
A type of copper cable line with multiple conductors similar to a telephone cable.

IN THE REAL WORLD

Don't Forget to Raise Your Hand

Depending on the implementation, various access methods can be used in physical star networks. The most common use either collision detection (like CSMA/CD), token passing (like Token Ring), or polling. We've already talked about the first two, so let's talk a little about polling. In polling, each computer communicates in turn, like in Token Ring, but with central control deciding which device gets to transmit.

Think about a well-behaved classroom. Everyone gets to talk, but first you have to raise your hand to be recognized by the teacher. The teacher makes note of who raised a hand, calls on each student, and then has the students raise their hands again.

Most polling schemes are similar. The central control contacts each device and determines which devices have data they need to transmit. Each of those devices gets a chance to transmit its data, and then all of the devices are polled again, over and over. Communication priority is based on various factors, such as how long since a device was last permitted to transmit and how often the device is making transmit requests when polled.

5.1.4 Mesh Topology

Mesh topology
A network topology in which all devices are connected to each other (net topology).

In a **mesh topology,** shown in Figure 5-8, sometimes called a *net topology* because it looks something like a fisherman's net, each device is connected to every other device. This design allows all the devices to continue to communicate if one connection goes down. It is the ultimate in network interconnection reliability.

Figure 5-8

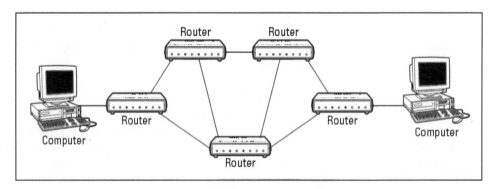

Mesh topology.

Mesh is rarely used as a local area network (LAN) topology, but often used to create a reliable wide area network (WAN) topology. The reliability comes from having multiple communication paths. The network (or inter-network) is able to compensate automatically for line breaks and failing devices. Many implementations can even compensate for changing traffic patterns and reroute packets to optimize communication speeds.

Take a look at Figure 5-9. Based on distance, you would probably say that the shortest path between Boston and New York is the direct link between the two. However, if this link is experiencing especially heavy traffic, the best link between the two might be to route traffic through Chicago, Miami, and then to New York. Thankfully, this routing process is transparent to the network users.

Different mesh topology implementations vary widely, depending on the underlying communication technology and physical connections. Some use dedicated lines run between the connection points, while others use leased (or even shared) public networks like the public telephone system. Connection speeds also vary. The one common factor in all mesh topologies is the fact that each node supports multiple connections and multiple paths.

Advantages of mesh topology include:

- Flexible variations can meet most network communication needs.

- Multiple communication paths provide fault tolerance and the ability to recover from failures.

Figure 5-9

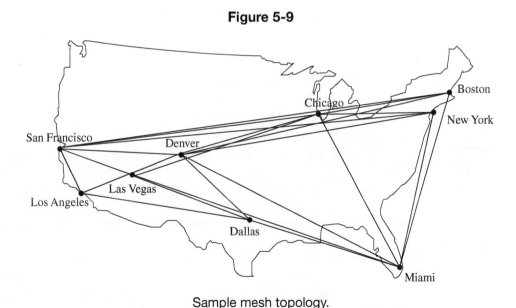

Sample mesh topology.

- They are able to choose routes based on factors such as traffic and congestion.
- Many implementations use leased hardware and lines, so maintenance and upkeep is handled for you (instead of by you).

  Disadvantages include:

- Designs are often very complex and may require the assistance of an outside consultant.
- Network hardware can be expensive and difficult to install.
- If managed internally, a mesh network is difficult to manage and maintain.
- Some billing methods are based on traffic volume and are potentially expensive.
- A mesh network can be difficult to troubleshoot.

You might be using a mesh network and not even know it. When using leased communications, you don't always know what happens when the traffic leaves your local network. The only things you ever deal with are the entry and exit points.

A well-known mesh network, possibly the best known and most used, is the United States **public switched telephone network (PSTN).** A fast-growing rival is the cellular phone network that has grown in recent years, but that's primarily a wireless mesh topology. The Internet has a partial mesh infrastructure, though not a true mesh because it doesn't have full connectivity between all nodes. You have multiple connections between major **nexus points** where several lines of communication come together, traffic routes can be updated automatically, and route determinations are often made on current conditions rather than physical proximity.

Public switched telephone network (PSTN)
A telephone network and infrastructure that includes the standard dial-up phone network.

Nexus points
The points where several lines of communication come together.

IN THE REAL WORLD

World Gone Wireless

AT&T, in a response to the U.S. Federal Communications Commission's request for comments regarding its National Broadband Plan, acknowledged the current obsolescence of the wire line telephone system. Using the informal term "POTS" (Plain Old Telephone System) interchangeably with the more professional "PSTN" (Public Switched Telephone Network) to refer to the obsolete system, the company asked the commission to consider a formal deadline for the transition of all wire line customers to a wireless system comprising broadband and IP-based connectivity, stating that carriers can no longer afford to maintain the old network while simultaneously building out the new systems.

IN THE REAL WORLD

It Depends!

The only blanket statement you can make about mesh topology access methods is "It depends." It depends on the underlying hardware used to build the mesh infrastructure. It depends on the OSI layer 2 protocol used to manage connections and traffic control. Before you can know how access is managed, you need to know what kind of mesh you have.

The most common access methods involve some version of collision detection, collision avoidance, or polling. We've already discussed collision detection and polling. Collision avoidance involves using careful timing to optimize communications and avoid collisions between network devices rather than reacting after the collisions occur.

The truth is that, in most cases, you won't care what kind of access method is used because you won't be directly responsible for its management or maintenance. Your only concerns will be your entry and exit points, the places where you connect to the mesh. Anything beyond that is out of your hands.

SELF-CHECK

1. List and briefly describe the four most common wired topologies.

2. Which topology is most often used in new networks and why?

Apply Your Knowledge   Examine your home and business network systems. Describe which topology is used in each and how you would expand that system to eventually include additional users.

Project 5.1

An important part of any network design is the network topology. In modern networks, the network topology can be either a wired or wireless topology. You can usually determine the physical topology through simple observation, by looking at the cable and connection devices used.

As part of documenting a network, you need to be able to draw simple network topologies and to recognize network sketches. Complete **Project 5.2: Recognizing Physical Topologies** in the online Networking Basics Project Manual to be able to identify recognize different network topologies.

5.2 COMPARING WIRELESS NETWORK TOPOLOGIES

802.11g
A wireless standard that uses the 2.4GHz frequency bank, like 802.11b, although transmitting at up to 54Mbps. Most 802.11g devices support and provide connectivity to 802.11b devices on the network because they are communicating within the same frequency band.

802.11n
A wireless standard developed to improve transmission rates offered by 802.11g and 802.11b devices. Although similar to 802.11g, the newer standard supports transmission rates up to 600Mbps.

Mode
In network topology, a wireless topology.

Wi-Fi
Wireless network.

Carrier Sense Multiple Access with Collision Avoidance (CSMA/CA)
A media access control method used in wireless networks to prevent data collisions.

Distributed coordination function (DCF)
A method of using CSMA/CA media access control.

Physical carrier sense method
Another term for DCF.

Wireless topologies are based on established radio-frequency communication technologies. Several IEEE standards have been defined, with 802.11b, 802.11g, and 802.11n the most common. The **802.11g** standard is downward compatible and supports 802.11b clients, while **802.11n** improves both by adding multiple-input multiple-output antennas (MIMO) while operating on both the 2.4GHz and the 5 GHz bands. The basic difference between the two primary topologies, referred to as **modes,** is whether or not you have a central access point that acts something like the central hub in a star topology. Another wireless topology you might see, though usually on a larger scale, is a wireless mesh.

Media access control in **Wi-Fi** is **Carrier Sense Multiple Access with Collision Avoidance (CSMA/CA),** which is similar to the contention-based CSMA/CD approach used by traditional Ethernet. With CSMA/CA, computers listen before they transmit; if no one else is transmitting, they proceed with transmission. Detecting collisions is more difficult in radio transmissions than in transmission over wired networks, so Wi-Fi attempts to avoid collision to a greater extent than traditional Ethernet. CSMA/CA has two media access control approaches.

One approach is the **distributed coordination function (DCF)** (also called **physical carrier sense method** because it relies on the ability of computers to physically listen before they transmit). DCF works well in traditional Ethernet because every computer on the shared circuit receives every transmission on the shared circuit. However, in a wireless environment, a computer at the extreme edge of the range limit from the AP (access point) on one side may not receive transmissions from a computer on the extreme opposite edge of the AP's range limit. All computers may be within the range of the AP, but may not be within the range of each other. In this case, if one computer transmits, the other computer on the opposite edge may not sense the other transmission and transmit at the same time causing a collision at the AP. The AP may be the only device guaranteed to be able to communicate with all computers on the WLAN. Therefore, the AP must manage the shared circuit using a controlled-access technique, not the contention-based approach of traditional Ethernet.

This technique is called the **point coordination function (PCF)** (also called the **virtual carrier sense method**). Not all manufacturers have implemented PCF in their APs. With this approach, any computer wishing to transmit first sends a request to transmit (RTS) to the AP, which may or may not be heard by all computers. The RTS requests permission to transmit and to reserve the circuit for the sole use of the

Point coordination function (PCF)
A method of using CSMA/CA media access control.

Virtual carrier sense method
Another term for PCF.

requesting computer for a specified time period. If no other computer is transmitting, the AP responds with a clear to transmit (CTS), specifying the amount of time for which the circuit is reserved for the requesting computer. All computers hear the CTS and remain silent for the specified time period.

The virtual carrier sense method is optional. It can always be used, never used, or used just for frames exceeding a certain size, as set by the WLAN manager. Controlled-access methods provide poorer performance in low-traffic networks because computers must wait for permission before transmitting rather than just waiting for an unused time period. However, controlled-access techniques work better in high-traffic WLANs because without controlled access there are many collisions.

5.2.1 Ad Hoc Mode

Ad hoc mode
A wireless network topology in which wireless devices communicate directly with each other, also called peer-to-peer mode.

Peer-to-peer mode
A wireless network topology in which wireless devices communicate directly with each other, also called ad hoc mode.

In **ad hoc mode,** wireless network devices communicate directly with each other, like in Figure 5-10. This term is also referred to as **peer-to-peer mode**. No central access point device is involved. No physical placement requirements exist, as long as the devices are in range of each other. Devices can also relay messages between each other, extending the network's range.

The advantages of ad hoc mode include:

• It is inexpensive with the hardware often preinstalled in the computer.

• It is easy to configure.

• It is easy to manage and maintain.

Figure 5-10

Ad hoc mode.

Disadvantages include:

- It has little security and is easily accessed by unauthorized computers.
- It is suitable to only very small networks.

You are more likely to encounter an ad hoc mode network in a home than in an office environment. When used, an ad hoc mode topology is most often implemented using a peer-to-peer architecture.

5.2.2 Infrastructure Mode

Infrastructure mode
A wireless topology in which wireless devices connect centrally to a WAP.

Wireless access point (WAP)
A central access point for wireless computers that also passes data to and from a wired network.

Infrastructure mode lets you combine wired and wireless networks through the use of a **wireless access point (WAP)**, as shown in Figure 5-11. The WAP provides a central access point for the wireless computers, but also passes data to and from the wired network. However, this configuration isn't the only possible one. Some small infrastructure mode networks are completely wireless, consisting of just a Wireless Access Point (WAP) and the wireless clients.

NETWORKING FACT

WAP vs. WAP
Wireless Application Protocol also uses the acronym WAP.

Figure 5-11

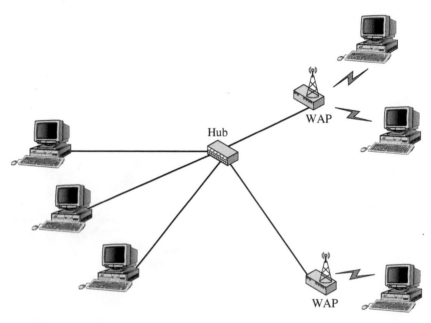

Infrastructure mode.

Wireless clients must be configured for either ad hoc or infrastructure mode. They can't operate in both at the same time. In infrastructure mode, the wireless computer is either configured to communicate through a specific WAP or will attempt to dynamically detect and then connect to a WAP. The WAP handles the process of moving data on and off the wired network.

The advantages of infrastructure mode include:

- It is inexpensive and easy to configure.
- It provides easy access between wired and wireless networks.
- It is scalable to meet requirements of large networks.
- Managing and maintaining it is easy.

    Disadvantages include:

- It is not secured by default.
- It has limited security options and is somewhat difficult to configure a secure network.
- It might allow unauthorized access to the network.

Infrastructure mode is commonly used as an inexpensive way of expanding existing wired networks to include new devices. Wireless-only infrastructure networks are commonly seen in home networks. When used in a home network, the WAP is often a wireless router and is used to connect the computers and to share a single Internet connection between the computers.

5.2.3 Wireless Mesh

Wireless mesh
A wireless topology made up of transmissions points with overlapping ranges.

A wireless mesh can take various forms. A **wireless mesh** is a set of WAPs or other transmission towers with overlapping ranges, like the example in Figure 5-12. The computer shown in the figure is in the range of three different WAPs and could potentially connect with any one of the three.

The network of cell phone towers in most regions of the United States is configured as a wireless mesh. The network is set up this way so you don't lose your call as you move out of the range of one cell tower and into the range of another. Wi-Fi hot spots are often set up as wireless meshes, in a hotel for example, so you can move through the hotel without losing your network connectivity.

In a LAN, you typically don't initially design the topology as a wireless mesh, but it becomes one as you add more WAPs. WAP range is typically 100 to 300 feet or more, depending on the device and manufacturer, so ending up with overlapping ranges is easy.

Figure 5-12

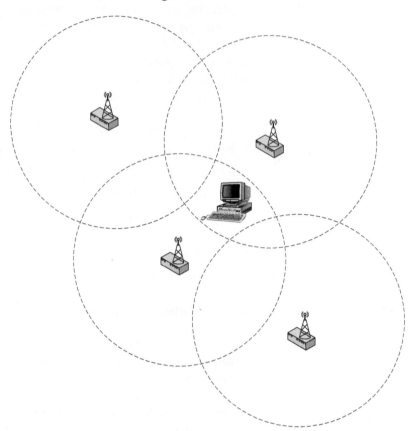

Wireless mesh.

Service set identifier (SSID)
A text string that identifies a WAP to wireless clients.

MAC address filtering
A WAP security method that allows or blocks wireless clients based on the MAC addresses encoded on their NICs.

IN THE REAL WORLD

Peek-a-boo!

Many organizations deploy WAPs without realizing the potential security hole that they represent. The WAP, by default, broadcasts its **service set identifier (SSID)**, a text string that identifies the WAP to wireless clients, so that client computers can discover the WAP and connect. Also by default, the WAP accepts connections from any wireless computer and broadcasts all data in clear text.

When implementing an infrastructure mode network, making use of available security features is important. With most WAPs, you can turn off SSID broadcasts so clients have to know the WAP ID before they can connect. Other features include **MAC address filtering** (so that the connection isn't allowed if the MAC address isn't on the list), en-crypted data transmissions, and user authentication before authorizing a connection. One of the most common activities in office buildings and around home networks (especially in apartments) is having someone piggyback on your Internet connection. Although you aren't responsible for their actions, having some activities traced back to your network could be embarrassing. You might wonder what the big concern is. After all, a little Internet time isn't that big a deal, even if they don't completely behave, is it? They're likely not logging on to your secure network or doing something illegal.

That is the problem. If an intruder is accessing, transmitting, or storing prohibited or illegal material, it could be quite embarrassing for you to explain to the authorities how your system was being used to access and transmit "exotic" images. You could even be liable for any damage that access caused!

Also, remember that the first step into your network is gaining a physical connection. After someone has a physical connection, he or she can use a variety of attacks to try to gain access to network servers. However, if a person is blocked from ever accessing the physical network, then the chance is that person doesn't even try.

Tips from the Professionals

The Mesh is Alive and Well!

Researchers are working on a new networking concept, which fully or partially replaces cables with wireless links. This wireless networking concept has generated commercial solutions and products featuring full-fetched wireless mesh networking functionalities.

The need for this new technology is the high flexibility of the network, which is able to self-adapt and self-configure on the fly depending on the specific operation conditions. Such capability minimizes the operational cost of network operation. Wireless mesh networking can overcome the limitations of both traditional wireless networks and classical IP-based solutions.

SELF-CHECK

1. List the two wireless network modes and describe how devices communicate in each.

2. When does an infrastructure mode network become a wireless mesh?

Apply Your Knowledge

1. Open Control Panel/Network and Internet.

2. Choose Network and Sharing Center.

3. Observe you network characteristics and list your active networks and connection types.

5.3 UNDERSTANDING OTHER TOPOLOGY ISSUES

Before leaving the topic of topology, we need to discuss a few additional issues. We need to talk about logical topologies and how they relate to physical topologies. We need to introduce hybrid topologies, including common examples of wired hybrid topologies. We also need to talk a little more about hybrid topologies that integrate wired and wireless topologies.

5.3.1 Understanding Logical Topology

Logical topology
A description of how devices on a LAN communicate and transmit data.

The physical topology describes how the network is structured. The **logical topology** describes how devices on the LAN communicate and transmit data. In current PC network technologies, you will see the network using one of two logical topologies, either bus or ring.

As illustrated in Figure 5-13, figuring out the logical topology for a physical bus or ring is easy. When a network is physically cabled in a bus, you can easily understand that it is sending data in a logical bus topology throughout the network. The data moves from device to device in a linear fashion. Likewise, a physical ring is easily interpreted as a logical ring.

When a network uses a physical star topology, media can be accessed and data sent in either a logical bus or a logical ring. It depends on the network connection devices used and the layer 2 protocol that is implemented.

Logical bus
A logical topology in which data travel in a linear fashion from the source to all destinations.

Logical Bus

In a **logical bus,** data travels in a linear fashion away from the source to all destinations. This is what you see in any recently implemented Ethernet network.

Figure 5-13

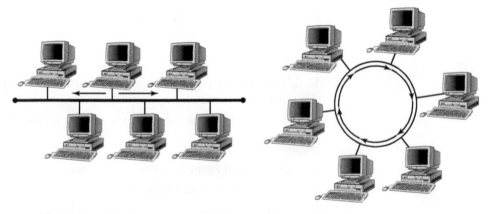

Logical bus versus ring.

Figure 5-14

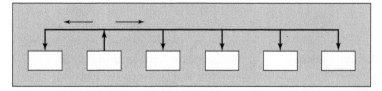

Ethernet hub.

In modern Ethernet networks, the physical layout is a star topology. At the center of the star is a hub. It is what happens inside that hub that defines the logical topology. As you can see in Figure 5-14, an Ethernet hub uses a logical bus topology inside to transmit data to all the segments of its star.

The advantages of a logical bus topology include:

- If a node is down, it does not bring down the entire network.
- It's the most widely implemented of the logical topologies.
- The necessary hardware is readily available and relatively inexpensive.
- The topology is easy to troubleshoot and maintain.
- Making additions and changes are easy without affecting other workstations.

Disadvantages are similar to those of any bus network:

- Collisions can occur easily.
- Only one device may access the media at a time.
- Performance degrades as more devices are added.

NETWORKING FACT

MAKING THE MOST OF YOUR LOGICAL BUS

The disadvantages of logical bus topology are reduced or eliminated by using switches instead of hubs in this topology.

10BaseT
A logical bus topology that uses a 10Mbps physical star topology.

10Base100
A logical bus topology that uses a 100Mbps physical star topology.

The original standard for this type of network was the **10BaseT** standard that defined a 10 Mbps star topology network. The most common current configuration is 100 Mbps Ethernet, occasionally referred to as **10Base100**. Most hubs can compensate for bandwidth differences, supporting both 10 Mbps and 100 Mbps devices connected to the same hub. Recent additions to the standards include Ethernet networks that support 1 Gbps on twisted-pair cable.

Logical Ring

In a logical ring, data travels in a ring from one device to another and back around to the beginning of the circle. In a Token Ring network, the most common implementation of the logical ring, devices are connected to a **Multistation Access Unit (MAU),** which is the central hub in a Token Ring network that is wired as a physical star.

The MAU, (pronounced "mauw" as in "mouse"), may look just like a regular hub. But as you can see in Figure 5-15, inside the MAU the data is passed from device to device using a logical ring. The MAU makes it possible for a network with a physical star topology to transmit data in a logical ring. If you connect a second MAU, the ring is extended to include both, continually expanding as you add more MAUs.

The advantages of a logical ring topology include those you would expect in a ring topology, including:

- There are no collisions because a token passing access method is used.
- Locating and correcting problems are easy with devices and cable.
- You can usually add devices without interrupting the network.
- In most implementations, failing devices can be automatically detected and isolated from the ring.

Disadvantages are also common to ring networks:

- A broken ring can stop all transmissions.
- A device must wait for an empty token before it can transmit.
- Necessary hardware is more expensive than that for a logical bus.

Multistation Access Unit (MAU)
A central hub connection device used in a Token Ring network.

Figure 5-15

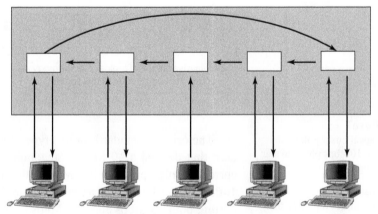

Multistation Access Unit (MAU).

Logical rings are most often seen in legacy networks that include (or included, at some time) an IBM host or in companies that were "IBM shops" that contracted or are contracting with IBM to supply their network hardware and maintain their network. Most of these legacy network segments now exist as part of a hybrid topology.

5.3.2 Using Wired Hybrid Topologies

A hybrid topology combines two or more different physical topologies in a single network. It often occurs simply as part of a network evolutionary cycle. As old networks are updated and replaced, older segments may be left with a legacy topology.

You will sometimes see extended star topologies, like the one you saw in Figure 5-7, referred to as a hybrid star-bus topology. By using this terminology, most networking professionals are referring to the connection between the hubs as a bus, but most networking professionals don't consider that description to be technically accurate. A situation that you often will see in Token Ring networks is two or more MAUs connected as shown in Figure 5-16. This is known as a **star-ring topology.** The network physically looks just like an extended star.

Most wired hybrids don't have a special name. They're just a combination of two or more bus, star, or ring topologies. There are, however, two relatively common hybrids you might encounter. One is using a vertical bus between floors in a building to connect LANs deployed on the different floors. The other is connecting LANs with a WAN mesh. In either, the LANs being connected will have their own internal bus, ring, star, or hybrid topology.

Star-ring topology

A physical topology that connects multiple MAUs to each other.

Figure 5-16

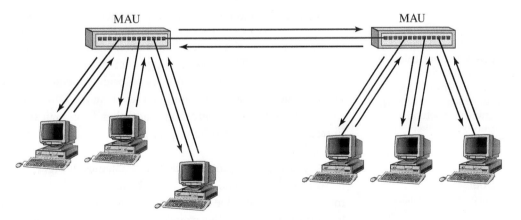

Star-ring topology.

Figure 5-17

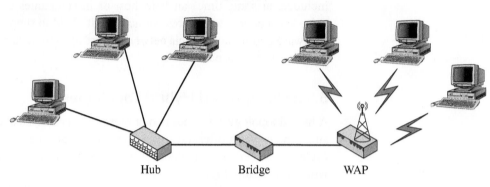

Hub   Bridge   WAP

Bridged network.

The advantages of using a hybrid topology include the advantages inherent in the topologies involved, but also include:

- It allows you to make use of legacy networks and hardware.
- It lets you scale out of your network without the expense of changing existing network segments.
- It provides greater flexibility in network design.

Disadvantages include:

- Network is more complex and more difficult to maintain.
- Communication problems can be difficult to isolate without sophisticated monitoring equipment.
- Specialized equipment is needed to connect the different topologies.

Bridge
A network communication device used to connect physical networks and provide a level of filtering between the networks.

One function of a **bridge** is to convert data packets between different level 2 protocols. Therefore, a bridge is most often used to connect different topologies into a hybrid network. A bridge operating in this role is invisible to devices operating at higher levels in the OSI model. If you were to connect an Ethernet logical bus and Token Ring logical star as shown in Figure 5-17, they would be seen as part of the same network segment for routing purposes.

Brouter
A network communication device that combines the functionality of routers and bridges.

If you wanted to connect the two topologies in Figure 5-17 as separate network segments, you would use a **brouter,** which combines bridge and router functionality. One cost-effective way to do this is to "grow your own" brouter. One way to do this would be to install both Ethernet and Token Ring NICs in a Windows Server computer and then configure the computer as a router.

IN THE REAL WORLD

Growing a Real-World Hybrid

In most organizations thinking that you will have the personnel or budget to tear out all of the old network cabling each time you go to expand or upgrade your network is unrealistic. Instead, you often end up with a mix of topologies resulting from whatever was popular when that network segment was deployed.

You might see something like the example in Figure 5-18. What we have here is three floors, connected by a vertical backbone running between them. Routers connect the floor LANs to the backbone. The first floor, the oldest in our example, is wired as a physical bus. The second

Figure 5-18

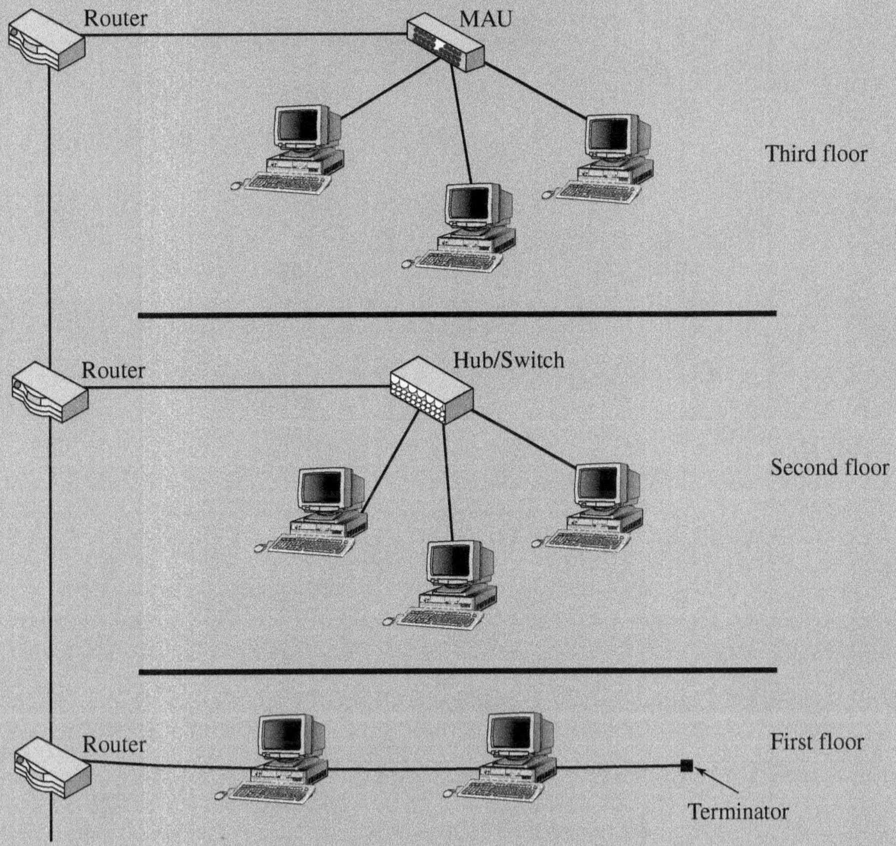

Router   MAU

Third floor

Router   Hub/Switch

Second floor

Router   First floor

Terminator

Original network.

(continued)

IN THE REAL WORLD   (continued)

is a logical bus network wired as star. The third floor is a logical ring, as shown in the drawing, but is wired using MAUs as a physical star.

Let's fast-forward a few years to the hybrid network shown in Figure 5-19. Problems with the network hardware on the first and third floors

Figure 5-19

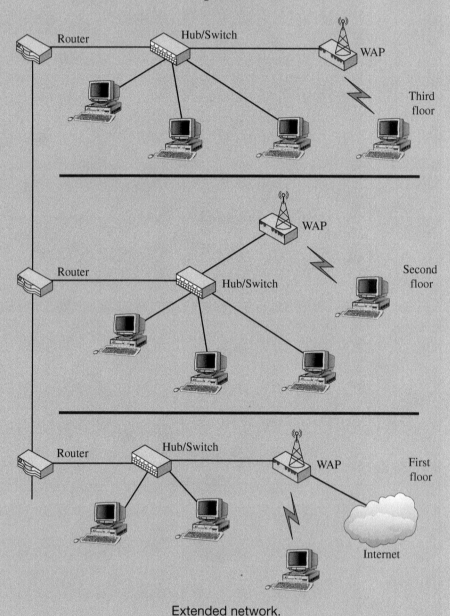

Extended network.

(continued)

have brought about a physical upgrade. Bus topologies are notoriously hard to troubleshoot. Ring network hardware has become more difficult to purchase and relatively more expensive than its logical bus counterparts. Both have been replaced by logical bus networks physically wired in a star topology.

That's not the only change. We also see WAPs in place on each of the floors. On the top two floors, the WAPs make deploying new computers easier because you don't have to run additional cable. On the first floor, we also see something else. This time, the WAP is also a wireless router and Internet proxy server. More accurately, it is a **network address translation (NAT)** server that enables Internet access for client computers using internally assigned **Private IP address**. (We will discuss NAT and Private IP addressing later in Chapter 7.) It is supporting multiple roles by providing:

Network address translation (NAT)
A server that enables Internet access for client computers using internally assigned Private IP address.

Private IP address
An address that can be used for addressing LANs, but cannot be used on the Internet.

- Infrastructure mode connections for wireless computers.
- Shared high-speed Internet connection for wired and wireless computers.
- Leased IP addresses to computers on the local LAN.
- Network address translation provided through the proxy to enable Internet access.
- Basic firewall protection filtering unwanted Internet traffic.

We also have something else happening here that might not be immediately apparent. It's very likely, in fact probable, that the range of these new WAPs all overlap, which means that the WAPs are potentially forming an effective mesh topology. Wireless computers could connect to any one of the WAPs, with the WAPs on the second and third floors offering redundancy for each other.

Are there any potential problems with this configuration? Unfortunately, yes, because the less control you have over your network, the less control you have over security. The network can become unbalanced with excessive traffic on some segments while little traffic is on others. When problems do arise (and they always do), isolating and correcting the cause can be difficult. A better design would be to assign each wireless computer a specific WAP as its primary network connection and implement security measures like authentication and MAC address filtering at the WAPs.

5.3.3 Combining Wired and Wireless Topologies

Probably the most common hybrids seen at this time are wired/wireless Ethernet hybrids. A WAP is designed with a wired Ethernet port so you can connect it directly to a wired hub. By doing so, you extend the logical bus to your wired computers, as well. You saw an example of this in Figure 5-11. The primary reasons for doing this are cost and convenience.

Some advantages of combining wired and wireless networks include:

- It allows for cost-effective scaling to meet growth requirements.
- Wireless NICs come preinstalled in most laptop computers.
- Because no cables are needed, you can extend the network into difficult-to-wire areas.

Some of the disadvantages are the same as you see in any hybrid topology, and include:

- Network is more complex than a single topology and it can be more difficult to isolate problems.
- Default WAP security settings are completely open and represent a potential security risk.
- Organization could lose sight of careful network planning.

Because extending a network using WAPs and wireless computers is so easy, some organizations have had a tendency to just let the network grow without careful planning and evaluation of network changes. Such uncontrolled growth makes for a poorly documented and poorly implemented network and could be a disaster in the making.

SELF-CHECK

1. When joining wired and wireless networks, what wireless mode is used and why?

2. Describe the physical structure of a logical bus and a logical ring.

Apply Your Knowledge *Note that this example is done on a Windows 7 Operating system laptop with a built in wireless card. The exercise will yield more examples if performed in a public area with free available Wi-Fi service.*

1. Follow the manufacturer's instructions to make sure your wireless device is turned on.

2. Open your Control Panel and click on Network and Internet.

3. Click Network and Sharing Center.

4. Record your current network status.

5. To see available networks to connect to click on Connect to a network.

6. Record the available wireless networks. Are they open or secured? What type of wireless security are they using, WEP, WPA, WPA2, etc.?

SUMMARY

Section 5.1

- There are four basic wired network topologies—bus, ring, star, and mesh.
- Each wired topology has its own advantages and disadvantages.

Section 5.2

- Wireless networks also have unique topologies.
- A physical star can actually be a logical bus or ring.

Section 5.3

- Hybrid topologies use elements of more than one basic topology in a single network.
- Wired and wireless devices can be used together in wired/wireless hybrids.

ASSESS YOUR UNDERSTANDING

UNDERSTAND: WHAT HAVE YOU LEARNED?

 Go to **www.wiley.com/go/ciccarelli/networkingbasics2e** to evaluate your knowledge of network topologies.

Measure your learning by comparing pre-test and post-test results.

SUMMARY QUESTIONS

1. Infrastructure mode is used in hybrid networks that include wired and wireless clients. True or false?

2. In which physical topology can a single break in the cable bring down the entire network?

   (a) Bus
   (b) Dual ring
   (c) Star
   (d) Mesh

3. What kind of device is used to connect bus network segments?

   (a) Bridge
   (b) Router
   (c) Repeater
   (d) Brouter

4. FDDI is an example of which physical topology?

   (a) Bus
   (b) Ring
   (c) Star
   (d) Mesh

5. Which of the following is a disadvantage of ad hoc mode?

   (a) The hardware required is prohibitively expensive.
   (b) Managing and maintaining it is difficult.
   (c) Clients cannot access resources on a wired network.
   (d) Laptop clients are not supported.

6. 10Base2 is an example of which physical topology?

   (a) Bus
   (b) Ring
   (c) Star
   (d) Mesh

7. A physical bus topology uses twisted pair cabling. True or false?

8. Which of the following is a disadvantage of a logical bus?

   (a) Performance degrades as more devices are added.
   (b) If a single node fails, it brings down the entire network.
   (c) The hardware is expensive and hard to come by.
   (d) The network must be brought down when adding nodes.

9. A MAU is used to wire which of the following?

   (a) Physical ring
   (b) Logical ring
   (c) Physical bus
   (d) Logical bus

10. You can use a bridge to connect a physical bus to a physical star. True or false?

11. When wiring multiple IEEE 802.3 coaxial cable segments, each one must have a different network address. True or false?

12. A MAU is wired internally as what?

    (a) A bus
    (b) A star
    (c) A single ring
    (d) A dual ring

13. Which of the following would be considered a legacy network?

    (a) A 10Base2 physical bus.
    (b) A 10Base100 logical bus.
    (c) An infrastructure mode network.
    (d) An ad hoc mode network.

14. A token is associated with which of the following?

    (a) A physical bus
    (b) A logical bus
    (c) Ad hoc mode
    (d) A logical ring

15. A hub is associated with which of the following?

    (a) A physical bus
    (b) A physical ring
    (c) A physical star
    (d) A physical mesh

16. A net topology is another name for which physical topology?

    (a) Bus
    (b) Ring
    (c) Star
    (d) Mesh

APPLY: WHAT WOULD YOU DO?

Your company occupies the first two floors in an office building. Each floor is configured as a 10Base2 LAN. The first floor has 20 nodes. The second floor has 45 nodes. Both are connected to a vertical backbone wired as a physical star.

1. What physical topology is used on both LANs?
2. What is the minimum number of cable segments on the first floor?
3. What is the minimum number of cable segments on the second floor?
4. Taken as a whole, what term best describes the network topology?
5. What symptoms would you see if a cable breaks on the second floor?

Your network is wired as shown in Figure 5-20.
You plan to use the same topology when you expand the network.

1. What term most accurately describes this topology?
2. How can you determine whether this is a logical ring or logical bus?
3. The wire leading to one node is accidentally cut. What should you expect as the effect of this?
4. Users on one star can't communicate with users on the other. What would most likely cause this?

Figure 5-20

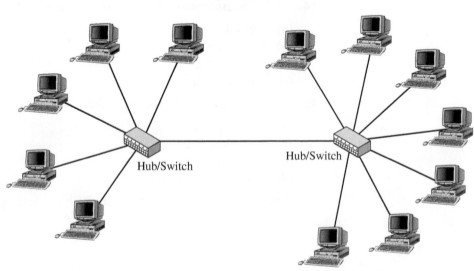

Sample network.

You support a small ad hoc mode network with five nodes. You are planning to add two additional computers in the near future.

1. Why is security a potential concern in this configuration?
2. What other term is used to refer to this topology?
3. What additional hardware is needed to add two computers?
4. What hardware would be needed if the network was configured as an infrastructure mode network?

BE A NETWORK DESIGNER

Designing Your Network Topology

Your office network is currently wired in a physical bus topology. Because of the age of the cable, how it is routed, and physical wear and damage over time, cable plant failures are occurring on an almost daily basis. You have been authorized to buy the equipment necessary to rewire the office, including new NICs (if necessary) and connection devices.

In two months, the office is expanding into additional adjoining floor space. This move is temporary until new offices can be made ready for move-in. This move-in is expected to happen in six or seven months. Only a few employees will be moving into the extra space, and you want to keep the cost and effort needed to give these employees network access to a minimum.

1. What happens if the cable fails in a physical bus network?
2. What kind of logical topology does the current network use?
3. What type of physical topology should you use when rewiring the current office area?
4. Why?
5. What logical topology should you use?
6. What kind of topology should you use to support the additional space you are moving in to in two months?
7. Why?
8. Describe the general steps you would need to take in two months to support the employees moving into the additional space.

KEY TERMS

10Base100	802.11g
10Base2	802.11n
10Base5	Ad hoc mode
10BaseT	BNC connector

Bridge

Brouter

Bus topology

Carrier Sense Multiple Access/Collision Avoidance (CSMA/CA)

Coaxial cable

Collision

Counter-rotating rings

Distributed coordination function (DCF)

Extended star topology

Fiber Distributed Data Interface (FDDI)

Gauge

Hybrid topologies

IEEE 802.5

Infrastructure mode

Legacy network

Logical bus

Logical topology

Logical topology

MAC address filtering

Mesh topology

Mode

Multistation Access Unit (MAU)

Network address translation (NAT)

Nexus point

Peer-to-peer mode

Physical carrier sense method

Physical topology

Point coordination function (PCF)

Private IP address

Public switched telephone network (PSTN)

Redundancy

Repeater

Ring topology

Service set identifier (SSID)

Star topology

Star-ring topology

Terminator

Thick Ethernet

Thicknet (RG-59 Coaxial Cable)

Thin Ethernet

Thinnet

Token Ring

Topology

Twisted pair cable

Virtual carrier sense method

Wi-Fi

Wireless access point (WAP)

Wireless mesh

6

NETWORK MEDIA AND DEVICES

What Do You Already Know?

- What are the types of cables commonly used in networks?
- What is a router?
- What is a bridge?
- What is a gateway?

 Go to **www.wiley.com/go/ciccarelli/networkingbasics2e** to assess your knowledge of network media and devices.

What You Will Find Out	What You Will Be Able To Do
6.1 How to choose network media.	Compare and contrast wired network media options.
	Describe appropriate applications for fiber-optic media.
6.2 Implementing network devices.	Identify the devices needed to implement an Ethernet or Token Ring network.
6.3 Implementing internetwork devices.	Select the appropriate connection device, given internetwork connectivity and feature requirements.
	Compare the appropriate use of bridges and routers.

INTRODUCTION

This chapter focuses on the physical network hardware. Before you can deploy a network, you need to collect the necessary hardware. Before you can get the hardware, though, you need to understand what you need and what it does. Today's technical marketplace offers a staggering variety of vendor and equipment options.

Your goals when selecting network hardware typically include meeting target goals for:

- Cost: You want to keep costs to a minimum without sacrificing quality.

- Scalability: Your choices need to be able to grow and expand as your organization grows, so interoperability and adherence to standards is important.

- Reliability: Downtime is annoying and expensive, so you want to be sure that you can rely on your choices.

- Management: Management and maintenance are a significant part of your ongoing costs, so it pays to keep the design as simple as possible.

Everything in your network is interrelated. When installing a new network, most of your hardware selections are driven by your topology choice. When expanding an existing network, you need to understand and consider existing hardware when making topology and hardware decisions for new network segments.

6.1 CHOOSING NETWORK MEDIA

A network's transmission media is a long-term investment. Unlike computer equipment, which is often replaced every two to five years, a company may use the same networking media for 10 to 15 years. Thus, choosing the correct media is crucial to having a functioning network.

Wireless networks are becoming more and more prevalent. We'll cover the media and devices required for them in Chapter 10. For now, we're going to focus on wired media. This means four basic media types:

- Coaxial cable (using copper wire)
- Shielded twisted pair (using copper wire)
- Unshielded twisted pair (using copper wire)
- Fiber optic (using glass or plastic)

When making your media selections, you should consider variations. The appropriate media type is determined by your physical topology, logical topology, and bandwidth requirements. Included with your media selection are the physical connectors used to connect to the network.

Copper cable is the oldest form of networking media. Furthermore, the vast majority of existing networks use some form of copper cabling. For higher-speed networks, many organizations are electing to use fiber-optic media, although copper can provide exceptional transmission rates—into the gigabit per second (Gbps) range.

Media is possibly the single most important long-term investment you will make in your network and should be chosen with great consideration. Your choice of media type will affect the type of network interface cards (NICs) installed, the speed of the network, and the capability of the network to meet the needs of the future.

There are also considerations relating to cable routing and placement. Let's start there.

6.1.1 Routing Your Cable Plant

Most regions have building codes that include specifications for network cable installation. These codes include items such as how or where cable can be routed, the use of **conduit,** and even the type of outer insulation the cable can have. One of the reasons many companies have a contractor install network cable for them is to make sure that all code requirements are met.

Conduit
Metal or plastic pipe used to contain network cable.

Even if not restricted by code requirements, installing network cable does have some common-sense guidelines (most of which happen to match up with typical code requirements). Where you route your cable can be significant and can directly impact reliability and safety. Cable insulation is another safety consideration.

Let's start with the obvious. When installing network cable, you want to avoid high traffic areas. In other words, don't put your cable where people will be walking. The reason why is two-fold—to protect the cable and to protect employees (or others walking through the work area). Overlooking loose cables is easy, and wherever you have loose cables, someone will eventually trip over them. However, it's just as hazardous for the cables. The constant movement and flexing as people walk over the cables eventually causes the internal conductors to break. The most common symptom is intermittent communication problems as the connection is made and lost.

Induction
The process through which a moving electrical current causes a voltage on a nearby wire.

As a result, cables are most often routed through suspended ceilings or through floors with a cable space for that purpose. When it does become necessary to cross a traffic lane, cables should be covered and protected. You need to protect network cables even when they are just running down a wall. The best way is to run the cables through conduit that contains only network cables, or at most, network cables and telephone lines. Do not run network cables through the same conduit as electrical lines. The copper wire cables can pick up a voltage through **induction.** The voltage can reach levels that can damage computer equipment or even cause injury.

Electromagnetic interference (EMI)
A source of interference caused by a strong magnetic field.

Radio frequency interference (RFI)
A source of interference that results from radio-frequency transmissions.

You also need to route your copper wire network cables to avoid sources of **electromagnetic interference (EMI)** or **radio frequency interference (RFI).** Both are sources of unwanted signals on your network cable that degrade signal quality. The interference levels depend on how your cables are routed and the type of cable used (more on cable types a little later).

EMI sources include any strong magnetic field, such as electric motors and fluorescent lights. Avoid routing cables near sources such as refrigerators, copy machines, or microwave ovens. When running past fluorescent lights, route the cable as far above the lights as possible and across, rather than with, the direction of the bulbs. RFI can be picked up from any radio frequency sources, including wireless transmitters if located too close to long cable lengths and microwave sources.

Fiber-optic cable is immune to problems with induction, EMI, or RFI. It is not, however, immune to physical damage. In fact, it is more fragile than copper wire cables, so you need to take extra care to avoid compression or vibration. Also, fiber optic is more expensive and more difficult to work with than copper wire.

Plenum
Teflon-based fire-retardant cable insulation.

Polyvinyl chloride (PVC)
A plastic commonly used as cable insulation.

What about insulation? Most codes require any cable routed through walls, floors, and ceilings and some require all cable, to have plenum insulation. **Plenum** is made from Teflon and is fire retardant, so in case of a fire, the cable won't help to spread the fire. The other insulation types you commonly see, such as **polyvinyl chloride (PVC)** plastic, not only burn, but give off toxic vapors while burning.

6.1.2 Using Coax

Coaxial cable (coax)
A type of Ethernet media consisting of a single copper conductor surrounded by insulation, a foil shielding, an outer jacket of PVC, or plenum.

Coaxial cable (coax) was the first type of networking media used in Ethernet LANs. Many networks still are using coaxial cable, though most are legacy networks.

Dielectric
The plastic insulator covering the central copper wire in coaxial cable.

Coaxial cable, as you can see in Figure 6-1, is constructed from one central copper wire that is covered with a plastic insulator, called a **dielectric,** and shielded from interference by a foil wrapping or braid. The outer jacket that protects the cable is either PVC or plenum. The foil or braided shielding in the coaxial cable must be grounded at one end to protect against EMI and help protect from RFI.

Figure 6-1

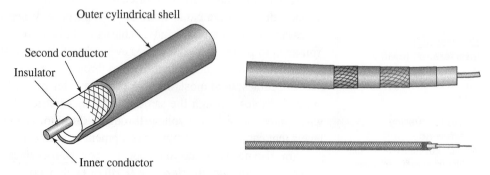

Coaxial cable.

Impedance
A measurement of opposition to varying electrical current.

Ohms
A unit of measurement for resistance of impedance.

All coax cables share the same basic structure, but vary in the size of the central copper core and cable **impedance,** measured in **ohms.** Higher impedance means higher resistance to a changing current, which is what you have in a data signal. Higher resistance means greater signal loss over a distance.

Recognizing Types of Coax

Many types of coaxial cable are used in various applications including networking and cable television. Each type of coax has specific characteristics that meet the needs of the type of transmission being carried. Table 6-1 shows the most common types of coaxial cable, comparing their impedance in ohms, common uses, and some of their basic characteristics. Many types

Table 6-1: Coaxial Cable Types

Classification	Impedance	Implementation	Description
RG-6	93 ohms	Cable TV	Like RG-59, but larger in diameter to accommodate higher bandwidth for cable TV transmissions.
RG-8	50 ohms	Thick Ethernet (Thicknet)	Solid copper core approximately 0.4 inches in diameter; must use a drop cable to attach to a device's NIC.
RG-11	75 ohms	Cable TV	Often has four layers of shielding.
RG-58/U	50 ohms	Thin Ethernet (Thinnet)	Solid copper core less than 0.2 inches in diameter.
RG-58 A/U	50 ohms	Thinnet	Like RG-58/U, but with a stranded copper core.
RG-58 C/U	50 ohms	Thinnet	Same as RG A/U, but used in military applications.
RG-59	75 ohms	ARCNET and Cable TV	Thick copper core with a large outer housing.
RG-62	93 ohms	ARCNET and IBM mainframes	Used in IBM 3270 systems to connect terminals to the mainframe.

Radio grade (RG)
A specification for coaxial cable used for network applications.

ARCNET
A low-level network protocol.

of coax use the **radio grade (RG)** classification, which defines the size of the copper center and the diameter of the outer jacket.

ARCNET was an early OSI layer 2 networking protocol, one that you are unlikely to ever see. The coax types most commonly used in networks are Thinnet and Thicknet. Thicknet is found only in legacy networks, but not used in new deployments. Thinnet is still used, but very rarely.

Comparing Ethernet Coaxial Cables

Thicknet (10Base5) was the original cabling used in Ethernet networks. It was typically used as a backbone and typically used a connection device known as a **vampire tap** to connect devices to the main cable through the use of a **drop cable** or DIX cable, a device cable specific to this network implementation. The name comes from the way that the cable usually dropped from a Thicknet cable running through the ceiling to the device. Figure 6-2 shows a common Thicknet cable with a vampire tap and a drop cable.

Vampire tap
A Thicknet cable tap that pierces the dielectric to connect to the inner core.

Drop cable
A Thicknet Ethernet device connection cable. Also called a DIX cable.

Thinnet (10Base2), developed after Thicknet, is smaller in diameter than Thicknet and much easier to work with. The connectors used with Thinnet, known as BNC connectors, can be either barrel connectors that attach one cable to another, or T connectors that attach devices to one cable. These connectors simply have to be connected and twisted into place to ensure their connection.

Advantages of Thinnet coaxial cable include:

- It's easier to install (than Thicknet).
- It's small in diameter.
- Its shielding, when grounded, reduces EMI and RFI.

Figure 6-2

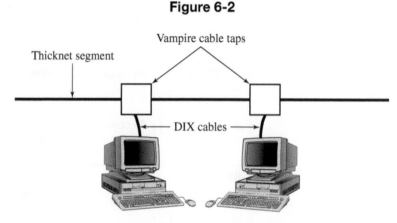

Thicknet client connections.

The disadvantages of using Thinnet include:

- If a cable breaks, the entire network goes down.
- The cable must be grounded to prevent interference.
- It's more expensive than twisted pair cable.
- The connectors and compatible NICs can be expensive.
- It does not support high-speed transmissions.

The shielding must be grounded on one end (and only one end) to be effective. Many implementations are not grounded, giving the false sense of security and protection. The cable must also be terminated at both ends.

Thinnet is considered antiquated by most network implementers, but its relative ease of use is appealing to some. A few manufacturers produced NICs that have both a coaxial cable connector and an unshielded twisted pair (UTP) connector, allowing you to change media as the network develops and the coaxial cable is phased out. NICs of this type have become uncommon and difficult to find, sometimes purchased as used equipment.

6.1.3 Using Shielded Twisted Pair (STP)

Shielded twisted pair (STP)
A cable that contains pairs of wire that are twisted periodically and covered with a foil or braid shield.

Shielded twisted pair (STP) consists of pairs of copper wires that are twisted together (see Figure 6-3). The pairs are covered in a foil or braided shielding, as well as an outer PVC jacket. As with coaxial cable, the shielding must be grounded to prevent the foil or braided shielding from becoming a magnet for electricity.

Figure 6-3

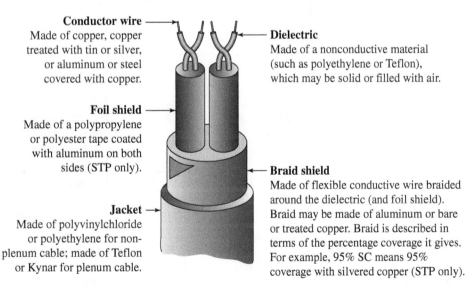

Conductor wire
Made of copper, copper treated with tin or silver, or aluminum or steel covered with copper.

Dielectric
Made of a nonconductive material (such as polyethylene or Teflon), which may be solid or filled with air.

Foil shield
Made of a polypropylene or polyester tape coated with aluminum on both sides (STP only).

Jacket
Made of polyvinylchloride or polyethylene for non-plenum cable; made of Teflon or Kynar for plenum cable.

Braid shield
Made of flexible conductive wire braided around the dielectric (and foil shield). Braid may be made of aluminum or bare or treated copper. Braid is described in terms of the percentage coverage it gives. For example, 95% SC means 95% coverage with silvered copper (STP only).

STP cable.

Cross talk
Signal changes caused on a wire by EMI from an adjacent wire.

STP is subject to near-end cross talk and EMI. **Cross talk** is the electromagnetic interference that occurs when the electrical signal on one wire changes the electrical properties of a signal on an adjacent wire. The twists in the pair provide cancellation, which is the process in which two wires are twisted together to prevent outside interference or cross talk.

The pairs are color-coded to make installation easier. For example, the color codes for 150 ohm STP-A cable are red and green wires for pair 1, and orange and black wires for pair 2.

Comparing STP Types

Type numbers
IBM STP category numbers.

Five types of STP are used in LAN implementations. STP is most commonly referred to by its IBM categories (**type numbers**). STP is commonly used in Token Ring networks, occasionally in legacy ARCNET networks, and rarely in Ethernet networks.

Unshielded twisted pair (UTP)
Cable that contains multiple pairs of wires that are twisted periodically to minimize interference.

Ethernet implementations usually use **unshielded twisted pair (UTP)** cable. The structure is similar, two or more pairs of twisted wires covered in a plastic jacket, but without the shield.

Table 6-2 compares the types of STP cabling, the number of pairs within each cable, the gauge of copper used, and their implementation. Cables used for voice-only and other non-networking applications are not included in the table.

Table 6-2: STP Cable Types

Type	Number of pairs	Gauge of copper conductor	Implementation
Type 1	2	22	Used in IBM's Token Ring networks for the main ring, or to connect nodes to the MAU.
Type 2	4	22	Used as a hybrid cable, one designed for multiple concurrent applications, for voice and data.
Type 6	2	26	Used as an adapter cable to connect a node to a MAU in Token Ring environments; can be used as a patch cable.
Type 8	2	26	Data cable that uses flat wire and is designed to run under carpets; prone to signal loss but adequate for short distances.
Type 9	2	26	Used between floors of a building; typically used in backbone implementations, and has a solid or stranded core and a plenum jacket.

IBM data connectors
Square, hermaphroditic connectors used in Token Rings.

RJ-45
A modular jack used for network connections.

The connectors developed for use with IBM cabling are known as the **IBM data connectors.** They are square, hermaphroditic connectors that are designed to interconnect with one another. Figure 6-4 shows you a data connector.

The IBM data connector is designed specifically for use in a ring topology. If you connect the cable to a port in a MAU, but not to a computer, the cable completes the circuit. When not connected, the cable internally connects the transmit to receive pair and receive to transmit pair, completing the circuit (and the ring). The most common cable configurations are to have IBM data connectors at both ends of the cable or an IBM data connector on one end and an **RJ-45** modular jack at the other. An RJ-45 modular jack looks a lot like phone plugs (R-11 jacks), although RJ-45 jacks are slightly larger.

Choosing STP Cabling

At one time, STP was the nearly exclusive choice when wiring a Token Ring network. This is no longer the case, since the introduction of MAUs and NICs designed to use UTP cable with modular connectors for RJ-45 jacks at each end.

Advantages of using shielded twisted-pair cable are:

- Shielding reduces EMI and RFI (if terminated).
- It can be used with RJ connectors, which are common and inexpensive, instead of with the IBM hermaphroditic connectors.

Figure 6-4

IBM data connector.

Figure 6-5

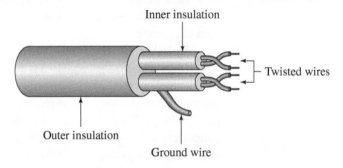

UTP cable.

The disadvantages of using shielded twisted-pair cable are:

- It must be properly grounded.
- It's more expensive than unshielded twisted pair.
- It's difficult to terminate.

Though not necessarily an advantage or disadvantage, STP is specifically designed for use with Token Ring, so is best matched to that use. However, terminating STP for IBM Token Ring networks takes time, primarily due to the fact that the cable is bulky and awkward, and the cable has to be grounded.

6.1.4 Using Unshielded Twisted Pair (UTP)

Unshielded twisted pair (UTP), shown in Figure 6-5, is the most common implementation of copper media today. It is made from twisted pairs of color-coded copper wires, but without insulation to protect against interference. Instead, the wire pairs within each cable have varied numbers of twists per foot to provide cancellation to help prevent interference.

The most common use of UTP that is not related to PC LANs is as telephone cable. As a network media selection, variations support Token Ring and Ethernet star topology networks.

Comparing UTP Types

Electronics Industries Alliance/Telecommunications Industry Association (EIA/TIA)
A standards body that defines UTP cable category standards.

Table 6-3 shows the UTP categories, the number of pairs in each, the grade of cable each uses, and how they are implemented. Standards defining UTP categories include **Electronics Industries Alliance/Telecommunications Industry Association (EIA/TIA)** 568-A and 568-B2. Backbone UTP versions, not listed in Table 6-3, have more than two pairs of wires, usually in multiples of 25 pairs.

Table 6-3: UTP Cable Categories

Type	Number of pairs	Transmission rate	Implementation
Category 1	2	Voice grade	Used in the telephone industry, but not suitable for data transmissions (though it has been used for short distances).
Category 2	2	4 Mbps	Can be used in data communications (Token Ring), but is rarely installed; no longer recognized under the 568- A standard.
Category 3	4	10 Mbps	Used for 10BaseT networks and for voice communication.
Category 4	4	16 Mbps	Used in IBM Token Ring networks.
Category 5	4	100 Mbps and higher	Used in Ethernet and 100BaseX networks. Certified to 100 Mbps.
Category 5e	4	100 Mbps and higher	Used in Ethernet and 100–1000BaseX networks. Certified to 1000 Mbps.
Category 6	4	100 Mbps and higher or 400 Megahertz (MHz) transmissions.	Used in Ethernet and 100BaseX networks. Certified to up to 10 Gbps.
Category 6e	4	10 Gbps or 625 MHz transmissions.	Standard cable for 10 Gigabit Ethernet **(10GBaseT).**
Category 7	4	700 MHz or up to 1.2 GHz in special applications.	Full-motion video and special government and manufacturing applications. Not currently used for LAN applications.

10GBaseT
A standard for 10Gbps Ethernet using UTP cable.

TIPS FROM THE PROFESSIONALS

Cat 5 and Cat 6

To help determine when CAT 5 or CAT 6 cable should be used, let's dig a bit deeper into their specifications.

Cat 5: Cat 5 cable contains four pairs of copper wire and supports speeds up to 100 Mbps. As with all other types of twisted pair EIA/TIA cabling, the maximum recommended run length for Cat 5 cable is 100m (328 feet). Although Cat 5 cable contains four pairs of copper wire, fast Ethernet communications only utilize two pairs.

Cat 5e, like Cat 5 supports networking speeds up to 1000 Mbps (1Gbps) over short distances by utilizing all four wire pairs, and is backward-compatible with ordinary Cat 5.

Cat 6: Cat 6 cable contains four pairs of copper wire as did Cat 5 and Cat 5e. Cat 6 utilizes all four pairs and supports speeds up to 1 gigabit per second (Gbps) and supports communications at more than twice the speed of Cat 5e. An enhanced version Cat 6a supports up to 10 Gbps speeds.

The UTP category number should be marked on the plastic jacket, as required by the Underwriters Laboratories (UL), the organization responsible for testing the safety of electrical wires, including the types of cable used in networks. Figure 6-6 shows the category marking on UTP cable.

In July of 2002, the EIA/TIA approved the Category 6 (Cat 6) standard called 568-B2.1, designed to support applications running at 1 Gbps or better. Cat 6 installations are generally considered more cost-effective than Cat 5 because of a greater variety of supported applications, higher potential

Figure 6-6

UTP cables showing labeling.

bandwidth, and longer lifespan without need for cable upgrade (because it should meet future needs).

Choosing UTP Cabling

When using UTP cabling, you need to consider the type of cable and connectors to use. Solid UTP, which consists of solid wires of copper twisted together, is used for permanent installations, such as within walls or raceways.

These permanent cable runs, referred to as **horizontal cross-connects,** are terminated at one end at a **patch panel** in the wiring closet and at the other end with, typically, an RJ-45 jack and wall plate.

Figure 6-7 shows a variety of RJ-45 jacks by different vendors. Jacks can be purchased for either the 568-A or 568-B standard, though some provide the color order for both standards within one plug.

UTP stranded cable consists of thin strands of copper within each individual wire. This type of UTP is more flexible than solid UTP and used for patch cords that connect devices to the RJ-45 jacks in the wall. Within the wiring closet, a patch cord is used between the patch panel and a hub or switch to connect the devices.

Advantages of using UTP include:

- It's inexpensive and easy to install.
- It's easy to terminate.
- It's widely used and tested.
- It's easy to maintain and troubleshoot.
- Patch cables come precut in most popular lengths.
- It supports many network types.

Horizontal cross-connects
Dedicated pathways for running cable through a building.

Patch panel
A wiring panel that simplifies wiring connections to multi-pair cables.

Figure 6-7

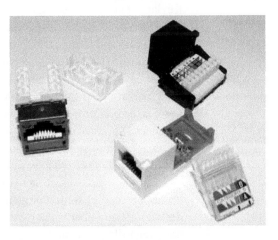

UTP connectors.

Disadvantages include:

- It's susceptible to interference.
- It's prone to damage during installation if mishandled.
- It's prone to physical damage if routed through traffic areas and not protected.
- Distance limits are often misunderstood or not followed.

UTP cabling is being installed in the vast majority of today's LANs with Cat 6 cable the most popular choice for new installations. Most existing installations are wired with either Cat 3 or Cat 5 cable. Although fiber-optic cabling might be used as the backbone cable between network segments, UTP is installed as the media to support connections to desktop computers and other devices.

6.1.5 Using Fiber Optic

Fiber-optic cable
A transmission media that uses glass or plastic fiber to carry light (laser) signals.

Attenuation
Loss of signal strength over distance.

Fiber-optic media offers several advantages over copper media and only a few disadvantages. **Fiber-optic cable** is constructed of a center core of silica, extruded glass, or plastic. It is designed to pass specific types of light waves over long distances with very little **attenuation,** the term for signal loss over distance. The center core of a multimode fiber-optic cable has a diameter of 125 microns (125μ), and is approximately the size of two human hairs. Fiber-optic cables can be purchased as single fibers or as pairs of up to 36 fiber strands. Pairs of fiber are needed to complete a full-duplex circuit.

Kevlar
Material used to protect the optical fibers in fiber-optic cables.

Figure 6-8 is a cross section of a typical fiber-optic cable. Outside the center core is cladding, which is reflective material that helps bend the light waves as they travel down the cable. **Kevlar,** the material used in bulletproof vests, is typically used to strengthen the cable and protect the glass fibers. Kevlar is extremely strong and resistant to damage.

Light-emitting diode (LED)
A light source typically used with fiber-optic cable.

Fiber-optic media is immune to EMI and RFI and typically not affected by lightning and electrical surges that can travel through copper media. Fiber optics can also support a higher bandwidth for longer distances without the use of a repeater than copper cable. Fiber-optic media transmits data using light, using either a laser light or a **light-emitting diode (LED)** as its light source. Laser is the preferred source for very long distance requirements (over several kilometers) because it typically emits a brighter light, but LED sources are preferred in most general LAN applications because they are more common, less expensive, more reliable, and have a longer projected lifespan.

Although many existing networks utilize a fiber-optic cable only as the backbone media, some companies are installing fiber-optic cable to the desktop. Plastic fiber is not currently accepted by the EIA/TIA 568-A standard, regardless, plastic fiber is widely used because the cables are usually less expensive and are less likely to be damaged during installation.

Figure 6-8

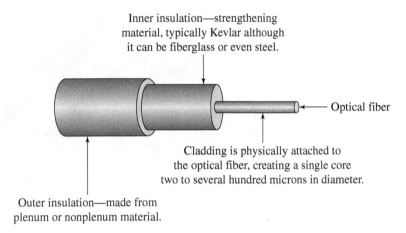

Inner insulation—strengthening material, typically Kevlar although it can be fiberglass or even steel.

Optical fiber

Cladding is physically attached to the optical fiber, creating a single core two to several hundred microns in diameter.

Outer insulation—made from plenum or nonplenum material.

Fiber-optic cable.

Recognizing Cables and Connectors

Multimode fiber
Fiber-optic cable that supports multiple concurrent communication signals.

Single-mode fiber
Fiber-optic cable that carries a single transmission signal.

SMA connector
A screw on fiber-optic connector.

Straight tip (ST) connector
A fiber-optic connector similar to a BNC connector.

Fiber-optic cables can come in various sizes that are identified by the size of the center core. The most common size for **multimode fiber,** which supports multiple transmission signals, is 62.5/125 microns. **Single-mode fiber,** which carries a single transmission signal, is more commonly used in long-distance applications, and has a core of 8/125 microns. Single-mode fiber can be implemented over three kilometers without needing a repeater. Several types of fiber-optic connectors are used, including SMA, ST, and SC.

There are two variations of the **SMA connector** screw-on connection shown in Figure 6-9. The 905 type has a straight connector. The 906 type has a connector that is smaller at the end so that two connectors can be joined with the use of a coupler. The difficulty in pairing two connectors to meet the needs of the dual-fiber interface has limited the use of the SMA connector in many new installations.

The **straight tip (ST) connector** uses a connection similar to that of the BNC connector. After you insert the connector, you twist and lock it into place. The ST is quick and simple to install, but is difficult to pair in dual-fiber installations. Figure 6-10 shows two ST connector variations.

Figure 6-9

SMA connector.

Figure 6-10

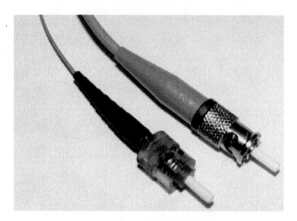

ST connectors.

The **subscriber connector (SC),** shown in Figure 6-11, is currently the most popular and is easy to recognize with its square tip. The SC connector is easy to install and is often coupled into duplex cables that form sets. A paired set may include keying, which prevents it from being installed incorrectly. In a keyed set, one connector is shaped slightly differently from its mate on the other end. In this way, the fibers are not crossed at installation.

The keyed set SC connector in Figure 6-11 has been adopted under EIA/TIA 568-A as the recommended fiber connector, referenced as 568-SC.

Justifying Fiber Optic

Fiber-optic cable can be used in many LAN architectures and applications, including Ethernet, 10Base-F, FDDI, and Optical Token Ring (Token Ring using fiber-optic cable) architectures.

Figure 6-11

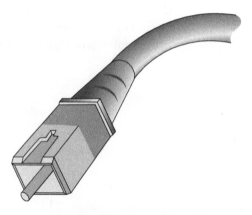

Keyed SC connector.

Advantages of using fiber-optic cable include:

- It can be installed over long distances.
- It provides large amounts of bandwidth.
- It's not susceptible to EMI or RFI.
- It cannot be tapped easily, so security is better.

Disadvantages of using fiber-optic cable are:

- It's the most expensive media to purchase and install.
- It requires appropriate conduit for outside use.
- You must match the cable type to the application.
- Strict installation guidelines must be met for the cabling to be certified.

Terminating fiber-optic cabling used to require extensive training, but today new techniques allow novices to learn how to terminate fiber in a matter of minutes. These new kits and fiber tips use specialized cutters and epoxy to ensure success, which has helped drive greater use in LAN applications.

IN THE REAL WORLD

A Cable Runs Through It

Wiring a home network is usually a simple matter, just a hub or switch, and a few device cables. Most office environments are much more challenging and complex. Typically, you can't have hubs spread around with cables running every which way. That configuration would lead to an unreliable network and a potential safety hazard.

When wiring an office, you usually have one central connection point, often the same room where you keep all of your network servers. That's where you would have all of your switches. The switches then go, not directly to the network devices, but to a patch panel like the type of panel used to wire a telephone system. Networking patch panels are typically designed with a set of jacks, often 100 or more, that are wired to connectors designed to let you attach your multi-pair cable used to wire the building.

How the multi-pair cable is routed depends on the building design. If raceways are available, these are used. Otherwise, the cable is run through the suspended ceiling. Either way, they eventually terminate with wall jacks. Prewired cables with RJ-45 connectors are then used to connect the devices to the jacks.

You might think that this setup would make for a troubleshooting nightmare, but in fact, it's designed to make troubleshooting as easy as possible. Indicator lights at the switch and patch panel give you the status of connections at that end. At the device end, you have indicator lights on the NIC. As for the run from the patch panel to the device jack, you can use an inexpensive continuity checker to test the line for breaks or shorts.

SELF-CHECK

1. List the UTP categories and typical application of each.
2. Contrast the structure of STP, UTP, and fiber-optic cable.

Apply Your Knowledge Look at the network cable connections in your home or office. Examine the cable coloring inside the RJ45 connector and determine if the color scheme used was ETA/IT 568A, 568B, or some generic custom color scheme

EIA/TIA 568A WIRING STANDARD	
PIN	**Wire Color***
1	White w/Green Stripe
2	Green w/White Stripe
3	White w/Orange Stripe
4	Blue w/White Stripe
5	White w/Blue Stripe
6	Orange w/White Stripe
7	White w/Brown Stripe
8	Brown w/White Stripe
For Cross Over Cable Wiring Wire ONE End using **568B** and one end as **568A** (Swap Orange and Green Pairs)	

EIA/TIA 568B WIRING STANDARD	
PIN	**Wire Color***
1	White w/Orange Stripe
2	Orange w/White Stripe
3	White w/Green Stripe
4	Blue w/White Stripe
5	White w/Blue Stripe
6	Green w/White Stripe
7	White w/Brown Stripe
8	Brown w/White Stripe
For Cross Over Cable Wiring Wire ONE End using **568B** and one end as **568A** (Swap Orange and Green Pairs)	

If you have some UTP cable available and a crimping set with RJ-45 terminals, then practice creating network cable with RJ-45 terminals by following these instructions:

1. Cut the outer jacket of the wire about 1.5" to 2" from the end and separate the pairs and align them in the wiring standard chosen order (either ETA 568A or ETA 568B). Begin flattening the wires to easily slip into the slots in the RJ-45 connector.

2. After you align all the wires and are ready to insert, you must trim them to approximately 1/2" in order to have as little untwisted wire in the connection as possible. Doing so is important to avoid near-end crosstalk interference (a form of interference caused by signals in nearby conductor wires).

3. Insert the wires into the connector making sure that each wire goes into its appropriate slot and extends all the way to the end of the connector underneath the gold crimping connectors. Look at the end of the connector to see the copper wires if you're using solid copper

cable, because if the wires don't extend to the end of the connector, the crimp will not make contact.

4. Press the cable and the jacket into the connector firmly so that the jacket will be crimped by the plastic wedge near the rear of the connector. Insert the connector using your crimping tool and crimp the cable. Crimp twice to confirm a good connection.

6.2 IMPLEMENTING NETWORK DEVICES

The transmission media carries the signal, but devices need a way of connecting to the media to transmit and receive. Most networks will also have a selection of other devices, as needed, to perform various functions on the network.

We're going to keep our focus primarily on wired networks and wired network devices for now. They include the network adapter or network interface card (NIC), central switch devices, and repeaters.

6.2.1 Using Network Interface Cards (NICs)

The NIC provides a device with the physical connection to the network. NICs can provide connections for any type of networking media, including wireless media. Not only do servers and workstations have NICs, so do network printers and all other network devices. Sample NICs are shown in Figure 6-12.

Device driver
Software that enables a computer's operating system to communicate with and control devices such as network adapters.

Specialized software, known as a **device driver,** lets the computer's operating system communicate with and control the NIC. Ethernet and Token Ring NICs have the Media Access Control (MAC) address hard-coded into the NIC by the manufacturer. The MAC address is unique so that data packets can be addressed appropriately to reach specific devices. If the NIC or the ROM chip containing the MAC address is replaced, the device's MAC address changes.

When selecting a NIC, check the following:

- The NIC must support the type of network you wish to connect to (Ethernet, Token Ring, etc.).
- The NIC must offer the right type of connector for the network media you're using (BNC, RJ-45, etc.).
- The NIC must support the available expansion slots (PCI for desktop or mini-PCI or PCMCIA for laptops).

To understand where a NIC fits in the process, think about the layers in the OSI networking model. When acting as a communication source device, the NIC:

- Receives the data packet from the Network layer
- Attaches its MAC address to the data packet

Figure 6-12

Network interface cards.

- Attaches the MAC address of the destination device to the data packet
- Converts data into packets (technically frames, but packets is also acceptable) appropriate to the network access method (Ethernet, Token Ring, FDDI)
- Converts packets into electrical, light, or radio signals to transmit over the network
- Provides the physical connection to the media

As a destination device, the NIC:

- Provides the physical connection to the media
- Translates the electrical, light, or radio signals into data
- Reads the destination MAC address to see whether it matches the device's own address
- Passes the packet to the Network layer if the destination MAC matches its own

The NIC's role is the same, no matter what type of device it is installed in or the type of media for which it is designed. If you are changing the network type or architecture, you typically have to replace the computer's NIC as part of the process.

6.2.2 Using Hubs

A hub is the central point of connection for cable segments in a physical star topology. Technically, a hub is a multiport repeater for use with twisted pair cable. Some hubs can also provide different services, depending on the sophistication of the hub. These specialty hubs include:

- **Managed hubs:** Hubs that support remote management and monitoring, such as remotely disabling a hub port.

- **Switched hubs:** Hubs that integrate functionality from switches (discussed later) into the hub.

- **Intelligent hubs:** Hubs with onboard processors that can perform various functions such as automatic error reporting, monitoring and reporting network traffic statistics, traffic buffering and collision avoidance, and so forth.

You need to know what services you want so that you can select your hub or switch accordingly.

Hubs create a logical bus wired as a physical star. They pass along all data that they receive, no matter which device it is addressed to, which can add to congestion on the network. Figure 6-13 shows a simple four-port hub connected to networking devices and creating a physical star topology. With simple hubs, collisions can occur at the hub, the same as on the cable in a physical bus. With managed hubs, these problems can be mitigated.

Advantages of using hubs include:

- They are cheap and readily available.

- They are easy to deploy and maintain.

- They can connect media operating at different speeds.

Figure 6-13

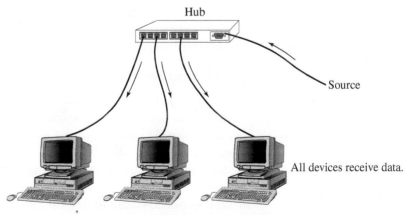

Hub and physical star.

Disadvantages include:

Collision domain
An area within an Ethernet network in which all devices in the domain compete for the cable, which may result in collisions.

- Simple hubs extend the **collision domain,** the segment in which collisions can occur, so collisions can still occur.
- Hubs can't filter the information passing through them so all packets transmit to all segments (all connected devices).

When choosing a hub for your Ethernet network, you will need to consider the following:

- **The type of media connection you'll need:** Typically, hubs provide one type of network connection, although some do provide another port of a different type. Some older 10BaseT hubs include one BNC port with their RJ-45 ports.
- **The number of ports you'll need:** Hubs are typically available in 4- to 48-port configurations. Linking most hubs together to create a single bus is also possible.
- **Speed:** A hub's speed depends on the type of network it is designed for use with, typically supporting both 10 Mbps and 100 Mbps, but 1 Gbps and faster hubs are available. Some hubs let you mix speeds, detecting the device speed and converting the signal as necessary, so that slower devices don't slow down the network as a whole.
- **Whether it's managed or unmanaged:** Managed hubs allow a network administrator to use software to view how the device is functioning from a remote workstation.
- **Whether there's an uplink port:** An uplink port lets you interconnect two hubs using a standard connection cable. The uplink port can be a separate port and identified as such or one that can be used as either a standard or uplink port, controlled by a switch.

Crossover cable
A cable used in place of an uplink port. This is accomplished by reversing the transmit and receive pair on one end of the cable.

Connecting hubs is possible without an uplink port by running a **crossover cable** between the hubs. A crossover cable is wired so that the transmit and receive pairs are reversed on one end. In other words, data transmitted at one end comes in as received data on the other. When using an uplink port, however, you use a standard cable, not a crossover cable.

6.2.3 Using Switches

Current switches often look and are commonly used exactly like hubs, but are in fact much more sophisticated devices. They are specific to the access method they are designed to support, so that an Ethernet switch is used in Ethernet networks only, a Token Ring switch in Token Ring networks, and so forth.

Switch
A connection device similar to a hub but more sophisticated including functionality that allows it to control and manage data transmissions.

Switches are actually multiport bridges that function at the Data Link layer of the OSI model. As shown in Figure 6-14, each port of a switch makes a decision whether to forward data packets to the attached network. The switch keeps track of all attached nodes' MAC addresses and the port

Figure 6-14

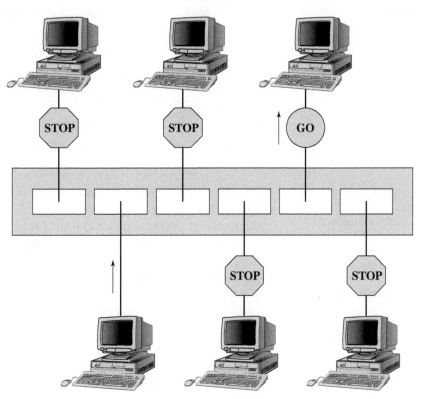

Switch and MAC address filtering.

to which each node is connected. With some switches, this can be a MAC address list if a hub is connected to the switch port instead of a single device. This information can help filter traffic and eliminate unwanted congestion.

Switches have become increasingly popular with network administrators and designers. Prices have become competitive with hubs, and though they are still more expensive than hubs, most of today's networks have switches installed in their wiring closets. Switches cut down on network traffic and keep the transmission of bandwidth-intensive data from affecting the entire network because each port on a switch is a separate collision domain.

Advantages of using switches include:

- They limit the collision domain.
- They can segment the network into multiple segments with separate collision domains.
- They support intelligent management capabilities including, in many servers, a built-in web server for remote management over the Internet.

Broadcast traffic
Traffic that is effectively addressed to every device on a network segment.

Virtual LANs (VLANs)
A LAN in which devices are logically configured to communicate as if they were attached to the same network.

Broadcast domain
A set of nodes configured to receive broadcasts as a group.

IEEE 802.1P
A standard that specifies how layer 2 switches can prioritize traffic and perform dynamic multicast filtering.

IEEE 802.1Q
A standard that defines VLANs.

Ring In
The inbound port used for connecting to MAUs.

Ring Out
The outbound port used for connecting to MAUs.

- They can limit broadcast traffic propagated between segments. **Broadcast traffic** goes out to every device on the network segment. If a response is required, every device can potentially respond, greatly increasing the amount of traffic generated.

Disadvantages include:

- They are typically more expensive than a hub of the same size.
- Some switches are complex and difficult to configure.
- Additional optional functionality can add to the potential complexity.

The most important advancement in switching that we've seen is the capability to create **virtual LANs (VLANs),** which is a LAN in which devices are logically configured to communicate as if they were attached to the same network, without regard to their physical locations.

One use of VLANs is to create **broadcast domains,** which are sets of nodes that receive broadcasts in a group, as if they were all on (and the only nodes on) the same physical segment. In the VLAN, ports are grouped into a single broadcast domain. Figure 6-15 shows how a VLAN allows devices to function as part of the same network segment, despite their physical location and connection.

This type of VLAN can be created at layer 2 using MAC addresses or at layer 3 using network addresses. VLANs are defined by the **IEEE 802.1P** and **IEEE 802.1Q** standards that specify the use of a router to pass packets between VLANs and to other networks. Routers do not typically pass broadcast packets.

Another use for VLANs is to segregate nodes by the functions they perform. This type is often used as a form of segregated network security.

6.2.4 Using Multistation Access Units (MAUs)

A MAU provides the function on a Token Ring network that a hub or switch provides on an Ethernet network. It provides the central connection that lets you wire a logical ring as a physical star, as shown in Figure 6-16.

The ring is created inside the MAU. When you connect additional MAUs, as shown in Figure 6-16, the ring is extended to the other MAUs. The ports used to connect the MAUs are typically labeled **"Ring In"** and **"Ring Out"**. With some older MAUs, you must physically complete the ring by connecting Ring Out on the last MAU back to Ring In on the first. With current MAUs, if the cable connecting the MAU were disconnected, the network would become two separate logical rings.

When no device is connected to a MAU device port, the signal passes on to the next port. When a device is connected, the ring includes the device. Each token (data packet) is received by every node in the path in order. If the device isn't the destination, it retransmits the token, so that the signal is constantly being boosted. This means that each device also acts as a repeater.

Figure 6-15

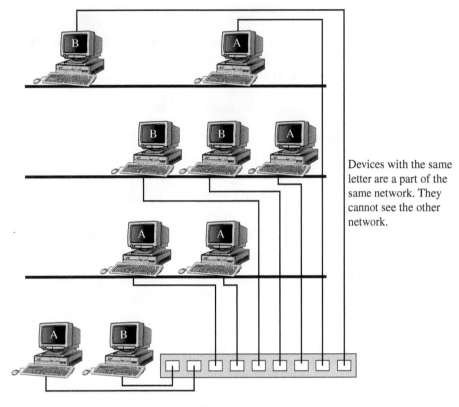

Devices with the same letter are a part of the same network. They cannot see the other network.

VLAN configuration.

Figure 6-16

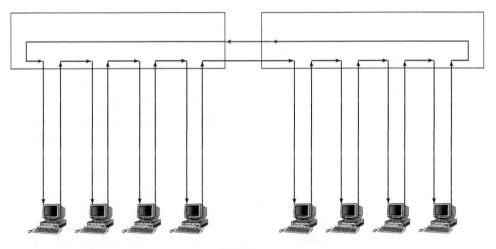

MAU star.

Advantages of using MAUs include:

- They are easy to install and configure.
- They have a long, reliable track record, often remaining in use for several years.
- MAUs are easy to troubleshoot and, in some instances, self-healing.

Disadvantages include:

- MAUs are more expensive than Ethernet hubs or switches.
- Compatible hardware, cables, and NICs are relatively expensive and sometimes hard to locate.
- Designed specifically for either 4 Mbps or 16 Mbps Token Ring, so the two cannot be mixed.
- MAUs are based on older technology and support a maximum bandwidth of 16 Mbps.

You cannot directly connect 4 Mbps and 16 Mbps MAUs. You cannot use a 4 Mbps NIC with a 16 Mbps MAU or vise versa. You can have both on your network, but on different cable segments connected by a bridge that manages the conversion between the two.

In most MAUs, a physical relay is used to open or close the connection to the device. Because of this relay, you often hear a series of "clicks" whenever the MAU is powered up or reset. Many MAUs support intelligent control that lets you remotely reset the MAU, view the status of the ports, and even enable or disable individual ports. Often, they can detect common communication problems, such as a device that fails to respond to a token, and automatically remove the device from the ring.

6.2.5 Using Repeaters

Repeater
A network device that amplifies a data signal. A repeater is used to connect network cable segments to extend a network.

Repeaters are networking devices that allow you to connect segments, thus extending your network beyond the maximum length of your cable segment. A repeater functions at the Physical layer of the OSI model and connects two segments of the same network. Some repeaters can connect segments of the same network that use different media types, such as an Ethernet segment using coaxial cable and another using Cat 5. A hub that includes a BNC connector is effectively a repeater of this type. Figure 6-17 shows a router used to extend a networks segment.

Simple repeaters are amplifiers, nothing more. They take the signal they receive, no matter how clean or dirty, and amplify it. Any unwanted noise is amplified along with the signal. More advanced repeaters have the ability to clean up the signal somewhat before retransmitting. Intelligent hubs acting also as repeaters can help to minimize collisions.

Comparing repeaters with other devices, except possibly hubs or switches, is difficult. With repeaters and the applications where they are used, you either

Figure 6-17

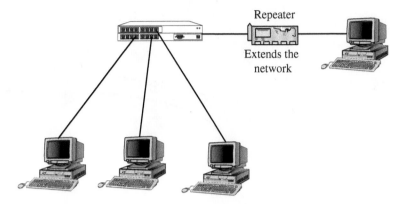

VLAN configuration.

need a repeater or you don't. Very rarely could you use a different device in place of a repeater, though a bridge might be substituted in some situations.

Advantages of using a repeater include:

- A repeater can connect different types of media (such as coax to twisted pair).
- Repeaters extend the distance a network can reach.
- Repeaters do not increase network traffic.

Disadvantages include:

- A repeater extends the collision domain.
- Repeaters cannot filter information, so the same information goes to all nodes.
- Repeaters cannot connect different logical network architectures.
- A network can include only a limited number of repeaters.

When installing a repeater, you should split the difference between network segments whenever possible. Consider the situation in Figure 6-18. You have a few devices at each end and 700 feet of 10Base2 Thinnet cable in between. The farther the signal goes on the cable before reaching a repeater, the more the signal drops and the more noise can get introduced with the signal. One possibility is shown on top. You could run the run a 300-feet length, a repeater, another 300-feet length, another repeater, and finally 100 feet. Below is a different solution. You would get a better network with a cleaner signal and better performance if you ran it as three lengths of 233 feet each with a repeater between each.

Though typically thought of as being used with Ethernet networks, most often with physical bus networks, this application of repeaters is not one that you might see. For example, a fiber-optic MAN backbone cable might include a repeater if a required segment run is longer than specified by the applicable fiber-optic standard. Even though supported, repeaters are rarely seen in Token Ring networks.

Figure 6-18

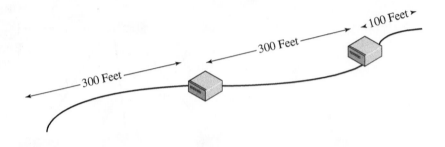

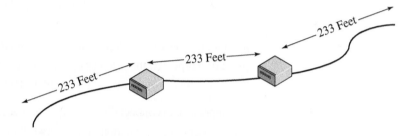

Repeater configurations.

 SELF-CHECK

1. What are the functional differences between a hub, switch, and MAU?
2. What is a virtual LAN (VLAN)?

Apply Your Knowledge Find and read the owner's manual for your home wireless router.

Each manufacturer has a slightly different method to log on and different options available. Log on to your router, and answer the following questions

1. What is the default IP address of your router?
2. What type of security is available (none, WEP, WPA)?
3. What is the SSID?
4. On what channel is it broadcasting?
5. Can you install MAC filtering?

IN THE REAL WORLD

Making the Connection

You're wiring an Ethernet network. Central connections are being made in a wiring closet. You want to try to keep down your costs and the network complexity, but you're concerned about collisions becoming a problem as the network grows. You also don't want to have to run to the wiring closet every time a user complains about a network problem.

What are you going to do? You actually have any number of solutions available, given these network requirements, and some of your decisions will be based on personal preference, but let's look at one possible solution.

One way to wire is to use managed hubs and intelligent switches. Each switch port connects to a hub with a cross-over cable. That hub represents a collision domain, that is, collisions can occur at the hub, but not between hubs. Traffic buffering at the switch prevents collisions between hubs. Note that by implementing VLANs on a switch, you would achieve the same results, with a lower cost and less equipment in your server closet.

How many switches do you need? Enough to provide a separate port for each hub and, possibly, a port for each network server. Because of the amount of traffic likely at some servers, they might each justify being connected as their own collision domain.

What about the hubs? How many ports do you need on each hub? For that, you need to consider your network traffic requirements. You'll want to use as few hubs as possible to keep the network easy to manage, but the fewer hubs you have, the more ports per hub and the larger the collision domain. Most users often have limited network access requirements, so you might be able to use hubs somewhere in the 32-port or higher range. For more active clients, drop that number down to 16 ports or even fewer.

6.3 IMPLEMENTING INTERNETWORK DEVICES

You can build a simple network with just NICs, hubs (or switches), and (if needed) repeaters. As networks grow and become more complex, additional devices are needed. The devices you need depend on the functionality required. Commonly used devices include bridges, routers, brouters, and gateways. As a quick word of warning, you need to be sure of your context when discussing gateways. In a TCP/IP network, the term *gateway* is used to refer to a router. In its classic definition, a gateway can be a much more sophisticated device.

Figure 6-19

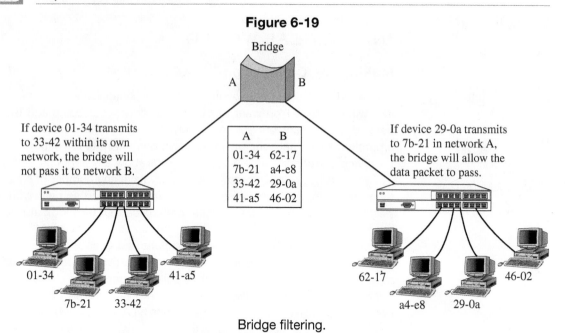

Bridge filtering.

6.3.1 Using Bridges

Bridge
A network communication device used to connect physical networks and provide a level of filtering between networks.

Bridges, like hubs, connect LAN segments, but like switches, they work at the Data Link layer of the OSI model. Because bridges work at the Data Link layer, they can use the MAC addresses to make decisions about the data packets they receive. A bridge provides four key functions:

- It builds a bridging table to keep track of devices on each segment.
- It filters packets that do not need to be forwarded to other segments based on their MAC address.
- It forwards packets whose destination MAC address is on a different network segment from the source.
- It divides one network into multiple collision domains, thereby reducing the number of collisions on any network segment.

Spanning Tree Protocol (STP)
A protocol used by bridges to decide whether to forward a packet.

Figure 6-19 illustrates how a bridge filters data. Bridges use the **Spanning Tree Protocol (STP)** to decide whether to forward a packet through the bridge and on to a different network segment. STP serves two functions. One is to determine a main bridge, called a root, when there is more than one bridge present. The root will make all the bridging decisions and deal with all bridging problems. The second function is to prevent **bridging loops,** which is when traffic gets stuck traveling between bridges and never reaches the destination computer.

Bridging loops
A condition in which packets are continually passed between bridges without ever reaching the destination computer.

In some situations you could use either a bridge or repeater to extend a network segment. The choice often comes down to determining which is more appropriate.

Advantages of using a bridge include:

- It limits the collision domain.
- It can extend network distances by boosting the signal.
- It can filter packets based on their MAC addresses.
- It can connect different types of media.
- Some can connect different types of network architectures.

Using a bridge to extend a network has an added advantage. Packets are processed by the bridge and retransmitted, not just amplified, providing a cleaner signal. Potential disadvantages include:

- Broadcast packets cannot be filtered, so their impact on traffic is not changed.
- It is more expensive than a repeater.
- It is more difficult to configure and creates a more complex network design.
- It can make troubleshooting communication failures more difficult.
- It is slower than a repeater because it must process the addresses and filter packets.

Encapsulation
The process of adding information to data as it passes through the layers.

Many bridges have the ability to convert between architectures or encapsulate data for passing through a foreign network type. **Encapsulation** is the process of wrapping a network packet inside another network packet, such as wrapping an Ethernet packet inside an FDDI packet. We have an example of using a bridge to convert between network architectures in Figure 6-20. A Token Ring network (logical ring) is connected to an Ethernet network (logical bus).

Figure 6-20

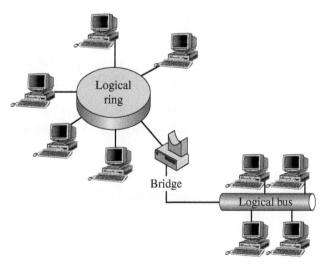

Connecting different architectures.

One thing you need to understand in this example is that both the Token Ring and Ethernet networks are part of the same network segment and would have the same network address. This means that for routing purposes, the two connected cable segments look like a single network segment to a router.

6.3.2 Using Routers

Router
A network communication device used to connect two or more networks or network types.

Routers connect different network segments that may be located in the same building or thousands of miles apart. They can connect different types of networks, such as Token Ring and Ethernet networks, or using different routed protocols including Internet Protocol (IP), Internetwork Packet eXchange (IPX), DECnet, and AppleTalk.

The router changes the packet's size, format, and addressing to fit the type of destination network on which the packet is being sent. They use the network address and the IP address in the TCP/IP environment, for example, to determine the best path for the packet to take to reach the destination quickly.

A router (or possibly a brouter) is usually not considered optional hardware. A network either does or doesn't have routing requirements. One situation where a router might be considered optional is when you use a router to segment a network as a way of reducing overall traffic requirements to improve network performance. Routers reduce broadcast traffic, except for a few examples, such as when supporting a broadcast domain or passing packets used to request automatic address assignments, when routers do block broadcast packets.

Advantages of using a router include:

- It limits the collision domain.
- It can connect networks using different media and architectures.
- It determines the best path for a packet to reach another network.
- It can filter or block broadcasts.

When used primarily to limit the collision domain or segregate traffic, you might consider a bridge as an alternate solution. Disadvantages to using a router include:

- It's more expensive than a bridge.
- It must be used with routable protocols.
- It can be difficult to configure and maintain.
- It makes troubleshooting communication problems more complex.
- It is slower than a bridge due to increased processing and routing updates sent between routers.

Figure 6-21

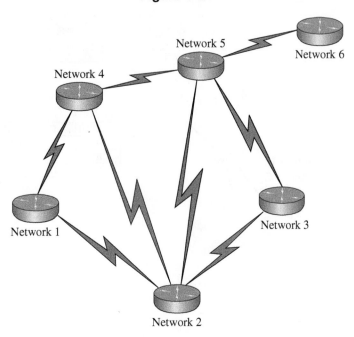

Determining best path.

Route
Path information between a
source and destination
computer.

Route
Path information between a
source and destination
computer.

Static routing
Manually configuring a route
that does not change unless it
is manually updated.

Dynamic routing
Automatically generating a
route that can adjust to
network conditions.

Routing table
A table stored in memory on
a router that keeps track of
known networks and the
appropriate port to use to
reach each network.

Brouter
A network communication
device that combines the
functionality of routers and
bridges.

A router determines the best path to a destination based on either static routing or dynamic routing and shares path information (the **"route"**) with other network routers. Figure 6-21 shows several networks connected with routers. Even though the data could travel from Network 1 to Network 6 through several paths, the router will determine the best path, based on the cost associated with getting there. The cost is based on an algorithm determined by the routing protocol being used, or the network administrator manually sets it.

With **static routing,** a network administrator manually configures a route into the router's routing table. **Dynamic routing** adjusts automatically to network topology or traffic changes based on information it receives from other routers. Whichever type of routing is used, the router determines the path for a packet by looking at the routing table, in which information about other networks is stored by the router. The **routing table** keeps track of known networks, the port on the router that should be used to send data to a particular network, and the "cost" for a data packet to get to that network.

6.3.3 Using Brouters

A **brouter** is a hybrid device that functions as both a bridge and a router. A brouter can work on networks using many different protocols. Any networking requirement that calls for a bridge or router can be filled by a brouter. Figure 6-22 shows a brouter acting as both a bridge and router.

Figure 6-22

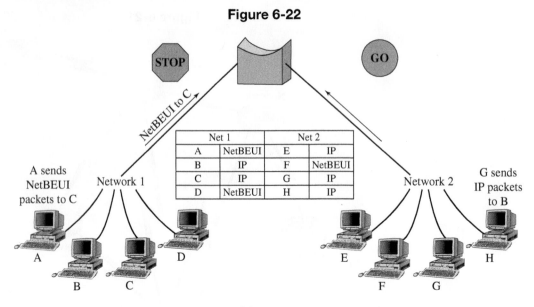

	Net 1		Net 2	
A	NetBEUI	E	IP	
B	IP	F	NetBEUI	
C	IP	G	IP	
D	NetBEUI	H	IP	

A brouter.

A brouter can be programmed to function in a specific way. If a brouter is forwarding data packets for a nonroutable protocol, such as NetBEUI, the brouter is functioning as a bridge. NetBEUI is a nonroutable layer 2 protocol. If a brouter is set to route data packets to the appropriate network for a routed protocol such as IP, it is functioning as a router.

Advantages of using a brouter include those of both a bridge and router. However, a brouter is not without its inherent disadvantages, also. The two primary disadvantages are cost and complexity, both exceeding either a router or bridge.

6.3.4 Using Gateways

Gateway
A network communication device used to connect dissimilar networks and devices.

Gateways, by classic definition, are devices that allow different types of network systems to communicate. The term *gateway* is used in a very general way in networking, and can mean a variety of things. If the term is used in reference to a device on the network, it means the device is providing some type of translation services to systems that could otherwise not communicate. Translation services can include address, protocol, and data translations. A router that also provides protocol translation can be considered to be acting as a gateway. Common gateway applications include:

- **Mail gateway:** Transfers mail between different types of e-mail services.
- **Host gateway:** Enables PCs to communicate natively with host computers.

Gateways tend to be expensive, are difficult to configure, and because of the processing overhead required, are often relatively slow devices. However, in some situations, they are your best solution.

As an example, consider the following situation. You have a network that includes a legacy Novell NetWare server that supports a proprietary server application. You have two options for accessing that server with Microsoft network clients. One is to install a NetWare client running in parallel with the built in Microsoft client. If the client computers are running with minimal resources, however, installing an additional client could severely degrade performance. There are also licensing concerns, because each client would require a separate license. The other option is to set up a Microsoft server configured as a NetWare gateway. The server can access

IN THE REAL WORLD

Routers

In this chapter we've talked about bridges, routers, and brouters as if they are separate, dedicated devices. In many applications, they are. Companies like Cisco Systems have made their mark in the technology world by providing network devices dedicated to performing specific functions on the network and doing it well. Actually, the devices are a combination of dedicated hardware and software designed specifically for that purpose. When you have critical, high-volume requirements, then a dedicated device is the way to go. However, it isn't your only option.

Most network operating systems, including Windows Server versions, let you create a router that is configured through the operating system. Need to connect to network segments? All you need to do is install network adapters in your server and enable routing. Need to bridge between Token Ring and Ethernet at the same time? No problem, as long as you have the right kind of NICs. Your software router is actually a brouter and can handle that for you, too. The necessary software ships with the operating system, so there's no additional software requirement.

If setting up a router through software is so easy and cheap, then why spend the money for a separate device? Two primary reasons: performance and features. Because Windows Server is a general-purpose operating system, it does a wide range of things relatively well, but doesn't do anything quite as well as dedicated software designed specifically for that purpose. Also, in order to be competitive and easier to justify the cost, dedicated routers include advanced management and maintenance features, making them more flexible that a software router.

the server resources and then reshare the resources to the Microsoft clients on the network. Also, because technically only one computer is accessing the NetWare server, only one client license is required.

SELF-CHECK

1. From the standpoint of collision zones and network segmentation, how do bridges and routers compare?

2. Contrast how bridges and routers filter traffic.

Project 6.1

Media is only part of the design decision when setting up a new network or expanding (or upgrading) an existing network. You must also select appropriate network devices, as needed, to meet communication, reliability, and configuration requirements.

Complete **Project 6.5: Choosing the Right Device** in the online Networking Basics Project Manual to understand how to choose appropriate network devices to meet network requirements.

SUMMARY

Section 6.1
- There are four types of network media used in wired networks: coax, STP, UTP, and fiber optic.
- The different media types (categories) have specific applications.

Section 6.2
- NICs, hubs, switches, and MAUs are devices needed to connect to the network.

Section 6.3
- A repeater can be used to extend a network.
- Bridges, routers, brouters, and gateways are used for internetwork connections.

ASSESS YOUR UNDERSTANDING

UNDERSTAND: WHAT HAVE YOU LEARNED?

 Go to **www.wiley.com/go/ciccarelli/networkingbasics2e** to evaluate your knowledge of network media and devices.

Measure your learning by comparing pre-test and post-test results.

SUMMARY QUESTIONS

1. A switch is effectively a multiport repeater. True or false?

2. What type of device do you use to configure a virtual LAN?
   (a) Hub
   (b) Switch
   (c) Bridge
   (d) Router

3. You need to connect two network cable segments. One is Token Ring and the other is Ethernet 10BaseT. Both need to be part of the same network segment. Which device should you use?
   (a) Hub
   (b) Switch
   (c) Bridge
   (d) Router

4. How does a router filter traffic?
   (a) By network address
   (b) By MAC address
   (c) By host name
   (d) By network architecture

5. A hub operates at the same OSI layer as what other device?
   (a) Repeater
   (b) Switch
   (c) Bridge
   (d) Router

6. What kind of media has a central copper core, dielectric, shield, and insulation?
   (a) STP
   (b) UTP
   (c) Fiber optic
   (d) Coaxial

7. Extruded glass is the only material used for fiber-optic cores. True or false?

8. By specification, a 10BaseT network will be wired with what kind of cable?
   (a) Thinnet
   (b) UTP
   (c) Fiber optic
   (d) Thicknet

9. Which STP cable type uses a flat wire, 26-gauge conductor?
   (a) Type 2
   (b) Type 6
   (c) Type 8
   (d) Type 9

10. Cat 6 UTP is certified up to what bandwidth?
    (a) 4 Mbps
    (b) 16 Mbps
    (c) 100 Mbps
    (d) 10 Gbps

11. You can use either an uplink port or a crossover cable to connect two hubs. True or false?

12. A bridge extends the collision domain. True or false?

13. How does a bridge filter traffic?
    (a) By network address
    (b) By MAC address
    (c) By host name
    (d) By network architecture

14. What connector type is most commonly used with fiber-optic network applications?
    (a) SMA
    (b) ST
    (c) SC
    (d) BNC

APPLY: WHAT WOULD YOU DO?

Your network is wired as shown in Figure 6-23. A fiber-optic cable is used as the vertical backbone. Each floor should be configured as a separate network segment.

1. What kind of device should you use to connect each floor to the backbone and why?

2. How many network segments (total) will you have when finished?

3. What would you use at the central connection point on each floor if each floor will be a single collision domain?

Figure 6-23

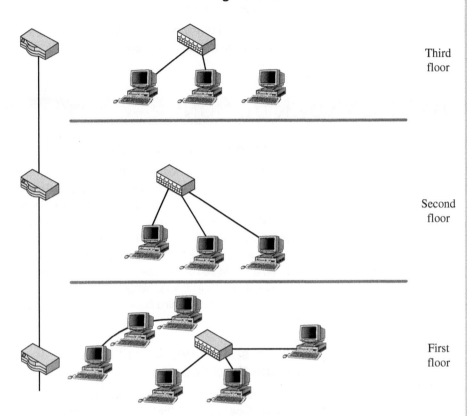

Third
floor

Second
floor

First
floor

A sample network.

4. What would you use at the central connection point on each floor if each floor will have multiple collision domains?

5. What would you use at the central connection point on each floor if you want to configure broadcast domains that include devices on different floors?

6. The first floor currently has two separate physical networks: a physical bus Ethernet network and a physical star Token Ring network. What are your options for connecting the networks?

7. What must you consider when selecting your connection device?

You are wiring a new Ethernet network. The network must route through several rooms, all on the same floor. Cable will route through raceways to a central patch panel in the server room. All PCs have 100 Mbps NICs installed.

1. What are your available copper wire cable options and the maximum bandwidth for each?

2. If cost is not a consideration, which option should you use and why?

3. What would be possible justifications for using fiber optic instead of copper wire cable?

4. What kind of connectors would you most likely use to connect the devices to a fiber-optic network?

BE A NETWORK DESIGNER

Designing a Physical Network

You are brought in to design a company's physical network. The company is preparing to move into new office space. The company leases offices on the first and third floors. They do not currently have a network in place.

The network design must support up to 150 nodes more or less evenly divided between the two floors. The network will include six secure servers that will be installed in the server room. The entire network should be treated as a single network segment, but with three collision domains, each with clients on both floors. You want to keep as much of the network support hardware on the third floor as possible.

Where should you install network connection devices for the third floor and why?

Each floor of the building has a wiring closet that can be used by anyone leasing office space on that floor. You will design the network, but the building management company requires that you hire a bonded contractor to physically run the cables. You cannot install any additional hardware in the wiring closet. Each floor has two patch panels, one for the vertical backbone and one for wiring the horizontal raceways for that floor.

Describe how you would wire device support for the third floor.

You have a secure server room already wired on the third floor. Currently, the only thing in the server room is a patch panel and 200 pair cable that is already run from the server room patch panel to the third floor cable closet patch panel. You do not have a securable server room on the first floor.

Explain how you would wire for first floor devices, keeping the vertical backbone pairs used to a minimum. Trace the wiring back to the third floor.

There is a vertical backbone in place. A 200-pair cable runs through all of the floors and is connected to a patch panel on each floor. Building management will make 16 pairs on the vertical backbone available to you to use however you wish.

The company's IT department authorizes the contractor to use only Cat 5e cable for horizontal runs. What are the potential adverse effects, if any?

KEY TERMS

10GBaseT

ARCNET

Attenuation

Bridge

Bridging loops

Broadcast domain

Broadcast traffic

Brouter

Coaxial cable (coax)

Collision domain

Conduit

Cross talk

Crossover cable

Device driver

Dielectric

Drop cable

Dynamic routing

Electromagnetic interference (EMI)

Electronics Industries Alliance/ Telecommunications Industry Association (EIA/TIA)

Encapsulation

Fiber-optic cable

Gateway

Horizontal cross-connects

IBM data connectors

IEEE 802.1P

IEEE 802.1Q

Impedance

Induction

Kevlar

Light-emitting diode (LED)

Multimode fiber

Ohms

Patch panel

Plenum

Polyvinyl chloride (PVC)

Raceway

Radio frequency interference (RFI)

Radio grade (RG)

Repeater

Ring In

Ring Out

RJ-45

Route

Router

Routing table

Shielded twisted pair (STP)

Single-mode fiber

SMA connector

Spanning Tree Protocol (STP)

Static routing

Straight tip (ST) connector

Subscriber connector (SC)

Switch

Type numbers

Unshielded twisted pair (UTP)

Vampire tap

Virtual LANs (VLANs)

7

TRANSMISSION CONTROL PROTOCOL/INTERNET PROTOCOL (TCP/IP)

What Do You Already Know?

- What is the most commonly used networking protocol?
- What protocols TCP/IP is named for?
- What is a hostname?

For additional questions to assess your current knowledge on TCP/IP protocol fundamentals go to **www.wiley.com/go/ciccarelli/networking basics2e.**

What You Will Find Out	What You Will Be Able To Do
7.1 Understanding TCP/IP fundamentals.	Understand the development of TCP/IP.
	Understand the relationship between TCP and IP.
7.2 How to manage IP addresses.	Identify IPv4 and IPv6 addressing requirements.
	Understand how IP addresses are organized.
7.3 How hostnames are used.	Understand how a system can translate a hostname to an IP address.
	Use DNS.
7.4 How to support TCP/IP.	Configure TCP/IP parameters on a Windows system.
	Understand when and how to use common utilities to test your TCP/IP configuration.

INTRODUCTION

Transmission Control Protocol/Internet Protocol (TCP/IP) is the most common protocol suite in current use. The Internet is based on this protocol, nearly all PC networks are founded on this protocol, and it is the current default protocol for current PC operating systems. Because of its widespread acceptance and use, you need to know how to configure TCP/IP **hosts** (computers on a TCP/IP network).

This chapter starts with a look at TCP/IP fundamentals and the two basic protocols from which it takes its name, Transmission Control Protocol (TCP) and Internet Protocol (IP). From there, we'll look at TCP/IP addressing. Address assignment is a critical part of network design and deployment, so you need to know something about how IP addresses are structured. We also need to spend some time with **name resolution** and how human-recognizable names (like www.busicorp.com) are resolved to numeric addresses. Finally, we look at configurable properties and some basic TCP/IP utilities.

7.1 UNDERSTANDING TCP/IP FUNDAMENTALS

Hosts
A network device on a TCP/IP network.

Name resolution
The process of mapping IP addresses to Internet host names.

To understand TCP/IP, you need to understand a bit about some of the goals in its development. The history of TCP/IP and the Internet are so closely tied that they cannot be separated. Both were developed as part of the electronic battleground of the cold war between the United States and Soviet Union. From its origins as a way to facilitate communication between a few university campuses, the Internet has grown into a world-wide phenomenon, helping drive the growth of the PC industry in the process and changing the way people communicate, collaborate, and do business.

TCP/IP is a suite of protocols, with TCP and IP at its fundamental base. We're going to take a look at each of these two protocols, including a quick breakdown of how the packets sent out on the network are structured. Although you might never need to know this information as a requirement for your job, it does help you understand keys points like how IP addresses are used to ensure packet delivery.

7.1.1 TCP/IP Design Goals

TCP/IP was first proposed in 1973 and was split into separate protocols, TCP and IP, in 1978. When the U.S. Department of Defense began to define the TCP/IP network protocols, their design goals included the following:

- TCP/IP had to be independent of all hardware and software manufacturers. Even today, this independence is fundamentally why TCP/IP makes such good sense in the corporate world: it is not tied to any specific company.

- It had to have good built-in failure recovery. Because TCP/IP was originally a military proposal, the protocol had to be able to continue operating even if large parts of the network suddenly disappeared from view, say, after an enemy attack.

- It had to handle high error rates and still provide completely reliable end-to-end service.

- It had to be efficient and have a low data overhead. The majority of IP packets have a simple, 20-byte header, which means better performance in comparison with other network protocols. A simple protocol translates directly into faster transmissions, giving more efficient service.

- It had to allow the addition of new networks without any service disruptions. This important design goal has helped fuel the growth and expansion of the Internet and PC networks.

As a result, TCP/IP was developed with each component performing unique and vital functions that allowed all the problems involved in moving data between machines over networks to be solved in an elegant and efficient way.

The popularity that the TCP/IP family of protocols enjoys today did not arise just because the protocols were there, or even because the U.S. government mandated their use. They are popular because they are robust, solid protocols that solve many of the most difficult networking problems and do so in an elegant and efficient way.

In meeting the design goals, the result was a protocol that had, and continues to have, several inherent benefits over other networking protocols. These benefits include:

- TCP/IP is a widely published open standard and is completely independent of any hardware or software manufacturer.

- TCP/IP can send data between different computer systems running completely different operating systems, from small PCs all the way to mainframes and everything in between.

- TCP/IP is separated from the underlying hardware and will run over Ethernet, Token Ring, and other networks.

Datagrams
A term used to refer to data packets at the OSI network level or equivalent level in other network models. Also known simply as a packet.

- TCP/IP is a routable protocol, which means it can send **datagrams** (TCP/IP network packets) over a specific route, thus reducing traffic on other parts of the network.

- TCP/IP has reliable and efficient data-delivery mechanisms.

- TCP/IP uses a common addressing scheme. Therefore, any system can address any other system, even in a network as large as the Internet.

The TCP/IP family continued to evolve and add new members. One of the most important aspects of this growth was the continuing development

Best effort transmission
A term used to refer to the connectionless transmission method used by IP.

Destination address
A 32-bit address field that identifies the host that should receive the datagram.

Protocol number
An IP header field that describes the type of protocol used in the datagram following an IP header.

Checksum
A value used to verify that a datagram has not changed during transmission.

Time to Live (TTL)
An IP header field whose value is used to limit the lifespan of a datagram based on the number of routers (hops) it crosses.

Hop count
Maximum number of routers the packet can cross, usually set to the default value of 32 hops.

Executioner
The current router when the TTL field counts down to zero.

Internet Control Message Protocol (ICMP)
A management and troubleshooting protocol that provides support through error and control messages.

Segments
(1) A physical network division within a larger physical network. (2) Term sometimes used to refer to datagram fragments.

of the certification and testing program carried out by the U.S. government to ensure that the published standards, which were free, were met. Publication ensured that the developers did not change anything or add any features specific to their own needs. This open approach has continued to the present day; use of the TCP/IP family of protocols virtually guarantees a trouble-free connection between many hardware and software platforms.

7.1.2 Internet Protocol (IP) and Transmission Control Protocol (TCP)

Internet Protocol (IP) operates at the Network layer of the OSI model, or more accurately, at the Internetwork layer of the DoD network model, but the two are effectively equivalent. In fact, IP is the main protocol at the layer. IP is what actually moves the data from point A to point B. IP is considered connectionless and does not exchange information in order to establish an end-to-end connection before starting a transmission. This type of communication is known as **best effort transmission.** It can't recover lost packets or even tell if a packet is lost in transmission by itself. That's one of the reasons other protocols are needed in the TCP/IP suite. IP's only job is to route the data to its destination.

During transmission, IP receives a datagram from a higher-level protocol like TCP (for connection-oriented transmissions) or User Datagram Protocol, or UDP, (for connectionless transmissions). IP adds its header to the datagram, consisting of information like the source and **destination addresses,** the **protocol number** (identifying the higher-level protocol in use), a **checksum** (to check for errors at the destination), and a code representing the enclosed higher-layer protocol. The information in the header provides the information needed for routing and delivery, including the **Time to Live (TTL)** field.

The TTL field is **hop count,** used to determine when to discard a packet as lost or undeliverable. The number is decremented by each router through which the packet passes. When it reaches 0, the current router (known as the **executioner**) sends an **Internet Control Message Protocol (ICMP)** time-exceeded message back to the original source.

Figure 7-1 is a simplified representation of how the IP header, upper layer header, and data fit together.

The data in the packet immediately follows this header information, which may correspond to a complete TCP segment, UDP datagram, or other IP-supported protocol data.

Transmission Control Protocol (TCP) serves to ensure a reliable, verifiable data exchange between hosts on a network. TCP breaks data into pieces called datagrams, or **segments,** wraps them with the information needed to identify it as a piece of the original message, and allows the pieces to be reassembled at the receiving end of the communications link. The most important information in the header includes the source and destination port

Figure 7-1

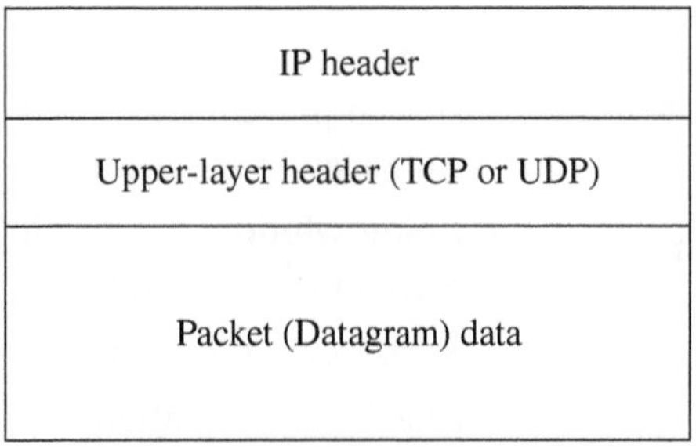

IP header
Upper-layer header (TCP or UDP)
Packet (Datagram) data

Datagram with headers.

numbers, a sequence number for the datagram, a control bit flag indicating how the segment should be handled, and a checksum.

TCP flags and their explanations are as follows:

- **ACK:** Stands for Acknowledge. The receiver will send an ACK that equals the sender's sequence number plus the Len, or amount of data, at the TCP layer.
- **S, SYN:** Synchronize is used during session setup to agree on initial sequence numbers. Note that sequence numbers are random.
- **F, FIN:** Finish is used during a graceful session close to show that the sender has no more data to send.
- SYN and FIN flags count as 1 byte. Think of the ACK as the sequence number of the next octet the receiver expects to receive.
- **R, RST:** Reset is an instantaneous abort in both directions (abnormal session disconnection).
- **P, PSH:**Push forces data delivery without waiting for buffers to fill. This is used for interactive traffic. The data will also be delivered to the application on the receiving end without buffering.
- **U, URG:** Urgent-Data is sent out of band.

To understand the role of the header, take a brief look at the TCP communication process. The first step in establishing the communications link is what is known as the "Three-Way Handshake." The client first sends a Synchronization TCP segment (Syn). The server responds with a second TCP segment containing both an acknowledgement of the communication request and synchronizing the connection (Syn/Ack). And finally the client responds again with a third segment acknowledging the connection requirements. The first two segments contain no application-layer data; the third of these segments may carry functional data, known as a payload.

Overflows
A condition where a destination system is sent more information than can be received.

Acknowledgement
A special packet type sent by a receiving system to acknowledge successful receipt of one or more datagrams.

Sequence number
Used by TCP to identify the order of each piece of information in a packet so that the packet can be reconstructed appropriately, despite any fragmentation or disordering that may have happened during data transmission.

Fragmentation offset
A field within the IP packet that specifies the distance, in eight-byte blocks from the beginning of the packet. The offset for the first fragment in a packet is set to 0.

Window
A TCP header field that identifies the numbers of segments that can be sent before the source host expects an acknowledgement from the recipient.

Key features of TCP communication include:

- Flow control that allows two systems to cooperate in datagram transmission to prevent **overflows** (when more data is sent than the destination can receive) and lost segments.

- **Acknowledgment** that lets the sender know that the recipient has received the information.

- Sequencing used to ensure that segments arrive in the proper order.

- Checksums that allow easy detection of corrupted segments.

- Retransmission of lost or corrupted segments that are managed in a timely manner.

TCP adds a certain amount of overhead compared to connectionless communication. However, where reliable delivery is a must, the overhead is an acceptable expense.

Fields in the TCP header support connection-oriented transmission. The source port number and the destination port number ensure that the data is sent back and forth to the correct application process running on each computer. Port numbers and their use are discussed in more detail later in this chapter. Two additional fields you should know about are the Window and Urgent Pointer.

The header is also designed to enable fragmented datagrams (datagrams broken into smaller pieces) and their reassembly. A **sequence number** and **fragmentation offset** value shows where the fragment fits as part of the complete datagram, allowing the datagrams to be rebuilt in the correct order in the receiving device.

A checksum value enables the protocol to check whether the data sent is the same as the data received.

The **Window** determines the number of segments transmitted before the sender expects an acknowledgment. Increasing this value helps improve efficiency in data transfers on a reliable network. The value is decreased

TIPS FROM THE PROFESSIONALS

Three-Way Handshake

The TCP Three-Way Handshake also presents a perfect target for hackers to cause a *Denial of Service (DOS)* attack known as a *SYN flood*. As soon as the server sends its SYN/ACK packet, it waits for a period of time for the client to send an ack and begin communication. The server has only a limited number of slots available for TCP to begin communications. If some evil person spoofs a legitimate user's IP address and sends only SYN packets, this will have the effect of using all the server's available connection slots, stopping any legitimate traffic from establishing a connection.

Urgent Pointer
A TCP header field that is used to identify higher-priority data that is interrupting a lower-priority transmission.

Out-of-band
A method in TCP that separates some information from the main data stream and designates it as urgent.

Telnet
A TCP/IP protocol and application that provides terminal emulation.

when network problems endanger the data's integrity so more segments need to be acknowledged until conditions improve.

The **Urgent Pointer** gives the location in the segment where the urgent data ends, assuming that the urgent data begins at the beginning of the segment. This allows **out-of-band** transmission of special data, which signifies to the receiving device that this data should be pushed ahead of any other that it has received but has not yet processed. Special data could be, for example, a keyboard break sequence in a **Telnet** (terminal emulation) session, which should immediately be processed by the receiving device.

As soon as the header is on the datagram, TCP passes the datagram to IP to be routed to its destination. The receiving device will perform a checksum calculation, and if the values do not match, an error has occurred somewhere

IN THE REAL WORLD

Routers and Routing

The IP portion of the TCP/IP protocol inserts its header in the datagram. It is then sent to the first router on the way to the destination or, if the source doesn't know the best route to take, to the host's default gateway. Each host on a TCP/IP network can have a default gateway. Its job is to forward datagrams toward their destination (if known) or to its default router, and so forth, until the destination is reached. Because routers don't know the location of every IP address, they have their own default gateways that act just like any TCP/IP host. Each router has a defined set of routing tables that help track routes to specific destinations.

Datagrams intended for the same destination may actually take different routes to get there. Many variables determine the route, and most modern routers are designed to compensate automatically for changing conditions such as excessive congestion or after detecting a failed route. Key to this process is the destination address, which includes both the address of the destination network and host.

Host address
A unique computer address on a network segment in a TCP/IP network.

The destination network is the network on which the final destination is located. The **host address** uniquely identifies the host device on that network. To ensure this unique identification, it is critical that each host (and network location) is uniquely identifiable within the network's scope. Part of the design process when deploying a TCP/IP network is determining what addresses will be used and how they will be assigned to the hosts.

along the line, and the datagram is silently discarded by the destination device. The source will resend any packet that is not acknowledged after a set timeout period.

SELF-CHECK

1. Describe the relationship between datagrams, IP header information, and TCP header information.

Apply Your Knowledge Describe some of the vulnerabilities of the TCP communication method.

Project 7.1

All TCP/IP hosts must have a unique IP address. The IP address can be assigned as a static address, one explicitly specified through the TCP/IP configuration properties, or as a dynamic address, where the host leases an address from a DHCP server.

Dynamic addressing is typically used for the majority of the hosts in a TCP/IP network, but you need to understand how to configure both dynamic and static addresses. You also have a number of potential security concerns when dealing with DHCP servers, especially in a Windows Active Directory network. Because of these security concerns, you will not be setting up and testing DHCP.

Complete **Project 7.2: Configuring TCP/IP Properties** in the online Networking Basics Project Manual to know how to configure a host for dynamic address assignment, configure static IP address parameters, and configure multihomed addresses.

7.2 MANAGING IP ADDRESSES

Each IP datagram destination includes an IP address and a destination port or socket number. They allow for successful delivery to any host on your LAN or, if connected to the Internet, potentially to any location in the world.

Each Ethernet network card (and any other NIC, for that matter) has its own unique hardware address, known as the media access control (MAC) address. This hardware address is predefined and preprogrammed on the NIC by the manufacturer of the board as a unique 48-bit number. Don't confuse this address, which is implemented as part of the Data Link layer of the OSI model, with the IP address, which is implemented at the Network

IP version 4 (IPv4)
The current IP version, which uses a 32-bit addressing scheme.

IP version 6 (IPv6)
A new IP version that uses a 128-bit address and provides a larger pool of addresses.

Dotted decimal notation
The decimal representation typically used for IP address and subnet mask values consisting of four decimal values separated by decimal points or "dots."

Class
A method of organizing available IPv4 addresses for assignment.

Internet Corporation of Assigned Names and Numbers (ICANN)
The organization that is responsible for maintaining IP network address and domain name registrations.

Private addresses
An address that can be used for addressing LAN devices, but cannot be used on the Internet.

Network Address Translation (NAT)
The process whereby transmissions can be routed appropriately from an outside system to internal systems with private IP addresses

Internet proxy servers
A server on a network that acts as an intermediary between systems to check and validate incoming requests to see if it can fulfill the request before passing it on to the server.

layer (or the Internet layer, the DoD networking model). The IP address is assigned, rather than hard-coded, and can be also be changed as necessary.

Our primary focus is on the current TCP/IP standard, known as **IP version 4, or IPv4.** Also in (currently limited) use is a new standard, **IP version 6 (IPv6)** developed to solve a looming problem—that the Internet is rapidly running out of available addresses. We take a brief look at IPv6, but only for comparison purposes and to let you know what's eventually coming your way.

7.2.1 Breaking Down IP Addresses

An IPv4 address is a 32-bit number, usually represented as a four-part decimal number with each of the four parts separated by a period or decimal point. For example: 192.168.10.1

You may hear this method of representation called **dotted decimal notation.** In the IPv4 address, each individual byte, or *octet* as it is usually called, can have a decimal value of 0 through 255.

The way these addresses are used varies according to the network's **class,** which is one way that the addresses are organized. The 32-bit IPv4 address is divided to create an identifier for the network, which all hosts on that network share, and for each host, which is unique among all hosts on that network. In addition, the address can be divided further to allow for a subnetwork address, which is a way of dividing an assigned network address among smaller networks for organizational and management purposes.

Some host addresses are reserved for special use. For example, in all network addresses, host numbers of all 0s and all 1s are reserved. An IPv4 host address with all host bits set to 0 in binary identifies the network itself, so 172.16.0.0 refers to network 172.16. An IP address with all host bits set to 1 in binary is known as a broadcast address. The broadcast address for network 172.16 is 172.16.255.255. A datagram sent to this address is automatically sent to every individual host on the 172.16 network.

The **Internet Corporation of Assigned Names and Numbers (ICANN)** is responsible for registering and maintaining IP address and Internet domain name registrations. In theory, you could get an IP address from ICANN. In real-world applications, you will most likely have to ask your Internet service provider (ISP) to secure an IP address on your behalf. However, registered addresses are only required if you are connecting to the Internet, and you need an address that is recognized by the Internet. For your local network, you have the option of using addresses that have been set aside as private addresses.

Internet routers don't recognize **private addresses,** so a computer with a private address cannot directly access the Internet. Services like **Network Address Translation (NAT)** and **Internet proxy servers** come into play then. As shown in Figure 7-2, they replace the computer's private address with a valid Internet address on outgoing packets. As packets come in destined for a local host, the Internet address is replaced with the host's private address.

Figure 7-2

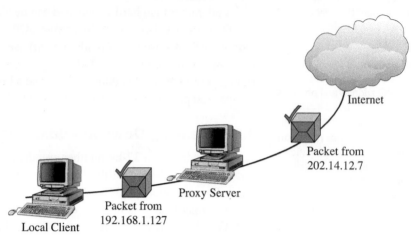

Address translation.

To get a better understanding of these processes, let's take a look at each of these separately.

NAT is the process of converting between one set of public IP addresses that are viewable from the Internet and a second set of private IP addresses that are hidden from people outside of the organization. NAT is transparent, in that no computer knows it is happening. If external intruders on the Internet can't see the private IP addresses inside your organization, they have a more difficult time attacking your computers. Most routers and firewalls today have NAT built into them, even inexpensive routers designed for home use. To do this conversion, the NAT on the firewall uses an address table to translate the private IP addresses used inside the organization into proxy IP addresses used on the Internet. When a computer inside the organization accesses a computer on the Internet, NAT changes the source IP address in the outgoing IP packet to its own address. NAT also sets the source port number in the TCP segment to a unique number. This unique number is then added to the NAT address table, where it is available to help locate the IP address of the actual sending computer in the organization's internal network. The NAT process makes it possible to hide the internal IP addresses from external systems. In fact, external systems see only one IP address for all systems within the organization.

How this works in practice is that the firewall is assigned a public IP address within the network domain assigned to the organization. All other systems on the network are assigned private IP addresses. Because these internal addresses are never used on the Internet but are always converted by the firewall, internal users aren't concerned about intruders discovering their internal IP address.

Similarly, Internet proxy servers act as an intermediary between systems to route requests to the appropriate system. A proxy server is a server that sits between a client computer and a real server. The proxy server intercepts packets that are intended for the server and processes them. The proxy server can examine the packet and decide to pass it on to the real server, or it can reject the packet. Or, the proxy server may be able to respond to the packet itself without involving the real server at all. For example, a web proxy often stores copies of commonly used web pages in its local memory store. When a user requests a web page from a remote web server, the proxy server intercepts the request and checks whether it already has a copy in its cache. If so, the web proxy returns the page directly to the user. If not, the proxy passes the request on to the real server.

Managing Address Classes

As you can see, having different classes of addresses, private and public, is helpful to securing a network. For IPv4 addresses, the internal bits assigned to each segment of the decimal-dot address help identify the network and the host. How these bits are used varies according to the network class of the address. The following classes of IP addresses offer a default set of boundaries for varying sizes of address.

IPv4 address classes are shown in Figure 7-3. Address classes A, B, and C are used for IP host addressing. Addresses in class D are used for multicasting, a way of sending one packet to multiple defined groups of computers.

Figure 7-3

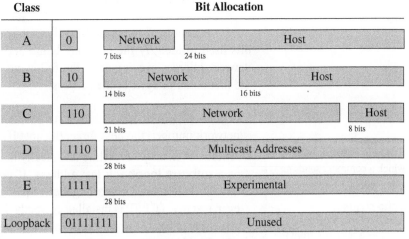

IPv4 address classes.

Let's take a closer look at each of these classes and their use.

Class A
A network address classification that defines, by default, up to 127 networks with up to 16,777,214 hosts each.

Class B
A network address classification that defines, by default, 16,384 networks with up to 65,534 hosts each.

Class C
A network address classification that defines up to 2,097,152 networks with up to 254 hosts each.

Class D
Network addresses set aside for multicast broadcast applications.

Class E
Network addresses set aside for experimental use.

- **Class A** was designed for very large networks only. The default network portion for Class A networks is the first 8 bits, leaving 24 bits for host identification. The high-order bit is always binary 0, which leaves 7 bits defining 127 networks. The remaining 24 bits of the address allow each Class A network to hold as many as 16,777,214 hosts. All possible Class A networks are in use; no more are available.

- **Class B** was designed for medium-sized networks. The default network portion for Class B networks is the first 16 bits, leaving 16 bits for host identification. The 2 high-order bits are always binary 10, and the remaining 14 bits define 16,384 networks, each with as many as 65,534 hosts attached. Class B networks are generally regarded as unavailable, but address conservation techniques have allowed some of these addresses to become available from time to time over the years.

- **Class C** was designed for smaller networks. The default network portion for Class C networks is the first 24 bits, leaving 8 bits for host identification. The 3 high-order bits are always binary 110, and the remaining 21 bits define 2,097,152 networks, but each network can have a maximum of only 254 hosts.

- **Class D** is the multicast address range and cannot be used for networks. These addresses have no network/host structure. They are taken as a complete address and used as destination addresses only, just like broadcast addresses. The 4 high-order bits are always 1110, and the remaining 28 bits allow access to more than 268 million possible addresses. Multicast addresses are used for managing broadcasts to defined groups of computers, such as streaming video out to specific computers on a network.

- **Class E** is reserved for experimental purposes. The first 4 bits in the address are always 1111.

Take another look at the bit values shown in Figure 7-3. Because the bits used to identify the class are combined with the bits that define the network address, we can draw the following conclusions from the size of the first octet, or byte, of the address:

- A value of 126 or less indicates a Class A address. The first octet is the network number, the next three, the host ID.

Loopback
A communication test in which a computer sends an echo request to itself.

Echo request
A TCP/IP message that requests a response from the host receiving the message.

- A value of exactly 127, while technically in the Class A range, is reserved as a software **loopback** test address. If you send an **echo request** to 127.0.0.1, it doesn't actually generate any network traffic. It does, however, test that TCP/IP is installed correctly. Using this number as a special test address has the unfortunate effect of wasting almost 17 million possible IP addresses, a case of early 1970s short-sightedness, much like the theory that 64KB of RAM should be enough for PCs.

- A value of 128 through 191 is a Class B address. The first two octets are the network number, and the last two are the host address.

- A value of 192 through 223 is a Class C address. The first three octets are the network address, and the last octet is the host address.

- A value of 224 through 239 is a Class D multicast address. Again, there are no network or host portions to multicast addresses.

- A value greater than 239 indicates a reserved Class E address.

7.2.2 Using Subnets

The IP addressing scheme provides a flexible solution to the task of addressing thousands of networks, but it is not without problems. The original designers did not envision the Internet growing as large as it has; at that time, a 32-bit address seemed so large that they quickly divided it into different classes of networks to facilitate routing rather than reserving more bits to manage the growth in network addresses. To solve this problem, and to create a large number of new network addresses, another way of dividing the 32-bit address was developed, called **subnetting.**

Subnetting
The process of dividing a network address into smaller networks.

When faced with the choice of whether or not to subnet your network, you must remember several of the advantages to subnetting. The following list summarizes the advantages of the subnetting solution:

- It minimizes network traffic, decreasing congestion because routers filter traffic by network address, keeping local traffic on the local network.

- It isolates networks from one another, requiring routers to provide connectivity between the subnets.

- It can improve performance by reducing the traffic in a network segment, especially in Ethernet networks where collisions have become a problem.

- It defines the limits of a broadcast domain because routers do not forward broadcast packets.

- It optimizes use of IP address space by letting you specify the number of hosts per network.

- It enhances the ability to secure a network through careful segmentation and the use, where needed, of firewalls between subnetworks.

An IP subnet modifies the IP address by using host ID bits as additional network address bits. In other words, the dividing line between the network address and the host ID is moved to the right, thus creating additional networks but reducing the number of hosts that can belong to each network.

When IP networks are subnetted, they can be routed independently, which allows a much better use of address space and available bandwidth. To subnet an IP network, you define a bit mask, known as a subnet mask, in which a bit pattern of consecutive 1s followed by consecutive 0s is logically ANDed with the IP address to produce a network address with all 0s in the host ID.

Working out subnet masks can be one of the most complex tasks in network administration and is not for the faint of heart. However, if you have two or more segments (or subnets), you will have to make some sort of provision for distributing IP addresses appropriately. One way is to assign different network class addresses (such as using multiple Class C addresses), but subnetting makes more efficient use of available addresses.

If you are using private addresses, which are discussed in some detail later in this section, you might well be able to use multiple network addresses, but you won't be able to do this in all networks. The possibility also exists that you might encounter a routed network that someone else has set up, so you need to understand at least the basics involved. The goal of this chapter is to introduce you to subnetting, but not to try to make you an expert in the process.

The subnet mask is similar in structure to an IP address, but it works a bit like a template that, when superimposed on top of the IP address, indicates which bits in the IP address identify the network and which bits identify the host. In binary, if a bit is on (set to 1) in the mask, the corresponding bit in the address is interpreted as a network bit. If a bit is off (reset to 0) in the mask, the corresponding bit in the address is part of the host ID. Often, you will use only one subnet mask throughout to subnet your network, as in Figure 7-4.

Variable Length Subnet Masking (VLSM), another subnetting option, is the practice of using more appropriate varied subnet masks with the same classful network for the different subnet sizes. A **classful network** is one subnetted to the default boundaries of network and host bits, based on the class of IP address.

Variable Length Subnet Masking (VLSM)

A subnetting option in which variable length subnet masks are used instead of all subnets having the same subnet mask.

Classful network

A network that is subnetted to define the boundary for the network and host bits.

Figure 7-4

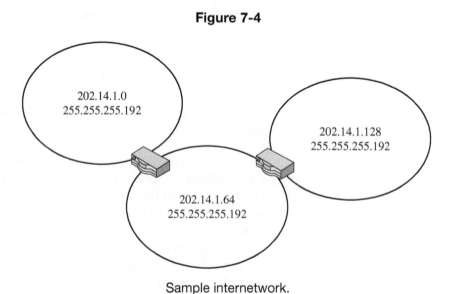

Sample internetwork.

Table 7-1: Default Subnet Masks

Class	Subnet Mask Bit Pattern	Subnet Mask
A	11111111 00000000 00000000 00000000	255.0.0.0
B	11111111 11111111 00000000 00000000	255.255.0.0
C	11111111 11111111 11111111 00000000	255.255.255.0

A subnet is only known and understood locally; to the rest of the Internet, the address is still interpreted as a classful IP address (and maybe even as a group of classful addresses) if an entity has administrative control over a contiguous block of such addresses. Table 7-1 shows how this works for the standard IP address classes.

Routers use the subnet mask to extract the network portion of the address so that they can compare the computed network address with the routing table entry corresponding to the mask used and send the data packets along the proper route on the network.

Classless Inter-Domain Routing (CIDR)

Classless Inter-Domain Routing (CIDR)
An alternative way of defining and specifying network addresses, using the format *network_address/ network_address_bits*.

The traditional way of representing addresses is with an IP address and subnet mask value. It has become common, however, to use the **Classless Inter-Domain Routing** (or **CIDR,** which is usually pronounced "cider") standard representation. CIDR networks are described as "slash x (/x)" networks; the x represents the number of bits in the IP address range used as the network address. The idea is that this is more easily represented and understood than the decimal values, though network administrators used to the original method often disagree. You can see an example of this in Table 7-2.

In CIDR terms, a network classified as a Class C network under the old scheme becomes a /24. The real purpose of CIDR is that you can define networks that fall between the old classifications, as shown in Table 7-2.

Subnetting a Class C Network

How do you find out the values that you can use for a Class C network subnet mask? The leftmost three octets in a Class C address are defined for you, leaving you with the rightmost octet for your own host and subnetting use. If your network consists of a single segment, you have the following subnet mask:

11111111 11111111 11111111 00000000

Table 7-2: CIDR vs. Subnet Mask Representations

InterNIC Network Type	Subnet Mask	Number of Usable IP Addresses
/8	255.0.0.0	16,777,214
/12	255.240.0.0	1,048,574
/16	255.255.0.0	65,534
/20	255.255.240.0	4,094
/21	255.255.248.0	2,046
/22	255.255.252.0	1,022
/23	255.255.254.0	510
/24	255.255.255.0	254
/25	255.255.255.128	126
/26	255.255.255.192	62
/27	255.255.255.224	30
/28	255.255.255.240	14
/29	255.255.255.248	6
/30	255.255.255.252	2

When expressed as a decimal number, this is: 255.255.255.0

Because all of your addresses must match these leftmost 24 bits, you can do what you'd like with the last 8 bits, given a couple of exceptions that we look at in a moment.

You might decide to divide your network into two equally sized segments, with, for example, the numbers 0 through 127 as the first subnet (00000000 through 01111111 in binary) and the numbers 128 through 255 as the second subnet (10000000 through 11111111 in binary). Notice how the numbers within each subnet can vary only in the last seven places. So, placing 1s in the mask where the bits should be identical for all hosts in a subnet, the subnet mask becomes 255.255.255.128. In binary this is:

11111111.11111111.11111111.10000000

As a quick tip, you can use the Windows Calculator in scientific mode (select View and then Scientific) to look at binary-to-decimal and decimal-to-binary conversions. Click **Bin** button and then type the bit pattern that you want to convert. Click **Dec** to display its decimal value. You can also go the other way and display a decimal number in binary form. Scientific mode works great for hexadecimal and octal numbering systems, as well.

Now let's get back to the exceptions mentioned earlier. The network number is the first number in each range, so the first subnet's network number is W.X.Y. 0 and the second is W.X.Y. 128 (the host address set to all 0s).

Table 7-3: Class C Network as Four Subnetworks

Network Number	First Address	Broadcast Address
X.Y.Z.0	X.Y.Z.1	X.Y.Z.63
X.Y.Z.64	X.Y.Z.65	X.Y.Z. 127
X.Y.Z.128	X.Y.Z.129	X.Y.Z.191
X.Y.Z.1292	X.Y.Z.193	X.Y.Z.225

The default router address is commonly the second number in each range—W.X.Y.1 and W.X.Y. 129—and is not required, but a lot of network administrators like to set them up that way. The broadcast address is the last address (the host address portion set to all 1s), or W.X.Y. 127 and W.X.Y. 255 in this case. The broadcast address is set by definition, so you can't play around with it. You can use all the other addresses within the range as you see fit on your network. Table 7-3 shows how you can divide a Class C network into four equally sized subnets with a subnet mask of 255.255.255.192. Doing so gives you 62 IP addresses on each subnet after you have accounted for the network and broadcast addresses.

In Figure 7-5, we've put in some real numbers (using addresses out of the private address range) to let you see how the addresses might be used in your network.

Keep in mind that except for the network address and broadcast address, there are no firm and fast rules as to how you use the other available addresses. However, you might find it worth your while to set up internal addressing standards.

Figure 7-5

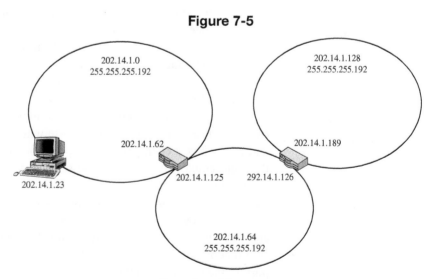

Sample address use.

Assigning Private Addresses

You will often use a private address when setting up your network and use public addresses only at those points where you are directly exposed to the Internet. The benefits? The most obvious one is that you don't need a registered address to set up your network. Also, these addresses are isolated from the Internet, so devices must access the Internet through a NAT server, proxy server, or other device to facilitate communication. This design provides a boundary between your network and the Internet and prevents hosts on the Internet from knowing the internal addressing scheme of your network.

The private address ranges are:

10.0.0.0 - 10.255.255.255 (10.0.0.0/8)

172.16.0.0 - 172.31.255.255 (172.16.0.0/16)

192.168.0.0 - 192.168.255.255 (192.168.0.0/24)

Request for Comment (RFC)

Documents by which the Internet is defined and through which Internet standards are published. All RFC documents are available from various websites for download and viewing.

The private address spaces listed with each class description are specified in **Request for Comment (RFC)** 1918 as being available to anyone who wants to use IP addressing on a private network but does not want to connect these networks directly to the Internet. As private addresses are those addresses that are not permitted to be routed by Internet routers, ISPs can be fined for passing traffic with these addresses as source or destination.

7.2.3 Using Ports and Sockets

Port numbers

A number that is used to identify the source or destination application during data communication.

In addition to the IP address, a packet also has **port addresses** or **port numbers.** Data travels from a port on the sending computer to a port on the receiving computer. A port is a numerical value that identifies applications associated with the data, source port for the source application, and destination port for the destination application. TCP/IP supports two types of ports, UDP and TCP ports, and within these each port is assigned a unique 16- bit number in the range of 0 through 65535 through a separately maintained list.

The very existence of ports and their numbers is more or less transparent to the users of the network because many server-side ports are standardized. Thus, a client application protocol will know which remote port it should connect to for a specific service. For example, all servers that offer Telnet services usually do so on TCP port 23 by default, and web servers normally run on TCP port 80. As a result, when you connect to the Internet to browse to a Web server, you automatically connect to port 80, and when you use Telnet, you automatically connect to port 23. The TCP/IP protocol suite uses a modifiable lookup table to determine the correct port for the data type. Table 7-4 lists some of the well-known port numbers for common protocols.

Table 7-4: Well-known Port Numbers

Port	Protocol
UDP port 15	Netstat
TCP port 20	FTP data
TCP port 21	FTP control
TCP port 22	SSH
TCP port 23	Telnet
TCP port 25	SMTP
TCP port 53	DNS zone transfers
UDP port 53	DNS queries
UDP port 69	TFTP
TCP port 70	Gopher
TCP port 79	Finger
TCP port 80	HTTP
TCP port 110	POP3
UDP port 111	RPC
TCP port 119	NNTP
TCP port 123	NTP
UDP port 137	NetBIOS name service
TCP port 143	IMAP4
UDP port 161	SNMP
TCP port 443	HTTPS
UDP port 520	RIP
UDP port 2049	NFS

Applications can also define their own port numbers with values of 1024 through 49151. These port numbers are used by TCP and UDP alike to be temporarily assigned to client application protocols when communicating with a remote device and its server application protocol. Ports from 49152 to 65535 are called *Ephemeral Ports*, and are generally divided into *Registered ports* (1024 through 49151) and *Dynamic ports* (49152 through 65535).

You may hear or see the terms socket and port used as if they are interchangeable terms, but they are not. The combination of an IP address, associated protocol, and a port number is known as a **socket.** A socket identifies a single network process in terms of the entire Internet or other end-to-end IP-based internetwork. Two sockets—one on the sending system

Socket

The combination of an IP address, an associated protocol like TCP or UDP, and a port number used for defining connections for connection-oriented communications.

and one on the receiving host—are needed to define a connection for connection-oriented protocols, such as TCP.

7.2.4 Looking Ahead to IPv6

A detailed discussion of IPv6 is beyond the scope of this course, but we
can't leave the subject of addressing without at least a mention. Careful
management of existing addresses and extensive use of private addressing
on LANs have kept the Internet from running out of address space, but
these solutions won't work forever. At some point, the address space has to
be extended. That process, at least the beginning of it, is going on now.

IPv6 uses a 128-bit addressing scheme, so the new address space supports 2^{128} (approximately 340 undecillion or 3.4×1038) addresses. It has
more than 79 octillion (that's 79,000,000,000,000,000,000,000,000,000 to
you and me) times as many available addresses as IPv4. That's enough IP
addresses for every grain of sand on earth! Also, instead of representing the
binary digits as decimal digits, IPv6 uses eight sets of four hexadecimal
digits, like so:

3FFE:0B00:0800:0002:0000:0000:0000:000C

When writing IPv6 addresses you can abbreviate these very long addresses by dropping leading 0s (zeros) like the 0 before the B in "0B00"
in the previous example. You can also drop any single grouping of complete zero octets, those having all zeros, between numbers as long as you
replace them with a double colon (::) and they are complete octets. If you
apply this rule to the above address, it would make the example address
look like so:

3FFE:B00:800: 2:: C

As with IPv4, several addresses are reserved for special uses. For example, the IPv6 address ::/0 is the default address for a host that has yet to
be assigned an address. The address ::1/128 is reserved for the local loopback (like 127.0.0.1 in IPv4). IPv6 also includes provisions for the old IPv4
hosts so they can be migrated to the new addressing scheme. This migration
is accomplished by using the address ::xxx . . . , where the last four sets of
digits refer to the old IPv4 address.

The details of how IPv6 addresses are implemented are beyond the
scope of the chapter, but suffice to say that addressing is significantly more
complicated. Every host has three different addresses, used to uniquely
identify it on the network, the network to which it belongs, and routing information. Several concepts and enhancements also are unique to IPv6, are
as follows:

Stateless address auto-configuration (SLAAC)
Allows systems on an IPv6 network to automatically configure their network address by sending and receiving a request for configuration information from a local router.

• **Stateless address auto-configuration (SLAAC):** This feature allows
systems to configure themselves automatically when connected to an

IN THE REAL WORLD

Utilizing IPv6 Protocols

Before leaving the discussion of IPv6, let's take a quick look at some new protocols that are introduced with this standard.

Internet Control Message Protocol for IPv6 (ICMPv6) provides important messaging services for the IPv6 network. This protocol sends error reports for packets that cannot be properly routed and messages about the status of the network.

Neighbor Discovery Protocol (ND) protocol allows IPv6 systems to recognize other systems on the network and find available routers. This protocol works on the Network layer. As a major change to IPv4, which relies heavily on the ARP protocol to help address individual nodes, this protocol allows each node using IPv6 to automatically set up its own address.

Internet Key Exchange (IKE) protocol is responsible for managing the IP security built into IPv6. This protocol provides the necessary management that allows IPv6 packet headers to provide protection of data while it is being transmitted.

Mobile IPv6 (MIPv6) allows mobility of systems by permitting them to maintain IP connectivity while they move from one network to another. This protocol works with ND to make sure that movement from one access point to another is smooth.

As you can see many exciting new protocols are introduced with IPv6, still, before implementing IPv6 on your network, you should be aware of several potential security pitfalls. First of all, most new operating systems are installed on systems with IPv6 on by default, which provides a potential inroad for unwanted network access through unsuspecting network users. When you introduce a new system to your network, take the time to disable the IPv6 protocol on IPv4 networks.

Secondly, although built-in security is a part of the IPv6 specification, unless your version of IPv6 implements the necessary protocols, you won't enjoy those requested security enhancements. When implementing an IPv6 network, make sure to do a complete security analysis of what your needs are and what your vendors offer.

Finally, for this discussion, the ICMPv6 protocol, while providing essential messaging for the network also provides a potential opportunity for overloading the network with messages, thus preventing other, legitimate traffic from being transmitted. In IPv4, you can prevent ICMP messaging, and remove the potential for this type of attack. In IPv6, ICMP is an essential component so you won't be able to just stop all such messaging.

The bottom line is, as with all networks, you must carefully plan out your implementation of IPv6 before introducing it to your environment.

IPv6 network. To do so, IPv6 makes use of the Internet Control message Protocol version 6 (ICMPv6), which answers a host's local link request with the appropriate configuration parameters.

End-to-end principle

This principle states that, whenever possible, communications protocol operations should be defined to occur at the end-points of a communications system.

Hop limit

The number of routers a packet can traverse between its system of origin and the destination.

Multicasting

The method by which a system can send a single packet to multiple recipients.

- Enhanced **end-to-end principle** support: The end-to-end principle suggests that whenever possible, communications protocol operations should occur at the end points of the communication cycle. In the case of IPv6, the end-to-end principle is enacted in several areas including the packet header in IPv6. This is simplified from IPv4, removing unnecessary components, and the TTL is now a **hop limit,** thus removing the need for routers to compute the time a packet has spent in a queue. Finally, IPv6 uses the MAC address to help build the host address, thus moving the responsibility for addressing to the end points of the communications channel.

- **Multicasting:** In IPv6, systems can transmit a single packet to multiple destinations. Although this feature is optional with IPv4 and requires the use of additional protocols in the TCP/IP stack, IPv6 has built in multicasting capabilities that eliminate the need for additional protocols.

TIPS FROM THE PROFESSIONALS

The First and Last Subnets

When calculating the number of subnets, we use the formula $2^{n}-2$, where "n" is the number of bits taken from the host (that's 2 to the power of n minus 2). So if we take 2 bits from the host, we get total of two subnets ($2^{4}-2$—see Table 7-5). In fact we get a total of four subnets, but according to IEEE Request For Comment, we cannot use the first subnet because all the subnet bits are turned "off" in the first subnet and we cannot use the last subnet, because all the subnet bits are turned "on" at the same time.

Cisco, along with creating CIDR notation, has configured its routers and does allow first subnet to be used by issuing an IOS command "ip subnet zero." Keep in mind that the subnet bits refer to the number of bits taken from the host. So we have to subtract all subnet bits on and all subnet bits off. In real life, we can use all the subnets, but the published rules of subnetting do not allow us to use first and last subnet. Note that the formula for calculating the number of hosts per subnet is the same, but we use the number of bits remaining in the host part of the IP address, $2^{h}-2$ (that's 2 to the power of h minus 2). The first IP address is the subnetted network designation, and the last IP address is the broadcast address for the subnet.

Table 7-5: Relationship Between Number of Subnets and Hosts Per Subnet

Additional Bits required	Subnet Address	Maximum Number of Subnets	Maximum Number of Hosts Class C	Maximum Number of Hosts Class B	Maximum Number of Hosts Class A
0	0	0	254	65,534	16,777,214
2	192	2	62	16,382	4,194,302
3	224	6	30	8,190	2,097,150
4	240	14	14	4,094	1,048,574
5	248	30	6	2,046	524,286
6	252	62	2	1,022	262,142
7	254	126	**Invalid**	510	131,070
8	255	254	**Invalid**	254	65,534

Most current operating systems include support for IPv6, which is provided at varying levels between the operating systems. As this support occurs, the migration is expected to be gradual over several years, with some industry pundits saying it is unlikely that IPv4 addresses will ever be fully retired.

SELF-CHECK

1. List the network address ranges and default subnet masks for the classes assigned as network addresses.

2. List the supported private address ranges by class.

Apply Your Knowledge As a network administrator, you have been assigned a Class C private network of 192.168.5.0 and told you need to subnet it into six subnets and you want to have 25 to 30 assignable IP addresses. Refer to Table 7-6.

See anything funny about those network numbers? Did you catch it? You weren't necessarily required to subnet the network. You probably could have just as easily used 192.168.10 through 192.168.17 (or a similar range) with the default class C subnet mask (255.255.255.0). Your class C network address is a private address.

1. What is the network address of each subnet?

2. How many available assignable IP addresses exist within each subnet?

3. What is the broadcast address of each subnet?

Table 7-6: Class C Network as Six Subnetworks

Network Number	First Address	Broadcast Address
192.168.10.32	192.168.10.33	192.168.10.63
192.168.10.64	192.168.10.65	192.168.10.95
192.168.10.96	192.168.10.97	192.168.10.127
192.168.10.128	192.168.10.129	192.168.10.159
192.168.10.160	192.168.10.161	192.168.10.191
192.168.10.192	192.168.10.193	192.168.10.223

4. How many assignable IP addresses would you have in each subnet if you simply used the suggested range of 192.168.10.0 through 192.168.17.0?

7.3 IMPLEMENTING NAME RESOLUTION

Not only do you need to concern yourself with IP addresses, you also have to worry about host names. Why? Most people find it easier to remember a textual name than a string of numbers. When they need to find a file server, remembering to look for file1.busicorp.local than for 192.168.11.152 is easier. TCP/IP provide different mechanisms for resolving host names as IP addresses and, conversely, IP addresses as host names.

A host name is typically the name of a device that has a specific IP address and on the Internet is *part* of what is known as a **Fully Qualified Domain Name (FQDN)**. An FQDN consists of a host name and a **domain name,** which is how names are organized on the Internet and in a large number of TCP/IP LANs. An example of an FQDN is hostname.company.com.

We start with a quick overview of host names and how they are organized. The process of finding the IP address for any given host name is known as name resolution, and it can be performed in several ways: a HOSTS file, a request broadcast on the local network, the Domain Name Service (DNS), and Windows Internet Name Service (WINS) for NetBIOS names.

Fully Qualified Domain Name (FQDN)
A name made up of a host name prepended to a domain suffix.

Domain name
A logical security boundary in a directory-based network.

7.3.1 Organizing TCP/IP Host Names

On the Internet, domains are arranged in a hierarchical tree structure. The following list includes some of the top-level domains currently in use, with several more not listed that have been added in recent years:

- **.com:** A commercial organization. Most companies end up as part of this domain.

- **.edu:** An educational establishment, such as a university.

- **.gov:** A branch of the U.S. government.
- **.int:** An international organization, such as NATO or the United Nations.
- **.mil:** A branch of the U.S. military.
- **.net:** A network organization.
- **.org:** A nonprofit organization.

For example, your local ISP is probably a member of the .net domain, and your company is probably part of the .com domain. The .gov and .mil domains are reserved strictly for use by the government and the military within the United States. The .com domain is the largest, followed by the .edu domain.

In other parts of the world, the final part of a domain name represents the country in which the server is located, such as .ca for Canada, .jp for Japan, .uk for Great Britain, and .ru for Russia. ICANN assigns all Internet domain names and makes sure that a name is not duplicated. Names are assigned on a first-come, first-served basis, but if you try to register a name that infringes on someone else's registered trademark, your use of that name will be rescinded if the trademark holder objects. Several companies handle the details for registering your domain name for you, at a price.

The unique host name, the part before the domain name, is under your control. Some names have become standard host names through their use, such using www for your web server. You should develop internal naming standards to make machines on your local network easier to recognize, such as using ftp for FTP servers, fs (or something similar) for file servers, or possibly user names for end-user computers. Be careful, though, because too descriptive a name on a sensitive server could lead an attacker directly to it.

7.3.2 Resolving with HOSTS

HOSTS
In TCP/IP terminology, a network device.

Several automatic conversion systems are available to translate an IP address into a host name, and **HOSTS** is one of the simplest. You create a file called HOSTS, located in a folder or directory, based on the requirements of your operating system, and enter a line in the file for every system. For example:

198.34.56.25 myserver.com #My server's information

198.34.57.03 yourserver.com

The problem, from an administrative standpoint, is that you must store this ASCII file on every single workstation on your network. When you make a change, you must change the contents of the HOSTS file on every single workstation on your network. This process is simple but painful inside a network. But what happens if you want to go outside of this network to other networks or to the Internet? The file would be too large and too complicated to manage. The HOSTS file method is used when you only have a few host devices that you need to manage.

7.3.3 Resolving with Domain Name System (DNS)

The Domain Name Service (DNS) is a more automated method for managing DNS names. You use DNS to translate host names and domain names to IP addresses, and vice versa, by means of a standardized lookup table. The system works just like a giant telephone directory. With some DNS systems, network administrators must maintain the table manually. With others, known as **dynamic DNS** systems, automatic updates are supported.

DNS is an essential part of large TCP/IP networks because it simplifies the task of remembering addresses; all you have to do is simply remember the host name and domain name. Figure 7-8 gives you an idea of how it works. You enter the URL http://www.microsoft.com in your web browser to go to the Microsoft home page. Your web browser has the TCP/IP protocol query a DNS server for the IP address of www.microsoft.com. If necessary, the request is forwarded to another DNS until an entry for the host name is found and returned. Your web browser connects to the Microsoft web server and downloads the home page.

A **DNS zone** is an administrative area or name space within a DNS domain. The DNS server with primary responsibility over that zone is said to be **authoritative** over the zone. You can configure additional, hierarchical zones to make the system easier to maintain. The DNS servers contain the **zone file,** or **DNS table,** containing the DNS records for that zone. Most records include a host name, a record type, and an IP address. Figure 7-6 shows entries from a DNS table taken from a small Windows Active Directory domain.

Dynamic DNS
DNS service that supports automatic DNS table updates.

DNS zone
An administrative division of DNS names for maintaining name resolution.

Authoritative
A server with primary responsibility for a DNS zone to which DNS table updates are made and used as the source for updating other copies of the zone table.

Zone file
A DNS mapping file that contains the DNS records for a specific zone.

DNS table
A DNS mapping file that contains DNS records.

Primary DNS server
An authoritative server for a DNS zone.

Secondary DNS server
A server that contains a copy of a zone database that is periodically updated from the primary DNS server.

Figure 7-6

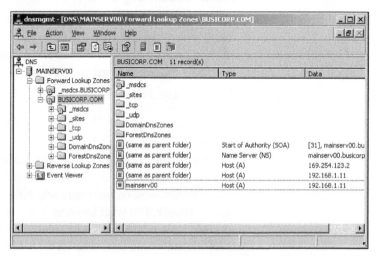

Sample DNS records.

Primary DNS servers are authoritative for the zone for which they carry the zone file, and **secondary DNS servers** have a nonauthoritative copy of the zone file updated from the primary server. Changes occur at the primary server that is authoritative for that zone.

The most common record type is the *address record*, also known as a **host record** or **A record,** which maps a host name to an IP address. Each zone can have a single **start of authority (SOA)** record, which describes the zone and authoritative server. Mail servers are mapped as **mail exchange (MX)** servers. DNS servers are mapped as **name server (NS) records.** The **canonical name (CNAME)** record, or **alias** record, lets you map additional names to the same IP address. For example, your web server has the host name www, and you want that machine to also have the name ftp so that users can use FTP to access a different portion of the file system as an FTP root.

DNSSEC (DNS Security Extensions) adds security to the Domain Name System, and is designed to protect the Internet from certain attacks, such as DNS cache poisoning. It is a set of extensions to DNS, which provide: a) origin authentication of DNS data, b) data integrity, and c) authenticated denial of existence.

7.3.4 Resolving with Windows Internet Naming Service (WINS)

Windows Internet Naming Service (WINS) was a service available in Windows Server versions earlier to Windows Server 2008. This service provided name resolution where NetBIOS was still in use. **NetBIOS** (pronounced "net-bye-ose") was an acronym formed from network basic input/output system, and was used to manage data exchange and network access. NetBIOS provided an application programming interface (API) with a consistent set of commands for requesting lower-level network services to transmit information from node to node. With NetBIOS, devices were recognized and accessed by their NetBIOS names.

NetBIOS is supposed to be no longer needed since Windows 2000, but that's not really the case. If you disable NetBIOS on your domain controllers, you won't be able to establish a two-way transitive trust between two Windows Server forests.

In legacy Windows Servers (earlier releases than Windows Server 2008), the WINS service support NetBIOS requirements. WINS mapped NetBIOS names to IP addresses. Because routers don't forward NetBIOS name resolution broadcast, broadcast couldn't be used to resolve names for devices on a different network segment. WINS allowed you to continue using the NetBIOS names that you had previously used to access the resources because WINS provided the cross-reference from NetBIOS name to an IP address. When you install and configure TCP/IP on a Windows system, you can specify one or more WINS server addresses. The computer

Host record

A DNS record that maps a host name to an IP address. It is the most common type of DNS record. Also known as the **A record.**

Start of authority (SOA) record

A DNS zone record that describes the zone and the authoritative server. A zone can have only one SOA record.

Mail exchange (MX) record

A DNS record used to identify a mail server.

Name server (NS) record

A DNS record that identifies a DNS server.

Canonical name (CNAME)

A record that is used to map duplicate host names to a single IP address.

Alias

Similar to the CNAME, a record that is used to map duplicate host names to a single IP address

Windows Internet Naming Service (WINS)

A service that is used for automated NetBIOS name-to-IP address resolution on a Windows network.

NetBIOS

An API command set used to control lower-level network services and node-to-node data transfers.

IN THE REAL WORLD

Active Directory and DNS

A DNS server is not a requirement for all TCP/IP networks. Smaller networks can often get away without a DNS server, with one major exception. A DNS server is a required part of a Windows Active Directory network. When you promote a Windows Server to the role of Active Directory domain controller, you must either identify a DNS server that will be authoritative for the domain or let the domain controller wizard configure the computer as a DNS server. Domain names, structured like Internet domain names, are used to define security boundaries in an Active Directory network. The concepts underlying Active Directory were introduced in Novell servers.

Host names identify client computers in most of the Active Directory management utilities. Hence, support for host name resolution is a key component.

One of the most common configurations is to either use an existing Windows DNS server or configure the domain controller as a DNS server. Often, network administrators configure all of the domain controllers as DNS servers to provide fault tolerance.

Tips from the Professionals

Browser Hijacking

The translation from user-friendly names to IP addresses for Internet browsing is made using large lookup tables where the interrelationship between the two addressing schemes is kept. Users generally are unaware that their own computer also has the capability of using a local database called a "hosts" file that is stored in **\Windows\system32\drivers\etc** to do the same thing.

Browser hijacking is the process where malicious software alters your computer's host files to force redirects in your Internet browser that you do not have control over. Browser hijacking is both annoying and dangerous, because the web pages you are redirected to are often used to download more malicious software to your device.

sends its NetBIOS name and IP address to the WINS server, and the WINS server uses this information to automatically update its mapping table.

As an additional note, if you have only limited NetBIOS name resolution requirements, you can use LMHOSTS files. **LMHOSTS** files are name resolution–mapping files, similar to HOSTS files, but used for NetBIOS names.

LMHOSTS
A text file used for NetBIOS name resolution.

SELF-CHECK

1. At minimum, what kind of records will you have in the DNS table for a host that is known by multiple names?

Apply Your Knowledge When do you need a WINS server on a TCP/IP network?

Project 7.2

Name resolution, associating computer names with IP addresses, is a critical function in a TCP/IP network. Name resolution lets you locate hosts by name.

Two types of name systems are used, DNS names and NetBIOS names. DNS names are the types of names used across the Internet. A DNS name consists of the host's unique name with the domain name as a suffix, like student00.busicorp.com.

The other types of name system used are NetBIOS names, which are simple text names used with NetBIOS applications and the NetBEUI network protocol, like STUDENT00.

Complete **Project 7.3: Comparing Name Resolution Options** in the online Networking Basics Project Manual to understand and be able to identify DNS and WINS resolution options and parameters.

7.4 SUPPORTING TCP/IP

Before leaving our discussion of TCP/IP, we need to talk a little about TCP/IP configuration and some of the most commonly used TCP/IP tools and utilities. Several parameters are available when configuring a TCP/IP host. IP address information is required. Other parameters you can configure include default gateway and the DNS server. You can also configure the host to receive configuration information automatically.

TCP/IP includes a wide array of tools and utilities. Most run as command line interface (text-based) commands, but graphical user interface (GUI) utilities have been developed for use in environments like Microsoft Windows and graphical Linux and Unix desktop environments. One advantage of TCP/IP is that many of the commands have the same command name and options when run from different operating systems. One thing that Windows administrators need to watch, however, is that unlike Windows and MS-DOS commands, TCP/IP optional parameters are sometimes case-sensitive.

7.4.1 Configuring TCP/IPv4Parameters

For Windows 7, you configure TCP/IP through the Network Sharing Center. Figure 7-7 shows the properties you might see for a typical wired local area network connection.

Select **Internet Protocol version 4 (TCP/IPv4)** and click **Properties** to view and configure TCP/IP properties. Figure 7-8 shows the General properties for a computer configured with a **static IP address,** one that has been entered manually for the computer. Other parameters include the subnet mask, default gateway, and DNS server addresses.

Click **Advanced** to configure additional TCP/IP parameters. The IP Settings properties, shown in Figure 7-9, let you configure additional IP

Static IP address
An IP address set manually on a system.

Figure 7-7

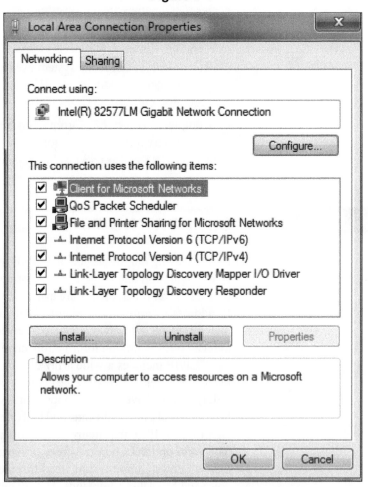

Local Area Connection Properties dialog box.

Multihomed
A TCP/IP host configured
with multiple IP addresses.

addresses, configuring the computer as a **multihomed** host. You can also configure additional default gateways and router metric information, which is interface speed information used in best route calculations.

The DNS properties are shown in Figure 7-10. Here, you can enter additional DNS server address information, as well as domain name suffix information for host name resolution. The **Register this connection's addresses in DNS** checkbox is used to enable dynamic DNS support, so the computer can register itself with the primary DNS server.

The WINS properties in Figure 7-11 are only necessary if you have NetBIOS name resolution requirements on a routed network. Remember, with networks using Windows Server 2008, you probably will not encounter WINS. You can list the WINS servers and NetBIOS support. If your network doesn't have any NetBIOS support requires, you can select **Disable NetBIOS over TCP/IP** to disable NetBIOS support.

Figure 7-8

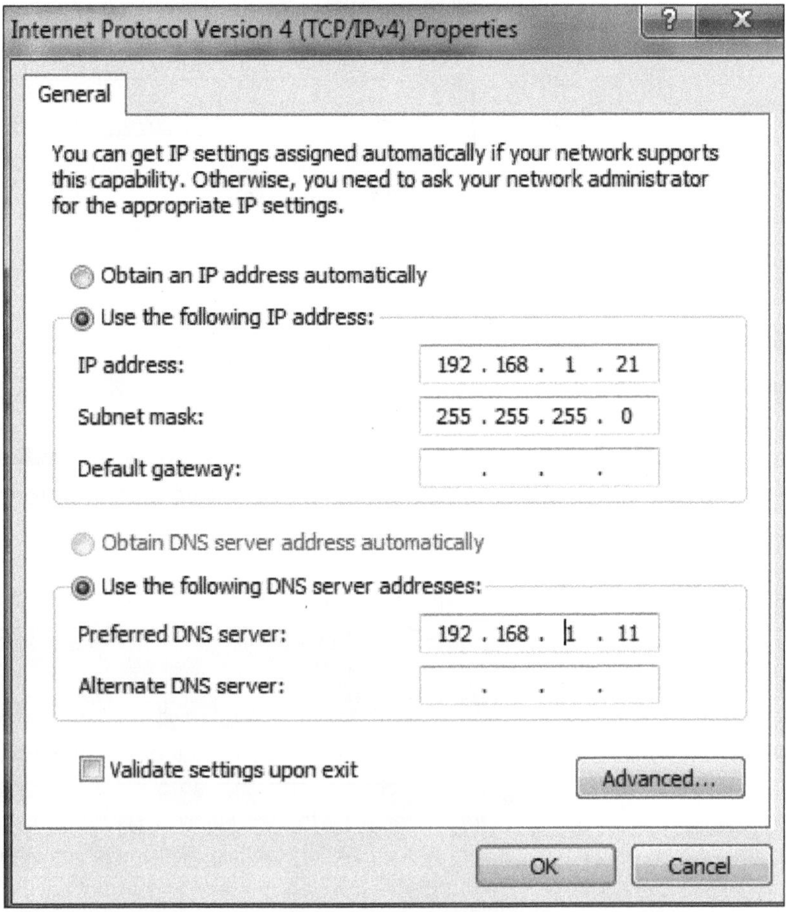

General tab of the TCP/IPv4 Properties dialog box.

Figure 7-9

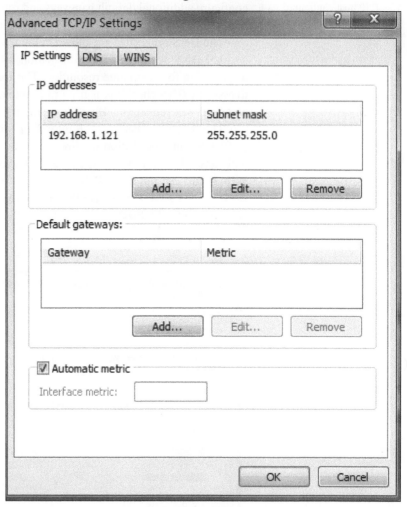

IPv4 Settings properties.

TIPS FROM THE PROFESSIONAL

WINS in Windows Server

Windows Server has used various configuration tools over time, introducing new components and removing or deprecating others. Windows 2008, for example, no longer uses WINS as a primary configuration option, viewing it as a Role or Feature. Windows Server 2000 saw WINS as a primary component. If you are working in a network using Windows 2000, you should be aware that you may need to configure systems to use WINS.

Figure 7-10

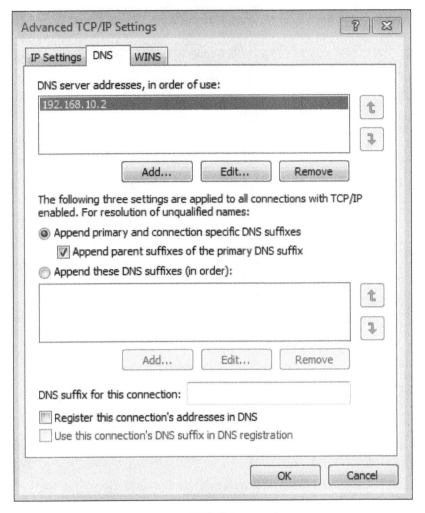

DNS Tab.

7.4.2 Configuring TCP/IPv6 Parameters

Windows 7 provides support for configuring your systems for IPv6 addresses using the same kind of properties definitions as you just saw in the section on IPv4 configuration. Let's step through the same configuration process for IPv6 as we did for IPv4.

Similarly to IPv4 configurations, you set up your IPv6 address through the Local Area Connections Properties dialog box (see Figure 7-7). Select **Internet Protocol version 6 (TCP/IPv6)** and click **Properties** to view and configure TCP/IP properties. Figure 7-12 shows the General properties for a computer configured with a static IP address for a IPv6 address, one that has been entered manually for the computer. Other parameters include the subnet prefix length, default gateway, and DNS server addresses.

Figure 7-11

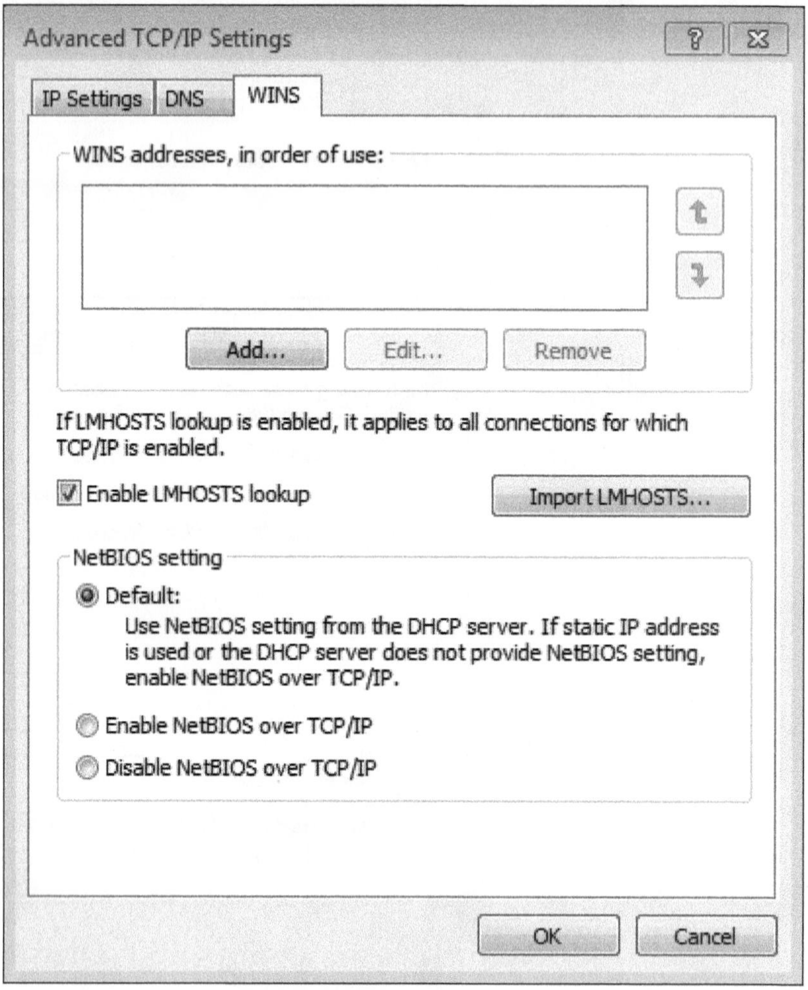

WINS Tab.

You can use the **Advanced** tab to configure this system to be multi-homed, as you did for the IPv4 address. Figure 7-13 shows the dialog box you would use to make these changes to your configuration.

You can configure DNS properties using the dialog box shown in Figure 7-14.

7.4.3 Automating IP Configuration

Although not especially complicated, TCP/IP configuration can be a daunting task if you have a very large TCP/IP network. In that case, you will often find it better to configure hosts to receive TCP/IP address and configuration information automatically, as shown in Figure 7-15.

Figure 7-12

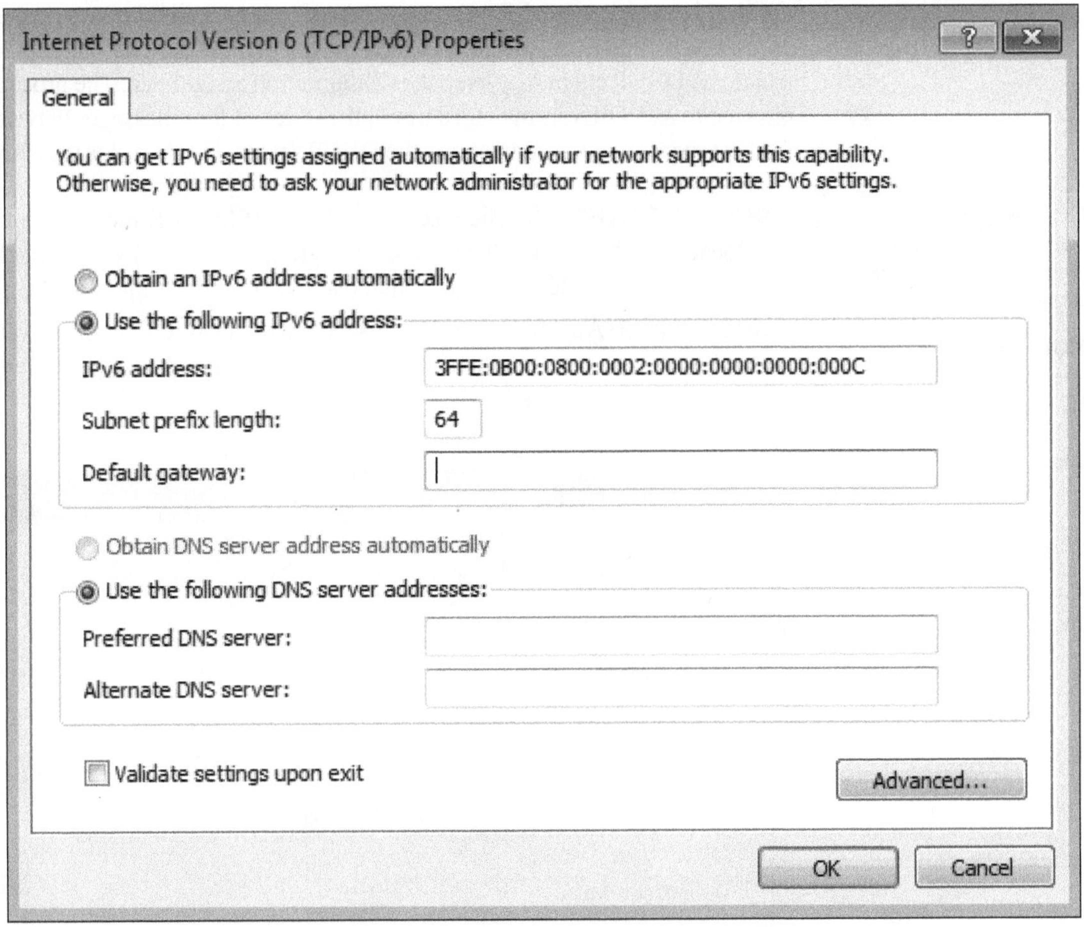

General tab of the TCP/IPv6 Properties dialog box.

Dynamic Host Configuration Protocol (DHCP)
A protocol and service used to provide IP addresses and TCP/IP configuration parameters.

You can also configure the system to obtain an IPv6 address automatically, as in Figure 7-16. A **Dynamic Host Configuration Protocol (DHCP)** server provides IP address and configuration information. For IPv4, the Alternate Configuration properties, shown in Figure 7-17 determine what the host will do if it is unable to receive an address from the DHCP server. For IPv4, by default, it will use Automatic Private IP Addressing (APIPA) to assign itself an IP address in the 169.254.0.0/16 address range. APIPA is a feature of Windows operating systems and provides a failover method to ensure that the host has an IP address.

The other option is to choose **User configured** and specify alternate IP address information to use if the host cannot get IP addressing information automatically.

The primary reason for using DHCP is to centralize the management of IP addresses. It can also assign DNS servers, default gateway addresses, subnet masks, and many other options.

When the DHCP service is used, DHCP scopes include pools of IP addresses that are assigned for automatic distribution to client computers on an as-needed basis, in the form of leases, which are periods of time for which the DHCP client may keep the configuration assignment. The process, referred to as DORA, is managed through a series of four messages between the host requesting the address and the DHCP server. The four messages are:

DHCPDISCOVER

A message sent by a client to start the IP address lease process.

DHCPOFFER

A message returned by a DHCP server offering a valid IP address lease to a requesting client.

- **DHCPDISCOVER:** The client sends a DHCPDISCOVER message to try to locate a DHCP server. The message requests the server location (its IP address) and includes the requesting host's MAC address and host name.

- **DHCPOFFER:** Any available DHCP server with a valid IP address available for lease responds with a DHCPOFFER message. Message contents

Figure 7-13

IPv4 Settings properties.

Figure 7-14

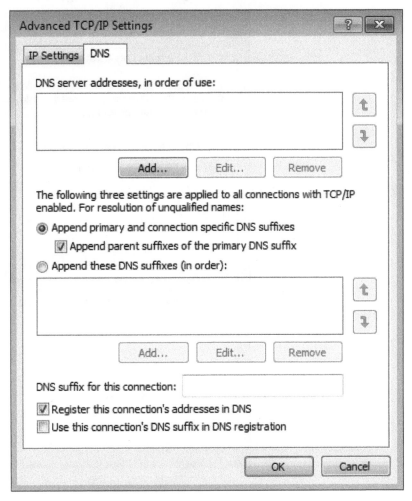

DNS properties.

includes requesting the host's MAC address, an available IP address and subnet mask, the lease period (how long the address is valid before is must be renewed), and the DHCP server's IP address.

- **DHCPREQUEST:** The client accepts an IP address offered by sending a DHCPREQUEST that includes the IP address of the server that offered the address. If the client receives multiple offers, it will accept the first address offered.

- **DHCPACK:** The server whose offer was accepted sends a DHCPACK message, acknowledging the client. The message will include a valid lease for the address and can include optional TCP/IP configuration settings.

Figure 7-15

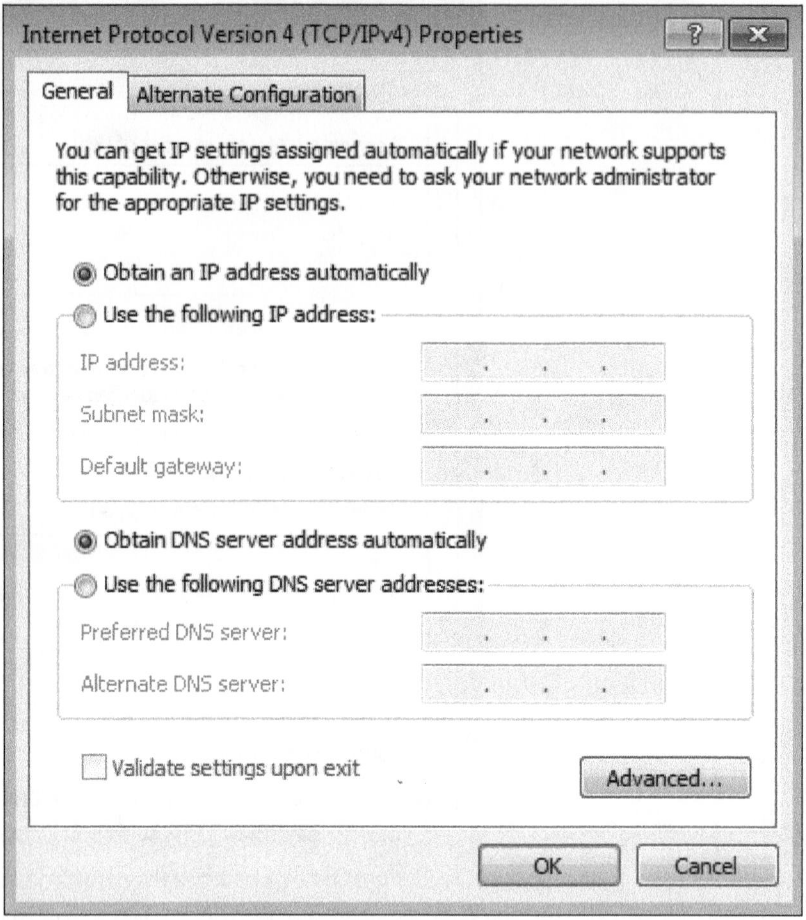

Internet Protocol Version 4 (TCP/IPv4) Properties   ? ✕

General | Alternate Configuration

You can get IP settings assigned automatically if your network supports
this capability. Otherwise, you need to ask your network administrator
for the appropriate IP settings.

◉ Obtain an IP address automatically

◯ Use the following IP address:

    IP address: .   .   .

    Subnet mask: .   .   .

    Default gateway: .   .   .

◉ Obtain DNS server address automatically

◯ Use the following DNS server addresses:

    Preferred DNS server: .   .   .

    Alternate DNS server: .   .   .

☐ Validate settings upon exit   [Advanced...]

[OK]   [Cancel]

Automatic IPv4 configuration enabled.

Because broadcast messages are used, if a router separates the DHCP server from any clients, the router must be configured to pass the DHCP broadcast. This configuration is referred to as being **BOOTP enabled.** In a Windows network, you can also configure one or more computers as **DHCP proxies or agents** to forward requests. If a server's offer is not accepted or some other problem occurs during the lease process, the DHCP server broadcasts a **DHCPNACK** message, cancelling the lease offer.

As long as the lease period is valid, the client will continue to use the IP address unless the address is released or the client renews the lease and receives a different address in the process. Clients attempt to renew their lease at 50 percent of the lease period. The address pools are centralized on the DHCP server, allowing all IP addresses on your network to be administered from a single server. Doing so saves loads of time when changing the IP addresses on your network. Instead of running around to every workstation

BOOTP enabled
A router that is configured to pass DHCP broadcasts.

DHCP proxy (agent)
A computer that is configured to forward DHCP broadcasts via a unicast directly to the DHCP server through routers.

DHCPNACK
A message broadcast by a DHCP server to cancel a lease offer.

Figure 7-16

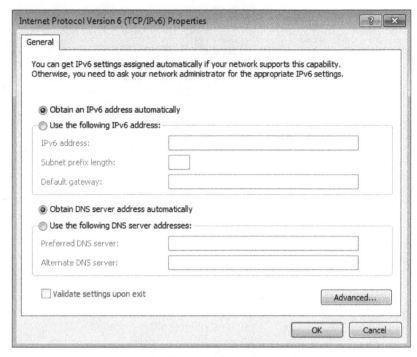

Automatic IPv6 configuration enabled.

and server and resetting the IP address to a new address, you simply reset the IP address pool on the DHCP server. The next time the client machines are rebooted, they are assigned new addresses. If the client workstation cannot locate the DHCP server on the network automatically APIPA addressing will be used, unless disabled. If disabled and no alternate address specified, the computer will have an address of 0.0.0.0.

7.4.4 Recognizing Common Utilities

TCP/IP utilities include a wide variety of management and troubleshooting tools. They include tools that let you trace the process of a packet through the network and test communication between TCP/IP hosts. They also let you force a host to release a leased IP address or request configuration information from a DHCP server. Some of the most commonly used utilities include:

- ping
- pathping
- tracert (traceroute)
- ipconfig (ifconfig)
- nslookup (dig)

Figure 7-17

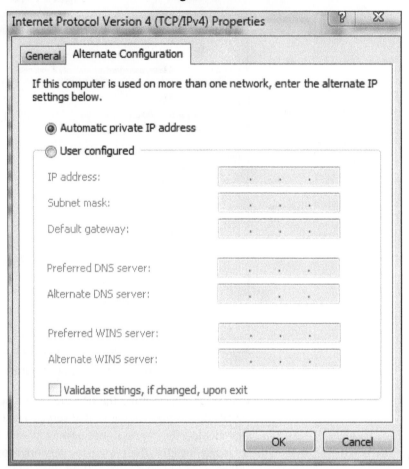

Alternate configuration properties.

We take a brief look at each of these utilities. A more advanced discussion of these utilities and command options is beyond the scope of this chapter. Additional information about TCP/IP utilities is available through the Windows Help system, Unix and Linux Help systems, and several online reference sources.

Using ping, pathping, tracert, and traceroute

ping
A TCP/IP utility that is used to test host-to-host communication. The same command is used for Windows and Unix/Linux.

The ping, pathping, tracert, and traceroute commands are all used for testing TCP/IP communications. The simplest of these, the Packet InterNet Groper or **ping** command is used to test communication between two host computers. In its simplest form, run:

ping *destination_host*

You can specify the destination host by host name or IP address. The command reports whether nor not the destination host responds and the round trip time. If you specify the destination host name, you can test both communications and DNS host name resolution.

The **pathping** command returns not only the destination host, but information about each of the routers encountered along the way.

You can also get route information from the **tracert** or **traceroute** commands. The tracert command is the Windows and MS-DOS version of the command. The same command is run as traceroute on Linux and Unix computers.

Using ipconfig, and ifconfig

The **ipconfig** command reports IP configuration information and lets you manage automatic IP address configuration. Run without any additional parameters, the command returns basic configuration information for the local host, including the host's DNS suffix, primary IP address, subnet mask, and default gateway. To get more detailed information, you can run:

ipconfig/all

This command returns more detailed information, including multi-homed addresses (if any), DHCP, DNS, and WINS server information, and the host's MAC address (or addresses, if it has multiple network adapters installed).

You can also use the ipconfg command to manage automatic IP address assignment. Keep in mind, when a system has an automatic IP address assigned, it is receiving the address from a DHCP server, which leases the address for a period of time. Sometimes, especially with laptop users, the lease period may be exceeded when the computer is not attached to the network. The DHCP server may then reassign that address to a different system. When the original system reattaches to the network, an IP address conflict can happen on the network. One or both systems will receive a broadcast message stating that there is an IP address conflict. You can use the ipconfig command to remove the conflict, as in the following:

ipconfig/release

After this command runs, the host will have an IP address of 0.0.0.0. As you may remember, this address is not recognizable for the network. To communicate on the network the system will need a valid IP address. To force the host to broadcast a DHCPREQUEST and lease a new IP address, run:

ipconfig/renew

For Linux and Unix systems, use **ifconfig** instead of ipconfig. Except for the command name, the command function and supported options are the same.

pathping
A TCP/IP utility used to track a packet from one host to another, including any routers along the way. This command is a Windows command-line.

tracert
A TCP/IP utility that is used to track a packet from one host to another, including any routers along the way. This is a Windows command-line command.

traceroute
A TCP/IP utility that is used to track a packet from one host to another, including any routers along the way. This is a Unix/Linux command.

ipconfig
A TCP/IP utility that can be used to view and manage IP address and configuration information. This is the Windows/MS-DOS version of the command. See also ifconfig.

ifconfig
A TCP/IP utility that can be used to view and manage IP address and configuration information. This is the Unix/Linux version of the command. See also ipconfig.

Using nslookup and dig

nslookup
A TCP/IP utility that is used to retrieve information from, test, and manage name servers. The same command is supported on both Windows and Unix/Linux.

dig
A Unix/Linux command that is equivalent to the nslookup command. See also nslookup.

The most common use of the **nslookup** and **dig** commands is troubleshooting DNS servers on your network. The nslookup command is supported on Windows NT and later, Unix, and Linux systems. The dig command is available on Unix and Linux systems, but not the Windows version of the TCP/IP protocol suite.

When you run nslookup without any additional parameters, it returns the host name and IP address of the default DNS server. It also returns an nslookup prompt (>). From here, you can run additional nslookup commands that let you test DNS server operations, such as requesting the IP address for specified host names. You can also view and set DNS server options.

The dig command is identical to the nslookup command, both in what it does and how it is used.

IN THE REAL WORLD

Multiple DHCP Servers

For most networks, one DHCP server physically will be able to meet the operational requirements of issuing IP address leases and configuration settings to clients. In fact, under normal operating conditions the load can be relatively light after the initial address assignments are made. Not only that, one DHCP server can be configured with multiple scopes and support multiple subnetworks from one central location, and log and the routers are configured to forward DCHP broadcasts.

So, why should you configure multiple servers? Fault tolerance. Your network depends on DHCP to provide IP addresses and configuration parameters. If you have only one DHCP server and it goes down, you might not notice right away. In fact, you might not even notice until leases start expiring, clients are unable to renew their address leases, and users start complaining that they can't access anything on the network.

If you set up multiple DHCP servers, they can cover for each other. The typical configuration is to put about 80 percent of a subnet's addresses on one server and 20 percent on the other. Should either one fail, the other should be able to handle IP addressing requirements, at least long enough for you to fix the failing server. When you do set up the servers, however, be careful not to overlap the **address scopes** (the addresses available for assignment) configured on the DHCP servers. If you do, you could end up with duplicate address assignments, and a whole other set of problems.

Address scopes
A set of addresses that is available for assignment through DHCP.

SELF-CHECK

1. What messages are passed, and in what direction, when a client successfully leases an IP address from a DHCP server?
2. How could you quickly determine whether or not a Windows XP computer configured for automatic IP address assignment received a valid address?

Apply Your Knowledge Using the ifconfig command on a Linux system is equivalent to using the ipconfig command on a windows system. Try it.

SUMMARY

Section 7-1
- TCP/IP was originally designed by the U.S. Department of Defense.
- The TCP/IP standard is widely published and is applicable regardless of the type of systems communicating.
- IP operates at the Network layer of the OSI model and is responsible for moving data between systems.
- TCP ensures reliable transmission and breaks transmissions into segments.

Section 7-2
- IPv4 is the current version of the Internet Protocol, and IPv6 makes room for many more addresses than IPv4.
- IPv4 addresses are written in a dotted decimal format, where each segment represents a component of the system's address.
- IPv4 has five classes of addresses, each with unique properties, each allowing for a different use, including public and private addresses and multicasting.
- NTS can be used to assign a single IP address to an organization while still allowing internal systems to communicate outside of the organization and receive appropriate transmissions from external systems without revealing their private address.

Section 7-3
- Domains are hierarchically structured on the Internet.
- The HOSTS file makes it possible to translate an IP address into a host name.
- DNS is an automated means of resolving IP addresses into host names.
- WINS is a service that was used in previous versions of Windows Server to perform NetBIOS name resolution.

Section 7-4
- You can configure a Windows system with a static IP address, or to request and automatically configure the address from a DHCP host.
- You can configure a Windows system with multiple IP addresses, for use if it is not possible to get an automated address.
- TCP/IP provides several utilities to assist in managing your IP address.

ASSESS YOUR UNDERSTANDING

UNDERSTAND: WHAT HAVE YOU LEARNED?

 Go to **www.wiley.com/go/ciccarelli/networkingbasics2e** to evaluate your knowledge of TCP/IP protocol fundamentals.

Measure your learning by comparing pre-test and post-test results.

SUMMARY QUESTIONS

1. You want to force a Windows XP client on a TCP/IP network to release a leased address. Which utility should you use?

   (a) ping
   (b) ifconfig
   (c) ipconfig
   (d) dig

2. What is a socket?

   (a) Another term for a port.
   (b) The combination of an IP address, protocol, and port number.
   (c) A link used for updating dynamic DNS.
   (d) Another term for a router.

3. In what order are messages sent during a successful DHCP lease?

   (a) DHCPREQUEST, DHCPOFFER, DHCPACK, DHCPDISCOVER
   (b) DHCPDISCOVER, DHCPREQUEST, DHCPOFFER, DHCPACK
   (c) DHCPREQUEST, DHCPDISCOVER, DHCPOFFER, DHCPACK
   (d) DHCPDISCOVER, DHCPOFFER, DHCPREQUEST, DHCPACK

4. A multihomed host must have two or more network adapters installed. True or false?

5. What does the TCP header Window field specify?

   (a) The number of segments that can be transmitted before an acknowledgement is required.
   (b) That the host is running some version of Microsoft Windows.
   (c) The maximum allowable datagram size.
   (d) Reassembly information for reassembling fragmented datagrams.

6. What is the primary name resolution method used on the Internet?

   (a) WINS
   (b) DNS
   (c) HOSTS
   (d) LMHOSTS

7. The IP address 201.220.102.14 is an example of an address from what address class?

   (a) Class A
   (b) Class B
   (c) Class C
   (d) Class D

8. A private address can be used on a local intranet, but not on the Internet. True or false?

9. The process of subdividing a standard class address into smaller network segments is known as what?

   (a) Segmenting
   (b) Subnetting
   (c) Fragmenting
   (d) Routing

10. What is the significance of the IP address 127.0.0.1?

    (a) It's a private Class B host address
    (b) It's a Class E address
    (c) It's used for loopback testing
    (d) It's assigned by default if a host cannot lease an address

11. Which of the following cannot be specified on the general properties when configuring TCP/IP configuration properties on a Windows XP computer?

    (a) Primary DNS server
    (b) Primary WINS server
    (c) Default gateway
    (d) Subnet mask

12. How would you use the CIDR specification format to specify the network address 192.168.10.0?

    (a) 192.168.10/24
    (b) 192.168.10/16
    (c) 192.168/32
    (d) 192.168/24

13. IPv6 supports a larger address pool than IPv4. True or false?

APPLY: WHAT WOULD YOU DO?

1. You are identifying TCP/IP configuration requirements for the network shown in Figure 7-18. You are to use the network address 192.168.12.0 for the entire network. Each subnet must support up to 55 hosts. All of the clients will share the proxy server for Internet access.

Figure 7-18

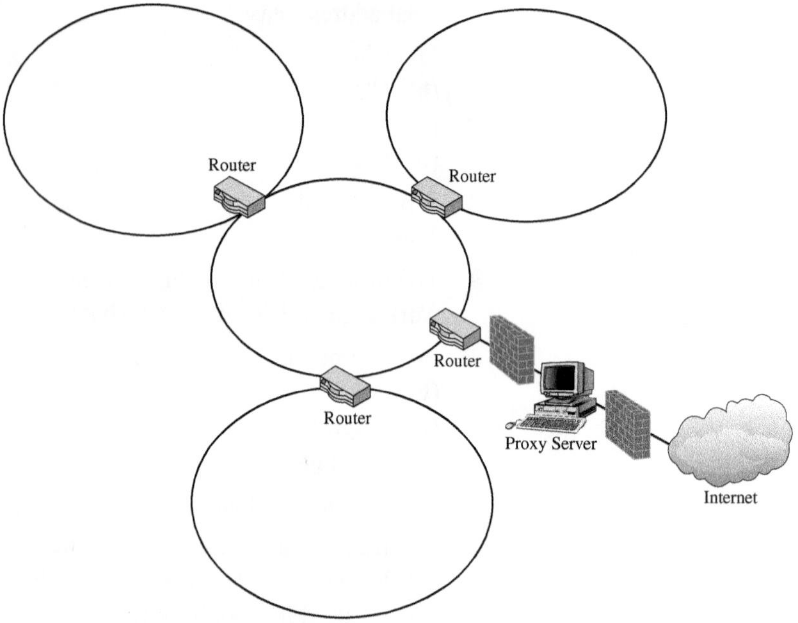

Sample network for configuration.

(a) What network addresses will you use?

(b) Why must you use different network addresses for each segment?

(c) What is the subnet mask?

(d) At minimum, how many public IP addresses will be required?

(e) Why?

(f) How can you keep the administrative overhead required to manage host IP addresses to a minimum?

(g) What are the configuration requirements for this to work?

2. You are configuring the network shown in Figure 7-19. The network addresses of selected static host addresses are shown. All hosts are running either Windows 7 or Windows Server 2008. TCP/IP is the only protocol in use on the network.

The standard configuration for end-user host computers is shown in Figure 7-20.

(a) After deploying the network, all end users in 172.18 /16 cannot communicate with any other hosts. What are possible causes?

(b) Each host has an IP address of 0.0.0.0. What does this address tell you?

(c) What could you run to force a computer to try again to lease an address?

Figure 7-19

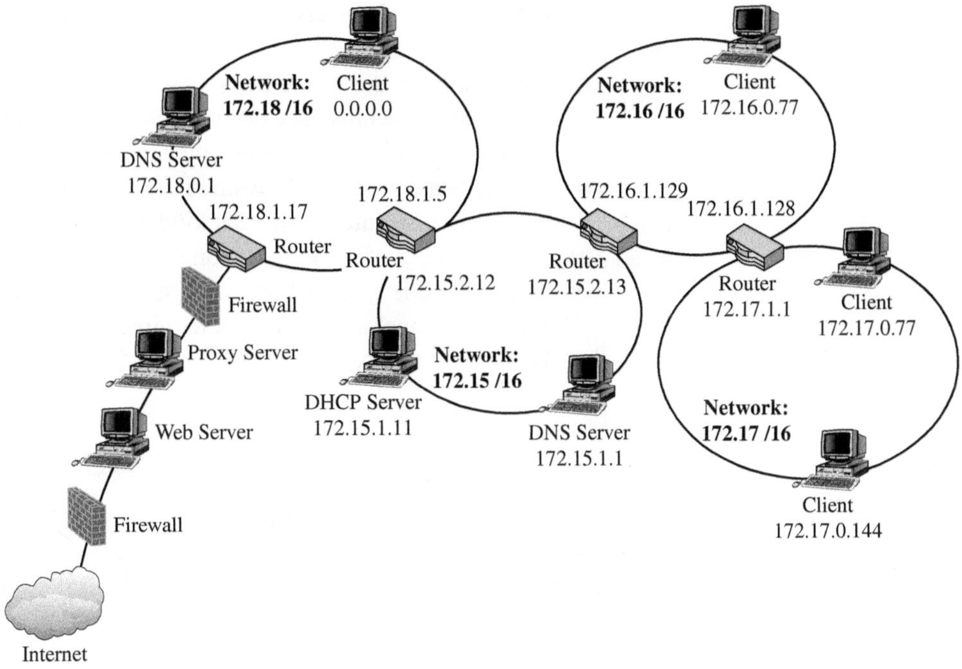

Routed LAN.

Figure 7-20

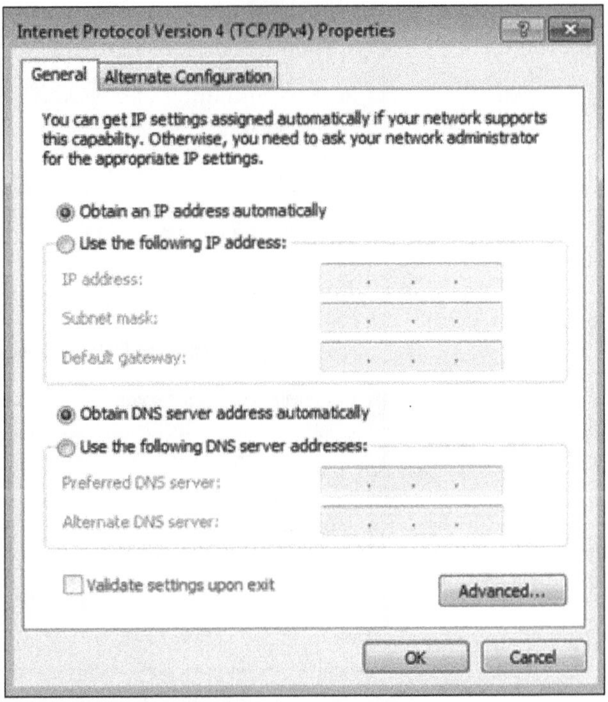

Standard client configuration.

(d) Why might you add a second DHCP server?

(e) If given multiple offers, how does a client determine which offer to accept?

(f) For what purpose are the DNS servers used?

(g) Under what circumstances would WINS servers also be required?

(h) What role would port numbers play in network operations?

(i) Port 21 is associated with what kind of activity?

(j) Port 80 is associated with what kind of activity?

(k) Why is each router configuration with two IP addresses?

(l) Figure 7-21 is from a host configured with a static IP address. What additional information is required?

(m) Why might this be necessary?

Figure 7-21

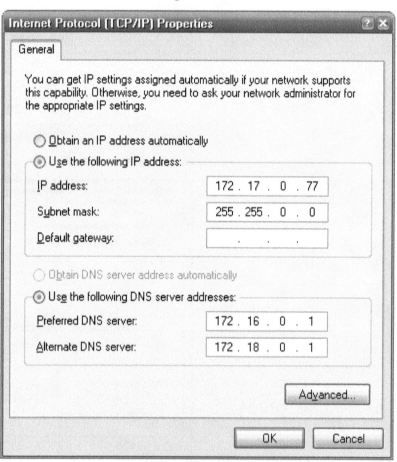

Custom client configuration.

BE A NETWORK ADMINISTRATOR

Building a TCP/IP network

You are designing a network that will eventually support up to 1,000 hosts. The network will be wired as a physical star using hubs as the central connection points. TCP/IP is the only protocol that will be used on the network. The network will be configured as a Windows Active Directory domain with a domain controller in each subnetwork. Network hosts will not have direct access to the Internet, but will be able to access Internet resources through four shared proxy servers. The network will also include two public web servers that will connect to the Internet through a firewall.

1. What guidelines should you use to configure subnetworks?

2. What type of network addresses should you use for configuring the subnetworks to support all of the hosts, but also minimize the complexity of the network?

3. What public IP address requirements are there on the network, if any?

4. Describe how you would manage IP address and TCP/IP property configuration for the majority of the hosts.

5. Describe how you would handle host name resolution requirements, assuming that there are no NetBIOS name requirements.

6. What is the role of routers, if any, in the network and what special configuration issues might you have?

7. What is the role of bridges, if any, in the network and what specific configuration issues might you have?

KEY TERMS

Acknowledgement

Address scopes

Alias

Authoritative

Best effort transmission

BOOTP enabled

Canonical name (CNAME)

Checksum

Class

Class A

Class B

Class C

Class D

Class E

Classful network

Classless Inter-Domain Routing (CIDR)

Datagrams

Destination address

DHCP proxy

DHCPACK

DHCPDISCOVER

DHCPNACK

DHCPOFFER

DHCPREQUEST

Dig

DNS table

DNS zone

Domain name

Dotted decimal notation

Dynamic DNS

Dynamic Host Configuration Protocol (DHCP)

End-to-end principle

Echo request

Executioner

Fragmentation offset

Fully Qualified Domain Name (FQDN)

Hop count

Hop limit

Host address

Host record

Hosts

HOSTS

ifconfig

Internet Control Message Protocol (ICMP)

Internet Corporation of Assigned Names and Numbers (ICANN)

Internet proxy servers

IP version 4 (IPv4)

IP version 6 (IPv6)

ipconfig

LMHOSTS

Loopback

Mail exchange (MX) record

Multicasting

Multihomed

Name resolution

Name server (NS) record

NetBIOS

Network Address Translation (NAT)

Nslookup

Out-of-band

Overflows

pathping

ping

Port numbers

Primary DNS server

Private Addresses

Protocol number

Request for Comment (RFC)

Secondary DNS server

Segments

Sequence number

Socket

Start of authority (SOA) record

Stateless address auto-configuration (SLAAC)

Static IP address

Subnetting

Telnet

Time to Live (TTL)

traceroute

tracert

Urgent Pointer

Variable Length Subnet Masking (VLSM)

Window

Windows Internet Naming Service (WINS)

Zone file

8

NETWORK SERVERS AND SERVICES FUNDAMENTALS

What Do You Already Know?

- What services are provided by a network?
- Which server-operating systems are available?

To assess your knowledge of network servers and services, go to **www.wiley.com/go/ciccarelli/networkingbasics2e**

What You Will Find Out	What You Will Be Able To Do
8.1 The basic services networks provide.	Identify the role of common network services.
8.2 The features available in Microsoft Windows Server versions.	Understand how Microsoft Windows Server versions differ from one another.
8.3 Mac OS X networking.	Compare and contrast Mac OS X Server and Microsoft Windows Server.
8.4 Networking with Unix and Linux NOS.	Compare and contrast Unix and Linux networking to other NOS.
8.5 The background of Novel Netware.	Recognize Novell NetWare features.
8.6 Network virtualization.	Justify the use of virtual machines.
8.7 Implementing basic network services.	Address issues relating to traffic flow and server placement.

INTRODUCTION

Network servers are a vital part of any network. Their maintenance and upkeep is the network administrator's primary task. To do so, you need to understand the role of basic network services, including the Network Operating System (NOS). We give you an overview of some of the most popular NOS options and compare and contrast their features and functionality. We also look at some basic design issues and server placement considerations.

8.1 CONSIDERING BASIC SERVICE REQUIREMENTS

We start with a look at basic service requirements. The primary functionality of a LAN is to enable shared services of different types. Service requirements vary by organization, but we can divide them into some general categories.

- **File and print services:** File and print services, which enable the sharing of files, programs, and printers, are among the most fundamental of services and are found on nearly every network from the smallest peer-to-peer home network to the largest enterprise.

- **Server applications:** These applications are specialized and typically present only when there is a specific need.

- **Network support services:** Most of the services included in this category are the background "nuts and bolts" that keep the network running smoothly.

Keep in mind that the details of what services are provided (or even needed) and how they are implemented can vary widely between different NOS. We're looking at services from a more general standpoint and keeping vendor-specific considerations to a minimum.

Servers are often deployed throughout the network, as shown in Figure 8-1. However, placement should not be random.

You need to consider requirements such as user access, traffic flow patterns, and so forth when deciding on server placement. All network configurations have a maximum bandwidth and with Ethernet networks, performance degrades and traffic levels (and collisions) increase as more computers are placed on a network.

Another issue that may arise when discussing network servers is their ability to scale. Scaling is the process of increasing the resources available to an NOS, server application, or other resource until it meets your needs.

Figure 8-1

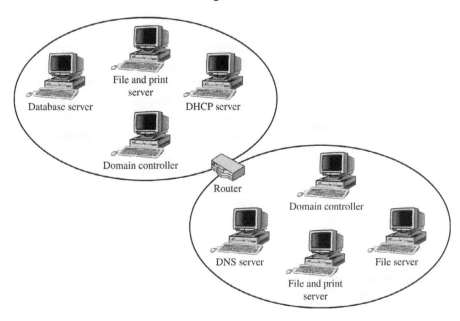

Network servers.

By saying that a product is scalable, manufacturers are usually implying two things:

- You don't have to initially buy more than you really need.
- It can grow as you grow.

When talking about servers and server applications, you can scale up, out, or both. When you scale up, you increase a server's hardware resources, which means adding more disk space, more memory, or maybe a faster (or additional) processor. When you scale out, you add more servers of the same type.

8.1.1 Using File and Print Services

For most organizations, especially in the early days of PC LANs, file and print services were the driving force behind justifying a network. Users need to share information for an organization to thrive. Because of this need, the most common types of network servers are file servers and print servers.

File servers make files and directories (file folders) available to network users. You can use file servers to share programs and files that users need to access, like templates and reference files. You can use them to store files for a project or design team. One of the primary reasons for having file servers is to give the users a central location for storing their own files and to ensure that the files are backed up regularly. The unfortunate truth is that files stored on a user's own local computer are seldom, if ever, backed up.

Print servers give users access to shared printers. They also let you manage user access, so that you can limit access to specialty printers, large format printers, or other print devices. You can also specify user priorities for printer use, that is whose **print jobs** (documents waiting to print) print first, and which users have permission to manage printers and print jobs. Typically, any user who can print to a printer can manage his or her own print jobs, but only those users given special permissions can manage other users' print jobs. Print job management tasks include suspending or canceling (deleting) print jobs, changing the order of print jobs in the queue, and so forth. Print devices controlled by a print server can be directly connected to the server or, in some cases, connected directly to the network and managed remotely by the print server.

Seeing a server supporting both file server and print server responsibilities is common, especially on smaller networks. If your server supports both, you need to carefully monitor hard disk use and available disk space. Some print jobs, especially those that include large, complex graphics can require very large files. These files are temporarily stored in a **print spooler** or **print queue** (temporary storage area) on the hard disk and can affect available disk space.

8.1.2 Introducing Server Applications

Server applications are usually deployed on an as-needed basis. The most common server applications are relational database applications and web servers. Web servers can host websites (for public access or for internal use) and **web services,** which are applications that are accessible from the Internet or local intranet. Web services accept parameters and return values formatted using **Extensible Markup Language (XML),** a format used for formatting data for transfer. It has become a standard for data transfers across the Internet. You may see other server applications, such as e-mail servers, servers designed to support group projects and other shared documents, or even team development servers that facilitate team-based software development.

Servers that support public access are sometimes deployed outside of the LAN on an isolated perimeter network known as a Demilitarized Zone (DMZ), as shown in Figure 8-2. A **firewall,** a network security device that filters network traffic, isolates the perimeter network from the rest of the LAN, acting like a gatekeeper that keeps the outside world out, but allows limited interaction with servers deployed on the network.

A **host-based firewall** is a firewall running on a single host or server. These firewalls restrict network traffic for only that server.

Print job
A document that has been prepared and is ready to print.

Print queue
A temporary storage location for print jobs waiting to print. Also known as a **print spooler.**

Web services
Specialized application that run on web servers and provide services to clients over the Internet.

Extensible Markup Language (XML)
A data format used for formatting data for transmission using defined schemata, similar in formatting to HTML used for web pages.

Firewall
A network security device that filters traffic into or out of a network or subnet.

Host-based firewall
A firewall on a host that controls traffic to and from that host.

Figure 8-2

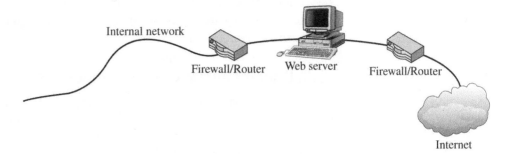

Network with a perimeter network.

FOR EXAMPLE

FIGURE 8-2

Often, you will have two firewalls, as in Figure 8-2, with one between the perimeter network and the internal LAN and another between the perimeter network and the Internet, so that you can control the traffic between the web server and Internet users.

Most server applications are resource-intensive. Often, they have special security and access requirements, with direct access to the servers strictly limited. Because of these security measures, most server application's documentation recommends that they are configured as the only application running on the server. However, even when recommended by the application's manufacturer, network administrators do not always follow these guidelines and may try to run multiple applications on the same server.

Because of the expense involved for both the server hardware and application software, having only one instance of a particular type of application server that is shared throughout the network is common. One exception is web servers. Companies commonly deploy multiple public web servers, often all hosting the same content, to improve user access

---

NETWORKING FACT

The Health Insurance Portability and Accountability Act (HIPAA) requires additional security measures be used for any hosts, server, or network that stores patient information. As a result, many medical data-processing companies, hospitals, and insurance companies use host-based firewalls to restrict access to servers that house HIPAA sensitive information.

performance and to provide fault tolerance should one server fail. Other server applications also usually support fault-tolerant configurations, but whether or not they are deployed depends on how critical the application is to business operations.

8.1.3 Understanding Network Support Services

Some support services are required. Others are optional, depending on your network configuration. This area is where servers might be called on to perform multiple duties, depending on the specific services they are hosting.

Servers that support network services include servers such as:

- Network control and management servers, which run the NOS, handle the control functions for the network, authenticate users, and take care of network background management tasks.
- Specialty authentication and authorization servers, such as Remote Access Dial In User Service (RADIUS) servers.
- Remote Access Servers (RAS, or Microsoft Routing and Remote Access Servers {RRAS}, Virtual Private Network (VPN) endpoints, and software-configured routers.
- Network protocol support servers, such as Domain Name System (DNS) and Dynamic Host Configuration Protocol (DHCP) servers.
- Servers providing shared or public resources.
- Network Address Translation (NAT) and Internet connection sharing servers.
- Specialized gateway devices, such as mainframe computer gateways for mainframe access.

This list is by no means complete for all of the types of servers you might see. As with application servers, the types of servers you have will depend on your network's specific requirements. For example, if you don't have any remote access requirements, you won't have a remote access server.

SELF-CHECK

1. What types of servers are most commonly found on PC LANs?
2. What is the role of application servers?

Apply Your Knowledge How and why would you need a DMZ for your network system? Using standard icons draw what a DMZ might look like connected to both your network and the Internet. How many and where might you place firewalls?

IN THE REAL WORLD

The Lure of False Economy

Computers have become relatively inexpensive in recent years, at least for typical end-user and home use systems. High-end computers built to support resource-intensive server applications can still be relatively expensive, depending on the application's specific requirements. Because of this high cost, network designers and administrators are sometimes tempted to deploy application servers as multi-use servers. Although doing so may save some money up front, it's usually not a good idea in the long run.

To begin with, multi-use servers can be difficult to set up and maintain. Most server applications are written with expectations that the application will be the only one running on the server. As a result, the application assumes that it has unlimited access to all of the server's resources. Convincing the application to share hardware resources usually requires custom configuration at both the operating system and server level. Typically, none of the applications run at truly optimum capacity.

You may have to deal with other issues. The applications can have different security requirements or support different levels of access. User access permissions granted to users of one application could allow them to accidentally (or maliciously) delete files for the other application. Recovery can be difficult, if not impossible.

As application requirements evolve over time (and they will), upgrading the server to meet the new requirements can be a daunting task. Performance of one or more of the applications might suffer, eventually reaching the point where you have to move it to a separate server and migrate any related data and configuration settings. Migration procedures are often complicated and riddled with pitfalls.

8.2 CONSIDERING MICROSOFT WINDOWS SERVER

Windows for Workgroups (WFW)
An early Microsoft Windows Desktop version that supported peer-to-peer networking.

Windows Server 2008, the latest version of Microsoft's NOS, is possibly the most popular NOS in use today. Microsoft introduced its first true NOS with Windows NT in 1993. Around the same time, Microsoft released a version of its Windows client operating system with built-in peer-to-peer networking, called **Windows for Workgroups (WFW).** Windows NT went pretty much unnoticed until version Windows NT 3.51 was introduced about a year later. Windows NT 3.51 was relatively stable, and by this time, hardware vendors had released computers using 486 and Pentium processors, which significantly improved the operating system's performance.

Because of its similarity to Windows 3.1 and its powerful networking features, Windows NT gained popularity. Microsoft began to put significant marketing muscle behind it, and Windows NT became a viable alternative in the NOS market previously dominated by Novell NetWare and the various flavors of UNIX. Windows NT was succeeded by Windows 2000 Server, Windows Server 2003, and Windows Server 2008.

The Windows server platform is the first choice of many developers because of the similarity in programming for all Windows platforms. Microsoft provides several tools and references to support developers for download and as free online references.

In addition, all current Windows products have built-in client software and the built-in capacity to operate in a peer-to-peer networking environment. That means you can build a simple network to share files, printers, and other resources without having to deploy Microsoft's Active Directory. The major drawbacks, however, are that peer-to-peer networks only work well with a small number of computers involved and the security management is very limited. We discussed the advantages and shortcomings of peer-to-peer networks in Chapter 5.

8.2.1 Exploring Windows Server Features

Although subtle differences between the desktop operating systems and their server counterparts do exist, the basic look and feel is the same. (See Figure 8-3 for an example of the Windows Server 2008 desktop.) Hence a novice administrator can easily learn the fundamentals of working with a Windows NOS. Analysts refer to this as a **shallow learning curve.**

Shallow learning curve
A term that refers to ease of learning because of associations with something the learner already knows.

Windows as a server platform is designed to work seamlessly with current Windows clients and, with additional client software, most down-level versions. However, it also has integrated support for Macintosh and UNIX clients, although some client features are limited.

Edition
A way of describing product variations for a specific Microsoft Server product and version.

A feature that is important to network designers and administrators is the level of scalability built into the Windows 2003 Server and Windows Server 2008 product families, which Microsoft refers to as different **editions.** These include one designed specifically for use as a web platform, its Standard edition designed for small to medium (and some large) businesses, and the two most scalable editions, Enterprise and Datacenter. The idea is that you only buy as much server functionality as you actually need, and that you can mix multiple editions on your network as appropriate.

Note that Microsoft doesn't look at Windows Server 2008 as a standalone product, but as part of a suite of server products including database, business productivity, IT management, program development, and security products. These products are sold as server applications designed specifically to run on Microsoft's server operating systems and optimized for that environment. They are also designed to interact relatively seamlessly with each other to provide a coherent application environment. Microsoft carries

Figure 8-3

Windows Server 2008 desktop.

its model of offering different product editions to meet different business needs to its server application products.

Windows Server 2008 has more built-in components and updated third-party drivers, but the main difference between 2003 and 2008 is Virtualization Management. Microsoft introduced a new feature with Windows Server 2008 64bit called Hyper-V (V for Virtualization). More and more companies are reducing hardware costs by running several virtual servers on one physical machine. We discuss virtualization in more depth a little later.

8.2.2 Supporting Interoperability

Windows Server has many tools for platform interoperability. UNIX Interoperability components in Windows Server 2008 R2 allow you to reduce costs by integrating UNIX and Microsoft Windows systems to deliver a complete solution. The interoperability of security and directory services, file and printer sharing, and re-use of UNIX code and IT skills across platforms delivers a simplified infrastructure and allows UNIX or Windows IT staff to manage both systems from one place.

Windows Server 2008 R2 UNIX interoperability components help you:

- Leverage existing skills, with either Windows or UNIX, to manage both platforms.
- Integrate applications to maximize existing investments while extending UNIX-based applications to Windows systems.
- Migrate applications from UNIX to Windows using a phased approach, reducing risk and expensive downtime.

Earlier versions of Windows Server can interoperate with NetWare. When Windows NT Server was first introduced in 1993, NetWare was the primary network operating system available. Three main programs facilitate the integration of Windows and NetWare, as shown in Table 8-1.

These products are supported on Windows Server 2000 and earlier and are compatible with NetWare version 4 and earlier. They can be used with IPX/SPX (Microsoft NWLink) only, with no support for TCP/IP.

Table 8-1: Windows Server and NetWare Interoperability

Windows Server Product	*How Windows and NetWare Are Integrated*
Gateway Services for NetWare (GSNW)	GSNW installs as a service on a Windows Server machine and translates requests for Windows resources into NetWare requests. GSNW allows multiple Windows NT and Windows 2000 clients to connect through a Windows NT server to NetWare servers using only Windows client software and protocols.
Client Services for NetWare (CSNW)	CSNW allows clients to directly access NetWare servers, but you must install it on every Windows workstation computer that needs access to NetWare resources. Additionally, all users who want to access NetWare resources need user accounts and rights on the NetWare servers they access.
File and Print Services for NetWare (FPNW)	FPNW is a method for providing files and printers hosted by Windows Server to Novell clients. When installed and configured on a Windows server, this service makes a Windows server look like a NetWare server to Novell clients.

8.2.3 Understanding Service Support

Windows Server 2008 supports a full range of network services. We look at a few key areas for comparison, including authentication, file and print services, application support, and a security overview.

Since Windows 2000 Server and Windows XP, all Windows products have been able to use **Kerberos** technology for authentication. Kerberos support is also built into clients (and network servers) running UNIX and Linux. Authentication also works in conjunction with Microsoft's Active Directory service when authenticating Kerberos clients. Essentially, every user that successfully authenticates to the Active Directory authentication system receives a unique identifier known as a ticket. From then on, that ticket is sent along with all transmissions to indicate exactly who sent the information.

The directory-based model used by Windows Server versions means that users log in one time to get access to all of a domain's resources. Access security is built around domains, which define the boundaries for security management, and are based around a directory structure containing objects representing network entities and containers used to organize them. You can also define and control security between domains, letting you build enterprise and extranet security models to meet your specific needs.

Windows Server's file and print services are designed to meet resource-sharing requirements for nearly any network. The major advantage to Windows Server over other server platforms is that it uses the familiar Windows interface and terminology. Windows even supports **caching,** keeping copies of files on the local computer that are updated whenever the client connects to the network. Caching is especially useful with remote access clients and telecommuters.

Windows Server uses the concept of folders (representing directories) and shares for its file sharing. To make files accessible to network users, the folders in which they are stored are **shared** to the network, making it available to network users. After a folder is shared, a client can access all the files within it (depending on the security settings, of course) and any folders within it as well. Additionally, Windows Server supports the sharing of printers in the same manner. When configured correctly, the client connecting to the printer can automatically install the driver for a printer shared under Windows Server.

Windows is arguably the platform with the most developer support. Third-party vendors write thousands of software titles for Windows. Developers can create these programs using the same development tools they use to write Windows client programs. Microsoft makes programming references readily available at no charge. Finally, a program that is certified as Windows Compatible must work on a range of Windows platforms, with various application certification levels supported. Many server applications run as services, giving them more direct access to the operating system and hardware resources, as a way to provide optimum performance.

Kerberos
A highly secure industry-standard authentication method. Developed for Unix and supported on most current NOS as an authentication method.

Caching
Local storage network resources. Cached files are refreshed, updating either the local copy or network copy, depending on which has the most recent changes, when the user connects to the network.

Sharing
A term that refers to making resources (specifically file and print resources) available to network clients.

Patch
A minor update that fixes small glitches that crop up from time to time, such as minor security or performance issues.

Windows Server Update Service (WSUS)
Microsoft's patch management tool for Windows Server. WSUS provides a number of features including targeting of patches to specific groups of machines, support for Microsoft products, and error reporting.

Group Policy Object (GPOs)
An Active Directory method for defining and distributing policy configuration information throughout the directory or to specific groups of users or computers.

One of the responsibilities every network manager faces is applying software **patches** to keep your operating system and other software updated. A software patch fixes issues that aren't significant enough to merit a new version of the software, but are important enough to require fixing. Most of the patches correct security flaws that computer hackers have uncovered.

Periodically, all the recently released patches are combined into a service pack. Although the most diligent network administrators apply all patches as they're released, many administrators just wait for the service packs.

For all versions of Windows, you can use Windows Update to apply patches to keep your operating system and other Microsoft software updated. You can find Windows Update in the Start menu. Windows Update automatically scans your computer's software and creates a list of software patches and other components that you can download and install. You can also configure Windows Update to automatically notify you of updates so that you don't have to remember to check for new patches.

For larger networks, you can set up a server that runs **Windows Server Update Services (WSUS)** to automate software updates. WSUS essentially lets you set up your own Windows Update site on your own network. You then control how software updates are delivered to the computers on your network. For more information, see: www.microsoft.com/windowsserversystem/updateservices.

That said, Windows Server has a full-featured security system. Where the security works, it works relatively well. You have detailed control over security configuration settings and can even configure different security schemes for different groups of users or computers. In an Active Directory network environment, you can use security definition policies, known as **Group Policy Objects (GPOs),** distributed and automatically applied to client computers (and to user accounts). The current Windows Server version is designed to be secure by default, with unused services disabled by default.

TIPS FROM THE PROFESSIONALS

Group Policy Objects

GPOs are assigned to Active Directory containers (sites, domains, or OUs). They are then applied to computers and users in those containers. GPOs can contain both computer and user sets of policies. The computer section of a GPO is applied during boot. The User section of a GPO is applied at user login. The GPOs are applied in the following order: first to Local Group Policy object (Local GPO), then GPOs linked to containers in this order: site, domain, and organizational units. Within each container the GPOs are applied from last to first (i.e. from the bottom of the list to the top of the list for each container).

IN THE REAL WORLD

What About Viruses?

Why do so many hackers spend time developing malicious attacks against Windows? Probably because it's the biggest target.

The vast majority of desktop and laptop computers worldwide run some version of Windows, which means attackers have a massive number of potential victims and self-propagating attacks are more likely to flourish. UNIX and Linux are, in many ways, more vulnerable. However, with such a smaller relative population, they haven't been a target in recent years. The same is true of Apple Macintosh OS X versions, which have seen very few attacks. The primary reason is the relatively small population, which means an attack would be much less effective and less likely to spread. This situation might change if the number of Linux and Macintosh systems in use continues to grow.

8.2.4 Understanding Group Policy

Group policy refers to a feature of Windows operating systems that lets you control how certain aspects of Windows and other Microsoft software work throughout your network. It has many features that you might expect to find in a management console such as Active Directory. Users and computers are controlled instead by group policy. For example, you must use group policy to control how often users must change their passwords and how complicated their passwords must be. As a result, group policy is an important tool for any Windows network administrator.

Group policy consists of a collection of GPOs that define individual policies. These policy objects are selectively applied to both users and computers. Each policy object specifies how some aspect of Windows or some other Microsoft software should be configured. For example, a group policy object might specify the home page that's initially displayed when any user launches Internet Explorer. Then, when a user logs on to the domain, that policy object is retrieved and applied to the user's Internet Explorer configuration.

Group policy objects can apply to either computers or users. A policy that applies to a computer will be enforced for any user of the computer. A policy that applies to a user will be enforced for that user no matter what computer he or she logs on to. As a network administrator, you'll be mostly concerned with policies that apply to users. But computer policies are useful from time to time as well.

To use group policy, you have to know how to do two things: (1) create individual group policy objects, and (2) apply—or link—those objects to user and computer objects. Both tasks can be a little tricky.

The trick to creating group policy objects is finding the particular setting you want to employ. Trying to find a specific group policy among the thousands of available policies can be frustrating. For example, suppose you want to force all network users to change their passwords every 30 days. You know there's a group policy that controls the password expiration date. You can use the Group Policy Management Console to find it.

After you've created a group policy object, you then link it to the users or computers you want it to apply to. Creating a policy that applies to all users or computers is simple enough. But things get more complicated if you want to be more selective—for example, if you want the policy to apply only to users in a particular organizational unit (OU) or to users that belong to a particular group.

CAREER CONNECTION

Enabling Group Policy Management on Windows Server 2008

Before you can work with group policy on a Windows Server 2008, you must enable group policy on the server. The procedure is simple enough and needs to be done only once for each server. Here are the steps:

1. Choose Start ⇨ Administrative Tools Server ⇨ Manager.
2. Click Features in the console tree.
3. Click Add Features. Be patient—it takes a few minutes for the list of features to populate.
4. Select the Group Policy Management check box and then click Next.
5. When the confirmation page appears, click Install. Be patient again—it may take a few minutes to install.
6. Click Close—you're done!

After you've completed this procedure, a new command titled Group Policy Management appears on the Start ⇨ Administrative Tools menu. You use this command to create and link Group Policy objects.

SELF-CHECK

1. What is the role of different Windows editions?
2. What kinds of authentication are supported by Windows Server 2003?
3. What is the difference between scaling up and scaling out?

Apply Your Knowledge Create a password policy on your local machine requiring complex passwords. Complex passwords are passwords of a minimum length–usually at least 8 characters, and containing upper- and lower-case letters, numbers, and/or special characters.

1. Open Control Panel and go to Administrative tools.

2. Open Local Security Policy.

3. In the console tree, click Password Policy (Security Settings/Account Policies/Password Policy).

4. In the details pane, right-click the policy setting that you want, and then click Properties.

5. Select the options that you want, and then click OK.

8.3 CONSIDERING APPLE MACINTOSH

The Apple Macintosh's biggest problem for the last several years has been one of perception rather than performance. Macintosh (Mac) opponents (read competitors) relied on embedded prejudices, wondering aloud how any system that easy and fun to use could be taken seriously for business. They also pointed to the larger catalog of business applications available for Windows PCs. They usually did this, of course, without mentioning how many of those applications were developed either by Microsoft or by application programmers working closely with Microsoft.

Some computer professionals who started out with command-line interfaces like UNIX shells were often frightened off by the Mac's graphical user interface (GUI) and the fact that no command line interface was available. If you couldn't click it, you couldn't run it. They preferred an operating system where you could dig down and "get your hands dirty" in the system internals. Never mind that these explorations into the OS often resulted in failure, with the problem worse when they finished than when they started.

The Macintosh interface is considered to be the easiest to use of all graphical user interfaces. It was the first computer to offer a reliable GUI desktop, shown in Figure 8-4. Developed in 1983 by Apple, the Macintosh

Figure 8-4

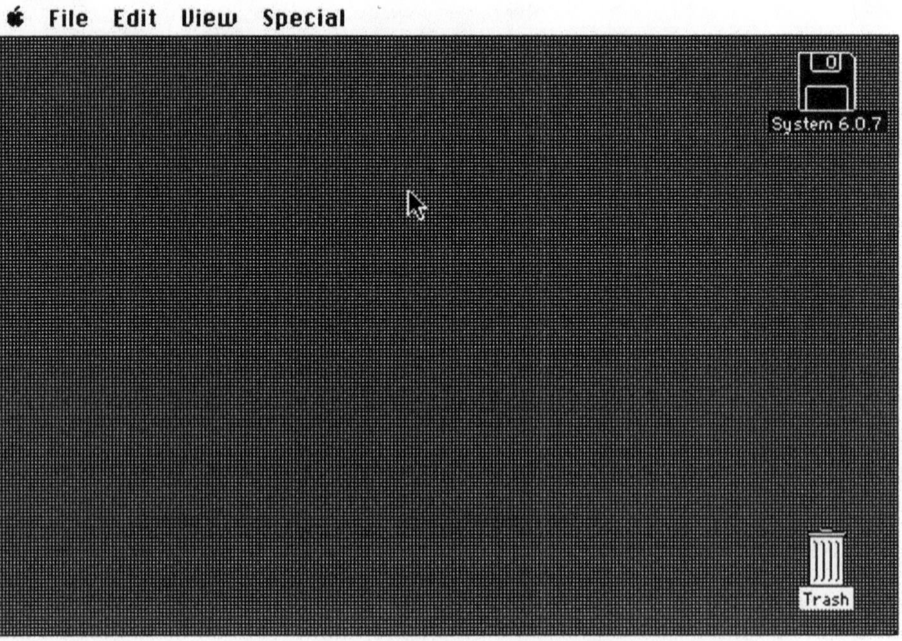

The original Mac desktop.

Operating System (or Mac OS) is seeing a resurgence of popularity with the introduction of several new models and aggressive advertising campaigns with head-to-head comparisons between Macs and PCs.

The Mac has always had a very loyal following, and with good reason. The Macintosh OS (combined with the Macintosh hardware platform) is a very user-friendly computer—maybe the most user-friendly interface available. Many people who have never used computers before, after comparing Macs with PCs, buy Macs. The Macintosh is especially well suited to multimedia applications and holds its own on office productivity applications.

Perhaps the most revolutionary change is Apple's switch from the Motorola processors it has used since the first days of the Mac to an Intel processor architecture, the one used by Windows PCs. What this means is that you can install both the Mac OS and Windows on the same computer in a **dual boot** configuration, and can decide at startup whether you want to run Windows or the Mac OS.

Dual boot
A computer configuration in which you can choose the operating system used to start the computer.

8.3.1 Exploring Mac Features

The Mac OS has gone through several major revisions so far, with each version having many more features than the one before it. Perhaps the best way to understand the Mac is to understand its operating system and the changes it has gone through over the years. The major Mac OS releases include:

- **System 1:** When the original Macintosh was released in 1984, the Mac OS interface was pretty bare. It contained the basic elements of the current Mac OS. It had no support for color, but it did have a very powerful GUI that made many people go out and buy it.

- **System 6:** System 6 was introduced around 1986 and introduced color to the operating system, displaying thousands or even millions of colors. This was when the PC was still struggling to show 256 colors. System 6 could switch between programs using a product known as Multifinder, but didn't support true **multitasking,** concurrent applications actively running at the same time.

Multitasking
Support for running concurrent applications.

- **System 7:** Macintosh System 7 added true multitasking support. In addition, it added support for **TrueType fonts,** which are automatically scalable fonts (and an important part of the current Windows interface), added the ability to share out a disk onto the network, and gave users the ability to use virtual memory, another feature key to the Windows family.

TrueType fonts
Automatically scalable fonts used with Mac and Windows.

- **System 7 Pro:** An improvement on System 7 that included digital signature technology, integrated e-mail, and speech recognition. Apple introduced the Keychain, which stored the various online passwords for a user so that only one password was required when a user went online.

Happy macked
A term referring to a Mac operating system that can be loaded and run from a single diskette.

System 7 Pro was not considered a major release because it couldn't be **happy macked** (meaning the operating system could not fit on a single floppy disk).

- **Mac OS 8:** 1997 brought a name change, actively promoting the Macintosh. System software was now to be known as Mac OS. Also, due to a partnership with Microsoft (and an infusion of capital from the same), Internet Explorer was installed as the default browser. Mac also increased its cross-platform connectivity with the introduction of an updated version of its PC Exchange product, which now had support for Windows 9x long filenames. Finally, the OS contained its own **Java Virtual Machine** for running Java applications.

Java Virtual Machine (JVM)
A software component that enables an operating system to run Java language applications.

- **Mac OS 9:** With Mac OS 9, Apple brought the Mac OS up to speed with Microsoft's multiuser offerings. It was now possible to specify different settings and environments for multiple users of the same Macintosh.

- **Mac OS X (OS 10):** Amid much hoopla, Apple introduced OS X, the current version and first major rewrite of the Mac OS in years, in 2001. The basic interface still looks the same; but the use of color, graphics, and moving graphics is much improved over previous versions. Also, it is based on a UNIX kernel, which makes it more stable, more scalable, and generally more powerful than previous versions. Also, for the first time, you can save directly to **Portable Document Format,** or **PDF,** a common document format that was developed by Adobe and has since become a de facto standard.

Portable Document Format (PDF)
The de facto document format originally developed and licensed by Adobe.

TIPS FROM THE PROFESSIONALS

It's a Jungle Out There

Note that since the original release of OS 10.0, named Cheetah, all the successive upgrades have been named for big cats: 10.1-Puma, 10.2-Jaguar, 10.3-Panther, 10.4-Tiger, 10.5-Leopard, 10.6-Snow Leopard, and 10.7-Lion.

The Mac OS X desktop is shown in Figure 8-5. It is considered a flexible, user-friendly and Internet-friendly interface. It is also supports a credible NOS version, Mac OS X Server.

In the mid 1990s, AppleTalk was supplanted by a networking scheme called Open Transport. The current generation of Macintosh computers uses industry-standard TCP/IP networking. The only protocol left over from the

Figure 8-5

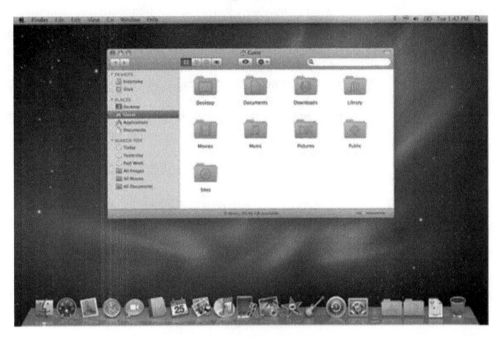

OS X (10.6 Snow Leopard) desktop.

TIPS FROM THE PROFESSIONALS

AFP

AppleTalk
A high level protocol developed and used by Apple.

AFP is a Presentation layer protocol. It's the part of **AppleTalk** that governs how files are stored and accessed on the network. AFP allows files to be shared with non-Macintosh computers. You can integrate Macintoshes into any network operating system that recognizes AFP. NetWare and all versions of Windows since Windows 95 use AFP to support Macintoshes in their networks.

AppleTalk Filing Protocol (AFP)
A protocol that supports file sharing, file transport, and end-user printer sharing.

AppleTalk days that is still in widespread use is **AppleTalk Filing Protocol (AFP),** used to enable file sharing.

As you would expect, the Mac OS X Server supports Mac clients but, with its latest versions, includes Samba so that Windows clients can authenticate to a Mac OS X Server and access server resources. Also, the Mac OS X Server can function beautifully as an Internet server because the core of Mac OS X is UNIX, and because of the kernel's close ties with TCP/IP.

8.3.2 Considering Mac OS X Server

Apple offers a dedicated network operating system known as Mac OS X Server, which is designed for PowerMac G3 or later computers. Mac OS X Server is based on a Unix operating system kernel known as Mach. Mac OS X Server can handle many network server tasks as efficiently as any other network operating system, including Windows 2000, NetWare, and Unix.

Mac OS X Server is the server version of the Mac OS X operating system, which is the current operating system version for client Macintosh computers.

The Mac OS X Server includes the following features:

- Apache Web server, which also runs on Windows and Linux systems.
- NetBoot, a feature that simplifies the task of managing network client computers.
- File services using AFP.
- WebObjects, a high-end tool for creating websites.
- QuickTime Streaming Server, which lets the server broadcast multimedia programs over the network.

8.3.3 Supporting Interoperability

As a server platform, the Mac OS is reliable and fairly scalable. It really can't compete with the largest UNIX or high-end Open Enterprise or Windows Server 2008 platforms in the enterprise, but it makes for a good workgroup and web server platform. In that respect, the Mac OS is compatible with many different clients.

Mac OS X, like all other current operating systems, supports TCP/IP for network and Internet connectivity. Still, the Mac isn't quite a flexible as a client, requiring the network server to provide a compatible computing environment. One aid to interoperability is that Microsoft provides a Mac version of its popular Office productivity suite.

8.3.4 Understanding Service Support

The Kerberos authentication mechanism handles the authentication for Mac OS X, which makes Mac OS X compatible with other popular networking environments. Additionally, Mac OS X includes a feature known as the keychain, mentioned earlier. The **keychain** is a storage location for all the passwords you might use on the Internet (website passwords, FTP passwords, etc.) or anywhere. When a user authenticates to the system, that procedure unlocks the keychain. From then on, any time the user revisits a

Keychain
A Macintosh operating system feature that supports online (Internet) passwords.

location that has credentials stored in the keychain, the keychain will automatically provide them on behalf of the user.

In addition to Kerberos and the keychain, Mac OS X and newer versions include support for Apple's **Open Directory.** Open Directory is a directory much like Microsoft's Active Directory and Novell's eDirectory. It allows all users to authenticate to a central database of users so a user has to authenticate only once to the Directory. From then on, the security settings stored in the Directory for that user dictate what parts of the network can be accessed and under which conditions.

Open Directory
A Mac directory-based networking model.

In addition to being a client, a Macintosh can be a file and print server using **AppleShare** as well as an Internet server using various Apple and third-party software. The advantage of having a Macintosh as a server is that it is extremely easy to administer. It is so easy, in fact, that many first-time users have no problems networking Macs and turning them into file (or other) servers. Also, in small companies where there isn't a budget for an IT staff or money for outsourced support, a Mac OS server can be managed by existing staff.

AppleShare
Apple's proprietary networking software.

Mac OS X has a unique position as far as application support is concerned. It can run older Mac OS applications as well as those written

IN THE REAL WORLD

Has the Mac's Time Finally Come?

The Mac has carved out a niche in some business areas. Since its original release, it has been the computer of choice for graphic applications, commercial artists, and publishing firms. Many multimedia developers consider it the only choice for music and video editing, because of its inherent strengths and the powerful multimedia applications available for the Mac.

However, something else has also been going on, a bit of a quiet revolution. Through marketing arrangements and special discounts, Macs have found a place as the recommended (and preferred) computer on many college and university campuses. Why does this make a difference? As these new graduates make their way into the job market with diploma in hand and Mac nestled in their briefcase, if they are called on to make any recommendations about computer hardware or software, they're going to recommend the Macintosh. That way, they can integrate a familiar environment into a primarily PC world. The ability of Macs to now run both the Mac OS and Windows via dual-booting is likely to accelerate this trend.

specifically for Mac OS X. Plus, it can run some UNIX and X Window System applications, provided they support the Mac OS kernel.

Apache Web Server
A popular open-source web server.

Many application developers are creating small business suite packages for Mac OS X Server. Mac OS X Server comes with the **Apache Web server,** the most popular UNIX-based (and possibly most popular overall) web server, and MySQL 4, making for a very powerful open source web platform for developing database-driven websites.

The Mac OS offers reliable security. Mac OS X has local user account security built in as part of the OS. Network security has also been taken into account. Many services that would be susceptible to a hack are turned off by default, making the Mac secure by default right out of the box. Additionally, many third-party security products (including some that implement Kerberos security) are available that can make the Mac OS extremely secure over the network.

SELF-CHECK

1. What is a keychain?
2. What is Open Directory?
3. What is the relationship between Mac OS X and UNIX?

Apply Your Knowledge Screen Capture is part of the Mac OS X operating system.

To capture the entire screen, press Command+Shift+3.

To capture part of a screen, press Command+Shift+4.

The cursor will then turn into a cross-hairs icon. Click and drag over an area to select it. When you release the mouse button, the image is taken, and you'll hear a snapshot sound.

You can capture a window or object by using this last method, or, follow these steps to get a more precise screenshot:

1. Press Command+Shift+4.

   Again, the cursor turns into the cross-hairs icon.

2. Press the spacebar.

   The cursor turns into a camera icon.

3. Move the camera cursor over the window or object that you want to capture.

   When you move the cursor over an object, it becomes highlighted.

4. After you highlight the window that you want, click the mouse anywhere on the window or object to take the screenshot.

Does your screenshot look like this?

8.4 CONSIDERING UNIX AND LINUX

Of the other network operating systems available, the various forms of UNIX (including Linux) probably have some of the most loyal supporters. It is the oldest of the network operating systems, though not always following the same model. Early UNIX networks would have a single UNIX server accessed by dumb terminals, not a network made up of intelligent devices.

Bell Labs developed UNIX, in part, in 1969. We say "in part" because there are now so many iterations, commonly called *flavors,* of UNIX that it is almost a completely different operating system. Although the basic architecture of all flavors is the same (32-bit kernel, command-line based, capable of having a graphical interface, as in X Window System), the subtle details of each may make one flavor better in a particular situation than another. Linux, although also sometimes described as a flavor or version of UNIX, is actually something different. It is a separate operating system that was written to look and act exactly like UNIX, but with a license structure to help it more quickly grow and evolve. Linux versions and variations include the source code so that you can create your own flavor. Throughout this section, statements made about UNIX features and functionality also apply to Linux, unless explicitly stated otherwise.

8.4.1 Exploring UNIX/Linux Features

UNIX flavors incorporate a kernel, which constitutes the core of the operating system and can access hardware and communicate with user interfaces.

UNIX versions are most often identified by their kernel version. The UNIX kernel is like the core operating system components of Windows Server and NetWare (sometimes also referred to as the operating system kernel).

UNIX supports two types of user interfaces: several versions of the command-line interface (know as **shells**) and the graphical interfaces (with **X Window System** probably the best known version).

Linux, whose popularity has grown rapidly in the last several years, was originally developed by **Linus Torvalds** at the University of Helsinki, Finland. He started his work in 1991 and released version 1 of the Linux kernel in 1994. Linux is now available in literally hundreds of different downloadable versions, known as **distributions,** all with one common feature. They are licensed using an **open-source license,** specifically called the **GNU public license,** which means you can modify it, as long as you include the source code when you redistribute it. The different distributions support different features sets, have different embedded applications, and have different hardware requirements. Check the requirements before starting installation. Recovering a computer from a failed installation attempt is sometimes difficult.

Some Linux distributions run on a wide variety of platforms, including Reduced (or Rapid) Instruction Set Computing (RISC) processors like MIPS and Alpha, and the Motorola processor traditionally used in Apple Macintosh. The vast majority of Linux distributions run on Intel processors, simply because those processors are the most common type in computers world-wide.

Like UNIX, Linux comes with network support for TCP/IP. Some versions also support other protocols. Hundreds of different distributions can be downloaded at no charge, but most businesses use one of the commercial versions, such as Caldera's OpenLinux, SUSe, and Red Hat. Red Hat Linux is one of the most portable versions of Linux, with code that runs natively on the Intel, Alpha, and SPARC processors. SUSe was acquired by and is now sold by Novell, including a number of server and office productivity programs written specifically for use with SUSe.

8.4.2 Understanding Service Support

UNIX can use multiple methods of authentication, but UNIX generally uses Internet standard protocols. Most often, UNIX will use **Lightweight Directory Access Protocol (LDAP)** or Kerberos for authentication. Client versions are also designed for use with NDS and Active Directory networks as well. Flexibility is one of the reasons for its continued popularity.

UNIX file and print services are TCP/IP-based. Therefore, protocols like FTP, NFS, and HTTP are used with standard file sharing. UNIX printing uses the **LPD/LPR** protocols to handle the print process and printer management. The UNIX software, called **Samba,** is also available; it makes UNIX appear as a Windows server for file sharing. It uses the standard Server Message Block (SMB) protocol—the same protocol that Windows networking uses. Samba is freely available on the Internet.

Shell
A Unix/Linux command-line interface.

X Windows System
A popular Unix GUI.

Distribution
A downloadable or otherwise distributable set of Linux installation files for a specific Linux flavor and kernel version. Most distributions include a suite of preinstalled applications.

Open-source license
A software distribution license under which you can modify the software but must distribute the source code with the modified software.

GNU (GNU not unix) public license
The specific open-source license that applies to most Linux distributions.

Lightweight Directory Access Protocol (LDAP)
A TCP/IP authentication protocol.

LPD/LPR
TCP/IP protocols that support network printer access in a Unix/Linux network environment.

Samba
A Unix/Linux SMB emulation.

UNIX has plenty of application support, mainly because it has been around so long. However, it is important to note that applications are usually made to run on the specific version and flavor of UNIX, or at the very least, a specific kernel version, and are not always forward or cross-platform compatible. For example, an application written for Sun Solaris may not run on SCO UNIX, even though they are both UNIX. However, UNIX applications that comply with the **POSIX** standard should run on most UNIX and Linux versions with little or no modification.

POSIX
A Unix application development standard.

A large amount of UNIX software, most of it identified as Linux software now, is available for free on the Internet. You can download and install it, but no technical support may be available. Also, quality and reliability varies and authors typically offer no guarantees.

Most Linux distributions include a full suite of productivity applications, such as a word processor, the X Window System graphical interface, and source code compilers. Entertainment software, such as media players, video editors, and even games, are also typically included in the mix. In addition, nearly all distributions include a web server and an assortment of

IN THE REAL WORLD

Computing on the Cheap

P-s-s-t. Wanna free computer? Yeah, free. What's the catch? Well . . .

Computer hardware is cheap. Used computer hardware is dirt cheap. In fact, ask around and you probably won't have too much trouble finding companies or individuals disposing of old computers when they upgrade, computers you might even get for free. However, without an operating system, a computer is little more than a large, heavy doorstop.

Have you priced operating systems lately? You can pay as much for a full copy of the latest Windows version as you might pay for a low-end computer with Windows already installed. And don't even think about going with a bootleg version. Microsoft has all sorts of protections to turn Windows off if you try to bootleg it, or track the copy back to you—and they do prosecute. Even then, you need applications. There's not much reason to have a computer without applications.

The answer? Linux. You can download it for free, most distributions come with a full suite of varied applications, and it runs on pretty much any computer you're going to find that can physically run. Laptop, desktop, wired network or wireless, it doesn't matter. Unless you have some kind of brand new, super hot hardware accessories, device drivers are probably also available. Remember, we're trying for free, so you won't have the latest and greatest.

Besides, all the cool geeks use Linux. Well, they have it on at least one computer.

web development tools. Most Linux setup programs let you choose which optional applications, if any, you want to install.

UNIX has existed for quite some time, and therefore many of the security issues have been discovered and their causes fixed. Even though new security issues are always popping up, fixes are usually easy to come by. Many of the users can come up with fixes themselves because the average UNIX administrator is extremely well versed at fixing his or her own problems.

SELF-CHECK

1. How is Linux related to UNIX?
2. What is a Linux distribution?
3. What is the significance of Linux being distributed under an open source license?

Apply Your Knowledge Do you use a version of Linux? Which version seems to be the most popular? List several current versions of the free open-source software, and their characteristics. If you have an older computer that you are not using, download and install one of these iterations (perhaps Ubuntu or Fedora). Note that you might want to wait until you have completed Project 8.1 on page 292 to create a virtual Linux appliance.

8.5 EXPLORING NOVELL NETWARE

Novell NetWare was one of the first PC networking products on the market. It was originally modeled on a paradigm based on mainframe computing environments with a focus on resource access and security. NetWare was once the king of network operating systems. Today, NetWare networks are rare, but you can still find them if you look hard enough. NetWare has always had an excellent reputation for reliability. In fact, some network administrators swear that they have NetWare servers on their networks that have been running continuously, without a single reboot, since Ronald Reagan was president.

Novell released the first version of NetWare in 1983, two years before the first version of Windows and four years before Microsoft's first network operating system, the now defunct LAN Manager. Over the years, NetWare has gone through many versions. Check out Table 8-2 for the most important versions.

Beginning in 2005, NetWare transformed itself into a Linux-based system called Open Enterprise System (OES). In OES, the core of the operating system is actually Linux, with added applications that run the traditional NetWare services such as directory services. (For more information, see "Linux" earlier in this chapter.)

Table 8-2: Comparing the Important Versions of NetWare

NetWare Version	Characteristics
NetWare 3.x	This version made NetWare famous. NetWare 3.x used a now outdated directory scheme called the *bindery*. Each NetWare 3.x server has a bindery file that contains information about the resources on that particular server. With the bindery, you had to log on separately to each server that contained resources you wanted to use.
NetWare 4.x	In 4.x, NetWare Directory Service, or NDS, replaced the bindery. NDS is similar to Active Directory. It provides a single directory for the entire network rather than separate directories for each server.
NetWare5.x	5.x introduced a new user interface based on Java for easier administration, improved support for Internet protocols, multiprocessing with up to 32 processors, and many other features.
NetWare 6.0	6.0 introduced a variety of new features, including a new disk management system called Novell Storage Services, web-based access to network folders and printers, and built-in support for Windows, Linux, Unix, and Macintosh file systems.
NetWare 6.5	Novell released its last major version of NetWare (6.5) in summer 2003. It included improvements to its browser-based management tools and was bundled with open-source servers such as Apache and MySQL.

8.6 VIRTUALIZATION AND VIRTUAL MACHINES

Virtualization is one of the hottest trends in networking today. The basic idea behind virtualization is to use software to simulate the existence of hardware. This powerful idea enables you to run more than one independent computer system on a single physical computer system. For example, suppose your organization requires a total of 12 servers to meet its needs. You could run each of these 12 servers on a separate computer, in which case you would have 12 computers in your server room. Or, you could use virtualization to run these 12 servers on just two computers. In effect, each of those computers would simulate six separate computer systems, each running one of your servers.

Virtual machine (VM)
A software simulated computer.

Each of the simulated computers is called a **virtual machine (VM)**. For all intents and purposes, each virtual machine appears to be a complete, self-contained computer system with its own processor (or, more likely, processors), memory, disk drives, CD-ROM/DVD drives, keyboard, mouse, monitor, network interfaces, USB ports, and so on.

Like a real computer, each virtual machine requires an operating system to do productive work. In a typical network server environment, each virtual machine runs its own copy of Windows Server 2008 (or an earlier version). The operating system has no idea that it's running on a virtual machine rather than on a real machine.

Here are a few terms you need to be familiar with if you expect to discuss virtualization intelligently:

- **Host:** The actual physical computer on which one or more virtual machines run.

- **Bare metal:** Another term for the host computer that runs one or more virtual machines.

- **Guest:** Another term for a virtual machine running on a host.

- **Guest operating system:** An operating system that runs within a virtual machine. By itself, a guest is just a machine; it requires an operating system to run. The guest operating system is what brings the guest to life. As far as licensing is concerned, Microsoft treats each virtual machine as a separate computer. Thus, if you run six guests on a single host and each guest runs Windows Server 2008, you need six licenses of Windows Server 2008.

- **Hypervisor:** The virtualization operating system that creates and runs virtual machines.

The two basic types of hypervisors are Type 1 and Type 2. A Type 1 hypervisor runs directly on the bare metal. A Type 2 hypervisor runs within an operating system, which in turn runs on the bare metal.

For production use, you should always use a Type 1 hypervisor because they're much more efficient than Type 2 hypervisors. However, Type 1 hypervisors are considerably more expensive than Type 2 hypervisors. As a result, many people use inexpensive or free Type 2 hypervisors to experiment with virtualization before making a commitment to purchase an expensive Type 1 hypervisor.

8.6.1 Looking at the Benefits of Virtualization

You might suspect that virtualization is inefficient because a real computer is inherently faster than a simulated computer. Although real computers are faster than simulated computers, virtualization technology has become so advanced that the performance penalty for running on a virtualized machine rather than a real machine is only a few percent.

The small amount of overhead imposed by virtualization is usually more than made up for by the simple fact that even the most heavily utilized servers spend most of their time twiddling their digital thumbs, waiting for something to do. In fact, many servers spend nearly all of their time doing nothing. As computers get faster and faster, they spend even more of their time with nothing to do.

Virtualization is a great way to put all of this unused processing power to good use. Besides this basic efficiency benefit, several other compelling benefits to virtualization are:

- **Hardware cost:** You can typically save a lot of money by reducing hardware costs when you use virtualization. For example, suppose you replace ten servers that cost $4,000 each with one host server. Granted, you'll probably spend more than $4,000 on that server, because it needs to be maxed out with memory, processor cores, network interfaces, and so on. So you'll probably end up spending $15,000 or $20,000 for the host server. And you'll end up spending something like $5,000 for the hypervisor software. But that's still a lot less than the $40,000 you would have spent on ten separate computers at $4,000 each.

- **Energy costs:** Many organizations have found that going virtual has reduced their overall electricity consumption for server computers by 80 percent. This savings is a direct result of using less computer hardware to do more work. For example, one host computer running ten virtual servers uses approximately one tenth of the energy used if each of the ten servers were run on separate hardware.

- **Recoverability:** One of the biggest benefits of virtualization is not the cost savings, but the ability to quickly recover from hardware failures. For example, suppose your organization has ten servers each running on separate hardware. If any one of those servers goes down due to a hardware failure—say a bad motherboard—that server will remain down until you can fix the computer. On the other hand, if those ten servers are running as virtual machines on two different hosts and one of the hosts fails, the virtual machines that were running on the failed host can be brought up on the other host in a matter of minutes.

    Granted, the servers will run less efficiently on a single host than they would have on two hosts, but the point is that they'll all be running after only a short downtime.

    In fact, with the most advanced hypervisors available, the transfer from a failing host to another host can be done automatically and instantaneously, so downtime is all but eliminated.

- **Disaster recovery:** Besides the benefit of recoverability when hardware failures occur, an even bigger benefit of virtualization comes into play in a true disaster recovery situation. For example, suppose your organization's server infrastructure consists of 20 separate servers. In the case of a devastating disaster, such as a fire in the server room that destroys all hardware, how long will it take you to get all 20 of those servers back up and running on new hardware? Quite possibly the recovery time will be measured in weeks.

In contrast, virtual machines are actually nothing more than files that can be backed up onto tape. As a result, in a disaster-recovery situation, all you have to do is rebuild a single host computer and reinstall the hypervisor software. Then you can restore the virtual machine backups from tape, restart the virtual machines, and be back up and running in a matter of days instead of weeks.

SELF-CHECK

1. What is a virtual machine?
2. Name some of the benefits of virtualization.

Project 8.1

Now let's create our first virtual machine.

You should have already installed VMWare Player during the pre-lab in the online Networking Basics Project Manual.

1. Download the latest Linux interaction of your choice, in this example Fedora 14 in ISO format. *(Note that .ISO is a file format used to create disk images).* ISO images may be directly loaded into VMWare Player to create a virtual appliance.
2. Click on the newly created VMWare Player Icon and open VMWare Player.
3. Choose the installer disk image file radial and browse to the location where you downloaded Fedora14.iso, then click Next.

   Choose Linux as your operating system and Fedora as the version. Click Next.
4. Accept the default name and location, but remember where you put it!
5. Leave the default Disk capacity and click Next.
6. Leave the default selections and click Finish.
7. Accept the default Removable hardware discovery. If asked to update and you have a current Internet connection, chose to update.

Congratulations! You now have a working virtual appliance running Fedora as a virtual machine on your host computer.

Note that you are running the operating system based on the ISO image. If you wish to have a more permanent installation, click on the "Install to Hard Drive Icon on the desktop."

8.7 IMPLEMENTING BASIC NETWORK SERVICES

Okay, you have the pieces and parts, you understand the basic network services available, but how do you put them together? How do you decide which NOS to use? What about client operating systems?

As networks continue to grow larger and more complex, network design and determining server placement can become almost as much an art as it is a science. A detailed look at network design issues is beyond the scope of this chapter, but while on the subject of NOS and network services, we should take the time to discuss a few fundamentals.

8.7.1 Deciding on the Basics

There's no better place to begin than the beginning. You've decided that you need a LAN. Maybe you already have a LAN, but you need a better one. Where do you go from here?

For our discussion, we're going to work from a few basic assumptions that apply to most networking environments:

- You have a (predominately) wired network.
- Your network is based on a physical star/logical bus topology.
- You have one or more WAPs to support wireless clients.
- You use Ethernet for network access and run TCP/IP as your network protocol.
- You need to access the Internet.
- The majority of your network clients run some version of Windows (though not necessarily the most recent).
- You have, or are considering using, one or more non-Windows computers.

Does this describe all LANs? Of course not, but it does cover the majority. Each LAN is uniquely matched to your organization's specific requirements.

During this discussion about implementing network servers, keep in mind that we are limiting our discussion to LANs only, including routed LANs made up of multiple subnetworks. WANs have additional considerations beyond those discussed here and require you to address issues that are beyond the scope of this chapter.

8.7.2 Thinking About Heterogeneous Networks

A *heterogeneous network* is one that has a mix of different hardware platforms, client types, and operating systems. In the early days of PC networking, heterogeneous network support could be a nightmare. Nonstandard equipment was common and different operating systems were not designed to work with each other.

Hardware and system software manufacturers have worked hard in recent years to try to reduce interoperability problems. Why? Primarily because it's good for business. Industry standards have been developed that define networking requirements and common network interfaces. Software manufacturers have integrated interoperability into their designs.

Keep in mind what is necessary for computers to communicate with each other. At the most basic level, requirements include:

- A physical connection to the network
- A common access method
- A common network protocol

The unprecedented growth of Ethernet and Wi-Fi networks covers the first two requirements. TCP/IP meets the third. However, those only give you a packet-level compatibility. It doesn't mean that a computer can understand the data inside the packet.

Data compatibility is a software issue. Sometimes, compatibility means services and service clients that are standardized across multiple platforms, like downloading files from an FTP server. Compatibility is provided across platforms by TCP/IP. Sometimes, it means having the appropriate client software, like the NetWare client so that you can access files on a NetWare file server or a SQL Server client that lets you access a Microsoft SQL Server database.

8.7.3 Thinking About Traffic Flow

Two of the biggest concerns about a network, and areas about which users are most likely to complain, are performance and reliability. People want the network to work, to be available when they need it, and get them what they want when they want it. One of the major issues impacting both of these is traffic flow.

Bandwidth is a particular issue for Ethernet networks; then again, available bandwidth is an issue in any networking environment. Bandwidth issues are more noticeable with Ethernet because you reach a threshold point where collisions become a critical concern and so much time is spent in trying to recover that the network grinds to a halt. Token Ring performance also suffers as the number of computers increases, but the change is more gradual given that a ring has a physical limit for the number of computers.

How do you keep collisions at a manageable level? You do it by creating collision zones, network segments where traffic is somewhat isolated to that segment and a limited number of devices are competing for time on the media. You can use routers, bridges, or switches to define collision zones. You can see a simple example of how this works in Figure 8-6, where we have a network that includes two routers and a bridge.

The bridge filters traffic by MAC address. The routers filter traffic by network address. With either, traffic local to the segment attached to the device remains on that segment and only traffic bound for a different segment is passed. Collisions impact each segment separately so their impact isn't passed through the device to other network segments.

Routers do provide additional traffic management over what bridges provide in one area. Bridges propagate broadcasts, packets addressed to all computers, to connected segments. Except for special cases, like DHCP traffic, routers block broadcasts, which helps minimize overall traffic volume.

Even though these devices help manage traffic, it comes with a cost. Bridge and router operations come with a certain amount of overhead. Depending on the device capacity and the amount of traffic it has to carry, a bridge or router can become a problem in itself. One way to avoid this problem is careful server placement.

Figure 8-6

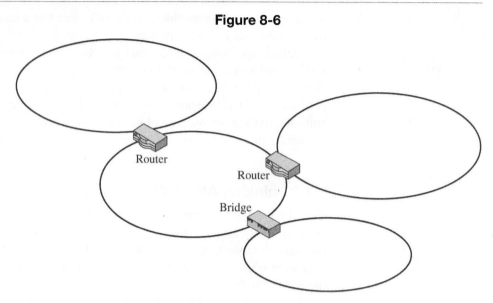

Sample routed/bridged network.

8.7.4 Thinking about Server Placement

One of the determining factors when placing servers in a routed (or bridged) network is how server placement is going to affect network traffic. The general rule is to place servers so that they are local to the devices that most often need access to them.

Placing File and Print Servers

Guidelines for placing file and print servers can also be used as good general guidelines for most types of servers. We'll look at file servers first. Consider the sample network in Figure 8-7. Accounting sits in one area in the office; sales, marketing, and operations in another; manufacturing and warehouse in a third; and then support and IT in a fourth. You've created subnetworks based on these physical divisions and put all of the file servers back physically with support and IT.

The problem with this design is that when any users (other than support and IT) need to access a server, the traffic has to cross at least one router. With accounting, it has to cross two routers, going through either operations or manufacturing. That traffic also increases the amount of traffic through those subnetworks and increases the likelihood that collisions could become a problem.

Figure 8-8 shows a more efficient network design. We've placed departmental file servers physically with the departments that need access them. By doing so, we're able to keep more of the traffic local to the network,

Figure 8-7

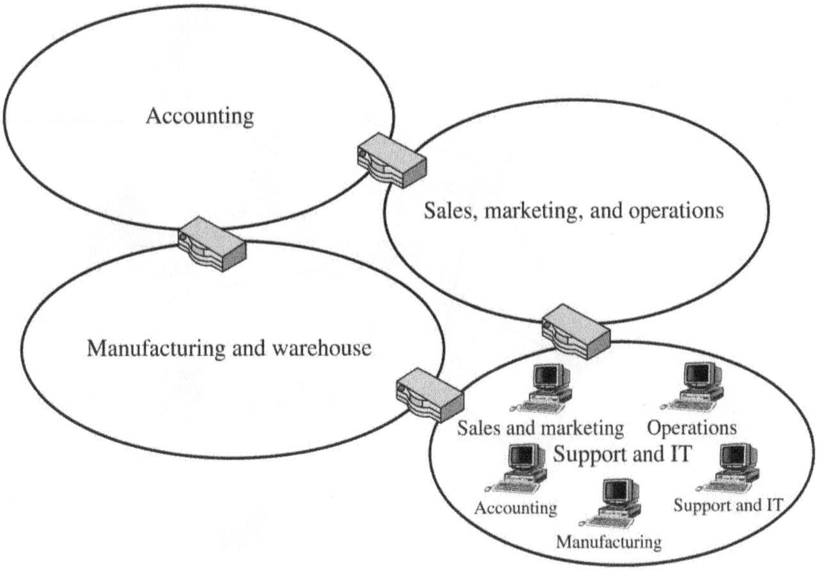

Network with centralized servers.

reducing the load on the routers and dropping the bandwidth use on the networks along the way.

Figure 8-9 shows the network from a logical design standpoint. Just because, for example, the accounting file server is physically part of the

Figure 8-8

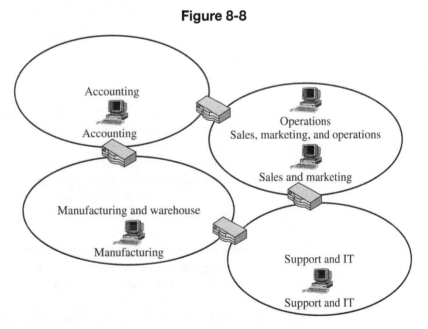

Network with distributed servers.

Figure 8-9

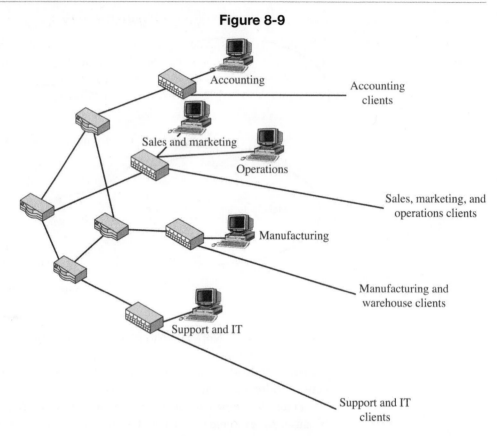

Physical network layout.

accounting subnetwork doesn't mean that it is physically located in that part of the building. What you are more likely to see is a situation like the one in Figure 8-9. Here, we have the file servers in a secure server room, indicated by the dashed line. The network hubs are also physically located the same room. Servers are connected to the appropriate hubs, with lines running out to the network clients.

Network routers are also located in the same secure server room, making wiring your network easier. It also simplifies things should you want to reconfigure your network in the future.

The concerns are similar with print servers as with file servers, placing them local to the users who need to access them. Print jobs can be very large, especially those that include complex graphics.

Along with server placement, you have to consider the placement of network-connected printers that use a separate printer server (some act as their own print server). With that configuration, you have the traffic from the client to the print server as it queues the print job, then across the network from the print server to the printer when it actually prints.

Placing Domain Controllers/Network Servers

NOS manufacturers generally provide guidelines for how many network servers you need and how they should be placed in common network scenarios. Network servers handle critical tasks such as user authentication and authorization control. Because of these critical tasks, NOS manufacturers typically recommend that any network, no matter how small, have two network servers. Employing two network servers provides fault tolerance should one of the servers fail.

In a routed network, manufacturers typically recommend that you place at least one network server, Active Directory domain controller for example, in each subnetwork. That keeps traffic associated with user login local. Login generates a significant amount of traffic for most NOSs and when you consider that most users typically log in about the same time each morning, the traffic that would generate through the routers could be significant. If the local server gets overwhelmed, a server on a different subnetwork could handle the login requests, but this is exception to the rule.

This configuration provides fault tolerance, though a failed server will result in an increase in traffic between subnetworks. It also helps ensure that user will be able to login even if a router is temporarily out of service. Without a local network server, a failed router could prevent users on that network segment from logging in. They might still be able to log in locally to their computers, but they wouldn't have access to network resources, including those on the local network, because no server would be available to authenticate the access requests.

Placing Support Servers (DHCP, DNS, WINS, etc.)

The number and placement of support servers like DHCP servers, name-resolution servers, and the like depends on factors relating to the number of clients on each subnetwork, client configurations, and security concerns. DHCP servers and DNS servers are a fact of life on most networks. With WINS servers, it depends on whether or not you have NetBIOS requirements.

With both DHCP servers and name resolution servers, you will typically want to have at least two to provide fault tolerance. A DHCP server can be configured with multiple address scopes and thereby support multiple subnetworks. The routers will need to be configured to support **BootP forwarding** to ensure they pass DHCP packets.

BootP forwarding
A router configuration option that enables routers to pass DHCP broadcasts.

As long as the name resolution requirements aren't excessive, the network might be able to get by with one DNS and one WINS server. One important point is that on networks that connect to the Internet, you want to isolate your DHCP and internal DNS servers from Internet hosts. The more information you expose about your network, the more you invite a potentially successful attack.

Placing Other Specialty Servers

Specialty servers include shared servers such as e-mail servers and application servers such as database servers. Because of the expenses involved, most small-to-medium networks make do with one of each of these servers types. On very large LANs, or when supporting a broad base of resource-intensive applications, you may need multiple servers, though not necessarily on different network segments. Take database servers for example. Some networks will have two database servers that host duplicate databases so that, should one of the servers fail, the other one can take over automatically without users ever realizing that a problem occurred.

That said, this group is the hardest for which to apply any general guidelines. Application servers, their capabilities, and their deployment requirements vary widely by the very natures. When provided, you should use any manufacturer guidelines when determining best placement.

IN THE REAL WORLD

Heterogeneous Application Compatibility

You've configured your Linux server to support Windows clients. Does this guarantee full file compatibility? Not necessarily. We've focused on network compatibility issues so far, but you also have to worry about file formats supported on the local computer.

Let's take a closer look at your Linux server. You deployed it for use as an internal web server to handle intra-office communication needs. The computer has a large hard disk, so you install and configure Samba so you can share directories to the network and use the Linux server as an additional file server. So far, so good.

You deploy the Linux server at your desk. You plan to use it as an additional network client, but you also want have it handy in case there are any problems. A user uploads a Microsoft Word file to the server that contains information you need. Will you be able to read the file?

The correct answer is a strong "it depends." Applications use their own, typically proprietary, internal file formats. That way, in order to read or modify the file, you need the same application or one that supports that file format. In the case of Linux, if you install the right distribution, you're in luck. One of the software packages often included with Linux distributions is an office productivity package (word processor, spreadsheet, etc.) that supports the same file formats as Microsoft Office Suite applications. If you have it installed on your computer, you can probably read the file.

8.7.5 Documenting Your Success

Let's be optimistic that you are successful in placing your network servers. What then? You need to recognize that networks are not static environments. The number, types, and placement of users changes with time. Network and client operating systems capabilities and requirements change as manufacturers release new versions. Business support needs evolve over time. Network server placement is not a situation where you can just consider the job done and not worry about it any more.

Baseline
Values collected for comparison against later performance statistics.

After you have your network set up like you want it, you should collect network performance statistics. You should save information such as typical and peak bandwidth usage, including when peaks occur during the day. Should you suspect network problems in the future, these **baseline** statistics give you something against which you can compare current network conditions. Relocating some of your servers or even deploying additional servers may be necessary. However, after you make any major changes to the network, you need to collect and save another set of baseline statistics.

SELF-CHECK

1. What is the general rule for server placement in a routed LAN?
2. How do bridges and routers filter traffic?

Project 8.2

In this project, you will review some key points about basic services and look at some options for setting up servers to support various basic services.

Complete **Project 8.3 Part A: Understanding Basic Services** in the online Networking Basics Project Manual to understand the services you will commonly find on most LANs.

SUMMARY

Section 8.1
- The primary functionality of a LAN is to enable shared services.
- Basic network services include file and print services, server applications, and network support services.

Section 8.2
- Windows Server 2008 is the latest Microsoft Network Operating System.
- Windows Server Operating System has a similar look and feel to Windows desktop operating system.

Section 8.3

- Macintosh interface is considered to be the easiest to use of all graphical user interfaces.
- Apple's network operating system is called Mac OS X Server.

Section 8.4

- Unix is the oldest network operating system.
- All Linux distributions are open source.

Section 8.5

- Novell NetWare was one of the first PC networking products on the market.
- Open Enterprise System is a Linux-based operating system that runs NetWare services.

Section 8.6

- Virtualization uses software to simulate the existence of hardware.
- Virtual machines are slower than physical machines, but far less costly.

Section 8.7

- Heterogeneous networks use a mix of hardware platforms, client types, and operating systems.
- Documenting your network will make it easier to maintain and expand the network over time.

ASSESS YOUR UNDERSTANDING

UNDERSTAND: WHAT HAVE YOU LEARNED?

 Go to **www.wiley.com/go/ciccarelli/networkingbasics2e** to evaluate your knowledge of network servers and services fundamentals.
Measure your learning by comparing pre-test and post-test results.

SUMMARY QUESTIONS

1. Tickets are used with which authentication method?

    (a) Kerberos

    (b) LDAP

    (c) NTLM

    (d) DHCP

2. Which of the following runs as a dedicated server only?

    (a) UNIX

    (b) Windows 2000 Server

    (c) Windows Server 2003

    (d) NetWare 6.5

3. The core components of the UNIX operating system are referred to as what?

    (a) Samba

    (b) Kernel

    (c) Directory

    (d) Source

4. Which of the following is an example of an application that could be deployed as a server application?

    (a) A word processor

    (b) A spreadsheet

    (c) A relational database management system

    (d) A media player

5. With which operating system version did the Macintosh OS move to a UNIX kernel base?

    (a) System 6

    (b) System 7

    (c) Mac OS 8

    (d) Mac OS X

6. Macs that are built on an Intel processor architecture can run both Mac OS and Windows. True or false?

7. Most application servers should be configured as the only application running on a server. True or false?

8. Which Windows server application gives Windows clients access to NetWare 4 server resources?

    (a) SFU
    (b) GSNW
    (c) CSNW
    (d) FPNW

9. The following is an example of what?

    OPERATIONS.BUSICORP

    (a) A typeless context
    (b) A common object name
    (c) A typefull context
    (d) A typefull distinguished name

10. Which statement is true of Linux, but not UNIX?

    (a) It supports both command line and GUI interfaces.
    (b) It is distributed under an open-source license.
    (c) It can use POSIX compliant applications.
    (d) It supports LDAP and Kerberos for authentication.

11. Which of the following lets a Mac OS X server provide shared file resources to Windows clients?

    (a) NFS
    (b) SFU
    (c) Samba
    (d) LDAP

12. Which server type would you most likely allow direct access to the Internet?

    (a) DHCP server
    (b) WINS server
    (c) Active Directory domain controller
    (d) Web server

APPLY: WHAT WOULD YOU DO?

1. You are updating a LAN and need to identify NOS requirements. The network currently has three Novell NetWare 3.2 servers. You have Windows clients that access the NetWare servers through a Windows 2000 Server running GSNW. You plan to replace the NetWare servers with new servers, eventually removing the NetWare servers from the network.

(a) What type of authentication is used between the Windows 2000 Server and the NetWare servers?

(b) What network-centric directory structure, if any, is currently being used?

(c) If you replace the NetWare servers with NetWare 6.5 servers, how would this impact the configuration for client access? Explain your answer.

2. You have a Windows Server 2008 Active Directory network. You are planning to make some changes to the network and the services it offers. The network is currently configured as a single LAN with two domain controllers, one DHCP server, three files servers, and a Microsoft SQL Server database server. You also have two web servers running Windows 2003 Server on a perimeter network that is separated from the main network by a Linux server configured as a router and firewall. (See Figure 8-10). Most network clients are running Windows XP Professional, but some are running Mac OS X. You plan to deploy a Mac OS X server that will be used to store digital video development projects and commercial artwork. Collisions are becoming a problem and you plan to divide the LAN into two subnetworks connected by a router. You are configuring a Linux computer to act as the router for the networks.

(a) What can you do to give PC users access to files on the Mac OS X server?

(b) What network protocol changes will you have to make to current network systems?

(c) After you subdivide the network, how many additional domain controllers will you be required to deploy, if any?

(d) Where should you place the domain controllers?

(e) How will this impact traffic through the router?

(f) What is the minimum number of DHCP servers needed in the new configuration?

(g) How will DHCP server configurations change after you deploy the router, assuming there are DHCP clients on both subnetworks?

(h) What special router configuration will be needed?

(i) The Linux server includes the software needed to configure it as an IP router. What additional special software would be required to support Windows and Mac OS X clients?

(j) What configuration changes would be needed on the clients?

(k) File sizes on the Mac OS X server will be very large. You want to minimize their impact on traffic through the router. How should you do this?

(l) What effect would the configuration changes have on the web servers?

Figure 8-10

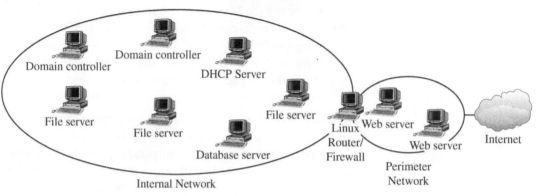

A sample network.

BE A NETWORK DESIGNER

You are designing a routed LAN that will have four subnetworks. The network will be configured as a Windows Active Directory domain. Most clients will receive their IP configuration information from DHCP servers. Clients will include a mix of computers running Windows XP, Windows 95, Mac OS X, and various Linux distributions.

One of your design goals is to keep the traffic through the routers to a minimum. Also, the network should be configured so that the clients will be able to reach any subnetwork, even if one of the routers fails. Your current plans do not include any wireless client support requirements. You are expected to minimize unnecessary costs.

Because of file and security requirements, you estimate that you will need at least three file servers. You plan to configure Windows XP clients as print servers as needed. You will have an internal web server and MySQL database server, both running on Linux computers.

1. Describe how you will configure network protocols up through the Network layer of the OSI model? Justify your choices.

2. In general, how will you determine the best placement for the file servers?

3. Describe how you will configure and deploy domain controllers and support for automatic IP address configuration, keeping the design requirements in mind.

4. The MySQL database server's primary role is providing content for the internal web server. How will you determine the best place to deploy these servers?

5. Your purchasing department got a great deal on 20 low-end desktop computers. The computers will come without an operating system.

The users who wll get these computers need basic office productivity applications and access to the internal web server. What is the least expensive way to meet these requirements?

6. Describe your network including router placement and domain controller placement. Explain how the design meets configuration requirements.

KEY TERMS

Apache Web Server

AppleShare

AppleTalk

AppleTalk Filing Protocol (AFP)

Baseline

BootP forwarding

Caching

Distribution

Dual boot

Edition

Extensible Markup Language (XML)

Firewall

GNU public license

Group Policy Object (GPOs)

Happy macked

Host-based firewall

Java Virtual Machine (JVM)

Kerberos

Keychain

Lightweight Directory Access Protocol (LDAP)

LPD/LPR

Multitasking

Open Directory

Open source license

Patch

Portable Document Format (PDF)

POSIX

Print job

Print queue

Samba

Shallow learning curve

Sharing

Shell

TrueType fonts

Virtual Machine (VM)

Web services

Windows for Workgroups (WFW)

Windows Server Update Service (WSUS)

X Windows System

CHAPTER

9

ENTERPRISE NETWORKING SERVICES

What Do You Already Know?

- How do companies connect their networks to the Internet?
- What is building-block network design?
- When do you choose equipment for a network design?

To assess your knowledge of enterprise network services and design go to **www.wiley.com/go/ciccarelli/networkingbasics2e.**

What You Will Find Out	What You Will Be Able To Do
9.1 Internet architecture.	Explain the Internet's hierarchical architecture.
9.2 Internet technologies.	Identify Internet technologies commonly found on PC networks.
9.3 Need analysis.	Identify critical tasks performed during needs analysis.
9.4 Technical design.	Explain the purpose and expected result of technical design.
9.5 Cost assessment.	Compare and contrast traditional and building-block network design processes.
9.6 Network deployment.	Compare options for implementing a network design.

INTRODUCTION

The larger and more complex your network, the more important it becomes that you spend the necessary time and effort in developing a network design before implementing the network. With smaller LANs, you can sometimes get away with just letting the network grow and evolve as your requirements change. With a large enterprise, you need to carefully consider all aspects of the network.

This chapter looks at wide area network (WAN) servers and services, as well as other WAN components, from the context of network design. A thorough understanding of the network design process will help you understand how to address issues such as service requirements and server placement.

The chapter starts with a discussion of the largest WAN in current use, the Internet.

This discussion includes a look at the Internet's hierarchical architecture and Internet technologies commonly found on PC networks. From there, the discussion moves on to the design process, including expected deliverables at the end of each phase. The chapter ends by talking a little about network implementation issues.

In general, any discussions about local area network (LAN) technologies and requirements, for the purpose of this chapter, include the backbone network (BN), if any. Also, any discussions of metropolitan area network (MAN) connectivity are lumped together with WAN connectivity. For the purposes of this chapter, the two are effectively the same.

9.1 LOOKING TO THE INTERNET

Why start a discussion about enterprise wide area networking with a look at the Internet? The Internet is the world's largest, most complex WAN. Any WAN you design and deploy will have some features in common with the Internet. Also, almost any WAN you might see includes Internet technologies.

The Internet is a network of networks—a set of separate and distinct networks operated by various agencies and organizations. The Internet exists only to the extent that these thousands of separate networks agree to use Internet protocols and to exchange data packets with one another.

National ISP
One of the ISPs that operates at the topmost level of the Internet and is responsible for transferring messages inside and between countries.

Network access points (NAPs)
A top-level Internet data exchange point maintained and operated by commercial communication enterprise or common carrier.

9.1.1 Introducing Internet Architecture

Why do you care about the Internet's architecture, or about its capacity? In the last few years, the Internet has rapidly replaced traditional WAN infrastructure designs, becoming the backbone of choice. If you're using, or even considering, the Internet as your corporate backbone, you need to know how it works.

The Internet is hierarchical in structure. At the top are the very large national Internet service providers (ISPs), such as AT&T and Sprint, which are

Figure 9-1

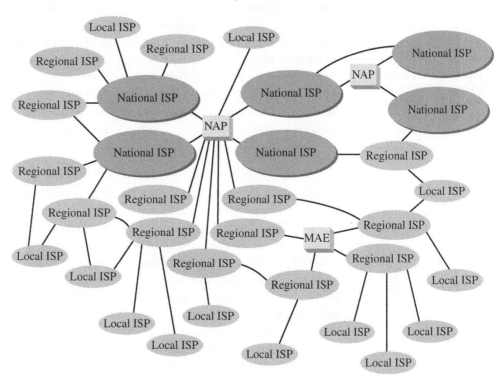

Internet hierarchy.

National Science Foundation (NSF)
The organization originally responsible for management of Internet.

Regional ISP
A mid level ISP that operates between national and local ISPs and provides services directly to some larger companies.

Local ISP
An ISP who sells Internet access to individuals.

Metropolitan Area Exchange (MAE)
Smaller NAPs created to link regional ISPs whose networks come together in major cities.

responsible for large Internet networks. These **national ISPs** connect together and exchange data at **network access points (NAPs)**, as shown in Figure 9-1.

In the early 1990s, when the Internet was still primarily run by the **National Science Foundation (NSF)**, the NSF established four main NAPs in the United States to connect the major national ISPs. This number has since grown to about a dozen NAPs in the United States with many more spread around the world. When the NSF stopped funding the Internet, the companies running these NAPs began charging the national ISPs for connections, so today the NAPs in the United States are all commercial enterprises run by various common carriers such as AT&T and Sprint.

National ISPs provide services for their customers and to **regional ISPs** such as BellSouth and EarthLink. These regional ISPs rely on the national ISPs to transmit their messages to national ISPs in other countries. Regional ISPs provide services to their customers and to **local ISPs,** who sell Internet access to individuals. As the number of ISPs grew, a new form of NAP called a **Metropolitan Area Exchange (MAE)** emerged. MAEs are smaller versions of NAPs and typically link a set of regional ISPs whose networks come together in major cities. Today there are about 50 MAEs in the United States.

In general, ISPs at the same level do not charge one another for transferring messages they exchange across a NAP or MAE. That is, a national ISP does not charge another national ISP to transmit its messages, and a regional ISP does not charge another regional ISP. This is called **peering,** which makes the Internet work and has led to the belief that the Internet is free, which is true to some extent. However, higher-level ISPs normally charge lower-level ISPs to transmit their data and local ISPs charge individuals for access. Also, most NAPs now charge national ISPs for access.

Peering
A term that refers to free message and data exchange between ISPs at the same hierarchical level.

9.1.2 Understanding Today's Internet

Several years ago, there was great concern that the Internet would reach capacity. The growth of traffic on the Internet was increasing significantly faster than the construction of new Internet circuits. Capacity wasn't reached, of course, due in part because companies could make money by building new circuits and charging for their use. Today, a large number of fiber-optic circuits have been built but not yet been turned on, held in reserve until needed to support further Internet expansion. Technological advances have also helped, such as new optical technologies that mean 10–20 times more data can be transmitted through fiber-optic cable than before. Many countries, companies, and universities are now building the **Next Generation Internet** using even newer, experimental, very high-speed technologies.

Next Generation Internet
A new higher speed Internet currently under development.

Today, the backbone circuits of the major U.S. national ISPs operate at ATM OC-48, or 4 gigabits per second (4 Gbps), and OC-192 (10 Gbps). A few are experimenting with OC-768 (80 Gbps) and OC-3072 (160 Gbps). (See Table 9-1.) This expansion is important because annual Internet traffic in the U.S. will reach 1,000 exabytes, or one zettabyte, which is one million million billion bytes of data by 2015. A zettabyte is roughly equivalent to 50 million Libraries of Congress.

As traffic increases, ISPs can add more and faster circuits relatively easily, but where these circuits come together at NAPs and MAEs, bottlenecks are becoming more common. Network vendors such as Cisco and Juniper are making larger and larger switches capable of handling these high-capacity circuits, but it is a daunting task. When circuit capacities increase by 100 percent, switch manufacturers also must increase their capacities by 100 percent.

9.1.3 Connecting WANs Through the Internet

At the most basic level, companies connect their networks to the Internet the same way you do, through an ISP. Larger companies might connect through a regional or even national ISP so that they can connect directly into a high-speed backbone circuit, but some larger local ISPs can also

Table 9-1: Connection Type-Speeds

Type	Cabling	Use(s)	Bit Speed	Byte Speed
ATM OC-3	Fiber optic	WAN	155.520 Mbps	19.440 MB/s
FDDI	Fiber optic	LAN	155.000 Mbps	19.375 MB/s
T4/DS4	RJ-45/Fiber optic	LAN/ WAN	274.176 Mbps	34.272 MB/s
ATM OC-12	Fiber optic	WAN	622.080 Mbps	77.760 MB/s
1000-Base SX (Gigabit)	RJ-45/Fiber optic	LAN/ WAN	1000.000 Mbps	125.000 MB/s
HDTV	N/A	N/A	1200.000 Mbps	150.000 MB/s
ATM OC-48	Fiber optic	WAN	2488.320 Mbps	311.040 MB/s
ATM OC-192	Fiber optic	WAN	9953.280 Mbps	1244.160 MB/s
Fast Gigabit	RJ-45/Fiber optic	LAN/ WAN	10000.000 Mbps	1250.000 MB/s
ATM OC-256	Fiber optic	WAN	13271.040 Mbps	1658.880 MB/s
ATM OC-48 WDM	Fiber optic	WAN	39813.120 Mbps	4976.640 MB/s
ATM OC-768	Fiber optic	WAN	39813.120 Mbps	4976.640 MB/s
ATM OC-3072	Fiber optic	WAN	159252.480 Mbps	19906.56 MB/s

Points of presence (POP)
The place at which an ISP provides services to its customers (i.e., the customer's connection to the ISP).

FOR EXAMPLE
Figure 9-2 shows a POP using a collapsed backbone network (BN) with a layer-2 switch.

provide this service. For small to medium-sized companies, they are probably using the same local ISPs that you use.

These multiple connections can be made because each ISP has one or more **points of presence (POP)**. A POP is simply the place at which the ISP provides services to its customers. To connect into the Internet, a customer must establish a circuit from his or her location (home or business) into the ISP POP. For individuals, the connection is through a remote access server (RAS), which checks the user ID and password to make sure the caller is a valid customer. Once logged in, the user can begin sending TCP/IP packets from his or her computer to the POP.

So, how do businesses connect? In the early days of using the Internet as a backbone, companies' options were somewhat limited and

Figure 9-2

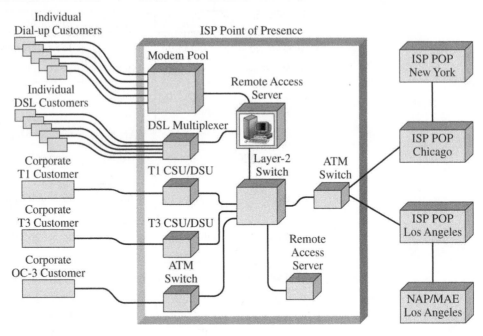

ISP points of presence.

often prohibitively expensive. One of the more common options was leasing T1 or T3 circuits into the ISP. This limitation has changed as communication technologies have improved and additional options have come available. Some of the most commonly used connection options now include:

- Digital subscriber line (DSL)
- Cable modem
- Fixed wireless

If some of these technologies sound familiar, they should. They're the same technologies used to provide high-speed home Internet access. Keep in mind that many companies do continue to use traditional WAN link technologies, such as point-to-point T1, ATM, or X.25 circuits, but using the Internet as a backbone is, at least for now, the preferred technology.

Asymmetric DSL (ADSL)

The most common type of DSL in use. ADSL includes a voice circuit and upstream and downstream circuits that operate at different speeds.

DSL

The biggest drawback with respect to DSL services is that they are not available in all locations and, even where available, connection bandwidth varies. In general, DSL services have advanced more quickly in Canada, Europe, Australia, and Asia than in the United States, owing to their newer telephone networks from the end offices to the customer.

The most common type of DSL in use today is **asymmetric DSL (ADSL)**. ADSL creates three separate channels over one **local loop circuit,** the connection between the customer and the telephone company's switching center. One channel is the traditional voice telephone circuit. A second channel is a relatively high-speed simplex data channel **downstream** from the carrier's end office to the customer. The third channel is a slightly slower duplex data channel primarily used for **upstream** from the customer to the carrier's end office. ADSL is called asymmetric because its two data channels have different speeds.

The size of the two digital channels depends on the distance from the **customer premises equipment (CPE),** the term used to refer to the customer's physical geographic location, to the end office. The shorter the distance, the higher the speed, because with a shorter distance, the circuit suffers less attenuation and higher-frequency signals can be used, providing a greater bandwidth. Table 9-2 lists the common types of ADSL.

A second common type of DSL is **very-high-data-rate digital subscriber line (VDSL)**. VDSL is an asymmetric DSL service designed for use over very short local loops of at most 4,500 feet, with 1,000 feet being more typical. It also provides three channels: the normal analog voice channel, an upstream digital channel, and a downstream digital channel. Table 9-3 lists the types of VDSL many industry experts anticipate will become common.

One problem is that VDSL has not yet been standardized, and five separate standards groups are working on different standards. Therefore, the exact data speeds and channels are likely to change as manufacturers, telephone companies, and the industry in general gain more experience and as the standards groups attempt to merge competing standards. Several companies are also developing symmetric versions of VDSL in which upstream and downstream channels have the same capacity.

Logical loop circuit
The connection between a carrier's central office and a customer.

Downstream
A circuit that carries traffic from a carrier or ISP to a customer.

Upstream
A circuit that carries traffic from a customer to a carrier or an ISP.

Customer premises equipment (CPE)
Communication equipment installed at the customer's location.

Very-high-data-rate digital subscriber line (VDSL)
Asymmetrical DSL currently under development and designed to carry high-speed traffic over shorter distances than standard ADSL.

Table 9-2: ADSL Bandwidths

Type	Maximum Length of Local Loop	Maximum Downstream Rate	Maximum Upstream Rate
ADSL T1 (G.Lite)	18,000 feet	1.5 Mbps	384 Kbps
ADSL E1*	16,000 feet	2.0 Mbps	384 Kbps
ADSL T2	12,000 feet	6.0 Mbps	640 Kbps
SDSL	18,000 feet	1.5 Mbps	1.5 Mbps

*E1 is the European standard services similar to T1 services in North America.

Table 9-3: VDSL Types

Type	Maximum Length of Local Loop	Maximum Down-stream Rate	Maximum Upstream Rate
1/4 OC-1	4,500 feet	13 Mbps	1.6 Mbps
1/2 OC-1	4,000 feet	26 Mbps	2.3 Mbps
OC-1	4,000 feet	52 Mbps	16 Mbps

Data Over Cable Service Interface Specification (DOCSIS)
Current dominant standard for cable modem digital communication services.

Hybrid fiber coax (HFC)
A cable network that uses both fiber-optic and wired coaxial cable.

Shared multipoint circuits
A circuit design in which several customers connect to the same circuit to share the available bandwidth.

Cable Modem

One alternative to DSL is the cable modem, a digital service offered by cable television companies. Several standards are competing, but the **Data Over Cable Service Interface Specification (DOCSIS)** standard is the dominant one. DOCSIS is not a formal standard but is the one used by most vendors of **hybrid fiber coax (HFC)** networks (i.e., cable networks that use both fiber-optic and coaxial cable). As with DSL, these technologies are changing rapidly.

Cable modem architecture is very similar to DSL—with one very important difference. DSL is a point-to-point technology whereas cable modems use **shared multipoint circuits,** as shown in Figure 9-3. With cable

Figure 9-3

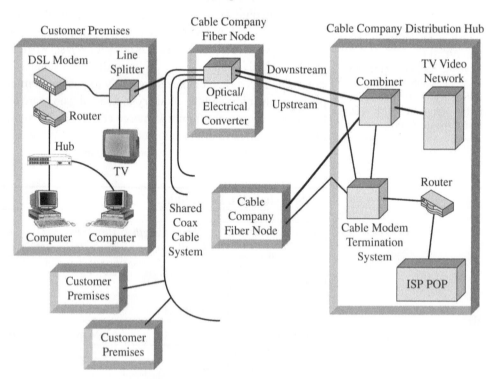

Multipoint circuits connections. Cable modem architecture. ISP = Internet service provider; POP = point of presence.

modems, each user must compete with other users for the available capacity. Furthermore, because the cable circuit is a multipoint circuit, all messages on the circuit go to all computers on the circuit. All the downstream Internet traffic for your neighborhood to all the cable modems in your neighborhood is encrypted using the DES encryption algorithm designed by the U.S. government. In addition to being encrypted, data sent from your computer to the Internet is never sent to other cable modems in your neighborhood. When using a cable modem, the cable company makes the connection to the ISP POP for you.

A few widely used standards are available in the cable modem industry. Unlike the telephone system, each cable TV company was able to build very different HFC cable plants because each cable company was a separate entity with no need to connect to other cable TV networks. In theory, cable modems can provide downstream speeds of 27 to 55 Mbps and upstream speeds of 2 to 10 Mbps, depending on the exact nature and quality of the

TIPS FROM THE PROFESSIONALS

Comparing DSL and Cable Service

In the area of download speeds, cable speeds are higher than DSL. Many cable companies are upgrading their network with fiber optics, so in some areas they are far superior to DSL.

- Basic DSL Internet Speeds: 768 Kbps to 1.5 Mbps
- High-End DSL Internet Speeds: 3 Mbps to 7 Mbps
- Basic Cable Internet Speeds: 4 Mbps to 6 Mbps
- High-End Cable Internet Speeds: 12 Mbps to 30 Mbps and higher

Security is always a concern, so the fact that DSL connection is never shared between your location and the nearest DSL hub or central office is an advantage for DSL. The bandwidth to your cable ISP is shared by you and all the other Internet users in your area using the same service, so if your area has a lot of users, your service can be negatively impacted.

An additional concern with having a shared Internet connection is that they are by nature less secure than having a dedicated connection. Shared mediums are more susceptible to eavesdropping, denial of service attacks, and service theft. However, cable companies use an encryption that does compensate for this susceptibility somewhat.

HFC cable plant. In practice, the speeds offered vary widely depending on the cable provider and factors such as when the current infrastructure was deployed. Because of these factors, service levels can even vary by neighborhood. As minimum expected rates, typical downstream speeds range between 1.5 and 2 Mbps and typical upstream speeds range between 200 Kbps and 2 Mbps, with higher rates available in most urban areas or where the infrastructure has been recently upgraded.

Fixed wireless
Another term for wireless DSL.

Wireless DSL
A wireless communication method that requires line of sight communication between communication transmitters.

Fixed Wireless

The most popular type of **fixed wireless** is **wireless DSL,** which requires a line of sight between the communicating transmitters. For this reason, it has limited application because it requires tall buildings or towers to be effective. The most common use today is to provide Internet access to multi-tenant buildings such as remote office buildings, apartment buildings, and hotels. Transmitters are used to connect the building to the ISP, and DSL is used inside the building to connect to the wireless transceiver, shown in Figure 9-4.

Figure 9-4

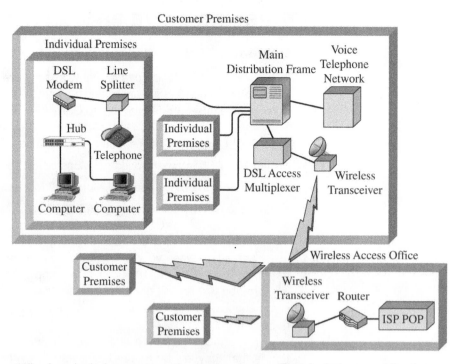

Wired and wireless connection technologies. Fixed wireless architecture.
DSL = digital subscriber line; ISP = Internet service provider; POP = Point of Presence.

Fixed wireless comes in both point-to-point and multipoint versions. The **point-to-point version** is designed to connect only two locations and is often used as a backbone between buildings owned by the same organization. The **multipoint version** is sometimes called point-to-multipoint because only one central receiver and all other locations communicate with it. The multipoint version is designed as an alternative to DSL and cable modems and is intended for use by an ISP supporting a small number of customers.

Like cable modems, the circuit is a shared circuit, so users must compete for the shared capacity, but most installations are limited to a few dozen users. Data transmissions for both versions generally range from 1.5 to 11 Mbps, depending on the vendor.

Other fixed wireless technologies such as satellite are also available. Most satellite technologies use the satellite for downstream and upstream transmissions, but a small number use traditional dial-up modems for upstream transmissions.

9.1.4 Including Internet Technologies in an Enterprise Network

The relationship between enterprise networks and the Internet doesn't end with connectivity issues. Internet technologies have a firm place on most networks, from the smallest LAN to the largest enterprise. The reason is simple. The protocol designed for the Internet, TCP/IP, is also the de facto standard for PC networking. Internet services built in the TCP/IP protocol suite are also available for use on your network.

Many of these services are occurring in the background. You might not even realize that they are there. For example, any time one computer communicates with another it needs to know its MAC address, which is hard-coded on the network adapter. TCP/IP uses **Address Resolution Protocol (ARP)** to find a computer's MAC address when its IP address is known. The flip side is also supported. **Reverse Address Resolution Protocol (RARP)** finds the IP address when the MAC address is known.

Some services are support services where inclusion might be considered to be optional, but only in the broadest definition of the term. Do you want to support automatic IP address assignments to network clients? You're going to need one or more DHCP servers (or other devices that provide IP address information based on DHCP services). Are you using domain names to name your clients (like mycomp.busicorp.com)? You are if you have a directory-based network like Microsoft's Active Directory, which means that you probably want to include DNS servers for name resolution.

Point-to-point version
A wireless DSL configuration used to directly connect two locations to each other.

Multipoint version
A wireless DSL configuration that is designed to enable ISP to support wireless customer connection as an alternative to DSL or cable modem connections. Also known as point to multipoint version.

Address Resolution Protocol (ARP)
A TCP/IP protocol that provides a device's MAC address based on its IP address.

Reverse Address Resolution Protocol (RARP)
A TCP/IP protocol that returns an IP address based on the device's known MAC address.

IN THE REAL WORLD

Private Web Sites

Probably as many different uses of private websites exist as companies deploying them on their networks. In many ways, websites are limited only by the designers' imaginations.

Probably the most common use of internal websites is as an informational tool. Any kind of information that is of general interest to employees, such as company news, can be posted to the website, making it immediately available to employees. Some companies have found this way cuts down the seemingly endless stream of company memos. The content presented to the employee can be tailored to individuals or by other means, such as by department, so that people only see what they need to see.

Some companies have set up websites as reference libraries. Consider a situation where your company provides its own customer support on its products. As a general rule, the more information a support person has available, the better able he or she is able to do his or her job. That means more efficiency, less time spent on each customer call, and, in many cases, a higher level of customer satisfaction.

Another way that websites are being used to improve communication while cutting down on paperwork is to have employees fill out forms online instead of on paper. For example, some companies require weekly timesheets. When employees fill them out on paper, not only does the employee enter the information, someone else probably needs to copy the same information into a database somewhere. By using a standard form that the employee can call up from the corporate website, the employee can fill out the information online and enter it directly into the tracking database without involving another set of hands.

World Wide Web
A term that refers to the collection of web servers on the Internet.

What about technologies that are truly optional? For most people, the Internet means one thing—the **World Wide Web,** the vast collection of Web servers strung around the world that provide access to nearly every type of information and service you can imagine. Many companies have brought that technology down to the local scale, setting up websites on their private intranets and communication tools. Other technologies are also finding their place on private networks, like streaming media, providing access to things like company informational meetings from employees' desktops.

SELF-CHECK

1. Describe the hierarchical structure of Internet ISPs starting at the highest level.

2. Compare the connection technologies used by ADSL and cable modems.

Apply Your Knowledge What is the speed of your Internet connection? A number of online services will test your connection speed for free. Try Speedtest (www.speedtest.net) and see what your download and upload speeds are.

9.2 CREATING A WIDE AREA NETWORK (WAN)

A WAN is a set of interconnected LANs. All of the factors that you must consider in LAN design must also be considered in WAN design. However, with an enterprise WAN, you must also consider device placement and traffic flows across wide area links.

A building's architect must accept that a building is no more stable or secure than its foundation. The same is true of a WAN, where the foundation is the individual LANs. The better designed and more reliable your LANs, the more reliable your WAN. Of course, the best designed LANs can't compensate for poorly selected links, inefficient bandwidth use, or inappropriate server placement.

9.2.1 Identifying Your Goals

First, what is it you want to do? At one level, the answer to this question is fairly easy—you want an efficient, reliable network. What does that mean? That means that the network and necessary network resources are available to the users. It also means that sufficient bandwidth is provided to ensure efficient access to those resources.

When designing a network, you should use well-defined design processes to identify your network goals. Using well-defined design processes provides you with a framework for identifying network needs and developing your network design—whether you are designing a new network or upgrading an existing network.

Traditional network design process
A network design process based on lengthy detailed analysis that often requires up to two years to complete a design.

9.2.2 Using the Traditional Design Process

The **traditional network design process** follows a very structured systems analysis and design process similar to that used to build application systems.

1. The network analyst meets with users to identify user needs and the application systems planned for the network.

2. The analyst develops a precise estimate of the amount of data that each user will send and receive, and uses this to estimate the total amount of traffic on each part of the network.

3. The analyst checks that the circuits can support this traffic. He or she designs it with a modest increase in traffic. The analyst obtains cost estimates from vendors.

4. One or two years later, the network is ready to be built and implemented.

Although expensive and time consuming, this traditional process works well for static or slowly evolving networks. In the real world, design and deployment has to occur on a faster scale because of the rate at which network technologies and user expectations change. Traffic has also become a more complicated issue. Not only do you need to consider traffic requirements, but also the rate of growth of these requirements. Flexibility, being able to rapidly scale your network to meet changing needs, is critical. This rapid rate of deployment and change is sometimes referred to as operating on **Internet time.**

9.2.3 Using the Building-Block Design Process

Many organizations now use a simpler approach to network design called the **building-block process.** The key concept is that networks that use a few standard components throughout the network are cheaper in the long run than networks that use a variety of different components on different parts of the network.

Rather than attempting to accurately predict user traffic on the network and build networks to meet those demands, the building-block process instead starts with a few standard components and uses them over and over again. The goal is simplicity of design. This strategy is sometimes called **narrow and deep** because a very narrow range of technologies and devices is used over and over again (very deeply throughout the organization). You end up with, in theory, a simpler design process and a more easily managed network built with a smaller range of components.

The basic design process involves three steps, shown in Figure 9-5, that are performed repeatedly. This process begins with **needs analysis,** during which the designer attempts to understand the fundamental current and future network needs of the various users, departments, and applications. This guess is likely to be educated at best. Users and applications are classified as typical or high volume. Technology needs, but not specific technology products, are identified.

The next step, **technology design,** examines the available technologies and assesses which options will meet users' needs. The designer makes

---

Internet time
A term that refers to the need for companies to be able to rapidly evolve as the industry and customer expectations change.

Building-block process
A network design process based on the concept that networks that use a few standard components are less expensive in the long run than networks that use a wide variety of components.

Narrow and deep
A term used to describe the building-block design strategy as having a narrow range of technologies used deeply (i.e., over and over) throughout an organization.

Needs analysis
The first step in the building-block design process, which is the process of understanding current and projected future network requirements.

Technology design
The second step in the building-block design process, in which available technologies are examined and assessed to determine their appropriateness in meeting network requirements.

Figure 9-5

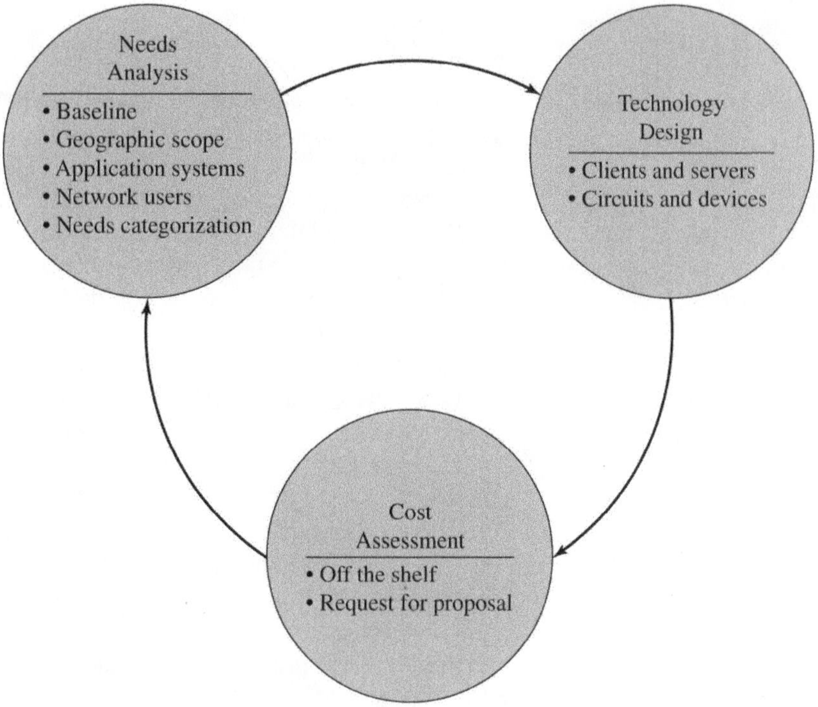

Building-block design process steps.

some estimates about the network needs of each category of user and circuit in terms of current technology (e.g., 10BaseT, 100BaseT, 1000BaseT, DSL, cable modem) and matches needs to technologies. Because the basic network design is general, it can easily be changed as needs and technologies change. The difficulty lies in predicting user demand so one can define the technologies needed. Most organizations solve this on the LAN level by building more capacity than they expect to need. At the WAN level, organizations try to match solutions closer to their needs because of the outside costs involved. By designing networks that can easily grow and then closely monitoring growth, they can expand the network ahead of the growth pattern.

In the third step, **cost assessment,** the relative costs of the technologies are considered and an attempt is made to get management to buy off on the plan. The process then cycles back to the needs analysis, which is refined using the technology and cost information to produce a new assessment of users' needs. This in turn triggers changes in the technology design and cost assessment and so on, until the design process is finished and the network is ready to deploy.

Cost assessment
The third step in the building-block design process, in which the relative costs of available technologies are considered.

IN THE REAL WORLD

Let's Build a Network!

Specific business requirements drive, in almost every case, the decision to design and deploy a WAN. After you leave the comfortable confines of your LAN, the world becomes much more complicated. Hence, a well thought-out network design becomes a critical issue.

When designing a WAN, you must look at the network as a whole, but to do so, you must look at each of the individual LANs in detail. As you identify LAN requirements, you can also identify the relationships between those LANs and wide area connectivity requirements.

One thing that you must realize and accept is that network requirements change quickly. When you design your network, you need to consider both current needs and future use requirements. That often means building a network that more than meets your current requirements so that you aren't constantly revising and upgrading the network once it is in place. As with nearly any type of project, the earlier in the process you make your changes, the easier they are to implement and the less they cost.

Consider the following situation. Busicorp's long-range business plan calls for growth through acquisition. Busicorp acquires another company and integrates that company's offices into the existing Busicorp WAN and Active Directory domain. If the company has a network, the plan calls for adding it with minimal interruption. If there isn't a LAN, your job is to build one. From a design standpoint, this situation means that you have to go through the network design process each time Busicorp makes a new acquisition. Because each newly acquired company is going to be different, it means going through the complete process from the context of that company's resources, requirements and relationship to the rest of the network.

Project 9.1

The network design process is usually treated as a series of design phases. Often, they are broken down into needs analysis, technology design, and cost assessment. However, none of these phases is completely isolated. Each impacts the other, and during the design process you often have to go back and forth between the design phases until you are finished.

Complete **Project 9.2: Understanding Network Design Requirements** in the online Network Basics Project Manual. This project focuses on network design phases, including the requirements of each and expected deliverables.

SELF-CHECK

1. Compare traditional and building-block design processes.
2. What are the three process steps in the building-block design process?

9.3 PERFORMING NEEDS ANALYSIS

The goal of needs analysis is to understand why the network is being built and what users and applications it will support. In many cases, the network is being designed to improve poor performance or enable new applications to be used. In other cases, the network is upgraded to replace unreliable or aging equipment, or to standardize equipment and technologies.

Often the goals in network design are slightly different between LANs (including BNs) on the one hand and WANs on the other. In the LAN environment, the organization owns and operates the equipment and the circuits. If major changes are needed, the organization bears the cost. Most network designers tend to err on the side of building too big a network—that is, building in more capacity than they expect to need. In contrast, in most WANs, the organization leases circuits from a common carrier and pays for them on a periodic or per-use basis. Most network designers tend to err on the side of building too small a network because they can lease additional capacity incrementally—but canceling a long-term contract for unused capacity is difficult.

The goal of the needs analysis step is to produce a **logical network design,** which is a statement of the network elements needed to meet the organization's needs. It focuses on the fundamental functionality needed instead of specific technologies or products. Those decisions are the responsibility of the technology design.

9.3.1 Analyzing Geographic Scope

The first step in needs analysis is to break the network into three conceptual parts on the basis of their geographic and logical scope. These are the access layer, the distribution layer, and the core layer. The **access layer** is the technology that is closest to the user—the user's first contact with the network—and is often a LAN or a remote access connection. The **distribution layer** is the next part of the network that connects the access layer to the rest of the network, such as the BN(s) in a specific building. The **core layer** is the innermost part of the network that connects the different distribution-layer networks to each other, such as WAN circuits connecting different offices together. The core layer is usually the busiest and most

Logical network design
The goal of the needs assessment design phase, which consists of a statement of the required network elements.

Access layer
The network technology—typically the LAN or remote access connection—closest to the user.

Distribution layer
The part of the network that connects the access layer to the rest of the network, as with a backbone network.

Core layer
The innermost part of a network, which connects distribution layer networks, as with WAN connections.

important part of the network. Not all layers are present in all networks; small networks, for example, may not have a distribution layer because the parts of the access layer connect directly together.

Starting with the highest level is easiest, so most designers begin by drawing a network diagram for international or countrywide WAN locations that must be connected. Details such as the type of circuit and other considerations will be added later. Next, the individual locations (LANs) connected to the WAN are drawn, usually in a series of separate diagrams. The designers gather general information and characteristics of the environment in which the network operates. For example, they must determine whether there are any legal requirements, such as local, state/provincial, federal, or international laws, regulations, or building codes that might affect the network.

Figure 9-6 shows the initial drawing of a network design for an organization with offices in four areas connected to the core WAN. The Toronto location, for example, has a distribution layer (implemented as a BN)

Figure 9-6

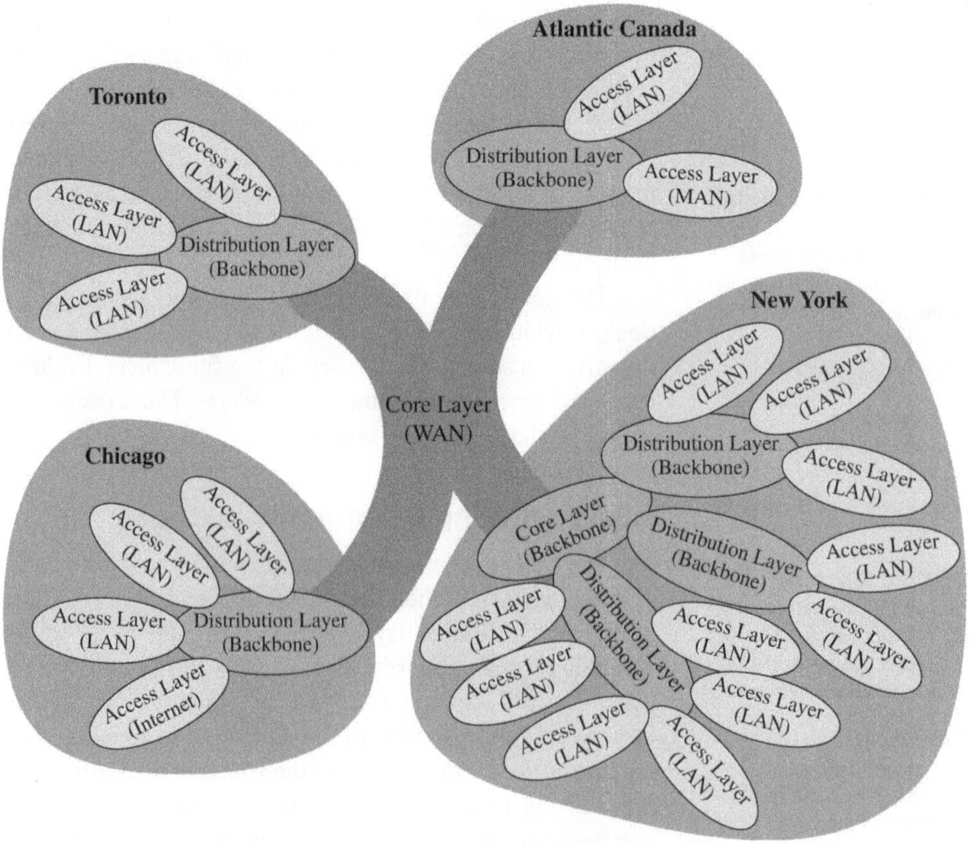

Initial network drawing. Geographic scope.

connecting three distinct access-layer LANs (for this example, three distinct LANs in the same office building). Chicago has a similar structure, with the addition of a fourth access part that connects to the Internet. Note that the organization has only one Internet connection, so all Internet traffic must route through the core network to the Chicago location.

The Atlantic Canada network section has two distinct access layers; one is a LAN and one access layer is a dial-up remote access. The New York network section is more complex, having its own core network component with a BN connected into the core WAN, which in turn supports three distribution-layer BNs. Each of these supports several access-layer LANs.

9.3.2 Analyzing Servers and Application Systems

Traditionally the primary reason to deploy a LAN has been to share resources. As LAN technologies matured, another justification was to reduce total cost of ownership (TCO) by centralizing management as support requirements and efforts compared to the distributed management required by individual LANs. The basic reasons remain the same with a WAN, but on a broader scale.

The basic servers on an enterprise WAN are the same as you see on any LAN, including:

- File and print servers
- Network support servers
- Application servers

File servers provide centralized file storage and access control. Print servers share printer resources to network users. Network support services include the network operating system (NOS) servers, such as Active Directory domain controllers, remote access servers, DHCP servers, DNS servers, network address translation (NAT) and other Internet access servers, specialized gateways, and other servers of this type. The difference is that you are going to need more servers, and projecting traffic patterns and bandwidth requirements is probably going to be more difficult. With some server types, like domain controllers, the best solution is often to have at least one of each type of server in each physical location. For others, like remote access servers, you may need only one or two servers placed in strategic locations.

When designing an enterprise network, you will start to see differences between it and a LAN when you add application server requirements into the mix. Because deploying and maintaining application servers is usually much more expensive, you are less likely to have one of each application server on every LAN. To start, review the list of applications that will be used on the network and identify the location of each. Next, add applications expected to deploy on the network in the future to the list.

In most cases, the applications will be relatively well defined. Specific internal applications (such as payroll and accounting) and external applications (such as web servers) may already be part of the existing network. As part of this process, review the organization's long- and short-range plans concerning changes in:

- Company goals and strategic plans
- Development plans for new products or services
- Sales projections and research and development projects
- New offices that must be served by the communications network
- Future commitments to technology

This list is just a guideline as to the types of changes that you need to consider. The network is closely tied to the business and its requirements, so any change to the business means a change to the network. For example, a major expansion in the number of offices or a major electronic commerce initiative will have a significant impact on network requirements.

You should also identify the hardware and software requirements of each application that will use the network. If possible, you need to identify the protocol each application uses. In today's network environment, for most applications that means either a protocol from the TCP/IP protocol suite or, in some cases, application-specific custom protocols. This knowledge will be particularly useful later when designers develop technological solutions. For example, if the main financial application payroll runs on an IBM mainframe, the network may need to support **Systems Network Architecture (SNA)** traffic (a proprietary IBM architecture used by IBM mainframes) and provide a gateway to translate it into more standard TCP/IP protocols. Another example you might see is a gateway to provide Windows clients with access to a legacy NetWare server, which also introduces IPX/SPX protocol requirements.

Systems Network Architecture (SNA)
An IBM proprietary network architecture used with IBM mainframe computers.

You also need to look back at geographic scope requirements. You need to consider where the servers are currently located, which users need to access those servers, and the traffic associated with that access. You may find that physically relocating one or more of the servers or deploying additional servers is more efficient, from the standpoint of user access and traffic control.

A good example is database servers. Having a database server that acts as the back-end data source for one or more applications is common. Some of the records on the database server will apply to the business as a whole while others, such as inventory levels or customer records, apply specifically to one geographic location.

A possible solution is shown in Figure 9-7. This database server deployment is based on the network design you saw in Figure 9-6. Let's assume that, because the only Internet connection (other than connections

Figure 9-7

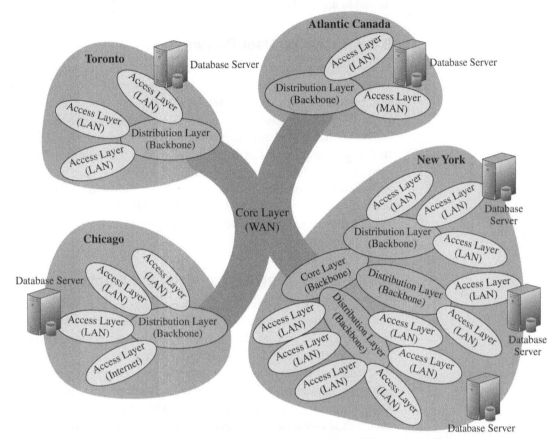

Geographic scope: LAN = local area network; MAN = metropolitan area network; WAN = wide area network.

Database server deployment.

possibly used for VPN links) is in Chicago, so that is where you plan to deploy all of the company's web servers. You keep a database server with a master copy of all of the data in Chicago. You place the database server on one of the access layer LANs.

However, each of the other locations also has database access requirements. Most of these requirements relate to data related to that region, so you deploy a database server with only **partitioned data,** a subset of the data that applies to that region. This plan reduces the traffic generated by user access. This configuration will generate some additional traffic because of the need to keep the data updated on each of the servers. For Toronto and Atlantic Canada, you place a database server on one of the access layer LANs. However, in New York, in order to minimize traffic on the core layer, you might choose an access layer LAN from each of the distribution layer

Partitioned data
A subset of data contained in a database.

backbones. If you look closely, you'll notice that traffic between LANs connected to any of the New York backbones must cross the core layer.

9.3.3 Analyzing User Requirements

In the past, application systems and shared servers accounted for the majority of network traffic. Today, much network traffic is produced by the discretionary use of the Internet, which also impacts application server traffic. Applications such as e-mail and web servers generate significant traffic, so the network manager is no longer in total control of the network traffic generated on his or her networks. This traffic growth is likely to continue in the future as network-hungry applications such as desktop videoconferencing become more common. In addition to understanding the applications, you must assess the number and type of users that will generate and receive network traffic and identify their location on the emerging network diagram.

9.3.4 Categorizing Network Requirements

So far, you've designed in terms of geographic scope, application systems, and users. You must additionally assess the relative amount of traffic generated in each part of the network. You've likely already started this process at some level, but now it becomes your focus.

With the building-block approach, the goal is a rough assessment of the relative magnitude of each application's network traffic requirements, both today and in the future, in comparison with the other applications. Likewise, each user is categorized as either a typical user or a high-traffic user. These assessments will be refined in the technology design stage of the process. Applications that require large amounts of multimedia data or those that load executables over the network are likely to be high-traffic applications. So are applications that are time sensitive or need constant updates, like financial information systems and order processing. The amount of traffic generated to support word processing applications or a web server's network access requirements are likely to be relatively minimal.

After the network requirements have been identified, organize them into **mandatory requirements** (things you must include), **desirable requirements** (things you should include), and **wish-list requirements** (things users want you to include). This information enables the development of a minimum level of mandatory requirements and a negotiable list of desirable requirements that are dependent on cost and availability. For example, desktop videoconferencing may be a wish-list item, but it will be omitted if it increases the cost of the network beyond what is desired. Look at the list at the bottom of Figure 9-8. This figure is focusing on one geographic location, with file server, mail server, and web server identified as mandatory applications. One wish-list item is also identified, videoconferencing.

Mandatory requirements Network requirements identified by needs analysis as items that must be included in the network design.

Desirable requirements Network requirements identified by needs analysis as items that should be included in the network design.

Wish-list requirements Network requirements identified by needs analysis as items that users would like to have but aren't really necessary.

Figure 9-8

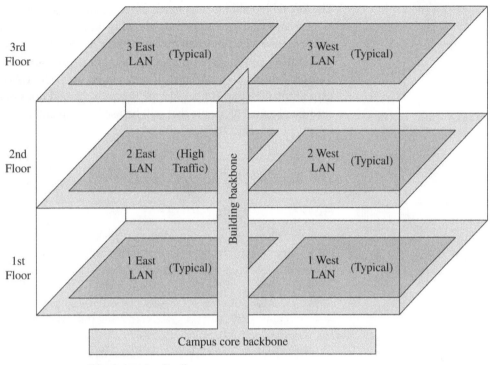

Mandatory Applications
File server
 –File sharing
Mail server
 –E-mail
Web server
 –Web applications for internal and external use

Wish-List Applications
 –Desktop videoconferencing (2 East and 2 West)

Network requirements.

At this point, the local facility network diagrams are prepared. For a really large network, there may be several levels.

FOR EXAMPLE

FIGURE 9-8

For an organization with campuses in multiple locations, the designer of the network in Figure 9-8 might choose to draw separate diagrams for each campus (Toronto, Chicago, Atlantic Canada, and New York, for example). Conversely, the designer might just add more detail to develop separate, more detailed diagrams for a single location, say New York. The choice is up to the designer, provided the diagrams and supporting text clearly explain the network's needs.

9.3.5 Compiling Your Deliverables

The key deliverable for the needs assessments stage is a set of logical network diagrams (like Figure 9-8), showing the applications, circuits, clients, and servers in the proposed network, each categorized as either typical or high traffic. You might also need an additional diagram showing the relationship and relative traffic requirements between the LANs. The logical diagram is the conceptual plan for the network and does not consider the specific physical elements that will be used to implement the network.

IN THE REAL WORLD

How Wide is Your Area?

Needs analysis, or network design in general, is not a one-time activity. A number of business activities and changes in company goals and strategies can force you to rethink your network.

Here's the situation. Busicorp has a WAN configured as a Windows Active Directory domain. The network is already in place and working well. You have sufficient bandwidth to meet the users' needs with a little room remaining for growth.

What happens when Busicorp acquires another company, one with its own LAN, in another geographic location? The company's long-range expansion plans call for you to integrate that LAN into the corporate enterprise. Rather than just throwing in another WAN link, you need to carefully consider the impact on your network.

Needs analysis issues include considering the connectivity requirements between the existing and new offices. You have to identify what servers are present in the new office, how they're being used, and whether or not existing offices will need access to them. You also need to determine what kinds of access users in the new office will need in the existing network.

Here's what you find. The network is set up as a Red Hat Enterprise Linux network with an additional Windows 2003 Server file server. The clients are running various operating systems with a mix of Fedora Linux and Windows versions from Windows 95 up. You need to keep the existing file server in place and upgrade and bring clients up to current levels, so you will need to add an Active Directory domain controller, allow for client access to both the Windows and Linux servers. Also, because it is a stand-alone LAN, you need some kind of WAN link to the rest of the enterprise. Initially, other than keeping the domain controller up-to-date and possibly e-mail messages, there will probably be little need for communication between this LAN and the rest of the network, though you can expect that to change as users settle into their new situation.

SELF-CHECK

1. What are the three conceptual layers in a network communication model?

2. How does analysis of network servers relate to geographic analysis?

Apply Your Knowledge What categories should you use to organize network requirements, from most to least critical?

9.4 DEVELOPING A TECHNOLOGY DESIGN

Physical network design
The result of the technology design process, which identifies the network hardware and software needed, typically as design diagrams.

After the needs have been defined in the logical network design, the next step is to develop a **physical network design** (or set of possible designs). The physical network design starts with the client and server computers needed to support the users and applications. If the network is a new network, new computers will need to be purchased. If the network is an existing network, the servers may need to be upgraded to the newest technology. After they are designed, then the circuits and devices connecting them (at the LAN and WAN level) are designed.

9.4.1 Designing Clients and Servers

The building-block approach specifies needs in terms of some standard units. Typical users are allocated the base-level client computers, as are servers supporting typical applications. Users and servers for applications needing more powerful computers are assigned more advanced computers.

Applications (both client and server) typically specify their minimum hardware requirements. When designing computer hardware, keep in mind that real-world requirements often exceed those minimums. With many server applications, calculating actual hardware requirements on a case-by-case basis may be necessary. The good news is that hardware costs continue to drop and you are likely to find that when you get ready to buy the hardware, you can afford more advanced servers for the same price, building in support for growth.

9.4.2 Designing Circuits and Pathways

At least for LAN hardware, the same built-in cost reductions apply for network circuits and devices. For the WAN, available technologies and associated costs tend to change a little more slowly. With either, two interrelated decisions in designing network circuits and devices are the fundamental

Capacity planning
The process of estimating the size and type of network circuits needed.

technology and protocols (e.g., Ethernet, ATM, TCP/IP), and the capacity of each circuit (e.g., 10 Mbps, 100 Mbps, 1,000 Mbps). These two are inter-related, because each technology offers different circuit capacities.

Designing the circuit capacity means **capacity planning,** estimating the size and type of the standard and advanced network circuits for each type of network (LAN, BN, WAN). For example, should the standard LAN circuit be 10BaseT, 100BaseT, or 10/100 switched Ethernet? Likewise, should the standard BN circuit be 100BaseT, 1000BaseT, or ATM OC-3?

Circuit loading
A term that refers to the amount of traffic a circuit must carry.

Average circuit traffic
A network's usual traffic requirements.

Peak circuit traffic
A network's maximum traffic requirements.

Capacity planning requires assessment of the current and future **circuit loading** (the amount of data transmitted on a circuit). This analysis can focus on either the **average circuit traffic** (usual traffic requirements) or the **peak circuit traffic** (maximum traffic requirements). Designing for peak circuit traffic is the ideal, but not always possible because of the related costs.

TIPS FROM THE PROFESSIONALS

Peak Banking Hours

In an online banking network, traffic volume peaks usually are in the midmorning (bank opening) and just prior to closing. Telephone companies normally have their highest peak volumes on Mother's Day.

Turnpike effect
A situation in which network use exceeds original estimates simply because the network and its services are available to the users.

Forecasts and estimates are inherently less precise than current network traffic information. One consideration is the **turnpike effect,** which results when the network is used to a greater extent than was anticipated because it is available, is very efficient, and provides new services. The annual growth factor for network use may vary from 5 to 50 percent and, in some cases, may exceed 100 percent for high-growth organizations. You often won't know the actual growth rate until the network is in place and you have real-world numbers to apply.

Although no organization wants to pay for more capacity than it needs, the usual working estimate is that upgrading a network costs 50 to 80 percent more than building it right the first time. Few organizations complain about having too much network capacity, but being under capacity can cause significant problems. Given the rapid growth in network demand and the difficulty in accurately predicting it, most organizations intentionally overbuild (build more capacity into their network than they plan to use), and then end up using this supposedly unneeded capacity (often within three years or less).

9.4.3 Selecting Design Tools

Network modeling and design tools can perform a number of functions to help in the technology design process. With most tools, the first step is to create a diagram or model of the existing network or proposed network design. Some modeling tools require the user to create the network diagram from scratch. That is, the user must enter all of the network components by hand, placing each server, client computer, and circuit on the diagram and defining what each is.

Network discovery
The process by which a network design tool identifies a component already present on an existing network.

Other tools support **network discovery.** In this case, the user provides some starting point, and the modeling software explores the network and automatically draws the diagram itself. After the diagram is complete, the user can then change it to reflect the new network design. Obviously, a network discovery tool only helps if you already have a network. Also, network discovery tools tend to be most helpful when the network is very complex.

Simulation
A mathematical technique for simulating real-world network conditions based on variable parameters.

After the diagram is complete, the next step is to add information about the expected network traffic and see if the network can support the level of traffic that is expected. **Simulation,** a mathematical technique in which the network comes to life and behaves as it would under real conditions, is used to model the behavior of the communication network. Applications and users generate and respond to messages while the simulator tracks the number of packets in the network and the delays encountered at each point in the network. Simulation models may be tailored to the users' needs by entering parameter values specific to the network at hand. However, a simulation is no better than the data provided. If the initial parameters aren't accurate, then the simulation will be invalid.

An accurate simulation can give you estimated response times throughout the network and, with good modeling tools, highlight potential trouble areas. The very best tools offer suggestions on how to overcome the problems that the simulation identified (such as subnetting a LAN or increasing a WAN link from T1 to T3).

9.4.4 Compiling Your Deliverables (Again)

The key deliverable is a set of one or more physical network designs. Most designers like to prepare several physical designs so they can trade off technical benefits against cost. In most cases, the critical part is the design of the network circuits and devices. In the case of a new network designed from scratch, defining the client computers with care is also

Figure 9-9

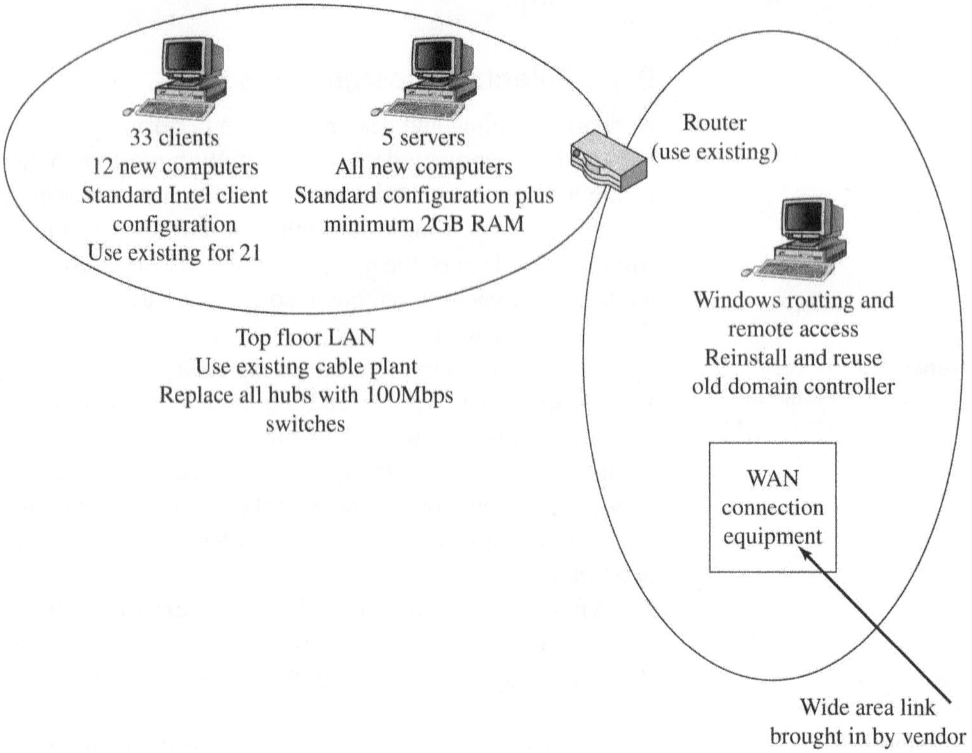

LAN/WAN design.

important because these computers will form a large portion of the total cost of the network.

You need to diagram the access level LANs and the connections that form your WAN. This time, you need to provide details like the type of protocols used, connection devices, number of client computers, and so forth. Figure 9-9 is a more detailed diagram for one of the LANs and the network in Toronto. Notice that it lists the number and types of devices, but doesn't include information like vendors. That comes later in the process.

Even though it doesn't specifically call it out here, the existence of a backbone implies at least one additional router used to connect the LANs to that backbone. As you get more details about the remote link requirements for the backbone, like the specific connection type, you would add those to the drawing.

This place is additionally where a good design tool can make your life easier. Most design tools will let you print your design diagrams, including equipment list. That way you avoid duplicating your effort.

FOR EXAMPLE

FIGURE 9-9

Notice that the drawing indicates that some of the existing equipment will be reused.

IN THE REAL WORLD

Getting Physical

You are designing an extension to the Busicorp WAN. The company is growing through acquisition. The most recent acquisition has a Red Hat Enterprise Linux server, a Windows file server running Windows 2003 Server, and an assortment of Linux clients and Windows clients running various versions of Windows client operating systems.

The general guidelines for the extension specify that the LAN should be made part of the Windows Active Directory domain. Initially leave the Linux server in place, although you will eventually phase it out. Bring up any clients running Windows XP or earlier to current operating system levels. The LAN will link through a VPN over the Internet through an ADSL link.

What does the physical design look like? Let's start with the LAN. Nothing in the design requires you to upgrade the cable plant on local LAN connection hardware, so you don't need to include it in the design. The design lists three Windows servers, an Active Directory domain controller, a routing and remote access (RRAS) and VPN endpoint, and access to the Linux server. You decide to deploy new computers running Windows Server 2003 as the domain controller and RRAS server.

What about the WAN requirements? One component overlaps with the LAN requirements, the RRAS server. You'll also need to identify a local ISP to provide the connection to the Internet. You'll need an ADSL line, provided either directly by the local telephone carrier or indirectly through the ISP, and the ADSL connection hardware, either from the telephone carrier, ISP, or purchased separately. Because the clients haven't had any contact with the rest of the network in the past, you determine that, at least initially, communications over the WAN link are minimal.

SELF-CHECK

1. What are your design requirements during capacity planning?
2. What is the ideal circuit design in relation to estimated circuit loading?
3. What is network discovery?

Project 9.2

During the technical design phase you work on creating the network's physical network design. During this process you identify the network devices that you need and determine their placement, which includes ensuring that the equipment can support the projected circuit load.

Often overlapping this process is cost assessment. During this phase, you identify the potential vendors and then have them provide cost estimates. Technical design and cost assessment often overlap. You might choose to adjust your physical design based on hardware availability and cost.

Complete **Project 9.4: Researching Network Hardware** in the online Network Basics Project Manual to understand the process of cost assessment in networking design.

9.5 SELLING YOUR PLAN

Before you can begin implementation, someone has to authorize the plan and the budget. You have to convince the decision makers that your plan is the best (read most cost-effective) design. That means performing a cost assessment to justify your design.

The purpose of this step is to assess the costs of various physical network design alternatives produced in the previous step. The main items are the costs of software, hardware, circuits, and personnel. All factors are interrelated with regard to cost.

9.5.1 Estimating Costs

Estimating the cost of a network is quite complex because many factors are not immediately obvious. Some of the costs that must be considered are:

- Circuit costs, including costs of circuits provided by common carriers or the cost of purchasing and installing your own cable.
- Internetworking devices and WAN connection devices.
- Hardware costs, including computers, hubs, switches, printers, and uninterruptible power supplies.
- Software costs for NOS, application software, middleware, and client applications.
- Network management costs, including special hardware, software, management personnel and training.
- Test and maintenance costs, including diagnostic software and onsite spares.
- Costs to operate the network.

Some estimates will be closer to actual costs than others. Hardware costs, for example, are relatively easy to estimate. Others, like personnel costs and training, are more difficult. In some organizations, you might be expected to break down the costs by department based on projected network use. This requirement makes the process even more complicated and, for a new network, could be little better than a rough guess.

9.5.2 Developing a Request for Proposal (RFP)

Request for proposal (RFP)
A thumbnail sketch of network requirements that is used to obtain general vendor recommendations and bids.

Even though most LAN components can be purchased off the shelf, organizations often develop a **request for proposal (RFP)** before making large network purchases. The term might vary between different organizations, but the concept is common throughout the corporate (and nonprofit, government, and any other organization type) world. It's a thumbnail sketch of what you need, specifying what equipment, software, and services are desired. You can use this request to go to your vendors and ask them to give you their best prices. Some RFPs are very specific about items and time frame. In other cases, items are defined as mandatory, desirable, or wishlist, or several scenarios are provided and the vendor is asked to propose the best solution. Figure 9-10 is a summary of the key parts of an RFP.

After the vendors have submitted their proposals, the organization evaluates them against specified criteria and makes its choices. Depending on the scope and complexity of the network, redesigning the network on the basis of the information in the vendors' proposals is sometimes necessary.

Multivendor environment
A network environment in which components and services are purchased or leased from multiple vendors.

One of the key decisions in the RFP process is the scope of the RFP. Will you use one vendor or several vendors for all hardware, software, and services? **Multivendor environments** tend to provide better performance

TIPS FROM THE PROFESSIONALS

Zoom in on RFPs

All the best RFPs start with a complete needs assessment. RFPs should focus on the result or impact expected. Outline the decisions that need to be made as a result of the proposal and list the specific areas that you would like additional information to assist in the decision-making requirements. Identify key requirements for success/failure avoidance such as budgetary constraints and delivery deadlines. RFPs are generally private documents created and issued by individual companies or organizations to have other organizations bid on contracts to implement, repair, or upgrade needed systems for their organization. You can see a public domain (open record) RFP from the U.S. Census Bureau at http://www.census.gov/procur/www/fssp/att05.html.

Figure 9-10

Information in a Typical Request for Proposal

- Background information
    - Organizational profile
    - Overview of current network
    - Overview of new network
    - Goals of new network
- Network requirements

    - Choice sets of possible network designs (hardware, software, circuits)
    - Mandatory, desirable, and wish-list items
    - Security and control requirements
    - Response-time requirements
    - Guidelines for proposing new network designs
- Service requirements

    - Implementation time plan
    - Training courses and materials
    - Support services (e.g., spare parts on site)
    - Reliability and performance guarantees
- Bidding process

    - Time schedule for the bidding process
    - Ground rules
    - Bid evaluation criteria
    - Availability of additional information
- Information required from vendor

    - Vendor corporate profile
    - Experience with similar networks
    - Hardware and software benchmarks
    - Reference list

Sample RFP.

and prices because one vendor unlikely makes the best (or least expensive) hardware, software, and services in all categories. The problem is that multivendor environments can be more difficult to manage. When failures occur (and they will), each vendor can blame the others.

9.5.3 Selling It to Management

One of the main problems in network design is obtaining the support of senior management. Management often sees the network as little more than a cost center, something on which the organization is spending a lot of money with little apparent change. The network keeps on running just as it did the year before.

One key to gaining the acceptance of senior management lies in speaking the management's language. Talking about switching from frame relay to ADSL is pointless because this terminology is meaningless from a business perspective. A more compelling argument is to discuss the growth in network use. For example, a simple graph that shows network usage growing at 25 percent per year, compared with network budget growing at 10 percent per year, presents a powerful illustration that the network costs are well managed, not out of control. Likewise, a focus on network reliability is an easily understandable issue. Depending on the applications that rely on the network, such as financial processing or customer sales, network downtime can cost hundreds or even thousands of dollars per hour.

9.5.4 Compiling Your Deliverables (One More Time)

Now we bring everything together. There are three key deliverables for this step. You'll have an RFP that goes to potential vendors. After the vendor has been selected, you need to revise the physical network diagram with the technology design complete and actual hardware filled in. Finally, you need to deliver the business case that provides support for the network design, expressed in business objectives.

IN THE REAL WORD

Signoff

Busicorp is expanding its WAN by connecting a newly acquired company's LAN. You've identified the physical requirements, which include two servers, a few new client computers to replace those that can't upgrade to the current Windows versions, a wide area link, and wide area connection hardware. On the software side, you need two licensed copies of Windows Server 2003 and client operating system licenses for each of the client computers you need to upgrade.

This is the basis of your RFP. You put together a formal list and send copies to Busicorp's list of approved vendors (who you refer to as the usual suspects). Because you've never had an office in this geographic location before, and because none of your current ISPs service that location, you also have to locate and contact new vendors for the wide area link. You want it done fast, and you want it done right the first time, so you call a few friends and locate a network consultant in the area to help you with the wide area requirements.

When the bids come back, you hand it off through your manager for approval. This situation is where approval is relatively easy because it falls under the company's public long-range expansion goals. Regardless, you still have to justify your design decisions to show that your choices are the most cost effective.

SELF-CHECK

1. Which network costs are usually the hardest to estimate?
2. What should you include on an RFP?

Apply Your Knowledge Draft a RFP based on the previous In the Real World section.

9.6 DEPLOYING YOUR WAN

After the design process is complete, you can finally order the pieces and parts and start deploying your new network (or network upgrades). Unfortunately, doing so is seldom a matter of just hooking everything up as it comes in. Hardware needs testing to make sure it's working properly, software needs to be installed, and you must manage any number of other details. One of the first things you should do, whether installing new or upgrading, is go back to your design documents and prepare an installation checklist. That way, you can make sure that everything gets done in the right order and nothing gets missed.

You can look at the process as having two broadly defined steps: deploying the LANs and then connecting them together. Even if these steps are happening at the same time, keeping your thought processes (and implementation procedures) organized is easier if you think of them as separate activities. If your LANs are not working properly, you might not be able to tell whether or not your remote links are working at optimum levels, or at all, in some cases.

9.6.1 Deploying Your LANs

There are two basic LAN scenarios. One is installing a new network, which means you don't have to worry about existing network users. The other is upgrading an existing LAN, which means you have to keep everything working while you bring in the new network.

New Network

When installing a new network, you need to be sure that you take care of all of the preliminaries that might require outside help, which includes things like registering your domain name, having the network cable run, and so forth. If you expect the users to walk into a turnkey operation where everything is ready to go, you need to have all of the software, including client applications, already installed and tested. To help with this task, different software packages are available that let you install one client computer as the model and duplicate that installation on the other clients. The most popular product of this type is currently Norton Ghost.

Existing Network

Things can get difficult with an existing network. Not only do you have the issue of trying to deploy all of your new hardware and software, you have to do it with minimal interference to the network users and current network operations. Some companies make the change as an all-at-once switch, but using a gradual, phased approach is more common.

Changing all at once requires careful timing and coordination. The switch is usually planned for a period when the network will be unused, or minimally used, and allows for sufficient time to complete the process. One way companies have done this is scheduling the upgrade over a long holiday weekend. Doing so is more difficult for multinational organizations, because many holidays are at least somewhat regional. Scheduling upgrades in different locales at different times may be necessary.

In a phased approach, you upgrade the network a little a time. Maybe you start with the infrastructure, swapping out hubs for higher-speed switches for example. Then you move on to the next phase, maybe replacing selected servers or exchanging client computers.

9.6.2 Connecting Your LANs

At this point, you need to connect your disconnected LANs into a WAN. A key part of any successful WAN deployment is testing—before you link, during the linkup, and after the LANs are connected.

The exact process involved, and the testing required, depends on how the LANs are connected. There is, however, one common factor. Any time you have wide area links, at least one third-party is going to be involved. That means that you aren't completely in control of the process. Take connections in Figure 9-11 by way of high-speed links through the Internet. The figure shows local distribution layers and the POP location for the ISP.

One possibility is that you have three offices, all in the same city, but far enough apart that you can't use local LAN technology for a backbone to link them. The other possibility is that the circuit load on each distribution layer BN is sufficient to justify a separate VPN link.

> **FOR EXAMPLE**
>
> **FIGURE 9-11**
>
> From this drawing, considering that each distribution layer has a separate connection through an ISP in New York, you can tell there are special connection requirements.

Figure 9-11

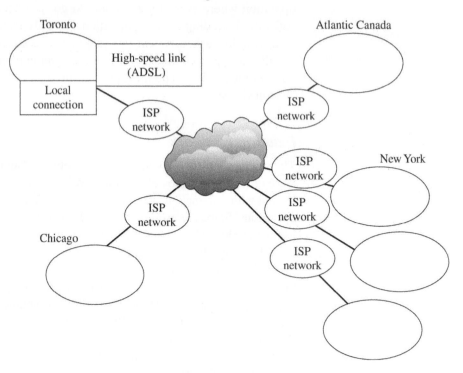

LAN connections.

Key components might include:

- Local connection device to the high-speed link
- High-speed carrier
- Internet service provider

Your point of contact for each of these components may well be a separate entity. Also, you have the same requirements at the other end, and usually have different carrier providers and different ISPs at each end of the link. In most cases, coordinating with each of these parties to get them together at the same time is your responsibility.

9.6.3 Remaining (Ongoing) Tasks

After the network is deployed and running, your first reaction is that you want to take a long break and get away from the network for a while. Unfortunately, if it's your network (that is, you didn't come in as a temporary resource to set up the network and leave), your job is just starting.

You'll want to do some things in the first few days after you get the network operational. You need to validate your design, make sure that the network you designed and deployed is really the network you want. Start by updating your final network design documents to include any changes made during the final implementation. Include detailed information about the equipment you install, like model numbers, serial numbers, the vendor and, if available, a contact name and number in case of trouble.

You should collect baseline performance statistics at various times and at various locations on the WAN. You want to collect traffic statistics for

IN THE REAL WORLD

D (Deployment)—Day(s)

After you have everything in place, you want to get the new company joined into the enterprise as quickly as possible. After weighing your options, you decide to set up as an all-at-once change over a holiday weekend (after bribing your coworkers with overtime and free food), leaving the office with a turnkey network.

Setup includes hardware installation, software installation, and management-related configuration tasks. Management tasks are beyond the scope of this course, so we'll leave those tasks alone except to say that they have to be done.

You can do some things in advance without seriously impacting the current network. You can go ahead and install the operating system on the new Windows Server 2008 computers. You can also install and test the wide area link. When you set up a domain controller, you need access to the domain, so you'll need to have the link and RRAS server in place before you finish setting up the domain controller.

You can set up the clients that you need to upgrade and the new clients you need to set up to run the Windows client installations and upgrades as unattended installations. Unintended installations mean that they run automatically without any human interaction, or minimal interaction. You still want to check each installation to make sure that the client is running properly. You need to configure the client computers to access both the Windows and Linux servers and set up network users and their access permissions for all of the local users. You should test everything, as much as possible, to make sure that it works.

As soon as you feel relatively sure that everything's done, you leave behind printed instructions that tell the users how to log on to the new network and (very important) change their passwords the first time they log on. You need to provide them with instructions about how to use the network and differences that they're going to see. Leaving at least one person on site to provide support, answer users' questions, and fix or replace anything that breaks would be worth your while.

Remember, on a project like this, *something always breaks*.

each LAN (and each subnet in a routed LAN) and for the WAN links. Compare these statistics to the projected estimates you developed during the design process. If you find significant variance, places in the network where traffic levels are much higher than expected, you need to come up with a quick resolution. Two of the most likely solutions are increasing the available bandwidth or moving some of the users or network servers to change traffic flow patterns.

One of your goals is ensuring that the network operates at acceptable levels. Your network users are sure to give you feedback if the network is running at less than top form. Some users will never be happy, no matter how well the network is performing, but the feedback you get from your users will often help you identify and correct bottlenecks and other performance problems.

From here on, the job comes down to regular upkeep and maintenance. Some periodic maintenance activities, like regular backups, can be at least partially automated. Others, like creating and deleting user accounts or managing access permissions, require your direct intervention. Details about regular maintenance procedures and available maintenance tools are beyond the scope of this chapter.

 SELF-CHECK

1. What is a turnkey network?
2. When upgrading an existing network, what is the advantage of scheduling the changes over a long holiday weekend?

SUMMARY

Section 9.1
- Any WAN you design and deploy will have some features in common with the Internet.
- Companies connect their networks to the Internet through an ISP.

Section 9.2
- With an enterprise WAN, you must also consider device placement and traffic flows across wide area links.
- The building-block process of network design starts with a few standard components and uses them over and over again.

Section 9.3
- The goal of needs analysis is to understand why the network is being built and what users and applications it will support.
- There are three components of needs analysis: access layer, distribution layer, and the core layer.

Section 9.4
- The physical design phase of network design consists of determining the specific equipment that will be used to build the network.

- Network modeling and design tools can perform a number of functions to help in the technology design process.

Section 9.5

- Cost assessment helps you justify your design.
- One of the main problems in network design is obtaining the support of senior management.

Section 9.6

- One of the first things you should do when deploying your network is go back to your design documents and prepare an installation checklist.
- A key part of any successful WAN deployment is testing—before you link, during the linkup, and after the LANs are connected.

ASSESS YOUR UNDERSTANDING

UNDERSTAND: WHAT HAVE YOU LEARNED?

 Go to **www.wiley.com/go/ciccarelli/networkingbasics2e** to evaluate your knowledge of transaction and locking support.

Measure your learning by comparing pre-test and post-test results.

SUMMARY QUESTIONS

1. When upgrading a network, you must make all of the technology changes at the same time. True or false?

2. How is an RFP used?

    (a) To organize network requirements by priority.

    (b) To illustrate the complete physical design.

    (c) To track items discovered during needs analysis.

    (d) To submit to vendors for bid and recommendations.

3. _____ requirements are your lowest-priority network requirements.

    (a) Mandatory

    (b) Desirable

    (c) Wish-list

    (d) Management-specified

4. What is the role of core layer network technology?

    (a) It provides the wide area links connecting distribution layer networks.

    (b) It acts as the backbone in a routed LAN.

    (c) It is the technology directly providing users with access to LAN resources.

    (d) It is the software and services operating on servers running the NOS.

5. What is circuit loading?

    (a) The process of testing a circuit to determine its maximum capacity.

    (b) The process of estimating network circuit requirements.

    (c) A reference to the amount of data carried on a circuit.

    (d) A reference to buying and installing more capacity than is actually needed.

6. You are typically more likely to overbuild when designing LAN technology requirements than when designing WAN technology requirements. True or false?

7. Identifying and locating application servers is part of which phase of the design process?

   (a) Needs analysis
   (b) Physical design
   (c) Cost assessment
   (d) Not a formal part of the design process

8. What are the connection points at the topmost level of the Internet's hierarchical structure?

   (a) MAEs
   (b) NAPs
   (c) POPs
   (d) Regional ISPs

9. When connecting to your local ISP, you connect through which of the following?

   (a) MAE
   (b) NAP
   (c) POP
   (d) NSF

10. Which term best describes cable modem connection architecture?

    (a) Point-to-point
    (b) Point of presence
    (c) Singlepoint circuit
    (d) Shared multipoint circuit

11. The narrow and deep design strategy refers to the expected outcome of the traditional network design process. True or false?

12. Which server type would you most likely need to deploy at each physical location in a WAN?

    (a) Log on and authentication
    (b) Mail service
    (c) Web server
    (d) Mainframe gateway

APPLY: WHAT WOULD YOU DO?

1. The following questions refer to the network graphic in Figure 9-12. The connections shown between the LANs are ATM links. Even though single links are shown from each LAN, the WAN is configured as a mesh with each LAN connecting by ATM to every other LAN.

   The network shown in Figure 9-12 is configured as a single Windows Active Directory domain with a single domain controller in each physical location. The database server on the Chicago LAN is accessed by users and applications from all locations.

Figure 9-12

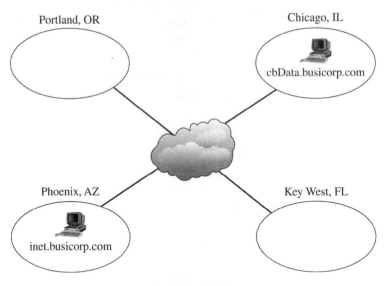

Sample WAN.

The company websites and the NAT server (inet.busicorp.com) that provides users with Internet access are located in the Phoenix office. Web server content is stored on the database server. Most of the content is relatively static. Updates are made on a weekly basis.

(a) How does NAT server location affect network traffic?

(b) What are the potential benefits of deploying additional NAT servers?

(c) What are potential drawbacks?

(d) How can you determine whether or not the change is cost effective?

(e) Regular business hours are 8:00 AM to 5:00 PM, local time at each location. Between 7:45 AM and 8:15 AM, local to Key West, traffic levels on the links between Key West and the other offices increases significantly and then drops back down to average levels. There is no significant difference in traffic levels between the other offices. To what is the traffic most likely related (justify your answer)?

(f) What is the probable cause?

(g) How should you resolve the problem?

(h) You need to reduce the circuit load in and out of the Phoenix location. You need to keep changes to the web servers to a minimum. The database server deployed in Chicago must host an accurate, up-to-date set of all corporate data. Based on what you know about the network, what should you do?

(i) How does this resolve the problem?

(j) What additional traffic will this solution generate?

2. The following questions refer to the network in Figure 9-13. Linux file servers are responsible for login and authentication. Clients are a mix of various Windows versions and Linux distributions. The network includes a small number of Windows-based application servers, identified in the figure.

The application servers are as follows:

- bdata.busicorp.com—Database server
- busiweb1.busicorp.com—Internal web server
- busiweb2.busicorp.com—Internal web server
- ms.busicorp.com—Internal mail server
- vs.busicorp.com—Streaming video server

You are redesigning the network to provide optimal performance. This includes determining what changes, if any, need to be made to the wide area links. Currently, the offices are linked by point-to-point T1 carrier circuits.

(a) From the standpoint of reliability and accessibility, what are the potential concerns about the current WAN configuration?

(b) What is the minimal change you can make to the network to minimize the potential impact of this shortcoming?

(c) How does this minimize the potential impact? Give a specific example.

(d) What kinds of information do you need to collect about the application servers?

Figure 9-13

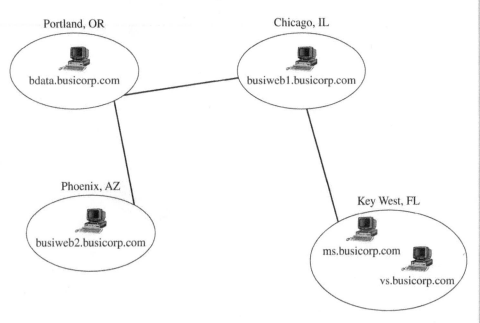

Sample heterogeneous network.

(e) What type of tools would enable you to predict the estimated circuit load changes if you relocate any of the application servers?

(f) Login and authentication is handled by Linux servers in Key West and Portland. How does this impact network traffic?

(g) How can you minimize average circuit traffic resulting from authentication requests?

3. The following questions refer to the network in Figure 9-14. The WAN links are VPN connections through the Internet. Even though only one connection is shown from each location, the WAN is configured as a mesh.

The network is configured as a Windows Active Directory domain. All of the clients run Windows 2000 Professional, Windows XP, or Windows Vista. Each location has a Linux computer configured as an internal Web site.

(a) You are looking to minimize connection costs. Connections in Portland and Chicago are made using ADSL. How does this affect the types of connections you must use in Phoenix and Key West?

(b) Why?

(c) What are potential concerns when using a cable modem to connect a LAN to the local ISP?

(d) What changes would be required if switching from a cable modem to an ADSL connection?

(e) If the new connection has similar available bandwidth, how would changing the connection type affect local LAN users?

(f) How can you avoid this effect?

Figure 9-14

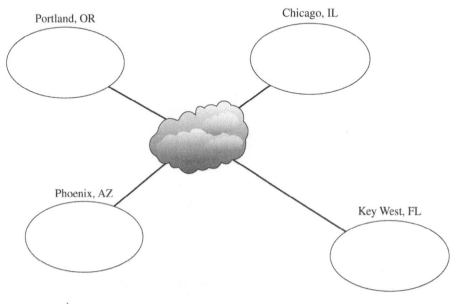

Portland, OR

Chicago, IL

Phoenix, AZ

Key West, FL

VPN WAN.

BE A NETWORK ENGINEER

Network Migration

Your company's network is currently configured as a set of stand-alone LANs. Some of the LANs are subnetworked. All of the LANs are configured with private IP addresses. Each is configured with the same class C address range.

Each LAN is configured as a Windows Active Directory domain. After connecting the LANs, you plan to reconfigure the network using a hierarchical structure with a root domain at the main office and child domains (subdomains) that are dependent on the root domain at the main office and each of the local offices. You plan to deploy new domain controllers at each location and repurpose the current domain controllers as file servers.

Network servers and application servers are duplicated at each location, which includes DHCP, DNS, mail, print, file, web, NAT, and database servers. You plan to use VPN connections over the Internet to connect the LANs. The final architecture will be a mesh configuration.

1. You want to use ADSL connections to the ISPs. What is required at each location?

2. What would prevent you from using the same vendors for each location?

3. You generate a combined list of all of the hardware required for the new network configuration. This list includes replacing any client computers that cannot be upgraded to current Windows versions. During which building-block network design phase would you identify these requirements?

4. Your company has a list of possible hardware and software vendors. How could you generate bids to find the best prices?

5. What changes, if any, will you need to make to the TCP/IP configuration for each LAN?

6. Why?

7. Based on what you know about the LAN configurations, what is the easiest way to make this change?

8. What cost reduction, if any, might be possible in the new network configuration?

9. In order to ensure a reliable network, how many domain controllers will you need?

KEY TERMS

Access layer

Address Resolution Protocol (ARP)

Asymmetric DSL (ADSL)

Average circuit traffic

Building-block process

Capacity planning

Circuit loading

Core layer

Cost assessment

Customer premises equipment (CPE)

Data Over Cable Service Interface
   Specification (DOCSIS)

Desirable requirements

Distribution layer

Downstream

Fixed wireless

Hybrid fiber coax (HFC)

Internet Time

Local ISP

Logical loop circuit

Logical network design

Mandatory requirements

Metropolitan Area Exchange (MAE)

Multipoint version

Multivendor environment

Narrow and deep

National ISP

National Science Foundation (NSF)

Needs analysis

Network access points (NAPs)

Network discovery

Next Generation Internet

Partitioned data

Peak circuit traffic

Peering

Physical network design

Point-to-point version

Points of presence (POP)

Regional ISP

Request for proposal (RFP)

Reverse Address Resolution Protocol (RARP)

Shared multipoint circuits

Simulation

Systems Network Architecture (SNA)

Technology design

Traditional network design process

Turnpike effect

Upstream

Very-high-data-rate digital subscriber line
   (VDSL)

Wireless DSL

Wish-list requirements

World Wide Web

CHAPTER

10

WIRELESS, REMOTE, AND WIDE AREA NETWORKING

What Do You Already Know?

- What is Wi-Fi?
- Why do you need to plan your LAN configuration?

For additional questions to assess your current knowledge of wireless, remote access, and WAN connectivity go to **www.wiley. com/go/ciccarelli/networkingbasics2e.**

What You Will Find Out	What You Will Be Able To Do
10.1 What is Wi-Fi.	Identify Wi-Fi standards.
	Compare wireless standards.
	Configure a network client.
10.2 How to implement remote access.	Understand which access type works for you.
	Configure a system for remote access.
10.3 Understand what is involved in joining LANs into WANs.	Plan your LAN configuration.
10.4 Understand what can be used to access wireless networks.	Take a look at access devices.
	Understand cloud computing.

INTRODUCTION

Traditional wired LANs meet the networking requirements of many, if not most, organizations. Several, however, have networking requirements that require the introduction of additional networking technologies. Wireless networking solutions are becoming increasing popular, especially with the rapid drop in associated costs. Remote access has long been a key part of many company's networking requirements. Wide area network (WAN) solutions used to create internetworks ranging from two connected LANs and up, are another important part of the networking mix for larger companies.

This chapter takes a look at these different network technologies with an eye on justifying their place in your network design. We also look at some of the special deployment and configuration requirements.

10.1 DEPLOYING WIRELESS NETWORKING

Wireless LANs (WLANs)
LANs connected over a large geographic area, traditionally defined by a LAN connected through the switched telephone network.

Several reasons are behind the rapid growth of **wireless LANs (WLANs).** Physically, it is often the easiest type of networking to deploy and maintain. In environments where you can't run the cable for a wired network, it might be your only available solution. In addition, nearly all laptop computers sold in the United States come preconfigured to support wireless networking.

We focus our discussion on Wi-Fi, which is the commercial name for a set of standards developed by the IEEE 802.11 standards group. A group of vendors selling 802.11 equipment trademarked the name Wi-Fi to refer to 802.11 because they believed that consumers were more likely to buy equipment with a catchier name than 802.11. Wi-Fi is intended to evoke memories of Hi-Fi, as the original stereo music systems were called.

10.1.1 Understanding Wireless Fundamentals

Digital Enhanced Cordless Telecommunications (DECT)
A cordless protocol primarily used for cordless phones.

DECT 6.0
The version of DECT that is used in the United States.

Voice over IP (VoIP)
The technology on which Internet-based telephone services are based.

The primary standards associated with wireless networking are the 802.11 family. Before we discuss them, let's take a quick look at one predecessor to current wireless transport standards, **Digital Enhanced Cordless Telecommunications (DECT),** or, as it is known in the United States, **DECT 6.0.** DECT was developed in Europe, but did not make use of communications frequencies available within the U.S. To make use of the standard, the DECT 6.0 standard was developed. In the 1990s several manufacturers introduced DECT in their wireless network products. However, at the time, the U.S. did not allow communications on the frequencies supported by DECT. To take advantage of the capabilities of DECT, manufacturers changed their development focus to wireless telephones. DECT is still used today for cordless telephones. DECT is also a primary component of **Voice over IP (VoIP)** solutions, which allows telephone communications by running VoIP on the server side and DECT on the handset side. DECT remains important in the telecommunications realm, but in wireless networks, the overarching standard family remains 802.11.

The 802.11 family of technologies is much like the Ethernet family. The 802.11 standards reuse many of the Ethernet 802.3 components and are designed to connect easily into Ethernet LANs. For these reasons, IEEE 802.11 is often called **wireless Ethernet.**

Identifying Basic Components

There are three basic component requirements for WLAN or Wi-Fi deployment. You will need a compatible network adapter for each network device. Additionally, if you are deploying an infrastructure mode WLAN (which are the most common type), you'll need one or more wireless access points (WAPs).

The third component is an assigned **frequency range**—the radio frequencies that the wireless devices can use, which replaces wired media. Most countries permit WLANs to operate in two frequency ranges that have been reserved for unlicensed transmissions. These frequency ranges are the 2.4 GHz and 5 GHz ranges, which are the ranges allowed by the North American standard. A potential problem is that a variety of consumer electronics items such as radio-controlled toys, baby monitors, telephones, and even microwave ovens use these same frequency ranges. Hence, they can all interfere with wireless networking devices.

Frequency range directly affects data rates. The larger the **bandwidth** (the frequency range available), the greater the capacity of the wireless circuit and the faster data can be sent. You can think of the frequency range like the width of a pipe carrying water. The wider the pipe, the more water it carries. The wider the frequency range, the more data it carries. The 2.4 GHz range has a smaller bandwidth than the 5 GHz range, so the 5 GHz range (potentially) transmits data faster than the 2.4 GHz range.

Data transmission is also affected by **attenuation,** the weakening of a signal the farther it is from its source. Higher frequencies suffer attenuation more quickly than lower frequencies. Because of this, transmissions in the 2.4 GHz range can travel father and through more walls and other sources of interference than can transmissions in the 5 GHz range. As interference increases and the signal strength weakens, the effective bandwidth that can be used decreases and the capacity and the data rate decreases, which means that wireless technologies that use the 5 GHz range have a shorter effective range than those using the 2.4 GHz range.

One potential problem with WLANs is security. Because anyone within range of a WAP can receive transmissions, eavesdropping is a serious threat. Well-designed WLANs encrypt transmissions so that only authorized computers can decode and read the messages.

Wireless Ethernet
A term used to refer to the 802.11 wireless standards.

IN ACTION:
UNDERSTANDING
WIRELESS
COMMUNICATIONS

Be able to identify components involved in Wi-Fi communications.

Frequency range
A set of radio frequencies available for a specific purpose or application.

Bandwidth
A term used to describe a frequency range or the capacity of a data transmission.

Attenuation
Loss of signal strength over distance.

Understanding Topology and Access Control

The Wi-Fi logical and physical topologies are the same as those used by Ethernet, using a physical star and logical bus when configured for infrastructure mode. There is a central WAP to which all devices direct their transmissions (star), but the radio frequencies are shared (bus) so that all computers must take turns transmitting.

Wi-Fi media access uses **Carrier Sense Multiple Access with Collision Avoidance (CMSA/CA),** which is similar to the CSMA/CD used by Ethernet. With CSMA/CA, computers listen before they transmit and if no one else is transmitting, they proceed with transmission. Detecting collisions is more difficult in radio transmission than in transmission over wired media, so Wi-Fi attempts to avoid collisions to a greater degree than traditional Ethernet. CSMA/CA simultaneously uses two media access control approaches.

The first media access control method used is the **distributed coordination function (DCF),** which is also called **physical carrier sense method (PCSM)** because it relies on the ability of the computer to physically listen before it transmits. With DCF, each packet is sent using stop-and-wait **automatic repeat request (ARQ).** After the sender transmits one packet, it immediately stops and waits for an **acknowledgement (ACK)** from the receiver before attempting to send another packet. When the receiver of a packet detects the end of the packet in a transmission, it waits a fraction of a second to make sure the sender has really stopped transmitting, and then immediately transmits an ACK (or **negative acknowledgement, or NAK**). The original sender can then send another packet, stop and wait for an ACK, and so on.

While the sender and receiver are exchanging packets and ACKs, other computers may also want to transmit. So when the sender ends its transmission, you might ask why doesn't some other computer begin transmitting before the receiver can transmit an ACK? The answer is that the physical carrier sense method is designed so that the time the receiver waits after the transmission ends before sending an ACK is significantly less time than the time a computer must listen to determine that no one else is transmitting before initiating a new transmission. Thus, the time interval between a transmission and the matching ACK is so short that no other computer has the opportunity to begin transmitting.

The other technique used is **point coordination function (PCF),** also called the **virtual carrier sense method (VCSM).** DCF works well in traditional Ethernet because every computer on the shared circuit receives every transmission on the shared circuit. However, in a wireless environment, not every transmission is received. A computer at the extreme edge of the range limit from the WAP on one side may not receive transmissions from a computer on the extreme opposite edge of the WAP's range limit. In the example in Figure 10-1, all of the computers are in range of the WAP,

Carrier Sense Multiple Access with Collision Avoidance (CMSA/CA)

An access method used on Wi-Fi networks that is similar to the CSMA/CD used on Ethernet networks, except that it makes more of an effort to avoid collisions between transmitting devices.

Distributed coordination function (DCF)

A media access method in which a device must physically listen before transmitting. Also known as physical carrier-sense method (PCSM).

Physical carrier sense method (PCSM)

See distributed coordination function (DCF).

Automatic repeat request (ARQ)

A stop-and-wait transmission method used by DCF.

Acknowledgement (ACK)

A special packet type sent by a receiving system to acknowledge successful receipt of one or more datagrams.

Negative acknowledgement (NAK)

A special packet type sent by a receiving system to indicate that a packet was not successfully received.

Figure 10-1

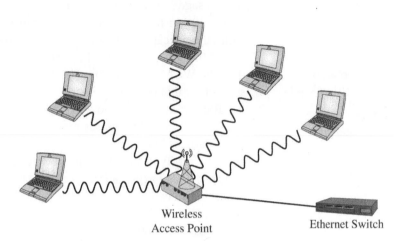

Wireless
Access Point

Ethernet Switch

Sample infrastructure network.

Point coordination function (PCF)
A wireless transmission method that uses RTS and CTS to control transmissions. Also known as virtual carrier-sense method (VCSM).

Virtual carrier sense method (VCSM)
See **point coordination function (PCF)**.

Hidden node problem
A situation in which a wireless client at one end of a WAP's range is not able to detect a client at the other end of its range.

Request to transmit (RTS)
A message type in a WAP, whereby a system requests to be permitted to transmit on the network.

Clear to send (CTS)
A signal sent by a WAP to inform a computer that it can send data.

IN ACTION:
Wi-Fi STANDARDS
Get to know what standards govern Wi-Fi communications.

but may not be within the range of each other. In this case, if one computer transmits, the other computer on the opposite edge may not sense the other transmission and transmit at the same time, causing a collision at the WAP. This is called the **hidden node problem** because the computers at the opposite edges of the WLAN are hidden from each other.

When the hidden node problem exists, the WAP is the only device guaranteed to be able to communicate with all computers on the WLAN. Therefore the WAP must manage the shared circuit using a controlled access-technique, not the contention-based approach of traditional Ethernet. With this approach, any computer wishing to transmit first sends a **request to transmit (RTS)** to the WAP, which may or may not be heard by all computers. The RTS requests permission to transmit and to reserve the circuit for the sole use of the requesting computer for a specified time period. If no other computer is transmitting, the WAP responds with a **clear to send (CTS),** specifying the amount of time for which the circuit is reserved for the requesting computer.

Wi-Fi is the fastest growing and most rapidly changing area in networking technologies today, so you can expect to see Wi-Fi applications to continue to change. Three 802.11 Wi-Fi transmission standards are currently in use and one that is under development that is designed to provide higher-speed WLAN networks. These are:

- 802.11a: Rarely used in PC networking applications.
- 802.11b: The original Wi-Fi standard.
- 802.11g: The updated Wi-Fi standard.
- 802.11n: High-speed standard currently in use.

Overlay network
A wireless network that parallels and overlaps a wired network.

Supported channels given for each of the standards is based on United States usage standards. Other countries may allow more or fewer channels, depending on frequency spectrum regulations. With each of these standards, the typical configuration is an infrastructure mode WLAN connected to an Ethernet-wired network, as shown in Figure 10-2. In this configuration, the WLAN is being used as an **overlay network,** one that provides support for mobile computers in the same areas and the wired network.

Bandwidth use is a potential concern, just as it is with Ethernet networks. PCF initially imposes more fixed cost delays than wired Ethernet when traffic is low because computers must request permission before they can transmit. Typically, Wi-Fi users experience few response time delays as long as the total network traffic remains below 85 to 90 percent of the total available bandwidth. Still, monitoring traffic patterns is still important. The response time delays increase slowly up to the 85 to 90 percent threshold. After this level is reached, the number of noticeable delays increases rapidly until the network is 100 percent saturated.

Figure 10-2

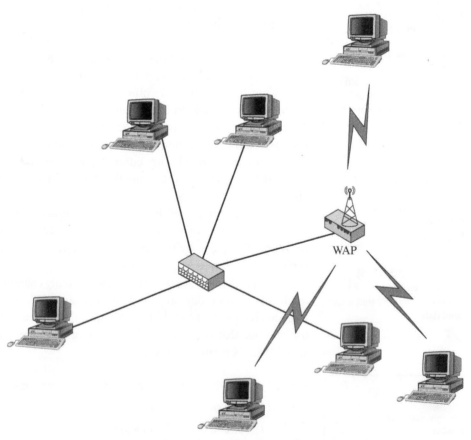

Sample overlay network.

802.16 WiMAX

A set of high-speed wireless communication standards.

802.16d fixed WiMAX

A high-speed wireless communication standard that is sometimes used for MAN connections or to connect public Wi-Fi WAPs to a central point for communication with the Internet.

802.16e mobile WiMAX

A high-speed wireless standard designed as an alternative for cell phones and computer hardware.

802.11a

The first high-speed wireless standard. Extends 802.11. 802.11a defines transmissions that utilize the 5GHz frequency band with 54Mbps of wireless throughput. The standard is not commonly used.

802.11b

The basis for most of the early wireless devices. 802.11b uses the 2.4GHz frequency band for communication and allows for up to 11Mbps of throughput to be transmitted.

802.11g

A wireless standard that uses the 2.4GHz frequency bank, like 802.11b, although transmitting at up to 54Mbps. Most 802.11g devices support and provide connectivity to 802.11b devices on the network because they are communicating within the same frequency band.

An additional set of commercial wireless standards is known as the **802.16** or **WiMAX** standards. WiMAX standards are not currently used in LAN configurations. The **802.16d fixed WiMAX** standard is used in some areas for wireless metropolitan area network (MAN) connections or for connecting Wi-Fi public access points to a central, shared connection to the Internet. The **802.16e mobile WiMAX** standard is designed to provide an alternative to current mobile Wi-Fi and cellular telephone standards. Theoretical ranges are up to 30 miles, with real-world effective ranges between 2.5 and 5.0 miles.

Looking at 802.11a

The IEEE **802.11a** standard provides high-speed wireless networking in the 5 GHz range. It provides eight channels for indoor use in the United States and one channel for outdoor use. The indoor channels are identified as 36, 40, 44, 48, 52, 56, 60, and 64, with 149 identifying the outdoor channel.

Each channel provides speeds of up to 54 Mbps under perfect conditions. The range, under perfect conditions, is rated at 50 meters (150 feet). In practice, it is usually less. The farther you are from the WAP, the lower the supported data rate. Typically, 54 Mbps is supported at no more than 50 feet between the WAP and networked devices. Under normal operating conditions, speeds of 26 Mbps to 34 Mbps are common, and the speed may even drop to 6 Mbps if interference is present.

Looking at 802.11b

The IEEE **802.11b** standard provides moderate speed wireless networking in the 2.4 GHz range. It provides three channels for indoor use in the United States. The channels are identified as channels 1, 6, and 11.

Each channel provides a maximum data rate of 11 Mbps. Only where significant interference exists or the signal begins to weaken because the user is moving far from the WLAN does the data rate change in an attempt to improve signal quality. Thus, for those users close to the center of the WLAN, 6 to 11 Mbps is common. The range under ideal conditions is 450 feet, although the actual range in practice is typically much less. The speed may drop to 1 Mbps in the presence of heavy interference.

The advantage over 802.11a is that 802.11b suffers less attenuation. The signal has a greater range with less decrease in speed as distance from the WAP increases. However, under optimal conditions, 802.11b supports lower speeds than 802.11a.

Looking at 802.11g

The **802.11g** standard supports high-speed wireless networking in the 2.4 GHz range. It provides three channels for indoor use in the United States, using the same channel numbers as 802.11b, 1, 6, and 11.

Each channel provides a maximum data rate of 54 Mbps. The range under ideal conditions is 450 feet. The actual range under normal conditions is less. The data rate can drop as low as 6 Mbps when significant interference is present.

802.11g is backward compatible with 802.11b, so 802.11b devices can communicate with an 802.11g WAP. In fact, you can deploy a WLAN that has 802.11g WAPs and any mix of 802.11b and 802.11g client devices, which means that it supports existing laptops that have built-in 802.11b NICs.

However, this mixed configuration is not without its potential problems. 802.11b devices are still limited to the 802.11b transmission maximum of 11 Mbps. As well, 802.11b devices become confused when 802.11g devices operate at high speed near them. Because of this, when an 802.11g device detects an 802.11b device nearby, the 802.11g device drops into a lower bandwidth operational mode.

Looking at 802.11n

802.11n
A wireless standard currently under development.

Multi-input multi-output (MIMO)
A technology that makes the use of multiple transceivers and receivers to improve the speed of communications.

The IEEE **802.11n** standard provides very high-speed wireless networking using both the 2.4 GHz and 5 GHz frequency ranges simultaneously by using multiple sets of antennas optimized to the different frequencies. Using **multi-input multi-output (MIMO)** antennas, the 802.11n standard can use both frequencies to increase the data speeds up to 600 Mbit/s, depending on the configuration of the device in use. To increase the data speeds, the 802.11n standard uses MIMO to allow up to four communications channels with through put of up to 40Mzh each.

The 802.11n standard was finalized in 2009, but was adopted by many organizations previous to ratification. It is also designed to be backward compatible with 802.11a, 802.11b, and 802.11g.

Bluetooth

Bluetooth
The commercial name for a WPAN standard. Refers to all devices that work through this protocol including headsets, keyboards, mouses, etc.

802.15
The IEEE standard for WPAN or Bluetooth devices.

Wireless Personal Area Network (WPAN)
The standard covering Bluetooth devices, also known as the IEEE 802.15 standard.

Bluetooth is the commercial name for the IEEE **802.15** standards, which calls it a **Wireless Personal Area Network (WPAN).** Bluetooth is a strikingly different type of wireless LAN from the others discussed earlier in this chapter. It is not intended as a general-purpose network in competition with 802.11wireless LANs. Its goal is to provide seamless networking of data and/or voice devices in a very small area (up to 10 meters or 30 feet, possibly to increase to about 100 meters or 300 feet with the next generation of technology). Bluetooth can be used to connect many different types of devices, such as keyboards to computers and headsets to mobile phones.

Bluetooth devices are small (about one-third of an inch square) and inexpensive. They are designed to replace short-distance cabling between devices such as keyboards, mice, and a telephone headset and base or to link your PDA to your car so that your door can unlock and automatically open as you approach. Bluetooth provides a basic data rate of 1Mps that can be divided into several separate voice and data channels.

10.1.4 Configuring Wi-Fi

Configuring a WLAN using Wi-Fi includes two parts. You need to configure the access point and each of the wireless devices. WAP configuration procedures and options can vary widely between manufacturers and different WAP applications. All WAPs can act as bridges when connecting to a wired Ethernet network. Most also act as broadband routers and network access servers, supporting shared high-speed Internet access.

Consider the configuration shown in Figure 10-3. The WAP provides shared Internet access and IP address and configuration information for all of the wireless computers. By default, it will also provide addresses for any wired computer in the connected network segment that is configured to receive an IP address automatically.

The design and implementation process begins with a site survey that determines the feasibility of the desired coverage, the potential sources of interference, the current locations of the wired network into which the WLAN will connect, and an estimate of the number of WAPs needed.

Figure 10-3

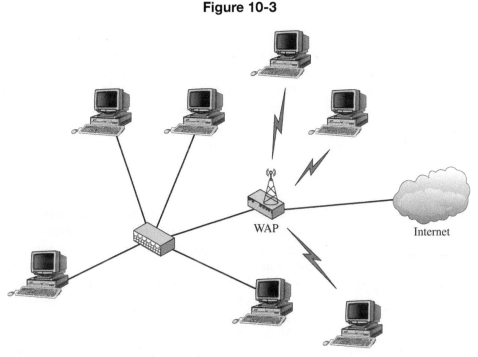

Sample network configuration.

Sources of interference include RFI sources (such as microwave ovens, cordless telephones, and industrial equipment) and walls. WLANs work best when there is a clear line of sight between the WAP and networked devices. The heavier the wall, or the more walls the signal must pass through, the greater the interference.

Configuring a WAP

The specific procedures for configuring a WAP are manufacturer, and sometimes model, specific. Although most will work "out of the box" without any special configuration, we don't recommend you do so because the WAP will broadcast its default Service Set Identifier (SSID) and not use any type of security. Doing so makes it easy for unauthorized users to connect to you network.

Most manufacturers let you connect to a USB port, through the local intranet, and sometimes through the public Internet to configure a WAP. Remote management is typically disabled by default and typically should not be enabled. Configuration options usually include:

- **Internet connection information:** IP address configuration, router name, and similar information.

- **Local network information:** DHCP configuration, including address scope available for assignment, routing configuration, and possibly simple dynamic DNS support.

Mixed mode
A wireless communication option supported by some WAPs that enables the device to work with both 802.11b and 802.11g at the same time.

- **Wireless configuration:** Mode (as 802.11b, 802.11g, or both in a **mixed mode and 802.11n**), SSID, channel used, and whether or not the SSID is broadcast.

- **Wireless security:** Wireless security mode and configuration, authentication requirements (if any), MAC filtering information, and, in some cases, more advanced or custom security settings.

- **Network security:** Which can include a built-in firewall and the ability to pass or block virtual private network (VPN) traffic.

Other options can include setting different types of Internet access restrictions by URL, address, domain, service, or TCP or UDP port information. Some WAPs have settings relating to application support, including Internet gaming support. Most let you set an administrator password to control access to WAP configuration settings.

IN ACTION:
CONFIGURING A
WIRELESS ROUTER

Set up your router to support wireless connection.

Figure 10-4 shows you a typical configuration screen. Notice from the menu across the top that this specific WAP supports a variety of configuration screens and a large number of configurable parameters.

Notice, in this case, the WAP is configured to provide DHCP support. The settings shown here are defaults for this model, and as you can see, it leaves the 192.168.1.1 through 192.168.1.99 unused by the scope and

Figure 10-4

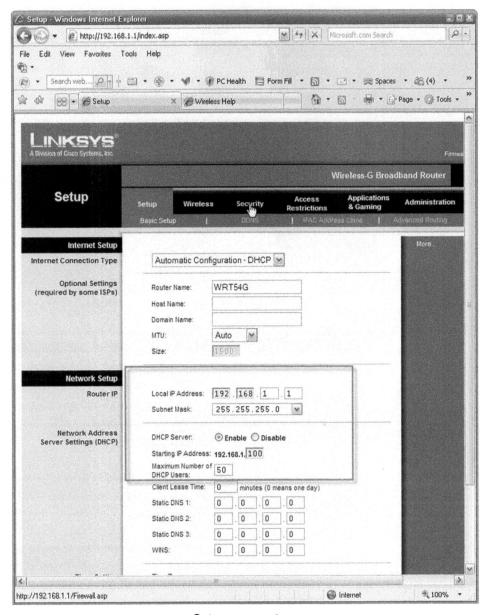

Setup parameters.

available for assigning through other means, such as static addresses. Also, it will support no more than 50 clients, so addresses above 192.168.1.150 will typically be available for other uses.

Figure 10-5 has typical wireless configuration parameters. This WAP has obviously not been secured. This configuration is set up for mixed mode as well, meaning it can support both 802.11b and 802.11g clients.

Figure 10-5

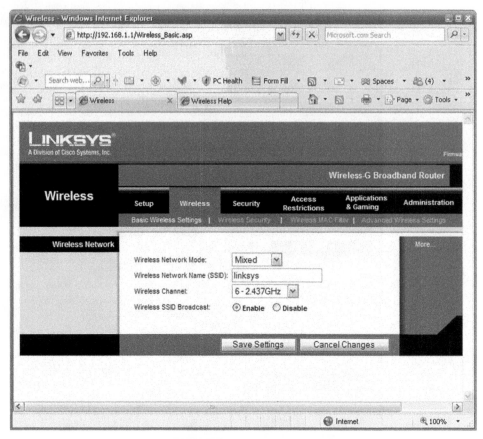

Wireless parameters.

Further, it is using its default SSID, and is broadcasting the SSID, making it easy for anyone in range to see and connect to the WAP. The WAP is using channel 6, which means any clients connecting to this WAP will also have to use channel 6.

Wireless security settings are beyond the scope of this course, but you should be aware that available options vary by manufacturer. Security configuration options should be one of your primary considerations when selecting a WAP.

Configuring Network Clients

Set up your router to support wireless connection. The options for configuring network clients vary by operating system type and version. Current Windows operating system versions are able to detect and automatically configure access to WAPs that broadcast their SSID and don't have any security configuration requirements. You can view a list of available networks and set the relative connection priority, using the first network if possible, then the next, and so on. The properties for a wireless connection are much the same as those for a wired, except for the Wireless tab, shown in Figure 10-6. From here, you can manually enter configuration information such as the WAP's SSID and information about authentication and encryption.

Some information, like the signal strength, can be helpful when troubleshooting wireless connections.

Figure 10-6

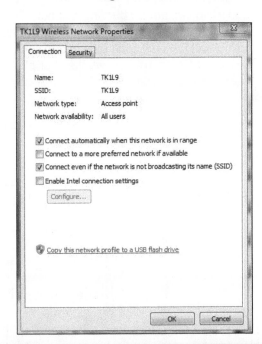

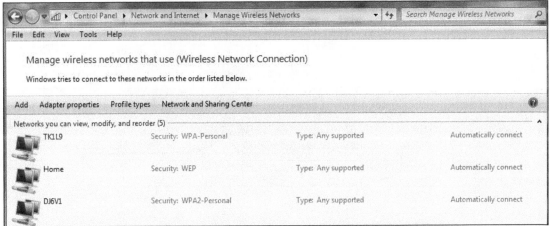

Connection wireless parameters.

IN THE REAL WORLD

Indiana University

The following is a true story that illustrates the potential effect of wireless interference.

"Most of the buildings at Indiana University have both wired and wireless network access. The Kelly School of Business at Indiana University has two major buildings: a modern building built in 2002 and an older building built in 1968. The new building was designed with wireless networks in mind; the old building was not. My office is in the old building.

One Wi-Fi access point is on the floor, which should provide sufficient coverage. However, concrete walls make it hard for wireless signals to penetrate. Figure 10-7 shows the floor plan, the position of the access point, and the data rates that are available at different locations on the floor.

Figure 10-7

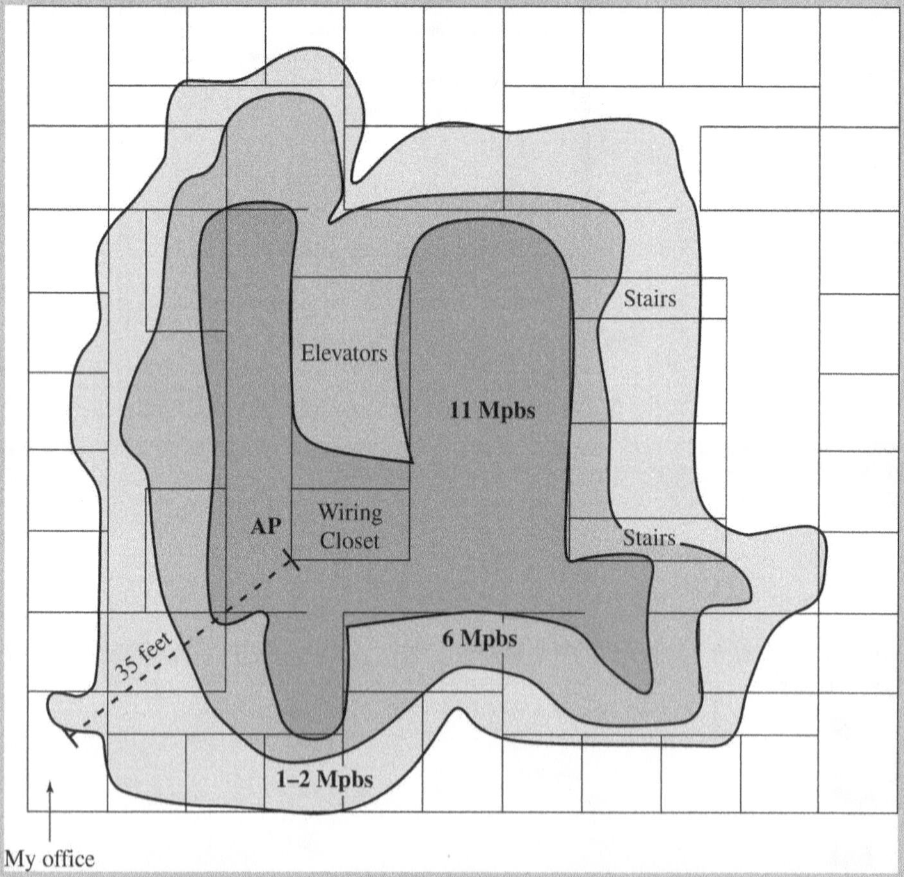

WLAN design.

(continued)

(continued)

My office is located about 35 feet from the access point (less than 12 meters), which is well within the normal range for high-speed access. However, because of the concrete walls, I am unable to receive a signal in most of my office."

SELF-CHECK

1. How does the access method used by Wi-Fi differ from that used by Ethernet?
2. What happens if an 802.11g device detects an 802.11b device nearby?

Project 10.1

Wireless networking has become the preferred network topology in several networking scenarios. Development of wireless networking technologies is moving more quickly than other technologies that relate to PC networking. As a result, if you aren't dealing with wireless networking now, you probably will be soon.

Complete **Project 10.2: Understanding Wireless Technologies** in the online Network Basics Project Manual to review various wireless technologies and some important considerations related to wireless access point (WAP) configuration.

10.2 IMPLEMENTING REMOTE ACCESS

Virtual private network (VPN)
An encrypted, secure, private communication path over a public carrier.

Nearly all network operating systems (NOS) support some option for remote client access. The details vary by NOS, but you typically have the option of either connecting through a dial-up connection or via the Internet through a **virtual private network (VPN)** connection.

During this section, we're going to take a look at remote access fundamentals, including an overview of remote access protocols, and a sample of how you might configure remote access. However, a detailed discussion of security issues relating to remote access is beyond the scope of this course.

10.2.1 Comparing Access Fundamentals

You must consider several factors when configuring remote access connection options. How many concurrent remote connections do you need to support? What are the clients' bandwidth requirements? Do client computers have Internet access available? Do they have modems?

Remote access requires one or more computers configured to provide access, usually called **remote access servers,** and one or more clients requiring access. The traditional access method is for clients to call in through the dial-up telephone network, more formally called the **Public Switched Telephone Network (PSTN) or Plain Old Telephone System (POTS).** Figure 10-8 shows an example.

Advantages of dial-up access include:

- **Readily available:** You can usually find a telephone line available in nearly any population center in the world.
- **Low initial cost:** Modems are cheap, and many computers come with a modem already installed.
- **No LAN hardware requirements for the client:** Because you're connecting through a modem, you don't need a NIC or any network cabling.

But, when you're considering dial-up access, you should also consider the disadvantages:

- **Variable incremental costs:** Your incremental costs, cost per connection, will depend on your long distance charges (if any) and how long you stay connected.
- **Low bandwidth:** For example, dial-up bandwidth in the United States is limited to no more than 56 Kbps and can be lower depending on line conditions.

Remote access servers
Any combination of hardware and software components that are used to permit access to a network from remote clients.

Public Switched Telephone Network (PSTN) or Plain Old Telephone System (POTS)
A telephone network and infrastructure that includes the standard dial-up phone network.

IN ACTION:
SELECTING ACCESS
TYPES FOR YOUR NEEDS

Benefits and drawbacks of using dial-up.

Figure 10-8

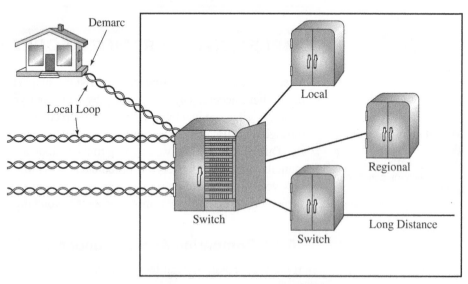

Central Office

Local connection to the PSTN.

- **Little communication security:** Tapping telephone conversations, even between computers, is relatively easy, and if not encrypted, easy to intercept and steal sensitive data.

Access security can also be a concern. How (or even if) user authentication is managed varies by NOS type and version. Some administrators go with default, minimal security configurations, making it relatively easy for unauthorized personnel to access your network.

In recent years access methods that rely on connecting through the Internet have become more popular. In that case, both the user and the remote access server must obviously have Internet access. A VPN connection is used, like the example in Figure 10-9.

Other methods have been used at different times, but nearly all have been phased out in favor of the Internet. Advantages of connecting through the Internet include:

- **Higher available bandwidth:** High-speed Internet connections ranging from around 300 Kbps up through several Mbps are readily available in most regions of the country.
- **Minimal incremental changes:** Most ISPs charge a flat monthly fee for unlimited access, and even most hotels provide access for free or at reasonable rates (typically $10 per day or less).

Figure 10-9

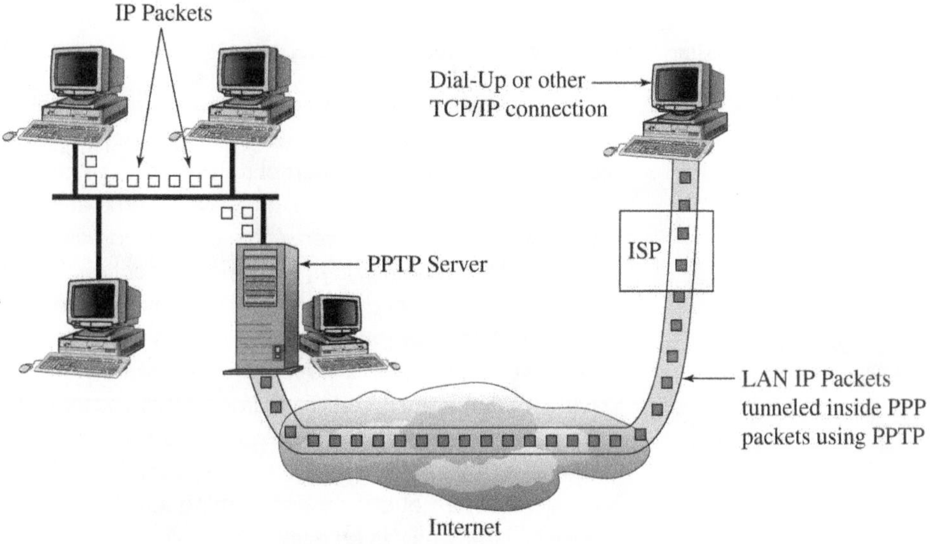

Remote access VPN connection.

- **Flexible security configurations:** VPN connection methods provide for a wide variety of authentication options and secure encryption methods.

Of course, there are disadvantages, including:

- **Internet access required:** Mobile users won't always have convenient Internet access available and might find themselves working, for example, from a public Wi-Fi hot spot.
- **More complex configuration requirements:** Internet access is more complex and administrators and users might possibly try to save time by cutting corners and skimping on security.
- **Not supported by all NOS:** Some older NOS provide native support for dial-in access only, and though some workarounds for configuring VPN access are available, they often aren't worth the time or expense involved.

In most configurations, from the user's standpoint very little difference between connecting locally or through a remote access connection exists. Users must be authenticated before they are allowed access to the network, and rights and permissions they've been granted determine their resource access. There are, however, a couple of significant potential differences. In some remote access configurations, users can access resources physically hosted on only the remote access server. The other difference is that if the user is connecting through a low bandwidth method (such as through a dial-up modem), the delays when copying or opening files from the network can be noticeable.

IN THE REAL WORLD

Cutting Costs with the Internet

Some companies have found it cost effective to get rid of the dial-in remote access services and switch to Internet VPN connections, paying for some employees' Internet connections as part of the deal. Many companies that allow, or even, encourage some employees to telecommute have traditionally covered the associated costs. If that connection involves a long-distance call, and long connection times to the company network, the connection charges can be quite expensive.

What these companies have found is that it is usually cheaper to pay a flat fee to cover the employee's Internet connection instead of paying for dial-up connection charges. Often, employees are able to get high-speed Internet connections, making them more efficient. Another added benefit is in employee satisfaction. After the employee has a high-speed Internet connection coming into the house, sharing it with the rest of the family is an easy matter.

10.2.2 Comparing Access and Authentication

A remote access protocol manages the connection between a remote computer and a remote access server. The primary remote access protocols used today are:

- Serial Line Internet Protocol (SLIP)
- Point-to-Point Protocol (PPP) and Point-to-Point Protocol over Ethernet (PPPoE)
- Point-to-Point Tunneling Protocol (PPTP)
- Layer 2 Tunneling Protocol (L2TP)

SLIP, PPP, and PPoE are used to create dial-up remote access connections. PPTP and L2TP are VPN protocols and are used not only with client remote access, but also when connecting LANs to create WANs.

Another consideration when configuring remote access is the authentication protocol used. Authentication protocol options vary by client and server. Authentication methods also vary by NOS and remote access server type. Authentication can be handled by the individual server using network authentication methods or with the remote access server handling authentication itself, or authentication can be centralized using **Remote Authentication Dial-in User Service (RADIUS)** or other centralized authentication methods. Microsoft has its own implementation of RADIUS technology, which it refers to as **Internet Authentication Service (IAS).**

Remote Authentication Dial-in User Service (RADIUS)
A centralized authentication method.

Internet Authentication Service (IAS)
A Microsoft implementation of RADIUS technology.

Serial Line Internet Protocol (SLIP)
An older access protocol originally designed for use with Unix computers. SLIP passes user names and passwords as clear text.

Comparing SLIP and PPP

Serial Line Internet Protocol (SLIP) was originally developed for use with UNIX, as a way for terminals to connect to UNIX servers. It is still sometimes used for that purpose with both UNIX and Linux servers.

It is being used less frequently because it lacks features when compared with other protocols. Although a low overhead is associated with using SLIP and you can use it to transport TCP/IP over serial connections, it does no error checking or packet addressing and can be used only on serial connections. SLIP does not support encrypted passwords and therefore transmits passwords in clear text, which is inherently not secure.

Setting up SLIP for a remote connection requires a SLIP account on the host machine and usually a batch file or a script on the workstation. When SLIP is used to log in to a remote machine, a terminal mode must be configured after login to the remote site so that the script can enter each parameter. If you don't use a script, you will have to establish the connection and then open a terminal window to log in to the remote access server manually. Many modern operating systems, such as Windows 2000 Server (and later), don't support inbound SLIP connections. Windows still supports outbound SLIP to allow connections to UNIX machines.

Point-to-Point Protocol (PPP)

A protocol that is used for remote connections over a variety of connection methods and that supports multiple network protocols.

Link Control Protocol (LCP)

A PPP subprotocol used to communicate between PPP hosts and clients to negotiate communication parameters.

Compression control protocols (CCPs)

A PPP subprotocol that manages data compression.

Encryption control protocols (ECPs)

A PPP subprotocol that handles negotiating encryption methods.

Network control protocols (NCP)

An IPX/SPX protocol that provides services in support of client/server connections.

IP control protocol (IPCP)

A PPP network control protocol that manages and configures TCP/IP over PPP support.

Dynamic Host Configuration Protocol (DHCP)

A protocol and service used to provide IP addresses and TCP/IP configuration parameters.

Point-to-Point over Ethernet (PPPoE)

A communication protocol that encapsulates PPP frames inside Ethernet packet.

Point-to-Point Protocol (PPP) implements TCP/IP connections over point-to point links (for example, dial-up and dedicated leased lines), but it also supports other network protocols, such as IPX. PPP encapsulates the packets of protocols being carried by PPP. Because it features error checking and can run over many types of physical media, PPP has almost completely replaced SLIP. It is most commonly used for remote connections to ISPs and LANs. PPP uses the **Link Control Protocol (LCP)** to communicate between PPP client and host. LCP tests the link between client and PPP host and specifies PPP client configuration. Through LCP, PPP also supports authentication negotiation, as well as negotiation of encryption and compression between client and server, using **compression control protocols (CCPs)** that handle data compression and **encryption control protocols (ECPs)** responsible for data encryption.

PPP can support several network protocols through the use of protocol specific **network control protocols (NCP)**. PPP can automatically configure TCP/IP and other protocol parameters through the use of the **IP control protocol (IPCP)** NCP. On the downside, high overhead is associated with using PPP, and it is not compatible with some older configurations.

From the technician's standpoint, PPP is easy to configure. After you connect to a router using PPP, the router assigns all other TCP/IP parameters usually with **Dynamic Host Configuration Protocol (DHCP)**. IP configuration information can be assigned over a LAN connection or a dial-up connection. When you connect to an ISP, you are most likely getting your IP address from a DHCP server.

Point-to-Point over Ethernet (PPPoE) is a way of encapsulating PPP frames over an Ethernet network. Though we mention it here for your reference, it is not used for configuring remote access clients. Instead, it is most often used to let network users share an "always on" high-speed Internet connection, like a DSL line or cable modem.

Comparing PPTP and L2TP

Point-to-Point Tunneling Protocol (PPTP) and **Layer 2 Tunneling Protocol (L2TP)** are both VPN protocols. You can use them to configure VPN connections through the Internet or to configure secure communications over a LAN connection. PPTP is the Microsoft-created protocol based on PPP that is used to create virtual connections across the Internet using TCP/IP and PPP. It is supported with Windows NT 4.0 and later servers and Windows 95 and later clients. L2TP was designed by the Internet Engineering Task Force (IETF) and supports both TCP/IP and non-TCP/IP protocols on VPNs by encapsulating them in an IP frame as a wrapper.

To use PPTP, you set up a PPP session between the client and server, typically over the Internet. After the session is established, you create a session that connects through the existing PPP session using PPTP.

Point-to-Point Tunneling Protocol (PPTP)
A Microsoft-developed protocol that is used for VPN connectivity.

Layer 2 Tunneling Protocol (L2TP)
An industry-standard VPN connection protocol.

Layer 2 Forwarding (L2F)
The Cisco Systems protocol on which L2TP is based.

The PPTP session tunnels through the existing PPP connection, creating a secure session. PPP packets are encapsulated inside IP packets for transmission. In this way, you can use the Internet to create a secure session between the client and the server. In most situations, you will likely want to encrypt the communications between the server and the remote client. Microsoft supports encryption through the Microsoft Point-to-Point Encryption (MPPE) protocol.

L2TP is a combination of Microsoft PPTP and Cisco's **Layer 2 Forwarding (L2F)** technology. It supports a variety of protocols, including IPX and AppleTalk. This support gives it the advantage of letting you connect non-TCP/IP clients to networks running protocols other than TCP/IP. L2F is supported on the Windows OS beginning with Vista. Other advantages include:

- Industry standard protocol, giving it broad-based support.
- Can authenticate both the user and client computer using certificates (a method of defining shared security) or a preshared key (a value known to the server and client).
- Supports stronger authentication methods than PPTP.

However, it isn't without its own disadvantages.

- Not compatible with some NAT devices (but in a Windows 2003 or 2008 Server, NAT is supported).
- Tunneling can reduce throughput.

Internet Protocol Security (IPsec)
An industry-standard security protocol that provides encryption and authentication for L2TP VPN connections.

Transport mode
An IPsec mode in which the data portion of a packet is encrypted for host-to-host communications.

Tunnel mode
An IPsec mode in which the entire IP packet is encrypted and then encapsulated in another IP packet for host-to-host, host-to-network, and network-to-network communications.

Internet Protocol Security (IPsec), an industry standard, provides security for L2TP. IPsec is a set of open standards designed to provide security for IP networks. It provides support for peer-computer authentication and data authentication and data encryption. It supports two modes of operation. When operating in **transport mode,** only the message portion of the IP packet is encrypted. It is used for host-to-host communications. Remote access connections always use transport mode. It also supports a **tunnel mode,** in which the entire packet is encrypted and then encapsulated inside another IP packet. It enables IPsec support for non-IPsec aware client operating systems. Tunnel mode can be used with host-to-host communications, but is also used with host-to-network and network-to-network communications. On a Windows network, IPsec is supported by Windows 2000 and later servers and Windows XP and later clients unless used for VPN access with the L2TP client software installed.

VPN connections using PPTP or L2TP can be used to configure a single remote workstation to connect to a corporate network over the Internet. The workstation is configured to connect to the Internet via an ISP, and the VPN client is configured with the address of the VPN remote access server, as shown in Figure 10-9. A VPN connection often connects remote workstations to corporate LANs when a workstation must communicate with a corporate network. PPTP is typically used when communicating over a dial-up or broadband PPP link through an ISP and the link must be secure.

Understanding Authentication Protocols

Several authentication protocols can be used with PPP and PPTP. If configured with support for multiple protocols, the server and client will negotiate the authentication protocol used while negotiating other communication parameters. Supported protocols include:

- **Password Authentication Protocol (PAP):** Based on a user name and password passed as clear text and authenticated against information stored on the server.

- **Shiva Password Authentication Protocol (SPAP):** Passes the password in a relatively easy to break encryption method.

- **Challenge Handshake Authentication Protocol (CHAP):** Industry standard using a challenge-and-response where the server sends a challenge to the client; the client returns a 128-bit response that is based on the original challenge and the user's password.

- **Microsoft Challenge Handshake Authentication Protocol (MS-CHAP):** Developed by Microsoft (originally supporting Windows 3.1) as its own CHAP version that sends two parallel hashes (values derived from the challenge, response, and a key value) during authentication, a LAN Manager hash and NT LAN Manager (NTLM) hash.

- **Microsoft Challenge Handshake Authentication Protocol version 2 (MS-CHAPv2):** Enhanced CHAP version with security improvements that include not using the LAN Manager hash, making it more secure than MS-CHAP.

- **Extensible Authentication Protocol (EAP):** Industry standard way of adding additional authentication protocols such as support for smart cards, which are specialized access and authentication security devices.

EAP-Transport Layer Security (EAP-TLS)
An EAP protocol extension designed for use with smart cards for authentication.

MD5-Challenge (MD5-CHAP)
A protocol designed for testing and troubleshooting EAP connections.

Public Key-based User to User or PKU2U was newly introduced with Windows 7. This authentication protocol allows users to share data between computers. Users use an online ID connected to their Windows user account to access shared files by authenticating through the PKU2U protocol.

Windows 2008 Server's implementation of EAP includes support for **EAP-Transport Layer Security (EAP-TLS),** designed for use with smart cards. It also includes **MD5-Challenge (MD5-CHAP),** which is a protocol designed for testing and troubleshooting EAP connections and should not be used when configuring your network security.

Because of security concerns, limit use of PAP and SPAP to clients or servers that don't support more secure authentication methods. You should avoid MS-CHAP as well, as it does not authenticate the server and the LAN Manager hash is not very secure and is easily broken. EAP and MS-CHAPv2 are preferred options, depending on the capabilities of your remote access server and the client operating systems supported. MS-CHAPv2 cannot be used with Windows 95 and older Windows clients because it doesn't send the LAN Manager hash needed by those clients. CHAP is required when using non-Microsoft clients that don't support EAP. CHAP and EAP, because they are both industry standard protocols, support a wide variety of client types. One potential disadvantage of CHAP is that passwords must be stored using reversible encryption.

You can implement additional, centralized support for authentication, especially when you have multiple remote access servers, by including a RADIUS server in your networking mix. The RADIUS server can use passwords provided by the NOS or can maintain its own password database. RADIUS is a de facto standard supported by several manufacturers, including Microsoft, to support authentication, authorization, and even provide logging for remote connections. One of the advantages of using RADIUS is that it supports several connection methods, including dial-up connections, VPN, and even computers connecting through WAPs on a wireless network.

10.2.3 Configuring Remote Access

The specific requirements for configuring remote access vary by network operating system, but the necessary parameters are very similar. We look at the requirements for Windows, by configuring remote access service, which are typical.

With Windows Server 2008, you set up remote access through Routing and Remote Access Service (RRAS). You can set up a server to support dial-up connections, VPN connections, or both. Dial-up connection support requires one or more modems. Some companies install modem banks, several dial-up modems built onto a device or interface card, so that one server can support several dial-up users. A separate phone is also needed. The number of modem ports and phone lines physically limits the number of concurrent users.

When configuring VPN connection support, you must identify the network interfaces that can be used, shown in Figure 10-10. You also identify how clients are issued IP addresses, either from an existing DHCP server or you can specify a range of addresses that can be issued directly by the RRAS server.

By default, the server will be configured to support MS-CHAP, MS-CHAPv2, and EAP. This is configured through the RRAS server properties, shown in Figure 10-11.

IN ACTION:
CONFIGURING FOR
REMOTE ACCESS

What you need to know when setting up your systems.

Figure 10-10

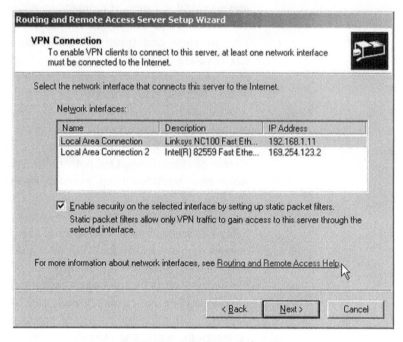

Available network interfaces.

Figure 10-11

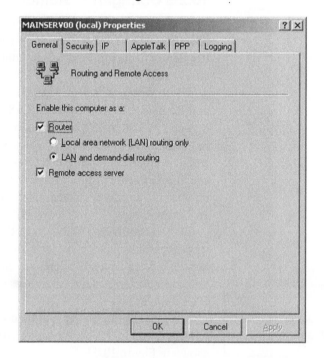

RRAS server properties.

To manage the authentication methods supported, activate the Security tab shown in Figure 10-12 and then click Authentication methods.

Authentication options are shown in Figure 10-13. Checked authentication methods are supported. To remove support for an authentication method, remove the check.

When configuring clients, you will typically configure the client as either a dial-up or VPN client, but you may have situations where you might configure a client to support both. On Windows computers, configure client connections through Network Connections. When configuring a dial-up connection, you will specify the company name, phone number, and who can use the connection. Client-side security is configured through the connection properties. The client connection's advanced security settings, shown in Figure 10-14, let you choose the authentication protocols supported by the client.

Configuring a VPN connection over the Internet is just as easy. You need to tell the computer whether or not it needs to dial the initial connection, for example, if it needs to dial in to an ISP before establishing the connection, and the name of the server to which it will connect. You also configure who can use the connection.

Figure 10-12

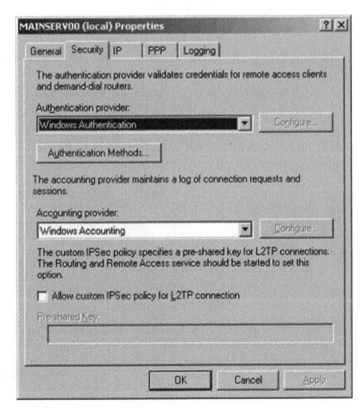

RRAS Security Tab.

Figure 10-13

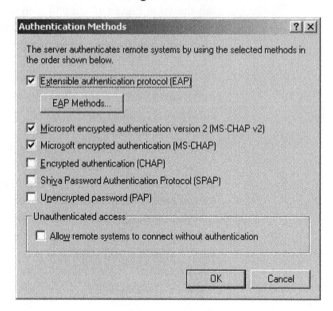

Authentication options.

Figure 10-14

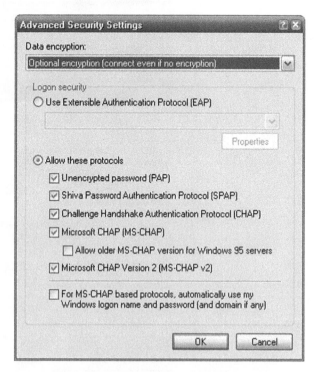

Dial-up client advanced security settings.

Figure 10-15

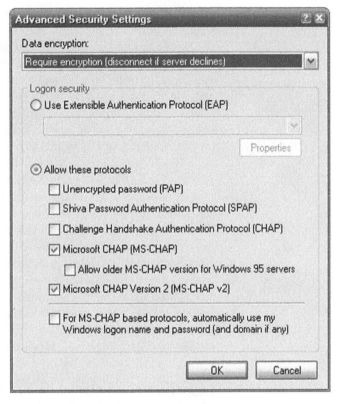

VPN client advanced security settings.

One difference with a VPN connection is security configuration settings. A detailed discussion of these settings is beyond the scope of this chapter, but we take a quick look at the default authentication protocols, shown in Figure 10-15.

By default, as you can see, only the more secure authentication protocols are supported.

IN THE REAL WORLD

Wired and Wireless Solutions

Many companies find a combination of wireless and wired networks to be an optimal solution. For example, one company provides laptops to all workers. When the workers are in the office, they can connect to the company corporate Intranet and, through that, the Internet using their wired connection. When they log in, corporate personnel use a single

(continued)

(continued)

user ID and password combination to authenticate and get access to all resources within the corporate domain.

However, many of the company personnel often find they need to be away from the office for various reasons: working at home on the weekends, traveling on business trips, checking e-mail during the lunch hour, etc. This company helps their personnel to continue to be productive by also providing a means for connecting to the corporate Intranet wirelessly: each worker is issued a laptop with wireless capabilities. Each worker can use whatever means available to access the Internet, including a Wi-Fi connection or a home wireless connection. As soon as a worker is on the Internet, he or she can use VPN to access the corporate Intranet using his or her assigned authentication method. In the case of this company, the workers use the standard user ID and password combination. However, to assist in keeping the passwords secure, this company requires users to use a variable password key, which changes once every five minutes. Workers are issued a password decryption device that provides the appropriate password. To access the corporate Intranet, the user first accesses their local installation of the VPN software. The user then directs the VPN software to connect to the corporate IntraNet and enters authentication information. To get the password, the user uses the variable password key device to get the current password. To be authenticated, the user must use the right combination of user ID and password.

Because the company provides this solution, workers are able to continue to be productive during most times they have to be out of the office.

SELF-CHECK

1. What are the two protocols that support VPN connections over the Internet?

2. What authentication protocols are supported for PPP connections?

Project 10.2

Windows Server 2008 Routing and Remote Access (RRAS) allows you to configure a server to support dial-up and VPN remote access connections. RRAS supports both PPTP and L2TP VPN connections. The same server can support multiple clients; however, a separate dial-up modem is needed for each dial-up client.

Complete **Project 10.3: Setting Up Remote Access** in the online Networking Basics Project Manual to understand how to enable RRAS on a computer running Windows Server 2008 and view its configuration.

10.3 JOINING LANS INTO WANS

By classic definition, a LAN becomes a WAN when traffic between the networks crosses through a public carrier. When using a VPN over the network to make your WAN connection, it works much the same as a VPN remote client, except that you are connecting a network instead of a single server, like in Figure 10-16. This method of connecting LANs has gained popularity of late, but several other connection methods are supported and still in common use.

No matter how the connection is made, the basic idea is the same. You need a router at each end with some kind of connection between them. Though simple in theory, the configuration details can vary widely depending on how the connection is made between the routers. Each carrier option and connection type has its own configuration requirements and special considerations.

10.3.1 Considering WAN Options

You need to consider a number of different variables when planning a WAN. You need to consider items such as:

• Number of LANs you need to connect
• Geographic location of the LANs

Figure 10-16

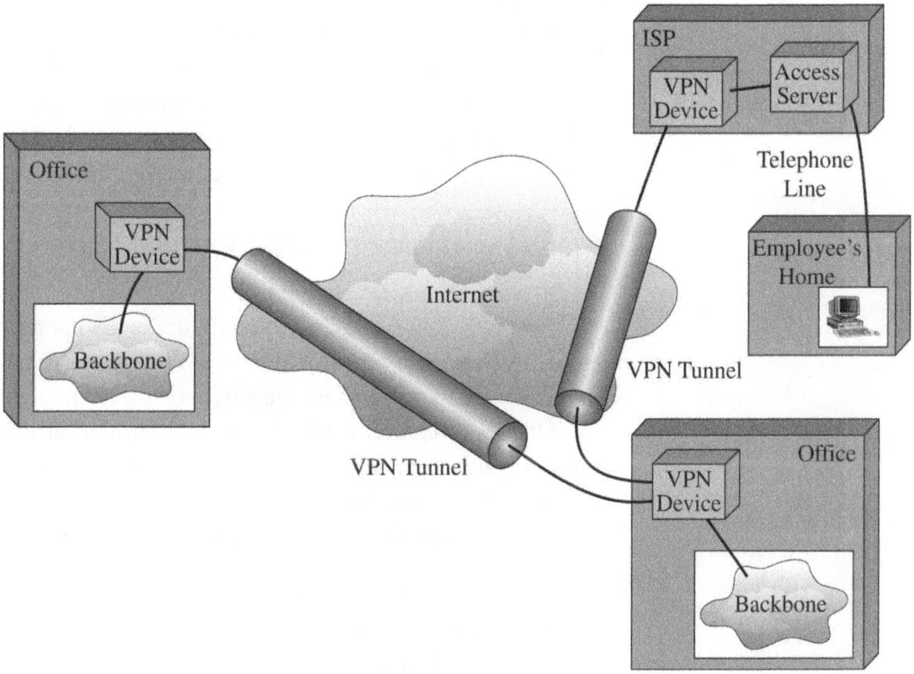

Internet VPN.

- Number of computers in each LAN
- Implementation budget
- Network operating system(s)
- Network servers and services
- Bandwidth requirements

Many WAN configurations are heterogeneous networks, requiring you to support a mix of network operating systems, server types, and client types. It might even include one or more mainframe computers.

Planning LAN Configurations

Deciding on computer placement can, in itself, be a complicated issue. Client computers are the easiest part; you need enough client computers to support your network users at each location. Servers are a different issue.

You need to consider the types of servers that you need and which users need access to those servers. Many NOS recommend that you place critical servers like Windows Active Directory domain controllers local on each LAN. For other types of servers, you want to place servers so that they are local to the majority of the clients that need to access them as much as possible. Why? Bandwidth between LANs is often a limited resource on a WAN, and you want to try to keep traffic between LANs to a minimum. However, this isn't a strict rule. Availability is another consideration. Do you need a full-time connection to the servers? Do you have only periodic connections?

Server placement can be something of a balancing act. You need to balance the cost and other requirements of placing multiple servers against the support requirements for accessing a server through a wide area link. You will have at least one device, a router, in every location. A router is a required device, managing the connection to other LANs.

Planning WAN Connections

WAN connections are supported over a wide variety of connection types. With many NOS, the easiest to configure is a VPN connection over the Internet. Technically, you set up both a VPN connection and NAT, to enable the network clients to share the single connection over the Internet.

Other connection methods are very similar, at least at the most basic level. A router connects to a circuit that carries the traffic. Another router at the other end of the connection completes the circuit. The connection can be made over one of three network types:

- Circuit-switched networks
- Dedicated circuit networks
- Packet-switched networks

One thing you need to understand is that these network connections can be used to connect network routers or, in many cases, to connect the network to the Internet to support a VPN connection.

10.3.2 Connecting with Circuit-Switched Networks

Circuit-switched networks are the oldest and simplest approach to MAN and WAN circuits. These services operate over PSTN; that is, the telephone networks operated by the common carriers such as AT&T, Verizon, CenturyLink, and so on.

Cloud architecture
A connection architecture in which you know your connection points but not the communication path inside the cloud.

Circuit-switched services use **cloud architecture.** The users lease connection points (e.g., telephone lines) into the common carrier's network, which is called the cloud, shown in Figure 10-17. A person (or computer) dials the telephone number of the destination computer and establishes a temporary circuit between the two computers. The computers exchange data, and when the task is complete, the circuit is disconnected (e.g., by hanging up the phone).

Cloud-based designs are simpler for the organization because they move the burden of network design and management inside the cloud from the organization to the common carrier. Network managers do not need to

Figure 10-17

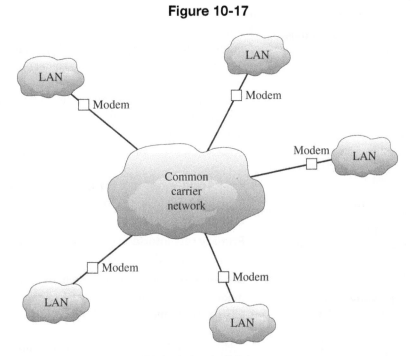

Dialed circuit services.

**Integrated services
digital network (ISDN)**
A circuit-switched network
communication method that
combines voice, video, and
data communication.

Narrowband ISDN
BRI and PRI ISDN
configurations.

**Network terminator
(NT-1 or NT-2)**
An ISDN connection device
that acts like a hub for ISDN
connections.

Terminal adapter (TA)
An ISDN client device that
performs the same role as a
network adapter for ISDN
connectivity. Also known as
an ISDN modem.

ISDN modem
See terminal adapter.

**Service profile identifier
(SPID)**
An NT-1/NT-2 unique
identifier.

**Basic rate interface
(BRI)**
An ISDN configuration that
has two B channels and one
D channel.

**Primary rate interface
(PRI)**
An ISDN configuration that
supports up to 23 64Kbps
B channels and one 64Kbps
D channel.

Broadband ISDN
A high-speed digital ISDN
that uses ATM circuits
carrying data at either
155.52Mbps or 622.08Mbps.

worry about the amount of traffic sent between each computer; they just need to specify the amount of traffic entering and leaving each computer and buy the appropriate size and number of connections into the PSTN. However, it comes at a price. Cloud-based designs can be more expensive because users must pay for each connection into the network and pay on the basis of the amount of time each circuit is used. You will learn more about cloud based computing in section 10.4.

To use POTS, the standard dial-up system, you need to lease a circuit into the network (i.e., a telephone line) and install special equipment (i.e., a modem) to enable your computer to talk to the PSTN. To transfer data to and from another computer on the network, you instruct your modem to dial the other computer's telephone.

A higher bandwidth option is to use **integrated services digital network (ISDN)**, which combines voice, video, and data over the same digital circuit. The original version is occasionally called **narrowband ISDN** and the most current referred to as broadband ISDN. ISDN is widely available from a number of common carriers in North America.

To use ISDN, you must lease connection points in the PSTN, which are telephone lines just like POTS. Next, they must have special equipment to connect their computers (or networks) into the PSTN. Users need an ISDN **network terminator (NT-1 or NT-2)** that functions much like a hub, and a NIC (called a **terminal adapter, TA** or even an **"ISDN modem"**) in all computers attached to the NT-1/NT-2. In most cases, the ISDN service appears identical to the regular dialed telephone service, with the exception that usually (but not always) each device attached to the NT-1/NT-2 needs a unique **service profile identifier (SPID)** to identify it. To connect to another computer (such as a remote router) using ISDN, you dial that computer's telephone number using the ISDN NIC in much the same way as you would with a modem on a regular telephone line.

Various ISDN configurations exist, each supporting different capacities. The configurations shown here are those supported in the United States. Europe and other regions can vary in the number of channels supported:

- **Basic rate interface (BRI):** Supports two 64 Kbps digital channels (called **B channels**) and one 16 Kbps control signaling channel (called a **D channel**).

- **Primary rate interface (PRI):** Offered to commercial customers and supporting 23 64 Kbps B channels and one 64 Kbps D channel.

- **Broadband ISDN:** Circuit-switched service using asynchronous transfer mode (ATM) circuits, discussed later in this chapter, to carry data at 622.08 Mbps and 155.52 Mbps.

Broadband ISDN is backward compatible and can accept transmissions from BRI and PRI circuits.

The three main problems with POTS and ISDN circuit-switched networks are as follows:

- Each connection goes through the regular telephone network on a different circuit. These circuits may vary in quality, meaning that although one connection will be fairly clear, the next call may be noisy.
- The data transmission rates on these circuits are usually low. Generally speaking, transmission rates range from 28.8 Kbps to 56 Kbps for dialed POTS circuits to 128 Kbps to 1.5 Mbps for ISDN circuits.
- You usually pay per use for circuit-switched services, which can get very expensive over time.

PSTN connection methods, especially POTS, are most commonly used for Internet connections and for remote access connections when the bandwidth requirements are minimal.

10.3.3 Connecting with Dedicated Circuit Networks

Dedicated circuit network
A connection method in which you lease circuits from common carriers at a flat rate.

With a **dedicated circuit network,** you lease circuits from common carriers. All connections are point to point, from one building in one city to another building in the same or a different city. The carrier installs the circuit connections at the two end points of the circuit and makes the connection between them. The circuits still run through the common carrier's cloud, but the network behaves as if you have your own physical circuits running from one point to another as in Figure 10-18.

Once again, the user leases the desired circuit from the common carrier (specifying the physical end points of the circuit) and installs the equipment needed to connect computers and devices (for example, routers or switches) to the circuit. This equipment may include **multiplexers** or a **channel service unit (CSU)** and/or a **data service unit (DSU);** a CSU/DSU is the WAN equivalent of a NIC in a LAN.

Channel service unit (CSU)
A dedicated circuit network connection device.

Data Service Unit (DSU)
A dedicated circuit network connection device.

Unlike circuit-switched services that typically use a pay-per-use model, dedicated circuits are billed at a flat fee per month, and the user has unlimited use of the circuit. Once you sign a contract, making changes can be expensive because it means rewiring the buildings and signing a new contract with the carrier. Therefore, dedicated circuits require more care in network design than do switched circuits, both in terms of locations and the amount of capacity you purchase.

Three basic architectures are used in dedicated circuit networks: ring, star, and mesh. These are effectively the same as the network topologies of the same names. In practice, most networks use a combination of architectures. For example, a distributed star architecture has a series of star networks that are connected by a mesh or ring architecture.

T carrier circuits are the most commonly used form of dedicated circuit services in North America today. Costs are a fixed amount per month,

Figure 10-18

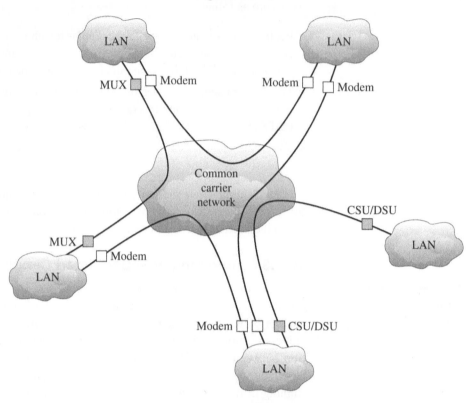

Dedicated circuit services.

regardless of how much or how little traffic flows through the circuit. Several types of T carrier circuits are available as shown in Table 10-1.

T1 lines are commonly used to carry data and voice transmissions. **T2, T3, and T4** lines are made by bundling multiple T1 lines. T3 or T4 are sometimes used by large corporations with high bandwidth requirements.

T1
The standard T-carrier circuit for carrying voice and data.

T2, T3, and T4
Bundles of T1 lines.

Table 10-1: T Carrier Service Characteristics

T Carrier Designation	DS Designation	Speed
FT1	DS0	64 Kbps
T1	DS1	1.544 Mbps
T2	DS2	6.312 Mbps
T3	DS3	44.376 Mbps
T4	DS4	274.176 Mbps

Table 10-2: SONET/SDH Services

SONET Designation	SDH Designation	Speed
OC-1		51.84 Mbps
OC-3	STM-1	155.52 Mbps
OC-9	STM-3	466.56 Mbps
OC-12	STM-4	622.08 Mbps
OC-18	STM-6	933.12 Mbps
OC-24	STM-8	1.244 Gbps
OC-36	STM-12	1.866 Gbps
OC-48	STM-16	2.488 Gbps
OC-192	STM-24	9.953 Gbps

Synchronous optical network (SONET)
An ANSI-standard high-speed U.S. fiber-based communication network.

Synchronous digital hierarchy (SDH)
The name under which SONET is marketed.

Fractional T1 (FT1) service is provided for companies that need high-bandwidth communications but don't require the bandwidth provided by a full T1 circuit. Companies lease a portion of the T1 line, usually in 65 Kbps multiples. Many companies that used to use FT1 lines have switched over to high-speed Internet instead.

Synchronous optical network (SONET) is the American standard (ANSI) for high-speed dedicated circuit services. A recently standardized and almost identical service that easily interconnects with SONET is marketed under the name **synchronous digital hierarch (SDH).**

SONET transmission speeds begin at the optical carrier level 1 (OC-1) of 51.84 Mbps. Each succeeding rate in the SONET fiber hierarchy is defined as a multiple of OC-1, with SONET data rates defined as high as OC-192, or about 10 Gbps. Table 10-2 presents the other major SONET and SDH services. Notice that the slowest SONET transmission rate (OC-1) of 51.84 Mbps is slightly faster than the T3 rate of 44.376 Mbps.

SONET and SDH are available only in limited areas with most availability restricted to major metropolitan areas.

Packet-switched networks
A cloud architecture carrier network that uses a fixed-rate connection plus per-packet charges to determine charges.

Packet assembly/ disassembly device (PAD)
A packet-switched network connection device.

10.3.4 Connecting with Packet-Switched Networks

With **packet-switched networks,** as with circuit-switched networks, you buy a connection into the common carrier cloud as shown in Figure 10-19. The user pays a fixed fee for the connection into the network (depending on the type and capacity of the service) and is charged for the number of packets transmitted.

The user's connection into the network is a **packet assembly/disassembly device (PAD),** which the customer or common carrier can own and operate. The PAD converts the sender's data into the Network layer and the Data Link layer packets used by the packet network and sends them through

Figure 10-19

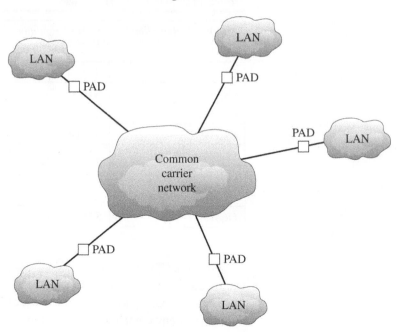

Packet-switched services.

the packet-switched network. At the other end, another PAD reassembles the packets back into the Network layer and Data Link layer protocols expected by the destination and delivers them to the appropriate computer. The PAD also compensates for differences in transmission speed between sender and receiver; for example, the circuit at the sender might be 1.5 Mbps whereas the receiver only has a 64-Kbps circuit.

X.25
The oldest packet-switched service in current use.

The oldest packet-switched service is **X.25**. X.25 offers various services, including datagram services for network communication. When packets arrive at the PAD, connecting the user's network to the packet-switched network, their Data Link (e.g., Ethernet) and Network layer (e.g., IP) packets are removed and X.25-specific packets are substituted. Packets are moved through the X.25 network in much the same way as in TCP/IP networks. When they arrive at the edge of the X.25 network, new destination protocols (e.g., Ethernet, IP) are created and the message is sent on its way. X.25 is sometimes called a reliable packet service because it provides complete error checking and guaranteed delivery on all packets transmitted.

Although common in Europe, X.25 is not widespread in North America. The primary reason is its transmission speed. For many years, the maximum speed into North American X.25 networks was 64 Kbps, but this maximum speed has increased to 2.048 Mbps, which is the European standard for ISDN. However, for many users, 2.048 Mbps is still not fast enough.

Asynchronous transfer mode (ATM)
A packet-switched network standard communication method that provides improved performance compared to X.25 and is scalable up to 39Gbps.

Asynchronous transfer mode (ATM), also standardized, is a newer technology than X.25. ATM is similar to X.25 in that it provides packet-switched services, but it has four distinct operating characteristics that differ from X.25. First, ATM performs encapsulation of packets, so packets are delivered unchanged through the network. Second, ATM provides no error control in the network; error control is the responsibility of the source and destination. ATM is considered an unreliable packet service.

Because the user's data link packet remains intact, the devices at the edge of the ATM network can check the error-control information in the packet to ensure that no errors have occurred and to request transmission of damaged or lost packets. Figure 10-20 illustrates the difference in error control between X.25 networks and ATM networks. The left side shows that when an X.25 packet leaves its source A and moves through node B, to node C, to node D, and finally to destination E, each intermediate node acknowledges the packet as it passes.

The right side of the figure shows how an ATM packet moves through node B, node C, node D, and on to destination E. When destination E receives the packet correctly, a single acknowledgment is sent back through the nodes to source A, as shown by the numbers 5, 6, 7, and 8. Some common carriers have started using the term fast packet services instead to refer to these services that do not provide error control—it sounds better for marketing!

ATM provides extensive information that enables the setting of very precise priorities among different types of transmissions: high priority for voice and video, lower priority for e-mail.

ATM is scalable; combining basic ATM circuits into much faster ATM circuits is easy. Most common carriers offer ATM circuits that provide the

Figure 10-20

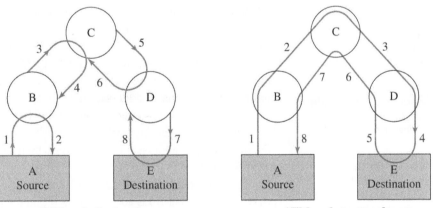

X.25 packet network   ATM packet network

Comparing X.25 (left) and ATM (right).

same data transmission rates as SONET: 51.84 Mbps, 466.56 Mbps, 622.08 Mbps, and so on up to 39 Gbps (which would be equivalent to OC-768). New versions called T1 ATM (1.544 Mbps) and T3 ATM (45 Mbps) are also available.

Frame relay

A transmission method that transmits data faster than X.25 but slower than ATM; it does not include any error control.

Frame relay is an even newer packet-switching technology that transmits data faster than X.25 but slower than ATM. It has sometimes been called a poor man's ATM. Like ATM, frame relay performs encapsulation of packets, so packets are delivered unchanged through the network. Like ATM, it is an unreliable packet service because it does not perform error control. It is up to the software at the source and destination to perform error correction and to control for lost messages.

Frame relay does not yet provide quality of service (QoS) capabilities, such as priority scheduling and other quality controls, but it is under development. Different common carriers offer frame relay networks with different transmission speeds. Most offer a range of CIR speeds that include 56 Kbps, 128 Kbps, 256 Kbps, 384 Kbps, 1.544 Mbps, 2.048 Mbps, and 45 Mbps.

Switched multimegabit data service (SMDS)

A packet-switched server that is under development.

Switched multimegabit data service (SMDS) is an unreliable packet service like ATM and frame relay. Like ATM and frame relay, SMDS does not perform error checking; the user is responsible for error checking. As with ATM and frame relay, SMDS encapsulates incoming packets.

SMDS is not yet standardized. At present, most (but not all) common carriers offer it. SMDS was originally aimed at MANs, particularly the interconnection of LANs. Recently, it has also made its way into the WAN environment. Regional telephone companies offer SMDS at a variety of transmission rates, ranging from 56 Kbps up to 44.376 Mbps. No widely accepted standards exist, so transmissions rates vary by carrier. The future of SMDS is uncertain because it is not standardized and offers no clear advantages over frame relay.

Multiprotocol Label Switching (MPLS)

A method in high performance networks that uses labels to route communications appropriately.

Label Switched Routers (LSRs)

Devices used with MPLS.

Forwarding Equivalence Classes (FEC)

Term used in MPLS to indicate sets of packets that use the same labels.

Another approach that improves QoS and the movement of packets with different layer-2 protocols is **Multiprotocol Label Switching (MPLS)**. With MPLS, routers called **Label Switched Routers (LSRs)** are used. The network manager defines a series of **Forwarding Equivalence Classes (FEC)** through the network of LSRs. Each FEC has a reserved data rate and a QoS.

When a packet arrives at the edge of the MPLS network, an edge LSR reads the destination address on the incoming packet. The edge LSR can be configured to use the IP address, the IP address and the source or destination port, or the address in any protocol understood by the LSR. The edge LSR accepts the incoming packet and attaches an MPLS label (packet that contains the FEC address). The edge LSR then forwards the packet to the next LSR as defined in the FEC.

This LSR reads the MPLS label and removes it from the incoming packet, consults its MPLS address table to find the packets next destination, attaches a new MPLS label with the new FEC address, and forwards the packet to the next LSR in the FEC.

This process continues until the packet reaches the edge LSR closest to its final destination. This edge LSR strips off the MPLS label and forwards the packet outside of the MPLS network in exactly the same format in which it entered the MPLS network.

The advantage of the MPLS is that it can easily integrate the layer-2 protocols and also provide QoS in an IP environment. It also enables traffic management by enabling the network manager to specify FEC based on both the IP address and the source or destination port.

10.3.4 Choosing a Connection Type

The connection type you use will depend on your connection requirements. You need to consider the data rates supported and also the costs involved. An overview of the currently supported connection methods is provided in Table 10-3.

IN THE REAL WORLD

Growing Your Network

WAN connection methods often evolve over time. A company might initially use a circuit-switched network method before it has an accurate idea of the bandwidth and connectivity requirements. It usually isn't long before the company upgrades to a faster connection method, either deciding that the initial choice isn't fast enough or because the remote office's needs outgrow the connection's capabilities.

Why not go with a faster connection from the beginning? Traditionally, the main reason has been cost. Not only are the lease costs relatively expensive for most dedicated circuit and packet-switched networks, the necessary hardware can be as or even more expensive. Add in the per-packet cost for packet-switched networks, and the costs continue to climb. Still, companies that need the bandwidth are often willing to pay the price. Companies that want the added security of an effectively private line are even willing to pay the added costs relating to secure connections. At least, that's the way it's always worked in the past.

This state of affairs is quickly changing, especially with smaller businesses. They are diving straight in with connectivity in the moderate to the low end of the high-speed range. How? With high-speed Internet connections—most often DSL lines or cable Internet connections. Connectivity in the 3 to 5 (and even higher) Mbps range is both readily available and relatively inexpensive. Furthermore, current Windows versions make configuring and maintaining their own VPN connections relatively easy for network administrators.

Table 10-3: Comparing Wide Area Connection Services

Type of Service	Nominal Data Rates	Effective Data Rates	Relative Cost	Reliability	Network Integration
Circuit-Switched Services					
POTS	33.6 Kbps to 56 Kbps	33 to 300 Kbps[1]	Low	High	Difficult
ISDN	128 Kbps to 1.5 Mbps	122 Kbps to 1.3 Mbps	Moderate	Moderate	Difficult
B-ISDN	155 Mbps to 622 Mbps	300 Mbps to 1200 Mbps[2]	High	Low	Difficult
Dedicated Circuit Services					
T Carrier	64 Kbps to 274 Mbps	53 Kbps to 218 Mbps	Moderate	High	Moderate
SONET	50 Mbps to 10 Gbps	48 Mbps to 9.1 Gbps	High	High	Moderate
Packet-Switched Services					
X.25	56 Kbps to 2 Mbps	50 Kbps to 1.5 Mbps	Moderate	High	Difficult
ATM	52 Mbps to 10 Gbps	84 Mbps to 16 Gbps[3]	High	Moderate	Moderate
Frame Relay	56 Kbps to 45 Mbps	56 Kbps to 44 Mbps	Moderate	Moderate	Moderate
SMDS	56 Kbps to 45 Mbps	45 Kbps to 36 Mbps	Moderate	Low	Difficult
Ethernet	1 Mbps to 40 Gbps	900 Kbps to 36 Gbps	Low	High	Simple
VPN Services					
VPN	56 Kbps to 2 Mbps	50 Kbps to 1.5 Mbps	Very low	Low	Moderate

Notes:
1. Assuming data compression and no noise
2. B-ISDN is full duplex
3. ATM is full duplex

SELF-CHECK

1. What are the connection methods supported for circuit-switched, dedicated circuit, and packet-switched networks?

2. What are the architectures supported by circuit-switched, dedicated circuit, and packet-switched networks?

Table 10-4 has some generally accepted guidelines for choosing a connection type based on bandwidth requirements.

When considering the costs involved, remember that you not only need to include the cost of circuit (and incremental costs, if appropriate), you also need to consider the cost of the connection hardware. With most methods, you can buy or lease the hardware from your carrier or purchase compatible hardware from a third-party vendor. Keep in mind, however, that if you buy your hardware from a third party, you need to make sure that is has a service department that will stand behind its equipment. If you run into problems in the future and have third-party hardware, you can expect the local carrier to blame any and all problems on the hardware.

Another consideration is the maturity of the technology. Although newer connection options might offer higher-speed connectivity, and maybe even at a lower cost, what kind of a track record does it have? Is the information available about reliability or, if problems do occur, the average time before they are repaired? The newest and fastest is not always the best, especially when you figure in the costs that come with down time.

Table 10-4: WAN Connection Recommendations

Network Needs	Recommendations
Low Traffic Needs (64 Kbps or less)	POTS if dial-up is acceptable VPN if reliability is less important Frame relay otherwise
Moderate Traffic Needs (64 Kbps to 2 Mbps)	VPN if reliability is less important T1 if network volume is stable and predictable Frame relay otherwise
High Traffic Needs (2 Mbps to 45 Mbps)	Ethernet if available T3 if network volume is stable and predictable Frame relay otherwise
Very High Traffic Needs (45 Mbps to 10 Gbps)	Ethernet if available SONET if network volume is stable and predictable ATM otherwise

10.4 ACCESSING A WIRELESS NETWORK

Wireless networking opens up a whole lot of possibilities from the tools you can use to access the networks, to what you can do within a wireless network. In this section we take a look at several devices that can be used to access wireless networks. We then get a brief understanding of a relatively new paradigm called cloud computing. But first, we look at access devices.

10.4.1 Access Devices

In today's networking world, users are using many different types of devices to access networks wirelessly. Company employees are using their cell phones to check e-mail as well as tablets to update work files as necessary. Students are using PDAs to research information for their school assignments and their phones to access on-line music. When considering wireless networking, you need to keep in mind the capabilities and requirements for using, managing and supporting these devices. Here we take a look at just a few of the current options.

Smartphones

Smartphone
A telephonic device that provides similar capabilities to a personal computer.

BlackBerry
A variety of smartphone.

iPhone
A variety of smartphone provided by Apple Inc.

A **smartphone** is a variety of cell phone that provides some computing capabilities. You can think of smartphones as a cell phone combined with a handheld computer.

Several different tools are available that allow users access to wireless networks. The primary difference between a smartphone and a mobile phone is that a smartphone comes with an independent operating system, thus giving it similar capabilities to a computer. Using this operating system, developers can create applications specific to the device. A few popular smartphone operating systems are:

- **BlackBerry:** This operating system was introduced in 1999 as an e-mail-ready pager. Today, however, the BlackBerry provides a cell phone as well as the same application capabilities as other smartphones. BlackBerrys support multitasking and built-in interoperability with various business applications like Microsoft Exchange and Lotus Domino, which allows for easily synchronizing with business tools like e-mail, calendaring, and contact lists.

- **iPhones:** The iPhone operating system was introduced in 2007 by Apple Inc. The iPhone was one of the first Smartphones that used a multi-touch technology and a web browser. With the multi-touch technology, the iPhone is able to interact with the user through touch and motion. You can manually enter commands through the touch interface and the iPhone can interpret your entry to access your requested action. The first generation of iPhone did not have the capability to use third-party applications. It wasn't till the second generation of the iPhone, introduced in 2008, that third-party applications were supported. Now iPhone users can directly download applications to their iPhone through Apple's Application store.

Android
A smartphone operating system that allows developers to create applications for smartphones.

• **Android:** The Android operating system was introduced in 2008. This operating system was developed with the backing of Google, which means the Android operating system was built in Google tools including maps, calendar, and Gmail (Google's e-mail solution).

Each of the Smartphone operating systems supports various applications including:

• **Productivity applications:** These types of applications include small versions of popular business productivity applications like the Microsoft suite of tools including Word, Excel, and PowerPoint.
• **Communications:** This type of application includes ways to communicate with other users including sending SMS text messages, e-mail messaging, and accessing social networks (like Twitter, Facebook, and MySpace).
• **Personal management:** This type of application includes software for managing personal budgets, planning (as in vacation, party, and wedding planning), and personal calendars.
• **Health and fitness:** This type includes software for tracking your exercise, calories, menus, and finding a great place to go for a bike ride.
• **Entertainment:** This type includes applications that allow you to find out when a movie is playing at your local movie theater, where to find your favorite cuisine, and many different games.

Most Smartphones are capable of downloading and installing applications without the use of a computer. However, many Smartphones have accessories that allow you to mimic a full computing experience.

Tablets

Tablets are another type of wireless device popular with network users. A tablet is a portable personal computer generally with a touchscreen input and a built-in wireless adapter. Similar to Smartphones, Tablets come equipped with an independent operating system that allows users to add applications based on their needs. Smartphones share many of the characteristics discussed in the preceding Smartphone discussion, with the exception that they're designed to allow input from pen-like devices as well as from touch screens. Users use tablets for a variety of applications, including taking notes in meetings, showing diagrams in closed sessions, updating files while traveling, and, of course, playing a game or two. Because tablets can be connected through wireless networking, users can be allowed access to network resources, like printers and fax machines, as well. The downside of using a tablet instead of a full computer is that the operating system on tablets tends to be lightweight as compared to the full feature PC.

The iPad is the current leader in tablet devices. Apple Inc. introduced the iPad in 2010. The iPad has spurred a great deal of interest in tablet computing. The iPad has a similar interface to the iPhone in that it supports multi-touch interactions. The iPad is most known for its audio/visual capabilities. Some of the big draws for this tablet is that users can read books, watch movies, listen to music, play games, and surf for web content.

Several other tablet systems are available including the HP Touchpad, Motorola's Xoom, Samsung Galaxy, and Toshiba's Tablet. Still other manufacturers are in the process of developing other tablet devices that will provide similar functionality to the iPad, but with unique operating systems. Manufacturers will build their devices around several different possible operating systems, including Mee-Go by Nokia and Android.

10.4.2 Cloud Computing

With cloud computing, organizations can purchase services from a service provider that has a large network of hardware capabilities to provide services to clients. From the client's perspective, cloud computing allows access to services, including software, utilities, storage, etc., as needed without the large expenditure of acquiring and maintaining a large infrastructure. Currently, cloud computing service providers provide the following types of services:

> **IN ACTION: CLOUD COMPUTING**
>
> Understand the basic components of cloud computing.

- **Software as a Service (SaaS):** With this type of service, the service provider hosts one or more application within their infrastructure that they make available to thousands of clients. SaaS potentially can provide all types of applications including specialized applications (like payroll or HR applications) or generalized applications like word processors.

- **Development services:** With this type of service, providers can host environments that allow developers to create software without maintaining a robust local environment. Google Maps provides one such service for developers.

- **Utility services:** Companies can access services that provide necessary utilities like virus protection and security monitoring.

- **Commerce services:** Many people are aware of eBay. Services like this provide an interface for merchants to make goods and services available for clients to bid on.

As you can see many different types of services can be available in a cloud computing environment. In general, you can think of cloud computing as being any service that is offered outside of a company and is available to users from many different areas. So, what is required for participating in cloud computing?

When looking at cloud computing, you need to consider three components: the front end, the back end, and middle ware. The front end refers to the client side. To access services in the cloud the front end must have:

- **Access to the network containing the cloud:** This access usually is to the Internet.

- **Some kind of client hardware:** This allows the client to provide input and receive output to and from the cloud. This can be a laptop or some other form of terminal (like a tablet).

- **Appropriate software to access the cloud services:** Many service providers allow access from something as simple as a browser, while others may require specialized client software.

On the back end lies the infrastructure including the servers, storage devices, applications, etc. Because of the nature of cloud computing, service providers generally warehouse robust systems capable of providing the processing power necessary to deliver services. Additionally, the service provider is responsible for ensuring services are available to clients at any point so they generally maintain a high level of redundancy. Furthermore,

IN THE REAL WORLD

You're in the Clouds

Would you believe most people who have used the Internet have already used some form of service in cloud computing? You have, too, if you have an e-mail account outside of your company, like Hotmail, Yahoo Mail, or Gmail. To get to any of these e-mail services, you have to use your own hardware, like your laptop, to access the network containing the services. Most of these services are available through the Internet. You also have to use special software to access the service, usually a web browser. On the back end the e-mail provider provides the e-mail capability along with the security features that allow you to access your e-mail account, and prevents others from unauthorized access. The service provider also provides all the storage necessary to store your e-mail until you clean out your inbox. As you can tell cloud computing is quite usable.

TIPS FROM THE PROFESSIONALS

No Silver Lining in This Cloud

Although cloud computing sounds like a great idea, it does have some concerns that prevent wide adoption. These concerns include security, privacy, and ownership. When considering service providers, take the time to find out how they plan on securing your data and restricting access to those you authorize. Additionally, how will they make sure unauthorized people cannot view your data when you're accessing it from the local coffee shop? Finally, if you plan on storing your data on the service provider's storage devices, consider who legally owns that data.

service providers have to be able to warehouse and maintain large quantities of client data. To this end they often have large storage facilities as well.

Between the front and back ends is the middleware. The middleware is responsible for allowing communications between systems within an interaction between the front and back ends. Middleware is a specialized software application that administers the interaction between the front end and back end. With the middleware a central server can monitor traffic and route requests appropriately.

SELF-CHECK

1. Name three types of applications available for a smartphone.
2. What services can you think of that you already access through cloud computing?

Apply Your Knowledge There are a number of smartphone models available today from various manufactures, but only a few operating systems.

Research and compare:

- BlackBerry OS
- Windows Mobile
- OS for iPhone
- Android OS

List your results in a spreadsheet with each operating system and a list of the most common or desirable functions. Which do you think is the most useful in an enterprise network?

SUMMARY

Section 10-1

- The 802.11 family is the primary set of standards associated with wireless networking.
- Wireless networking requires a compatible network adapter on each device, one or more wireless access points, and an assigned frequency range.
- Configuring a WLAN using Wi-Fi depends heavily on the requirements of the equipment manufacturers.

Section 10-2

- Remote access generally requires one or more remote access server and a set of clients requiring access.
- Requirements to configure a system to support remote access is highly dependent on the networking operating system.

Section 10-3

- LANs become WANs when traffic between networks crosses through a public carrier.
- Cloud-based architecture designs allow organizations to move the burden of network design and management to a common carrier.

Section 10-4

- Various smart devices are available today that provide smaller, handheld platforms on which to perform many computer type activities, including accessing wireless networks.
- Cloud computing uses three components, a front end, a back end and middleware, responsible for managing communications between the front and back ends.

ASSESS YOUR UNDERSTANDING

UNDERSTAND: WHAT HAVE YOU LEARNED?

 Go to **www.wiley.com/go/ciccarelli/networkingbasics2e** to evaluate your knowledge of wireless, remote access, and WAN connectivity.
Measure your learning by comparing pre-test and post-test results.

SUMMARY QUESTIONS

1. Which packet-switched connection method supports the highest bandwidth connections?

(a) X.25

(b) Frame relay

(c) ATM

(d) T service

2. SONET optical carrier levels are measured in multiples of what speed?

(a) 16 Kbps

(b) 51.84 Mbps

(c) 45 Mbps

(d) 622.08 Mbps

3. Standard dial-up remote access connections use which of the following?

(a) POTS

(b) X.25

(c) ISDN

(d) T1

4. MS-CHAP is the most secure authentication protocol supported for Windows PPP clients. True or false?

5. What is the current Wi-Fi standard?

(a) 802.16e

(b) 802.11a

(c) 802.11b

(d) 802.11g

6. Secure remote access connections can be established over the Internet by using a VPN. True or false?

7. Which protocol is used for Windows client dial-in remote access to a Windows server?

(a) PPP

(b) SLIP

(c) PPTP

(d) L2TP

8. Which PPP subprotocol includes network-protocol specific support protocols that support network protocol configuration?

(a) LCP

(b) EAP

(c) NCP

(d) CCP

9. By classic definition, a LAN becomes a WAN when connections cross a public carrier. True or false?

10. What is the industry standard protocol for configuring VPN connections?

(a) PPTP

(b) L2TP

(c) SLIP

(d) MPPE

APPLY: WHAT WOULD YOU DO?

1. You are designing a remote access solution for a company with three sets of requirements:

- Field service personnel need as flexible a connection method as possible that will work from nearly any location—five users total.

- Telecommuters need a full-time connection to the company network that supports at least 1 Mbps—three users total.

- Researchers need to have high-speed access (at least 2 Mbps) when possible, but sometimes need to connect from remote locations—two users total.

In addition, you need to keep hardware purchases to a minimum. User counts represent current requirements. Field engineers seldom need to be online for more than a few minutes at a time. Telecommuters need nearly full-time access during working hours. Researcher time requirements vary depending on whether they are gathering information or processing the data.

(a) For which type of user is a dial-up access most appropriate?

(b) Least appropriate?

(c) For which type of user is a VPN over the Internet most approprate?

(d) Least appropriate?

(e) When configuring support for field service personnel, what is needed at the client end?

(f) At the network end?

(g) When configuring support for telecommuters, what is needed at the client end?

(h) At the network end?

(i) How can you determine the number of modems that will be required at the network end, if any?

2. A company is putting in a second office at a remote location. The office will be set up as part of the same Windows Active Directory domain as the main office. The initial office configuration will include client computers, a domain controller, a DNS server, and file and print servers. A DHCP server in the main office will provide IP configuration information for client computers in the remote office.

(a) What are the major factors affecting the connection bandwidth requirements?

(b) What are the requirements to configure a connection between the offices?

(c) From the standpoint of IP address assignment at the remote office, how would you be able to tell if the link fails?

(d) How could this problem be avoided?

(e) You configure the network with a single connection. What are your options to correct the problem if the connection becomes saturated as the remote office grows?

BE A NETWORK ADMINISTRATOR

Building a WAN

You are designing a WAN solution that will connect five offices at various locations in the United States. Reliability and access to data in any location are critical concerns, and a failure at any one location should not prevent other locations from communicating. You want to be able to specify the exact topology used to connect with remote offices with a determinate path between the offices. The offices need full-time connections.

You estimate the current peak bandwidth requirements as 1 Mbps between each office and the other four offices. Requirements can vary from month to month and are their highest at end of quarter and end of year. You want to be able to predict connectivity costs in advance.

1. How well does a circuit-switched solution meet your requirements (explain your answer)?

2. How well does a direct circuit solution meet your requirements (explain your answer)?

3. How well does a packet-switched solution meet your requirements (explain your answer)?

4. What kind of topology would you use? Describe the connection and hardware requirements at each location.

5. The link between two offices fails. Based on your answer to question 4, how does this impact the network?

KEY TERMS

802.15

802.11a

802.11b

802.11g

802.11n

802.16 WiMAX

802.16d fixed WiMAX

802.16e mobile WiMAX

Acknowledgement (ACK)

Android

Asynchronous transfer mode (ATM)

Attenuation

Automatic repeat request (ARQ)

Bandwidth

Basic rate interface (BRI)

BlackBerry

Bluetooth

Broadband ISDN

Carrier Sense Multiple Access with Collision Avoidance (CMSA/CA)

Channel service unit (CSU)

Clear to send (CTS)

Cloud architecture

Compression control protocols (CCPs)

Data Service Unit (DSU)

DECT 6.0

Dedicated circuit network

Digital Enhanced Cordless Telecommunications (DECT)

Distributed coordination function (DCF)

Dynamic Host Configuration Protocol (DHCP)

EAP-Transport Layer Security (EAP-TLS)

Encryption control protocols (ECPs)

Forwarding Equivalence Classes (FEC)

Frame relay

Frequency range

Hidden node problem

Integrated services digital network (ISDN)

Internet Authentication Service (IAS)

Internet Protocol Security (IPsec)

IP control protocol (IPCP)

iPhone

ISDN modem

Label Switched Routers (LSRs)

Layer 2 Forwarding (L2F)

Layer 2 Tunneling Protocol (L2TP)

Link Control Protocol (LCP)

MD5-Challenge (MD5-CHAP)

Mixed mode

Multi-input multi-output

Multiprotocol Label Switching (MPLS)

Narrowband ISDN

Negative acknowledgement (NAK)

Network control protocols (NCPs)

Network terminator (NT-1 or NT-2)

Overlay network

Packet assembly/disassembly device (PAD)

Packet-switched networks

Physical carrier sense method (PCSM)

Plain Old Telephone System (POTS)

Point coordination function (PCF)

Point-to-Point over Ethernet (PPPoE)

Point-to-Point Protocol (PPP)

Point-to-Point Tunneling Protocol (PPTP)

Primary rate interface (PRI)

Public Switched Telephone Network (PSTN)

Remote access servers

Remote Authentication Dial-in User Service (RADIUS)

Request to transmit (RTS)

Serial Line Internet Protocol (SLIP)

Service profile identifier (SPID)

Smartphone

Switched Multimegabit Data Service (SMDS)

Synchronous Digital Hierarchy (SDH)

Synchronous Optical Network (SONET)

T1

T2, T3 and T4

Terminal adapter (TA)

Transport mode

Tunnel mode

Virtual carrier sense method (VCSM)

Virtual private network (VPN)

Voice over IP (VoIP)

Wireless Ethernet

Wireless LANs (WLANs)

Wireless Personal Area Network (WPAN)

X.25

11

NETWORK SECURITY

What Do You Already Know?

- What are the primary goals of network security?
- What is Malware?
- Why is antivirus software so important?

 To assess your knowledge of network security fundamentals, go to **www.wiley.com/go/ciccarelli/networkingbasics2e.**

What You Will Find Out	What You Will Be Able To Do
11.1 Why network security is important.	Justify the need for security management. Identify common threats and their potential impact.
11.2 How user access insures that only authorized users have access to your network.	Understand user and group accounts. Configure access permissions and user rights.
11.3 Why configuring network security is important.	Explain how to protect a network using firewalls. Compare wireless security configuration options. Describe data encryption options and how they are used.
11.4 What computer security is.	Identify the most common types of malicious software. Explain the role of antivirus software and other security suite software.

INTRODUCTION

Network security is a broad subject and growing more expansive with nearly every passing day. The people trying to attack your computers and the people trying to protect them are in an ongoing race. Our discussion is limited to an overview of the subject, focusing on a few key topics.

Not only could the subject of security more than fill a book, most of the topics introduced in this chapter could easily justify a book in itself. Our discussion of security starts by explaining why security is important and with a look at risk analysis. Next, we move on to practical subjects that apply directly to security: management activities like managing user accounts, resource access permissions, user rights, and guidelines for managing passwords. The chapter looks at network threats with an emphasis on threats originating from the Internet and how you can use firewalls to protect a network. The chapter introduces the subject of data encryption and encryption options. It discusses wireless networking and wireless configuration options. It also looks at auditing and why logs can be important. Finally, it talks about malicious software and ways to protect a computer from its effects.

Most of our examples in this chapter focus on the Windows family of operating systems and Windows networks. Despite anecdotal evidence to the contrary, a debate is ongoing as to whether or not Windows is inherently any less secure than any other operating system (OS). Each OS, many services, and most server applications have their own unique flaws. The reason that Windows and Windows applications are so often the target of choice is because so many Windows PCs are out there as potential targets in comparison to any other OS.

11.1 UNDERSTANDING THE NEED FOR SECURITY

If you're connected to the Internet, your computer is likely under attack. Attempts to identify and exploit your computer's weaknesses are probably ongoing. Even if your network doesn't have Internet access, you might have someone trying to break into secure (or insecure) systems. Why? For some, it's the thrill of the chase, the excitement they get slipping through security protections. For others, it is money. Not only is corporate espionage rampant, but also information such as valid names, e-mail addresses, and even credit card numbers are worth a great deal when passed into the wrong hands. You'll even find people who attempt to justify their actions for personal reasons, such as revenge against a company or person who wronged them in some way, either real or imagined.

You have two very broad security goals as a network professional. One is to prevent attacks and unauthorized access to data. The other is to detect these occurrences when they do happen, taking whatever steps are necessary to recover, minimize the damage, and prevent it from happening in the future.

Figure 11-1

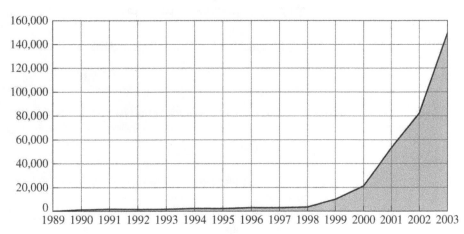

Reporting security incidents.

11.1.1 Understanding the Problem

Computer Emergency Response Team (CERT)
A group established to respond to computer security problems.

Computer security has become increasingly important over the last several years. Security incidents have increased, especially when the Internet is involved. The number of Internet security incidents reported to the United States **Computer Emergency Readiness Team** (US-CERT) has doubled nearly every year (see Figure 11-1). More recent summaries show the number of incidents declining slightly, but the financial impact of each incidence increasing. Numerous worldwide organizations use the name "CERT" to deal with cyber security response, with the first organization CERT® Coordination Center (CERT/CC), established at Carnegie Mellon University in 1988. Although the US-CERT is independent of these groups, it often coordinates with them on security incidents. When the Department of Homeland Security (DHS) created US-CERT, the CERT/CC was instrumental in providing the expertise necessary for protecting critical infrastructure and coordinating response to cyber attacks. Through US-CERT, DHS and the CERT/CC work jointly on these activities.

Security breach
A computer incident that includes somehow bypassing or avoiding security measures.

NETWORKING FACT

Approximately 95 percent of the respondents to a 2005 Computer Security Institute/FBI Computer Crime and Security Survey reported that they had detected **security breaches** in the last 12 months. About 90 percent reported they suffered a measurable financial loss due to a security problem, with the average loss about $200,000. Most recent results reported by various organizations indicate that this 95 percent is still accurate for attempts to breach security, though some industry experts believe successful attempts have fallen off slightly. In 2007 the Computer Security Institute separated from the FBI in its reporting, becoming a purely commercial operation, and as a result the responses to its surveys and the accuracy have diminished.

TIPS FROM THE PROFESSIONALS

CSI Computer Crime and Security Survey (2010)

The 15th edition of its annual CSI Computer Crime and Security Survey (June 2010) with only a 6.4 percent response rate had these key points:

1. Malware infection continued to be the most commonly seen attack, with about two-thirds of respondents reporting it, and it appeared to be on the rise.

2. Respondents reported markedly fewer financial fraud incidents than in previous years, with less than 9 percent saying they'd seen this type of incident during the covered period.

3. Of the approximately half of respondents who experienced at least one security incident last year, a little more than 45 percent of them reported they'd been the subject of at least one targeted attack.

4. Fewer respondents than ever (i.e., 77) were willing to share specific information about dollar losses they incurred.

5. Respondents said that regulatory compliance (e.g., Health Insurance Portability and Accountability Act (HIPAA) and Health Information Technology for Economic and Clinical Health (HITECH), breach notification laws, Sarbanes-Oxley, Payment Card Industry Data Security Standard (PCI DSS), international privacy/security laws, Federal Information Security Management Act (FISMA), and Gramm–Leach–Bliley Act (GLBA) efforts have had a positive effect on their security programs.

6. By and large, respondents did not believe that the activities of malicious insiders (as opposed to non-malicious insiders) accounted for much of their losses due to cybercrime.

7. Slightly more than half of the respondents said that their organizations do n ot use cloud computing. Ten percent, however, say their organizations not only use cloud computing, but also have deployed cloud-specific security tools.

Health Insurance Portability and Accountability Act (HIPAA)
A law passed in the United States that defines requirements for protecting patient data.

Protecting customer privacy also drives the need for increased network security. In 1998, the European Union passed strong data privacy laws that fined companies for disclosing information about their customers. In the United States, organizations are required to comply with the data protection requirements of the **Health Insurance Portability and Accountability Act (HIPAA),** and a California law providing fines up to $250,000 for each unauthorized disclosure of customer information. The Health Information Technology for Economic and Clinical Health (HITECH) Act, enacted as part of the American Recovery and Reinvestment Act of 2009, was signed into law on February 17, 2009, to promote the adoption and meaningful use of health information technology. Subtitle D of the HITECH Act addresses the privacy and security concerns associated with the electronic transmission of health information, in part, through several provisions that strengthen the civil and criminal enforcement of the HIPAA rules.

11.1.2 Recognizing the Problem

For many people, security means preventing unauthorized access, such as preventing an attacker from breaking into your computer. Security is much more than that, however. Often called the CIA Triad, three primary goals exist in providing security: confidentiality, integrity, and availability. **Confidentiality** refers to the protection of data from unauthorized disclosure of customer and proprietary data. **Integrity** is the assurance that data have not been altered or destroyed. **Availability** means providing continuous access to the critical data and the operation of the organization's hardware and software so that staff, customers, and suppliers can be assured of no interruptions in service.

Figure 11-2 identifies some potential threats to a computer center, data communication circuits, and attached computers. In general, your goals in response to security threats are ensuring business continuity and preventing unauthorized access.

Business continuity planning refers primarily to ensuring availability, with some aspects of data integrity. One concern is **disruptions,** which are the loss of or reduction in network service.

Disruptions may be minor and temporary, affecting only a few users. They can be caused by device failures, such as a failing hub or switch, or by a result in the data destruction. For example, a virus (a malicious program that attaches itself to another program and then propagates copies of itself) may destroy files that users need. Once again, hardware could be the cause. A hard disk crash may result in needed files being destroyed.

Other disruptions can be catastrophic. Natural or manmade disasters such as fires, floods, earthquakes, mudslides, tornadoes, or terrorist attacks can destroy large parts of the buildings and networks in their path. Especially active viruses can overwhelm a network and all of its computers.

Unauthorized access relates primarily to confidentiality, but also to integrity, because someone with unauthorized access may change important data. Unauthorized access is external attackers gaining access to organizational data files and resources from across the Internet. However, most unauthorized access incidents involve employees, if not as the attacker, then as the source for passwords or other information.

Unauthorized access might have only minor effects. A curious intruder may explore the system, gaining knowledge that has little value, and perhaps leaving behind some sort of calling card. A more serious intruder might be a competitor bent on industrial espionage who attempts to gain access to

Confidentiality
A term that refers to protection of data from unauthorized disclosure.

Integrity
The assurance that data has not been altered or destroyed.

Availability
A term that refers to providing continuous access to the critical data and the operation of an organizations hardware and software so that there is no interruption of service.

Business continuity planning
Ensuring availability and integrity; keeping the business running when disruptions occur.

Disruptions
Interruptions of or reductions in network service.

Unauthorized access
Access by unauthorized personnel that violates confidentiality and/or integrity.

Figure 11-2

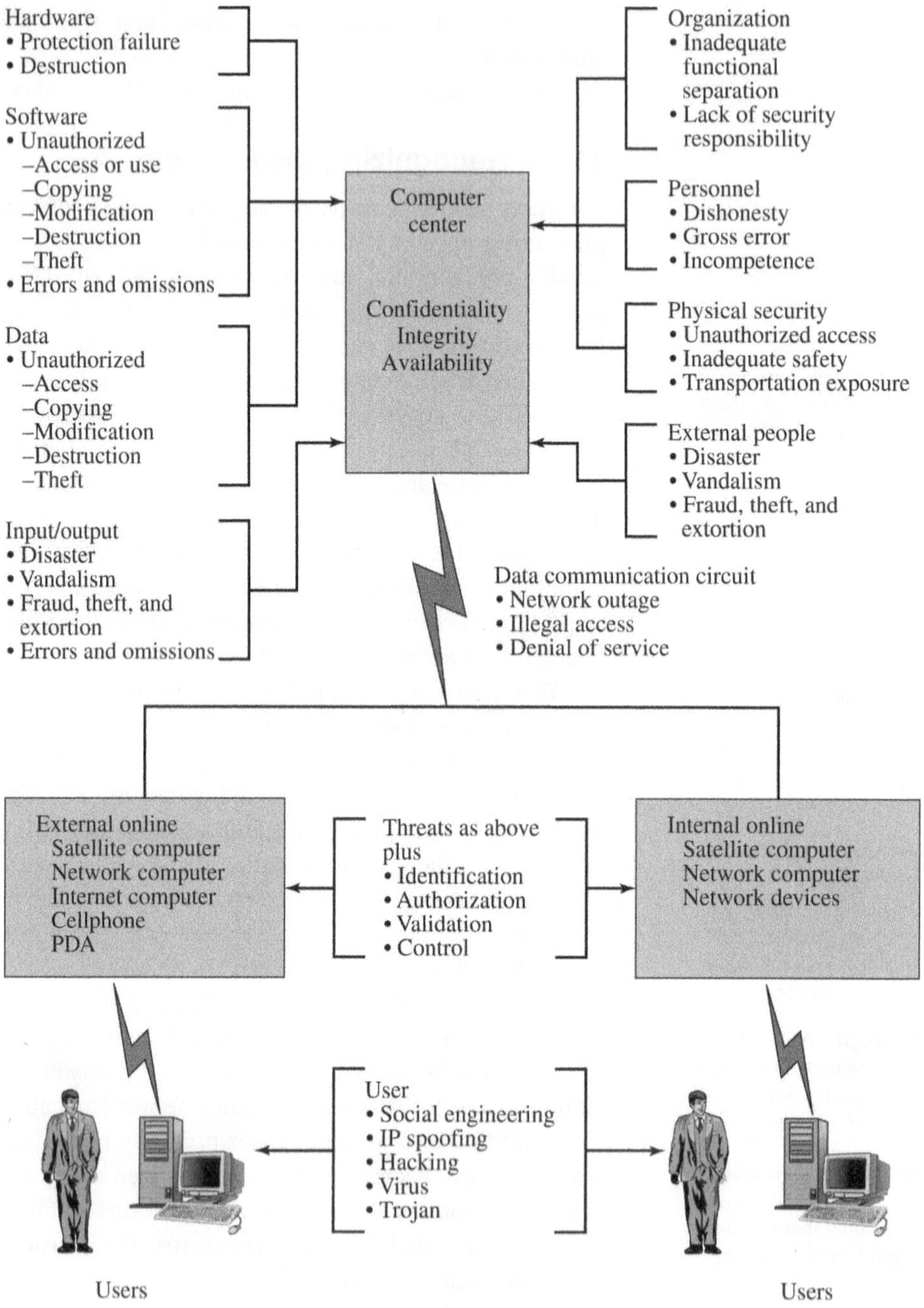

Hardware
• Protection failure
• Destruction

Software
• Unauthorized
  −Access or use
  −Copying
  −Modification
  −Destruction
  −Theft
• Errors and omissions

Data
• Unauthorized
  −Access
  −Copying
  −Modification
  −Destruction
  −Theft

Input/output
• Disaster
• Vandalism
• Fraud, theft, and
  extortion
• Errors and omissions

Computer
center

Confidentiality
Integrity
Availability

Organization
• Inadequate
  functional
  separation
• Lack of security
  responsibility

Personnel
• Dishonesty
• Gross error
• Incompetence

Physical security
• Unauthorized access
• Inadequate safety
• Transportation exposure

External people
• Disaster
• Vandalism
• Fraud, theft, and
  extortion

Data communication circuit
• Network outage
• Illegal access
• Denial of service

External online
  Satellite computer
  Network computer
  Internet computer
  Cellphone
  PDA

Threats as above
plus
• Identification
• Authorization
• Validation
• Control

Internal online
  Satellite computer
  Network computer
  Network devices

User
• Social engineering
• IP spoofing
• Hacking
• Virus
• Trojan

Users

Users

Types of risks.

information on products under development or the details and price of a bid on a large contract. Worse still, the intruder could change files to commit fraud or theft, or could destroy information to injure the organization.

TIPS FROM THE PROFESSIONALS

Data Breaches in 2009–2010

According to the 2009–2010 Data Breach Investigations Reports conducted by the Verizon Business RISK team in cooperation with the United States Secret Service:

Most data breaches continue to originate from external sources. Though still a third of our sample, breaches linked to business partners fell for the first time in years. The median size of breaches caused by insiders is still the highest, but the predominance of total records lost was attributed to outsiders. Ninety-one percent of all compromised records were linked to organized criminal groups. A growing percentage of cases and an astounding 94 percent of all compromised records in 2009 were attributed to Financial Services.

(The current report may be found at: http://www.verizonbusiness. com/resources/reports/rp_data-breach-investigations-report-2011_en_ xg.pdf.)

11.1.3 The Risk Analysis Process: Assessing Security Risks

One key step in developing a secure network is to conduct a risk assessment. Doing so assigns levels of risk (how likely they are to occur and the amount of damage they could cause) to various threats to network security by comparing the nature of the threats to the controls designed to reduce them.

Identifying Network Assets

Network assets
Any hardware or software of value on a network.

Start by identifying **network assets,** which are any things of value on the network (hardware or software). Probably the most important asset on a network is the organization's data. Typical assets are listed in Figure 11-3.

Now, consider the related costs. For example, suppose someone stole a database server worth $8,000. You could easily replace the computer and software and that problem would be solved in a few days. Go a step further. Suppose that database contained archival records for a hospital. Even if the data can be recovered from backups, the cost could easily run into millions of dollars from lawsuits alone resulting from the possible disclosure of confidential information. If the attacker were able to steal or corrupt the

Figure 11-3

Hardware	• Servers, such as mail servers, web servers, DNS servers, DHCP servers, and LAN file servers • Client computers • Devices such as hubs, switches, and routers
Circuits	• Locally operated circuits such as LANs and backbones • Contracted circuits such as MAN and WAN circuits • Internet access circuits
Network software	• Server operating systems and system settings • Application software such as mail server and web server software
Client software	• Operating systems and system settings • Application software such as word processors
Organizational data	• Databases with organizational records
Mission-critical applications	• For example, for an Internet bank, its website is mission-critical

Types of assets: DNS = Domain Name Service; DHCP = Dynamic Host Control Protocol; LAN = local area network; MAN = metropolitan area network; WAN = wide area network.

Network assets.

backups, the costs quickly magnify, including the costs to research and re-enter all of that information manually.

Mission-critical application
An information system that is vital to an organization.

An important type of asset is the **mission-critical application,** which is an information system that is vital to an organization's survival. This application should not be permitted to fail, and if it does fail, the network staff drops everything else to fix it.

For example, an Internet bank has no brick-and-mortar branches, so its websites are mission-critical applications. If they crash, the bank cannot conduct business with its customers.

After you have a list of assets, you should evaluate them based on their importance. There will rarely be enough time and money to protect all assets completely, so focusing the organization's attention on the most important ones is important.

Identifying Threats

A threat to the network is any potential adverse occurrence that can do harm, interrupt the systems using the network, or cause any loss to the organization. Threats may be listed in generic terms, such as theft of data or destruction of data, but being specific is better. Use actual data from the organization being assessed in your descriptions, such as theft of customer credit card numbers or destruction of the inventory database.

After you identify the threats, you can rank them according to their probability of occurrence and the estimated cost. Figure 11-4 summarizes common threats and their likelihood of occurring, along with a typical cost estimate, based on several surveys (primarily the 2005 CSI/FBI Computer Crime and Security Survey).

These survey results are taken from a number of different businesses, so the threat and possible cost for any particular type of business can vary. They are meant to provide general guidelines. An Internet bank, for example, is more likely to be a target of fraud and to suffer a higher cost if it occurs than a restaurant with a simple website.

When considering possible threats, most people first think about unknown attackers breaking into a network across the Internet, which does happen. Unauthorized access continues to be a problem. Figure 11-4 identifies one likely event as a virus infection (more than 80 percent of organizations).

Interestingly, more companies often suffer unauthorized access by their own employees than by outsiders. Unauthorized access and attacks like data theft, whether from internal or external sources, can have far-reaching consequences. The cost to recover afterward can be very high, both in dollar cost and bad publicity. Over the years, several major companies have had their networks broken into and have had proprietary information such as customer credit card numbers stolen. Winning back the customers can be an even greater challenge than fixing the security breach.

You should get two messages from Figure 11-4. First, security threats are expensive. Based on relative probabilities of the different threats, you can see that the threats to business continuity have a greater chance of occurring than unauthorized access. The most common threat with fairly high cost is a virus. Still, given the cost of fraud and theft of information, even a single event can have a significant impact.

Figure 11-4

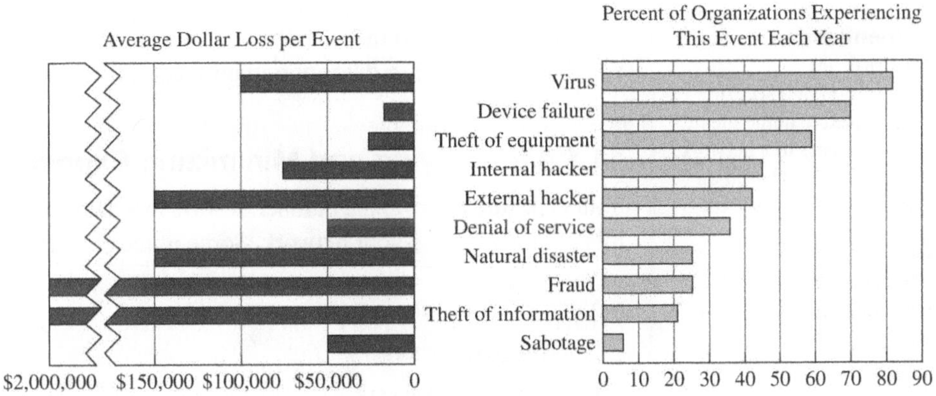

Potential threats.

IN THE REAL WORLD

Cybercrime Arrests

Over the past several years the Secret Service has successfully investigated several of the largest cybercriminal cases in the United States. In 2010, the Secret Service arrested more than 1,200 suspects for cybercrime violations. These investigations involved more than $500 million in actual fraud loss and prevented approximately $7 billion in additional losses.

For example in 2010, Albert Gonzalez received a 20-year prison sentence for his role in the TJX and Heartland Payment System breaches. Maksym Yastrzemski was given a 30-year prison sentence in Turkey as the seller of payment card data for Gonzalez and other cybercriminals.

Additionally, Vladislov Horohorin, also known as BadB, was arrested in Nice, France on a Secret Service warrant and is being extradited to the United States. BadB was an original founder of the CarderPlanet criminal forum and he had been the largest and well-known trafficker of stolen payment card data for nearly a decade. In a joint investigation with the Netherlands High Tech Crime Unit, the Secret Service provided investigative assistance that led to the take down of the Bredolab Botnet and the arrest of the Botherder nicknamed "Atata" by Armenian authorities.

The second important message is that the greatest threat of unauthorized access is not from the outside intruder coming at you over the Internet, but rather from your own employees. This has been true since the early 1980s when the FBI first began keeping computer crime statistics and security firms began conducting surveys of computer crime, which is any criminal activity involving or directed against computers. However, in recent years, the number of external attacks has increased at a greater rate while the number of internal attacks has stayed relatively constant. Even these attacks often involved, at least indirectly, an internal employee. External attacks are often expedited by compromised **authentication credentials,** supplied by users who haven't used **due diligence** in protecting their passwords.

Authentication credentials
Information or a security device used to authenticate a user's access to a network, most commonly based on user name and password.

Due diligence
The care exercised by a reasonable person to avoid harm or loss.

11.1.4 Identifying and Minimizing Exposure

Your exposure refers to the number of ways in which someone (or something) might gain access to your network. Some of the most common risks include:

- Network client computers
- Unprotected servers
- Remote access servers
- The Internet

IN THE REAL WORLD

Sometimes It's Just Stupidity

This situation is made up, using Busicorp as a fictitious example. If it sounds familiar, you're right. Multiple cases like this example have happened in recent years. However, the names have been changed to protect the innocent (and the stupid).

An employee, overwhelmed by the pressure of end-of-year analysis and reporting, copies some customer files to his laptop. The idea is that he can work on them at home and bring the finished reports back with him in the morning. He dozes off on the train home and when he wakes up, the computer is missing.

The problem is that those customer records included personal information like addresses, Social Security numbers, mother's maiden name, and so on. In short, all of the information that someone needs to steal a person's identity. Within a few days, Busicorp's customers report a rash of identity thefts (and even more that go undetected for weeks).

Who's responsible? The employee, obviously, for copying the records to his laptop and not guarding it more carefully, but it doesn't end there. Busicorp is also at fault for not better protecting the data and preventing the employee from copying it off in the first place.

Network computers are often left unwatched and unguarded when not in use, especially at night. Who's to say that the new janitor didn't apply for the job with the specific goal of stealing corporate information for sale to the highest bidder? All it might take is someone forgetting to log off at the end of the day. Barring that, many users have very bad security habits, like "hiding" their password under the keyboard or in the top desk drawer.

Unprotected servers can be another risk. Critical servers should be physically secured, kept under lock and key or other security mechanism, at all times. Data theft or destruction is much easier if you're sitting at the server's keyboard. In some cases thieves have walked out of the building with servers, or at least their hard drives, tucked under one arm.

Any time you open your network to remote access you take a calculated risk. When you set up a remote access server, you must put security measures in place to ensure that only authorized personnel have access. The tools available to you vary by operating system, but include things like limiting the numbers from which calls are accepted, having the server call back to provide access instead of allowing the user to dial in and connect, and requiring secure authentication based on user name and password or other authentication mechanisms.

CAREER CONNECTION

Do You Need Security?

Most small networks are in small businesses or departments where everyone knows and trusts everyone else. Folks don't lock up their desks when they take a coffee break, and although everyone knows where the petty cash box is, money never disappears.

Network security isn't necessary in an idyllic setting like this one, is it? You bet it is. Here's why any network should be set up with at least some minimal concern for security:

Even in the friendliest office environment, some information is and should be confidential. If this information is stored on the network, you want to store it in a directory that's available only to authorized users. Remember these important points:

- **Not all security breaches are malicious.** A network user may be routinely scanning through his or her files and come across a filename that isn't familiar. The user may then call up the file, only to discover that it contains confidential personnel information, juicy office gossip, or your résumé. Curiosity, rather than malice, is often the source of security breaches.
- **Sure, everyone at the office is trustworthy now.** However, what if someone becomes disgruntled, a screw pops loose, and he or she decides to trash the network files before jumping out the window? What if someone decides to print a few $1,000 checks before packing off to Tahiti?
- **Sometimes the mere opportunity for fraud or theft can be too much for some people to resist.** Give people free access to the payroll files, and they may decide to vote themselves a raise when no one is looking.
- **If you think that your network doesn't contain any data that would be worth stealing, think again.** For example, your personnel records probably contain more than enough information for an identity thief: names, addresses, phone numbers, Social Security numbers, and so on. Also, your customer files may contain your customers' credit card numbers.

> **Trojan horse**
> A program that is expected to do one thing but actually does something else. The name is a reference to classical Greek literature.

- **Attackers who break into your network may not be interested in stealing your data.** Instead, they may be looking to plant a **Trojan horse** program on your server, which enables them to use your server for their own purposes. For example, someone may use your server to send thousands of unsolicited spam e-mail messages. The spam won't be traced back to the attackers; it will be traced back to you.
- **Finally, remember that not everyone on the network knows enough about how Windows and the network work to be trusted with full access to your network's data and systems.** One careless mouse click can wipe out an entire directory of network files. One of the best reasons for activating your network's security features is to protect the network from mistakes made by users who don't know what they're doing.

Hacker
An expert in problem solving with a computer who sometimes gains illegal access to and sometimes tampers with information in a computer system.

Smart card
Sometimes called an integrated circuit card (ICC), it is any pocket-sized plastic card with embedded integrated circuits, usually containing security information such as encryption keys to facilitate access control mechanisms.

Just as remote access is a known threat, so is connecting to the Internet. As soon as you connect your network to the Internet, you've opened a potential door that **hackers,** individuals trying to break into your system, can start picking away at. Some of these attacks are designed to gain access to the network while others are designed to bring it down, either crashing the network or tying it up to the point that no one can get access to it.

There's also the risk of what might follow you home from the Internet. Two of the most common sources of viruses and other malicious programs are files downloaded from the Internet and e-mail attachments. Never download a file unless you are certain of its source, and even then, you should scan the file for viruses before opening or executing it. One thing that many people don't realize is that most multimedia files are a form of executable file and have become a common mechanism for distributing viruses.

SELF-CHECK

1. Based on industry surveys, what is the most likely source of unauthorized access?
2. What is a mission-critical application?
3. What should you consider when assigning levels of risk?

Apply Your Knowledge   Look at the scenario described in "Sometimes It's Just Stupidity." Then look at the Veterans' Affairs (VA) case from May 2006. (In May, VA officials said a laptop computer containing the personal information of about 26.5 million veterans and active duty members of the military was stolen from the home of a VA employee. And a laptop was stolen from a VA subcontractor's Reston, Virginia office.)

List ways that this loss could have been mitigated or prevented in order of cost and ease of implementation.

11.2   IMPLEMENTING USER ACCESS SECURITY

Biometric scan
A security scan based on a user's identifiable physical characteristic.

User account
A user identified to a computer or network.

Network security begins with user access security. All user access attempts should be authenticated, either by a user name and password or other security mechanisms such as a **smart card** or **biometric scan** based on characteristics like the user's thumb print or retina.

A network is no more secure than its **user accounts,** and user account security should be first and foremost in your mind. You manage access to network resources through a user account and the rights given to that account. The network administrator is charged with the daily maintenance of these accounts. Common security duties include renaming accounts and resetting forgotten (or compromised) passwords. You can also specify where users can log in, how often they can log in, at what times they can log in, how often their passwords expire, and when their accounts expire.

11.2.1 Managing User Accounts

Domain account
A Windows Active Directory user account used for domain authentication and resource access authorization.

Local account
A user account used by the local computer for authorization and resource access authentication.

Active Directory users and computers
A Windows Active Directory utility used to manage organizational units, users, groups, computers, and other domain objects.

All network operating systems have some method for creating and managing user accounts. Each user should have his or her own account for accessing the network, and the company should have a written policy in place emphasizing the importance of not sharing account information with anyone else.

In a Windows Active Directory domain, you have two types of user accounts. **Domain accounts** give users access to domain resources and are required for domain login. Member computers, both clients and servers, also have **local accounts.** These accounts don't give you access to the network, but do let you access resources local to the computer. Local administrator accounts give you full access to the computer, including configuration information and the permission to install applications.

Active Directory accounts are managed using the **Active Directory Users and Computers** utility, shown in Figure 11-5. Each user account will be contained in an organizational unit (OU) or other domain container.

Figure 11-5

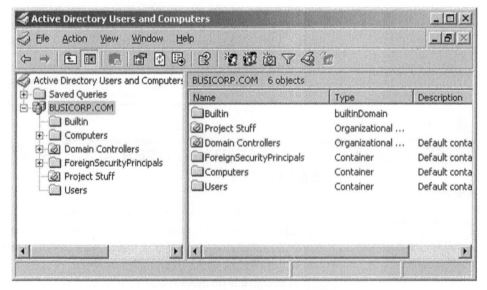

Active Directory users and computers.

Maintenance accounts
A user account created explicitly for the purpose of performing maintenance tasks.

Administrator
A user name often associated with a maintenance account that has unlimited access to a computer or network. See also **supervisor, root,** and **superuser.**

Root
A name that may be given by the network operating system to a special user account known as a maintenance account that has unlimited access to a computer or network.

Superuser
A Unix or Linux user account that has unlimited access to a computer or network.

When you create a user account, you will also assign an initial password. Typically, the account will be configured to force the user to change the password the first time it's used to log into the domain.

User accounts are also organized into groups, which are sets of users. Rights and access permissions can be granted individually to users or to a group, in which case they also apply to the group's members.

Special user accounts are known as **maintenance accounts** because they are used for system and network management and maintenance. The network operating system (NOS) will create one or more of these accounts by default, giving them names like **administrator, supervisor, root,** or **superuser,** depending on the NOS. These names are well known, so one of the first things you should do (if possible) is rename these accounts. You can also create additional maintenance accounts, as necessary. Users should use these accounts for login only when performing maintenance functions and use a standard user account at all other times. Why? Think what could happen if you leave your desk for an extended time with the computer logged in as an administrator. The possible result could be devastating.

Windows manages maintenance accounts through group membership. Several predefined groups are designed to let users perform specific functions, such as backing up data, managing user accounts, or even administering the network. You can see some of these listed in Figure 11-6.

Figure 11-6

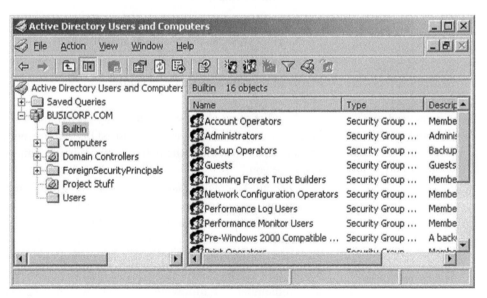

Built-in groups.

Users should be added to these groups only when they need the additional rights and permissions granted in order to do their jobs.

When a user account is no longer needed (like when the user leaves the company), the account should be either deleted or disabled so that it can't be used for access. The advantage of disabling an account is that it can be renamed and assigned to a new user, making it easy to set up access for the employee's replacement. You should also disable an account if the user will be gone for an extended period, like on vacation.

11.2.2 Managing Passwords

Crack
A term used for the process of guessing or compromising a password.

Strong password
A password that is designed to be difficult to guess or crack.

Managing passwords involves ensuring that all passwords for user accounts follow security guidelines so that they cannot be easily guessed or **cracked,** as well as implementing features of your network operating system to prevent unauthorized access.

Generally speaking, a **strong** or **complex password** is a combination of alphanumeric and special characters that is easy for you to remember and difficult for someone else to guess. They should be at least eight characters, if not more. Here are some passwords that you should never use:

- The word password
- Proper names
- Your pet's name
- Your spouse's name
- Your children's names
- Any word in the dictionary
- Important dates, such as birthdays, anniversaries, etc.
- Any of the above with a leading or trailing number
- Any of the above spelled backward

Weak password
An easily guessed password.

This list of **weak passwords** is only partial, but it should give you an idea of what you want to avoid. Most NOSs can be configured to prevent users from using some of them, like using your user name or the word password, for you.

Difficult-to-crack passwords should include a combination of numbers, uppercase letters, lowercase letters, and special characters (not just letters, not just numbers, not just special characters, but a combination of all three). Special characters are those that cannot be considered letters or numbers (for example, $ % ^ # @). An example of a strong password is tqbf4#jotld. Such a password may look hard to remember, but it is not. You may remember the following sentence, which uses every letter in the English alphabet: The quick brown fox jumped over the lazy dog. Take the first letter of each word, put the number 4 and a pound (#) symbol in the middle, and you have a strong password.

Auditing tool
Utilities designed to automatically review and test network security.

Crack program
A program designed to find weak, easily compromised passwords.

To check passwords, you can use **auditing tools,** such as a **crack program** that tries to guess passwords. If you are using strong passwords, the crack program should have great difficulty guessing them. Here are a few examples of strong passwords:

- run4!cover
- iron$steel4
- tpwb2m,k? (This PassWord Belongs 2 Me, oKay?)

All NOSs include functions for managing passwords so that the system remains secure and passwords cannot be easily hacked with crack programs. These functions include automatic account lockouts and password properties like password expiration.

In an Active Directory domain, these functions are set through group policy. To have them apply to the domain, you configure password policy through a group policy object (GPO) linked to the domain and include password policies and account lockout policies.

Hackers (and users who forget their passwords) attempt to log in by guessing the password. To ensure that a password can't be guessed by repeatedly inputting different passwords, most NOSs allow an account to be disabled, or locked out, after a set number of unsuccessful login attempts. After it's locked, the user cannot log in to that account even if the correct password is entered. This security measure prevents a potential hacker from running an automated script to continuously attempt logins using different character combinations. However, it doesn't prevent an intruder from intercepting cracking the password with specialized tools, so account lockout still leaves some potential security holes. **Account lockout policies** supported by Windows are shown in Figure 11-7.

Account lockout policies
Policies controlling account lockout configuration parameters.

After a lockout is activated, to log in successfully the user must ask the network support staff to unlock the account if the network operating system doesn't unlock it after a preset period. In high-security networks, having an administrator manually unlock a locked account might be advisable rather than letting the network operating system do it automatically. That way, the administrator is always notified of a possible security breach. The problem is, however, that this policy could leave your network more vulnerable to some types of denial of service attacks (discussed later in the chapter).

You also have control over password policies. The default policies for a Windows Server 2003 Active Directory domain are shown in Figure 11-8.

The policy settings shown here are for Windows, but most NOSs support the same restrictions, though they might identify them by different names. Let's take a quick look.

Figure 11-7

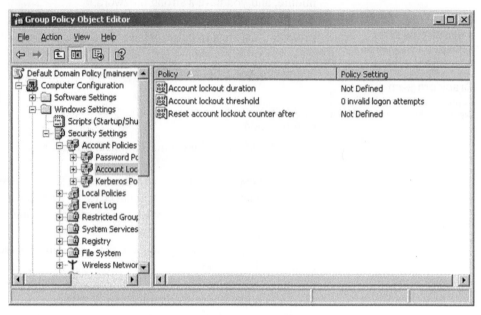

Account lockout policies.

Figure 11-8

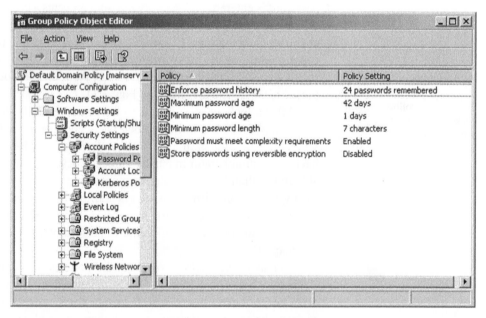

Default password policies.

Enforce password history
The number of passwords the system will remember to prevent a user from reusing.

Enforce password history determines how many different passwords will be remembered, preventing the user from reusing them. For example, with the current setting, a user would have to come up with at least 25 unique passwords, the 24 remembered passwords plus the current password.

Maximum password age
The maximum time between password changes.

Maximum password age sets password expiration. After the specified period, the password expires and can no longer be used. In Figure 11-7, the maximum password age is set to 42 days. Most companies use a value between 30 and 60 days. The network will begin warning the user to change his or her password a few days before it expires. Why force changes? The longer a user keeps the same password, the more likely it is to get compromised.

Minimum password age
The minimum time that must pass between password changes.

Minimum password age sets the minimum time between password changes. Why? To prevent the user from sneaking past the password history. Even set to a value as short as one or two days, it becomes more effort than it is worth to repeatedly change passwords until the user can get back to using a favorite password.

Minimum password length
The minimum number of characters a password must contain.

The user's password must be at least equal to, but can be longer than, the **minimum password length.** Passwords should be long enough to make for secure passwords, but not so long as to be difficult to remember.

Password must meet complexity requirements
A Windows password policy that forces users to use stronger passwords.

The **password must meet complexity requirements** policy forces users to use strong passwords. The password must be at least six characters long (unless overridden by a longer value specified in the minimum password length) and include at least three of the following:

- English uppercase characters
- English lowercase characters
- Numbers (0 through 9)
- Non-alphabetic "special" characters (such as !, @, #, %, and so on)

Store passwords using reversible encryption
A Windows password policy that should be left disabled unless required (e.g., when using CHAP for authentication).

The **store passwords using reversible encryption** is a policy supported by some NOSs as a default option. Typically, this policy is disabled in a Windows network and should remain disabled unless required. It is required when using the Challenge-Handshake Authentication Protocol (CHAP) and with Microsoft Internet Information Services (IIS) Digest Authentication.

11.2.3 Managing Access Security and User Rights

You can secure files that are shared over the network in two ways:

- At the share level
- At the user (group) level

In a network that uses share-level security, you assign passwords to individual files or other network resources (such as printers) instead of assigning rights to users. Early Windows workgroup configurations used it as a way to manage security. You then give these passwords to all users who need access to these resources. With this type of security, the network support staff has no way of knowing who is managing the resources.

Current Windows versions and most other NOSs typically use user-level security. Rights to network resources are assigned to specific users or groups. In a workgroup environment, this is managed separately on each computer. In a client-server or directory-based network, permission management is more centralized, but can also rely on rights assigned at the computer hosting the resource. Typical file share permissions are shown in Figure 11-9.

One thing to keep in mind is that denied permissions take precedence over granted permissions. If you deny a permission to a user, you can't give

Figure 11-9

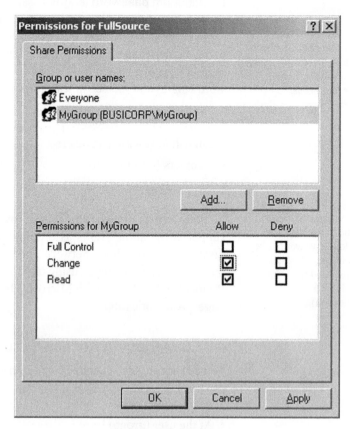

Share permissions.

Figure 11-10

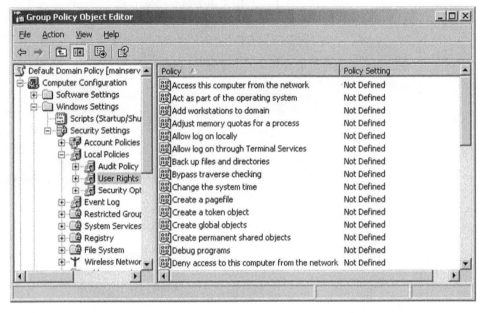

User rights.

the user rights to the resources. If you deny a permission to a group, it is denied to all of the group's members.

You can also manage user rights, which determine what a user can do. One way rights are assigned is through group membership in management groups. Individual rights can also be granted to individual users or to groups. Figure 11-10 shows a partial list of user rights supported by Windows operating systems. These rights can be set on an individual computer, but more commonly, you set user rights policies for groups of computers through GPOs linked to OUs and, if appropriate, associated with computer groups.

TIPS FROM THE PROFESSIONALS

A Caution on Deny Permissions

Use the deny permissions sparingly or not at all. The IT world is rife with stories of the new network administrator who in an effort to secure his or her networks, used the deny permission on the "Everyone" group, forgetting that even though they were a member of the administrative group with full access, they were also automatically a member of the Everyone group, and thus were locked out of their own system.

IN THE REAL WORLD

Understanding the Exceptions

As with most rules, there are exceptions to the guidelines for managing user passwords. Why? Some types of user accounts call for special management procedures.

Some applications and services can be configured to launch in the security context of a user account. One example of this is the Microsoft SQL Server. When Busicorp installed the SQL Server, the network administrator set up a user account specifically for that purpose. Two months later, the SQL Server crashed. More correctly, the SQL Server would no longer start.

After some investigation, the reason turned out to be rather simple. Take a look at Figure 11-11. Notice that you can override some password

Figure 11-11

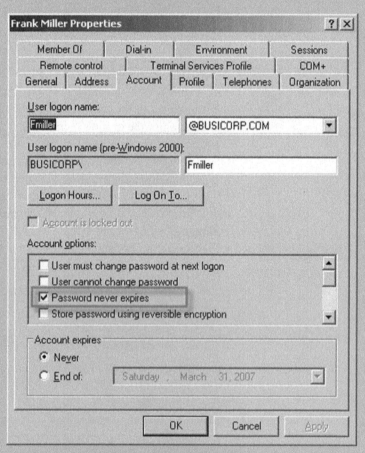

Sample user properties.

(continued)

(continued)

restrictions through user properties, including maximum password age. This has been done in Figure 11-11, by checking the password never expires property in the Account properties.

When the network administrator set up the user account, he forgot one detail. He didn't check the password never expires. Two months later, the password expired, the user can't be authenticated, and the SQL Server can't start.

You have a great deal of flexibility when setting user rights. For example, you might set one set of rights for domain controllers, another for member servers, and yet another that applies to client workstations.

SELF-CHECK

1. What are the guidelines for Windows complex passwords?
2. What is the advantage of user-level security over share-level security?
3. Why is it more efficient to manage groups than to manage users?

Apply Your Knowledge Create some passwords that you think are strong, and then check them at the Microsoft Security and Safety Center (www.microsoft .com/security/pc-security/password-checker.aspx):

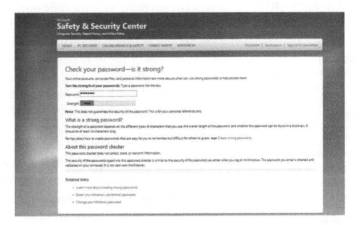

The preceding example uses the password P@$sw0rd, which Microsoft considers weak as it is a derivation of one of the most common passwords used.

11.3 CONFIGURING NETWORK SECURITY

Hardening
The process of making a network or computer more secure.

Firewalls
A network security device that filters traffic into or out of a network or subnet.

Directed attacks
An attack that is under the direct control of a hacker.

WinNuke
An early hacker program that sent TCP/IP packets with invalid header information.

Stop error
The Microsoft term for a terminal failure or crash resulting in a "Blue Screen."

Blue Screen of Death
A visual indication of stop error. You must reboot the computer to clear the error.

IP spoofing
The process of sending packets with a fake source address.

Ping of Death
A type of DoS attack that sends oversized ping packets to the target computer.

Denial of service (DoS)
An attack that attempts to disrupt a network or its servers by flooding them with packets.

When talking about securing your network, we're looking at two general areas. You need to protect your network, but you also need to protect the individual computers on your network. The two are very closely related.

The first concern, which we've already discussed, is controlling network access through user authentication, access permissions, and rights assignments. The next is controlling communications in, out, and through the network. You also need to configure network computers to ensure that they are secure, which sometimes means adding special security programs. This process of making the network and individual computers more secure is sometimes referred to as **hardening.**

What it takes to make a network safe depends on your goals. Is your primary focus keeping the network running efficiently? Then you might need to focus on subnetting or configuring collision domains. Worried about keeping information in or out? Then you could be looking at **firewalls,** which filter network traffic based on various criteria. Worried about someone intercepting data from the network? If so, then encryption might be necessary.

11.3.1 Identifying Network Attacks

Network attacks that are directed by a hacker are called **directed attacks.** One of the first identified attack "tools" was **WinNuke,** a Windows program that sends special TCP/IP packets with an invalid TCP header. Windows 95/98 and Windows NT/2000 computers would crash when they received one of these packets because of how they handled bad data in the TCP header. Instead of returning an error code or rejecting the bad data (Microsoft calls it out-of-band data), it resulted in a **stop error,** commonly referred to as the **Blue Screen of Death (BSoD).** Figuratively speaking, the hacker causes the computer to blow up, or to be nuked. Patches and service packs for the affected Microsoft products have long since quelled the threat that out-of-band data once posed, but hackers have continued to fine-tune their attacks.

IP spoofing is the process of sending packets with a fake source address, pretending that the packet is coming from within the network that the hacker is trying to attack. The address can be considered stolen from the hacker's target network. A router (even one that filters individual packets) is going to treat this packet as coming from within the network and will let it pass; however, a firewall can prevent this type of packet from passing into the secured network. Figure 11-12 shows a hacker attempting an IP spoof.

The **Ping of Death** is a type of **denial of service (DoS)** attack. A DoS attack prevents any users, even legitimate ones, from using the system. Normally, when you ping a remote host, four normal-sized **Internet Control Message Protocol (ICMP)** packets are sent to the remote host to see

Figure 11-12

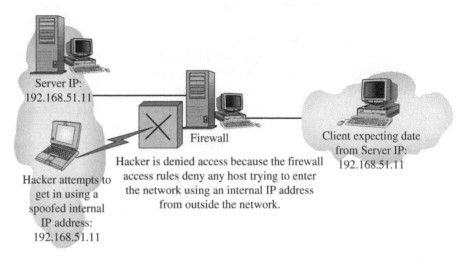

Server IP:
192.168.51.11

Firewall

Client expecting date
from Server IP:
192.168.51.11

Hacker is denied access because the firewall
access rules deny any host trying to enter
the network using an internal IP address
from outside the network.

Hacker attempts to
get in using a
spoofed internal
IP address:
192.168.51.11

IP spoofing.

Internet Control Message Protocol (ICMP)
A management and troubleshooting protocol that provides support through error and control messages.

> ### FOR EXAMPLE
> #### FIGURE 11-12
> Notice that the hacker with the spoofed IP address is denied access to the network by the firewall.

if it is available. In a Ping of Death attack, a very large ICMP packet is sent to the remote host, whose buffer is flooded by this packet. Typically, this causes a system to reboot or hang. Patches to prevent a Ping of Death attack from working are available for most operating systems.

SYN flood
A DoS attack that uses a flood of SYN packets.

SYN flag
Bits internal to a SYN packet carrying status and other information.

SYN packet
A packet used when initializing a TCP/IP communication session.

A **SYN flood** is another specialized DoS attack. In normal communications, a workstation that wants to open a TCP/IP communication with a server sends a TCP/IP packet with the **SYN flag** set to 1. The server automatically responds to the request, indicating that it is ready to start communicating. Only new communications use SYN flags and a new **SYN packet** is used only if you lose your connection and must reestablish communications. To initiate a SYN flood, a hacker sends a barrage of SYN packets and the receiving computer tries to respond to each SYN request for a connection until the victim machine cannot respond to any other requests because its buffers are overfilled. At that point, it rejects all packets, including valid requests for connections. Patches that can help with this problem are available for the various NOSs.

There are also other types of DoS attacks, in which an attacker attempts to disrupt the network by flooding it with messages. One common feature

Distributed denial-of-service attack (DDoS)
A DoS attack in which the attacker controls multiple attacking systems.

DDoS agent
Software placed on a computer that enables it to be used as a message source in a DDoS attack.

DDoS handler
Software used during a DDoS attack to control the agents.

Black box system
A proprietary system in which you know what a system does but not the hardware or software it contains.

Packet filtering
The ability of a router or firewall to discard packets that don't meet certain criteria. This is a key feature of firewalls.

Port filtering
Involves passing or blocking packets based on the port address.

is that most attackers use tools that enable them to put false source IP addresses on the incoming messages so that it is impossible to quickly recognize a message as a real message or a DoS message, making the attack harder to prevent.

A **distributed denial-of-service attack (DDoS)** is even more disruptive. With a DDoS attack, the attacker breaks into and takes control of many computers (sometimes thousands) on the Internet and plants software on them called a **DDoS agent.** The attacker then uses software called a **DDoS handler** to control the agents. The handler issues instructions to the computers under the attacker's control, which simultaneously begin sending messages to the target site. In this way, the target is deluged with messages from many different sources, making it harder to identify the DoS messages and greatly increasing the number of messages hitting the target.

11.3.2 Adding Firewalls

Connecting your private network (where only authorized users have access to the data) to a public network (where everyone connected has access to the data) introduces the possibility for security break-ins. A firewall helps to protect a private network from unauthorized users on a public network.

Firewalls are usually a combination of hardware and software. The hardware is typically a computer or a dedicated piece of hardware (often called a black box) that contains two network cards. One connects to the public side, the other, to the private side. The software controls how the firewall operates and protects your network. It examines each incoming and outgoing packet and rejects any suspicious packets. In general, firewalls work by allowing only packets that pass security restrictions to be forwarded through the firewall.

Firewalls can be placed on top of an existing operating system or be self-contained. **Black box systems** are proprietary systems that have external controls and are not controlled by the operating system. Windows supports configuring routers to act as firewalls; third-party firewalls run on both Windows and UNIX/Linux. Novell makes its own firewall product, BorderManager, which runs on NetWare.

One key feature of firewalls is **packet filtering,** which is the ability of a router or a firewall to discard packets that don't meet certain criteria. Another is **port filtering,** passing or blocking packets based on the port address. The applications that must communicate through the firewall help to determine its configuration for port filtering. For example, to support a web server, you'll typically need to open port 80 and possibly port 443. Port 80 is used with Hypertext Transfer Protocol (HTTP), used by web servers to communicate, and port 443 is used with Secure Sockets Layer (SSL), for secure communications.

Many firewalls use **dynamic packet filtering** to ensure that the packets they forward match sessions initiated on their private side. A **dynamic state**

Dynamic packet filtering
A firewall filtering method that passes packets that match sessions initiated on the internal network.

Dynamic state list
A list of communication sessions between stations inside and outside the firewall that is maintained on the firewall. Also known as a **state table.**

State table
See **dynamic state list.**

Demilitarized zone (DMZ)
A protected area of a network between the internal network and the Internet that is bounded by one or two firewalls. Also known as a **perimeter network.**

Perimeter network
See **demilitarized zone.**

Screened subnet
A subnet that is isolated from the rest of the network by a firewall.

list (also known as a **state table**), held on a firewall, keeps track of all communications sessions between stations inside the firewall and stations outside the firewall. This list changes as communications sessions are added and deleted. Dynamic state lists allow a firewall to filter packets dynamically.

In dynamic packet filtering, only packets for current (and valid) communications sessions are allowed to pass. Someone trying to play back a communications session such as a login (known as a replay attack) to gain access will be unsuccessful if the firewall is using dynamic packet filtering with a dynamic state list because the data sent would not be recognized as part of a currently valid session. The firewall will filter out (or "drop") all packets that don't correspond to a current session using information found in the dynamic state list. For example, a computer in Network A requests a Telnet session with a server in Network B. The firewall in between the two keeps a log of the communication packets that are sent each way. Only packets that are part of this current communication session are allowed back into Network A through the firewall.

Figure 11-13 shows a failed attempt to infiltrate a network that is protected with a dynamic state list. The firewall was waiting for a specific order of packets, and the hacker's packet was out of sequence.

Firewalls are often configured as part of a **demilitarized zone (DMZ),** also called a **perimeter network,** which is an area protected by one or two firewalls. When used on the intranet to isolate a segment, it is called a **screened subnet.** One standard DMZ setup has three network cards in the

Figure 11-13

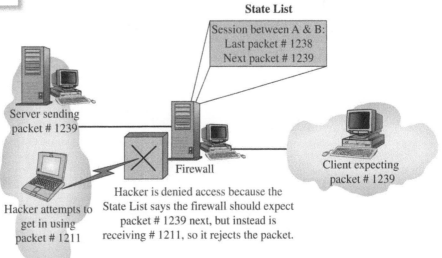

State List

Session between A & B:
Last packet # 1238
Next packet # 1239

Server sending packet # 1239

Client expecting packet # 1239

Firewall

Hacker attempts to get in using packet # 1211

Hacker is denied access because the State List says the firewall should expect packet # 1239 next, but instead is receiving # 1211, so it rejects the packet.

Dynamic packet filtering.

FOR EXAMPLE

FIGURE 11-13

Notice that the hacker attempts to insert a packet into the communication stream but fails because the packet did not have the correct packet number. There are ways around this, but a discussion of hacker techniques in that detail is beyond the scope of this chapter.

firewall computer, as shown in Figure 11-14. The first goes to the Internet. The second goes to the network segment where the aforementioned servers are located, the DMZ. The third connects to your intranet.

People outside your network primarily access your web servers, FTP servers, and mail-relay servers, so you should place them in the DMZ. When hackers break into the DMZ, they can see public information only. If they break into a server, they are breaking into a server that holds only public information. The corporate network is not compromised. Also, no e-mail messages are vulnerable because only the relay server, a waypoint for transferring the message, can be accessed. All actual messages are stored and viewed on e-mail servers inside the network. As you can see in Figure 11-15, the e-mail router, the FTP server, and the web server are all in the DMZ, and all critical servers are inside the firewall.

Another common configuration is to use two firewalls. One sits between the internal network and the perimeter network, and the other between the perimeter network and the Internet. Traffic destined for the internal network must pass through two networks.

The exact configuration you use depends on your particular network support and protection requirements.

Figure 11-14

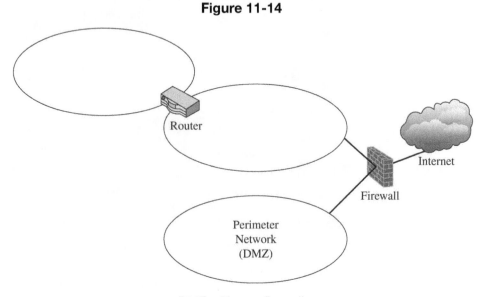

DMZ with one firewall.

Figure 11-15

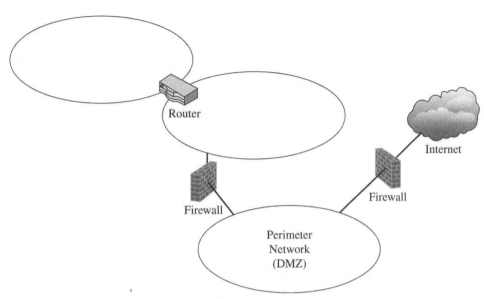

DMZ with two firewalls.

11.3.3 Adding Encryption

Encryption is the process of encoding data, while decryption is the process of decoding encrypted data. Encrypted data is sent over the network and decrypted by the intended recipient. Generally speaking, encryption works by running the data (represented as numbers) through a special **encryption formula** or **encryption algorithm** (with the value used in the encryption called a **key**) used to encrypt and decrypt the data. The NSA has had classified encryption tools and formulas as munitions since 1979 and therefore regulates them. The agency is concerned that unfriendly nations, terrorists, and criminals will use encrypted communications to plan crimes and go undetected.

One way to measure an encryption algorithm is by its **bit strength** (key length). Until 1998, only software with 40-bit strength and less could be exported. By special consideration, the U.S. Department of Commerce has increased that limit to 56-bit strength and then 128-bit strength .

In internal networks, some encryption is necessary, such as when communicating with a secure server, which can be done automatically by many modern network operating systems and server applications. Encryption is also used by many e-mail systems, giving the user the option to encrypt individual or all e-mail messages. Third-party software packages can provide data encryption for e-mail systems that don't natively have the ability to encrypt. Encryption is also typically used for data transmission over virtual private networks (VPNs) to keep the data private when using the Internet to connect remote users securely to internal networks. Finally, encryption

Encryption algorithm
Values used for data encryption. Also known as an **encryption formula.**

Encryption key
The table or formula that defines which character in the data translates to which encoded character.

Bit strength
A measure of encryption strength based on the number of bits in a key.

has become important with the advent of e-commerce, online banking, and online investing. Buying products and handling finances online would not be possible if the data sent between all involved parties over the Internet were not encrypted.

Encrypting Data

The encryption process involves taking each character of data and comparing it against a key. For example, you could encrypt the following string of data in any number of ways:

The quick brown fox

For sample purposes, let's use a simple letter-number method. In this method, each letter in the alphabet corresponds to a particular number. (You may have used this method as a kid when you got a decoder wheel in your Cracker Jack or breakfast cereal box.) If you use a straight alphabetic-to-number encryption (for example, A=1, B=2, C=3, and so on), the data translates into the following:

20 8 5 17 21 9 3 11 2 18 15 23 14 6 15 24

You can then transmit this series of numbers over a network, and the receiver can decrypt the string using the same key in reverse. From left to right, the number 20 translates to the letter T, 8 to H, 5 to E, and so on. Eventually, the receiver gets the entire message:

The quick brown fox

Most encryption methods use much more complex formulas and methods. Our sample key was about 8 bits long; some keys are extremely complex and can be a maximum of 128 bits long. The larger the key (in bits), the more complex the encryption—and the more difficult it is to crack.

To encode a message and decode an encrypted message, you need the proper encryption key or keys. Encryption keys fall into two categories: symmetric and asymmetric.

Using Shared Key Encryption

Shared keys are also known as **symmetric or session keys.** In shared key encryption technology, both the sender and receiver have the same key and use it to encrypt and decrypt all messages.

International Business Machines (IBM) developed one of the commonly used private key systems, called **Data Encryption Standard (DES).** In 1977, the United States made DES a government standard, defined in the **Federal Information Processing Standards Publication 46-2 (FIPS 46-2).**

DES uses lookup table functions and is incredibly fast when compared with public key systems. A 56-bit private key is used. In a challenge to break the DES, several Internet users worked in concert, each tackling a portion of the 72 quadrillion possible combinations. The key used in the

---

Shared key encryption
Encryption based on a single key used for both encryption and decryption.

Symmetric key encryption
Encryption based on a single key used for both encryption and decryption.

Data Encryption Standard (DES)
A private key encryption system originally developed by IBM.

Federal Information Processing Standards Publication 46-2 (FIPS 46-2)
A U.S. government publication that defines DES as a government standard.

challenge was broken in June 1997, after searching only 18 quadrillion keys out of the possible 72 quadrillion. The plain-text message read, "Strong cryptography makes the world a safer place."

Advanced Encryption Standard (AES)
A symmetric-key encryption standard adopted by the U.S. government using three block ciphers, each of which consists of a 128-bit block size.

> ### NETWORKING FACT
>
> Because of this challenge showing the relative weakness of the DES cipher, in 1997, a worldwide call for submissions of encryption algorithms was issued by the U.S. Government's National Institute of Standards and Technology (NIST). Five algorithms were selected into the second round, from which Rijndael was selected to be the final standard. **Advanced Encryption Standard (AES)** is a symmetric key encryption technique, which in 2001 replaced the commonly used Data Encryption Standard (DES) and is defined in the November 2001 Federal Information Processing Standards Publication 197 (FIPS-197).

Using Public Key Encryption

Public key encryption
Encryption based on separate sender and receiver keys.

Public key
An encryption used by the sender to encrypt data, based on the receiver's private key.

Private key
An encryption known to the receiver only in public key encryption.

Public key, or **asymmetric encryption,** uses two keys to encrypt and decrypt data: a public key and a private key, as shown in Figure 11-16. The receiver's **public key** encrypts a message to the receiver. The message is sent to the receiver, who can then decrypt the message using the **private key.**

Figure 11-16

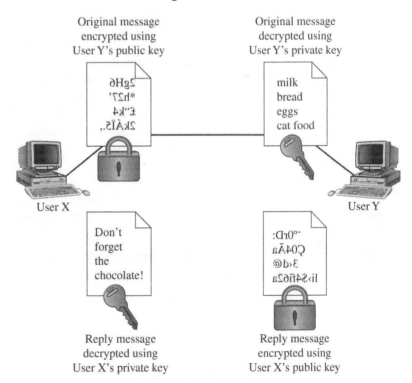

Public key encryption.

TIPS FROM THE PROFESSIONALS

Digital Certificates

You might have seen the term *digital certificate* come up before in the context of security and mentioned during discussions about encryption.

Basically, a **digital certificate** is an electronic document that uses a digital signature to bind a public key with identity information. The certificate can be used to verify that a public key belongs to an individual. A trusted authority issues it to a company, computer, or person, and it proves they are who they say they are. Windows (and other NOSs) have the ability to generate certificates for internal use or for testing communications. For identification to the world at large, you need to obtain a certificate from an accepted **certificate authority.** You might do this, for example, if you have a public e-commerce site so that your customers can validate who you are. Along with identifying information, the certificate has a specific lifespan and is valid only during that period.

Digital certificate
A secure identifier issued to a company, computer, or person that proves they are who they say they are.

Certificate authority
A trusted organization or a software service that can grant certificates.

This communication is one way. If the receiver wants to send a return message, the same principle is used. The message is encrypted with the original sender's public key (the original sender is now going to be the receiver of this new message) and can only be decrypted with their private key. This encryption process achieves the objective of **confidentiality,** because only the intended receiver and holder of the private key can read the message. However this system is also used in reverse to show **authentication.** If the sender uses his or her private key to encrypt the message, then the receiver (and everyone else) would decrypt the message using the sender's verified public key and be assured that the message came from that particular sender.

Rivest, Shamir, and Adleman (RSA)
A public key encryption algorithm.

Asymmetric keys
The public and private keys used in public key encryption.

Rivest, Shamir, and Adleman (RSA) encryption is a public key encryption algorithm named after the three scientists from the Massachusetts Institute of Technology (MIT) who developed it. They created a commercial company in 1977 to develop **asymmetric keys** and received several U.S. patents. Their encryption software is used in several networking products.

11.3.4 Implementing Wireless Security

While we're talking about network security, we should spend a little time looking at wireless security. Wireless networking has become a popular option because it is inexpensive and easy to configure. One problem, however, is that most default configurations leave gaping holes in your network security. In the best case, all that happens is someone "borrows" your signal for free Internet access. In the worst, the connection gives them time to hack into your network undetected and unobstructed.

You secure your wireless network through wireless access point (WAP) configuration parameters and by implementing Wired Equivalent Privacy (WEP), Wi-Fi Protected Access (WPA), or 802.1x as security mechanisms.

Configuring the WAP

There are literally hundreds of different WAPs and each uses a different method to configure its internal software. Figure 11-17 shows an example. For the most part, they follow some general patterns. You need to configure its IP address scheme to match your network's.

Some important parameters include:

- **SSID:** This is the name of the wireless network that this AP will advertise. In a network with only one WAP, you can think of the SSID as the "name" of the AP. WAPs come with a default SSID, usually based on the

Figure 11-17

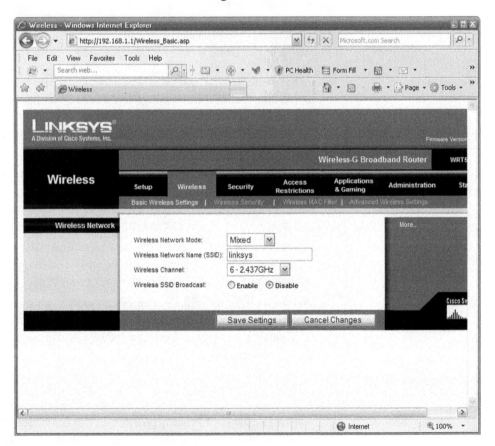

WAP configuration parameters.

TIPS FROM THE PROFESSIONALS

WPA vs. WPA 2

Wi-Fi Protected Access (WPA) was created to replace Wired Equivalent Privacy (WEP) in securing wireless networks when it was discovered that serious flaws made WEP very easy compromise.

Although WPA is much harder to crack, doing so was still possible with the use of more advanced tools. WPA2 addresses this problem with the introduction of the AES algorithm. Theoretically, passphrases created with the AES algorithm are virtually impossible to compromise.

1. WPA2 is the improved version of WPA.
2. WPA only supports Temporal Key Integrity Protocol (TKIP) encryption while WPA2 supports Advanced Encryption Standard (AES). AES is a symmetric key encryption standard that has been adopted by the U.S. government.
3. Theoretically, WPA2 is less susceptible to intrusion or hacking than WPA.
4. Because WPA2 uses the AES, it requires more processing power than WPA, which uses the less secure (TKIP).

manufacturer's name, and usually well known by people looking for a WAP to link into. One of the first things you should do is change the SSID. If you want to keep the network secure, you should also disable SSID broadcast, as shown in Figure 11-17, to prevent the WAP from announcing itself.

- **Operating mode:** WAPs can operate in either Access Point mode or Bridging mode. Access Point mode allows the WAP to operate as a traditional access point to allow a wireless client transparent access to a wired network. Two WAPs set to Bridging mode provide a wireless bridge between two wired network segments and filter traffic by MAC address.

- **Password:** Every WAP has some kind of default password that is used to access the WAP's configuration. For security reasons, you should change this password as soon as you are able to connect to and configure the WAP.

- **Wireless channel:** 802.11 wireless networks can operate on different channels to avoid interference. Most wireless WAPs can be set to work on a particular channel from the factory, so for security reasons, you should change it as soon as you can.

Wired Equivalent Privacy (WEP)
A security scheme that can provide basic security for 802.11b, 802.11g and 802.11n networks.

WAPs can also support Wireless Equivalent Privacy, Wi-Fi Protected, and 802.11x to further secure your network. Some support a combination of them.

Wired Equivalent Privacy (WEP) provides basic security for a wireless 802.11b or 802.11g local area network. The WEP protocol is used to encrypt data being transmitted over a wireless 802.11b network. It is a

Figure 11-18

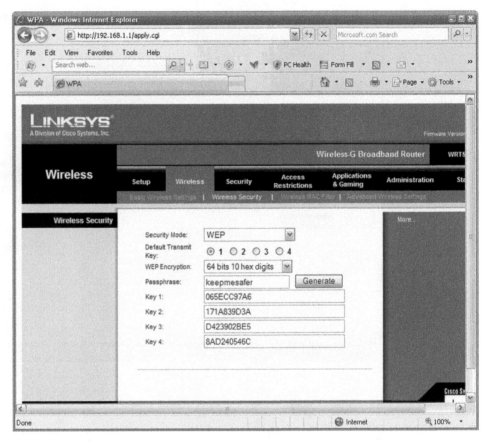

WEP configuration.

lower-layer security protocol, and it encrypts the data before transmission using an algorithm known as RC4. To encrypt the data, a string of characters known as a key is used. The key is made up of a random number known as the Initialization Value (IV) plus a string of text chosen by the administrator or user that sets up WEP on a device, as shown in Figure 11-18. The keys used to encrypt the data stream are usually 40, 64, or 128 bits long.

Wi-Fi Protected Access (WPA) is a standard that improves upon the original design of WEP. It was designed to be compatible with WEP-enabled hardware and software and can usually be implemented with a simple software upgrade. In order to provide this enhanced security, WPA adds two main components as shown in Figure 11-19: TKIP and user authentication. **Temporal Key Integrity Protocol (TKIP)** encrypts the keys so they are more difficult to intercept by an eavesdropper. WPA's user authentication uses the Extensible Authentication Protocol (EAP), which is a form of public key encryption, to ensure that the user using the wireless network is a valid user.

Wi-Fi Protected Access (WPA)
A wireless security standard that uses TKIP and user authentication.

Temporal Key Integrity Protocol (TKIP)
An encryption algorithm used to encrypt keys used with WPA.

Figure 11-19

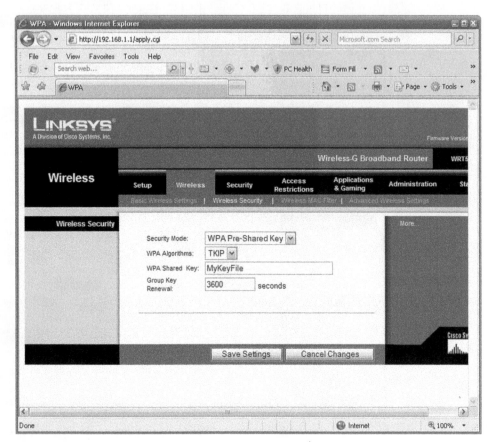

WPA configuration.

802.1x
A wireless security standard method for authenticating users.

Supplicant
An 802.1x term that refers to a client needing authentication.

Authenticator
A term that refers to a WAP during 802.1x authentication.

The **802.1x** standard is an open framework designed to support multiple authentication schemes. Before a client (known as a **supplicant** in 802.1x parlance) can communicate on a wireless network, it asks the WAP (known as an **authenticator**) for permission to enter and provides its credentials. The WAP passes those credentials to a centralized authentication server (like a RADIUS server). The server sends back an accept message to the access point if the authentication method is successful, and the access point will allow the user to connect to the wireless network. Note that 802.1x will allow no access to any wireless ports of any kind (except for 802.1x/EAP during authentication) until the user is authenticated. Also, encryption is not required for use with 802.1x. It is an authentication method only, but it can provide significant security measures, even without WEP keys.

Some manufacturers have added RADIUS authentication as an authentication option with or without 802.1x, using their own nonstandard implementations. This added authentication requires you to provide the RADIUS server's IP address, port, and either a shared key or a WEP encryption key.

TIPS FROM THE PROFESSIONALS

The Problem with WEP

Do not use WEP and expect a secure wireless network! Researchers have now shown that they can break 104-bit WEP, a common 802.11b/g/n security mechanism, in as little as one minute. A team at the Technische Universität Darmstadt said that they can grab the key with a 95 percent probability of success in as little as two minutes using a 1.7GHz Pentium-M machine to do the calculations.

With the right tools and some time, anyone can crack WEP by gathering enough information from the airwaves, which is then used to figure out the pass-phrase protecting the wireless link. The more packets gathered, the better the chance of success.

Here's how the attack works. In order to find the key, an attacker has to have enough traffic to analyze. The researchers forced the protected network to start generating packets. After they have 40,000 packets to analyze, they have a 50 percent success rate in grabbing the key; an additional 20,000 packets nudges the success rate up to 80 percent. Reaching the 95 percent threshold requires 85,000 data packets. As they were able to generate 764 packets per second, they were able to hit the 85,000 mark in 1:51.

Understanding VPN Security

Virtual Private Networks (VPNs) allow users to connect to your network remotely via the Internet. Prior to VPN technology, the only way to provide private remote network connections was through actual private lines, which were (and still are) very expensive. For example, to set up a remote office you could lease a private T1 line from the phone company to connect the two offices. This private T1 line provided excellent security because it physically connected the two offices and could be accessed only from the two endpoints.

VPN provides the same point-to-point connection as a private leased line, but does it over the Internet instead of through expensive dedicated lines. To create the tunnel that guarantees privacy of the data as it travels from one end of the VPN to the other, the data is encrypted using special security protocols.

Internet Protocol Security (IPSec)
A security protocol used for VPN security.

The most important of the VPN security protocols is called **IPSec,** which stands for Internet Protocol Security. IPSec is a collection of standards for encrypting and authenticating packets that travel on the Internet. In other words, it provides a way to encrypt the contents of a data packet so that only a person who knows the secret encryption keys can decode the data. And it provides a way to reliably identify the source of a packet so that the parties at either end of the VPN tunnel can trust that the packets are authentic.

Referring to the OSI network model, the IPSec protocol operates at the Network layer, which means that the IPSec protocol has no idea about what kind of data is being carried by the packets it encrypts and authenticates. The IPSec protocol concerns itself only with the details of encrypting the contents of the packets (sometimes called the payload) and ensuring the identity of the sender.

Layer 2 Tunneling Protocol (L2TP)
A security protocol used for VPN security.

Another commonly used VPN protocol is **Layer 2 Tunneling Protocol (L2TP).** This protocol does not provide data encryption. Instead, it is designed to create end-to-end connections called tunnels through which data can travel. L2TP is actually a combination of two older protocols, one (called Layer 2 Forwarding Protocol, or L2FP) developed by Cisco, and the other (called Point-to-Point Tunneling Protocol, or PPTP) developed by Microsoft. Note that PPTP is still often used in Microsoft systems.

Most VPNs today use a combination of L2TP and IPSec, called L2TP over IPSec. This type of VPN combines the best features of L2TP and IPSec to provide a high degree of security and reliability.

11.3.5 Using Auditing and Logs

Client and network operating systems have different built-in tools that help you monitor system and network activity. Two key areas are auditing and logs.

Auditing
The process of watching key activities and recording specific successful and failed activities.

Audit policies
Windows policies used to control auditing.

Auditing is the process of watching key activities you've identified and recording, depending on how it is configured, successful and failed attempts. Commonly audited activities include user login attempts, changes to system or network security, and attempts to access critical or sensitive files. Available Windows **audit policies** are shown in Figure 11-20.

Perhaps the best way to understand the role of audits in network security is to consider an example. You have a set of sensitive data files in a secure directory. Users should be able to view the files, but not modify or delete them. You configure access permissions to limit user access, but you also want to know if any user attempts to delete any of the files. You set up auditing to track failed delete attempts on the files. If a user does try, the attempt, along with a time stamp and user name, is recorded.

Logs give you a way of reviewing what's been happening on a system. Most operating systems and applications keep a variety of logs. Installation logs record what happened during OS or application installation, error logs keep track of detected errors, and so on. Windows family operating systems keep one set of logs available for easy access, collectively known as **event logs,** shown in Figure 11-21. They are accessible through the Event Viewer, part of the Administrative Tools.

Event logs
One of several logs that the Windows family operating systems keep to give you a way of reviewing what has been happening on a system.

The logs you see depend on how your computer is configured and the applications it supports. Entries include informational messages, warnings, errors, and successful and failed audit entries. The logs, at minimum, include:

- **Application log:** Application-related messages for applications that support the functionality, like Microsoft SQL Server.

Figure 11-20

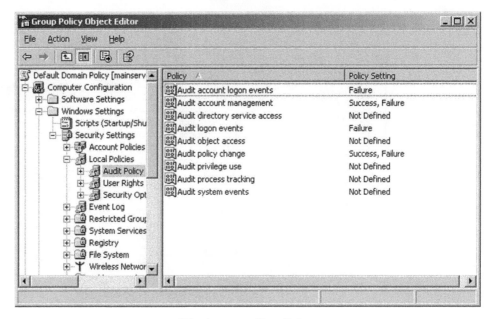

Windows audit policies.

- **System log:** System-related messages relating to system hardware, the operating system, and system services.
- **Security log:** Security messages including audit success and failure entries. You must be an administrator to view the security log's contents.

Figure 11-21

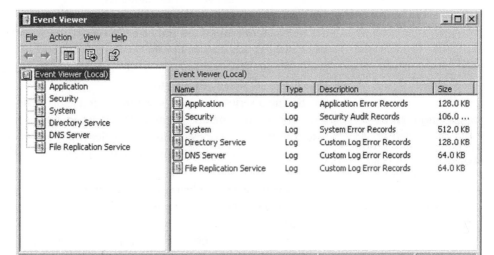

Windows event logs.

Figure 11-22

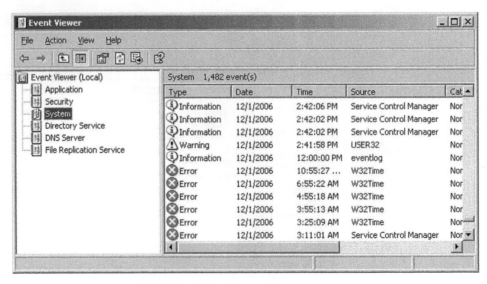

Sample system log entries.

Others vary by computer. All domain controllers will also have a Directory Service log recording Active Directory events. Computers configured as DNS servers will have a DNS service log. Some applications even add their own logs, though most write information to the Application log.

In Figure 11-22, you see the contents of the system log. Entries with an "i" are informational, things such the normal starting and stopping of various services. Warnings are indicated by an exclamation (!). These events aren't critical, but you should review them because they could represent a problem that could get worse. An "X" indicates an error, such as a failing device or a service that failed to start.

Seeing a series of errors occurring over a short period of time is common. These errors are due to **cascading failures,** where one failure directly results in the next. For example, if a service fails to start, any services that depend on that service will also fail to start. Each of these failures will write an error the system log.

You can open individual entries to get information about that entry. Take a look at the example in Figure 11-23. The exact contents of the error will vary.

Review the contents of each of the event logs periodically, watching especially for warning and error entries. You may also want to save the log's contents to provide a security trail.

Cascading failures

A situation in which one failure is the direct cause of other failures. Cascading failures are seen after a service fails, causing any dependent services to also fail.

Figure 11-23

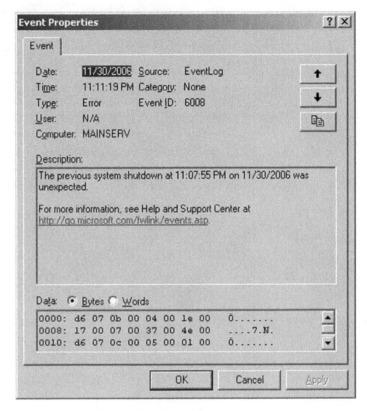

Detailed log entry.

TIPS FROM THE PROFESSIONALS

Be Careful What You Monitor For

You can set up an audit policy so that user or system activity in specified event categories is recorded. You can monitor security-related activity, such as who accesses an object, if a user logs on to or logs off of a computer, or if changes are made to an auditing policy setting. However trying to audit and monitor too many events is inherently dangerous for two reasons. First and foremost the more you audit, the slower the system becomes, and the quicker your storage space fills up with logs. When the space for log storage fills up, it can cause difficulties, including shutting down your server.

Secondly, the task of reading and understanding the sheer volume of generated logs can be near impossible, and may result in you missing critical information that is obscured by the other events. Monitor only selected events, and if you suspect that an intrusion or activity that is outside policy happened, then monitor that specific type of event, user, or computer.

IN THE REAL WORLD

All By Ourselves

Busicorp is worried about corporate espionage. It has a large research and development (R & D) department that needs occasional access to the rest of the network, but other departments should be prevented from peeking around in R & D servers and clients.

One way to accomplish this security scenario is to set up a screened subnetwork like the one shown in Figure 11-24. You set up a subnet and deploy all of the R & D computers. You install a firewall between that subnet and the rest of the company intranet.

Figure 11-24

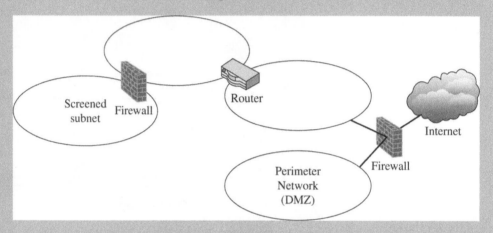

Sample LAN.

After the firewall is in place, you have control over traffic into and out of the screened subnet. You can set up different types of filter criteria, as necessary, including setting different criteria on incoming and outgoing traffic. For example, you could limit incoming traffic so that the only traffic allowed is that generated as a response to a message issued from inside the screened subnet.

SELF-CHECK

1. What typically happens during a DoS attack?
2. What typically happens during a DDoS attack?
3. From an operational standpoint, what is the difference between shared key and public key encryption.

Apply Your Knowledge PING is a useful tool for testing connectivity, but can also be used to stress you network system to test for weaknesses. You should be familiar with the switches listed in this table.

Switch	Function
-t	Pings the specified host until stopped. To see statistics and continue type Control-Break. To stop type Control-C.
-a	Resolves addresses to host names.
-n < count >	Sets number of echo requests to send.
-l < size >	Sends packets of a particular size.
-f	Sets the "Don't Fragment" flag in outgoing packets.
-i < TTL >	Specifies a Time To Live for outgoing packets.
-v < TOS >	Specifies type of service.
-r < count >	Records the route for count hops.
-s < count >	Timestamps count hops.
-j < host-list >	Loose source route along host-list.
-k < host-list >	Strict source route along host-list.
-w	Sets a long wait period (in milliseconds) for a response.

Stressing your network system: **Do Not Do This on a Live Production Network as it will affect network traffic!**

1. Press Ctrl+Alt+Delete and choose Start Task Manager from the resulting window.

2. Choose the Networking Tab to observe your network connection.

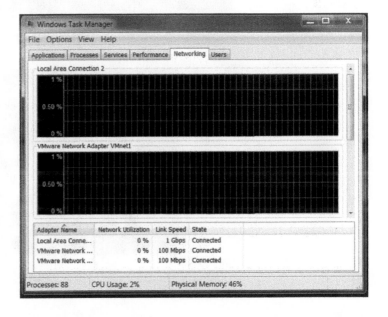

3. Open a command prompt by holding the Flag key and R key to open the run window. Type "cmd" and click OK.

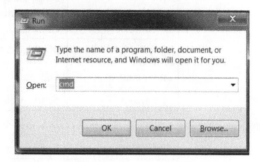

Do this on both the attack computer and the target computer.

4. Find the IP address of both computers by typing "ipconfig" at the command prompt.

Attack Computer.

Target.

5. Ping the target computer to confirm connectivity.

6. Now type: Ping –l 65500 –t 192.168.27.195 and watch the network performance on both the target and attack computer.

(Note that typing this will send packets of 65500 bytes in size and will continue until you manually stop the activity.)

To stop packets being sent type "Ctrl+C".

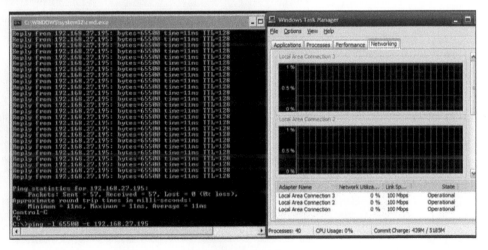

Attack computer.

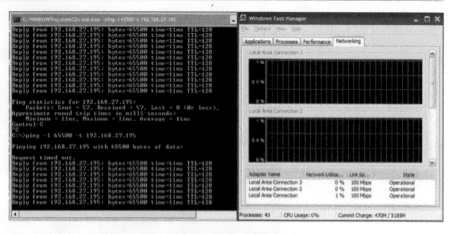

Attack computer running ping.

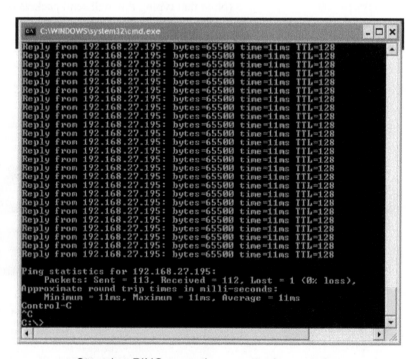

Stopping PING operation on attack computer.

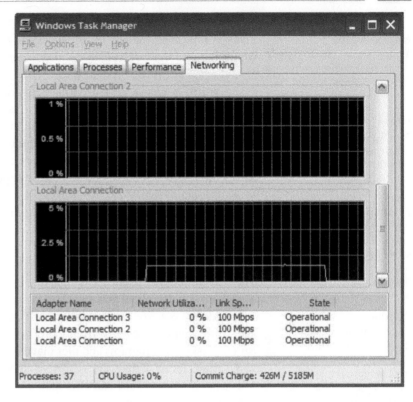

Target Computer Task manager monitoring networking.

11.4 CONFIGURING COMPUTER SECURITY

Malware
Malicious or annoying and unwanted software.

Signature
A code within a virus by which it can be identified.

Polymorphic virus
A type of encrypted virus that includes a scrambled virus body, a decryption routine that first gains control of the computer, and a mutation engine randomizing decryption routines that change each time a virus infects a new program.

Part of securing your network is securing the computers on the network. Several types of malicious software are waiting to infect unprotected computers, including viruses, worms, and Trojans (or Trojan horses). Other potential risks include spyware that gathers information about your activities and adware that makes you more susceptible to pop-up ads.

11.4.1 Understanding Malicious Software

You must also pay special attention to avoiding malicious software, sometimes called **malware,** such as viruses. Some are harmless, such as nuisance messages, but others are serious, causing destruction of data. Viruses can be recognized by their **signature,** code within the virus by which it can be identified, but some **polymorphic viruses** change their appearances with each infection as they spread, making detection more difficult.

Macro viruses
Viruses that are contained in documents or spreadsheet files.

Worm
A self-propagating form of malicious software.

Trojan horse
A program that is expected to do one thing but actually does something else. The name is a reference to classical Greek literature.

Rootkit
A program that can hide itself, along with other programs, files, and processes from the operating system, anti-virus software, and other security software.

Spyware
Software that monitors, records, and sometimes sends out computer activity usually without the users knowledge.

Most viruses attach themselves to other programs or to special areas of disks. As the files execute or are accessed, the virus spreads. **Macro viruses,** viruses that are contained in documents or spreadsheet files, can spread when an infected file is opened.

A **worm** is special type of virus that spreads itself without human intervention, copying itself from computer to computer. Worms spread when they install themselves on a computer and then send copies of themselves to other computers, usually by e-mail or through security holes in software. Part of the concern with worms is that they can quickly spread themselves across the Internet and to any connected computer, which makes them difficult to contain or remove.

A Trojan, or **Trojan horse,** is a program that appears to be one thing, but is actually another. When you execute the program, it does its damage. A Trojan could easily erase disk partition information, causing you to lose all of the information on a disk, before you have any idea what's happening. The only good thing about a Trojan is that it can't spread itself. The victim has to actively download and copy and then execute the program.

A **rootkit** is a program that hides itself, as well as other programs, files, and even running processes, from the operating system. The rootkit itself isn't the risk—the programs and files that the rootkit is hiding are. It is used with various forms of malware to prevent antivirus programs from detecting and removing them. They can also open a backdoor into the system, a way for someone to sneak in.

Spyware collects information about a user's activities, such as files opened, programs run, and websites visited. It is sometimes used to track employees' activities. Some types of spyware are more malicious, not only collecting information but also sending it to a collection site. Spyware of this type is sometimes used to steal sensitive information such as credit card numbers.

TIPS FROM THE PROFESSIONALS

Protection from Spyware and Adware

Both spyware and adware can be annoying in that they clog up your computer's workings and can noticeably slow it down. They're also dangerous because they track your activities and can provide your private information to unauthorized individuals without your permission or knowledge. To help ordinary users defend themselves from this malware, several organizations publish free software to detect, remove, and prevent future infection of spyware and adware. Spybot Search and Destroy is one such free application that performs this service. Check out http://www.safer-networking.org/en/home/index.html.

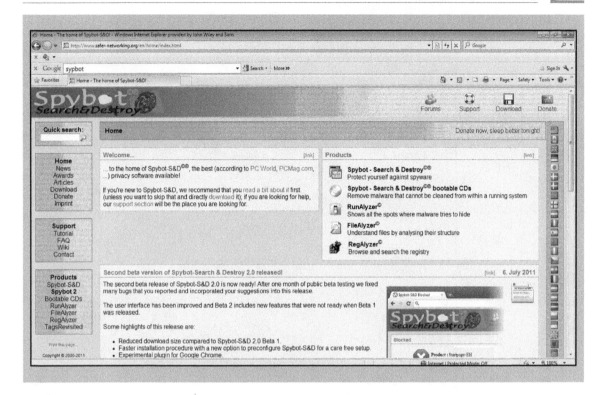

Adware

Software that makes a computer more easily locatable by and more susceptible to pop-up and other online ads.

Push

The process of transferring data from a source to a destination, where the transfer is initiated by the sender, without receiving a request from the receiver.

Adware is normally not dangerous, but can be annoying. It acts something like a beacon, advertising your computer's existence and location to the Internet. Adware causes an ongoing flow of pop-up ads and browser windows to open spontaneously on the desktop. Adware usually infects a computer by enticing the user to visit (or be redirected to) a Web site that **pushes** (like downloading, but initiated by the source) the adware onto your computer.

11.4.2 Protecting Networked Computers

The following guidelines apply to both networked and stand-alone computers that connect to the Internet, dial into another computer, or to which files are copied from removable media.

One key to avoiding malicious software and preventing the spread of viruses is to not copy or download files of unknown origin, or at least to check every file you do copy or download. The same goes for e-mail attachments. If you don't recognize the source, don't open the attachment. The other is to install antivirus software on every computer. Several different packages are available, supporting different feature sets and working with various degrees of success. As a general rule, though, go with a well-known manufacturer.

What about the features you need? At minimum, your antivirus software should be able to scan the computer, both the hard disk and memory, before it installs. You should be able to configure it to run periodic scans to

Figure 11-25

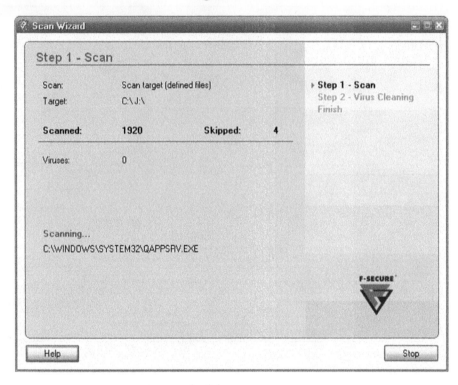

Antivirus scan.

keep the hard disk clean and should support on-demand scanning, like the scan shown in Figure 11-25. It should also scan both the message content and attachments of both incoming and outgoing e-mail messages.

A critical concern is how extensive a database of malware signatures the program has and how often it is updated. Some experts estimate that as many as ten new viruses appear daily. Identifying the virus signatures and keeping antivirus software updated is a constant struggle. This is one area where you do sometimes see cooperation, with different manufacturers sharing information with each other about emerging threats.

Most antivirus products currently on the market include the antivirus program as part of a security suite that includes features such as:

- A firewall that lets you set filter parameters for that computer.
- Intrusion detection software that warns you when another computer tries to connect to your computer.
- Browser monitoring software that warns you of suspicious activities such as attempting to redirect you to another website or trying to download a file to your computer.

- Spam filters to detect and block unwanted e-mails.
- Application controls that prevent one program from launching another without your knowing.

Most manufacturers and computer dealers install some version of antivirus software, usually one with a license that expires in six months to a year, on new computers. Many of the larger ISPs, especially those offering high-speed Internet access, offer security suites at no charge to their subscribers. Why? Avoiding virus infections and other attacks are good business for the ISP, too. Furthermore, offers of those kinds of additional perks make for satisfied customers in a competitive market where word-of-mouth is often the most efficient advertising.

IN THE REAL WORLD

The Sony BMG Copy Protection Scandal

For most of the public at large, the first introduction to the term rootkit came about as result of the outcry over an action taking by Sony BMG music, commonly known as the Sony BMG CD copy protection scandal. Here's what happened.

Starting in 2005, Sony BMG placed a rootkit on some of its music CDs. When someone played the CD on a computer running Windows, the rootkit installed on the computer. Actually, two different programs were used, placed on a total of about 100 different titles. The problem is that Sony didn't warn anyone about what it was doing. The CD packaging or the CD itself didn't have any specific mention of the rootkit, other than some vague language about security rights management.

Sony's goal was copy protection, a way to prevent customers from sharing the music from the CDs on the Internet. The actual result was quite different. The rootkit opened several security holes, making the computers more susceptible to viruses and interfering with computer operations. In addition, lawsuits were brought against Sony BMG claiming that the rootkit itself violated the software license under which it was developed.

An outcry ensued and Sony BMG released a utility that supposedly removed the rootkit. What it actually did was unhide the files and unmask the rootkit, but it didn't remove it. Sony BMG finally released a utility to completely remove the rootkit and all associated files. Sony BMG also recalled the CDs on which the "protection" was installed, paying retailers to remove them from their shelves. Despite this action, Sony BMG still had to deal with suits brought in Texas, California, and New York, not to mention the customer satisfaction issues.

Why mention this cautionary tale? If you aren't careful, some of the actions you take in pursuit of security can go too far, especially if they affect networks or computers outside of your network.

SELF-CHECK

1. What are the most common types of malicious software?
2. What is the potential risk from Adware?
3. Why is it important that an antivirus program update its signatures?

Apply Your Knowledge Download and install Spybot Search and Destroy; run the program and list how many intrusions it finds.

Installing:

Find where you downloaded spybotsd162.exe and double click on it to begin the installation.

1. Click Next on the Welcome screen
2. Accept the License Agreement and click Next
3. Accept the default location and click Next
4. Deselect all the radials
5. Accept the defaults and click Next
6. Install Program
7. Leave the radials selected to run program and click Finish
8. Accept the Legal Stuff
9. Update, then Start using the program by selecting Check for Problems

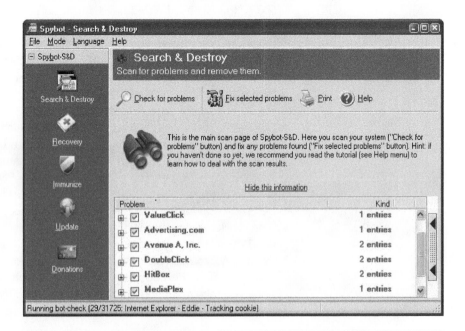

SUMMARY

Section 11.1

- Confidentiality, integrity, and availability are the three primary goals of providing network security.
- Network security helps to ensure business continuity.
- Risk assessment defines how vulnerable your network is to potential security breaches.
- During risk assessment, ranking threat by likelihood and potential cost is important.

Section 11.2

- User authentication helps to prevent unauthorized access to you network.
- User accounts should be deleted or disabled when they are no longer needed.
- The strength or weakness of a password refers to how easily it could be guessed or cracked.

Section 11.3

- Firewalls protect private networks from unauthorized users on a public network.
- Firewalls can be configured to create a perimeter network, or DMZ, around a private network.
- Encrypting data prevents it from being intercepted and used by unintended recipients.

Section 11.4

- A worm is a type of virus that installs itself on one computer and then sends copies of itself to other computers.
- Malware is any type of malicious or unwanted software.
- Antivirus software installed on each computer can help to prevent viruses from spreading to the network.

ASSESS YOUR UNDERSTANDING

UNDERSTAND: WHAT HAVE YOU LEARNED?

 Go to **www.wiley.com/go/ciccarelli/networkingbasics2e** to evaluate your knowledge of network security fundamentals.

Measure your learning by comparing pre-test and post-test results.

SUMMARY QUESTIONS

1. Which of the following is an example of a strong password?
   (a) dictionary
   (b) bluegreen2
   (c) cu&tin=bronze
   (d) ahtraM

2. Which of the following could be used to detect someone trying to guess a user's password?
   (a) Account lockout
   (b) Password history
   (c) Password age
   (d) Reversible password encryption

3. Which of the following encryption algorithms are used with WEP security?
   (a) DES
   (b) RC4
   (c) RSA
   (d) DHA

4. Which of the following refers to a network segment isolated for security reasons?
   (a) WPA
   (b) DES
   (c) TKIP
   (d) DMZ

5. Which of the following is a malicious application designed to monitor and record a user's activity on a computer?
   (a) Spyware
   (b) Rootkit
   (c) Worm
   (d) Signature

6. A Trojan horse is a program that appears to be one thing but is actually another. True or false?

7. Unauthorized access is most often the result of an incursion by an individual from outside an organization. True or false?

8. Which of the following requires you to store passwords using reversible encryption?

   (a) EAP

   (b) CHAP

   (c) MS-CHAPv2

   (d) WPA

9. Ping of Death is an example of which of the following?

   (a) Malware

   (b) WinNuke attack

   (c) DoS attack

   (d) SYN flood

10. Which of the following might an attacker employ to make a DDoS attack harder to detect or block?

    (a) IP spoofing

    (b) Dynamic filtering

    (c) WinNuke

    (d) A DES algorithm

11. You can deploy publicly accessible computers within a network segment configured as a perimeter network. True or false?

12. You suspect that a device driver failed to initialize during system startup. Which Windows Event Log should you check?

    (a) Application

    (b) Security

    (c) Directory service

    (d) System

13. You want to limit traffic into and out of your network to ports 80 and 443. What type of device should you deploy?

    (a) Firewall

    (b) NAT server

    (c) Switch

    (d) Bridge

14. Based on CERT surveys, what is the most prevalent risk to computers deployed on a network that is connected to the Internet?

    (a) Unauthorized access by employees

    (b) Unauthorized access by outside attackers

    (c) Virus infection

    (d) Hidden spyware

15. A smart card is an example of a biometric device. True or false?

APPLY: WHAT WOULD YOU DO?

1. The following questions refer to the sample network in Figure 11-26.

   Your network has experienced several problems, including virus infections and attempted break-ins. You are reconfiguring the network to improve network security.

   (a) What are the potential points of access to your network?

   (b) Your company has two public web servers. Where should they be deployed?

   (c) Why?

   (d) You want a record of failed attempts to log in locally to a secure member server. How can you do this?

   (e) The member server is running Windows 2000 Server. Where should you check to see if there have been any login attempts?

   (f) You want to configure Network A as a screened subnet. What do you need to do?

2. The following questions refer to the password policies shown in Figure 11-27.

   Password policies for the busicorp.com domain are shown in Figure 11-27. These policies apply to all domain computers.

   (a) What is the minimum password length?

   (b) How often must users change passwords?

   (c) What can be done so that you never have to change a user's password?

   (d) How can you increase the time a user must wait before changing his or her password?

Figure 11-26

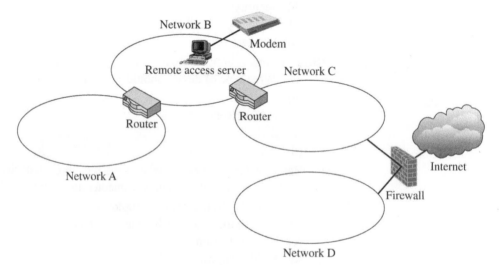

Sample network.

Figure 11-27

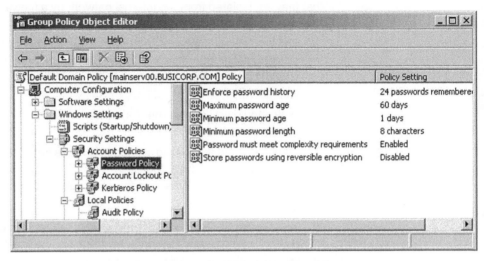

Busicorp domain password policies.

(e) In the list below, identify the values a user could enter as a password.

- ThisIsMyPassword
- il2ra0t
- *abcABC123#*
- *44o%45%0*
- *tQbFjOtF2times*
- $#@@47&!%

BE A NETWORK SECURITY ENGINEER

Securing a Network

You were recently hired as the network administrator for Busicorp. The network is a routed LAN with three subnetworks connected in a mesh configuration using three Linux computers configured as routers. The network is set up as a single Windows Active Directory domain.

You plan to add a WAP to one of the subnets to make it easier to support laptop computers. A single WAP will have sufficient range to cover the office and beyond to the street outside. You are concerned about external access to your network and want to make the wireless subnet as secure as possible.

You have a mail relay server and a web server that you want to deploy so that they are isolated from the internal network by a firewall. You also want to protect them from the Internet with a second firewall.

1. The web server supports an e-commerce application through which customers can purchase and download documents. Why should you install a certificate from a recognized certificate authority on the web server?

2. Why should you deploy the web server on perimeter network instead of one of the internal subnets?

3. You have been authorized a budget to make improvements to network security. You want to make sure that you use the money as efficiently as possible. What two things should you do first?

4. Why?

5. You disable SSID broadcast on your WAP. What else can you do to make it more difficult for someone to locate and identify your WAP?

6. Your WAP supports WEP and WPA. Which should you use?

7. Why?

8. Sketch your network. Show the location of the firewalls, routers, web server, and the Internet.

KEY TERMS

802.1x

Account lockout policies

Active Directory Users and Computers

Administrator

Advanced Encryption Standard (AES)

Adware

Asymmetric keys

Audit policies

Auditing

Auditing tool

Authentication credentials

Authenticator

Availability

Biometric scan

Bit strength

Black box system

Blue Screen of Death (BSoD)

Business continuity planning

Cascading failures

Certificate authority

Computer Emergency Response Team (CERT)

Confidentiality

Crack

Crack program

Data Encryption Standard (DES)

DDoS agent

DDoS handler

Demilitarized zone (DMZ)

Denial of service (DoS)

Digital Certificate

Directed attacks

Disruptions

Distributed denial-of-service attack(DDoS)

Domain account

Due diligence

Dynamic packet filtering

Dynamic state list

Encryption algorithm

Encryption key

Enforce password history

Event logs

Federal Information Processing Standards Publication 46-2 (FIPS 46-2)

Firewalls

Hacker

Hardening

Health Insurance Portability and Accountability Act (HIPAA)

Integrity

Internet Control Message Protocol (ICMP)

Internet Protocol Security (IPSec)

IP spoofing

Layer 2 Tunneling Protocol (L2TP)

Local accounts

Macro viruses

Maintenance accounts

Malware

Maximum password age

Minimum password age

Minimum password length

Mission-critical application

Network assets

Packet filtering

Password must meet complexity requirements

Perimeter network

Ping of Death

Polymorphic virus

Port filtering

Private key

Public key

Public key encryption

Push

Rivest, Shamir, and Adleman (RSA)

Root

Rootkit

Screened subnet

Security breach

Shared key encryption

Signature

Smart card

Spyware

State table

Stop error

Store passwords using reversible encryption

Strong password

Superuser

Supplicant

Symmetrical key encryption

SYN flag

SYN flood

SYN packet

Temporal Key Integrity Protocol (TKIP)

Trojan horse

Unauthorized access

User account

Weak password

Wi-Fi Protected Access (WPA)

WinNuke

Wired Equivalent Privacy (WEP)

Worm

NETWORK MANAGEMENT

What Do You Already Know?

- What is the role of a network administrator?
- What is a backup routine?
- What is a redundant system?

 To assess your knowledge of network management go to **www. wiley.com/go/ciccarelli/networkingbasics2e.**

What You Will Find Out	What You Will Be Able To Do
12.1 **Recognizing network management requirements.**	Justify the network management function in an organization.
12.2 **Managing reliability.**	Use backups, fault tolerant disk systems, and redundancy to help ensure reliability.
	Given a data scenario, design appropriate backup and restore routines.
12.3 **Controlling configuration management.**	Identify requirements for managing users.
	Describe how to implement automated software distribution and updates.
12.4 **Monitoring networks.**	Identify tools and procedures to network and server performance.
12.5 **Understanding management systems.**	Explain the functions and features of Simple Network Management Protocol (SNMP) network management systems (NMS).
12.6 **Managing individual servers.**	Describe the proper use of server management tools.

INTRODUCTION

Network management is the process of operating, monitoring, and controlling the network to ensure it works as intended and provides value to its users. When discussing network management, you need to consider some general management areas:

- Managing the network as a whole
- Managing individual servers
- Managing client computers
- Managing users

Network management is obviously an extremely broad subject area. There is no way we can address all aspects of network management in a single chapter. Even if you limit yourself to a homogeneous network with a single network operating system (NOS), the subject can fill several volumes.

Our goal in this chapter is to focus on some key management areas and relate them to the types of tasks you might be called upon to perform in a network support role. We start by looking at network management requirements and ways these might be met. From there, we move on to two fundamental management activities, managing backups and managing redundancy. We look at configuration management and automating software distribution, as well as network and server monitoring. You will also be introduced to tools that are specific to TCP/IP based networks. Finally, we provide a brief introduction to server and server application management tools.

12.1 RECOGNIZING NETWORK MANAGEMENT REQUIREMENTS

Network management
The process of operating, monitoring, and controlling a network to ensure that it works as intended and provides value to its users.

Firefighting
A term that refers to reacting to network problems as they arise rather than relying on planned network management activity.

Effective network management starts with a good network design. Without a well-planned, well-designed network and without a well-organized network management staff, operating the network becomes extremely difficult. Unfortunately, many network managers spend most of their time **firefighting**—dealing with breakdowns and immediate problems. If managers do not spend enough time on planning and organizing the network and networking staff, they are destined to be reactive rather than proactive in solving problems.

12.1.1 Identifying Management Requirements

Since the late 1980s, network management requirements have changed dramatically. There has been an explosion in the use of microcomputer-based networks with more than 90 percent of most organizations' total computer processing power residing on microcomputer-based LANs. Since the early 1990s, the number of computers attached to LANs has grown by almost 40 percent per year. In addition, the number of Internet-based servers (e.g., web servers, e-mail servers, and FTP servers) has grown dramatically.

Where mainframes are still part of the network mix, mainframe networks remain important, but the real future of network management lies in the successful management of multiple clients and servers communicating over local area networks (LANs), wide area networks (WANs), and the Internet. Part of the underlying management headache is that individual departments often initially deployed LANs, WANs, and web servers as separate networks and applications. Their initial goals were to meet the needs of their individual owners. Integration, and integrated management, came later.

Modern network management encompasses management requirements at every level of the network. It means understanding the needs of heterogeneous hardware and software systems, as well as the wants and needs of a diverse network user population. The bottom line, in every case, is working to keep the network working, and working well.

12.1.2 Justifying Network Administration

Network administrator
An individual who is responsible for network management and support.

As a **network administrator,** the professional responsible for managing the network, you have the responsibility of ensuring uninterrupted network service to users. Having well-honed troubleshooting skills may be a great asset for a desktop support person, but it is not enough for a network administrator. You need to know about problems before they exist. How is this possible? Solid planning, the right monitoring tools, and detailed documentation will help you stay a step ahead.

Why is network management important? Network management represents the culmination of the past, current, and future work on a network. In essence, network management is the glue that ensures that legacy systems continue to operate with existing and new systems. And in the end, this glue should be transparent to users in your organization.

Even the simplest of today's networks are complex entities that change minute by minute. The challenge for a network administrator or information technology (IT) team is to have all the tools necessary to identify those changes and determine whether a change warrants an intervention. Doing so means considering everything in proper context. For example, you might find that a network server is operating near full capacity. However, if the server is under heavy load only in the morning when everyone is logging in, you might determine that you don't need to take any kind of immediate action. But if the server is under heavy load most of the time, then you would need to take a closer look.

Well-planned and executed network-management procedures and policies can help reduce the total costs of operating a business. Networks perform several roles, one of which is the automation of processes that were once done by hand. For example, organizing addresses and addressing envelopes for a mass mailing is a task that once would have taken several days. Now it takes only a few minutes with a database of addresses and a functioning network. If the network is down, it could take hours or days to retrain staff or reorganize a department to use a manual system. That means that the problem can probably be fixed before the alternative method can be in place, but that time (and money) is still lost. Network **downtime,** unplanned loss

Downtime
A period of time during which a network is unavailable to users, typically unplanned.

CAREER CONNECTION

What Does a Network Administrator Do, Anyway?

Network administrators administer networks, which means that they take care of the tasks of installing, configuring, expanding, protecting, upgrading, tuning, and repairing the network. Network administrators take care of the network hardware, such as cables, hubs, switches, routers, servers, and clients, as well as network software, such as network operating systems, e-mail servers, backup software, database servers, and application software. Most importantly, network administrators take care of network users by answering their questions, listening to their troubles, and solving their problems.

- **Equipment upgrades:** The network administrator should be involved in every decision to purchase new computers, printers, or other equipment. In particular, the network administrator should be prepared to lobby for the most network-friendly equipment possible, such as new computers that already have network cards installed and configured and printers that are network ready.
- **Configuration:** The network administrator's job includes considering what changes to make to the cabling configuration, what computer name to assign to the new computer, how to integrate the new user into the security system which rights to grant the user, and so on.
- **Software upgrades:** Every once in a while, operating system vendors release a new version of their network operating system. The network administrator must read about the new version and decide whether its new features are beneficial enough to warrant an upgrade. In most cases, the hardest part of upgrading to a new version of your network operating system is determining the migration path—that is, how to upgrade your entire network to the new version while disrupting the network or its users as little as possible. Upgrading to a new network operating system version is a major chore, so you need to carefully consider the advantages that the new version can bring.
- **Patches:** Between upgrades, vendors release patches and service packs that fix minor problems with their server operating systems. The network administrator must ensure that these patches and service packs are installed throughout the network on a timely and consistent manner.
- **Performance maintenance:** One of the easiest traps that you can get sucked into is the quest for network speed. The network is never fast enough, and users always blame the hapless network manager. So the administrator spends hours and hours tuning and tweaking the network to squeeze out that last two percent of performance.
- **Ho-hum chores:** Network administrators perform routine chores, such as backing up the servers, archiving old data, freeing up server hard drive space, and so on. Much of network administration is making sure that things keep working and finding and correcting problems before any users notice that something is wrong.
- **Ordering:** Ordering equipment and understanding equipment requirements is 15% of a networking administrator's role.
- **Software inventory:** Network administrators are also responsible for gathering, organizing, managing software licenses, and tracking the entire network's software inventory. You never know when something is going to go haywire on Joe in Marketing's ancient Windows 2000 computer and you're going to have to reinstall that old copy of WordPerfect. Do you have any idea where the installation discs are?

of network resources, can have a serious adverse effect on a company's finances, but solid network management can help prevent downtime.

Understanding your role in network administration is important, especially as networks grow and evolve. You have to check your ego at the door, especially when networks are organized around smaller entities. For example, when management is organized around departments, or WAN management is primarily delegated at the LAN level, administrators must work together and keep each other informed about their activities.

Key to integrating LANs, WANs, and the Internet into one overall organization network is for LAN, WAN, and web managers, if the roles are filled by different individuals or teams, to recognize that they cannot make independent decisions without considering their impacts on other parts of the organization's network. These managers must work from a single overall communications and networking goal that best meets the needs of the entire organization. This may require some network managers to compromise on policies that are not in the best interests of their own departments or networks.

TIPS FROM THE PROFESSIONALS

Establishing Routine Chores

Much of the network administrator's job is routine stuff—the equivalent of vacuuming, dusting, and mopping. Or if you prefer, changing the oil and rotating the tires every 3,000 miles. Yes, it's boring, but it has to be done. Here are some of the routine, ho-hum tasks you do as an administrator:

- **Backup:** The network administrator needs to make sure that the network is properly backed up. If something goes wrong and the network isn't backed up, guess who gets the blame? On the other hand, if disaster strikes, yet you're able to recover everything from yesterday's backup with only a small amount of work lost, guess who gets the pat on the back, the fat bonus, and the vacation in the Bahamas?
- **Protection:** Another major task for network administrators is sheltering your network from the evils of the outside world. These evils come in many forms, including hackers trying to break into your network and virus programs arriving through e-mail.
- **Licensing:** Software is intellectual property and licenses provide the right to use the software and define conditions of use. In today's world of easy access to software of questionable origin, it is particularly important to keep track of all software installed in your network system, and maintain proof of purchase for end user use. Make sure you maintain software licenses in a separate log for audit purposes.
- **Cleanup:** No matter how much storage your network has, your users will fill it up sooner than you think. The network administrator gets the fun job of cleaning up the attic once in a while.

12.1.3 Considering Network Management Strategies

For a network management strategy to be well planned and implemented, having the information about the network readily available and regularly reviewed and analyzed is critical. **Latency** (network performance delays) and **bottlenecks** (areas with less than optimal performance) can be identified as they occur. The less acceptable, but more common, alternative is that users report performance delays that might have already grown into much bigger problems.

You must also stay abreast of changes on the network. This also includes keeping users informed about their responsibilities in maintaining a healthy network. Many times, users don't understand everything that goes into building and maintaining a network. Although they typically don't need to know the gory details, it's helpful to explain to users networking basics such as accessing the server, software errors, and the backup process.

You must also consider how network support is organized. Although technical support is only part of the administration and management team, it is critical that it be responsive, reliable, and predictable. Set guidelines for response times based on priority and impact on overall network performance.

One approach adopted by some IT departments is to provide support in levels, depending on the problem, as shown in Figure 12-1. This approach helps ensure that support professionals understand what is expected of them and that problems are directed to the appropriate personnel.

The first level of support, **end-user support resources,** involves creating documentation for your users. This support can include resources from vendors, how-to articles, and a list of remedies for common problems called **FAQ (frequently asked questions).** Key concerns include making sure that the documentation is written at a level that the users can understand, and that it is readily available and that easy to use.

If users are unable to resolve the problem on their own, they will request the front-line services of the Level 1 support team. **Level 1 support personnel** are responsible for resolving desktop application issues,

Latency
Network performance delays.

Bottlenecks
Network or computer components responsible for loss of performance.

End-user support resources
First level support consisting primarily of user documentation.

FAQ (frequently asked questions)
Common problems and their remedies.

Level 1 support personnel
Personnel responsible for handling minor problems, typically by phone or email messages.

Figure 12-1

End-User Support Resources
Level 1: Desktop Support
Level 2: Diagnostic and Network Support
Level 3: Vendor or Software Engineering Support

Support levels.

assisting with software installation or configuration, and troubleshooting basic network connectivity. Typically, Level 1 support utilizes e-mail or the phone whenever possible to provide a cost-effective support model. Remote desktop control applications allow Level 1 support to view the steps performed by the user or take control of the user's computer when necessary. If all else fails, Level 1 support staff may be called on to provide on-site support, although it's provided as a last resort.

Level 2 support staff
Personnel responsible for resolving more serious problems, and who are more skilled and experienced than Level 1 support staff.

Level 3 support staff
Personnel responsible for resolving serious problems, often requiring on-site resolution, who are more skilled and experienced than level 2 staff.

Level 2 support staff (and **level 3 support staff,** at some companies) are more skilled and experienced in troubleshooting. They have more in-depth knowledge of desktops, networks, and specialized network devices such as firewalls and routers. These levels of support staff have to know how to deal with dozens of software applications and hardware types because the cause of a technical problem can be very different depending on the network scenario.

Though some network administrators might also have a technical support role, it isn't true of all organizations. In some organizations, network administrators aren't so much the next step up in support, but rather a separate support path. Larger networks have more than enough going on to keep a network administrator or network support team busy full time. It's not unusual for technical support to work in parallel with network support and put their heads together on particularly difficult problems. Often, the difference is that technical support personnel are more generalists, needing to know a little about a lot of different subject areas. Network support personnel have in-depth, special knowledge about the network operating systems used, network technologies, and the applications and services provided on the network.

When all internal support resources are exhausted, the IT staff might turn to outside resources for help. Vendors may be contacted for specific troubleshooting support or to report an undocumented software problem. Or, in the case of customized applications, the software engineering group may need to get involved to determine whether changes need to be made directly to the software. If the latter occurs, you will need to have an alternative solution ready for your users because it may take months before the software engineers or vendors are able to provide a fix.

Why the delay before going for outside help? The trend in recent years, after an initial period, is to provide support on a fee-based, per-incident system. These charges can be significant, in part to ensure that you only call when you have a serious problem. However, most manufacturers often also have extensive online, automated support resources. These resources are designed to not only answer most of your questions, but provide access to downloaded resources such as device drivers, program fixes, updates, and the like. One example is Microsoft's TechNet, which includes a massive, searchable documentation database.

As shown in Figure 12-2, TechNet includes items such as detailed installation and configuration instructions.

Figure 12-2

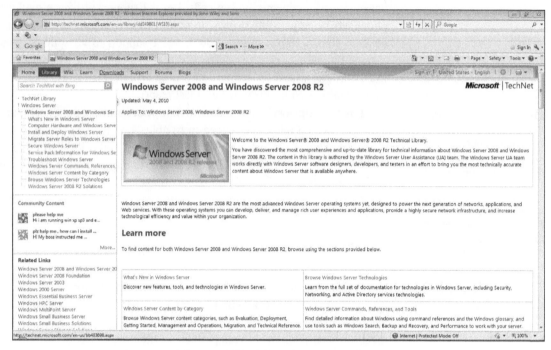

Microsoft TechNet documentation.

IN THE REAL WORLD

Instant Credibility

How does a company know in advance whether or not a job candidate really knows anything about network administration? Consider this situation. A smaller-sized company has just lost its network administrator to a higher bidder. The administrator has left suddenly, choosing to use up accrued vacation time during his two weeks' notice. You need a new administrator who can come in ready to dig into the task. The problem is, you don't really have anyone who is really qualified to even ask the right questions.

One thing you can use to evaluate potential candidates is professional certifications. Although some certifications are probably as much a test about how well you can cram for exams and take tests, many exams commonly force you to apply knowledge rather than just parrot back information. Nearly all of the major manufacturers have certifications based on the networking products and server applications.

You have a few Cisco brand routers on your network? Maybe you want to require an entry-level Cisco certification. Your network is based

(continued)

(continued)

on Windows Active Directory? Microsoft has various levels of Windows certifications that relate to networking applications. Are you interested in seeing if they know anything at all? CompTIA has a general networking certification, and another set of certifications targeted at client and end-user support.

As a computer professional, what does all this mean to you? Despite the bad press that some certifications have gotten over the past several years, they are still one of the best tools for evaluating whether a job candidate has any credibility. They can help you land that first, important job in your professional career path. After you get there, then it is up to you to prove that you do know what you're talking about.

SELF-CHECK

1. In general terms, what is a network administrator's role?
2. Why is it critical to avoid unplanned downtime?

Apply Your Knowledge   Windows Task manager is one of the most useful tools included in the Microsoft Operating System suite. It is the first tool in monitoring and troubleshooting individual computers.

To quickly open Task Manager:

1. Press Ctrl+Alt+Delete on your keyboard.
2. Choose *Task Manager* at the bottom of the list, and observe the Task Manager window. First, the Applications Tab shows all applications presently open on the computer.
3. *The Process Tab* shows each process or thread that is active and the amount of CPU usage that it is occupying. The Processes tab is really the heart of Task Manager. This tab has the most useful information when it comes to troubleshooting and identifying issues, and it provides the most effective tools for resolving those issues.
4. *The Services Tab* shows the different services installed on the computer and whether they are running. PID is Process Identifier Number.
5. *The Performance Tab* graphically shows the performance of the CPUs (in this case 4 on a Quad Computer) and the Memory usage. It may be customized to show more indices.
6. The Network tab shows network activity to and from the computer.
7. *The User Tab* lists all users currently logged on to the computer. In this case it is only one to the desktop, but in the case of a server there can be numerous. This tab allows you to disconnect particular users as desired.

Finally, network management would not be complete without up-to-date, accurate, and complete network documentation. Documentation begins with your network design or, when building a support organization for an existing network, a complete network inventory. Documentation also includes a network diagram depicting connections, devices, and network IP information, as well as reports on network performance and security, log files, user problem reports, configuration documentation, and even administrator journal entries.

12.2 MANAGING RELIABILITY

Whether you are currently managing a network or are taking over a network from another administrator, ensuring that the basic components for protecting and managing the network are in place is important. Initially, you will need to evaluate some basic systems that will ensure that there will be no loss of data in the event of a hardware failure or catastrophe such as a fire or natural disaster. Although you have the goal of providing continuous, uninterrupted service to users, reaching that goal won't mean much if some or all of the user data is lost.

Fault tolerance
The ability of equipment or network resources to continue operating even after a failure.

Two key concepts define the first objectives that a network administrator should achieve. **Fault tolerance** is found in networks that are able to withstand a partial failure and continue to operate, albeit with some impact on performance. Ensuring the highest levels of fault tolerance requires redundancy. **Redundancy** is a system of duplicating a service or function that already exists on a network. **Redundant systems** either perform the same function as primary systems or are available as quick replacements. Redundant systems might provide an exact duplicate of the primary system's hardware, software, and data. In other cases, they might be configured to perform the same function, but not require duplicate hardware. For example, Microsoft recommends deploying multiple domain controllers that maintain duplicates of the Active Directory database in case of a failure. However, the domain controllers can (and often do) have different hardware and even different software configurations.

Redundancy
1. Duplicate data paths.
2. Duplication of resources.

Redundant systems
Systems that duplicate resources provided by primary network systems.

How you implement these fault tolerance and redundancy solutions depends on your network's specific requirements. You should consider backup systems to be a requirement in any network environment. Redundant systems should be considered on a case-by-case basis, depending on how critical server resources are to network operations.

Backup
The process of copying data stored on a computer and saving an exact duplicate of the data on another storage device.

12.2.1 Managing Backups

A **backup** refers to the process of copying data stored on a computer and saving an exact duplicate of the data on another storage device. Backups of data can include operating systems, user files, applications, and anything that is stored on a hard disk. A backup can be as simple as copying a document onto a removable disk or CD for storage, or can involve special backup software, hardware, and storage media.

Typically, backups of servers and other computers that maintain important data are performed on dedicated hardware using special software. Most operating systems, and even some applications, include integrated backup software. This software can be a part of the operating system, like the **Windows Backup** utility, or a separate product that ships with the operating system, as is the case with most Linux distributions.

Windows Backup
A Microsoft Windows backup utility.

Backups are a critical part of network management. They are your best protection against hardware failure and data loss. Regardless of the size of the company, whether it is a one-person home office or a multi-server network, backups can become the lifeblood in the event of a disaster. Backups have the following characteristics:

- They provide an inexpensive storage option.
- Removable media (tapes) allow for off-site storage. Additional backup options include RAID arrays, online (Internet) backups, and optical.
- Large amounts of data can be backed up at once.
- Entire data sets can be recovered in case of serious failure.
- Files that are accidentally erased can be individually restored.

Backup destination
The location at which backed up data is stored.

You have various options for storage media as your **backup destination.** Two of the most common are backing up to a network share or backing up to magnetic tape. Backups via the Internet are becoming more common due to the increasing volume of data and the cost of backup devices and media.

The advantages of backing up to a network share include:

- Storage is readily available
- Backups are easy to configuration
- It is simple to set up fully automated backups

Tape drives are used to store large amounts of information at a relatively low cost. Most drives use Small Computer System Interface (SCSI) communications, although high-end systems use fiber-optic connections for the best performance when transferring data. They also have the advantage of being removable media, making it possible to keep a recent backup copy offsite in case of catastrophic failure or natural disaster.

Although the whole purpose of a backup is to be able to restore the data when necessary, you may find yourself in a situation in which the restore does not work. You need to understand, when using tapes as your backup media, that they have a limited lifespan and must be replaced periodically. Tape drives also need regular maintenance. You need to clean the tape drive regularly and should make sure you have access to another tape drive that is the same model as your backup drive, should your tape drive fail.

Understanding Backup Types

Archive bit
A bit associated with a data file. When set, it indicates that the file has changed and needs to be backed up.

Different types of backups vary in the amount of time required and amount of data backed up. The **archive bit,** depending on the type of backup you are running, helps determine the files you need to back up. When a file's archive bit is set on, it indicates that the file has changed and needs to be backed up. Most backup systems support the following types of backups:

Full backup
Another term for normal backup.

Normal backup
A backup operation that backs up all specified data and resets the archive bit as each file is backed up. Also known as a full backup.

- **Normal:** Normal backups are also referred to as **full backups.** Normal backups are used to back up all data, whether or not all the files have changed since the last backup. This type of backup is used the first time a backup is performed on a server and then periodically to back up all data.

- **Differential:** Differential backups use the archive bit to determine whether a file has changed since the last normal backup. The backup does not reset the archive bit when it runs. Differential backups take longer than incremental backups on subsequent runs because all changed data is backed up each time. They require less time to restore data because you restore the full backup and most recent differential backup only.

- **Incremental:** Incremental backups use the archive bit to determine whether a file has changed since the last full or incremental backup. The archive bit is reset as each file is backed up. Incremental backups take less time than differential backups on subsequent backups. However, data restoration takes more time because the normal backup tape and all incremental tapes made since the last normal backup are needed.

Some backup systems support other backup types, such as daily backups, which backup those files changed on a specific data based on the file's last modified property, whether or not the archive bit is set.

Planning Backup and Recovery

When planning your backup strategy, the normal backup usually takes place at an off-peak time, such as over the weekend. You can configure the backup to run after everyone has left for the weekend. Because normal backups back up all data, the backup can take a long time to complete. In companies that require support over the weekend, the backup strategy needs to be carefully planned to back up all data without interfering with the company's normal functions.

Figure 12-3

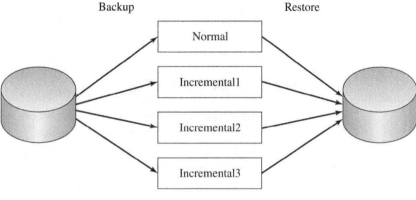

Incremental backups.

Between normal backups, use either incremental or differential backups to minimize data loss in case of a failure. The type of backup you run and the frequency depends on factors such as how long you can allow for backups to run and how quickly you need to recover the data should a failure occur.

Consider the situation in Figure 12-3. You run a normal backup over the weekend and incremental backups nightly. Should a failure occur on Thursday afternoon, you would have to restore from the normal backup and the three incremental backups made since that normal backup (in order).

Compare the situation shown in Figure 12-3 to Figure 12-4. You run a normal backup over the weekend and differential backups nightly. Recovery from the same failure means restoring from the normal backup and one differential backup, the one made Tuesday. Differential backup 3 would not have occurred yet.

Figure 12-4

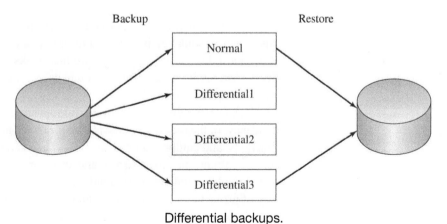

Differential backups.

As a general rule, if your priority is getting the backups to run as quickly as possible, use incremental backups. If your emphasis is on restoring data with minimal time or effort, use differential backups. Keep in mind that any data not backed up will have to be recreated or reposted.

12.2.2 Managing Redundancy

Redundancy can be applied almost anywhere in a network, from hard disks to network cables. For instance, the dependence on Internet access for business transactions and communication has prompted many companies to add redundant Internet connections. Most of these companies use two separate providers for more reliable service.

 CAREER CONNECTION

Using Redundancy

Under what circumstances do you need to implement a redundancy solution? They include:

Redundant Array of Independent (or Inexpensive) Disks (RAID)
A disk configuration that provides improved disk performance, disk fault tolerance, or both.

- You should add redundancy to critical servers in the form of a **Redundant Array of Independent (or Inexpensive) Disks (RAID)** solution.
- You should add redundant features to any component that must always be running.
- You should use redundancy for business-critical functions such as a database server or Internet access that clients depend on.
- If you would lose your job if the network goes down, then you need to add redundancy wherever possible.

The two general redundancy categories are disk-level and server-level. Disk-level redundancy is designed to protect a computer against data loss if one hard disk fails (or two or more hard disks, in some configurations). Server-level redundancy protects you in case any critical component, or the entire computer, fails.

If money weren't a problem, networks would be designed with full redundancy. In the real world, cost is a major factor in deciding what services, functions, and equipment need (or at least get) redundancy. The centralized services found on client-server and directory-based networks make the server an ideal candidate for redundancy, because it is the most cost-effective way of protecting data. Adding redundancy to one or a few servers than to an office of workstations is much cheaper.

Redundancy at the Disk Level

RAID 1
A fault-tolerant configuration based on two hard disk drives, with both containing the same data. Data is protected in the event of the failure of a single hard disk. See also **disk mirroring** and **disk duplexing.**

Disk mirroring
A RAID 1 configuration based on two hard disks being connected to the same disk controller.

Disk duplexing
A RAID 1 configuration based on two hard disks connected to different disk controllers.

RAID 5
A fault tolerant configuration based on three or more hard disks in which data and parity information are striped across the hard disks. Data is protected in the event of the failure of any one hard disk. Also known as **disk striping with parity.**

Disk striping with parity
See **RAID 5.**

The most common way of providing disk-level redundancy is through implementation of some type of fault tolerant RAID solution. A fault tolerant solution is one that protects your data in case of a disk failure. There are several defined RAID configurations, but the two fault-tolerant ones most commonly used in PC networks are RAID 1, which defines disk duplexing and disk mirroring, and RAID 5, which defines disk striping with parity. The Newer RAID 6 and RAID 10 are less commonly used because of cost and complexity.

With **RAID 1,** you have two hard disks, both with identical data, as in Figure 12-5, which means that 50 percent of the storage capacity is lost to providing fault tolerance. If either drive fails, the computer will continue to operate, using data from the other disk drive. With **disk mirroring,** both hard disks are connected to the same disk controller, making it a possible point of failure. With **disk duplexing,** the hard disks are connected to separate disk controllers.

RAID 5, shown in Figure 12-6, requires at least three hard disks. This is also known as **disk striping with parity.** The equivalent of one disk's storage capacity is lost to fault tolerance, so this method becomes more efficient the more disks you use. Data is written in blocks striped across the hard disks. Each set of data will also include parity data that is used to detect and correct from data errors, including the loss of one hard disk. In fact, the only noticeable difference when a hard disk is lost is a possible loss of performance during reads because of the need to regenerate the missing data.

RAID 6, is essentially an extension of RAID 5 that allows for additional fault tolerance by using a second independent distributed parity scheme (dual parity).

Figure 12-5

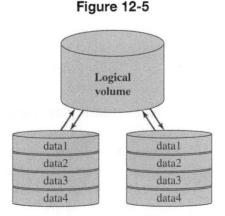

RAID 1 configuration.

Figure 12-6

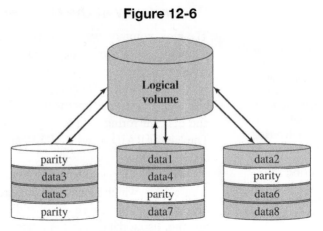

RAID 5 configuration.

RAID 10, requiring four or more disks, is accomplished by creating two RAID 1 mirror arrays and then striping data across them. Again, a single disk can fail and the array should continue to function. Four or more disks are required, and only half the total disk space is usable (the rest being taken up by redundant data).

If one hard disk fails in a RAID 5 configuration, the data is still available. To recover from the failure, you would need to replace the failing disk. Some configurations are **hot-swappable,** meaning that you can replace the disk without shutting down the disk subsystem or interrupting access to the data. After the failed disk is replaced, its data is regenerated.

Hot-swappable
A device that can be replaced without powering off.

The other configurations are essentially variations on or combinations of these RAID configurations, with some offering better performance, better protection, or both. RAID disk subsystems implement the RAID configuration through hardware. Many operating systems, including Windows Server versions, also support RAID configurations implemented through software. These solutions are typically less expensive than RAID disk subsystems, but also usually deliver poorer performance. If performance, as well as fault tolerance, is a critical issue, you should consider a hardware-based RAID solution.

Redundancy at the Server Level

Several other options are available for implementing server-level redundancy. Your available options will depend somewhat on your NOS, your server operating systems, and in some cases, the server applications that you are running. However, even with the different available variations, we can look at server redundancy by focusing on a few key features.

Redundancy options also fall more into the realm of fault tolerance, where all of the servers of a particular type are active on the network. When one server fails, the others take up the additional load. Examples include an Active Directory network with multiple domain controllers or deploying multiple Domain Name Service (DNS) servers on your network. The servers can cover for each other because they all contain the same data.

You use a similar configuration when providing fault tolerance for Dynamic Host Configuration Protocol (DHCP) servers. However, you cannot configure duplicate scopes on your DHCP servers. Instead, one server will have primary responsibility for a subnet. You configure a small percentage of those addresses as an address scope on a separate DHCP server to keep things running smoothly if the primary DHCP server fails. However, because a second server contains what is typically a much smaller address pool, this solution is only temporary.

Configurations used in PC-networks typically use either warm redundancy or hot redundancy. With **warm redundancy,** you have the hardware, operating system, and software in place, but the data on the redundant server isn't synchronized with the main server. With **hot redundancy,** you have identical hardware, software, and data. The difference between the two is that hot redundancy allows for immediate or near immediate switch-over between the servers. With warm redundancy, you must first synchronize the data on the redundant server, and then switch over through a process known as **failover.**

There are also two types of failover. **Automatic failover** is required when you must minimize the downtime while switching between servers. The primary server's failure is detected automatically and the switch is made automatically to the redundant (also called the secondary or alternate) server without any type of administrator intervention. With **manual failover,** administrator intervention is required to switch between the primary and redundant server. Manual failover is typically required when you must perform other actions, such as synchronizing the redundant server, as part of the process.

You'll find that many NOSs, such as Windows Server 2008, support multiple options for implementing server redundancy. Some third-party solutions also work with nearly any NOS or server application. However, from a cost standpoint, you should first use any options included with your NOS whenever possible.

As a general rule, the more automated the process and the faster the failover, the most expensive. Before you can determine whether or not a solution is worth the expense, you must consider the cost of downtime and how long it is likely to take you to finish failover when choosing your configuration option.

Warm redundancy
A redundant configuration with duplicate hardware and software but where data on the redundant hardware is not kept in sync with the primary server.

Hot redundancy
A redundant configuration with duplicate hardware, software, and data, in which the data is kept in sync with the primary server to allow for immediate failover.

Failover
The process of switching over to a redundant computer.

Automatic failover
A failover process in which an error is detected automatically, and the configuration switches over to the redundant server without administrator intervention.

Manual failover
A failover process that requires administrator or operating intervention, typically because it is necessary to synchronize the data on the redundant computer.

Project 12.1

The first instruction you read when opening new software is to make a backup. Unfortunately few users, including new network administrators, do this. That is, until they lose all their data on a failed hard disk once. All Windows Operating Systems include a backup utility.

1. To back up particular data or your entire hard disk, go to My Computer and right-click on your local drive, then select Properties. Next, click on the Tools tab and click the **Back up now** button.

2. If, as is common, you have not previously backed up your system, you will configure the backup utility here.

3. Select where you will store your backup data.

4. You can have Windows choose what to backup, or you can choose for yourself which files or drives you would like to back. (Windows Default will not backup Program Files, anything formatted with the

(continued)

(continued)

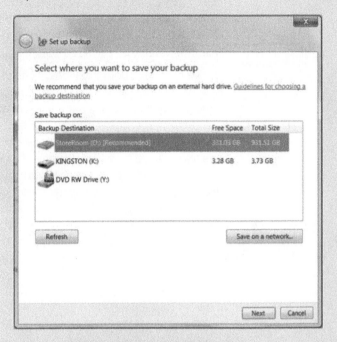

FAT file system, files in the Recycle Bin, or any temp files that are 1GB or more. For this exercise, we will designate which files to back up.)

5. Note that the default setting also includes a **System Image** backup.

6. You will get a confirmation screen showing what will be backed up.

7. You can then watch the progress of you backup.

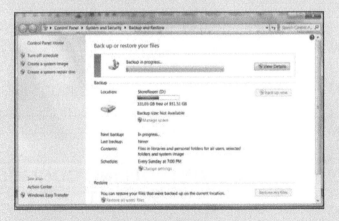

8. When the backup is complete, you will see the backup files and image folder, if you created one, in the location you indicated during setup.

IN THE REAL WORLD

Setting Backup Schedules

Nearly anyone who has used computers for any length of time has a horror story to tell about data loss. The same has happened to homeowners, who often never think about computer failures, suddenly lost their financial records, family photos, and other difficult-to-replace items.

Now, scale that out to a business. One of the primary motivations for bringing in a network is to make sharing data easier for users. Users are told to keep their files on network file servers instead of on their local computers. Database servers hold all of a businesses' critical data about inventory, sales and payment records, customer information, and financial accounting. Sudden loss of this data could be devastating. How often you need to back up data depends on how critical and volatile that data is.

Frequent backups can be critical. Busicorp has a Web site supporting Internet-based customers and sales. Customer orders and credit card and electronic payments post directly to a database server that provides the data backend for the web applications. How often do you need to back up the database? A near-constant running backup, maybe even ongoing updates keeping a redundant server synchronized, could be the appropriate answer. Why put in the effort? If that database fails, that information is lost. Not only have you probably lost those sales, you've likely lost those customers, who are going to find a different source for what they need in the future. What about the website? It is only hosting programs, not changing data, so you may only need to backup the website once a week or less.

 SELF-CHECK

1. Describe the three types of backups that are most commonly used in backup plans.
2. Describe RAID 1 and RAID 5 disk subsystems.
3. When would you need to implement automatic failover?

12.3 CONTROLLING CONFIGURATION MANAGEMENT

Configuration management means managing the network's hardware and software configuration, documenting it, and ensuring it is updated as the configuration changes. This management includes both server

Configuration management
Management of the network's hardware and software configuration.

and client configurations, including variations to support different roles and requirements.

Several things can fall under this general category. We're going to focus on two: managing user configurations and managing client software. Device configuration management, ways of centralizing device monitoring and control, is discussed separately, later in this chapter.

12.3.1 Understanding User Management

One of the most common configuration activities is adding and deleting user accounts. When new users are added to the network, they are usually categorized as being a member of some group of users, such as faculty or students, as in Figure 12-7. Each user group can have its own access privileges, which define what file servers, directories, and files they can access. Rights and permissions assigned to groups are also applied to group members unless explicitly blocked.

Log-in scripts
A series of commands that execute when a user logs in or a computer starts up.

You can also provide users and groups with their own **log-in scripts**, which specify commands to run each time the user logs in. Some network operating systems, including recent Windows Server versions, also support separate scripts associated with the client computer instead of the user. These scripts execute at computer startup.

In a network that uses a peer-to-peer or workgroup configuration, you must manage users separately on each computer. One of the reasons that client-server and directory-based networks are preferred is that they support

Figure 12-7

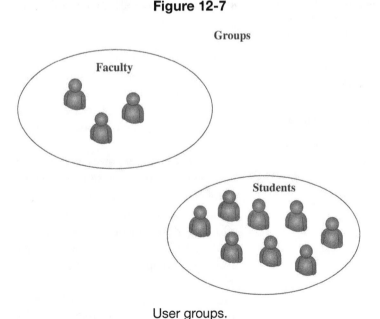

Groups

Faculty

Students

User groups.

centralized user management. User account information, including assigned rights and access permissions, are centrally stored on network servers.

The goal is to manage, whenever possible, at the group level, and make changes at the individual user level only when absolutely necessary. That lets you make better use of available time and effort, making a change once and having it apply to a group of related users.

12.3.2 Understanding Software Management

Another common activity is automatically installing or updating the software on the client computers attached to the network. Every time a new application system is developed or updated (or when a new version is released), each client computer in the organization must be updated. Traditionally, this meant that someone from the networking staff had to go to each client computer and manually install the software. For a small organization, this problem is time consuming although not a major issue. For a large organization with hundreds or thousands of clients, it can be a nightmare.

Electronic software distribution (ESD) A process by which software and updates are distributed automatically to network computers. Also known as automated software delivery and sometimes desktop management.

Electronic software distribution (ESD), sometimes called **desktop management** or **automated software delivery,** is one solution to the configuration problem. ESD enables network managers to install software on client computers over the network without physically touching each client computer. **Desktop Management Interface (DMI)** is the emerging standard in ESD software.

Some ESD packages provide Application-layer software for the network server and all client computers. The server software communicates directly with the ESD application software on the clients and can be instructed to download and install certain application packages on each client at some predefined time. Most can even test for and install application prerequisites, if necessary.

Desktop management See **electronic software distribution.**

Automated software delivery See **electronic software distribution.**

With some NOSs, this functionality is built into the operating system, so a separate ESD application is not required. You can, for example, configure software distribution over a Microsoft Active Directory network. You even have the option of associating the application with either the user or the client computer.

Desktop Management Interface (DMI) An emerging ESD software standard.

ESD software greatly reduces the cost of configuration management over the long term because it eliminates the need to update each and every client computer manually. An additional overhead is required for configuring software distribution, but it is usually minimal in comparison to the effort required to manually update every network client. Most versions also produce and maintain accurate documentation of all software installed on each client computer, supported at various levels of automation. This documentation makes it easier for network administrators to track software use and to avoid accidentally violating software licenses by installing an application on too many client computers.

IN THE REAL WORLD

Automatic Updates

If you have a small network, you may think that ESD is something that you don't need. After all, you don't spend that much time doing software installs or upgrades and you might even be able to let the users do it themselves. You don't need it, right? It's just not worth the effort.

Not so fast . . .

Your network could be using ESD and you might not even realize it. Do you have any computers running Windows? Do you enable automatic updates? If so, then you are using ESD. Windows Update streams software patches, security fixes, and other necessary changes to your operating system gradually as they come available. The only real requirements are that you have a genuine (valid) copy of Windows (yes, they do check) and an Internet connection. The typical configuration is to have your computer contact the Microsoft Update site and download the updates automatically.

Microsoft isn't the only company updating its software automatically. Do you use Adobe's Acrobat reader to view PDF files? Current Acrobat versions default to checking with Adobe's website for updates and letting you know if it finds anything. So do Corel's graphics programs.

Still consider ESD optional? What about anti-virus software? Anti-virus software has become a fact of life. Connecting to the Internet, even just to receive e-mail, without protection, is a risk. You would have a difficult time finding a new computer that ships without antivirus software already installed. However, the software is no better than its threat database. The risks keep changing, which means that the software needs constant updates to remain a viable protection. That means ESD.

SELF-CHECK

1. What is the primary advantage of organizing users into groups?
2. For what purpose is ESD used?

Apply Your Knowledge   Microsoft Windows and many other Applications now have the ability to automatically update anytime you are connected to the Internet.

To configure Windows Updates:

1. Click Start/All Programs/Windows Update.

   (If the icon is not available there, you can go to Control Panel/System and Security/Action Center/Windows Update to get to the same screen.)

2. Choose Change settings from the Windows Update window.

3. Here you can customize when, who, and how to allow windows to update itself.

12.4 MONITORING YOUR NETWORK

Performance monitoring
The process of collecting performance information about a network or individual computers.

After the basic components of the network are installed and running, it is time to get into the next phase of network management. **Performance monitoring** involves several tasks, each of which is intended to be completed with the same goal in mind—to stay informed about the health of the network. This process includes evaluating the performance of the network, servers, and workstations. Performance monitoring is also a critical procedure for identifying and correcting network problems. The faster the problems can be identified, the sooner a solution can be decided on and appropriate action taken.

Performance monitoring involves several tasks:

- Setting baselines for network performance
- Analyzing network traffic performance
- Assessing server hardware and software performance

Two levels of activity are referenced here—network monitoring activities that include the network as a whole and activities associated with individual computers, typically key network servers and application servers.

12.4.1 Establishing a Baseline

Baselining
The process of collecting performance baseline information.

Performance baseline
Performance information used as a point of comparison for network and computer performance analysis. It often includes typical and peak performance values.

If you don't know how the network performs under normal conditions, determining if it is performing poorly will be difficult. **Baselining,** or establishing a **performance baseline,** is a way to set a starting point for evaluating performance. Baselines vary on different networks because of the number of variables involved. Performance can be affected by the network protocol, the speed of the workstations and servers, and the speed (bandwidth) of the network infrastructure. The baseline for a network can be an average of performance measures, or can be based on separate values collected to represent typical and peak usage requirements.

After you have this information, you can compare network performance to expected norms. If the comparison indicates a significant decrease in the efficiency of the network, the network administrator knows there might be a problem. Without baseline information for this type of analysis, the network administrator might not know when the network is performing poorly until the network comes to a screeching halt.

12.4.2 Analyzing Network Performance

Network communication is a very complicated process. Nowhere is this more evident than when collecting data on network traffic. Analyzing network performance is a two-part process. The first step is to collect data as it is transmitted on the network. You collect data by running a network analysis program that will intercept all information transmitted on the network, whether or not it is intended for you.

The second part of the process involves you, the network administrator. Your responsibility is to evaluate the information for any interesting information. This may include but not be limited to:

- **The types of traffic on the network:** Some network-management protocols and network activities can create a lot of additional, possibly irrelevant, traffic. One thing that might help is disabling unneeded services and, if not required, NetBIOS support.

- **Frequently used protocols:** Some protocols are less efficient than others. Typically a network is designed to have one primary protocol, usually TCP/IP. If your analysis of protocols in use reveals an excessive amount of another type of traffic, such as AppleTalk, you may want to determine the source of the traffic, and determine whether the traffic can be controlled, replaced with a more efficient protocol, or completely eliminated.

- **Frequency of collisions:** Collisions, which occur on Ethernet networks, are indicative of a network that is saturated with too many devices competing for access. A switch might be a solution to the problem of excessive collisions. Each port on a switch can segment the network into separate collision domains. Another solution might be to subnet your LAN. Collisions can also occur in a wireless network. Laptops and workstations will experience collisions when the computers are too far away to hear the other workstation's transmission.

- **The percentage of frames with errors:** As frames are received on a device, they are checked for errors. Ethernet frames may have errors because of garbled data or because of fragmentation. Packet errors often indicate that a network interface card (NIC) is malfunctioning. The solution is to identify and replace the failing NIC.

- **The devices transmitting the most packets:** Workstations or other devices transmitting an unusually high number of frames in comparison to other computers may deserve your attention. The high transmission number could be due to valid requirements, or could be an indication of a hardware problem or even of a virus (or other malicious code) infection.

EtherPeek
A network monitoring application.

Several tools are available for collecting data on network performance. One is WildPacket's **EtherPeek** software, a performance-monitoring program.

Figure 12-8

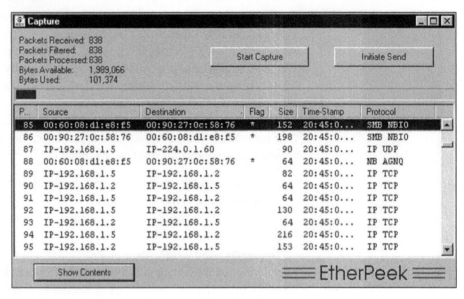

EtherPeek.

In Figure 12-8, EtherPeek displays details about several packets it has captured off the Ethernet network. Of special importance are the type of packets and the source of the packets. Alone, the type of packet and who sent it may not be of much interest during the analysis, but when calculating thousands of packets, this information can be critical. From just these two characteristics, you can determine the most heavily used protocol and the source address that is sending out the most packets. The results may be helpful in identifying a protocol problem or a network device that is transmitting a large number of packets unexpectedly.

You can use the Protocol Summary report, shown in Figure 12-9, to determine which protocol causes the majority of the traffic on the network.

You can save the data collected from your capture of packets to use later to compare to other reports. You can also perform the capture several times during the day to determine peak usage on the network.

EtherPeek is just one of several applications available. More advanced monitoring devices, known as **network sniffers,** use a combination of hardware and software to monitor network activity and can provide even more detailed information. These devices are also known as protocol analyzers or packet sniffers. No matter what they're called, they perform pretty much the same function.

However, you don't necessarily have to buy a separate monitoring application or tool. Microsoft supports a program named Network Monitor

Network sniffer

A device designed to collect network performance information and capture and log network packets. Also known as a packet sniffer or protocol analyzer.

Figure 12-9

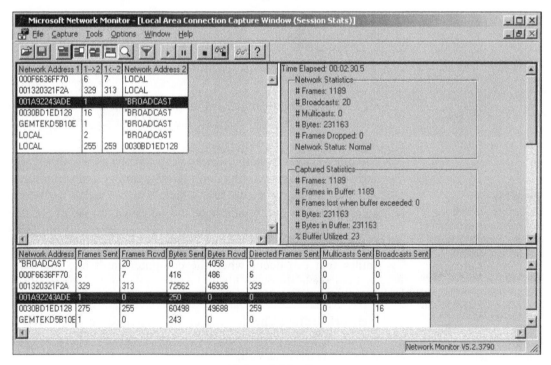

Protocol	Percentage		Packets
IP		85.919%	720
NetBIOS		7.399%	62
Loopback		4.654%	39
IP ARP		0.716%	6
Cisco DP		0.716%	6
NetWare		0.597%	5

Scale Down | Scale Up | 5x | Packets: 838 | Items: 6 | Sort... | Details...

Protocol summary.

with the Windows Server family products. Network Monitor can collect network traffic statistics and collect and save network packets. A sample capture is shown in Figure 12-10.

Figure 12-10

Microsoft Network Monitor - [Local Area Connection Capture Window (Session Stats)]

File Capture Tools Options Window Help

Network Address 1	1-->2	1<--2	Network Address 2
000F6636FF70	6	7	LOCAL
001320321F2A	329	313	LOCAL
001A92243ADE	1		*BROADCAST
0030BD1ED128	16		*BROADCAST
GEMTEKD5B10E	1		*BROADCAST
LOCAL	2		*BROADCAST
LOCAL	255	259	0030BD1ED128

Time Elapsed: 00:02:30.5

Network Statistics
  # Frames: 1189
  # Broadcasts: 20
  # Multicasts: 0
  # Bytes: 231163
  # Frames Dropped: 0
  Network Status: Normal

Captured Statistics
  # Frames: 1189
  # Frames in Buffer: 1189
  # Frames lost when buffer exceeded: 0
  # Bytes: 231163
  # Bytes in Buffer: 231163
  % Buffer Utilized: 23

Network Address	Frames Sent	Frames Rcvd	Bytes Sent	Bytes Rcvd	Directed Frames Sent	Multicasts Sent	Broadcasts Sent
*BROADCAST	0	20	0	4058	0	0	0
000F6636FF70	6	7	416	486	6	0	0
001320321F2A	329	313	72562	46936	329	0	0
001A92243ADE	1	0	250	0	0	0	1
0030BD1ED128	275	255	60498	49688	259	0	16
GEMTEKD5B10E	1	0	243	0	0	0	1

Network Monitor V5.2.3790

Network Monitor.

The version that ships with Windows is limited to capturing traffic originating from or destined for computer on which Network Monitor is running. A more advanced version of the application ships with Microsoft's **Systems Management Server (SMS)** product. That version of Network Monitor can capture and store any network traffic, no matter the source or destination, as long the computer on which it is running has a network adapter that supports promiscuous mode. **Promiscuous mode** is a mode of operation that allows a network adapter to intercept and read the complete contents of any packet on the network.

You need to realize that network monitoring tools and similar applications are also a potential security hazard. Unauthorized capture of network traffic could enable a person to collect valid computer names and IP addresses, some user information, and for applications that require clear text authentication, authentication credentials. A user interested in gathering such information could install the version of Network Monitor that ships with SMS, leave the laptop running and collecting data all day, and review the information later, possibly selling it to the highest bidder.

Systems Management Server (SMS)
Microsoft's SNMP management console product.

Promiscuous mode
A mode of operation that allows a network adapter to intercept and read the complete contents of any packet on a network.

12.4.3 Monitoring Network Computers

Network administrators often view servers as the nerve center of the network. When performance lags or a problem occurs, it usually involves the server, and not the network protocol or cables. On the server, particular areas should be monitored regularly. These areas include:

- **CPU usage:** You monitor CPU usage closely. If CPU usage frequently holds at more than 90 percent, the CPU is a potential performance bottleneck.

- **Memory usage:** System memory usage is also a critical performance factor. This usage includes both RAM memory and virtual memory provide through a **swap file,** which is drive space for temporary storage of data that typically would be saved in memory. Excessive **paging,** the processes of moving data between the swap file and RAM memory, can adversely affect system performance. Also watch for **faults** that can occur when the computer can't find the data it is looking for in the swap file and could indicate that you need a larger swap file.

- **Network traffic:** The demand on the server can be measured by the amount of traffic it is sending and receiving. A high volume of traffic can affect CPU usage as well.

- **Disk read/write:** Excessive reads and writes to the hard disk can indicate that you need a faster hard disk or may need to spread the load between

Swap file
Disk space set aside to emulate computer memory. A swap file is used to supplement memory.

Paging
The process of moving data between system RAM and the swap file.

Fault
A term that refers to the error reported when data cannot be found in memory.

Disk queue
Disk operations waiting
to be processed.

System Monitor
A Microsoft Windows
monitoring application;
previously called
Performance Monitor.

Performance Monitor
A Microsoft Windows,
monitoring application now
called **System Monitor.**

multiple hard disks. Also watch the **disk queue,** the number of disk accesses waiting to be serviced. Disk performance problems could be due to excessive paging, indicating that more RAM is needed.

Many products are available for monitoring server performance. Besides the built-in utilities that come with most server products, other products are available to monitor servers. HP Openview, IBM Tivoli, and Micromuses' NetCool are all very powerful products.

Windows **System Monitor** (called **Performance Monitor** in older Windows versions) is shown in Figure 12-11. Performance information is collected through performance counters, which are grouped into performance objects. For example, the processor-performance object contains all of the performance counters associated directly with the system processor. Some server applications will also add their own unique performance counters during installation.

You can monitor real-time activity, as shown in Figure 12-11, or log the data for later analysis. You can also log performance data to gather baseline

Figure 12-11

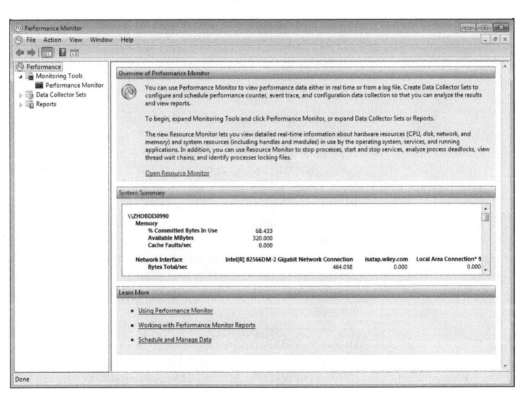

System Monitor.

data for individual servers. As with network baseline data, you can use the data later for comparison if you suspect a performance problem (or some other type of issue).

System Monitor defaults to the local computer, the computer on which it is running, but you can also collect performance counter information from other computers on the network. You can use System Monitor to compare computers side-by-side at the same time. When comparing two (or more) computers use an instance of System Monitor running on a completely separate computer. The utility does not put a significant load on a computer's resources, but if doing a comparison, it could skew the results.

Alert
A response to a Windows performance threshold value being met or exceeded.

Another feature of System Monitor is the ability to define **alerts.** System Monitor sets a threshold value based on a performance counter. When the threshold is exceeded by going either too high or too low (depending on how it is defined), the alert is triggered (fires). When this happens, you can have the computer:

- Log an entry in the application event log, so that you have a record of the alert and when it occurred.
- Send a network message to a specific computer.
- Start a performance log that you've already defined so that it can collect and record detailed statistics.
- Run a program, such as a utility designed to clear up the problem that caused the alert to fire.

Alerts are closely related to the Windows log files that record various entries relating to warnings, errors, and other activities. By default, a log entry is written when any alert occurs. If the logs fill up and can't accept any more entries, alerts stop firing.

Another particularly useful tool from Microsoft is their Microsoft Baseline Security Analyzer. Microsoft Baseline Security Analyzer (MBSA) is an easy-to-use tool that helps small and medium-sized businesses determine their security state in accordance with Microsoft security recommendations and offers specific guidance on important updates and security patches. Using it will assist in your security management process to detect common security misconfigurations and missing security updates on your computer systems.

Built on the Windows Update Agent and Microsoft Update infrastructure, MBSA ensures consistency with other Microsoft management products including Microsoft Update (MU), Windows Server Update Services (WSUS), Systems Management Server (SMS), System Center Configuration Manager (SCCM) 2007, and Small Business Server (SBS).

IN THE REAL WORLD

Using Alerts

You're the network administrator for Busicorp. You came into the job with the network already in place, and it was a mess. You and your staff spend nearly all of your time putting out fires with very little time for monitoring or advanced planning. You know that the network has some risk areas, not to mention the intermittent problems that you can't quite get a handle on. What can you do?

If you have some idea of the potential problem areas or types of problems you might need to watch for, you can use alerts to help you bring things under control.

Here's the situation. You have an application server that barely meets operational requirements. You suspect that requirements exceed resources during peak use, but you're not even sure when that is. You set up an alert that monitors processor activity. You set the threshold at 90 percent. When it fires, you have the alert write an entry to the application log and send a network message to your computer. After you configure the alert, you can go ahead with your normal day.

When the alert fires, you can do a quick check to see what else is happening on the network, who's attached to the application server, and other related activity. In case you're away from your desk, you can review the event logs to see when the alert fired to help you figure out what else was going on at the time. This way, you're able to document the problem and have a better chance of resolving it. You might even use the information as part of your justification for upgrading the server.

One last thing: Don't forget to disable or delete the alert when it's no longer needed. Otherwise, the alert will continue to fire every time the threshold is exceeded.

SELF-CHECK

1. Compare the roles of Microsoft's Network Monitor and System Monitor.
2. What is the justification for baselining?

Apply Your Knowledge

1. Download and install Microsoft Baseline Security Analyzer from: http://technet.microsoft.com/en-us/security/cc184923, on the download screen pick the operating system appropriate download, (i.e. MBSASetup-x86-EN.msi for a 32 bit system).
2. Run it directly from the Microsoft website or find where you saved it and double click on the .msi file to run.

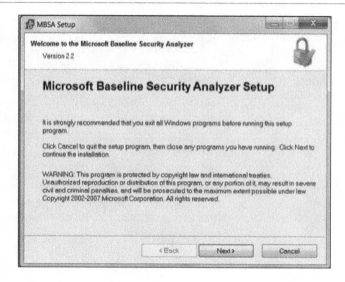

3. Click next, accept the license agreement, and click next again.
4. Accept the defaults and wait until it completes installing.
5. Open the program from the Start menu.
6. Scan your computer.

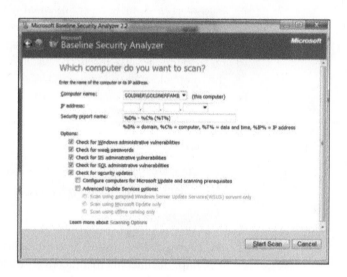

7. Observe the results.

12.5 USING MANAGEMENT SYSTEMS

Network management system (NMS)
A network monitoring device that uses hardware and software to monitor and maintain a network.

A **network management system (NMS)** uses a combination of hardware and software to monitor and manage devices on the network. Network administrators rely on the network management system for up-to-date information on the health of the network. Whether it is performance, inventory, configuration changes, or notification of network failures, a complete NMS can reduce the time involved in managing the network. More advanced NMS products can include additional functionality, such as a built-in ESD component. Unlike a monitoring program that runs on a server, NMS software will monitor network devices from one workstation, regardless of the vendor of the network device.

A network management model includes objects that represent elements of a network device, such as a port on a hub or system information. These objects and the corresponding attributes that provide details about them can all be monitored and changed remotely. Hubs that have been designed to participate in an NMS have several objects. An object such as an Ethernet interface can be asked to provide detailed information about its configuration and performance. NMS products take configuration management to a level undreamed of in earlier management products.

In order for the network management system to gather information about a device, it has to know about the device's attributes. Attributes can include make, model, software versions, performance information, configuration settings, and the technical support contact information. The device can temporarily record many of the performance attributes for use by the NMS. If the value for the attribute exceeds a certain percentage, or

Threshold
A target value used as reference to determine whether an activity or performance counter is out of expected tolerance.

threshold, the network management system can alert the network administrator of a possible problem. This is like the Windows Performance Monitor alerts discussed earlier in this chapter.

12.5.1 Managing TCP/IP Networks

Managing TCP/IP networks was once an easy task where network administrators could use simple tools to test network devices. As the TCP/IP networks have grown into complex networks, simple utilities such as Ping have become inadequate for managing the network or can't be used due to security restrictions enforced by firewalls.

Simple Network Management Protocol (SNMP)
A TCP/IP protocol for remote configuration monitoring and management.

In 1990, RFC 1157 defined the **Simple Network Management Protocol (SNMP),** which was created to help network administrators manage their growing networks. Network administrators can use SNMP to manage all kinds of network devices from many different vendors, as long as the vendor creates software that is compliant with SNMP. SNMP provides network administrators with a level of control that was previously unavailable.

Objects
1. A directory-based network entity.
2. SNMP management variable.

Management information base (MIB)
A collective term for all management information object on a network.

MIB file
A file that details how to access an object and that contains information about the object and how to manage it.

Management console
SNMP management software's user interface, or the computer on which the management software is installed.

Agent
An SNMP component that collects MIB information and delivers it to the management console.

Get command
A command used by an SNMP management console to retrieve information from a device.

Set command
A command used by an SNMP management console to manage device configurable parameters.

Trap command
A command used by SNMP to force an object to notify the management console based on system failures or performance problems.

SNMP is now included as a standard part of the TCP/IP protocol suite. When implemented on a network, it can record specific details about hardware and configurations and IP protocol information. In the event of a failure or performance problem, the information can be used to alert the network administrator.

The SNMP protocol is only one component of the SNMP management model. The model also includes:

• Manageable devices

• A network management console

• Management information base (MIB) agents

The SNMP protocol gathers management information from the manageable network devices. Each manageable device, such as a switch, router, or computer, has information on certain variables that are stored in a database. The variables, called **objects,** include history, hardware, configuration, and status. The objects are all defined in RFC 1155 (on management information). All of the management information objects that exist on the network are collectively known as the **management information base (MIB).** Each SNMP-compatible device created by a vendor must have a corresponding **MIB file** that details how to access the object information for that device. Due to the demand for centralized network management, most companies include SNMP functionality on their equipment. Hubs, routers, switches, workstations, and servers that are manageable can respond to SNMP commands. Without the MIB file, the **management console,** the SNMP management software's user interface, and the SNMP software will not be able to recognize the device's objects.

Object information, the device status, and other variables stored in the database must be collected and transferred to the management console when requested. When a request for information is made or a configuration change is sent to a device, the agent software running on the device, shown in Figure 12-12, uses the MIB to collect object information from the database. The **agent** collects MIB information about a managed device and provides the information to the management console. The agent can respond to a request or update the database with information that is received from the management console.

Unlike other network-management protocols, SNMP is relatively simple and reliable because it uses only three basic commands. Administrators use the **get command** to request information from the agent on a manageable device. When the network administrator wants to change a configuration setting on a device, he or she uses the **set command.** The set command changes the value of a configuration setting, rather than initiating the command on the device.

The last SNMP command, the **trap command,** sets a manageable device to automatically notify the management console of a system failure or

Figure 12-12

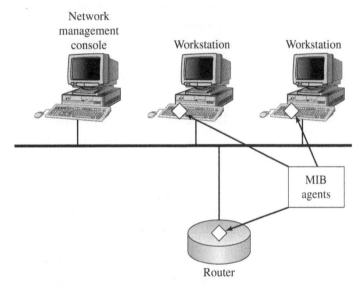

Agent software.

 CAREER CONNECTION

Using the Get Command

Here's how an administrator would use the get command to get information about a device:

1. From the network management console, the administrator sends a GetRequest, as shown in Figure 12-13, for system information from a device.

Figure 12-13

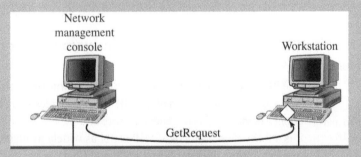

GetRequest.

2. The device receives the IP packet and passes the SNMP data to the agent.
3. The SNMP agent collects the system information and puts it in the right format.
4. The SNMP agent sends back a GetResponse with the system information.
5. The management console receives the GetResponse with the device's system information enclosed and updates the device information in the management console software.

performance problem. When information from a trap is received, it can commonly trigger an attention-getting alarm or alert on the network management console. However, because SNMP uses an unreliable protocol, the management console possibly may not receive a trap. As a precautionary measure, polling was added to the function of the management console. At regular intervals, the console will poll manageable devices for problems.

12.5.2 Remotely Monitoring a Network

Polling process
The process by which an NMS device collects data.

Network administrators who rely heavily on SNMP for critical system information run the risk of burdening the network with SNMP traffic. On large enterprise networks that have thousands of manageable devices, network performance can be seriously affected by the SNMP commands transmitted between the network management console and the manageable devices as part of the **polling process,** the process of gathering information about managed devices and their current status. The problem is further compounded on enterprise networks when the SNMP traffic has to travel over WAN connections.

RMON
A remote monitoring function supported by some devices and used with an SNMP management console to reduce traffic requirements.

RMON, a remote monitoring function that is supported by some devices, can help ease this problem. RMON is part of the management information base and it has its own objects. Each object has detailed summary information about the network and devices on the network. Network devices capable of running the RMON functions are called RMON probes. RMON probes do not communicate with the managed devices directly. Instead, the RMON probe collects data from the network in promiscuous mode. As data is transmitted on the network, the RMON probe collects the information on what is being transmitted and by whom. The management information collected by the RMON probe can then be sent to the network management console. Traffic is reduced because the RMON information from that network segment of the internetwork is communicated directly between the RMON device and the network management console.

12.5.3 Using Common Management Information Protocol

Common Management Information Protocol (CMIP)
A command protocol developed in response to and as an alternative to SNMP.

The ISO developed **Common Management Information Protocol (CMIP)** in response to the limitations of SNMP. CMIP provides more detailed information about a device, and is in general a more complex protocol than SNMP. Because it is a fairly new protocol, CMIP is not as widely available as SNMP. Cisco is one vendor that does support SNMP and CMIP in most of its products.

12.5.4 Implementing Network Management Systems

Implementing a network management system (NMS) on a network requires careful and thorough planning. You need to document your plan and everything that you do while implementing the network management system.

As part of implementing an NMS, the management console station should be selected by following certain criteria. First, you need to determine the management software that you will use. If you will primarily be supporting Cisco products, you may decide to use CiscoWorks management software. In a primarily Windows networking environment, you might choose SMS, mentioned earlier in this chapter. Otherwise, many other products are available, including Castle Rock's SNMPc, Hewlett-Packard's Open-View, and Computer Associates' NetworkIT, among others. These programs offer at a minimum these basic functions:

- They allow discovery of nodes.
- They provide support for both IP and IPX.
- They offer a graphical view of managed devices (which can be useful in network planning).
- They enable you to generate reports.
- They send alerts in the form of an audible alarm, an e-mail message, or contact via a pager.

In addition to deciding on hardware and software for your management console, you must determine what kind of security will be used on the

IN THE REAL WORLD

Taming the Beast

Busicorp's expansion plan has, for years, relied on growth through acquisition of other related businesses. While Busicorp has been acquiring businesses, it has also been acquiring their networks, which means that you have to find a way to integrate these diverse networks with your existing corporate WAN with as little adverse impact as possible.

This is a situation where knowledge is power. The more you know, the better your design decisions as you prepare to integrate the LAN. The problem is that gathering a network inventory is a long, complex, and boring process. Even with checklists to guide your research, overlooking items that could make a difference is easy. Depending on the size of the LAN, going through every configuration parameter on every networked computer is probably impossible.

In this type of situation, a quality network management system becomes your best friend. An NMS is specifically designed to analyze the network and dig out the detailed information for you, then let you generate custom reports that lay out that information in a easy to understand and use format. You can even make remote changes to configuration parameters, if necessary, to help it merge more easily into your WAN.

Network operations center (NOC)
A physically secure location where IT professionals review and manage all tickets, the weather, global political occurrences, financial market changes, Internet threats, etc.

console. The management console is often capable of collecting configuration information from network devices, including login names and passwords. Also, the network management console gives whoever uses it the ability to view, change, and delete configuration settings on devices. As a result, the management console should be in a physically secure location such as the **network operations center (NOC).**

SELF-CHECK

1. What is a network management system (NMS)?

2. What is the possible risk of an unauthorized NMS on a network?

Apply Your Knowledge What is required for a computer to collect data using RMON?

12.6 MANAGING INDIVIDUAL SERVERS

Just as there are a wide variety of network management tools, there are also a variety of server and server application management tools. The primary difference is that these tools are specific to the NOS or server application. Each networking product includes it own suite of management tools, which can even vary widely between different versions of the same product.

12.6.1 Understanding Local Management

We start by discussing management from the standpoint of local management. Each commonly used NOS provides either a management console interface or a set of management tools. In the case of Microsoft Windows Server, the majority is grouped together as Administrative Tools.

Even though the exact tools vary, we can use Windows as a general example. The concepts discussed, if not the specific tools, apply to other NOSs and to most server applications.

The management tools fall into two general categories: tools used to manage the server and tools used to manage the network. The tools used to manage the server, in the case of Windows, are generally the same as those

Computer Management
A Windows local management utility.

used to manage Windows client computers. They include tools like **Computer Management,** shown in Figure 12-14, that lets you view and manage computer devices and storage media. On member servers (not domain

Figure 12-14

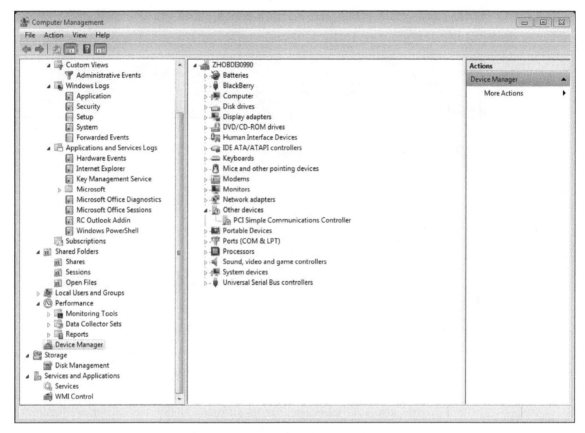

Computer Management utility.

controllers), you can also manage user and group accounts local to that computer. The example in Figure 12-14 is from an Active Directory domain controller, so local accounts are not supported. Domain controllers support domain user and group accounts only. When you promote a computer into the domain controller role, any local accounts are deleted.

Network management tools are tools that let you view and manage network resources. One of the tools that gets the most use in an Active Directory domain is **Active Directory Users and Computers,** shown in Figure 12-15. This is the primary tool for managing domain users and groups, member computers, domain controllers, and other domain resources.

Other NOSs, like Novell Network or Linux and UNIX, have their own equivalents to these management utilities. The same is true of many server applications. For example, most database management systems include some kind of utility that lets you manage not only the database and its contents, but also database users.

Active Directory Users and Computers

A Windows Active Directory utility used to manage organizational units, users, groups, computers, and other domain objects.

Figure 12-15

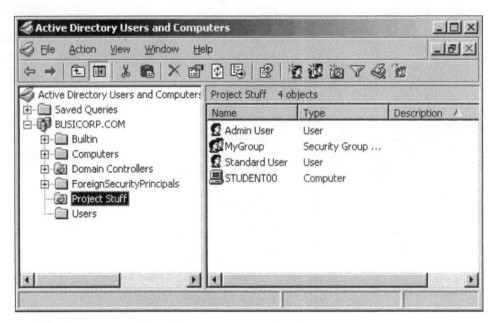

Active Directory Users and Computers.

12.6.2 Understanding Remote Management

Remote management is another area that varies widely, with many features and available tools specific to different NOSs and server applications. Rather than discussing specific remote management tools and utilities, we look at the various ways that they can be implemented.

Probably the most common way of supporting remote management is through management tools that can be installed on a client computer. These tools are usually available for most network servers and server applications. They let you manage the network as if sitting at the network servers. The same, or very similar, utilities are used. Information is retrieved from the network server and displayed at the client. Changes made at the client are then sent back over the network and written to the servers. These tools can even, in most cases, be used over remote links. A network administrator might be able to fix problems at odd hours from home with a laptop that has the management utilities installed.

Perhaps the biggest drawback of these types of tools is that they are a potential security risk. Even though they usually require you to log on as an administrative user (or superuser, in the case of UNIX and Linux), there is a risk in installing them on a client computer that is too openly accessible. Some network administrators are more careful about protecting their authentication criteria than others, and you should never assume that no compromised administrator accounts are on your network. You should do your best to restrict access to client computers that have management tools installed.

Another method you will see is to open a remote command prompt, such as through Secure Shell (SSH) terminal emulation, and run command-line management utilities. Because of the inherent risk involved, however, you should disable support for remote command prompts unless there is a specific requirement.

TIPS FROM THE PROFESSIONALS

Why SSH Replaced Telnet

Telnet, a TCP/IP protocol for accessing remote computers, transmits both user name and password in plaintext, and is just like painting them on the side of your building so that anyone can access and control your network devices.

Secure Shell (SSH) is the industry standard replacing Telnet. SSH commands are encrypted and secure. SSH uses a digital certificate to authenticate the connection between the client and the server and encryption protects passwords and the communication itself. SSH1 uses RSA encryption keys, and SSH2 uses Digital Signature Algorithm (DSA) keys to secure both the connection and authentication. SSH helps protects against packet sniffing, spoofing, and "man-in-the-middle" attacks.

A third way is to use tools that were primarily designed for user support and troubleshooting. These remote control utilities, of which there are both versions that ship with various operating systems and a wide variety of third party products, let you take over a system as if you were sitting at its keyboard. Actual screen information is sent to your computer and your keystrokes are applied at the remote computer.

The ability to remotely control a network server or server application is considered a significant security risk and should be avoided if at all possible. If your server's operating system supports a remote control functionality, it should be deleted or disabled. You should also monitor critical network resources for the possible introduction of third party remote control applications.

The capability for remote control as a support (or management) tool is built into many operating systems. Several third-party products are available, often sold as giving you an easy way to access your office computer from home. One problem with most of them is that no permanent record is made of the remote control session. Until a problem is detected, you may have no way of knowing who, or even if, someone has been breaking into a computer through remote control.

Servers aren't the only computers at risk. If someone can get access to a user's computer through a remote control program, not only do they have access to that computer, they probably have access to your network as a whole. Anything done on the network is done in the context of the local computer, usually without any indication that an outside individual was involved.

Project 12.2

Remote Desktop Connection allows you to access a computer running Windows from another computer running Windows.

To allow remote connections on the target computer:

1. Open System by clicking the Start/Control Panel/System and Maintenance/System.

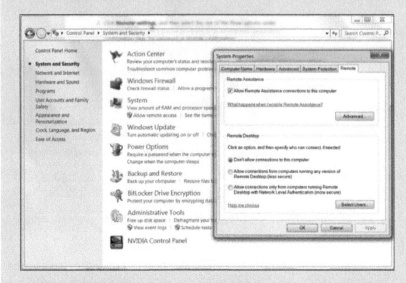

2. Click **Remote settings**, and then select one of the three options under "**Remote Desktop**." If you are prompted for an administrator password or confirmation, type the password or provide confirmation. Note that you might get a warning message about a computer set to sleep or hibernate after a period of unuse.

3. Click **Select Users**. If you are an administrator on the computer, your current user account will automatically be added to the list of remote users and you can skip the next two steps.

4. In the **Remote Desktop Users** dialog box, click **Add**.

5. In the **Select Users or Groups** dialog box, do the following:

    a. To specify the search location, click **Locations**, and then select the location you want to search.

    b. In **Enter the object names to select**, type the name of the user that you want to add, and then click OK.

6. To use Remote Desktop from your work computer:

Open Remote Desktop Connection by clicking the **Start** button ⊙, clicking **All Programs**, clicking **Accessories**, and then clicking **Remote Desktop Connection**.

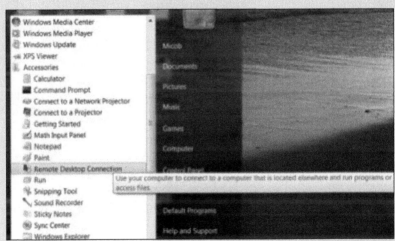

7. In **Computer,** type the name of the computer that you want to connect to, or its IP address. Click **Connect.**

IN THE REAL WORLD

The Lure of Remote Management

Think about this. You're a network administrator for Busicorp. You're also the person in charge, and you supervise the other administrators and computer technicians throughout the company and across the country. You're also the person who has to cover if any of the other administrators are unavailable. Because the company supports web-based retailing and 24/7 operations, critical support requests can sometimes come in at odd hours.

Your company invested in a support application that helps streamline the process. Users can report problems through an intranet website. Automated monitoring programs watch critical applications to make sure they are performing at optimum levels. When problems are detected, depending on the time and location, a network administrator is paged automatically. As time passes without the problem getting resolved, it gets escalated up the line, also automatically, until it finally reaches you—at 3 o'clock in the morning in the middle of a snowstorm.

The good news is, the problem is at the local office, so you can actually do something about it yourself. The bad news is, the problem is at the local office, so you're expected to do something about it yourself. Remote management tools can become an important part of your support mix in this type of situation.

Let's assume you've done everything right and you've got it all set up. You've installed ever possible management utility you can on your laptop. The network is set up with a remote access server that lets you connect through a secure VPN over the Internet. You even have a high-bandwidth Internet connection into your home. That means that, instead of getting dressed and slogging your way into the office, you can attach from your home and have a chance of resolving the problem without ever changing out of your pajamas.

Just be careful that you don't lose that laptop.

SELF-CHECK

1. What is the potential risk of installing management utilities on a client computer?
2. What kinds of support utilities can be used through a Telnet connection?
3. Why shouldn't you enable remote control applications on network servers?

SUMMARY

Section 12.1

- A network administrator has the responsibility of ensuring uninterrupted network service to users.
- Having information about the network be readily available and regularly reviewed and analyzed is critical.

Section 12.2

- Most operating systems include integrated backup software.
- Redundancy can be applied almost anywhere in a network.

Section 12.3

- Configuration management includes managing the configuration of both servers and client computers.
- Group level configuration allows you to make changes to many users at once.

Section 12.4

- A performance baseline helps you evaluate network performance.
- Monitoring allows you to analyze real-time network activity.

Section 12.5

- NMS products combine hardware and software to monitor and manage devices on the network.
- SNMP protocol gathers management information from network devices.

Section 12.6

- Network operating systems provide either a management console interface or a set of management tools.
- Remote management tools retrieve information from a server and display it on a client computer.

ASSESS YOUR UNDERSTANDING

UNDERSTAND: WHAT HAVE YOU LEARNED?

 Go to **www.wiley.com/go/ciccarelli/networkingbasics2e** to evaluate your knowledge of network management.

Measure your learning by comparing pre-test and post-test results.

SUMMARY QUESTIONS

1. Windows XP automatic updates are an example of which of the following?

   (a) ESD
   (b) NMS
   (c) SNMP
   (d) NOC

2. For what purpose is an SNMP trap command used?

   (a) To detect unauthorized agents.
   (b) To remotely disable a managed device.
   (c) To set device configuration parameters.
   (d) To have a device send a notification in case of a failure.

3. RAID 5 is an example of which of the following?

   (a) Automatic failover remote systems.
   (b) Fault tolerant disk subsystem.
   (c) Network monitoring device.
   (d) Software distribution method.

4. A company's LANs, WANs, and Internet websites can be managed separately without consideration for each other. True or false?

5. Which type of backup is used to back up changed data only, resetting the archive bit during the backup?

   (a) Daily
   (b) Normal
   (c) Incremental
   (d) Differential

6. Redundant systems with automatic failover are designed to enable the network to continue to provide a service without interruption and without direct human intervention. True or false?

7. For most day-to-day management tasks, it is more efficient to manage groups than to manage individual users. True or false?

8. Which of the following statements best describes a performance baseline?

   (a) A performance baseline provides a starting point for evaluation.
   (b) A performance baseline should be collected any time a problem is suspected.
   (c) A performance baseline must be taken when the network is inactive with no users connected.
   (d) A performance baseline should be taken only during peak use periods.

9. Which of the following could you use to capture network traffic for later analysis?

   (a) An SNMP management console
   (b) A network sniffer
   (c) Windows System Monitor
   (d) A remote control utility

10. A high percentage of frames detected with garbled data and other errors is usually an indication of what?

    (a) An active Ethernet network
    (b) An inefficient network protocol
    (c) A failing network adapter
    (d) Unauthorized network access

APPLY: WHAT WOULD YOU DO?

1. You are a network administrator. You've been hired to take over a mid-sized company's network that includes four locations connected by WAN links. Each local network is a routed LAN. Various network and client operating systems are currently in use on the network.

   You have almost no documentation for the network. You cannot find any kind of network inventory. Network failures are common.

   (a) Why is it important to document the network?
   (b) You do not have personnel available to perform a physical inventory. You decide to use a network management system (NMS) that is based on SNMP. What is required for the management console to be able to recognize a network device?
   (c) Who is responsible for providing this information to the company that developed the NMS?
   (d) From the context of SNMP management, what is an object?
   (e) During device polling, what is the role of an agent?
   (f) What types of information can be collected about a managed device?
   (g) What are the commands supported by SNMP and their use?

2. You are tasked with minimizing network downtime and the time required to recover after a failure. You have reviewed the current network management procedures and are developing guidelines to improve management.

   (a) You run a full backup on Saturday night and an incremental backup each weekday evening. The network fails during the day Wednesday. Which backups will be necessary to recover the computer and in what order should they be applied?

   (b) You run a full backup on Saturday night and a differential backup each weekday evening. The network fails during the day Wednesday. Which backups will be necessary to recover the computer and in what order should they be applied?

   (c) What type of backup minimizes the time required to run backups?

   (d) Why?

   (e) Your network includes a database server. You have a redundant server configured with warm redundancy. If the primary server fails, what must you do before you can fail over to the redundant server?

   (f) You have a file server that stores critical company files including product design documents, build lists, and manufacturing inventory requirements. The server has a RAID 5 disk subsystem with four hard disks. What happens if one hard disk fails and how would you recover?

   (g) What happens if two disks fail and how would you recover?

BE A NETWORK MANAGER

Network Management

You are looking to improve management of the network shown in Figure 12-16. The wide area links are VPN links over the Internet. Though not shown to that detail in the figure, each location is configured as a routed LAN.

The network is configured as a Windows Server 2008 Active Directory network. Each remote location is configured as a separate domain. All servers run Windows 2003 Server or Windows Server 2008. Client computers include a mix of various Windows versions, Mac OS X, and different Linux distributions. All network devices are designed for use with SNMP management consoles.

1. What kinds of baseline traffic should you collect on the network as a whole?

2. You initially decide to set up Microsoft SMS on the Chicago network. What is the possible impact on traffic across the wide area links?

Figure 12-16

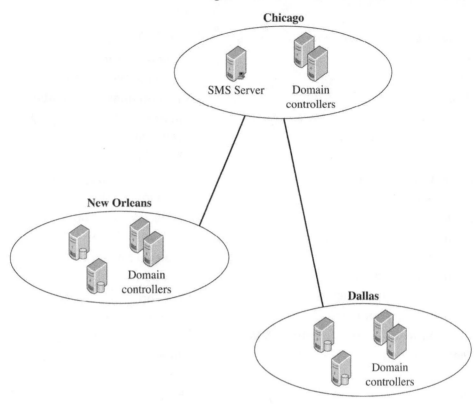

Sample network.

3. Why should you collect performance baseline information for individual application servers?

4. You want to keep your investment in third-party management tools to a minimum. What can you use to collect baseline data for application servers?

5. You are concerned about disk space on network file servers. You want to find out as soon as possible if free space falls below a threshold level and create a record of the occurrence. You also want to run a custom application that will clear unnecessary temporary files from the servers. What should you do?

6. Currently, server backups use network shares as their destination. The shares are physically located on file servers in Chicago. What is the potential risk in case of catastrophic failure? How could you avoid this?

7. You discover that a user was able to install Network Monitor from the SMS server to his laptop. What is the potential risk?

KEY TERMS

Active Directory Users and Computers

Agent

Alert

Archive bit

Automated software delivery

Automatic failover

Backup

Backup destination

Baselining

Bottlenecks

Common Management Information Protocol (CMIP)

Computer Management

Configuration management

Desktop management

Desktop Management Interface (DMI)

Disk duplexing

Disk mirroring

Disk queue

Disk striping with parity

Downtime

Electronic software distribution (ESD)

End-user support resources

EtherPeek

Failover

FAQ (frequently asked questions)

Fault

Fault tolerance

Firefighting

Full backup

Get command

Hot redundancy

Hot-swappable

Latency

Level 1 support personnel

Level 2 support staff

Level 3 support staff

Log in scripts

Management console

Management information base (MIB)

Manual failover

MIB file

Network administrator

Network management

Network management System (NMS)

Network operations center (NOC)

Network sniffer

Normal backup

Objects

Paging

Performance baseline

Performance Monitor

Performance monitoring

Polling process

Promiscuous mode

RAID 1

RAID 5

Redundancy

Redundant Array of Independent (or Inexpensive) Disks (RAID)

Redundant systems

RMON

Set command

Simple Network Management Protocol (SNMP)

Swap file

System Monitor

Systems Management Server (SMS)

Threshold

Trap command

Warm redundancy

Windows Backup

GLOSSARY

10Base2	A bus topology Ethernet network that uses thin coaxial cable. Also known as Thin Ethernet or Thinnet thin coaxial cable.
10Base5	A bus topology Ethernet network that uses thick coaxial cable. Also known as Thick Ethernet or Thicknet.
10Base100	A logical bus topology that uses a 100Mbps physical star topology.
10BaseT	A logical bus topology that uses a 10Mbps physical star topology.
10GBaseT	A standard for 10Gbps Ethernet using UTP cable.
802.11g	A wireless standard that uses the 2.4GHz frequency bank, like 802.11b, although transmits up to 54Mbps. Most 802.11g devices support and provide connectivity to 802.11b devices on the network because they are communicating within the same frequency band.
Acceptance stage	The final stage of the standardization process in which a solution is adopted as a standard.
Access point	A designated point of entry within a network where wireless devices send and receive transmissions.
Access Protocols	Communications procedures used at the Data Link layer on all networks.
ACK	A special Acknowledgement packet type sent by a receiving system to acknowledge successful receipt of one or more datagrams.
Ack	Acknowledgement message sent by the receiving computer in a connection-oriented transmission.
Acknowledgement	A special packet type sent by a receiving system to acknowledge successful receipt of one or more datagrams.
Active Directory	Microsoft's directory-based network architecture.
Ad hoc mode	A wireless network topology in which wireless devices communicate directly with each other, also known as peer-to-peer mode.
Address scopes	A set of addresses that is available for assignment through DHCP.
Addressing	How computers are able to identify and recognize each other on a network.
Alias	Similar to the CNAME, a record that is used to map duplicate host names to a single IP address.
American National Standards Institute (ANSI)	The coordinating organization for the U.S. national system of technical and non-technical standards.

Application layer (DoD and Internet)	Combines the OSI model Application, Presentation, and Session layers.
Application layer (OSI)	The network layer that houses the applications that allow users to access the network.
Application server	A server on a network whose primary function is to hold and manage application executables, files, and data.
Application service providers (ASPs)	Companies that develop and sell applications that are used over the Internet.
ARCNET	Acronym for Attached Resource Computer Network. ARCNET is an outdated networking protocol that was used in the 1980s for office automation tasks.
Attenuation	Loss of signal strength over distance.
Audit	The action of tracking and recording network activity, usually in regard to user activity.
Authentication mechanisms	Ways that the network can validate who is and who isn't allowed access to the network.
Authoritative	A server with primary responsibility for a DNS zone to which DNS table updates are made and used as the source for updating other copies of the zone table.
Backoff	A random amount of time each system on a network must wait before attempting to transmit when a collision has been sensed.
Bandwidth throttling	The method by which client demand for access to a web server can be regulated to manage access in times of high demand.
Bandwidth	The capacity on a given network for data transmission.
Best effort transmission	A term used to refer to the connectionless transmission method used by IP.
Bluetooth	A peripheral connection standard that allows devices such as cell phones, pagers, and PDAs to communicate.
BNC connector	A type of RF connector used to connect coaxial cables.
BOOTP enabled	A router that is configured to pass DHCP broadcasts.
Bridge	A network communication device used to connect physical networks and provide a level of filtering between networks.
Broadcast domain	A set of nodes configured to receive broadcasts as a group.
Broadcast traffic	Traffic that is effectively addressed to every device on a network segment.
Brouter	A network communication device that combines the functionality of routers and bridges.
Bus topology	A single main cable to which all devices are attached.
Canonical name (CNAME)	A record that is used to map duplicate host names to a single IP address.
Carrier Sense Multiple Access with Collision Avoidance (CSMA/CA)	A media access control method used in wireless networks to prevent data collisions.

Checksum	A value used to verify that a datagram has not changed during transmission.
Class	A method of organizing available IPv4 address for assignment.
Class A	A network address classification that defines, by default, up to 127 networks with up to 16,777,214 hosts each.
Class B	A network address classification that defines, by default, 16,384 networks with up to 65,534 hosts each.
Class C	A network address classification that defines up to 2,097,152 networks with up to 254 hosts each.
Class D	Network addresses set aside for multicast broadcast applications.
Class E	Network addresses set aside for experimental use.
Classful network	A network that is subnetted to define the boundary between the network and host bits.
Classless Inter-Domain Routing (CIDR)	An alternate way of defining and specifying network addresses, using the format network_address/network_address_bits.
Client/server network	Network model that connect multiple PCs, called clients, to a single computer, called a server, which distributes data and resources to the network.
Client operating system	The control program installed on the client PC.
Cloud Networking	A service that combines LAN, WAN, and management functionality necessary to offer IT-related capabilities as a service to clients.
Coaxial cable (coax)	A type of Ethernet media consisting of a single copper conductor surrounded by insulation, a foil shielding, and an outer cladding of plastic or plenum coating.
Collision domain	An area within an Ethernet network in which all devices in the domain compete for the cable, which may result in collisions.
Complex passwords	A user password that is designed to be difficult to guess, typically requiring at least three of the following: uppercase letters, lowercase letters, numbers and non-alphanumeric characters, and to be of a minimum significant length, like six characters.
Conduit	Metal or plastic pipe used to contain network cable.
Connection	The process of having the two computers recognize each other and open a communication channel between them.
Connectionless transmissions	Transmissions in which no response from the receiver is required.
Connection-oriented transmission	Transmissions that require an acknowledgement of receipt from the receiving computer.
Counter-rotating rings	The two rings in the dual ring topology that send data, each in a different direction.
Cross talk	Signal changes caused on a wire by EMI from an adjacent wire.

Crossover cable	A cable used in place of an uplink port. This is accomplished by reversing the transmit and receive pair on one end of the cable.
Data compression	Resizing the data to speed transmission.
Data encryption	Security measure to prevent data from being read by unintended recipients
Data Link layer (OSI Model)	The layer of the OSI model responsible for transmitting data over the network cable, also called the Network Interface layer.
Data presentation	Formatting data so that it is readable by the recipient.
Data separation	The process of "bookmarking" packets to allow for sessions to be recovered.
Datagram	A term used to refer to data packets at the OSI network level or equivalent level in other network models. Also known as a segment.
De facto standard	An unofficial standard that emerged through common usage in the marketplace.
Decapsulation	The process by which header and trailer information are stripped from a data packet.
Decentralized resource sharing	A term referring to sharing resources from peer servers and individual user's computers rather than from centralized sources.
Demand Priority Access Method	This media access method places the responsibility for network access control to the hub from the workstation. The hub is responsible for determining the priority for routing communications over the network.
Department of Defense (DoD) model	Alternate name for the TCP/IP model referring to its having been designed by the U.S. Department of Defense.
Destination Service Access Point (DSAP)	The first byte of the LLC extended two-byte address which indicates whether the destination address is for a single or group of computers.
Determinant Access Method	This network method makes it possible to trace packets as they pass through the network.
Device driver	Software that enables a computer's operating system to communicate with and control devices such as network adapters.
Device numbers	A random number selected by a device in an AppleTalk network that uniquely identifies that system on the network.
DHCP proxy	A computer that is configured to forward DHCP broadcasts through routers.
DHCPACK	A message sent by a server to acknowledge the client's acceptance of an address lease that includes the valid address lease and, possibly, optional TCP/IP configuration settings.
DHCPDISCOVER	A message sent by a client to start the IP address lease process.
DHCPNACK	A message broadcast by a DHCP server to cancel a lease offer.
DHCPOFFER	A message returned by a DHCP server offering a valid IP address lease to a requesting client.

DHCPREQUEST	A message sent by a client to accept a DHCP lease offer and, at the same time, inform any other servers that their offers were declined.
Dialog control	The service responsible for determining which computer is sending and which is receiving at any given time throughout the session.
Dielectric	The plastic insulator covering the central copper wire in coaxial cable.
Dig	A Unix/Linux command that is equivalent to the nslookup command. See also nslookup.
Directory-based networks	A centralized network architecture model that provides support for centralized user, security, and resource management. Also known as a directory services architecture.
Directory object	A directory services network entity, such as a user or computer.
Directory services network	A network model in which everything on the network, including users, computers, and shared resources, is maintained in a centralized directory. Also known as a directory-based network.
Distributed coordination function (DCF)	A method of using CSMA/CA media access control.
DNS table	A DNS mapping file that contains DNS records.
DNS zone	An administrative division of DNS names for maintaining name resolution.
Domain controller	Directory-based network server responsible for maintaining the directory of network objects and managing user authentication and authorization.
Domain member	A directory object assigned to a domain, typically referring to a user or computer.
Domain tree	A group of hierarchically related domains.
Domain	A logical security boundary in a directory-based network.
Dotted decimal notation	The decimal representation typically used for IP address and subnet mask values consisting of four decimal values separated by decimal points or "dots."
Drop cable	A Thicknet Ethernet device connection cable. Also called a DIX cable.
Dumb terminal	A screen and a keyboard with all data storage, processing, and control occurring at the mainframe.
Dynamic DNS	DNS service that supports automatic DNS table updates.
Dynamic Host Configuration Protocol (DHCP)	A protocol and service used to provide IP addresses and TCP/IP configuration parameters.
Dynamic routing	Automatically generating a route that can adjust to network conditions.
Dynamic Service Discovery	A feature of the IPX/SPX suite of protocols that permits all systems to recognize resources available on the network.
Echo request	A TCP/IP message that requests a response from the host receiving the message.

Economies of scale	This microeconomic term refers to the increase in efficiency of production as the quantity of goods increases.
Electromagnetic interference (EMI)	A source of interference caused by a strong magnetic field.
Electronics Industries Alliance/ Telecommunications Industry Association (EIA/TIA)	A standards body that defines UTP cable category standards.
Encapsulation	The process by which processing instructions are added to a data packet as it passes from computer to computer over a network.
Enterprise networks	A large network that contains multiple servers and typically integrates wide area links.
Ethernet	A protocol defining the wired connections within a network. Most commonly used networking standard with support for speeds ranging from 10 Mbps to 10 Gbps in current implementations.
Executioner	The current router when the TTL field counts down to zero.
Extended star topology	A star network with multiple hubs connected to the central hub.
Extranet	A private network that allows specific external users access over the Internet.
Fiber Distributed Data Interface (FDDI)	A dual ring topology that uses fiber-optic cable.
Fiber optic	Cables consisting of thin transparent plastic or glass fibers that transmit information using light (laser) signals.
Fiber-optic cable	A transmission media that uses glass or plastic fiber to carry light (laser) signals.
File server	A server on a network whose primary function is to serve as a repository for network user files.
File Transfer Protocol (FTP)	A transmission protocol used for sending files.
Flow control	The process that limits the number of transmissions sent at one time to avoid overloading the receiving device.
Forest	A logical group of domains.
Formal standard	A standard developed by an official industry or government body.
Fragmentation offset	A field within the IP packet that specifies the distance, in eight-byte blocks from the beginning of the packet. The offset for the first fragment in a packet is set to 0.
Frame	The data packet combined with its header and trailer information.
Full-duplex communication	A type of communication in which data flows in both directions at the same time.

Fully Qualified Domain Name (FQDN)	A name made up of a host name prepended to a domain suffix.
Gateway	A connection device that is used to connect networks and devices that would not otherwise be able to communicate with each other.
Get nearest server	A method by which clients search out the nearest server on the network in order to determine what services are available.
GNS response	The method by which servers respond to a GNS broadcast by clients searching for the closest server.
Half-duplex communication	A type of communication in which data flows in both directions, but only in one direction at a time.
Handshaking	The process used by computers for establishing a connection to each other.
Header	The set of information that is added to the beginning of a data packet.
Heterogeneous Networking	Environments that have a mix of hardware platforms, operating systems, and server applications.
Hidden costs	Refers to the operational costs of running a network that are not readily apparent.
High-level protocol	The rules for how data is transferred from one device to another.
Hop	The intervening routers in a path of routers through a network.
Horizontal cross-connects	Dedicated pathways for running cable through a building.
Horizontal relationship	Communication from one device to another on the same layer.
Host address	A unique computer address on a network segment in a TCP/IP network.
Host name	A unique identifier assigned to a device on a network used to access the device.
Host name resolution	A process through which a hostname identification is connected to an IP address, thus allowing communications between systems and devices on a network.
Host record	A DNS record that maps a host name to an IP address. It is the most common type of DNS record. (Also known as the host record.)
Host-based networks	A network architecture that relies on a central server to control all communications and clients that were capable of very minimal processing.
Hosts	A network device on a TCP/IP network.
Host-to-Host layer (DoD)	The TCP/IP model layer responsible for controlling the communication between network devices.
Hub	A connection device that allows multiple connections to the network.
Hybrid network	A network architecture that makes use of a combination of other types of architectures.
Hybrid topologies	Networks that use more than one topology in its physical structure.

Hypertext transfer protocol (HTTP)	A linking protocol that is used for accessing web pages over the Internet
IBM data connectors	Square, hermaphroditic connectors used in Token Rings.
Identification of choices stage	The second stage of the standardization processes in which potential solutions are identified.
IEEE 802.1	A standard the defines VLANs.
IEEE 802.1P	A standard that specifies how layer 2 switches can prioritize traffic and perform dynamic multicast filtering.
IEEE 802.5	IEE standard name for Token Ring topology.
ifconfig	A TCP/IP utility that can be used to view and manage IP address and configuration information. This is the Unix/Linux version of the command. See also ipconfig.
Impedance	A measurement of opposition to varying electrical current.
Induction	The process through which a moving electrical current causes a voltage on a nearby wire.
Information utilities	Companies that sell information services.
Infrastructure mode	A wireless topology in which wireless devices connect centrally to a WAP.
Institute of Electrical and Electronics Engineers (IEEE)	A professional society in the United States that includes a Standards Association (IEEE-SA) that develops various standards, but is best known for its standards for LANs.
International Organization for Standardization (ISO)	The ISO makes technical recommendations about data communication.
International Telecommunications Union— Telecommunications Group (ITU-T)	The technical standards-setting organization of the United Nations.
International Telecommunications Union (ITU)	The standards organization that makes technical recommendations about telephone, telegraph, and data communication interfaces on a worldwide basis.
Internet Control Message Protocol (ICMP)	A management and troubleshooting protocol that provides support through error and control messages.
Internet Corporation of Assigned Names and Numbers (ICANN)	The organization that is responsible for maintaining IP network address and domain name registrations.

Internet Engineering Task Force (IETF)	The standards organization that sets the standards that govern how much of the Internet operates.
Internet layer	The layer of the TCP/IP model responsible for addressing devices and routing data.
Internet model	A five-layer network model most commonly used.
Internet Packet Exchange (IPX)	The Network layer protocol used by the IPX/SPX suite of protocols, responsible for addressing and routing.
Internet Protocol (IP)	The protocol used to assign unique addresses to devices on the Internet.
Internet proxy servers	A server on a network that acts as an intermediary between systems to check and validate incoming requests to see if it can fulfill the request before passing it on to the server.
Internet service providers (ISPs)	Companies providing Internet access for a fee.
Internetwork layer	Another name for the Internet or Network layer in the TCP/IP model.
Intranet	A closed private LAN used for internal communication.
IP version 4 (IPv4)	The current IP version, which uses a 32-bit addressing scheme.
IP version 6 (IPv6)	A new IP version that uses 128-bit address and provides a larger pool of addresses.
ipconfig	A TCP/IP utility that can be used to view and manage IP addresses and configuration information. This is the Windows/MS-DOS version of the command. See also ifconfig.
Kevlar	Material used to protect the optical fibers in fiber-optic cables.
Light-emitting diode (LED)	A light source typically used with fiber-optic cable.
Listen before transmit method	The process by which a system senses traffic on the network before attempting to transmit at the end of the backoff period.
LLC type 1	Connectionless service on the LLC sublayer.
LLC type 2	Connection-oriented service on the LLC sublayer.
LMHOSTS	A text file used for NetBIOS name resolution.
Logical address	The unique network identifier assigned to a computer.
Logical bus	A logical topology in which data travel in a linear fashion from the source to all destinations.
Logical Link Control (LLC)	Provides the interface between the media-access method and Network layer protocols.
Logical topology	A description of how devices on a LAN communicate and transmit data.
Long DDP	Used to send packets between different networks when routing services are required within an AppleTalk network.

Long-haul transmission lines	Telephone cables within a wide area network used to transmit over long distances.
Loopback	A communication test in which a computer sends an echo request to itself.
Low-level protocol	A system of rules for how network connection is achieved.
MAC address filtering	A WAP security method that allows or blocks wireless clients based on the MAC addresses encoded on their NICs.
MAC address	The unique identifier of the network interface card attached to a computer.
Macintosh Plus	An Apple computer that offered an early version of peer-to-peer networking.
Mail exchange (MX)	A DNS record used to identify a mail server.
Manchester Encoding	A special type of unipolar signaling in which the signal is changed from high to low or from low to high in the middle of the signal.
Media Access Control (MAC)	Sublayer is responsible for the connection to the physical media and physical address.
Media Access Unit (MAU)	A unit in a Token Ring topology which passes packets to computers on the network.
Media player	Small portable digital device used for playing audio and video files.
Member server	A directory-based network server.
Mesh topology	A network topology in which all devices are connected to each other (net topology).
Messaging Server	A server on a network whose primary function is to manage messages between network devices, for example, e-mail and broadcast messaging.
Mode	In network topology, a wireless topology.
Multimode fiber	Fiber-optic cable that supports multiple concurrent communication signals.
Multiplexing	A communication method that allows multiple signals to transmit simultaneously across a single physical channel by varying length of transmission, frequency used, or both.
Multiserver network	A network that implements multiple servers in various roles.
Multistation Access Unit (MAU)	A central hub connection device used in a Token Ring network.
Name resolution	The process of mapping IP addresses to Internet host names.
Name server (NS)	A DNS record that identifies a DNS server.
Net topology	A network topology in which all devices are connected to each other (mesh topology).
NetBIOS	An API command set used to control lower-level network services and node-to-node data transfers.
Network adapter	The hardware that enables a computer to connect to a network.

Network address translation (NAT)	The process whereby transmissions can be routed appropriately from an outside system to internal systems with private IP addresses.
Network administrator	An IT expert specializing in the upkeep and support of networks.
Network architecture	A method of describing the logical design of a network of computers and how they interact.
Network Interface Card (NIC)	Another name for a network adapter.
Network Interface layer (DoD)	The layer responsible for routing data inside a single network.
Network layer (Internet)	The layer responsible for addressing devices and routing data.
Network layer (OSI)	The layer that handles routing of packets from one computer to another.
Network number	Used to identify devices on a network.
Network system	The path over which servers and clients communicate.
Network topology	Describes the physical connections between devices on a network.
Network	Computers connected in such a way that they can communicate with each other.
Nexus point	The point where several lines of communication come together.
Node	A uniquely identifiable device.
Nonreturn to zero	This telecommunications binary code schema represents 1s and 0s with separate significant voltage conditions (for example, 1 as positive voltage and 0 as no voltage). No other conditions are recognized in this code.
nslookup	A TCP/IP utility that is used to retrieve information from, test, and manage name servers. The same command is supported on both Windows and Unix/Linux.
NWLink	A Microsoft protocol that allows Windows computers to serve as NetWare clients.
Object model	A directory model in which all network models are treated as objects that can be clearly defined and described.
Ohms	A unit of measurement for resistance of impedance.
Organizational unit (OU)	A directory services container used to organize and hold other directory objects.
Out-of-band	A method in TCP that separates some information from the main data stream and designates it as urgent.
Overflows	A condition where a destination system is sent more information than can be received.
Patch panel	A wiring panel that simplifies wiring connections to multipair cables.
pathping	A TCP/IP utility used to track a packet from one host to another, including any routers along the way. This is a Windows command-line command.
Peer layer communication	Another name for horizontal relationships.

Peer server	The PCs in a peer-to-peer network that act as both client and server.
Peer-to-peer mode	A wireless network topology in which wireless devices communicate directly with each other (ad hoc mode).
Peer-to-peer network	A small network architecture in which individual computers are connected directly to one another and can act as both a server and a client.
Phase 1	A type of AppleTalk network in which one physical network and one logical zone is supported.
Phase 2	A type of AppleTalk network in which one physical network and multiple logical zones are supported.
Physical address	The unique identifier of the network card attached to a computer.
Physical carrier sense method	Another term for DCF.
Physical layer (Internet)	The TCP/IP layer responsible for how applications on both ends process data.
Physical layer (OSI)	The layer that control the rules for data transmission, including electrical currents, types of cables, and transmission speed.
Physical topology	The layout of the cables connecting the network devices.
ping	A TCP/IP utility that is used to test host-to-host communication. The same command is used for Windows and Unix/Linux.
Plenum	Teflon-based fire-retardant cable insulation.
Point coordination function (PCF)	A method of using CSMA/CA media access control.
Polyvinyl chloride (PVC)	A plastic commonly used as cable insulation.
Presentation layer (OSI)	The layer that control the rules for data transmission, including electrical currents, types of cables, and transmission speed, translating between application and network formats.
Primary DNS server	An authoritative server for a DNS zone.
Print jobs	Files sent to the print server by a network user, waiting to access the printer.
Print queue	A collection of files awaiting access to the printer on a printer server.
Print server	A server on a network whose primary function is to control network user access to shared printers.
Private addresses	An address that can be used for addressing LANs but cannot be used on the Internet.
Process layer (DoD)	The layer responsible for how applications on both ends process data.
Protocol number	An IP header field that describes the type of protocol used in the datagram following an IP header.
Protocol stack	The group of protocols surrounding a data packet that is added and removed as the data stack moves through the layers of the OSI model.

Protocol suite	Several network protocols grouped together, like TCP/IP.
Protocol	The way in which devices communicate on a network, things like signal strength and format.
Public switched telephone network (PSTN)	A telephone network and infrastructure that includes the standard dial-up phone network.
Raceway	Dedicated pathways for running cable through a building.
Radio frequency interference (RFI)	A source of interference that results from radio-frequency transmissions.
Radio grade (RG)	A specification for coaxial cable used for network applications.
Redundancy	Duplicate transmission paths.
Regional carriers	Regional telephone companies.
Reliable transport method	A transmission that ensures the error-free receipt of packets.
Repeater	An electronic amplifier used to increase the strength of an electronic signal as it moves through the cables.
Request for Comments (RFC)	The documents in which formal standards are published.
Resource servers	Any server that provides shared resources to a network.
Return to zero	This telecommunications code always returns to 0 volts after each bit before going to +5 volts (for a 1) or 5 volts (for a 0) for the next volt.
Ring in	The inbound port used for connecting to MAUs.
Ring out	The outbound port used for connecting to MAUs.
RJ-45	A modular jack used for network connections.
Root domain	The uppermost domain in a domain tree and the root of the domain hierarchical structure.
Route	Path information between a source and destination computer.
Router	A network communication device used to connect two or more networks or network types.
Routing protocol	The protocol used by routers to define how the routing path is chosen.
Routing table	A table stored in memory on a router that keeps track of known networks and the appropriate port to use to reach each network.
Routing	The process of determining the path required to deliver packets to their destination.
Secondary DNS server	A server that contains a copy of a zone database that is periodically updated from the primary DNS server.
Segment	(1) A physical network division within a larger physical network. (2) A term sometimes used to refer to datagram fragments

Sequence number	Used by TCP to identify the order of information in a packet so that the packet can be reconstructed appropriately, despite any fragmentation or disordering that may have happened during data transmission.
Sequence Packet Exchange (SPX)	The Transport layer protocol of the IPX/SPX suite of protocols responsible for providing connection delivery services and control of flow.
Server applications	Specialized applications that run on server NOSs and provide resources or special services to network clients.
Server operating system	The control program installed on the server. Also known as a network operating system.
Server	A computer that stores and provides resources and data to the network.
Server-side scripting	A method of providing a unified look and feel for web pages through the hosting server.
Service Advertisement Protocol (SAP)	The method by which servers announce their availability through broadcast messages upon the network.
Service set identifier (SSID)	A text string that identifies a WAP to wireless clients
Session layer (OSI)	The network layer that controls the communication.
Share-level security	A security method used in peer-to-peer networking, with access permissions based on password-protected resource shares.
Shielded twisted pair	A cable that contains pairs of wire that are twisted periodically and covered with a foil or braid shield.
Short DDP	Used to send packets to computers on the same network within an AppleTalk network.
Simple file sharing	A Windows XP files sharing method in which all workgroup members have the same access permissions.
Simple Mail Transfer Protocol (SMTP)	A communication protocol used to define how e-mail is sent and received.
Single point of failure	In the context of networking architectures, a term that refers to a resource that, when it fails, causes the network as a whole to fail.
Single-mode fiber	Fiber-optic cable that carries a single transmission signal.
SMA connector	A screw on fiber-optic connector.
Smartphone	Any device capable of placing phone calls and advanced computing functions including web browsing, e-mail transmission, media playing, document view, and schedule maintenance.
Source Service Access Point (SSAP)	The second byte of the LLC extended two-byte address indicates the address of a single computer.
Spanning Tree Protocol (STP)	A protocol used by bridges to decide whether to forward a packet.

Spooler file	A file on a print server that contains the list of print files waiting to be printed.
Spooling	The process by which files waiting to be printed on a print server are ordered to provide access to the printer.
Stack	A group of protocols that work together at different layers of the OSI model.
Star topology	A network topology in which network devices are connected to a single hub.
Star-ring topology	A physical topology the connects multiple MAUs to each other.
Start of authority (SOA)	A DNS zone record that describes the zone and the authoritative server. A zone can have only one SOA record.
Static IP address	An IP address set manually on a system.
Static routing	Manually configuring a route that does not change unless it is manually updated.
Straight tip (STP) connector	A fiber-optic connector similar to a BNC connector.
Subnet mask	A portion of the IP address that identifies the host address for the system.
Subnetting	The process of dividing a network address into smaller networks.
Subscriber connector (SC)	The most popular and easiest to use fiber-optic connector, recognizable by its square tip. SC connectors are typically used in a keyed pair.
Switch	A connection device similar to a hub but more sophisticated including functionality that allows it to control and manage data transmissions.
Telnet	A software application that allows a user to log on to a remote computer as if the user were sitting at that computer and using its resources.
Terminator	A passive device attached to each end of a coaxial cable in a bus topology to absorb the signal when it reaches the end of the line.
Thick Ethernet	See 10Base5.
Thicknet	See 10Base5.
Thin Ethernet	See 10Base2.
Thinnet	See 10Base2.
Time to Live (TTL)	An IP header field whose value is used to limit the lifespan of a datagram based on the number of routers (hops) it crosses.
Token Ring	A topology in which a data packet is sent around a ring of computers until it reaches its intended destination.
Topology	The structure of a network.
Total Cost of Ownership (TCO)	The complete cost of operating a network including the costs of hardware, software, maintenance, and administration.
traceroute	A TCP/IP utility that is used to track a packet from one host to another, including any routers along the way. This is a Unix/Linux command.

tracert	A TCP/IP utility that is used to track a packet from one host to another, including any routers along the way. This is a Windows command-line command.
Twisted pair cable	A type of copper cable line with multiple conductors similar to telephone cable.
Type numbers	IBM STP category numbers.
Unshielded twisted pair (UTP)	Cable that contains multiple pairs of wires that are twisted periodically to minimize interference.
Urgent pointer	A TCP header field that is used to identify higher-priority data that is interrupting a lower-priority transmission.
Vampire tap	A Thicknet cable tap that pierces the dielectric to connect to the inner core.
Variable Length Subnet Masking (VLSM)	A subnetting option in which variable length subnet masks are used instead of all subnets having the same subnet mask.
Virtual carrier sense method	Another term for PCF.
Virtual hosting	The method by which one system is able to serve as a host for multiple domain names, thus allowing several systems to share a single IP address and the host system to share resources, such as memory, processor cycles, etc.
Virtual LANs (VLANs)	A LAN in which devices are logically configured to communicate as if they were attached to the same network.
Virtual private networks (VPN)	A private communication path over the public Internet acting as a secure network within a larger or public network.
WAN switch	A connectivity device specific to LANs and used to connect to long-haul transmission media.
Web server	A specialized application server whose primary function is to server content to clients through the Internet.
Wi-Fi	An abbreviation for wireless network.
Window	A TCP header field that identifies the numbers of segments that can be sent before the source host expects an acknowledgement from the recipient.
Windows for Workgroups 3.11	An early Microsoft Windows version that supported peer-to-peer networking.
Windows Internet Naming Service (WINS)	A service that is used for automated NetBIOS name-to-IP address resolution on a Windows network.
Wired networks	Consist of PCs and servers, which are physically connected by cables.
Wireless access point (WAP)	A central access point for wireless computers that also passes data to and from a wired network.
Wireless mesh	A wireless topology made up of transmissions points with overlapping ranges.
Wireless networks	Use radio transmission instead of cables to communicate.

Wireless Personal Area Networks (WPANs)	Describes short distance wireless networks.
Workgroup name	A name used to uniquely identify a workgroup on a network.
Workgroup	A logical peer-to-peer network grouping.
Zone file	A DNS mapping file that contains the DNS records for a specific zone.
Zones	A logical group of clients within an AppleTalk network, used to route broadcasts appropriately within the given zone, and prevent other broadcast messages from crowding network traffic.

INDEX